# The T&T Clark Handbook of
# Edward Schillebeeckx

# The T&T Clark Handbook of Edward Schillebeeckx

### EDITED BY
Stephan van Erp and
Daniel Minch

LONDON • NEW YORK • OXFORD • NEW DELHI • SYDNEY

T&T CLARK
Bloomsbury Publishing Plc
50 Bedford Square, London, WC1B 3DP, UK
1385 Broadway, New York, NY 10018, USA

BLOOMSBURY, T&T CLARK and the T&T Clark logo are trademarks of
Bloomsbury Publishing Plc

First published in Great Britain 2020

Cover design: Terry Woodley
Cover image © Krisanapong Detraphiphat / GettyImages

A catalogue record for this book is available from the British Library.

A catalog record for this book is available from the Library of Congress.

ISBN:  HB:    978-0-5676-6243-9
       ePDF:  978-0-5676-6245-3
       ePub:  978-0-5676-6244-6

Typeset by Integra Software Services Pvt. Ltd.
Printed and bound in Great Britain

# Contents

## PART III  THEOLOGICAL THEMES

# Contributors

**Christiane Alpers** (Katholische Universität Eichstätt-Ingolstadt) is a Research and Teaching Fellow in Theology at the Catholic University Eichstätt-Ingolstadt. Her current research focuses on Erich Przywara's interpretation of Ignatian spirituality as well as on political theological responses to the current crises of the European Union. Her recent publications include *A Politics of Grace: Hope for Redemption in a Post-Christendom Context*. T&T Clark Studies in Edward Schillebeeckx (T&T Clark, 2018).
E-mail: christiane.alpers@ku.de

**Lieven Boeve** (KU Leuven) is Professor of Fundamental Theology at the Faculty of Theology and Religious Studies, KU Leuven, Belgium. He is also Director-General of the Office of Catholic Education Flanders. His most recent book is *Theology at the Crossroads of University, Church and Society: Dialogue, Difference and Catholic Identity* (Bloomsbury, 2016).
E-mail: lieven.boeve@kuleuven.be

**Erik Borgman, O.P.** (Tilburg University) is a lay Dominican. He is Full Professor for Public Theology and Academic Director of the Tilburg Cobbenhagen Center at Tilburg University. He has written extensively on the theology of Edward Schillebeeckx and is the author of the biography *Edward Schillebeeckx: A Theologian in His History. Part I: A Catholic Theology of Culture (1914–1965)* (Continuum, 2003). Currently he is the chair of the Edward Schillebeeckx Foundation (www.schillebeeckx.nl). His most recent book is *Leven van wat komt: Een katholiek uitzicht op de samenleving* (Meinema, 2017).
E-mail: e.p.n.m.borgman@uvt.nl

**Dries Bosschaert** (KU Leuven) is a Postdoctoral Researcher of the Fund for Scientific Research–Flanders (FWO) at the Faculty of Theology and Religious Studies, KU Leuven. His research focuses on the history of the church and theology in the twentieth century, including significant people and networks of theological renewal, the Second Vatican Council, and the relation between theology, culture, and labor. He is the author of the article "Understanding the Shift in *Gaudium et Spes*: From Theology of History to Christian Anthropology," *Theological Studies* 78 (2017), 634–58.
E-mail: dries.bosschaert@kuleuven.be

**Thijs Caspers** worked at the Tilburg Cobbenhagen Center (Tilburg University) as a researcher until the beginning of 2018. His research focused on the meaning of the Catholic faith for Dutch society. In 2018 he published two books in relation to this research: *Thuis zijn in het onbekende* (Abdij Van Berne, 2018) and *Eigen zinnen* (Abdij Van Berne, 2018). Currently he is working as an independent researcher and entrepreneur.
E-mail: thijscaspers@gmail.com

**Edmund Kee-Fook Chia** (Australian Catholic University, Melbourne) teaches at the Australian Catholic University, where he serves as Director of the Interreligious Dialogue Network. He researches in the areas of Asian Theology and Theologies of Religion, and he previously headed the ecumenical and interfaith office of the Asian Bishops' Conferences. He is the author of *World Christianity Encounters World Religions* (Liturgical Press, 2018).
E-mail: edmund.chia@acu.edu.au

**Stephan van Erp** (KU Leuven/Radboud University Nijmegen) is Professor of Fundamental Theology at the Faculty of Theology and Religious Studies at KU Leuven, and head of the Research Unit Systematic Theology and the Study of Religion. He is the coordinator of the Interfaculty Centre for Catholic Thought (InFaCT) at KU Leuven. He also holds the Edward Schillebeeckx Chair at the Radboud University Nijmegen. He is the managing editor of the Dutch-Flemish journal *Tijdschrift voor Theologie*.
E-mail: stephan.vanerp@kuleuven.be

**Julia Feder** (Creighton University) is Assistant Professor of Theology at Creighton University in Omaha, Nebraska. Her research focuses on theological anthropology, suffering, and soteriology. Her current book project, titled *Trauma and Salvation: A Theology of Healing*, draws upon the writings of Teresa of Avila and Edward Schillebeeckx to construct a contemporary posttraumatic soteriology. Her work has been published in *Theological Studies*; *Philosophy, Theology, and the Sciences*; the *Journal of Religion and Society*; and *Anthropology News*.
E-mail: juliafeder@creighton.edu

**Joris Geldhof** (KU Leuven) is Professor of Liturgy and Sacramental Theology at the Faculty of Theology and Religious Studies, KU Leuven, and currently the president of Societas Liturgica, an international scholarly association of liturgists worldwide. He has recently published the book *Liturgy and Secularism: Beyond the Divide* (Liturgical Press, 2018).
E-mail: joris.geldhof@kuleuven.be

**Anthony J. Godzieba** (Villanova University) is Professor of Theology and Religious Studies at Villanova University and former editor of *Horizons: The Journal of the College Theology Society*. His work in systematic, foundational, and philosophical theologies is published widely in various collections and journals. His most recent book is *A Theology of the Presence and Absence of God* (Liturgical Press, 2018).
E-mail: anthony.godzieba@villanova.edu

**Roger Haight, S.J.** (Union Theological Seminary) is Scholar in Residence at Union Theological Seminary in New York. He works in the area of fundamental theology. His current research probes the relationship between theology and science with an emphasis on evolution as in his recent article: "Spirituality, Evolution, Creator God," *Theological Studies* 79 (2018), 251–73. His latest book is *Spiritual and Religious: Explorations for Seekers* (Maryknoll, 2016).
E-mail: rogerdhaight@gmail.com

**Mary Catherine Hilkert, O.P.** (University of Notre Dame) is Professor of Theology at the University of Notre Dame, where she specializes in the areas of theological anthropology, fundamental theology, and feminist theologies and spirituality. She is the co-editor (with Robert Schreiter) of *The Praxis of the Reign of God: An Introduction to the Theology of Edward Schillebeeckx* (Fordham University Press, 2002); and author of *Naming Grace: Preaching and the Sacramental Imagination*; and *Speaking with Authority: Catherine of Siena and the Voices of Women Today* (Continuum, 1997).
E-mail: mhilkert@nd.edu

**Mary Ann Hinsdale, I.H.M.** (Boston College) is currently Associate Professor of Theology at Boston College. She specializes in theological anthropology, ecclesiology, and feminist theologies and theory. A former president of the Catholic Theological Society of America, she is the author of *Women Shaping Theology* (Paulist Press, 2006), and co-editor of the *T&T Clark Handbook of Theological Anthropology* (forthcoming, 2020).
E-mail: maryann.hinsdale@bc.edu

**Leo Kenis** (KU Leuven) is Emeritus Professor of Church History and the History of Theology at the Faculty of Theology and Religious Studies, KU Leuven. His research has focused on the history of Catholic theology during the nineteenth and twentieth centuries. He has been the editor of various academic book series and of the journal *Louvain Studies* and the editor (with Ernestine van der Wall) of *Religious Modernism in the Low Countries* (Peeters, 2013).
E-mail: leo.kenis@kuleuven.be

**Philip Kennedy, O.P.** (University of Oxford) is a member of the Faculty of Theology and Religion of the University of Oxford, a Senior Research Fellow in Modern Theology at Mansfield College, and a tutor for graduates at Campion Hall. His current research focusses on Christology. Among his books is *Christianity: An Introduction* (I.B. Tauris, 2011).
E-mail: philip.kennedy@mansfield.ox.ac.uk

**Michael E. Lee** (Fordham University) is Associate Professor of Theology and affiliated member of the Faculty of Latin American & Latino Studies at Fordham University. His research focuses on Roman Catholic theology, liberation theologies, Christology, and spirituality. His most recent publication is *Revolutionary Saint: The Theological Legacy of Oscar Romero* (Orbis Books, 2018).
E-mail: fmilee@fordham.edu

**Kathleen McManus, O.P.** of the Sisters of St. Dominic of Blauvelt, NY, has served as Associate Professor of Theology and as Director of the MA in Pastoral Ministry program at the University of Portland. She also held the Robert J. Randall Distinguished Professorship in Christian Culture at Providence College. She is currently working on a book entitled *Suffering and the Vulnerable Rule of God: A Feminist Epistemology*.
E-mail: kmcmanusop@gmail.com

**Jürgen Mettepenningen** (KU Leuven) is a Guest Lecturer at the Faculty of Theology and Religious Studies of the KU Leuven. He has published a number of articles and books concerning

"nouvelle théologie," among which is the monograph *Nouvelle Théologie – New Theology: Inheritor of Modernism, Precursor of Vatican II* (Bloomsbury, 2010).
Email: jurgen.mettepenningen@kuleuven.be

**Anton Milh, O.P.** (KU Leuven) is a Doctoral Researcher of the Fund for Scientific Research–Flanders (FWO) at the Faculty of Theology and Religious Studies, KU Leuven. He specializes in the history of religious orders and congregations in Flanders in the first half of the twentieth century, especially the Dominicans, Franciscans, and Capuchins. He is co-editor (with Mathijs Lamberigts and Mark De Caluwe O.P.) of a book on the recent history of the Dominicans in Flanders entitled: *Predikbroeders in woord en daad. Dominicanen in Vlaanderen in de twintigste eeuw* (Halewijn, 2016).
E-mail: anton.milh@kuleuven.be

**Daniel Minch** (University of Graz) is Assistant Professor of Dogmatic Theology at the University of Graz. He is part of the Institute of Systematic Theology and Liturgical Studies at the Faculty of Catholic Theology. Minch's research interests include theological hermeneutics, the economic dimensions of contemporary political theology, eschatology, and theologies of hope. He is the author of *Eschatological Hermeneutics: The Theological Core of Experience and Our Hope for Salvation.* T&T Clark Studies in Edward Schillebeeckx (T&T Clark, 2018).
E-mail: daniel.minch@uni-graz.at

**Martin G. Poulsom, S.D.B.** (University of Roehampton) is a Senior Lecturer in Systematic Theology at the University of Roehampton, London. His principal area of research looks at faith in creation. He is currently focusing on the relation between science and faith, and on the challenge of climate change. He writes principally from a perspective of theology *sequela* Schillebeeckx; he has published the monograph *The Dialectics of Creation* (Bloomsbury, 2014).
E-mail: martin.poulsom@roehampton.ac.uk

**Bernard P. Prusak** (Villanova University) is Professor for Historical and Systematic Theology at Villanova University. His areas of research and teaching are historical and systematic theology, with emphasis on Christology and the church, and with a special interest in the Second Vatican Council. He is the author of *The Church Unfinished: Ecclesiology Through the Centuries* (Paulist Press, 2004).
E-mail: bernard.prusak@villanova.edu

**Elizabeth M. Pyne** (Fordham University, London Centre) is currently an instructor at Fordham University's London Centre. Her research interests lie in theological anthropology, eco-theology, and political theology. She engages the intersections of these topics with diverse resources in critical theory, feminist and queer studies, and the ecological humanities.
E-mail: epyne@fordham.edu

**Karim Schelkens** (Tilburg University/KU Leuven) is Associate Professor in the History of Church and Theology at Tilburg University and Guest Professor at KU Leuven. He has served as Secretary General of the European Society for Catholic Theology from 2013 to 2018, and is

the head of a research program on the Transition of Catholicism in Late Modernity. His research focuses on religious biography, as well as on the Second Vatican Council and preconciliar *ressourcement* movements, on which he has published numerous monographs and edited volumes, including a critical edition of the *Council Notes of Edward Schillebeeckx*.
E-mail: k.schelkens@uvt.nl

**Laura Tack** (KU Leuven) is a Postdoctoral Researcher at the Faculty of Theology and Religious Studies, KU Leuven, where she completed a doctorate in theology. She has published on the hermeneutics of the Gospel of John, the visual imagery for revelation in Paul's Corinthian correspondence and the *Wirkungsgeschichte* of biblical themes in visual culture. As a biblical scholar and art historian, she has a keen interest in the changing conceptions of time in early and medieval Christian art and literature.
E-mail: laura.tack@kuleuven.be

**Daniel Speed Thompson** (University of Dayton) is Associate Professor of Religious Studies at the University of Dayton. He is the author of *The Language of Dissent: Edward Schillebeeckx on the Crisis of Authority in the Catholic Church* (University of Notre Dame Press, 2003). His current research focus is on Catholic intellectual life and curricula at Catholic universities, and on religion and science.
E-mail: dthompson3@udayton.edu

**Pim (Wilhelmus G.B.M.) Valkenberg** (Catholic University of America) is Professor of Religion and Culture at the School of Theology and Religious Studies, Catholic University of America in Washington DC. He studied in Utrecht and then taught systematic theology in Nijmegen between 1987 and 2007. His field of expertise is interreligious dialogue, specifically Christian–Muslim relations. Among his latest publications are *World Religions in Dialogue* (Anselm Academic, 2017), and *Renewing Islam by Service* (CUA Press, 2015).
E-mail: valkenberg@cua.edu

# Acknowledgments

This new addition to the *T&T Clark Handbook* series provides both a comprehensive introduction to the theology of Edward Schillebeeckx and new insights into Schillebeeckx's legacy for contemporary theology. A volume of this size and scope is notoriously difficult to put together, and even more difficult to do well. We believe that what we are presenting here is a truly excellent collection of chapters by exceptionally talented scholars. In order to complete this endeavor, many people have contributed their time and talent to help us reach the finish line. We certainly could not have done this without all of the support provided by a number of people on several continents. Here, we the editors would like to heartily thank everyone who helped us to bring this project to fruition. First and foremost, our warmest thanks go to Anna Turton, Sarah Blake, and everyone at Bloomsbury for their patience and support throughout this long process. We sincerely hope that this volume is a proud addition to the *Handbook* series, and we could not have done it without you. In the planning stages we received a great deal of insight and help from several people who deserve particular praise, including Robert J. Schreiter, Mary Catherine Hilkert, Erik Borgman, and Leo Kenis. Bob and Cathy have long been the source of much inspiration to students and researchers in "Schillebeeckx studies," and their volume, *The Praxis of the Reign of God*, has been the standard work in the field. We hope that this *Handbook* expands on and complements their work, and we have done our absolute best to live up to their example. Thanks also go to Erik and Leo for their help in planning the volume, and especially for their contributions and suggestions on specific texts. This *Handbook* has been a collaborative effort from the beginning, and so we would also like to sincerely thank Jacob Benjamins, Anton Milh, Anne Siebesma, and Huub Stegeman for their assistance with proofreading and careful recommendations, Thomas Aquinas Quaicoe for his work on the Index, and the members of the Research Group Fundamental and Political Theology at KU Leuven for contributing to a critical scholarly and collegial atmosphere for our work. This volume has been part of a research project funded by the Fund for Scientific Research–Flanders (FWO), and we wish to gratefully acknowledge their support. Additional thanks go to Mary Ann Hinsdale and Kathleen McManus who have co-organized special sessions on the theology of Edward Schillebeeckx with us at the annual convention of the Catholic Theological Society of America. We are honored to have such a wonderful forum in which to engage with many of the authors represented in this volume, and so thanks also to the members of the CTSA for facilitating the critical flow of ideas and Catholic scholarship in general. Finally, we would like to thank Brian Heffernan and Huub Stegeman for their careful work in translating several of the chapters in this volume from Dutch into English. It is only through the work of so many that we have been able to reach this point, and we are sincerely grateful.

Stephan van Erp
Daniel Minch

# Abbreviations

Listed below are the standard citations and abbreviations for the *Collected Works of Edward Schillebeeckx*, edited by T. Schoof and C. Sterkens (London/New Delhi/New York/Sydney: Bloomsbury T&T Clark, 2014), in eleven volumes. Because of the large amount of secondary material that refers to the older editions and translations of Schillebeeckx's work, the original page numbers will be cited in square brackets […] after the page numbers used in the Collected Works *(CW)*. Full bibliographic information for the volumes and individual essays cited is listed below.

| | |
|---|---|
| *Christ* | *Christ: The Christian Experience in the Modern World* |
| *Christ the Sacrament* | *Christ the Sacrament of the Encounter with God* |
| *Church* | *Church: The Human Story of God* |
| *CW* | *Collected Works of Edward Schillebeeckx* |
| *Essays* | *Essays: Ongoing Theological Quests* |
| *GFM* | *God the Future of Man* |
| *IR* | *Interim Report on the Books Jesus and Christ* |
| *Jesus* | *Jesus: An Experiment in Christology* |
| *RT* | *Revelation and Theology* (volumes I and II) |
| *UF* | *The Understanding of Faith: Interpretation and Criticism* |
| *WC* | *World and Church* |

Standard abbreviations for additional publications:

| | |
|---|---|
| *AAS* | *Acta Apostolicae Sedis* |
| Arch. | Personal Archives of Edward Schillebeeckx, Katholiek Documentatie Centrum at Radboud University Nijmegen, Archive number: 656 |
| BETL | Bibliotheca Ephemeridum Theologicarum Lovaniensium |
| *Council Notes* | *The Council Notes of Edward Schillebeeckx 1962–1963. Edited by Karim Schelkens. Instrumenta Theologica 34. Leuven: Peeters Press, 2011.* |
| *ST* | *Thomas Aquinas, Summa Theologiae* |
| *TGL* | *Tijdschrift voor geestelijk leven* |
| *TvT* | *Tijdschrift voor Theologie* |

*Theol. woordenboek Theologisch woordenboek,* 3 volumes. Edited by H. Brink, G. Kreling, A.H. Maltha, and J.H. Walgrave. Roermond: J.J. Romen & Zonen, 1952–1958.

## The *Collected Works of Edward Schillebeeckx* (by volume number with individual essays cited)

Schillebeeckx, Edward. *Christ the Sacrament of the Encounter with God.* Translated by Paul Barrett and Lawrence Bright, *CW* vol. 1. London: Bloomsbury T&T Clark, 2014.

Schillebeeckx, Edward. *Revelation and Theology.* Translated by N.D. Smith, *CW* vol. 2. London: Bloomsbury T&T Clark, 2014.

- "Revelation, Scripture, Tradition and Teaching Authority," 3–17 [I 3–26]
- "What is Theology?," 65–118 [I 95–181]
- "The Bible and Theology," 119–37 [I 184–214]
- "The Liturgy and Theology," 157–59 [I 240–44]
- "Scholasticism and Theology," 161–85 [I 245–84]
- "The Concept of 'Truth'," 189–205 [II 5–29]
- "The Non-Conceptual Intellectual Dimension in our Knowledge of God According to Aquinas," = "The Non-Conceptual Intellectual Dimension," 207–38 [II 157–206]
- "The Non-Conceptual Intellectual Element in the Act of Faith: A Reaction," = "The Non-Conceptual Intellectual Element," 239–68 [II 31–75]
- "Salvation History as the Basis of Theology: *Theologia* or *Oikonomia*?," = "*Theologia* or *Oikonomia*?," 271–88 [II 79–105]

Schillebeeckx, Edward. *God the Future of Man.* Translated by N.D. Smith, *CW* vol. 3. London: Bloomsbury T&T Clark, 2014.

- "Towards a Catholic Use of Hermeneutics," = "Catholic Use of Hermeneutics," 1–29 [2–44]
- "Secularization and Christian Belief in God," 31–54 [52–88]
- "Secular Worship and Church Liturgy," 55–69 [92–114]
- "The Church as the Sacrament of Dialogue," 71–84 [118–38]
- "Church, Magisterium and Politics," 85–99 [142–64]
- "The New Image of God, Secularization and Man's Future on Earth," = "The New Image of God" 101–25 [168–203]

Schillebeeckx, Edward. *World and Church.* Translated by N.D. Smith, *CW* vol. 4. London: Bloomsbury T&T Clark, 2014.

- "Humble Humanism," 15–24 [19–31]
- "Priest and Layman in a Secular World," 25–57 [32–76]
- "The Sorrow of the Experience of God's Concealment," 59–72 [77–95]
- "Church and World," 73–87 [98–114]
- "The Ecclesial Life of Religious Man," 109–25 [140–62]
- "Man and His Bodily World," 177–205 [230–68]

Schillebeeckx, Edward. *The Understanding of Faith: Interpretation and Criticism.* Translated by N.D. Smith, *CW* vol. 5. London: Bloomsbury T&T Clark, 2014.

- "The Interpretation of the Future," 1–11 [1–13]
- "The Context and Value of Faith-Talk," 13–18 [14–19]
- "Linguistic Criteria," 19–40 [20–44]
- "Theological Criteria," 41–68 [45–77]
- "Correlation Between Human Question and Christian Answer," 69–88 [78–101]
- "The New Critical Theory," 89–107 [102–23]
- "The New Critical Theory and Theological Hermeneutics," 109–35 [124–15]

Schillebeeckx, Edward. *Jesus: An Experiment in Christology.* Translated by Hubert Hoskins and Marcelle Manley, *CW* vol. 6. London: Bloomsbury T&T Clark, 2014.

Schillebeeckx, Edward. *Christ: The Christian Experience in the Modern World.* Translated by John Bowden, *CW* vol. 7. London: Bloomsbury T&T Clark, 2014.

Schillebeeckx, Edward. *Interim Report on the Books Jesus and Christ.* Translated by John Bowden, *CW* vol. 8. London: Bloomsbury T&T Clark, 2014.

Schillebeeckx, Edward. *The Church with a Human Face.* Translated by John Bowden, *CW* vol. 9. London: Bloomsbury T&T Clark, 2014.

Schillebeeckx, Edward. *Church: The Human Story of God.* Translated by John Bowden, *CW* vol. 10. London: Bloomsbury T&T Clark, 2014.

Schillebeeckx, Edward. *Essays: Ongoing Theological Quests, CW* vol. 11. London: Bloomsbury T&T Clark, 2014.

- "Experience and Faith," 1–34
- "The Search for the Living God," 35–50
- "Theological Interpretation of Faith in 1983," 51–68
- "Liberating Theology: Reflecting on J.-B. Metz's Political Theology" = "Liberating Theology," 69–84
- "Discontinuities in Christian Dogmas," 85–109
- "Theological Quests," [from *Theologisch testament*, pp. 69–137], 111–61
- "Culture, Religion and Violence: Theology as a Component of Culture," = "Culture, Religion and Violence," 163–82
- "Towards a Rediscovery of the Christian Sacraments: Ritualising Religious Elements in Daily Life," = "Towards a Rediscovery of the Christian Sacraments," 183–210

# Chapter 1

# Introducing Edward Schillebeeckx

## *A Theologian for Our Time*

Stephan van Erp and Daniel Minch

The Flemish Dominican, Edward Cornelis Florent Schillebeeckx, began his life during the German occupation of Belgium in 1914. Neutral Belgium once again became the battlefield of Europe, and the site of some of the most intense fighting as well as the first large-scale poison gas attacks. As a young man, Schillebeeckx joined the Dominican Order and thereby became a part of a long tradition of theology in the Catholic world. He himself contributed greatly to the Catholic theological tradition, especially during and after the Second Vatican Council. He became an internationally renowned scholar, a bestselling author in multiple languages, a controversial flashpoint, and a representative of the Catholic Church in the Netherlands all at once. It is no exaggeration to say that he is one of the most influential Christian thinkers of the twentieth century, and certainly one of the most important post-conciliar Catholic theologians in the world. This is to say that Schillebeeckx is clearly a worthy subject for a *T&T Clark Handbook*. His theological oeuvre is both broad and deep, and there is an international community of scholars who continue to carry on his work, both explicitly through "Schillebeeckx studies" and implicitly after having been influenced by him. The present is also an opportune time for this volume to appear.

There are two "forerunners" of sorts to this volume, but neither has the same aims nor quite the same scope as what we have brought together here. Most well known, of course, is the revised and expanded second edition of *The Praxis of the Reign of God*, edited by Mary Catherine Hilkert and Robert J. Schreiter.[1] This "Introduction" to Schillebeeckx's theology has the distinct advantage of bearing Schillebeeckx's own *Imprimatur* in the form of a theological prologue.[2] It provides eleven chapters that indeed introduce the main themes in Schillebeeckx's work which were considered most crucial at the time. Second, there is the volume *Edward Schillebeeckx and Contemporary Theology*, edited by Lieven Boeve, Frederiek Depoortere, and Stephan van Erp.[3] This volume markedly contains a brief but inspirational note from Schillebeeckx to the scholars

---

[1]  Mary Catherine Hilkert and Robert J. Schreiter, eds., *The Praxis of the Reign of God: An Introduction to the Theology of Edward Schillebeeckx*, 2nd ed. (New York: Fordham University Press, 2002).

[2]  Edward Schillebeeckx, "Prologue: Human God-Talk and God's Silence," *The Praxis of the Reign of God: An Introduction to the Theology of Edward Schillebeeckx*, ed. Mary Catherine Hilkert and Robert J. Schreiter, 2nd ed. (New York: Fordham University Press, 2002), ix–xviii.

[3]  Lieven Boeve, Frederiek Depoortere, and Stephan van Erp, eds., *Edward Schillebeeckx and Contemporary Theology* (London: T&T Clark, 2010).

who attended a conference in his honor on December 3–6, 2008.[4] He had been too ill to attend himself, and he died just over a year later, on December 23, 2009. *Edward Schillebeeckx and Contemporary Theology* is less of an overview of Schillebeeckx's own work than a constructive application of his theological legacy to the contemporary context, such as it was in 2009.

Times change, and so do the needs and interests of theologians. The previous volumes represent the collective efforts of what we can broadly call "first generation" and "second generation" Schillebeeckx scholars. The first generation—represented especially by Erik Borgman and two former holders of the Edward Schillebeeckx Chair at Radboud University Nijmegen, Robert Schreiter and Mary Catherine Hilkert—studied with Schillebeeckx or were also active in the last decades of his scholarly career. The second generation—which includes many notable theologians, including one of the editors of the current volume and current holder of the Schillebeeckx Chair, Stephan van Erp—came of age in the 1990s and early 2000s, during a period when Schillebeeckx's theological legacy was being called into question or somewhat suppressed by the ecclesial climate of the time. Today, a new generation of Schillebeeckx scholars is just now finding their footing in the world of theology. This "third generation" of young theologians represents both continuity and discontinuity with their mentors and teachers, including Schillebeeckx himself. Like the previous generations, they generally share concern for fundamental theological issues, as well as the environment, the role of women in the church, and the advancement of social liberation for all peoples. However, they have also been shaped by the global War on Terror, the uncertainty of the Great Recession, the ongoing sex abuse crisis and accompanying crises of authority and faith, and now the seemingly global resurgence of xenophobia, racism, and authoritarianism. This volume can certainly not address all of these issues, but we should be aware that these things lay behind and between the lines for many of the authors.

Above all, it is important that this volume represents all three generations of scholarship. Schillebeeckx himself never intended to found a "theological school," but it appears that one has grown quite organically on its own. It is therefore opportune to include everyone in a conversation about Schillebeeckx's theology and his relevance for the twenty-first century. This volume seeks to look back at the sources and trends that influenced Schillebeeckx, to carefully examine the content and development of his theology, and to meaningfully point the way toward the future and the ongoing reception of his work. We have been aided in this task by the recent publication by Bloomsbury of the *Collected Works of Edward Schillebeeckx* series, edited by Ted Schoof and Carl Sterkens with Robert Schreiter and Erik Borgman. The eleven volumes that have been published to date present amended translations of many of Schillebeeckx's most important works, including his Christology. These updated volumes have given English-speaking scholars a sturdy point of reference for their work, and even newly published material that was previously available only in Dutch.[5] Hopefully this series will continue to collect and make Schillebeeckx's work more widely available in several different formats.

---

[4] Edward Schillebeeckx, "Letter from Edward Schillebeeckx to the Participants in the Symposium 'Theology for the 21st Century: The Enduring Relevance of Edward Schillebeeckx for Contemporary Theology,'" *Edward Schillebeeckx and Contemporary Theology*, ed. Lieven Boeve, Frederiek Depoortere, and Stephan van Erp (London: T&T Clark, 2010), xiv–xv.

[5] See especially Schillebeeckx, *Essays, CW* vol. 11 (London: Bloomsbury T&T Clark, 2014). This volume includes several previously untranslated sections and difficult to access articles.

As scholars who stand in the tradition of Edward Schillebeeckx, we also look beyond him to the wider and deeper waters of the Catholic faith tradition. The great Dominican family influenced him, and it is notable that several Dominicans are authors here—from Dominican sisters to lay Dominicans (formerly the "third order") and young friars. Both lay and religious scholars are represented, as well as scholars of many nationalities working on different continents. The American contingent is quite strong, both because this is a volume aimed at the English-speaking world and because the reception of Schillebeeckx's work has historically been very extensive in the United States and Canada.

# I. A life in church and theology: Edward Schillebeeckx (1914–2009)

Before we turn to the structure and content of this volume, it is important to first speak about who Edward Schillebeeckx was and how he became one of the most important theologians of the modern age.

Edward Schillebeeckx was born on November 12, 1914 in Antwerp, Belgium. He was the sixth child in a large Catholic family of fourteen. In those days, such large families were quite common in Catholic circles, and the church played a central role in the life of the Schillebeeckx family. Even in primary school, young Edward was already an excellent student, and it was decided early on to send him to the Jesuit college and boarding school in Turnhout. For his further education, he chose the Dominicans who, as he put it, were "an order of grace and reason," and he entered the Dominican friary in Ghent.[6] Growing up in such a religious context did not, however, mean that the events in the world passed him by. He had strong views on the role of the church in the world, and, according to his biographer Erik Borgman, these views were actually what drew him to the Dominican Order in the first place. He chose a religious order that saw its role not so much over-against the world, but rather completely in and for the world.[7] It is precisely young Edward's orientation toward the world that caused Borgman to argue that the leitmotiv of his theology was a "theology of culture"—a theology of the world and its history.

Schillebeeckx studied philosophy and theology, a combination that was and still is quite common for seminarians. His philosophical teacher was Dominicus De Petter, the founder of the *Tijdschrift voor Filosofie*. In those days, De Petter was a well-known philosopher in the Low Countries thanks to his article "Impliciete Intuïtie" in which he confronted neo-Thomist philosophy—at that time still the "official" philosophy of the church—with the modern philosophies of Descartes and Kant.[8] De Petter taught Schillebeeckx about classical metaphysics

---

[6] Edward Schillebeeckx, *Theologisch testament: Notarieel nog niet verleden*, 2nd ed. (Baarn: Nelissen, 1995), 19–23, at 22.

[7] Erik Borgman, *Edward Schillebeeckx: A Theologian in His History*, trans. John Bowden (London/New York: Continuum, 2003), 29–37.

[8] Dominicus De Petter, "Impliciete intuïtie," *Tijdschrift voor Philosophie* 1 (1939), 84–105; Stephan van Erp, "Implicit Faith: Philosophical Theology After Schillebeeckx," *Edward Schillebeeckx and Contemporary Theology*, ed. Lieven Boeve, Frederiek Depoortere, and Stephan van Erp (London: T&T Clark, 2010), 209–23. See also Chapter 3 in this volume.

and Thomas's epistemology, but he also presented these in the context of the philosophical debates on knowledge and the role of the subject conducted by Edmund Husserl and the existentialist philosophers. Schillebeeckx was fascinated by philosophy, in particular that of Thomas Aquinas, and much of his earlier work was of a much more a philosophical nature. Thomas was a vital and indispensable part of the Dominican tradition, and philosophers like De Petter pointed out the need to rid his philosophy of neoscholastic misinterpretations. De Petter was also clear about the need for a modern interpretation of Aquinas. Schillebeeckx played an important part in this effort by writing about Thomas's philosophy of God, knowledge, and language and, in keeping with Dominican tradition, mainly reading Thomas himself rather than later interpretations of his work.[9] In that sense, Schillebeeckx was typical of his age. Theology was undergoing a process of development that could be characterized as both *ressourcement* and *aggiornamento*.

This combination of *ressourcement* and *aggiornamento* would also determine his approach in his dissertation on Thomas's doctrine of the sacraments. The subtitle of this rather impressive academic treatise can be translated as "a theological reflection on St. Thomas's teaching on the sacraments in light of the tradition and contemporary sacramental problematic" (*Theologische bezinning op S. Thomas' sacramentenleer in het licht van de traditie en van de hedendaagse sacramentsproblematiek*). The dissertation is a first indication of the main thrust of his later theology: trying to interpret the encounter with God, between tradition and situation.[10] Even this dissertation already shows Schillebeeckx's major talent for being able to first engage in a thorough historical an biblical analysis of the concept of "sacrament" before he moves on to a consideration of the Thomist theology of the sacraments. He then opens the way to the reformation of liturgical praxis that so many longed for in his days. He would elaborate on his insight with regard to the sacraments in his later books on marriage and Christology.[11] Schillebeeckx used "sacrament" as the impetus to come to philosophical, theological, and liturgical-practical innovations. He raised important questions, such as the difference between Platonic and Aristotelian interpretations of the sacraments and the historical Incarnation as the foundation for liturgical symbolic acts.

In 1958, Schillebeeckx was appointed as Professor of Dogmatics and the History of Christianity at the Catholic University of Nijmegen in the Netherlands (now Radboud University Nijmegen). This was a period in which the Catholic Church in Flanders and the Netherlands flourished, an age sometimes referred to as "the abundant Roman-Catholic life" ("Het Rijke Roomsche Leven"), an indication of the fact that Catholic identity was still a strong determining factor in the life of ordinary Catholics.

---

9  These essays have been collected in Edward Schillebeeckx, *RT, CW* vol. 2 (London: Bloomsbury T&T Clark, 2014).

10 Henricus Edward Schillebeeckx, *De sacramentele heilseconomie. Theologische bezinning op S. Thomas' sacramentenleer in het licht van de traditie en van de hedendaagse sacramentsproblematiek* (Antwerp/Bilthoven: 't Groeit/H. Nelissen, 1952). A French translation was published in 2004: Edward Schillebeeckx, *L'économie sacramentelle du salut: réflexion théologique sur la doctrine sacramentaire de saint Thomas, à la lumière de la tradition et de la problématique sacramentelle contemporaine*, Studia Friburgensia 95 (Fribourg: Academic Press, 2004).

11 Edward Schillebeeckx, *Christ the Sacrament, CW* vol. 1 (London: Bloomsbury T&T Clark, 2014); Edward Schillebeeckx, *Marriage: Human Reality and Saving Mystery*, trans. N.D. Smith, vol. 1 & 2 (New York: Sheed and Ward, 1965).

This was also the period in which the church announced that it would take time to reflect on the challenges of the modern age by means of an ecumenical council: the Second Vatican Council (1962–1965). The expectations that many people had for this Council led to a theological enthusiasm which, among other things, moved Schillebeeckx in 1961 to start a new theological journal for Flanders and the Netherlands: *Tijdschrift voor Theologie*. In the introduction to the very first issue, he wrote: "There is much talk of what is new in Catholic theology these days. This should not baffle us or raise our suspicion. What is meant is not a different theology, but the old theology of the church itself which has possessed itself more strongly of the realities of faith."[12] This first issue also contained a visionary document by the Dutch bishops on the challenges of the Council which they expect would bring an "internal renewal and reformation of catholic life."[13] The document concludes by explicitly mentioning "professor dr. E. Schillebeeckx" and thanking him for his contributions to this text, which are indeed unmistakable. He would go on to play an important role as advisor to the Dutch bishops.[14]

Eventually, Schillebeeckx would have both words of praise and criticism for the Council. In particular, he praised the church's openness to the world and the modern age, the importance of scripture as a symbol of the church, the recognition of freedom of religion, and the theological emphasis on salvation for people within history—all of which he believed were important gains. But he was also critical because he feared that the Council would become an excuse to shy away from real and enduring innovations, or that the dogmatic implications of the Council documents would not be examined further. He feared that instead the main emphasis would be given to the "pastoral" aspects of the Council, but in the wrong sense of the word: merely "pastoral" as psychological and consoling. He also suspected that some would abuse the Council documents, and thereby lead to further polarization between progressive and conservative members of the church. He believed that the Council had only been the start of something much larger, and that its documents should really form the basis for the work that had yet to be done. In 1965, together with Karl Rahner, Yves Congar, Hans Küng, and Johann Baptist Metz he founded the international theological journal *Concilium* to further expand on the ideas of the Council.

Schillebeeckx remained active as the Dutch bishops' advisor during the Dutch Pastoral Council (1966–1970). The bishops hoped to use this pastoral council to consider the results of the Second Vatican Council and its implications for the Dutch Church. This council would gain national and international notoriety for its discussion on priestly celibacy, particularly when during the final session, it was decided to abandon celibacy. In the Netherlands, this would form the starting point of a far-reaching polarization between progressive and conservative Catholics. From that moment on, Schillebeeckx was seen as an exponent of the progressive side, even though he himself counseled restraint and would always point out the validity of more traditional ideas. As a result of the discussion in church and society, politics became an important subject of his theology. He developed this theopolitical part of his work partially under the influence of Jürgen Habermas's critical theory of society and Johann Baptist Metz's political theology,

---

[12] "Ter Oriëntering," *TvT* 1 (1961), 1.

[13] "De Bisschoppen van Nederland over het concilie," *TvT* 1 (1961), 71–90, at 72.

[14] He commented on this later, for example in Edward Schillebeeckx, *I Am a Happy Theologian: Conversations with Francesco Strazzari*, trans. John Bowden (London: SCM Press, 1994), 17.

although his "political" concerns were more fundamentally a product of his theological concerns about "the world."

Shortly after the Second Vatican Council, Schillebeeckx's theology changed quite dramatically. As he himself acknowledged, this was the result of the introduction of contemporary philosophical hermeneutics into theology. According to Schillebeeckx, hermeneutics is a method for interpreting the Christian message in general, and scripture in particular, from within the modern frame of reference while staying true to the Word of God. Moreover, hermeneutics is an instrument for the justification and explanation of the Christian interpretation of reality to people who have different faiths and worldviews.[15] Hermeneutics actually served to make Schillebeeckx's theological intent more explicit, which on the one hand aimed for a proper understanding of tradition, and, on the other, to make it relevant to contemporary people in the contemporary situation. Hermeneutical reflection could now serve to explain the theological motives of this intent. After all, such reflection allowed Schillebeeckx to point to a new theological foundation, notably that experience and interpretation also could function as ways in which God reveals Godself in history.

Schillebeeckx's integration of hermeneutics is therefore not simply a theological appreciation of the contextuality and historicity of the Christian message. To him, it is also the way in which revelation can be thought of, and it is actually the form that it takes in the world. He saw context and interpretation in sacramental terms—as instances in which the presence of God could be experienced. This made the interpretation of contemporary history into a primary source for his theology—a *locus theologicus*—and interpretations of revelation are themselves stories about the salvific Christ Event. Therefore, hermeneutics is more than a methodology in his theological reflection. It is an essential part of the fabric of reality itself, and it is essentially related to the process and structure of revelation within creation.

The discovery of history, experience, and interpretation as sources of theology had a major impact on the direction of his thought. After 1968, he repeatedly distanced himself from the neo-Thomism of De Petter's metaphysics and therefore also the approach and the ideological background of his own publications prior to the Council. This was the main reason he abandoned the series *Theological Soundings* after volume five (*The Understanding of Faith*), even though ten volumes had originally been planned. He believed that hermeneutics would be needed to make these texts suitable for use in our day and age.

After the Council, he intensified his teaching in Nijmegen and lectured about hermeneutics and Christology.[16] Meanwhile, he had started preparations for a book on Christology which was meant to be the first of three volumes. He read a great amount of exegetical literature for this first volume, which would be entitled *Jesus, the Story of One Who Is Alive* (1974), and which appeared in English as *Jesus: An Experiment in Christology.*[17] With this exegetical-

---

[15] Edward Schillebeeckx, *UF, CW* vol. 5 (London: Bloomsbury T&T Clark, 2014).

[16] For more on Schillebeeckx's lectures and the development that can be traced in them, see Ted Schoof, "E. Schillebeeckx: 25 Years in Nijmegen, I," *Theology Digest* 37 (1990): 313–32; Ted Schoof, "E. Schillebeeckx: 25 Years in Nijmegen, II," *Theology Digest* 38 (1991): 31–44. See also Chapter 9 of this volume by Daniel Minch.

[17] Edward Schillebeeckx, *Jezus, het verhaal van een levende*, Baarn 1974; ET: Edward Schillebeeckx, *Jesus, CW* vol. 6 (London: Bloomsbury T&T Clark, 2014).

historical study, Schillebeeckx agreed with the conclusions of the Council that scripture should form an integral part of the life of the church and of theology. It resulted in a systematic theology firmly based on exegesis. The second volume of the trilogy carried the title *Justice and love, Grace and liberation* (1977) in Dutch. In English, it was known as *Christ: The Christian Experience in the Modern World* (UK version), and *Christ: The Experience of Jesus as Lord* (US version). This volume is generally considered to be one of the most important of Schillebeeckx's works, and together with the first they are two of the most important Christological books of the twentieth century.[18] In *Christ* he discusses the other books of the New Testament apart from the four gospels, and addresses issues around grace, salvation, and the mystery of human suffering. Moreover, he elaborates his political theology in a discussion with Johann Baptist Metz.

Around the same time, he had set a new theological course in Christology which won international recognition and fame; the church had begun an investigation into the orthodoxy of his theology. In 1968, questions had been raised about his work, and following the publication of his first *Jesus* book, an investigation was started, after which the Sacred Congregation for the Doctrine of the Faith decided to ask him a number of questions about the work in 1976.[19] Those questions mainly concerned the historical-critical method, the alleged primacy of the humanity of Jesus, the role of Jesus as a prophet as a denial of his messianic qualities, the Trinity and the virginal conception of Jesus. Schillebeeckx did not limit himself to answering the Congregation's questions, but also wrote an "intermezzo" after the second volume of the trilogy: *Interim Report.*[20] It would take well over a year after the final discussions in Rome in 1979 for this investigation to be concluded.[21] In a letter of November 20, 1980, Schillebeeckx was asked to publish his answers, and to declare his intent to obey doctrinal authority with regard to some of the doubts the Congregation still had, in particular about his idea of the relation between revelation and experience.

In 1982, he was awarded the prestigious Erasmus Prize, which recognizes significant contributions to European society and culture. This was an important appreciation of his work from an entirely different part of society than that of the Catholic Church. In this he joined such notable recipients such as Marc Chagall, Romano Guardini, Martin Buber, Claude Lévi-Strauss, Simon Wiesenthal, Mary Robinson, and many others. He pushed on to new territory with his next publication on ministry in the church, particularly priestly ministry. This again gave rise to problems with the doctrinal authorities. The Congregation for the Doctrine of Faith sent him a letter, dated June 13, 1984, in which it asked him to renounce what he had written in the late

---

[18] Edward Schillebeeckx, *Gerechtigheid en liefde: Genade en bevrijding*, Baarn 1977; ET: Edward Schillebeeckx, *Christ, CW* vol. 7 (London: Bloomsbury T&T Clark, 2014).

[19] Ted Mark Schoof, ed., *The Schillebeeckx Case: Official Exchange of Letters and Documents in the Investigation of Fr. Edward Schillebeeckx, O.P. by the Sacred Congregation for the Doctrine of the Faith, 1976–1980*, trans. Matthew J. O'Connell (New York: Paulist Press, 1984). Also see the special issue of *Tijdschrift voor Theologie*: "De zaak Schillebeeckx: reflecties en reacties," *TvT* 20 (1981), and especially Chapter 13 of this volume by Leo Kenis and Lieven Boeve.

[20] Edward Schillebeeckx, *Tussentijds verhaal over twee Jezusboeken*, Bloemendaal 1978; Edward Schillebeeckx, *IR, CW* vol. 8 (London: Bloomsbury T&T Clark, 2014).

[21] The letter containing the final judgment of the Congregation is included in *The Schillebeeckx Case*, 141–44.

1970s, largely in reaction to what he and many others had seen as ecclesiastical emergency.[22] He would have to agree to the doctrine of the church as formulated in a letter the Congregation had sent to the bishops of the Catholic Church, concerning issues with regard to ministers of the Eucharist, *Sacerdotium ministeriale* of August 6, 1983. He promised to address the issue in a new book, which he did in 1985 with a monograph entitled *The Church with a Human Face* (*Pleidooi voor mensen in de kerk*), which ends with a declaration:

> Greater confidence from the leaders of the church in the Spirit of God which also plays an inscrutable role in the community of the church, and indeed outside it, in secular events, would help our Christian communities to show more gospel-inspired vitality, with the permanent but restrained oversight (*episkope*) of the pastoral ministry of the church's *magisterium*.[23]

In response to this, Joseph Ratzinger, now prefect of the CDF issued a notification dated September 15, 1986, in which he claimed Schillebeeckx persisted in holding to an idea of priestly ministry that the Congregation regarded as in violation of church doctrine.[24] However, an explicit condemnation of Schillebeeckx was never issued.

By the time this took place Schillebeeckx had retired from his position as professor in Nijmegen.[25] In his farewell lecture, he unfolds a vision for a theology that moves critically between "tradition" and "situation." The tradition of faith, he writes, is a tradition which is "fraught with religious meaning *that possesses transformative, innovative, liberating, ultimately redemptive power.*"[26] The situation is "the current context which offers an answer, or various answers, to the question of how Christians, qua Christians, are in fact situated in this secular modern culture and society and how they deal with its intellectual and experiential categories."[27] According to Schillebeeckx, an important theological problem arises between tradition and situation which forever requires new answers and new reflection: "a perennial dialectics between the universality of the gospel, which challenges every culture critically and transcends it, and its concrete manifestation in particular cultures. Only in concrete particularity can the gospel reveal the universality of salvation coming from God."[28]

After his books on theology of ministry and two collections of sermons and shorter writings, he published two more major works. The first, *Church: The Human Story of God*,

---

22 Edward Schillebeeckx, *Basis en ambt: Ambt in dienst van nieuwe gemeentevorming*, Bloemendaal 1979.
23 Edward Schillebeeckx, *CHF, CW* vol. 9 (London: Bloomsbury T&T Clark, 2014), 249 [266–67].
24 Congregation for the Doctrine of the Faith, *Notification on the book Pleidooi voor mensen in de kerk. Christelijke identiteit en ambten in de kerk (Nelissen, Baarn 1985), by Professor Edward Schillebeeckx, O.P.* (September 15, 1985), http://www.vatican.va/roman_curia/congregations/cfaith/documents/rc_con_cfaith_doc_19860915_libro-schillebeeckx_en.html.
25 His farewell lecture has been published as Edward Schillebeeckx, "Theological Interpretation of Faith in 1983," *Essays, CW* vol. 11 (London: Bloomsbury T&T Clark, 2014), 51–68.
26 Ibid., 55. Emphasis original.
27 Ibid., 56.
28 Ibid., 57. For an extensive discussion of this theological problem, see Chapter 10 by Daniel Minch in this volume.

was the long anticipated third volume of his *Jesus* trilogy.[29] Although it does deal with the church, as its title promises, this only takes up about one-third of the book. He gets to the topic only after he has recapitulated and reformulated his anthropology and hermeneutics, and after he has discussed some important Christological concepts, such as the resurrection and the meaning of the "Kingdom of God" in the light of what the situation of religious pluralism and ideological pluralism. It is a very readable book which is still very popular among students, and it serves as an excellent introduction to his entire oeuvre. Schillebeeckx's final work is fittingly entitled *Theological Testament* (*Theologisch testament*), which incidentally has the rather paradoxical subtitle, roughly translated "a first draft of an ongoing past" (*Notarieel nog niet verleden*).[30] Apart from a short autobiography of about sixty pages, it also contains several short essays on dogma, creation and grace, eschatology, and the doctrine of God. From this brief description it is clear that the heart of Schillebeeckx's theology lies within dogmatics. Despite all of his work on hermeneutics and his political engagement, in the end he was still trying to express the nature of the relationship between God and humanity. He believed that hermeneutics and politics formed an integral part of this theological task. This concern was again demonstrated in an article published in *Tijdschrift voor Theologie* in 2000 on ritual studies and sacramentality, which would turn out to be one of his final academic articles.[31] In some sense, he returned to his first interest in a theology of the sacraments. In fact, he announced that he was working on a new book on the sacraments in the final decade of his life. He spent a great deal of time preparing and writing notes for the book, but unfortunately it ultimately never appeared.

On December 23, 2009, Edward Schillebeeckx quietly passed away after a long illness with a feeling of gratitude. The occasion of his death drew quite a bit of media attention, not just in the Netherlands, but also in the rest of the world. He was eulogized in newspapers, academic journals, and in Catholic periodicals both in print and online. This served as yet another reminder of how his work continues to be highly appreciated and that so many recognize his influence on their own work. At the time of his death, his longtime friend Hadewych (Dory) Snijdewind O.P., who cared for him during his illness, was with him. She recorded his last words: "Dory, God is calling me."[32] At 5:15 p.m., Edward Schillebeeckx answered God's call one final time after a life of faithful service to the church and to the Lord.

---

[29] Edward Schillebeeckx, *Mensen als verhaal van God*, Baarn 1989; ET: Edward Schillebeeckx, *Church*, *CW* vol. 10 (London: Bloomsbury T&T Clark, 2014).

[30] The second half of *Theologisch testament* (pp. 69–137) has been translated as Edward Schillebeeckx, "Theological Quests," *Essays*, *CW* vol. 11 (London: Bloomsbury T&T Clark, 2014), 111–61. For the events during Schillebeeckx's final years, see Ted Schoof, "Edward Schillebeeckx: de laatste twintig jaar," *Trouw aan Gods toekomst: de blijvende betekenis van Edward Schillebeeckx*, ed. Stephan van Erp (Amsterdam: Boom, 2010), 144–52.

[31] Edward Schillebeeckx, "Naar een herontdekking van de christelijke sacramenten: Ritualisering van religieuze momenten in het alledaagse leven," *TvT* 40 (2000): 164–87; ET: Edward Schillebeeckx, "Towards a Rediscovery of the Christian Sacraments," *Essays*, *CW* vol. 11 (London: Bloomsbury T&T Clark, 2014), 183–210.

[32] Edward Schillebeeckx, *Verhalen van een levende: Theologische preken van Edward Schillebeeckx*, ed. Hadewych Snijdewind (Nijmegen: Valkhof Pers, 2015), 439.

# II. State of Schillebeeckx research

In 2010, Robert Schreiter found that there had been at least eighty-two dissertations on Schillebeeckx's work.[33] To that number, we can add at least fourteen completed dissertations since 2008 (with around nine more currently in preparation). There have been two recent conferences on Schillebeeckx's work, one in Nijmegen commemorating his one hundredth birthday in August of 2014: "Grace, Governance and Globalisation: Theology and Public Life." This conference may in fact have marked a deliberate *political* turn in the interpretation and reception of Schillebeeckx's theology. Another conference, "The Authority of the Church in Politics," on the future of Catholic political theology was held in Leuven in 2016. There continue to be regular seminars and conference panels organized in Leuven and at the Catholic Theological Society of America, involving international and intergenerational groups of scholars. This collaboration looks to be on the increase as we enter a new phase in international and interdisciplinary cooperation between individual scholars and universities alike.

In terms of published monographs, there have been several recent attempts to either explicate or recontextualize Edward Schillebeeckx's work. Robert Schreiter has noted that of the dissertations on Schillebeeckx, the most popular topics include Christology, method and hermeneutics, soteriology, experience, revelation, and suffering.[34] In the first few years of this decade, the most prominent published studies include Edmund Kee-Fook Chia's application of Schillebeeckx's work to interreligious dialogue, specifically from the perspective of Asian theology; Steven M. Rodenborn's comparison of Johann Baptist Metz and Schillebeeckx's respective eschatological positions; Martin Poulsom's more Thomistically oriented study explores his theology of creation; Kathleen Dolphin's detailed study of the practical theology present in Schillebeeckx's sermons; Carsten Barwasser's assessment of Schillebeeckx's theology of culture; and Jennifer Cooper's work on the theological anthropology that is implicit in Schillebeeckx's early thought.[35] There have been significant edited volumes from European

---

[33] Robert Schreiter, "De invloed van Edward Schillebeeckx—De dissertaties over zijn werk," *Trouw aan Gods toekomst: De blijvende betekenis van Edward Schillebeeckx*, ed. Stephan van Erp (Amsterdam: Boom, 2010), 153–65.

[34] Schreiter, "De invloed van Edward Schillebeeckx," 158.

[35] Edmund Kee-Fook Chia, *Edward Schillebeeckx and Interreligious Dialogue: Perspectives from Asian Theology* (Eugene, OR: Pickwick Publications, 2012); Steven M. Rodenborn, *Hope in Action: Subversive Eschatology in the Theology of Edward Schillebeeckx and Johann Baptist Metz* (Minneapolis, MN: Fortress Press, 2014); Martin G. Poulsom, *The Dialectics of Creation: Creation and the Creator in Edward Schillebeeckx and David Burrell* (London: Bloomsbury T&T Clark, 2014); Kathleen Dolphin, *Praxis-Oriented Theology and Spirituality in the Sermons of Edward Schillebeeckx* (Lewiston, NY: The Edwin Mellen Press, 2014); Carsten Barwasser, *Theologie der Kultur und Hermeneutik der Glaubenserfahrung: Zur Gottesfrage und Glaubensverantwortung bei Edward Schillebeeckx OP* (Berlin: LIT, 2010); Jennifer Cooper, *Humanity in the Mystery of God: The Theological Anthropology of Edward Schillebeeckx* (London: T&T Clark, 2011). For a more full review and assessment of the literature, see Christiane Alpers and Daniel Minch, "Edward Schillebeeckx in de hedendaagse theologie," *TvT* 54 (2014), 398–409.

perspectives and from scholars from the global South, which illustrate the breadth and diversity of the reception of his work.[36] More recently, the *T&T Clark Studies in Edward Schillebeeckx* series has brought us two important volumes on Schillebeeckx studies, representing both junior (third generation) and senior scholars (first and second generation) in the field.[37] Recent monographs touch subjects such as suffering and intercultural theology, as with the work of Kevin P. Considine; Christiane Alpers's work explores public theology in a post-liberal and post-Christian context; Daniel Minch's in-depth analysis of the hermeneutical-eschatological structure of human subjectivity and contemporary economics; and Bernhard Kohl's assessment of suffering in search of a "negative anthropology."[38] These monographs come alongside many journal articles and book chapters, as well as numerous master's and bachelor's theses by students all over the world. The work goes on, and Schillebeeckx's ideas and language have slowly become part of the vernacular of Catholic theology, from his calls for orthopraxis and liberation, to his explication of Jesus as the "eschatological messiah," and especially his now famous dictum: *extra mundum nulla salus*—there is no salvation outside of the world.

All of this is to say that the field of Schillebeeckx studies is wide, and fairly diverse. It is not dominated by a small, dwindling number of hold-outs from the 1970s and 1980s. Schillebeeckx never strictly stayed in one area of theology. His exegesis is also fundamental theology, and his methodological works contain Christological insights. He never wrote an "anthropology," but theological anthropology is everywhere in his writings. Further, there are elements of political theology in his work on mysticism and even the "nature/grace" debate. He is at once a rather unsystematic thinker, and a true systematic theologian who seeks to hold together all of the strands of Catholic thought available to him in order to come to the most complete understanding of the divine mystery. Even with such a comprehensive approach, God remains "a limit-concept without content for us."[39] We are compelled to continue to talk about this mystery of faith; however, we can only "talk in a stammering way about God, but in doing so in fact talk about the reality of God and not just about conceptions of God."[40] There is, therefore, an essential tension

---

[36]   Thomas Eggensperger, Ulrich Engel, and Angel F. Méndez Montoya, eds., *Edward Schillebeeckx: Impulse für Theologien im 21. Jahrhundert/Impetus Towards Theologies in the 21st Century* (Ostfildern: Grünewald, 2012); Helen F. Bergin, ed., *From North to South: Southern Scholars Engage with Edward Schillebeeckx.* (Hindmarsh: ATF Theology, 2013).

[37]   Stephan van Erp, Lieven Boeve, and Martin G. Poulsom, eds., *Grace, Governance, and Globalization,* T&T Clark Studies in Edward Schillebeeckx (London: Bloomsbury T&T Clark, 2017); Stephan van Erp, Christopher Cimorelli, and Christiane Alpers, eds., *Salvation in the World: The Crossroads of Public Theology,* T&T Clark Studies in Edward Schillebeeckx (London: Bloomsbury T&T Clark, 2017).

[38]   Kevin P. Considine, *Salvation for the Sinned-Against: Han and Schillebeeckx in Intercultural Dialogue,* Missional Church, Public Theology, World Christianity 5 (Eugene, Oregon: Pickwick Publications, 2015); Christiane Alpers, *A Politics of Grace: Hope for Redemption in a Post-Christendom Context,* T&T Clark Studies in Edward Schillebeeckx (London: T&T Clark, 2018); Daniel Minch, *Eschatological Hermeneutics: The Theological Core of Experience and Our Hope for Salvation,* T&T Clark Studies in Edward Schillebeeckx (New York: T&T Clark, 2018); Bernhard Kohl, *Die Anerkennung des Verletzbaren: eine Rekonstruktion der negativen Hermeneutik der Gottebenbildlichkeit aus den Anerkennungstheorien Judith Butlers und Axel Honneths und der Theologie Edward Schillebeeckx',* Erfurter theologische Studien 110 (Würzburg: Echter, 2017).

[39]   Schillebeeckx, *Church,* 72 [74].

[40]   Ibid., 75 [77].

in Schillebeeckx's work between reality, expression, and interpretation. This applies to human experience, and in a special way to humanity's ability to experience salvation coming from God, and to then mediate that experience to others. The first Christians had this basic experience of salvation in their encounter with Jesus of Nazareth. One of the most important questions for Christian faith continues to be that of how we in the present can continue to experience this same salvation, despite the intervening centuries of history and all of the many human failures and tragedies that have come with that history.

# III. Content and structure of this *Handbook*

We have divided this *Handbook* into four main parts in order to best and most clearly present the fine work of our authors. The four parts are structured thematically as well as chronologically. The aim of the sections is to present the reader with an in-depth consideration of different aspects of Edward Schillebeeckx's life and theology, since the two are inextricably linked with one another. His formation as a young theologian and relationship to his context is essential for understanding how and why his work developed as it did. As we will see, history and theology cannot be separated, and so even strictly "dogmatic" considerations never remain merely at the level of theory.

Part I, "Sources," presents chapters on the various influences on Schillebeeckx in his work and in his life as a Dominican theologian. Wilhelmus Valkenberg (Catholic University of America) begins this volume with his chapter on the role of Thomas Aquinas in Schillebeeckx's thought. It is well known that Schillebeeckx wrote his dissertation under the direction of his confrere Marie-Dominique Chenu on Thomas's sacramental theology, and therefore Valkenberg rightly focuses on Schillebeeckx's early work. He also, however, aims to show how Thomas shaped major themes in Schillebeeckx's theology that were broadly consistent across the whole of his career, and not merely in one early "phase" that faded away after the Second Vatican Council. Similarly, Stephan van Erp (KU Leuven/RU Nijmegen) and Dries Bosschaert (KU Leuven) have crafted a chapter on the importance of another of Schillebeeckx's early influences, namely, his philosophy teacher and confrere, Dominicus De Petter. De Petter was an important figure in twentieth-century Catholic philosophy, and he taught his students in Leuven modern philosophical sources, including Immanuel Kant and Edmund Husserl, while also developing his own "realist metaphysics" as a challenge to the dominant, but rapidly deteriorating, neoscholastic synthesis. Karim Schelkens (Tilburg University/KU Leuven) and Jürgen Mettepenningen (KU Leuven) have provided us with an important and finely detailed account of Schillebeeckx's reception of *nouvelle théologie*, the movement of "returning to the sources" of theology which was especially active in France and Belgium prior to the Second Vatican Council. The authors locate Schillebeeckx in this movement and provide important background on the Jesuits and Dominicans who led the charge for theological renewal, especially the school for Dominicans outside of Paris, Le Saulchoir, which was led by Chenu until 1942. The importance of the Dominican Order in the renewal of Catholic life in the twentieth century should not be underestimated. In the chapter by Erik Borgman (Tilburg University) and Anton Milh (KU Leuven), the authors make it clear that Schillebeeckx was, first and foremost, a Dominican. This tradition shaped his faith life as well as his theology, and they delve into his often-neglected writings specifically on the subject of "Dominican spirituality." This is an especially important contribution for international audiences, because it contextualizes Schillebeeckx in both his time and faith tradition. Finally, Anthony J. Godzieba (Villanova University) provides an illuminating chapter on Schillebeeckx's phenomenology of experience. Specifically, Godzieba examines the "phenomenological context" of his theological reception of Martin Heidegger and Maurice Merleau-Ponty. This relates directly to how Schillebeeckx would later controversially apply this phenomenological framework to his explication of Jesus's resurrection. This aspect of Schillebeeckx's theology has often been misunderstood or misinterpreted, and Godzieba's valuable contribution helps to contextualize and clarify Schillebeeckx's faith in the resurrection.

Part II, "The Second Vatican Council and Its Aftermath," takes up the subject of Schillebeeckx's activity during and after the Second Vatican Council as a vocal member of the Dutch and the World Church. These chapters explore his influence on the Council as an advisor to the Dutch bishops, his activity in the Netherlands, and, most dramatically, the various Vatican investigations into his orthodoxy. This section also looks at the "turn" in Schillebeeckx's thought toward continental philosophy that began to become evident in his work in the late 1960s. He began to more explicitly engage with hermeneutic and existential philosophy, linguistic analysis, and historical critical biblical scholarship in order to make the content of Christian faith understandable to modern people. Joris Geldhof (KU Leuven) and Leo Kenis (KU Leuven) begin this section with a detailed theological and historical account of Schillebeeckx's activities on the eve of the Council, especially on behalf of the Dutch bishops. His contributions to the preparations are set within Schillebeeckx's overall sacramental worldview, which remained an essential part of his work at the Council and in the years afterward. Stephan van Erp (KU Leuven/RU Nijmegen) then provides substantial insight into Schillebeeckx's theological activity at the Council itself, and in particular his influence on the debates concerning the relationship between the church and the world. Schillebeeckx saw the proposed drafts of what became *Gaudium et spes* as an opportunity for an ongoing rapprochement between the two, rather than as providing a definitive status quo. In line with Schillebeeckx's reconsideration of the church-world relationship, Daniel Minch (University of Graz) explores the "hermeneutical turn" in Schillebeeckx's thought, and in particular his integration and methodological use of philosophical hermeneutics and critical theory. In the first of two chapters, Minch contextualizes this hermeneutical turn by showing the concern for authentic and faithful mediation of Christian faith which arose during and after the Council. Minch also shows the development of Schillebeeckx's teaching on the subject of theological hermeneutics in the courses he offered in Nijmegen, which illustrates the remarkable consistency in his call for both "theory" and critical "praxis." This chapter is followed by a second, more "synthetic" presentation of Schillebeeckx's overall hermeneutical framework, and the role it plays in his Christology. Minch tracks the full integration of critical theory, including the work of thinkers like Theodor Adorno and Jürgen Habermas in Schillebeeckx's attempts to mediate the perceived gap between theory and praxis, especially when confronted by concrete suffering in history. Minch then examines the key terms "tradition" and "situation" in Schillebeeckx's mature theology.

Returning to the direct historical results of the Council, Erik Borgman (Tilburg University) and Thijs Caspers give an account of the aftermath in the Netherlands. Schillebeeckx was the leading Dutch theologian in the period immediately following the Council, and so, Borgman and Caspers show the role that he played in the rapidly modernizing and secularizing Dutch context. Central to Schillebeeckx's theology is the need to make Christian faith, and specifically Christology, intelligible to modern people. Laura Tack (KU Leuven) delves more deeply into the issue of Christology, and specifically Schillebeeckx's use of historical critical sources in his bestselling *Jesus* volumes. This significant and detailed chapter highlights the consistent use of the Bible by Schillebeeckx for fundamental theology. His work becomes more sophisticated in the way he approaches the Bible up until his first *Jesus* book. Historical criticism ultimately forms part of Schillebeeckx's fundamental theological framework, and Tack helps to contextualize how he integrated this discipline and how it was viewed by his contemporaries. The final contribution to Part II comes from Leo Kenis (KU Leuven) and Lieven Boeve (KU Leuven). The authors offer the most complete and concise explanation to date of the three investigations of Schillebeeckx by the Congregation for the Doctrine of the Faith. The second case, regarding his *Jesus* volumes, is most well known, but the authors provide important insights into the investigations which preceded and followed that famous case. Despite the strong optimism following the Second Vatican Council coming from many quarters of the church, this chapter shows clearly how slow structures were to change, and the real conditions in which theology continued to be scrutinized by the magisterium.

Part III, "Theological Themes," deals with doctrinal and fundamental topics which were central to Schillebeeckx's work throughout his career. This is a substantial and diverse set of chapters, dealing with his thinking on traditional doctrines such as redemption, grace, and the role of Mary in the church. Although Schillebeeckx is often cast as having been deeply "philosophical" or "political," his theology was, in fact, always deeply marked by his commitment to the Catholic tradition. This is evident in Philip Kennedy's (University of Oxford) contribution on Schillebeeckx's theology of God. Kennedy proceeds from two "pillars" which act as the foundation of his theology: belief in God the Creator, and belief in Jesus Christ who is concentrated creation and in whom people find salvation. Kennedy expertly outlines the main points which ground Schillebeeckx's theology, making this a truly foundational essay especially for this section on doctrine. Martin G. Poulsom (University of Roehampton) provides a deeper reflection on Schillebeeckx's theology of creation, his "creation faith." Poulsom locates the source of Schillebeeckx's understanding of creation in his reading of Thomas Aquinas, marking Schillebeeckx as a deeply traditional Catholic thinker. Poulsom then moves forward to show how the insights articulated in Schillebeeckx's creation faith can help us today in the midst of the contemporary ecological crisis. Joris Geldhof (KU Leuven) then explores what he calls "Schillebeeckx's Sacramental Theology of the Sacraments," situating the individual sacraments within an overarching sacramental worldview. This chapter provides English audiences with an important assessment of Schillebeeckx's dissertation (which has yet to be translated into English). Geldhof goes on to explore Schillebeeckx's later reflections on the role of liturgy, the Eucharist, and the "sacraments of life" in Christian faith, and how these fit with his earlier sacramental worldview.

In two chapters, Mary Catherine Hilkert (University of Notre Dame) details the development of Schillebeeckx's theological anthropology. This is particularly important because Schillebeeckx himself never wrote a specific work on the subject, and so Hilkert makes this vital, yet implicit, concept explicit. Her careful work encompasses both the "early" and "later" Schillebeeckx. Her first chapter begins, roughly, in the late 1950s when Schillebeeckx was appointed in Nijmegen, and takes the reader up to the end of the 1960s. The shift in his thinking toward hermeneutics and Christology becomes evident in her second chapter. Hilkert clearly elucidates the connection between soteriology, Christology, and anthropology that is present in Schillebeeckx's Christological trilogy. In Christiane Alpers's (Katholische Universität Eichstätt-Ingolstadt) chapter on "Christ and Grace," she argues for the importance of grace in Schillebeeckx's theological synthesis. She also contests the view that he too easily adapted the Christian message to the modern world by drawing on Schillebeeckx's own arguments. Alpers makes a significant comparison on this issue to the views of Henri de Lubac, a contemporary of Schillebeeckx's who is often held up as a counter-example with regard to modernity.

Bernard P. Prusak (Villanova University) has written a comprehensive summary of Schillebeeckx's controversial views on the resurrection of Jesus. Prusak provides insight into how Schillebeeckx's interpretation of the resurrection changed and evolved based on clarifications that he wrote in subsequent works following his 1974 book, *Jesus: An Experiment in Christology*. This includes changes in his thought due to a turn to matters concerning ministry and ecclesiology in the 1980s. Julia Feder (Creighton University) has crafted an excellent assessment of Schillebeeckx's writings on Mary and Mariology. Her contemporary perspective shows both the merits and shortcomings of Schillebeeckx's approach, as she illuminates an area of his work that has been often neglected, especially in English language scholarship. Kathleen McManus provides a chapter on the eschatological reality of the Reign of God. McManus details how histories of suffering can be viewed in light of eschatological salvation, and she applies Schillebeeckx's category of negative contrast experiences to marginalized groups, especially impoverished women who experience violence in everyday life. She shows the dialectic between suffering and resistance that Schillebeeckx believed revealed God's presence and solidarity with God's people.

Given Schillebeeckx's experiences with the Congregation for the Doctrine of the Faith and his later ecclesiological focus, it is significant that Daniel Speed Thompson (University of Dayton) has written a chapter explicitly exploring the issues of magisterium and authority in Schillebeeckx's theology. Thompson sketches out the contours of his thought on apostolicity and the continuity of authority within the Catholic tradition. He fills in the details of Schillebeeckx's call for a more humble approach to authority, or "ecclesiology in a minor key," and he connects this with the contemporary ecclesiological practice of Pope Francis. Mary Ann Hinsdale (Boston College) presents a chapter on Schillebeeckx's later theology of ministry. She begins by drawing parallels between the crisis in ministry experienced in Schillebeeckx's context, and the contemporary crises of ministry and authority that has resulted from the sex abuse crisis. In this light, she focuses on the shifts in his theology that occurred in the 1980s, and which affected his approach to issues of ecclesial leadership and ministry. Hinsdale then shows how Schillebeeckx's later methodology and theology of ministry can be useful in confronting the crisis of ministry experienced by Christians today.

Finally, Part IV, "Theology of Culture," approaches topics that are pertinent for everyday Christians and their experience of faith within modern society. Roger Haight (Union Theological Seminary) takes up the issue of how salvation in Christ can be meaningfully experienced in the contemporary, "postmodern" world. Haight argues that Schillebeeckx's Christology is based on principles derived from historicity, negativity, and praxis. These allow for us to construct a plausible and faithful Christological answer to the very real human questions concerning salvation. Michael E. Lee (Fordham University) takes up the problem of liberation and salvation, and explicitly with reference to Schillebeeckx's interaction with liberation theology. This is an important contribution that aims to illustrate the common roots of Schillebeeckx's theology and Latin American liberation theology in *nouvelle théologie*. Lee then provides insight into concrete contacts between Schillebeeckx and liberation theology, as well as Schillebeeckx's own desire for a "European" theology of liberation that was proper to the Western European context. Edmund Kee-Fook Chia (Australian Catholic University, Melbourne) attempts to break us out of "the European context" by looking to the reception of Schillebeeckx's ideas in Asian theology and theology of religious pluralism. Chia presents Schillebeeckx's Christology as a useful and constructive response to maximalist readings of *Dominus Iesus*, and the problems that this document has engendered for interreligious dialogue and pluralism in a globalized world. Rounding out this section and this volume, Elizabeth M. Pyne (Fordham University, London Centre) reads Schillebeeckx's theology in light of the contemporary ecological crisis. Pyne argues that Schillebeeckx's theology provides a constructive image of humanity in relation to the natural world. From this model, she argues for a "politics of nature" that is consonant with Christian faith in creation, and which can serve as a starting point for addressing the contemporary crisis as an imperative of the gospel.

Together with our contributors, we have aimed to create a truly forward-looking *Handbook* which is still suited to the times. We hope that the chapters that we have assembled here will provide a solid introduction into the life and work of Edward Schillebeeckx, but we also hope that it will also deepen the reflections of scholars who are already familiar with his work. This is meant to be a point of reception and study of Schillebeeckx's theological legacy, as well as a point of dissemination in order to provide guidance in well-traveled areas and inspiration to open up new fields of study. As we said before, Schillebeeckx did not consciously wish to create a theological "school" (although that has happened anyway), nor did he presume to write "for all time," as it were. He was aware of his own contextual limitations, but nonetheless something in his work resonated beyond that context, and this *Handbook* illustrates the ways in which that resonance has changed and grown over the decades since he first became a "household name" for theologians. We cannot predict what the future will hold for Schillebeeckx's theology, or whether or not he will be confirmed as a "theological classic" with perennial resonance for generations. What we can see, however, is that he has, in his own words, provided us with a fruitful "starting point for doing theology in the 21st century."[41] It was his wish, however, that this should *only* be seen as a starting point. Judging by the reception history of his work thus far, it is already far more than just a starting point, but rather a well-spring, a point of inspiration, and a stimulus for new theologians to follow his methodology and his example as a person of faith, in the knowledge that "every human action for justice, peace, and the integrity of creation is at the same time the gift of the silent God."[42]

---

[41]  Schillebeeckx, "Letter from Edward Schillebeeckx," xiv.
[42]  Ibid., xv.

# PART I

# Sources

# Chapter 2

# The Thomistic Roots of Schillebeeckx's Theology

## Pim Valkenberg

This chapter will look at the role of Thomas Aquinas (1225–1274) as an important source for Edward Schillebeeckx's theological oeuvre. Such a choice would seem to be almost redundant if one considers the fact that Schillebeeckx was a Dominican friar who wrote his doctoral dissertation on Aquinas's teaching on the sacraments. Yet I remember quite vividly a conversation in which Schillebeeckx showed some surprise at the suggestion that Aquinas was still an important influence in his writings. He clearly suggested that Aquinas once might have been an important source for his early work, yet because of the sharp turning points in his life and academic writings he would now no longer consider Aquinas as an important source.

## I. "Fault Lines": The importance of discontinuity in Schillebeeckx's theological identity

*"Breuklijnen"* ("Fault Lines") is the title of a small volume of essays, edited by Schillebeeckx in his function as editor in chief of the Dutch periodical *Tijdschrift voor Theologie*.[1] The volume was dedicated to his fellow Dominican, colleague, and close companion Ted Schoof on the occasion of his retirement from the Faculty of Theology at the Catholic University of Nijmegen in 1994. Schoof's task was teaching the history of theology, in line with his acclaimed survey of Catholic theology between 1800 and 1970, published in Dutch under the programmatic title *Aggiornamento: The breakthrough of a new Catholic theology*.[2] The metaphors used in these two book titles clearly suggest a significant change between the beginning of the theological careers of these two Dominican friars and their present status after the Second Vatican Council. Both Schillebeeckx and Schoof would attest that Thomas Aquinas had been an important theological source for them, yet they would also say that other theological and non-theological approaches

---

[1] Edward Schillebeeckx, Bas van Iersel, Marga van Keulen, Herman Wegman, and Ad Willems, eds., *Breuklijnen: grenservaringen en zoektochten. 14 essays voor Ted Schoof bij zijn afscheid van de theologische faculteit Nijmegen* (Baarn: H. Nelissen, 1994).

[2] Ted Mark Schoof, O.P., *Aggiornamento: De doorbraak van een nieuwe katholieke theologie* (Baarn: Het Wereldvenster, 1968). ET: Ted Mark Schoof, *A Survey of Catholic Theology, 1800–1970*, trans. N.D. Smith (Eugene, OR: Wipf and Stock, 2008).

would have taken his place as primary source of inspiration for their post–Second Vatican Council writings. In the case of Schillebeeckx, such a fault line can be clearly detected in the preface to the original edition of his book *Jesus: An Experiment in Christology*, where he writes about a gap between academic theology and the concrete needs of the ordinary Christian.[3] In order to bridge this gap, Schillebeeckx decided to make a new start in his approach to Jesus of Nazareth, entering into a discussion of the historical and critical methods used by contemporary exegetes as basis of his theology.[4] The new situation of the Christian faithful in the Netherlands required a clear break with traditional speculative Christology *ad mentem sancti Thomae*.

Even though this break did not imply relinquishing Thomas Aquinas, as I will argue in the remainder of this chapter, it was a sign of the self-understanding of Dutch theologians in the 1970s and 1980s: new times require radical new approaches to the Christian tradition. This is what Schillebeeckx himself explained in his hermeneutical reflection in the *Breuklijnen* book: the Christian faith can remain true only if it is co-determined by shifts and rifts in the formulation of its dogmatic statements.[5] Against an older tradition that saw the development of dogma as a steady unfolding of the truth, Schillebeeckx judged that the sharp turns in Catholic theology after the Second Vatican Council required a strong emphasis on discontinuity.

There is another reason why Schillebeeckx stressed discontinuity, rather than continuity, in his own theological development. In his reflections on identity, Paul Ricoeur has explained how human beings develop a self-image by constructing a narrative identity in constant interaction with otherness.[6] Such a narrative engenders discontinuity in order to express the way in which historical events and encounters influence the self-awareness of the person telling the story of his life.[7] In the case of Schillebeeckx and the Thomistic roots of his theology, one may even paradoxically state that the Thomistic tradition in the line of Marie-Dominique Chenu O.P., which taught him to take history seriously, caused him to think less of Thomas Aquinas and his influence during the second part of his life. In hindsight, however, the biographer tends to construe more continuity in order to show how, through the vicissitudes of life, the human being who is the special object of his interest succeeded in maintaining a personal identity. In that sense, I want to show in this article how Thomas Aquinas was not only a formative and explicit influence in Schillebeeckx's early theological career, but remained an implicit influence

---

[3] "Woord vooraf" in Edward Schillebeeckx, *Jezus, het verhaal van een levende* (Bloemendaal: H. Nelissen, 1974), 5. ET: Edward Schillebeeckx, *Jesus, CW* vol. 6 (London: Bloomsbury T&T Clark, 2014), xxv.

[4] See the reflections by Schillebeeckx's friend and colleague Bas van Iersel in "Van bijbelse theologie naar bijbelse theologen," *Meedenken met Edward Schillebeeckx*, ed. Hermann Häring, Ted Schoof, Ad Willems (Baarn: H. Nelissen, 1983), 54–68.

[5] "Mede dankzij verschuivingen en breuken in dogma-formuleringen blijft het dogma waar." Schillebeeckx, "Breuken in christelijke dogma's," *Breuklijnen: grenservaringen en zoektochten*, 15–49, at 26. ET: Edward Schillebeeckx, "Discontinuities in Christian Dogmas," *Essays, CW* vol. 11 (London: Bloomsbury T&T Clark, 2014), 93.

[6] Paul Ricoeur, *Soi-même comme un autre* (Paris: Éditions du Seuil, 1990), 167–98; see also Marianne Moyaert, *In Response to the Religious Other: Ricoeur and the Fragility of Interreligious Encounter* (Lanham MD: Lexington Books, 2014), 99–101.

[7] See Ricoeur, *Soi-même comme un autre*, 176.

during the rest of his theological journey, even if Schillebeeckx himself thought that he had left scholastic theology behind.[8] In this respect, his theological biographer Erik Borgman writes: "I think that the opposition that he construed in this way is too schematic. What he discovered as the basis of his theology in his 'Louvain period' through Thomas Aquinas and Domien (Dominicus) De Petter certainly continues to be present in his later work."[9]

## Schillebeeckx as a student with the Dominicans

In a certain sense, the Thomistic roots of Edward Schillebeeckx could be taken for granted since Thomism was the officially recommended way of studying philosophy and theology for Catholics since Leo XIII's encyclical *Aeterni Patris* in 1879. If Thomas Aquinas was the *doctor communis* for all Catholics, he certainly was the default teacher among the Dominicans in the first half of the twentieth century. Yet it was not so clear from the beginning that young Edward would join the Dominicans, since he started in 1926 at the Jesuit College in Turnhout in Flanders.[10] However, Schillebeeckx was not happy with the spiritual environment there, and he decided to join the Dominican Order in 1934. Having made his profession a year later, he began to study philosophy in Ghent where Dominicus De Petter was the master of students.[11] After his philosophical studies and a period of military service due to the approach of the Second World War, Schillebeeckx began his theological training at the Dominican study house in Louvain (Leuven) in the summer of 1940. Even though Schillebeeckx did not think very highly of his theological teachers there, one of them taught him to locate the work of Thomas Aquinas in its historical context.[12] This historical approach to Thomas Aquinas was strengthened considerably when Schillebeeckx started to study with Marie-Dominique Chenu, among others, at Le Saulchoir, the house of studies of the Parisian province of the Dominicans. Two characteristics of Chenu's work made a great impression on Schillebeeckx: his meticulous scholarship in medieval history, and his pastoral engagement in contemporary culture. Yet this combination of scholarship and engagement is not only typical of Chenu and Schillebeeckx, but of Thomas Aquinas as well.[13]

---

[8] In my own research about the Scriptural roots of Thomas Aquinas I came to a similar conclusion about the continuity of implicit influence in cases where the lack of explicit influence suggests otherwise. See W.G.B.M. Valkenberg, *Words of the Living God: Place and Function of Holy Scripture in the Theology of St. Thomas Aquinas*, Thomas Instituut Utrecht 6 (Leuven: Peeters, 2000).

[9] Erik Borgman, *Edward Schillebeeckx: A Theologian in His History*, trans. John Bowden (London: Continuum, 2003), 197.

[10] Borgman, *Edward Schillebeeckx*, 25.

[11] The importance of De Petter for Schillebeeckx merits a separate chapter. See the next chapter in this volume by Stephan van Erp and Dries Bosschaert.

[12] This teacher was Raymond-Marie Martin. See Borgman, *Edward Schillebeeckx*, 52.

[13] Borgman, *Edward Schillebeeckx*, 104: "In the portrait that Chenu painted of him with much accuracy, Thomas was described as a theologian who tried to express the faith for his own time on the basis of the contemporary situation. By doing this, according to Chenu he performed the task which as a theologian *par excellence* he had to do. In this sense, Thomas Aquinas was a model theologian precisely as a thinker bound to medieval conditions."

# The sacramental economy of salvation

Another way to express the main focus of Edward Schillebeeckx in his theological formation in the tradition of Thomas Aquinas is his abiding interest in the relation between God and world, and his looking for ways to detect God's presence everywhere in creation. Thus, his theology can be characterized as a "theology about reality."[14] It is not difficult to see how the dissertation about the sacramental economy of salvation fits into this broader perspective. Schillebeeckx published this dissertation, using his religious name Henricus (after Heinrich Suso, the thirteenth-century Dominican mystic) as *De sacramentele heilseconomie* in 1952.[15] The subtitle of this book characteristically indicates that it engages in a theological reflection on Aquinas's theology of the sacraments in the light of the tradition and of the contemporary theological and pastoral challenges. In his preface, Schillebeeckx indicates that the published book forms the first part of a larger project that elaborates on a number of issues that could only be touched upon in this book of almost 700 pages. In fact, a summary of the second, more explicitly Christological part of the project was published a few years later as *Christus, sacrament van de Godsontmoeting* (*Christ the Sacrament of the Encounter with God*).[16] This later book was not just a summary, but also indicated a change in Schillebeeckx's methodology. In the preface to the first Dutch edition, he indicates that speculative theology needs to be a synthetic view of salvation in Christ as revelation of the saving Trinitarian God. Such a speculative theology must be based on and interfused with a thorough biblical reflection. In this sense, Schillebeeckx adds, the systematic theologian must learn to practice theology again in the way that Thomas Aquinas did it as a biblical theologian, albeit on the basis of different exegetical methods.[17] It is surprising to find the methodology, followed by Schillebeeckx in his *Jesus: An Experiment in Christology* (1974) prefigured in a scholastic study fifteen years before. It is even more surprising to find this methodology being based on Aquinas as a Scriptural theologian, which was a discovery that most of us made almost half a century later.[18]

Some of this shines through in the first pages of the *Sacramentele heilseconomie* where Schillebeeckx engages in a discussion about the place of the theology of the sacraments in Aquinas's

---

[14]  A.R. Van de Walle, "Theologie over de werkelijkheid: Een betekenis van het werk van Edward Schillebeeckx," *TvT* 14 (1974), 463–90.

[15]  Henricus Schillebeeckx, *De sacramentele heilseconomie. Theologische bezinning op S. Thomas' sacramentenleer in het licht van de traditie en van de hedendaagse sacramentsproblematiek* (Antwerp/Bilthoven: 't Groeit/H. Nelissen, 1952). This book has been translated into French as Edward Schillebeeckx, *L'économie sacramentelle du salut: Réflexion théologique sur la doctrine sacramentaire de saint Thomas, à la lumière de la tradition et de la problématique sacramentelle contemporaine*, Studia Friburgensia 95 (Fribourg: Academic Press, 2004). Unfortunately, it has not yet been translated into English.

[16]  The first and second editions of this book had a somewhat different title: *De Christusontmoeting als sacrament van de Godsontmoeting.* The third edition was published as Edward Schillebeeckx, *Christus, sacrament van de Godsontmoeting* (Bilthoven: H. Nelissen, 1959) and translated into English as *Christ the Sacrament, CW* vol. 1 (London: Bloomsbury T&T Clark, 2014).

[17]  Schillebeeckx, "Woord vooraf bij de eerste uitgave," *Christus, sacrament van de Godsontmoeting,* 7. To my knowledge, this preface is not printed in the English translations of this book since it is replaced by a "Foreword" written by Cornelius Ernst, O.P.

[18]  I was only vaguely aware of this when I wrote my own contribution to this discovery in *Words of the Living God.*

*Summa theologiae.*[19] In these pages he discusses an interpretation that sees the third part of Aquinas's *Summa,* containing the theology about Christ and the sacraments, as an appendix that comes after the main structure of the *exitus* of all creatures from God and the *reditus* of human beings toward God has been completed in the first and second parts.[20] Quite the contrary, the Flemish Dominican argues, the history of salvation made possible by Christ and enjoyed in His sacraments is an essential part of the movement of human beings toward God.[21] Christ and the sacraments belong together in the return of creatures to God: the sacraments are an extension of God's incarnation, so that Christ in his humanity is the main sacramental instrument of our salvation.[22]

This discussion shows as in a nutshell how Schillebeeckx conceives his entire theological project along the lines of the history of salvation in the line of the French *Nouvelle théologie* and of his dissertation director Chenu in particular, while at the same taking seriously the philosophical and metaphysical grounding of such a project. In this respect, it is no coincidence that Schillebeeckx writes his dissertation about the sacraments as encounter with God incarnate in Christ, since this is the place where the historical and the human dimensions of the Christian faith are paired with their supernatural and metaphysical foundations.[23] The structure of *Christ the Sacrament of the Encounter with God* shows how Schillebeeckx uses the category of "encounter" as a way to start with the human dimensions of the sacrament. Consequently, the book starts with a biblical exploration of these dimensions, and only gradually shifts to a more technical discussion of the theology of the sacraments in Thomas Aquinas by using the category of sacramental saving efficacy.[24] While explicit references to Thomas Aquinas are no longer ubiquitous in this book, it is quite evident how the entire project of the *Sacramentele heilseconomie* finds its inspiration in a historical and contextual interpretation of Saint Thomas Aquinas.

# II. Non-conceptual dimension of our knowledge of God

Many articles that Schillebeeckx wrote in the years before and after his move from Belgium to the Netherlands in 1957 have been collected in the five volumes of the series *Theologische Peilingen* ("Theological Soundings"), published between 1964 and 1972.[25] Some of them have been written in order to explain Thomas's theological insights for a broader public, for instance

---

[19] Schillebeeckx, "Ter inleiding: Situering van het sacramentstractaat in de thomistische geloofssynthese," *De sacramentele heilseconomie,* 1–18.

[20] The interpretation in terms of the neo-Platonic movement of *exitus* and *reditus* has often been associated with Marie-Dominique Chenu. For recent discussions, see Brian Johnstone, "The Debate on the Structure of the *Summa Theologiae*," *Aquinas as Authority*, ed. Paul van Geest, Harm Goris, Carlo Leget, Thomas Instituut Utrecht, 7 (Leuven: Peeters, 2002), 187–200; and Mark D. Jordan, "Structure," *The Cambridge Companion to the Summa Theologiae*, ed. Philip McCosker and Denys Turner (Cambridge: Cambridge University Press, 2016), 34–47.

[21] Schillebeeckx, *De sacramentele heilseconomie,* 14–15.

[22] Ibid., 16, with reference to Thomas Aquinas, *Compendium theologiae*, 239.

[23] See Borgman, *Edward Schillebeeckx,* 211–16.

[24] Schillebeeckx, *Christ the Sacrament,* 36 [60].

[25] "Theologische Peilingen" can be translated as "Theological Soundings"; three of the translated volumes are newly available as volumes 2, 4, and 5 of the *Collected Works.*

the article on "the Sources of Theology according to Aquinas" that was written for a theological dictionary in 1957.[26] Others contain a rather technical exposition of Aquinas's theology, such as an article on the "Non-Conceptual Intellectual Dimension in Our Knowledge of God According to Aquinas" that was deemed to demand so much of the reader that it was relegated to an appendix in the original English translation.[27] A short summary of this article will give a better insight in the way in which Thomas Aquinas functions as a basic theological source for Edward Schillebeeckx in the 1950s.[28]

In the article about the non-conceptual intellectual dimension in our knowledge of God according to Aquinas, Schillebeeckx tries to correct a certain one-sided development in the Thomistic tradition that asserts that in thinking or speaking about God we no longer use creaturely concepts but somehow grasp God in a notional way. This Thomistic tradition was criticized by philosophers such as Joseph Maréchal who held, on the basis of a Kantian epistemology, that we cannot grasp God conceptually or by way of an intellectual intuition. There is, however, in the knowing subject a dynamism of the spirit that reaches beyond the conceptual content of knowledge. Schillebeeckx ends this *status quaestionis* as follows:

> Maréchal ... considered his thesis to be based on Aquinas's works, and for this reason it has seemed to me to be profitable to find out to what extent Aquinas himself accepted an aspect in our knowledge of God that transcends our concepts, and whether he looked for this non-conceptual dimension in the dynamism of the spirit or in a certain objective dynamism of the content of being which is not open to concepts as such. It may at the same time become clear to what extent the historical teaching of Aquinas differs from the later Thomist tradition influenced by Scotus.[29]

This quotation clearly shows how Schillebeeckx's use of Thomas Aquinas as source of his theology entirely fits into the *Nouvelle Théologie* approach in the 1950s: against the background of a great familiarity with the Thomistic tradition, he looks for a renewal of this tradition on the basis of a historical approach to Thomas Aquinas in dialogue with contemporary philosophy.

---

[26] Published in Dutch as "De bronnen van de theologie volgens Thomas," the first part of chapter six ("Hoogscholastiek en theologie") in *Openbaring en theologie*, Theologische peilingen, 1 (Bilthoven: H. Nelissen, 1964), 159–70; English translation in the first part of the chapter "Scholasticism and Theology" in *RT, CW* vol. 2 (London: Bloomsbury T&T Clark, 2014), 161–73 [I 245–84].

[27] Schillebeeckx, "Het niet-begrippelijk kenmoment in onze Godskennis volgens Thomas van Aquino," originally published in *Tijdschrift voor Philosophie* 14 (1952) 411–53; also in *Openbaring en theologie*, 201–32. ET: Edward Schillebeeckx, "The Non-Conceptual Intellectual Dimension in our Knowledge of God According to Aquinas," *RT, CW* vol. 2 (London: Bloomsbury T&T Clark, 2014), 207–38 [II 157–206].

[28] Both the original Dutch version of *Openbaring en theologie* and the second volume of the Collected Works, *Revelation and Theology*, contain a second article about "The Non-Conceptual Intellectual Element in the Act of Faith: A Reaction," placed immediately after the article about the non-conceptual intellectual dimension in our knowledge of God according to Aquinas. This second article was originally published in *Tijdschrift voor Theologie* in 1963, and it is in fact a critical discussion of Max Seckler's book: *Instinkt und Glaubenswille nach Thomas von Aquin* (Mainz: Matthias-Grünewald, 1961).

[29] Schillebeeckx, "The Non-Conceptual Intellectual Dimension," *RT*, 210 [II 161–62].

In the main part of his article, Schillebeeckx gives an analysis of Aquinas's discussion of human knowledge of God in *Summa Theologiae* I q.12 a.12, in order to see whether there is in our knowledge of God any real contact with God that goes beyond our concepts. This leads him to an extensive interpretation of the famous threefold way in which we may be able to know something about God: the way of affirmation because we are part of God's creation; the way of negation because God is completely different from all creatures; and, finally, the way of eminence by which God infinitely transcends our knowledge. Schillebeeckx emphasizes that we do not know God's existence or how God is, yet there is a likeness with God that cannot be grasped conceptually but only by some participation in God. In technical terms: "The *act of signifying* goes further than the *ratio nominis,* but it exceeds this *ratio* in the direction indicated by its content itself, in such a way that the reality is really envisaged, but not conceptually grasped."[30] While Aquinas clearly states that concepts such as "goodness" cannot be ascribed to God, he also says that God is good in an absolute sense. Therefore, there must be a human knowledge of God that is more than purely conceptual. What we know about God is how God is not, and how other things relate to God. Therefore, there is an anthropological basis in the creature's pointing to God, even though this tendency escapes our precise conceptual definition. At this point, Schillebeeckx's interpretation of Aquinas seems to come close to that of Maréchal who has deeply influenced Karl Rahner's interpretation of Thomas Aquinas. Even though Schillebeeckx is influenced by De Petter rather than by Maréchal in his interpretation of Aquinas, it is clear that they share a common interest, namely to create space for a non-conceptual moment in our knowledge of God over against a neoscholastic interpretation that was one-sidedly conceptualist in nature.[31]

However, Schillebeeckx also notices that there is a certain fluctuation in Aquinas's statements, and therefore he tries to give a historical reconstruction of his sources and the development of his insights. Since the structure of our knowledge of God is closely connected with the so-called analogy of God, Schillebeeckx carefully looks at the sources of the idea of analogy, starting with Aristotle and Alexander of Aphrodisias, continuing with Arabic and Jewish philosophers, and ending with the works of the early scholastic doctors in the twelfth and early thirteenth centuries. He distinguishes three stages in Aquinas's teaching about the ontological analogy of God, and he shows how his position on the absence of a distinction between the divine attributes in God is opposed not only to the position defended by John Duns Scotus, but also to the later Thomistic interpretation influenced by Scotus. In the final pages, Schillebeeckx comes back to the discussion of the analogy in our naming God. His basic point is that in using names for God we transfer names to God on the basis of the real relationship of creatures to God, yet we do not attribute any concept to God. We attribute names to God that signify perfection in creatures, but the analogy is to be found in the names and not in the concepts. Toward the end of this rather long and complicated article in which many sentences are dotted with Latin phrases, Schillebeeckx discusses the question where our attribution of names for God begins: if we call God "good," is our language derived from the way in which God is good or from the way in which we know about goodness in creatures? His answer highlights the importance of the creaturely dimension in Thomas Aquinas:

---

[30] Ibid., 216 [II 171].
[31] Borgman, *Edward Schillebeeckx*, 227.

In other words, for our knowledge of God, the creaturely concept always remains the *prius* from which we can objectively only aim at and mean the ontological *prius,* without however ever conceptually grasping and understanding God. Analogy is a manner of *predication* and it moves therefore on the level of the *impositio nominis.* That is why, for our *explicit* knowledge, the creaturely reality is always the *prius* to which we have to refer in order to know anything about God. If we mean the implicit content, then the name "goodness" applies primarily to God. If, however, we mean the explicit conceptual contents, then these apply primarily to the creature, but it should be understood that—because of the implicit, real content—an objective view is opened onto what God really is.[32]

In other words, knowing and naming God always starts with human concepts since we have been created by God and therefore participate in God's being in a creaturely way.

I am convinced that this rather technical and difficult exposition of Aquinas's thinking by Schillebeeckx in 1952 nevertheless touches upon a characteristic of Schillebeeckx's theology that shows his enduring indebtedness to Thomas Aquinas: the importance of creation as relation of everything to God. On the one hand, this means that we—as creatures—can only have a limited knowledge of God. On the other hand, it means that this knowledge is always related to our creaturely situation. In a final quotation from Schillebeeckx's article: "Again and again, whenever he asked what we really know of God, Aquinas gave the same answer—firstly, *'quid not est'* and then, in immediate association with this, *'qualiter alia se habent ad ipsum.'* In other words, the *modus divinus* of a perfection can only be *negatively* and *relatively* situated."[33]

David B. Burrell has written extensively on this negative aspect of Aquinas's approach to our God-talk in his book *Aquinas: God and Action.* He often refers to Joseph Pieper's saying that "creation is the hidden element in the philosophy of St. Thomas."[34] One of the consequences of this attention to creation is that both the fundamental distinction between Creator and creatures is emphasized, and their concomitant relatedness. This causes our language about God to be predominantly characterized by negativity—because of the fundamental distinction—but at the same time by universal relatedness. Of course, it would be nonsensical to say that Aquinas is not interested in the church, but nevertheless it is significant that he did not develop an ecclesiology. If theology is about God and everything related to God, as the famous phrase at the beginning of the *Summa Theologiae* has it, then it makes sense not to limit Christian theology to church-related matters. To my mind, this is precisely the way in which Schillebeeckx builds on what

---

[32]  Schillebeeckx, "The Non-Conceptual Intellectual Dimension," *RT*, 237 [II 204].

[33]  Ibid., 218 [II 174]. I have quoted this same statement in Pim Valkenberg, *Sharing Lights on the Way to God: Muslim-Christian Dialogue and Theology in the Context of Abrahamic Partnership,* Currents of Encounter 26 (Amsterdam/New York: Editions Rodopi, 2006), 215, in order to substantiate my own approach to Thomas Aquinas as influenced by David Burrell and the "Utrecht Hypothesis."

[34]  David B. Burrell, *Aquinas: God and Action* (Notre Dame, IN: University of Notre Dame Press, 1979); the reference to Pieper in *Faith and Freedom: An Interfaith Perspective* (Malden, MA/Oxford: Blackwell, 2004), xix, 116; and in "Act of Creation with Its Theological Consequences," *Aquinas on Doctrine: A Critical Introduction,* ed. Thomas Weinandy, Daniel Keating, John Yocum (London: T&T Clark, 2004), 27–44, at 34; and finally in "Providence," *The Cambridge Companion to the* Summa Theologiae, ed. Philip McCosker and Denys Turner (Cambridge: Cambridge University Press, 2016), 156–67, at 158.

Thomas Aquinas has taught him. Being both Dominicans, the ecclesial dimension of Christian theology was important to them, yet the "worldly" dimension that relates speaking about God with the entire creation and with all human beings was certainly as important.[35]

# III. No salvation outside of the world

As I have argued at the beginning of this chapter, it is possible to show how Thomas Aquinas is still an important interlocutor in the theology of Edward Schillebeeckx even after the deep changes in his theology since the 1980s. The easy way to show this is to point to a few places where Schillebeeckx explicitly talks about the importance of Aquinas and his analysis of human language about God. This is the case, for instance, in his book *Church: The Human Story of God,* written in the late 1980s.[36] Yet explicit references to Thomas Aquinas can also be found in much later works, such as an article about *Christian Identity: Challenging and Challenged,* published (in Dutch) in a volume in honor of his ninetieth birthday in 2005.[37] In a similar way, one could look at the final article that Schillebeeckx contributed to the journal that he founded forty years before. This article goes back to where Schillebeeckx started his publications: the theology of the sacraments.[38] Even though his interlocutors are to be found mainly in the fields of ritual studies and performance analysis, Thomas Aquinas still functions as source of inspiration for a paragraph on signification and causation.[39]

Yet the more challenging way to trace Aquinas's influence on Schillebeeckx is to point to the manner in which the theology of creation broadens the perspective such that it goes in a totally different direction for Schillebeeckx compared to Aquinas, yet remains faithful to the angelic doctor's basic theological intuition. There is no better way to show this than to point, once again, to the trilogy about Jesus, published between 1974 and 1989. The English titles of the three books—*Jesus* (1979), *Christ* (1980), and *Church* (1990)—give the impression of a project conceived well in advance and executed accordingly. Yet this is not how Schillebeeckx proceeds; he changes his publication plans because of changing priorities derived from his pastoral intuitions. We have seen these changes at work in *Christ, the Sacrament of the Encounter*

---

35  In this sense, I think that some of my colleagues who can be seen as representatives of Schillebeeckx's approach to theology in the Dutch theological arena are faithful not only to Edward Schillebeeckx, but also to Thomas Aquinas in their endeavor to develop the cultural, secular and public dimensions of theology.

36  Edward Schillebeeckx, *Church, CW* vol. 10 (London: Bloomsbury T&T Clark, 2014), 73–74 [76–77].

37  Edward Schillebeeckx, "Christelijke identiteit, *uitdagend* en uitgedaagd: Over de rakelingse nabijheid van de onervaarbare God," *Ons rakelings nabij: Gedaanteveranderingen van God en geloof,* ed. Manuela Kalsky, André Lascaris, Leo Oosterveen, Inez van der Spek (Nijmegen/Zoetermeer: DSTS/ Meinema, 2005), 13–32. French translation with some additions in "L'identité chrétienne: défi et mise au défi: À propos de l'extrême proximité du Dieu non-expérimentable," *Angelicum* 82 (2005), 849–67.

38  Edward Schillebeeckx, "Naar een herontdekking van de christelijke sacramenten: Ritualisering van religieuze momenten in het alledaagse leven," *Tijdschrift voor Theologie* 40 (2000), 164–87; ET: Edward Schillebeeckx, "Towards a Rediscovery of the Christian Sacraments," *Essays, CW* vol. 11 (London: Bloomsbury T&T Clark, 2014), 183–210.

39  Schillebeeckx, "Towards a Rediscovery of the Christian Sacraments," 200–2.

*with God,* in *Jesus: An Experiment in Christology,* and they are on display again in *Church.* The *Foreword* states the following:

> This book is about the life of men and women and their bond with God as God has become visible above all in Jesus of Nazareth, confessed as the Christ by the Christian churches—which are increasingly aware that they live in a secular world amidst other religions. The book was originally intended to be an *ecclesiological third part* of the trilogy I announced some time ago. It was to be the completion of *Jesus* (1974, English translation 1979) and *Christ* (1977, English translation 1980). And so it is, but not from the perspective that I originally planned.[40]

Thomas Aquinas did obviously not write about Christians living in a secular world amid other religions. Yet I am convinced that his idea about what theology is and what it covers inspired Schillebeeckx to write not about the church as place of encounter with God's salvation but about the world as place of encounter with God's salvation: not *Extra Ecclesiam Nulla Salus,* but *Extra Mundum Nulla Salus.*[41] I have often thought about this new adage ("no salvation outside of the world") as a way to appreciate the truth in the old adage ("no salvation outside of the church"), namely, that Christians confess that they really encounter God in the place and the history of their coming together, yet at the same time they now realize better than ever that God is not bound to limit Godself to our home turf. The motto from Amos in Schillebeeckx's book expresses this well: "As I brought Israel out of Egypt, so I brought the Philistines from Caphtor, and Aram from Kir."[42] One might call this a radical theology of religions, but I believe it is even more radical since it is a theology of the world as place for the encounter with God, in a way not dissimilar from Karl Barth's reflections on World and Church in his famous *Römerbrief.*[43] This radicalism is again not dissimilar from what Thomas Aquinas says about theology: that it is about God and everything else as it relates to God.[44] Theology is not specifically about religious or pious things, but it is in principle about everything as related to God as creator and as final goal of the universe. In that sense, Jesus Christ, the church, and the sacraments are all relevant for Schillebeeckx as possible places for encounter with God. But other religions and the world at large is no less a place where God can be encountered, and in that sense the entire creation can become a sacrament. Even though Thomas Aquinas is hardly mentioned anymore, it is his theological acumen that allows Schillebeeckx to take this broad vision on the entire creation as place for the encounter with God.

---

[40] Schillebeeckx, *Church,* xxi [xiii].

[41] On "what theology is and what it covers" according to Aquinas (*ST* I. q.1), see my contribution: Pim Valkenberg, "Scripture," *The Cambridge Companion to the* Summa Theologiae, ed. Philip McCosker and Denys Turner (Cambridge: Cambridge University Press, 2016), 48–61; on "No Salvation Outside the World," see Schillebeeckx, *Church,* 5–15 [5–15].

[42] Amos 9:7, in Schillebeeckx, *Church,* 170 [171]. The "motto" is not included in the Bloomsbury edition's first pages. See Edward Schillebeeckx, *Mensen als verhaal van God* (Baarn: Nelissen, 1989), opposite of the title page.

[43] Karl Barth, "'Ein Wort and die draußen' (Rom. 11:11–24)," *Der Römerbrief,* new ed. (Zürich: Theologischer Verlag, 1989), 419–33.

[44] Thomas Aquinas, *ST* I q.1 a.7: *Omnia autem pertractantur in sacra doctrina sub ratione Dei, vel quia sunt ipse Deus, vel quia habent ordinem ad Deum ut ad principium et finem.*

# Chapter 3

# Schillebeeckx's Metaphysics and Epistemology

## *The Influence of Dominicus De Petter*

Dries Bosschaert and Stephan van Erp

Around the time that Edward Schillebeeckx was studying philosophy and theology with the Dominicans, the church's view on the philosophical foundations of theology began to shift. This was partially the result of various developments in modern philosophy. Besides emerging discussions on the diversity of interpretations of Thomism, there were other philosophical traditions evolving, most notably Maurice Blondel's philosophy of action, Edmund Husserl's phenomenology, and Martin Heidegger's development of an existential phenomenology. These advances had consequences for theology as well. Influenced by the philosophical work of his fellow Jesuit, Joseph Maréchal, Karl Rahner wrote his *Geist in Welt* in 1939, wherein he presented a new style of philosophy of religion by rereading the philosophy Thomas of Aquinas through the lens of Kantian epistemology.[1] Probably the best description of the consequences of these philosophical developments for theology can be found in *Le Saulchoir: A School of Theology* (*Une école de théologie: Le Saulchoir*), by Marie-Dominique Chenu, which gave a short history of the study house and a summary of the theological philosophical methodologies employed there.[2] This was a key text for the "*ressourcement,*" or the return to the historical sources of the Christian tradition of the mid-twentieth century.

From 1946 to 1947, Schillebeeckx studied at Le Saulchoir, the Dominican house of studies of the French province located outside of Paris. There, he was taught by Chenu and Yves Congar, and it was especially Chenu's interpretation of Thomas Aquinas that influenced Schillebeeckx. During his studies in France, he also attended lectures by Maurice Merleau-Ponty and Albert Camus in Paris, while among his teachers in the history of philosophy was Louis Lavelle, whose phenomenological philosophy had been a formative influence on Dominicus De Petter, O.P. (1905–1971). De Petter had been Schillebeeckx's philosophy teacher at the *philosophicum* in Ghent in the 1930s, and perhaps the most profound philosophical influence on Schillebeeckx's theology, arguably even after the latter's turn to critical theory, when he stated that he had left De Petter's Thomism behind.[3] In this chapter, we will discuss the

---

[1] Karl Rahner, S.J., *Geist in Welt*, Sämtliche Werke 2 (Freiburg im Breisgau: Herder, 2017).

[2] Marie-Dominique Chenu, O.P., *Une école de théologie: Le Saulchoir* (Paris: Cerf, 1985); Thomas F. O'Meara and Paul Philibert, *Scanning the Signs of the Times: French Dominicans in the Twentieth Century* (Adelaide: ATF Theology, 2013), 23.

[3] Edward Schillebeeckx, *Jesus, CW* vol. 6 (London: Bloomsbury T&T Clark, 2014), 580–81 [618–19].

theological and philosophical background that shaped De Petter's philosophy, his distinctive approach in comparison with Maréchal and the phenomenologists of his time, and De Petter's influence on Schillebeeckx's thought.

# I. The Thomist matrix of Catholic metaphysics (1907–1931)

With the promulgation of *Pascendi Dominici gregis* in September 1907, two months after the Holy Office's decree *Lamentabili sine exitu*, Pope Pius X hoped to settle the "modernist crisis." While focusing strongly on the new "erroneous" advancements in exegesis, he also offered a classical remedy for overcoming these from a philosophical point of view:

> We do decree anew, and confirm, and ordain that [all the ordinances of Leo XIII on scholastic philosophy] be by all strictly observed. In seminaries where they may have been neglected let the Bishops impose them and require their observance, and let this apply to the Superiors of religious institutions. Further let Professors remember that they cannot set St. Thomas aside, especially in metaphysical questions, without grave detriment.[4]

Thus, by the time the anti-modernist oath was installed three years later, the philosophical standard of the Roman Catholic Church seemed to have been defined by Neothomism. This originated from Leo XIII's encyclical *Aeterni patris* (1879) as a means to integrate the insights of modern philosophy in a Catholic metaphysical system, but by the twentieth century its original motivation seemed to have been lost. The first wave of Neothomism gave the impression of the existence of only one official branch of interpretation, developed mainly in Rome at the Gregorian University, the Dominican *Angelicum*, and the *Pontificia Accademia Romana di San Tommaso d'Aquino*. During a second wave, various Western European figures, schools, and institutes also embarked on Leo XIII's project and began to develop their own trajectories. They did so within the given boundaries of the time, but with their own particularities.[5] Exemplary of this second wave were, among others, the "School of Paris," centered around Msgr. Maurice Le Sage d'Hauteroche d'Hulst (1841–1896), the *Institut Catholique de Paris*, and the Dominican administered Faculty of Theology in the Swiss city of Fribourg.

Joannes (John) De Petter had been influenced by two waves of Belgian Thomism. He was born in Leuven, Belgium, in 1905, and, while he had wanted to become a missionary in the

---

[4] Pius X, *Pascendi dominici gregis* (September 8, 1907) 45, http://w2.vatican.va/content/pius-x/en/encyclicals/documents/hf_p-x_enc_19070908_pascendi-dominici-gregis.html. Published in *AAS* 40 (1907), 593–650.

[5] The idea of two schools of Neothomism was introduced in Roger Aubert, "Aspects divers du néo-thomisme sous le pontificat de Léon XIII," *Aspetti della cultura cattolica nell'età di Leone XIII: Atti del convegno tenuto a Bologna, il 27–28-29 dicembre 1960*, ed. Giuseppe Rossini, Quaderni di storia (Rome: Lune, 1961), 133–227. A further elaboration of this second wave regarding the Belgian context can be found in Philippe Chenaux, "De Mercier à Maritain: Une seconde génération thomiste belge (1920–1930)," *Revue d'histoire ecclésiastique* 92 (1997), 475–98.

central African colony of the Belgian Congo, his parents decided otherwise. First, he had to complete studies at the Higher Institute of Philosophy in Leuven.[6] In July 1923 he obtained his licentiate in philosophy with a thesis on Louis Lavelle. Traces of Lavelle's focus on the metaphysics of being defined by the subject and the act of being can be found in De Petter's later works. His thesis supervisor was Simon Deploige (1868–1927), a specialist in natural law and its sociological, political, and economical consequences. Deploige was connected with Mgr. Désiré-Joseph Mercier (1851–1926), who had become the Archbishop of Mechelen (Malines) in 1906. As one of his oldest disciples and secretaries, Deploige succeeded Mercier as President of the Higher Institute of Philosophy.

Around this time, the students at the Institute were also taught by Léon Noël and Nicolas Balthasar. The former had been appointed as professor in 1906, replacing Mercier.[7] Noël (1879–1953) had obtained his Magister degree with a thesis on free will and gave ample attention to Kant's distinction between theoretical and practical reason. In his further studies he focused on questions regarding epistemology. Particularly interesting in this regard is his description of the existence of a "Leuven school" that was open to the study of modern philosophies, in order to formulate answers based on the Catholic intellectual tradition, which primarily focused on the nature of knowledge.[8] His study of Edmund Husserl's thought influenced De Petter's interest in phenomenology. Nicholas Balthasar (1882–1959) also taught metaphysics at the Higher Institute.[9] After his doctoral studies at the Gregorian, he was appointed at the Faculty of Theology in 1907. He was mainly concerned with the nature of metaphysical knowledge, and, according to Louis De Raeymaeker, he could even be considered to be the "founder of the metaphysical school of Leuven."[10]

After his studies in Leuven, De Petter was introduced to a different branch of Belgian Thomism, namely, Thomism as it was understood and developed by the Dominican Order. Since the revival of Neothomism, the order of Thomas Aquinas had taken it as their main mission to promote the thought of their most famous member, especially through the centers in Rome, Fribourg, Paris, and Nijmegen. In the Belgian context, the intellectual life of the order was formed at several study houses. Although Le Saulchoir was not a Belgian center, it exerted an influence on the Belgian Dominicans and was originally founded in Kain, near Tournai, Belgium. It was established there in 1904 by the French Dominicans after they were expelled from France, but it was transferred in 1937 to Étiolles, near Paris when the Dominicans returned. This house of studies was known for its historical and contextual study of the texts of Thomas Aquinas and its interest in the ideas of Maurice Blondel. Here, Dominicans such as Pierre Mandonnet and Ambroise Gardeil laid the foundations for the most famous names connected to this house, namely, Marie-Dominique

---

[6]   Louis De Raeymaeker, "Les origines de l'Institut Supérieur de Philosophie de Louvain," *Revue philosophique de Louvain* 49 (1951), 505–633.

[7]   See Georges Van Riet, "L'épistémologie de Mgr Léon Noël," *Revue philosophique de Louvain* 35 (1954), 349–415.

[8]   See Léon Noël, "Le bilan de l'Ecole de Louvain," *Chronique de l'Institut supérieur de Philosophie* 1 (1914), 6–29.

[9]   Nicolas Balthasar, *L'être et les principes métaphysiques, UCL Bibliothèque de l'Institut supérieur de philosophie* (Louvain: Institut supérieur de philosophie, 1914).

[10]   Louis De Raeymaeker, "In memoriam le Chanoine Nicolas Balthasar," *Revue philosophique de Louvain* 55 (1959), 495.

Chenu and Yves Congar.[11] For De Petter however, the two study houses of the Belgian province were more important: the *philosophicum* in the city of Ghent and the *theologicum* in Leuven. Here he undertook his training after entering the order in 1923. De Petter again embarked on a mission to study the epistemological themes in metaphysics, specifically by focusing on the thought of Joseph Maréchal. This time, his professor of philosophy was the Dominican Mannes Matthijs. Although Matthijs never taught Schillebeeckx directly, Schillebeeckx later spoke of him fondly as "the man through whose loving philosophical influence I had finally become a Dominican."[12] Despite his overall theological focus, Matthijs was also engaged in bringing Thomist metaphysics into dialogue with modern epistemology.[13]

# II. Integrating "modern" perspectives (1931–1942)

In 1931, De Petter was appointed professor of philosophy at the *philosophicum* in Ghent. He had already shown his commitment to the development of Thomist metaphysics in his first publications in the newly founded "Thomistic Journal for Catholic Cultural Life" (*Thomistisch Tijdschrift voor Katholiek Kultuurleven*, established in 1930).[14] However, the journal's direction and specific focus on culture after the war, which was developed by his fellow Dominican Jan Hendrik Walgrave, prevented De Petter from fully elaborating his own ideas in depth. He favored a view of philosophy as an autonomous and specialized discipline, independent of theology, and highly technical in nature. This approach made De Petter an inspiring figure in the philosophical education of the Belgian Dominicans. Moreover, his appointment as *Magister fratrum studentium* in 1935 and as regens in 1939 at the *theologicum* in Leuven presented him with the opportunity to influence a whole generation of young Dominicans. It is therefore not surprising that Henricus Paulus Timp, Alfons Norbertus Luyten, and Guido Andreas De Brie approached De Petter with their idea to start a new journal in order to promote Thomist

---

[11] See esp. G. Alberigo, M.-D. Chenu, E. Fouilloux, J.-P. Jossua, J. Ladrière, *Une école de théologie. Le Saulchoir*, Théologies (Paris: Cerf, 1985).

[12] Erik Borgman, *Edward Schillebeeckx: A Theologian in His History*, trans. John Bowden (London/New York: Continuum, 2003), 39.

[13] Wilhelmus Matthijs, "Thomisme, moderne philosophie," *Geloof en wetenschap* 3 (1928), 185–96; see also Cees E.M. Struycker Boudier, *Wijsgerig leven in Nederland en België 1880–1980*, vol. 2: *Dominicanen* (Nijmegen: Katholiek Studiecentrum), 207–08, 288–89.

[14] Dominicus De Petter, "Nieuwe richting in de thomistische kennis en zekerheidsleer," *Thomistisch Tijdschrift voor Katholiek Kultuurleven* 1 (1930), 76–83; Dominicus De Petter, "De openbaring van het hedendaags wijsgerig leven," *Thomistisch Tijdschrift voor Katholiek Kultuurleven* 2 (1931), 77–93; Dominicus De Petter, "Nota over de wording van het Cartesianisme," *Thomistisch Tijdschrift voor Katholiek Kultuurleven* 2 (1931), 283–87; Dominicus De Petter, "Is de traditionele bewijsvoering voor Gods bestaan ontoereikend?," *Thomistisch Tijdschrift voor Katholiek Kultuurleven* 3 (1932), 87–90; Dominicus De Petter, "De filosofie der 'Geisteswissenschaften'," *Thomistisch Tijdschrift voor Katholiek Kultuurleven* 3 (1932), 277–81. For information about the journal, see Leo Kenis, "Van 'christelijk humanisme' naar 'zonder complexen christelijk'," *Predikbroeders in woord en daad: Dominicanen in Vlaanderen in de twintigste eeuw*, ed. Mathijs Lamberigts, Mark De Caluwe, Anton Milh (Antwerp: Halewijn, 2016), 146–62.

philosophy for a Dutch-speaking readership.[15] They envisioned a Dutch counterpart for journals such as *Revue néoscolastique de Philosophie, Bulletin Thomiste*, and *Revue des sciences philosophiques et théologiques*. At first, De Petter was reluctant, ultimately only joining the project on two conditions: his responsibility would be limited to the editorial aspects and not include the organizational administrative aspects, and the journal would be written entirely in Dutch and would thus not be in competition with the existing francophone journals. De Petter was not the only one who was hesitant. After a round of consultations by Timp with the Belgian and Dutch Dominicans it became clear that the older generation was especially skeptical about the potential for this type of journal. Most of their concerns were focused on the feasibility of the journal, but some also questioned the motivations and orientation of the project. In particular, the Dutch Dominican Michael Vincentius Kuiper, professor at the *Angelicum* and the Theological Faculty of Fribourg and a Hegel specialist, expressed his suspicions concerning the philosophical "openness" of both De Petter and the envisaged journal.

The students and their magister persisted and published a *prospectus* in five languages as an international announcement of their plans. This triggered a new wave of opposition. On the one hand, their aim to become the main journal for Belgian and Dutch philosophy had offended Johannes Diderik Bierens de Haan and Ferdinand Sassen of the Dutch journal *Algemeen Nederlands Tijdschrift voor Wijsbegeerte en Psychologie*. Given the Thomistic inclination of the editorial board, they objected in particular to any Dominican claim to represent the "openness" of Dutch philosophy. On the other hand, the new journal faced strong criticism from Dominican superiors, in particular the Master General, Martin Stanislas Gillet. He objected most strongly to the "positive constructive spirit" that was part of the motivation for the journal. Gillet misunderstood this phrase, but based a large part of his opposition to the journal on the assumption that it meant "positivist" and therefore in opposition to "speculative" theology, rather than as "positive theology" which complements and enables speculative theology. Moreover, in Timp's letters from Rome, he warned the Leuven Dominicans about an anonymous complaint to the Dominican *Curia Generalitia* and the rather suspicious interest in the project shown by the famous Dominican and Neothomist, Réginald Garrigou-Lagrange. After the initial hesitation of his provincial, De Petter finally received permission to write a report in order to explain the motivation for the new journal to the Magister General. His arguments highlighted the journal's aim to stimulate the academic life of the Flemish Dominican Province and specifically the need for a Thomistically oriented journal for the Dutch-world. The arguments seem to have reassured the Magister General, who permitted the project to go ahead.

The attempt at philosophical renewal undertaken by the young Dominicans was, contrary to the establishment of a Neothomist *philosophia perennis*, actually in line with a general tendency to confront philosophy and theology with contemporary challenges and currents of thought. The first issue of the journal *Tijdschrift voor Filosofie* (then spelled as *Tijdschrift voor Philosophie*) appeared in 1939, shortly after other well-known Dominican publications of the late 1930s. In 1935, Congar published two pastorally oriented critiques of contemporary theology, while in the same year, his confrere Chenu contributed to the same discussion with a publication in the *Revue des sciences philosophiques et théologiques*, wherein he argued for a

---

[15]  A full history of the journal can be found in Guido Andreas De Brie, *Hoofdstukken uit het Tijdschrift voor Filosofie*. See note 30 below.

living theology capable of taking into account human existence and its historicity.[16] As rector of Le Saulchoir, Chenu returned to this topic in a speech for the feast of the patron saint of the institute, Thomas Aquinas. The 1937 printed version of *Le Saulchoir: A School of Theology* spread rapidly among theology students looking for renewal, although it had not been intended for formal publication or audiences outside of the school itself.[17] While influential for theological renewal in Belgian, the publications by Congar and Chenu are mostly considered to be part of the French theological renewal or "*nouvelle théologie*" movement.[18] From that point of view, Louis Charlier's *Essai sur le problème théologique* is often considered a Belgian elaboration on the same concerns.[19] In line with the courses taught by René Draguet at the Leuven Faculty of Theology, this Belgian Dominican also reflected on the task of theology and especially its relation to revelation, rationality, and the particularities of its method.[20] Charlier had been teaching at the Leuven *theologicum* since 1927, and belonged to the same milieu as De Petter. While De Petter was also concerned with the development of current thinking, he approached it mainly from a philosophical point of view. He highlighted this in his two first publications for the newly founded *Tijdschrift voor Filosofie*. When the first issue of the journal appeared in 1939, it included De Petter's first controversial publication "Impliciete intuïtie" ("Implicit Intuition").[21] The second issue, published in 1940, included the "Intentionaliteit en identiteit" ("Intentionality and Identity").[22]

---

[16] Yves Congar, "Une conclusion théologique à l'enquête sur les raisons actuelles de l'incroyance," *Vie Intellectuelle* 37 (1935), 214–49; Yves Congar, "Déficit de la théologie," *Sept* (January 18, 1935).

[17] Marie-Dominique Chenu, "Position de la théologie," *Revue des sciences philosophiques et théologiques* 24 (1935), 232–57. See also Christian Bauer, *Ortswechsel der Theologie: M.-Dominique Chenu im Kontext seiner Programmschrift: 'Une école de théologie: Le Saulchoir'*, 2 vols. Tübinger Perspektiven zur Pastoraltheologie und Religionspädagogik (Berlin: LIT, 2010).

[18] See also Janette Gray, "Marie-Dominique Chenu and Le Saulchoir: A Stream of Catholic Renewal," *Ressourcement: A Movement for Renewal in Twentieth-Century Catholic Theology*, ed. Gabriel Flynn and Paul D. Murray (Oxford: Oxford University Press, 2012), 205–18.

[19] Louis Charlier, *Essai sur le problème théologique*, Bibliothèque Orientations: Section scientifique (Thuillies: Ramgal, 1938). For the case of Charlier, see Henry Donneaud, O.P., "Gagnebet's Hidden Ressourcement: A Dominican Speculative Theology," *Ressourcement: A Movement for Renewal in Twentieth-Century Catholic Theology*, ed. Gabriel Flynn and Paul D. Murray (Oxford: Oxford University Press, 2012), 95–110; Jürgen Mettepenningen, "L'Essai de Louis Charlier (1938): Une contribution à la nouvelle théologie," *Revue théologique de Louvain* 39 (2008), 211–32.

[20] For the case of Draguet, see Ward De Pril, "De bijdrage van René Draguet en Louis Charlier aan de reflectie over de speculatieve theologie," *Theologie als geloofsvertolking: Historische en theologische reflecties over het proefschrift van Piet Schoonenberg*, ed. Leo Kenis and Jürgen Mettepenningen (Leuven: Peeters, 2016), 81–96.

[21] Dominicus De Petter, "Impliciete intuïtie," *Tijdschrift voor Filosofie* 1 (1939), 84–105. This publication was republished as Dominicus De Petter, "Impliciete intuïtie," *Begrip en werkelijkheid: Aan de overzijde van de conceptualiteit* (Hilversum/Antwerp: Paul Brand, 1964), 25–43.

[22] Dominicus De Petter, "Intentionaliteit en identiteit," *Tijdschrift voor Filosofie* 2 (1940), 515–55. This publication was republished as De Petter, "Intentionaliteit en identiteit."

# III. De Petter's theory of implicit intuition: Renewal and controversy

De Petter's article for the first issue of *Tijdschrift voor Filosofie* was clearly groundbreaking, and it formulated a position, quite distinctive from other versions of twentieth-century Thomism.[23] According to Schillebeeckx himself, one had the choice in Catholic theology at the time between the metaphysics of either Maréchal (who Rahner chose) or De Petter (who he himself chose).[24] Maréchal argued that the validity of abstract concepts is founded in a non-intellectual dynamic of the mind. Knowledge, then, is considered a projective act in which the concept transcends itself toward the infinite.[25] Maréchal's metaphysics was based on Kantian epistemology, which denies the possibility of knowing the *Ding an sich*, the thing-in-itself. The *Ding an sich* functions merely as the transcendental limit of knowledge. De Petter criticized Maréchal for finding a solution to the antinomy of concept and reality outside the intellectual act itself, and therefore ultimately denying true knowledge of reality itself. Although Maréchal tries to bridge the gap between reason and reality through a transcendental dynamic of the mind, he needs a non-intellectual stopgap in order to do so. De Petter, in turn, proposed to ground his realist metaphysics on an intellectual act, which he called "implicit intuition." In his article, which uses this concept as its title, De Petter tries to conquer the so-called "critical problem," defined by the antinomy of concept and reality.[26]

## Correcting Kant: Intuition as the intellectual grasping of being

"Implicit intuition," as De Petter defines it, is the direct intellectual grasping of the real or the concrete. "Intuition," therefore, should not be understood as a sudden, accidental insight, which at best can be trained as if it is a certain type of sensibility or something to which one can "open one's mind." Nor should it be understood as a preparatory phase, from which all knowledge develops. Neither is implicit intuition a pre-reflexive given, which precedes active and conscious

---

[23] For the different positions in twentieth-century Thomism, see Fergus Kerr, *After Aquinas: Versions of Thomism* (Malden, MA/Oxford, Blackwell Publishing, 2002).

[24] Edward Schillebeeckx, "The Concept of 'Truth'," *RT, CW* vol. 2 (London: Bloomsbury T&T Clark, 2014), 189–200 [II 5–22].

[25] Cf. Karl Rahner, *Hearers of the Word*, rev. Johann Baptist Metz, trans. Ronald Walls (London/Sydney: Sheed and Ward, 1969), 59: "Consciousness grasps its particular object in a pre-concept of being (as we wish to designate this process of reaching out to grasp the 'more') and hence of the absolute breadth of its possible objects. In each particular cognition it always reaches out beyond the particular object, and thus grasps it, not just as its unrelated, dead 'thisness,' but in its limitation and reference to the totality of all possible objects. This is because consciousness, by being close to the particular in order to know it, also always reached out beyond the particular as such. The pre-concept is the condition for the possibility of the universal concept, of the abstraction which in turn is what makes possible the objectification of the datum of sense perception and so of conscious subsisting-in-oneself."

[26] For an English interpretation of De Petter's metaphysics, see Philip Kennedy, *Deus Humanissimus: The Knowability of God in the Theology of Edward Schillebeeckx* (Fribourg: University Press Fribourg Switzerland, 1993); cf. also Robert J. Schreiter, "Edward Schillebeeckx," *The Modern Theologians: An Introduction to Christian Theology in the Twentieth Century*, ed. David F. Ford, 2nd ed. (Oxford: Blackwell, 1997), 152–61.

knowledge. It is performed by the intellect, De Petter claims, but implicit intuition also enables the intellectual act to be a true grasping of reality. Therefore, implicit intuition is not an epistemic characteristic that is present in the intellect. It is a condition for knowledge that needs to be realized by the intellect itself. Thus implicit intuition is not merely the capstone of a naïve realist philosophy. The intellect and the abstract concepts it forms play an essential part in the act of the implicit intuition. Implicit intuition is "a moment of intuition which is essentially included in the intellectual act, from which it has received its most essential meaning and in which it could be discovered through reflective effort."[27]

De Petter's setup for a Kantian-influenced, but nevertheless realist, metaphysics is an attempt to conquer every dualism between the knowing subject and the known object, despite the difference between reality's concrete particularities and the intellect's abstract and necessarily unifying constructions. According to him, both the reality of concrete particularities and the intellectuality of abstract constructions are themselves an expression of the unity of being. The unity of being is, in turn, also the most fundamental and constitutive unity of the intellect, albeit implicitly and inadequately expressed in abstract concepts. This inadequacy, however, he argues, is a characteristic of the concept and the intellect, not of the unity of being itself.

In short, De Petter argues that implicit intuition is an indispensable aspect of the intellectual act, which nevertheless grasps the reality that is primary to the intellect. This reality-grasping aspect of the intellect becomes explicit only in the formation of knowledge through abstract concepts, which are expressions of truth—a truth that always presupposes the unity of being. Being is implied in the abstract expression, whereas the abstraction in itself cannot express this being. A concept is called "abstract," because it does not encompass concreteness. In relation to the concrete, abstraction is forever imperfect. It is imperfect compared to the unity that constitutes the concrete, which is the unity through which the abstract and the concrete can be understood together in the singularity of their being. De Petter claims that this singularity of being is the constitutive foundation of the unity of knowledge (truth), which is forever implicitly and non-conceptually implied in the intellect which makes itself explicit. This can only become clear through the activity of the intellect itself when it expresses itself through the act of judgment and the formation of abstract concepts.

The being that is expressed with the abstract concept guarantees the objectivity of the concept, De Petter stipulates. The abstraction has to be integrated into an ontological consciousness, because the unity of concept and reality is performed by the intellect, not by the abstract concept itself. The human mind can only form these concepts because of the ontological consciousness that is implied in the intellect. The realization of the inadequacy of the abstract concept diffusely explains how the abstract concept is the expression of an intellectual identity. Through this realization of the difference between the ontological consciousness and the abstracting intellect, the intellect finds the explanation for this difference in itself. This is the full meaning of the term "implicitness."

According to De Petter, being is pure act. By "being," he means the fundamental constitutive act of the consciousness of being by which the intellect intrinsically and totally performs itself and forms the basic principle of its activity and self-realization. Being is not a static condition, but an ever-changing current of events and relations. Yet, the metaphysical unity expressed by

---

[27]   De Petter, "Impliciete intuïtie," 101–02.

the term "being" is a unity that is present in the fluid reality of the multiple, individual beings; even if it is a unity which can only be established in metaphysical reflection, as a principle for structuring, used by the human intellect in reality. Although the unity present in multiplicity can be found only by means of philosophical reflection and is not part of a spontaneous and explicit knowledge, this does not mean that it is only a metaphysical concept—that is, only used logically and formally—and not something which is present in reality. According to De Petter, metaphysical unity is being as act. The act of knowledge implicitly confirms its own foundation, as being itself. Being as such is not the *quod* of the act of knowledge, but the *quo*—the internal principle from which every conceptual expression derives its intellectual meaning and value.

## Correcting Thomas: Epistemic judgments are intellectual and real

Abstract expression is part of an explicit judgment which lays claim to the epistemic truth because of its movement from the abstract to the concrete. Yet De Petter questions how this movement is possible. The abstraction itself cannot complete the movement into the concrete. This, he claims, is only possible because of an implicit moment in the expression. In principle, this implicitness is identical in the judgment and the concept, but in the judgment (e.g., A is B), only that which is implied by the abstraction is to some extent made explicit by means of the copula "is." However, the copula "is" can only function as the bridge between the abstract and the concrete if, apart from the standard copulative value, it is also given a judicative value. After all, if the term "being" denotes the implicit consciousness of being, this term has a judicative value. According to De Petter, this is so because only the consciousness of being has the objective value of judgment.

A judgment therefore is not merely conceptual, but it also consists of a retracing of the abstract content to a concrete reality. The act of abstraction does not include the concreteness of the actual being, however. Therefore, in order to be meaningful, a judgment consists of a supplementary act by which the abstract content of a judgment is traced back to concrete reality. The structure of a judgment corresponds to that particular function: it consists of a predicate, as that which has to be traced back to the concrete, and a copula, as that which brings about the tracing. Now that the meaning and the function of a judgment have been defined as a supplement to the abstraction, what needs to be explained is how a judgment connects the abstract content with the concrete. This is the question regarding the foundation of a judgment, to which the answer can be found in the moment of intuition of a judgment.

According to De Petter, the solution of traditional Thomist philosophy for the problem of reaching the concrete from the abstract by means of a judgment is untenable. This solution is the *conversio ad phantasmata*, or reaching the concrete through a judgment by means of a reflection on the contents of sensory perception on which the abstractions are dependent. De Petter questions whether it can be taken for granted that, because of the dependence of the abstractions upon sensory contents, a judgment could retrace those sensory contents in the abstract concept, and in doing so, reach the concrete again. For De Petter's rigid realism, the act of the imagination is not an option for connecting a judgment with the particular. The intellect cannot grasp concreteness in any other quality than that which is characteristic to it, that is, its intelligibility. The antinomy of the peculiar function of a judgment, of connecting the abstract and the concrete, is replaced by an antinomy of the sensory and the intellectual. Sensory perception does not grasp the concrete as concreteness. Although it experiences it as concreteness, the objectivity of an object can only be grasped by the intellect. Sensory perception, however, has to be regarded as a link between the concrete and the intellect. Otherwise, if the intellect was not able to fully grasp concreteness itself through the sensory perception, then it could not define the function of sensory perception as a full experience of concreteness.

In the last section of his article, De Petter identifies the unity of being with God, and the implicit intuition with the divine act that is pure intellect in itself. Without offering any satisfying explanation, De Petter concludes his article by saying that his theory of implicit intuition provides the necessary complementary value of the Augustinian doctrine of illumination to the Aristotelian-Thomist doctrine of knowledge.[28] What else, he wonders, could manifest itself so completely in inadequate beings that create equally inadequate abstract concepts?

# Controversy

Soon after publication of De Petter's article on implicit intuition, controversy broke out. On February 4, 1942, both Chenu's book *Le Saulchoir* and Louis Charlier's *Essai sur le problème théologique* were placed on the Index of Forbidden Books.[29] Ten days later the Belgian province of Dominicans received a letter from the Master General explaining that, in order to avoid further condemnations, a number of actions should be taken. In particular, De Petter was to be removed from his position as regent of studies and as director of *Tijdschrift voor Filosofie*. In addition, the publication of the journal was to be halted. De Petter's provincial attempted to protect him, and, while the provincial accepted his resignation as regent of studies, he refused De Petter's resignation as professor of anthropology and metaphysics. Moreover, he managed to obtain a mere suspension of the journal for only a few months. On March 6 of that same year, De Petter wrote a letter to the Master General in which he submitted to the actions and expressed his loyalty to the teachings of Aquinas.

In addition to these immediate actions, the Master General also ordered a visitation of the Belgian province by Mannes Matthijs. Matthijs, a former professor and supervisor of De Petter, ended up writing a positive report concerning the Belgian study houses, which provoked a number of critical remarks by the Master General. The visitation's presentation of De Petter in particular seemed "maybe somewhat too indulgent" to the Master General.[30] According to him, De Petter's independent philosophical style had caused confusion among the readers of the journal. Especially grave was that, according to him, "these 'new' theories, expressed in similar terms, did *not* preserve Thomist doctrine in its integrality."[31] The Master General, therefore,

---

[28] De Petter, "Impliciete intuïtie," 103–4.

[29] Etienne Fouilloux, "L'affaire Chenu. 1937–1943," *Revue des sciences philosophique et théologiques* 98 (2014), 261–352.

[30] "Le rapport est fort conciliant et peut-être même un peu trop indulgent." Martin Stanislas Gillet, "*Réflexions sur le rapport du T.R.P. Matthijs*, 01.06.1942 (Document 35)," in Guido Andreas De Brie, *Hoofdstukken uit het Tijdschrift voor Filosofie*, 34. *Hoofdstukken uit het Tijdschrift voor Filosofie* is a manuscript written and edited by De Brie and held in the archives of *Tijdschrift voor Filosofie* at the Institute of Philosophy in Leuven. It concerns the history of the journal, including De Brie's personal recollections and a collection of the most important documents in its history as appendices.

[31] "J'estime que des théories "nouvelles", proposées en termes pareils, ne maintiennent *pas* la doctrine thomiste intégralement." Ibid., 35.

decided to take three actions concerning the journal. He allowed it to continue to be published until the end of the Second World War, he appointed Matthijs as the new editor in chief, and every article on Thomas Aquinas was to be submitted to a Roman censor. In the following years only one article was rejected, namely, De Petter's "Nieuwe wendingen in de metafysiek" ("New Turns in Metaphysics"). The argumentation of the Master General caused De Petter to stop publishing:

> In a word, not only is this new metaphysics of P.D.P. [De Petter] not a reconsidered Thomism, nor an implicit Thomism anymore; it is the total and explicit overthrow of the metaphysics of S. Thomas and the whole Thomist tradition. [...] Either P.D.P. will have to change his mind and method, or he will have to give up teaching and writing, and so will all those who think or rethink Thomism like him.[32]

## IV. De Petter as a teacher and Magister (1942–1971)

The fact that De Petter stopped publishing during this period did not mean that he ceased his efforts to promote the development of Thomist metaphysics within the Dominican Order. He had always been concerned with the education of a new generation of Dominicans and particularly in these years of public silence he was responsible for the formation of his best-known student, Edward Schillebeeckx. As a student at the Dominican *studium* in Ghent, Schillebeeckx followed the philosophy courses of the regent of studies, De Petter. Not only would he later assume this function at the *studium* himself, but Schillebeeckx would also acknowledge his self-understanding as an apprentice of De Petter:

> As a student, I could witness his development into a true philosopher, as it were; and in his philosophical genesis, he also took me into his confidence. We spent hours talking about philosophy, with him as the teacher and me as the questioning, critical young student. During this process he gave me all sorts of dispensations with regards to obligations of monastic life and for books that were on the church's Index or otherwise forbidden.[33]

The outbreak of the Second World War also prompted De Petter to take political action, more particularly in 1943 in the case of Paul S. Trop. The Jewish Trop was arrested by the Germans and charged with possession of explosives, taking part in the resistance, and failing to wear the yellow Star of David. De Petter hid his wife and children in order to keep them from being arrested as well. In addition, De Petter managed to have the last charge against Trop, not wearing

---

[32] "M.S. Gillet to M. Matthijs, 20.06.1942 (Document 45)," *Hoofdstukken uit het Tijdschrift voor Filosofie*, 42.

[33] Edward Schillebeeckx, *Theologisch testament: Notarieel nog niet verleden*, 2nd ed. (Baarn: Nelissen, 1995), 24. We can find a reference to the De Petter in: Edward Schillebeeckx, *I Am a Happy Theologian: Conversations with Francesco Strazzari*, trans. John Bowden (London: SCM Press, 1994), 7. See also Erik Borgman, *Edward Schillebeeckx*, 52–7.

the distinctive yellow badge, dropped. Consequently, Trop's trial had become a political matter and thus had to be held in Belgium rather than in Germany. In collaboration with the prison director, De Petter helped Trop escape during a prison transfer. He was then reunited with his wife and children in a monastery, where they remained until the end of the war. In 1971 De Petter was honored as a "righteous among the nations" and a year later a tree was planted for him at Yad Vashem. Moreover, *Tijdschrift voor Filosofie* had to be cautious because of the German occupation of Belgium. Their decision to continue publishing during the war resulted in mandatory censorship by the German administration. Only the publication of "Das Problem von Lachen und Weinen" by the "half-Jew," Helmuth Plessner drew a German reprimand.[34] The publication of *Notes sur l'existence* by the Jewish French philosopher Jean Wahl passed the censorship unnoticed.

After the Second World War, a new era seemed to be dawning for De Petter. Only one year after the war, Manuel Suárez was elected as the new Master General of the Dominican Order. De Petter's provincial, Walterius J.H. Gobert, who had also recently been elected, concluded that he could now send his professor of metaphysics to Rome to obtain his Magister title at the *Angelicum*. However, precisely at that time, the professors of the *Angelicum* were involved in a dispute with the Jesuits of the study house of *La Fourvière* in France over the correct use of Thomas Aquinas in theology. Given that this debate had erupted over acceptability of a historical interpretation of Aquinas and that one of the main players was Garrigou-Lagrange, it bore a strong resemblance to the tensions over *Tijdschrift voor Filosofie* and De Petter's publications some years earlier.[35] As a result, De Petter's application was postponed indefinitely. In 1949, his application was renewed, but his publications first had to be examined again. This task was given to Michael Browne, professor at the *Angelicum* and later Master General of the Order. In May of 1949, he asked the Belgian Dominican to send him French summaries of all his Dutch publications. These would be added to the notes he had already taken himself while attending a lecture by De Petter at a conference in Amsterdam on *L'intuitif implicite dans l'acte de connaissance*.[36] The promulgation of Pius XII's encyclical *Humani generis* on August 12, 1950, seems to have held up the results of the examination. Indeed, the encyclical, which was motivated by the debates concerning the "*nouvelle théologie*," dealt exactly with the "new" theories and philosophies that obstructed "correct" interpretation of Aquinas and endangered Catholic metaphysics in general. Only two years later, De Petter was allowed to take the exam to obtain his *Magister* title. At the end of 1952, he traveled to Rome to meet his jury. Among them was Master General Suárez, who had made sure that the exam was planned so that he could personally attend. After the successful completion

---

[34] Helmuth Plessner, "Das Problem von Lachen und Weinen," *Tijdschrift voor Filosofie* 2 (1940), 317–84.

[35] The debate had been caused by some of the conclusions in the published doctoral thesis: Henri Bouillard, *Conversion et grâce chez S. Thomas d'Aquin: Étude historique,* Théologie (Paris: Aubier, 1944). An overview of the most important contributions to the debate can be found in Marie-Michel Labourdette, Marie-Joseph Nicolas, and Raymond-Léopold Bruckberger, *Dialogue théologique: Pièces du débat entre 'La Revue thomiste' d'une part et les R.R. P.P. de Lubac, Daniélou, Bouillard, Fessard, von Balthasar, S.J., d'autre part* (Saint-Maximin: Les Arcades, 1974).

[36] Dominicus De Petter, "L'intuitif implicite dans l'acte de connaissance," *Proceedings of the Tenth International Congress of Philosophy (Amsterdam, August 11–18, 1948)*, ed. Evert Willem Beth, Hendrik Josephus Pos, and J.H.A. Hollak (Amsterdam: North-Holland, 1949) 352–55.

of the exam, he even wrote to De Petter to let him know that he now considered the case closed. This did not mean that the past had been totally forgotten, however, as before he could return to Belgium on January 12, De Petter also had two short and tense encounters with Kuiper.

After the war, De Petter had once again begun to publish. First, he published a number of articles in *Tijdschrift voor Geestelijk Leven* on religious life and on Theresia of Lisieux. The focus of the journal on religious life and spirituality allowed De Petter to return to theological debate by dealing with less sensitive themes. However, in 1948, he resumed publishing on philosophical topics, dealing mostly with anthropology from a Thomist point of view. It is striking that these publications, of which "Persoon-zijn onder thomistische-metafysische belichting" and "Personne et personnalisation" were the first, were not published in *Tijdschrift voor Filosofie*, but in the journals *Studia Catholica* and *Divus Thomas*.[37]

De Petter remained involved in the development of metaphysics until the end of his life. On the one hand, De Petter remained active as editor in chief of *Tijdschrift voor Filosofie* until the age of sixty-five. Up to that point, the journal had been the unique responsibility of the Dominicans. A proposal by the Higher Institute for Philosophy to integrate this journal as their main platform after the split of the university into separate Flemish and Walloon universities came at the opportune moment. Consequently, late in 1970, the professors of philosophy André Wylleman, Urbain Dhondt, and Samuel IJsseling were added to the editorial board. On the other hand, De Petter had continued his efforts for the development of (Thomist) metaphysics. The clearest indication of this was the publication of his study *Begrip en werkelijkheid* in 1964.[38] Published in the years in which the Second Vatican Council seemed to open a new era for the Catholic Church, this volume was a collection of De Petter's most distinctive publications. In addition, De Petter also continued teaching metaphysics to a new generation, particularly Dominican students. In 1967, when a new Centre for Ecclesial Studies was established that brought together the educational programs of different religious orders and congregations, De Petter was appointed as teacher of metaphysics. In 1970 he was also asked to assume the responsibility for the Higher Institute for Philosophy course on philosophy of religion that had previously been taught by Albert Dondeyne. De Petter was supposed to have started teaching this course in the academic year 1971–1972, but on April 6, 1971 Dominicus De Petter died of heart failure.

After De Petter's death, his close associate De Brie helped to promote the intellectual reception of his fellow Dominican. His metaphysical ideas were brought together in the publication *Naar het Metafysische* ("Towards the Metaphysical"), a collection of unpublished course notes and personal notes.[39] The book is a synthesis of De Petter's metaphysical thought as it was presented to his students with both a critical reflection on the metaphysics of Kant and Husserl's phenomenology, and an effort to transcend classical Thomist metaphysics by questioning the idea of the *esse commune*. De Brie had also envisaged publishing a second volume, presenting

---

[37] Dominicus De Petter, "Persoon-zijn onder thomistisch-metafysische belichting," *Studia Catholica* 28 (1948), 43–64; Dominicus De Petter, "Personne et personnalisation," *Divus Thomas* 52 (1949), 116–78.

[38] Dominicus De Petter, *Begrip en werkelijkheid: Aan de overzijde van de conceptualiteit* (Hilversum/Antwerp: Paul Brand, 1964).

[39] Dominicus De Petter, *Naar het metafysische,* Filosofie en Kultuur (Antwerp/Utrecht: Uitgeverij De Nederlandsche Boekhandel, 1972).

a number of the anthropological texts written by De Petter in the later phases of his career, but unfortunately this second volume was never completed.

## V. De Petter's ambivalent influence on Schillebeeckx

In the first volume of his Christological trilogy, Edward Schillebeeckx explicitly dissociated himself from De Petter's theory of implicit intuition. According to Schillebeeckx, this type of metaphysics leaves no space for history and time, and, for that matter, no space for context. The answer, he writes, to the Christological question of whether God's salvific acts are present in Jesus of Nazareth, should be demonstrable in historical experiences. He himself regards this as a clear break with De Petter and even with Thomas Aquinas. He argues that Aquinas was able to confirm the implicit participation of the totality of being in each and every particular experience and each and every separate abstract expression as self-evident, because it was also a socio-cultural reality, and therefore part of people's experiences there and then. Schillebeeckx believes, however, that in a secularized society that offers different religious options, the idea of *participation* that lies behind the metaphysics of the implicit intuition needs to be replaced by the idea of *anticipation*, so as to recognize that being is becoming in history. Consequently, Schillebeeckx adds, every universal truth claim will have to justify itself to critical reason, to which it can only present itself as a hypothesis. Therefore, "[d]emonstrating the personal, socio-political, secular, historical relevance of the Christian faith (in a critical approach to society and culture) becomes an indirect test of faith-motivated statements."[40]

Schillebeeckx's Christology would therefore involve a clear break with the metaphysics of unity of his fellow Dominican and philosophical teacher, but also with that of Thomas Aquinas, for philosophical and social-cultural reasons. At this point, one could wonder whether Schillebeeckx has allowed contextuality and culture to fully determine and change the metaphysical foundations of (his) theology, or, at least, the way in which he justifies the relation between the context and the content of faith. In the first part of his last monograph *Church: The Human Story of God*, where he meditates on the word "God" and the experiences it expresses and produces, Schillebeeckx describes philosophical reflection on God as a distant context in which people use the word "God." According to him, philosophical traditions used to be rational and theoretical explorations of a presupposed belief in God.[41] In this sense, he argues, it must be acknowledged that religions are the primary contexts of the use of the word "God." That is, within a "context of worship and reverence."[42] So, Schillebeeckx's concerns in his last book apply not only to the internal differences of religious traditions or differences between religious traditions, but also to the difference of contexts in which philosophy and theology emerge.

After De Petter's attack on Thomist epistemology, and after his criticism of unifying metaphysical systems of participation and recognition of philosophy emerging from a context different from theology, it is important to ask if, starting in the 1970s, Schillebeeckx really was far

---

[40]  Schillebeeckx, *Jesus*, 581 [619].
[41]  Edward Schillebeeckx, *Church, CW* vol. 10 (London: Bloomsbury T&T Clark, 2014), 61–63 [62–64].
[42]  Ibid., 61 [62].

removed from Thomist philosophy as a foundation or natural conversation partner for theology.[43] It is possible that this is the consequence of Schillebeeckx's anticipation of the challenges for theology that would follow shortly after the end of his own scholarly career: religious pluralism, non-foundationalism and postmodern thought, and the attention given to otherness and difference. Like non-foundationalists and postmodern thinkers, Schillebeeckx seems to reject "metaphysics" or first philosophies in favor of historical experience. But is there no independent phenomenology or type of metaphysics that could incorporate history and particular experiences into a theology that confirms the unity of creation and the continuity in the history of salvation, despite the discontinuities with which human beings have responded to that history?

De Petter's metaphysics may well provide the answer to these questions. His stress on the performance of the intellect as a necessity for the confirmation of being implied in every intellectual judgment is thoroughly historical. De Petter does not claim that the intellect constructs being as such, nor does he support the type of phenomenology which claims that without the performing transcendental subject, there is no being, because being by definition would be being-as-it-is-perceived. On the contrary, De Petter advocates a strong realism, without claiming that being *as* being is fully available in concepts or judgments, although the performance of the intellect is necessary to understand that the totality of being lies at the origin of every intellectual act. Intellectual judgment reveals its origin by being inadequate and diffuse, or in other words, by implying that which it cannot reveal through its performance of grasping the real.[44] In De Petter's later works, he expresses a strong aversion to the concept of the *esse commune*, precisely because it ignores the historicity of the performing intellect. The contingency of beings, he claims, defies a full confirmation of their unity, and the experience of their contingency can only negatively point at a unity that is absolute and fully transcendent.

It is this last statement that led to Schillebeeckx's conclusion that De Petter's metaphysics is a metaphysics of participation, which offers a worldview founded on a concept of absolute Being. According to Schillebeeckx, this is undesirable for a contemporary culture in which the pluralism and historicity of events and ideas should be confirmed rather than transcendentally grounded. But Schillebeeckx himself, in contrast with his own criticism of De Petter's metaphysics, has been perfectly capable of combining a metaphysics of participation—in the form of a theology of creation—and a theology of historical experience in which the contingency of our historicity is fully acknowledged.[45]

To conclude, we would like to point out Schillebeeckx's own struggle with a metaphysical ambivalence that is integral to every experience of practiced faith, and which has led to reflexive forms of both positive and speculative theology. In the collection of articles published as *Revelation and Theology*, Schillebeeckx defines positive theology as seeking insight into the development of revelation in the Bible and the mystery of Christ into dogmatic theology.[46] According to him,

---

[43]  Despite the strong analytical Thomist tradition in contemporary theology, see, for instance, John Haldane, *Faithful Reason: Essays Catholic and Philosophical* (London/New York: Routledge, 2004), 3–15; and Fergus Kerr, *After Aquinas: Versions of Thomism* (Malden, MA/Oxford: Blackwell, 2002), 74–76.

[44]  Cf. David Tracy, "On Longing: The Void, the Open, God," *Longing in a Culture of Cynicism*, ed. Stephan van Erp and Lea Verstricht (Zürich/Berlin: LIT, 2008), 15–32.

[45]  See also Chapter 15 in this volume by Martin Poulsom, on Schillebeeckx's theology of creation.

[46]  On "positive theology," see Edward Schillebeeckx, "What Is Theology," *RT, CW* vol. 2 (London: Bloomsbury T&T Clark, 2014), 79–82 [I 118–23].

a necessary condition for understanding this development is the reconstruction of historical experiences of salvation and the communal, ecclesial life shaped by those experiences. This reconstruction, however, makes use of a reason that is illuminated by faith and allied with the history of faith. Neither the illumination of reason alone nor historical continuity on its own can fully grasp revelation in history. Therefore, theology should not overstate its demand for intelligibility. Here, he concludes:

> Theology is always a "stammering" in the face of the transcendent mystery of faith ... this humility is not merely a question of words, but also, something that must be apparent in the manner in which theology is practised. The attention of theology must always be directed to the mystery of salvation that is announced and not to the human means which help us to approach it ... In the content of faith there is both a tendency towards incarnation in human thought and a fundamental resistance to rationalisation. On the one hand, theology should not sink into so-called "evangelism", which is only aware of the mystery and the "folly of faith", nor should it tend towards an uncontrolled incarnation, which is only conscious of the meaningful intelligibility of faith ... Throughout history, therefore theology is always passing through a crisis or growth, as a result of which its true face is always appearing in a purer form "until we all attain to the unity of the faith" (Eph 4:13).[47]

---

[47] Schillebeeckx, "What Is Theology?," *RT*, 114–15 [I 176–77].

# Chapter 4

# Schillebeeckx and Theological Ressourcement

## Historical Notes on Schillebeeckx's Reception of Nouvelle Théologie

### Karim Schelkens and Jürgen Mettepenningen

The legacy of Edward Schillebeeckx is difficult to fully grasp or to adequately categorize. His theological enterprise has developed over the course of several decades, and as a theologian he was always in conversation with the context of his time, searching for answers in the rapidly changing environment of the twentieth century.[1] This contribution, however, does not so much focus on Schillebeeckx as one in dialogue with his context, but more on his indebtedness to the theological ressourcement movement of the *nouvelle théologie*. While this is underinvestigated in academic literature, it is clear that both on the level of theological ideas and intuitions, and on the factual level of direct contact and influences—certainly within his own religious order, the Dominicans—Schillebeeckx's oeuvre is molded by this intellectual horizon. This chapter seeks to contribute to the understanding of Schillebeeckx's reception of the ressourcement movement. In order to do so, we will start with a brief survey of the historico-theological setting of the "new theology" movement in France. We will also trace connections to the context of Schillebeeckx's native country of Belgium. In the second part, we will highlight elements of Schillebeeckx's indebtedness to this movement as of the 1950s, in a period when the insights of French theologians rapidly spread beyond the borders of "*la fille aînée de l'église*." Although Schillebeeckx really began his career in earnest once he moved northward, from Belgium to the Netherlands, it is clear that his theological roots were southern: Congar, de Lubac, and Daniélou. Not only did all of these figures become prominent voices at the Second Vatican Council, and not only were all of them later promoted to the cardinalate, but they also all served as *maîtres à penser* for one of the most influential theologians of the Low Countries.

---

[1]  Some sections of this chapter previously appeared in Jürgen Mettepenningen, *Nouvelle Théologie – New Theology: Inheritor of Modernism, Precursor of Vatican II* (London/New York: T&T Clark, 2010). The material is included here within the new context of this chapter.

# I. "Nouvelle théologie" as an intellectual horizon: Dominicans and Jesuits

## From the Dominicans in Paris …

Whoever is acquainted with post-reformation Catholic history will be predisposed to think that the following deals with the age-old struggle between the scholastic theologians of the Order of Preachers and the Society of Jesus in the seventeenth and eighteenth centuries. This is, however, not the case, even if the controversy on divine grace is never far off. Between the eighteenth and the twentieth centuries lies the age of Enlightenment and the Romantic era, both of whom have drastically reshaped the situation of Catholics and Catholic theology to the extent that members of the two orders no longer were arrayed to combat one another's insights, but rather joined efforts to reposition themselves theologically in a new era. That era was the one following the modernist crisis of the early twentieth century, and immediately afterward, the devastating experience of the First World War, which deeply shocked the self-evident and sometimes complacent confidence that ultramontane Catholics often still placed in "authority." In these post-crisis years, the bipolar starting point of the so-called *nouvelle théologie* might be set in 1935.

On January 18 of that year, the French Dominican friar Yves Congar, professor at the study house of the French Dominicans, Le Saulchoir, published an opinion piece in the Catholic newspaper *Sept*. The article was entitled *Déficit de la théologie*.[2] Congar used the piece to formulate his critique of the practice of theology. According to him it had become little more than a technical matter and had lost sight of its relationship with the faith and life of ordinary men and women. He bluntly compared the prevailing neoscholastic theology with a "wax mask": an expressionless face, lacking genuine connection with life. Congar called for a theology rooted in faith and life, as he made clear in a second article published in June of the same year in *Vie Intellectuelle*.[3] He was not alone. In that same year his confrere Marie-Dominique Chenu published an article on the *Position de la théologie*,[4] a contribution that served as a blueprint for the third chapter of his book *Une école de théologie: le Saulchoir*, which appeared two years later.[5] In line with Ambroise Gardeil, Le Saulchoir's founding father, Chenu too called for a reform of Catholic theology.[6] It ought to become "faith *in statu scientiae*" or "faith in

---

[2]  Yves Congar, "Déficit de la théologie," *Sept* (January 18, 1935).

[3]  When asked for his observations, Congar declared that the gap between faith and everyday life was due to the rise in secularization. Yves Congar, "Une conclusion théologique à l'enquête sur les raisons actuelles de l'incroyance," *Vie Intellectuelle* 37 (1935), 214–49.

[4]  Marie-Dominique Chenu, "Position de la théologie," *Revue de science philosophique et théologique* 24 (1935), 232–57.

[5]  Marie-Dominique Chenu, *Une école de théologie. Le Saulchoir* (Kain: pro manuscripto, 1937); new edition: Marie-Dominique Chenu, *Une école de théologie: le Saulchoir*, ed. Giuseppe Alberigo and Étienne Fouilloux, Théologies (Paris: Cerf, 1985), 91–173.

[6]  Chenu alludes to Ambroise Gardeil, *Le donné révélé et la théologie*, Bibliothèque théologique 4 (Paris: Cerf, 1909). Chenu provided a foreword to Gardeil's second edition: Marie-Dominique Chenu, "Préface pour la deuxième édition, in Ambroise Gardeil," *Le donné révélé et la théologie*, 2nd ed. (Paris: Cerf, 1932), vii–xiv.

its intellectual mode," and the framework within which the theologian functioned was to be much broader than that provided by neoscholasticism.[7] He insisted that it was not necessary to cut out the contingent historical context in order to engage in authentic theology. Indeed, the opposite was the case: the historical perspective focuses its research on the said reality and its concretization. With this vision in mind, Chenu fashioned a project together with his colleagues at Le Saulchoir, which was intended to provide a survey of the "history of theology in the West." The work would pay specific attention to the relationship between theology, cultural and spiritual life.[8] While the project was never realized, its prevailing tone was representative of its three promoters and their work.

In 1938, one year after the appearance of *Une école de théologie*, the Belgian Dominican Louis Charlier published an *Essai sur le problème théologique*.[9] Although he had not studied at Le Saulchoir, Charlier's ideas were remarkably close to those of Chenu. Charlier was a professor at the theologate in Leuven (or "Louvain" in French and as the University town was generally known at the time), whose work caused something of a stir and was the subject of a considerable number of book reviews.[10] This publication offered food for thought as, similar to the theology of John Henry Newman which had also influenced Congar, Charlier distinguished between the "conceptual dimension" of God's self-disclosure in revelation (the primary aspect of neoscholastic thought) and the "real dimension" thereof (which he considered to be lacking in theology). According to Charlier, revelation was first and foremost a living reality, and only appeared in a second instance in concepts, formulae, or dogmatic propositions. In themselves, these could never be said to enjoy any form of independence from lived reality. All of these attempts to renew theological language were rapidly experienced as an attack on neo-Thomism, the overarching framework of Catholic intellectual life as of the late nineteenth century.[11] An official response from the Vatican came when both Chenu's and Charlier's works were placed on the Index of Forbidden Books in February 1942.[12]

---

[7] Chenu, "Position de la théologie," 233; Chenu, *Une école de théologie*, 145.

[8] See the folder on "Chenu, Congar, Féret: Projet d'histoire de la théologie. Kain années 30" in the Archives of the French Province of the Dominicans. It was published by Michael Quisinsky, *Geschichtlicher Glaube in einer geschichtlichen Welt: Der Beitrag von M.-D. Chenu, Y. Congar und H.-M. Féret zum II. Vaticanum*, Dogma und Geschichte 6 (Berlin: LIT, 2007), 47–51. On Féret, also see Quisinsky, "Henri-Marie Féret OP (1904–1992): Auf dem Weg zu einer 'konkreten und geschichtlichen Theologie'," *"Mutig in die Zukunft": Dominikanische Beiträge zum Vaticanum II*, ed. Thomas Eggensperger and Ulrich Engel, Dominikanische Quellen und Zeugnisse 10 (Leipzig: St. Benno, 2007), 65–103.

[9] Louis Charlier, *Essai sur le problème théologique*, Bibliothèque Orientations. Section scientifique 1 (Thuillies: Ramgal, 1938).

[10] Jürgen Mettepenningen, "*L'Essai* de Louis Charlier (1938): Une contribution à la nouvelle théologie," *Revue théologique de Louvain* 39 (2008), 211–32.

[11] It should be observed here that neo-Thomism was not one monolithic strand of thought, but was in fact marked by internal plurality and by historical evolution. For more background, see the recent book by Rajesh Heynickx and Stéphane Symons, eds., *What's So New About Scholasticism? How Neo-Thomism Helped Shape the Twentieth Century* (Berlin/London: Walter De Gruyter, 2018).

[12] Cf. *Acta Apostolicae Sedis* (*AAS*) 34 (1942), 37. See also Étienne Fouilloux, *Autour d'une mise à l'Index*, in *Marie-Dominique Chenu, Moyen-Âge et modernité*, Les Cahiers du Centre d'études du Saulchoir 5 (Paris: Cerf, 1997), 25–56.

This prohibition marked the "end of the beginning," and a number of historians have described it as the closure of the first stage of what became *nouvelle théologie*.[13] Within the context of formal magisterial rejection, the expression "*nouvelle théologie*" was first coined. The credit goes to Pietro Parente, who made it clear on the front page of the Vatican newspaper that the Francophone representatives were no less than *novi heretici*.[14] The Italian theologian argued that the writings of these "new heretics" had discredited neoscholasticism and brought along an (exaggerated) interest in the human subject, in personal experience, religious sentiment, and the notion of historical development. Mariano Cordovani, who ranked among the "court theologians" of Pope Pius XII, agreed. He sharply criticized this "modern theology" during a lecture at the Angelicum in 1940, on the feast day of Thomas Aquinas.[15] Moreover, the words of Parente and Cordovani were applauded by the Dominican authorities, among them Réginald Garrigou-Lagrange, professor at the Angelicum. Suspicion spread rapidly, and the superiors of the Dominican priory in Leuven—where Charlier had taught—likewise considered it fitting to remove Dominicus De Petter from his teaching assignment in 1942. This is not just a detail: De Petter, who had caused something of a stir in 1939 with the publication of an article on "implicit intuition" in the first issue of the journal *Tijdschrift voor Philosophie*, would become one of the theologians who most influenced

---

[13] The idea that *nouvelle théologie* evolved in a number of phases can be found with authors such as Rosino Gibellini, Tharcisse Tshibangu, and Étienne Fouilloux. In 1980, Tshibangu described it as a crisis in two phases. See Tharcisse Tshibangu, *La théologie comme science au XXème siècle* (Kinshasa: Presses universitaires, 1980), 79–110. Six years later, René Guelluy suggested that the Dominican contributions of 1935–1942 served as the antecedent to *Humani generis*. See René Guelluy, "Les antécédents de l'encyclique 'Humani generis' dans les sanctions romaines de 1942: Chenu, Charlier, Draguet," *Revue d'histoire ecclésiastique* 81 (1986), 421–97. In a series of articles published between 1989 and 1992, Jean-Claude Petit agreed with Guelluy. See Jean-Claude Petit, "La compréhension de la théologie dans la théologie française au XXe siècle. La hantise du savoir et de l'objectivité: l'exemple d'Ambroise Gardeil," *Laval théologique et philosophique* 45 (1989), 379–91; Jean-Claude Petit, "La compréhension de la théologie dans la théologie française au XXe siècle. Vers une nouvelle conscience historique: G. Rabeau, M.-D. Chenu, L. Charlier," *Laval théologique et philosophique* 47 (1991), 215–29; Jean-Claude Petit, "La compréhension de la théologie dans la théologie française au XXe siècle. Pour une théologie qui réponde à nos nécessités: la nouvelle théologie," *Laval théologique et philosophique* 48 (1992), 415–31. In 1994 and 1998 respectively, Rosino Gibellini and Étienne Fouilloux confirmed that "*nouvelle théologie*" should be divided into two phases, although the precise dating of each phase differs from scholar to scholar. See Rosino Gibellini, *Panorama de la théologie au XXe siècle*, Théologies (Paris: Cerf, 1994), 186–96; Tshibangu, *La théologie comme science au XXème siècle*, 79–110; Étienne Fouilloux, *Une Église en quête de liberté: La pensée catholique française entre modernisme et Vatican II (1914–1962)* (Paris: Desclée De Brouwer, 1998), 193–300. While Fouilloux appears to suggest that the movement consisted of even more phases, Jürgen Mettepenningen has proposed four phases. See Fouilloux, "'Nouvelle théologie' et théologie nouvelle (1930–1960)," *L'histoire religieuse en France et Espagne*, Collection de la Casa Velázquez 87, ed. Benoît Pellistrandi (Madrid: Casa de Velázquez, 2004), 411–25; Jürgen Mettepenningen, *Nouvelle Théologie – New Theology*.

[14] Pietro Parente, "Nuove tendenze teologiche," *L'Osservatore Romano* (February 9–10, 1942), 1.

[15] Mariano Cordovani, "Per la vitalità della teologia cattolica," *Osservatore Romano* (March 22, 1940), 3. This text is also included in *Angelicum* 17 (1940), 133–46.

Schillebeeckx.[16] On the other hand, one should refrain from too hastily ranking De Petter among the theologians belonging to the *nouvelle théologie* current. Such an identification, it has recently been pointed out, starts from the problematic premise that *nouvelle théologie* was an overarching current under which various historians, theologians, and philosophers can be filed.[17]

In any case, here too, the critique of neoscholasticism was difficult to ignore, and in general the "new theologians" of the years 1935–1942 reacted against neoscholasticism by insisting on a return to the "historical Thomas Aquinas," a demand that fit within the emerging historical interest in the Middle Ages.[18] Instead of referring to authoritative commentaries on Thomas from the sixteenth and seventeenth centuries, they returned to the sources—to Thomas himself—creating a *ressourcement* in which the "authentic" thirteenth-century Thomism took pride of place over the (neo-)Thomistic system. Scholasticism was not abandoned completely—such would imply the dismissal of the accepted foundations of orthodoxy and, more than likely, one's own dismissal—rather it was supplemented.

## … To the Jesuits in Lyon

Having been confronted with the relegation of their writings on the Index and the critique of the Order's superiors, the Dominicans withdrew into the background. But the ressourcement movement did not end there; henceforth it was the Jesuits who took the lead, with a series of three remarkable publications. The first of these was Henri Bouillard's reworked doctoral dissertation,

---

[16]  Dominicus De Petter was a Belgian Dominican. In 1931 he was appointed to the Dominican study house of Ghent. In 1938 he was one of the main founders of the *Tijdschrift voor Philosophie.* His most notable publications were Dominicus De Petter, "Impliciete intuïtie," *Tijdschrift voor Filosofie* 1 (1939), 84–105; Dominicus De Petter, "Intentionaliteit en identiteit," *Tijdschrift voor Filosofie* 2 (1940), 515–55. For more information, see Désiré Scheltens, "De filosofie van P.D.M. De Petter," *Tijdschrift voor Filosofie* 33 (1971), 439–506. More recently, also see Stephan van Erp, "Geïmpliceerde transcendentie: De Petters 'impliciete intuïtie' als bevestiging van het zijn van de zijnden én het Zijn zelf," *Subliem niemandsland: Opstellen over metafysica, intersubjectiviteit en transcendentie,* ed. Wil Derkse, Arie Leijen, and Bruno Nagel (Best: Damon, 1996), 295–310; Dries Bosschaert, "Een intuïtie voor vernieuwing: Over Dominicus De Petter (1905–1971)," *Predikbroeders in woord en daad: Dominicanen in Vlaanderen in de twintigste eeuw,* ed. Mathijs Lamberigts, Mark De Caluwe, and Anton Milh (Antwerp: Halewijn, 2016), 245–69. See also Chapter 3 in this volume.

[17]  On this issue and on De Petter's philosophical position, see: Dries Bosschaert, "Dominicus De Petter O.P., a Forgotten Victim of the Crisis Caused by the *Nouvelle Théologie*?," *Ephemerides Theologicae Lovanienses* 93 (2017), 633–56.

[18]  In 1989, Johan Van Wijngaerden has pointed out that the measures against De Petter ought to be understood against the background of the sanctions against his confrere and fellow community member. See Johan Van Wijngaerden, *Voorstudie tot het denken van E. Schillebeeckx. D.M. De Petter o.p. (1905–1971): Een inleiding tot zijn leven en denken. Deel 1: Een conjunctureel-historische situering,* unpublished Master thesis (K.U. Leuven, 1988–1989), 114–17. It is equally clear that the withdrawal of Leuven professor René Draguet's teaching assignment in July 1942 was linked to the condemnation of Charlier's *Essai.* Cf. Ward De Pril, *Theological Renewal and the Resurgence of Integrism: The René Draguet Case (1942) in Its Context,* BETL 266 (Leuven: Peeters, 2016).

published in 1944 under the title *Conversion et grâce chez Saint Thomas d'Aquin*.[19] In the book's concluding observations, he wrote that "a theology lacking topicality was a false theology."[20] This type of statement could easily be interpreted as an attack on neoscholasticism. The same goes for the 1946 article by Jean Daniélou published in the journal *Études*, under the title *Orientations présentes de la pensée religieuse*.[21] Not only was Daniélou explicit in arguing that Thomism had a relative value, he also insisted that a return to the Bible, liturgy, and patristics was to be preferred over a theology that owed its existence to "a single medieval theologian." The commotion that followed the article caused the dismissal of Daniélou as editor of *Études*. The third publication, which appeared in the same year, was Henri de Lubac's *Surnaturel*.[22] Based on a historical study, de Lubac wanted to present a sort of essay in which "contact between Catholic theology and contemporary thought could be restored," as he later stated in his *Mémoire sur l'occasion de mes écrits*.[23] Here the seventeenth-century debates on grace and on the correct interpretation of Augustinian theology did in fact filter through. Nevertheless, the traditional divisions on the subject were no longer crucial. Like his colleagues at Le Saulchoir, De Lubac did not hesitate to pepper his overview with barely concealed critique of neoscholasticism. In his opinion, the latter swallowed up the mystery of faith, and left no genuine room for the experience of the supernatural.

Their desire to inject theology with a new lease of life, grace and its associated return to the sources of the faith inspired the Jesuits of Lyon to establish the series *Sources chrétiennes* and *Théologie*, in 1942 and 1944, respectively.[24] Both series were based at the Jesuit house of studies located on the Fourvière hill in the city of Lyon.[25] It was not long before the Lyon scholasticate and the series became vehicles of the *"nouvelle théologie,"* and soon de Lubac emerged as a central figure.[26] Fergus Kerr has convincingly argued that de Lubac's *Surnaturel* served as

---

[19] Henri Bouillard, *Conversion et grâce chez saint Thomas d'Aquin: Étude historique*, Théologie 1 (Paris: Aubier, 1944). Bouillard defended his dissertation at La Fourvière in 1941. On his theology, see Michel Castro, "Henri Bouillard (1908–1981): éléments de biographie intellectuelle," *Mélanges de science religieuse* 60 (2003), 43–58; and Michel Castro, "Henri Bouillard (1908–1981): éléments de biographie intellectuelle," *Mélanges de science religieuse* 63, no. 2 (2006), 47–59; Karl H. Neufeld, "Von Gott reden: Henri Bouillard 1908–1981," *Stimmen der Zeit* 199 (1981), 786–88; Thomas G. Guarino, "Henri Bouillard and the Truth-Status of Dogmatic Statements," *Science et Esprit* 39 (1987), 331–43; Eileen Scully, *Grace and Human Freedom in the Theology of Henri Bouillard* (Bethesda, MD: Academica Press, 2007).

[20] Bouillard, *Conversion et grâce chez saint Thomas d'Aquin*, 219.

[21] Jean Daniélou, "Les orientations présentes de la pensée religieuse," *Études* 79 (1946), 5–21.

[22] Henri de Lubac, *Surnaturel. Études historiques*, Théologie 8 (Paris: Cerf, 1946).

[23] Henri de Lubac, *Mémoire sur l'occasion de mes écrits*, Œuvres completes 33 (Paris: Cerf, 2006), 34.

[24] Excellent studies on both theologians are written by Bernard Sesboüé, *Yves de Montcheuil (1900–1944): Précurseur en théologie*, Cogitatio fidei 255 (Paris: Cerf, 2006); and Patrice Boudignon, *Pierre Teilhard de Chardin: Sa vie, son œuvre, sa reflexion*, Cerf Histoire (Paris: Cerf, 2008).

[25] On Fourvière, see Étienne Fouilloux, "Une 'école de Fourvière'?," *Gregorianum* 83 (2002), 451–59; Fouilloux, *Une Église en quête de liberté*, 172–91; Dominique Avon, "Une école théologique à Fourvière?," *Les jésuites à Lyon: XVIe-XXe siècle*, ed. Étienne Fouilloux and Bernard Hours (Lyon: ENS, 2005), 231–46.

[26] On de Lubac and the difficulties he was facing at the time, see Bernard Comte, "Le Père de Lubac, un théologien dans l'Église de Lyon," *Henri de Lubac. La rencontre au cœur de l'Église*, ed. J.-D. Durand (Paris: Cerf, 2006), 35–89, especially 73–81; Étienne Fouilloux, "Autour d'un livre (1946–1953)," *Henri de Lubac. La rencontre au cœur de l'Église*, ed. J.-D. Durand (Paris: Cerf, 2006), 91–107, especially 93–95. For a more general study, see Joseph A. Komonchak, "Theology at Mid-Century: The Example of Henri de Lubac," *Theological Studies* 51 (1990), 579–602.

a symbol in the struggle for historical theology. Even if this was unintentional, it became a landmark of critique upon the traditional approaches of Catholic theology that had heretofore relied on scholastic deductions and conclusions, and used Denzinger's collection of ecclesial fragments as its primary source. Kerr even went on to argue that *Surnaturel* brought about the greatest crisis of twentieth-century Thomism.[27]

For the Jesuits, a return to the sources of faith was regarded as the best antidote to Rome's prescribed orientation toward neoscholasticism. The embrace of historical reasoning called for Catholic theology to abandon the a-historical strand of Thomism and to criticize meta-historical "magisteriumism." In short, a kind of "source theology" was being advocated for. But just as Charlier and Chenu did in 1942, de Lubac and the Fourvière Jesuits met with stiff opposition. Once again, the famous voice of neoscholasticism, Garrigou-Lagrange, reacted. In February 1947, he published an article *La nouvelle théologie où va-t-elle?*[28] The answer to the question was clear: *nouvelle théologie* was a new form of Modernism. Garrigou-Lagrange firmly stated that the weapons used in the past to combat Modernism should again be used to suppress its resurgence.

History seemed to repeat itself. Alarmed by these allegations, the Jesuit authorities took action, and here too, not only Frenchmen were involved, but also churchmen from Schillebeeckx native soil. It was the Belgian Jesuit Jean-Baptiste Janssens, the Order's recently elected Superior General, who set up an inquiry into the orthodoxy of the teaching at Lyon-Fourvière.[29] The screening of the faculty was led by his former Leuven colleague and close confidant, Édouard Dhanis. Dhanis traveled to Lyon in 1949 and in June 1950, and his visit resulted, among other things, in the transfer of Henri de Lubac and Henri Bouillard from Lyon to Paris. This would have been a full-fledged promotion had the circumstances been otherwise. In parallel with this discretely organized inquiry and the resulting sanctions, a war now raged between the Roman Dominicans (with the *Revue thomiste* as their mouthpiece) and the Jesuits of Lyon (speaking through the *Recherches de science religieuse*).[30]

Slightly before the appearance of Garrigou-Lagrange's article charging the ressourcement theologians with Modernism, Pius XII—who likely had prior knowledge of the study—entered the debate. On September 17, 1946, he addressed the Jesuit general congregation,[31] and five days later, he did the same in front of the general chapter of the Dominicans.[32] The pope insisted that enough had been said about *nouvelle théologie* and that the time had come to end the debate. His words fell on deaf ears, and even provided the debate with new ammunition and publicity. Ultimately, Pius XII promulgated *Humani generis* in 1950: the encyclical can be understood as

---

[27] Fergus Kerr, *After Aquinas: Versions of Thomism* (Malden, MA: Blackwell, 2002), 134.

[28] Réginald Garrigou-Lagrange, "La nouvelle théologie où va-t-elle?," *Angelicum* 23 (1946), 126–45.

[29] Jürgen Mettepenningen and Karim Schelkens, "'*Quod immutabile est, nemo turbet et moveat*': Les rapports entre H. de Lubac et le P. Général J.-B. Janssens dans les années 1946–1948. À propos de documents inédits," *Cristianesimo nella storia* 29 (2008), 139–72.

[30] For an insight into the polemics surrounding "nouvelle théologie", see Fouilloux, *Dialogue théologique? (1946–1948)*, 153–95; Fouilloux, *Autour d'un livre (1946–1953)*; Aidan Nichols, "Thomism and '*nouvelle théologie*'," *The Thomist* 64 (2000), 1–19.

[31] Cf. "Il venerato Discorso del Sommo Pontifice alla XXIX Congregazione Generale della Compagnia di Gesù," *Osservatore Romano* (September 19, 1946), 1; see also, *AAS* 38 (946), 381–85.

[32] Cf. "Fervido Discorso del Sommo Pontifice ai Capitolari dell'Ordine dei Frati Predicatori," *Osservatore Romano* (September 23–24, 1946), 1; see also, *AAS* 38 (1946), 385–89.

Rome's final serious defense of neoscholasticism as a normative framework determining not only the style and method, but also the orthodoxy of Catholic theology.[33] The contents of *Humani generis* ran in a striking parallel to Pius X's encyclical against Modernism: *Pascendi dominici gregis*. On the other hand, *Humani generis* nowhere explicitly mentions the *nouvelle théologie*, even when it clearly targeted this particular movement.[34] The pope attacked historicism, for example, insisting that it places so much emphasis on particular facts that it thereby destroys the foundations of the universal truth of faith.

# II. The reception of the movement: From the 1950s to the Council

As had happened in 1942 with the Dominicans, the Jesuit scholars were also curtailed by a Roman censure. But again, this did not mark the end of their theological enterprise. As of 1950, *nouvelle théologie* swiftly sailed into new waters, and in the period between *Humani Generis* and the Second Vatican Council, it crossed the borders of France. In the German-speaking world the likes of Karl Rahner and Hans Urs von Balthasar picked up its insights,[35] while in the Low Countries it was received by young scholars such as Edward Schillebeeckx and Piet Schoonenberg.[36] Schillebeeckx and Schoonenberg would eventually become colleagues at the Catholic University of Nijmegen. In his 1948 doctoral dissertation, the Jesuit Schoonenberg made it clear that a correct reading of Augustine was crucial in the turn from neo-scholastic theology to theology as an articulation of the living faith.[37] For Schoonenberg, this meant picking up the new evolutions in Christological thought, which were set out by Belgian theologians such as Émile Mersch and exegetes such as Stanislas Lyonnet, a fellow Jesuit who was professor in exegesis at the Biblicum in Rome. In a series of four books on *The Faith of Our Baptism*, authored between 1955 and 1962, Schoonenberg elaborated an extensive approach of the creed, built upon the sources of faith: the Bible and

---

33  Pius XII, *Humani generis* (August 12, 1950) http://w2.vatican.va/content/pius-xii/en/encyclicals/documents/hf_p-xii_enc_12081950_humani-generis.html.

34  The encyclical does not mention "*nouvelle théologie*" by name, yet it does condemn thirteen matters it refers to as "new" and which were targeted at the movement.

35  Bernard Sesboüé, *Karl Rahner*, Initiations aux théologiens (Paris: Cerf, 2001), 193–95; Rudolf Voderholzer, "Die Bedeutung der sogenannten 'Nouvelle Théologie' (insbesondere Henri de Lubacs) für die Theologie Hans Urs von Balthasars," *Logik der Liebe und Herrlichkeit Gottes: Hans Urs von Balthasar im Gespräch*, ed. W. Kasper (Ostfildern: Matthias Grünewald, 2006), 204–28.

36  Cf. Jürgen Mettepenningen, "Edward Schillebeeckx: herodero y promotor de la 'nouvelle théologie'," *Mayéutica* 78 (2008): 285–302; Jürgen Mettepenningen, "Christus denken naar de mensen toe: de 'nouvelle théologie' christologisch doorgedacht door Piet Schoonenberg," *TvT* 46 (2006), 143–60.

37  Piet Schoonenberg, *Theologie als geloofsvertolking: Het proefschrift van 1948*, ed. Leo Kenis and Jürgen Mettepenningen, Documenta libraria 36 (Leuven: Peeters, 2008). See also, Jürgen Mettepenningen and Leo Kenis, eds., *Theologie als geloofsvertolking: Historische en theologische reflecties over het proefschrift van Piet Schoonenberg*, Annua Nuntia Lovaniensia 73 (Leuven: Peeters, 2016).

Patristics.[38] Here too, theology entered a period of return to its ancient sources, moving away from neoscholasticism. While in France the ressourcement movement was silenced, it did have connections with the work of the worker priests (*prêtres-ouvriers*), who carried out its pastoral aspect.[39] In any case, the internationalization of the movement allowed for the presence of non-Francophone voices, which were more widespread by the time the Council opened. Nonetheless, it should be noted that *nouvelle théologie* was not well received in countries such as Italy and Spain.[40]

Ultimately, the renewals that had been fought for in the decades prior were picked up and broadly embraced by the Second Vatican Council—described by Bruno Forte as "the council of history."[41] We will not discuss the Council at length here, but we may point to the fact that it constituted a key moment of reception and rehabilitation of *nouvelle théologie*. In this regard, two documents may be singled out in particular. For starters, the dogmatic constitution *Dei verbum* contained definite echoes of "*nouvelle théologie*" on the level of the acceptance of historical reasoning and "return to the sources," as well as its reframing theology of revelation. Studies of the initial conciliar draft on revelation have helped to clarify that the Council made a definitive step beyond framing revelation in a "propositional" manner, and that the Council resolutely opted for an approach that embraced historical contingency. That sensitivity can be felt even more strongly in another constitution, which was promulgated only toward the end of the Council. Many of those involved in ressourcement theology played an active role in the redaction and drafting of a new and unique document: *Gaudium et spes*, the Pastoral Constitution on the Church in the Modern World.[42]

This influence was not a coincidence: many of the renewal movements of the preconciliar era (the liturgical movement, ecumenical movement, patristic movement, etc.) left their mark on the Council's teachings.[43] As for *nouvelle théologie*, its impact could already be felt in John XXIII's opening statement to the council, where he made a clear distinction between the lived truth and the timely formulations of truth. Several representatives of "*nouvelle théologie*" were present

---

[38]  Piet Schoonenberg, *Het geloof van ons doopsel. Gesprekken over de Apostolische Geloofsbelijdenis*, vol. 1: *God, Vader en Schepper. Het eerste geloofsartikel* ('s-Hertogenbosch: Malmberg, 1955); ET: Piet Schoonenberg, *Covenant and Creation* (London/Sydney: Sheed and Ward, 1968); vol. 2: *Jezus, de Christus, de Zoon Gods. Het tweede geloofsartikel* ('s-Hertogenbosch: Malmberg, 1956); vol. 3: *De Mensgeworden Zoon van God. Het derde geloofsartikel*, 's-Hertogenbosch: Malmberg, 1958; vol. 4: *De macht der zonde. Inleiding op de verlossingsleer* ('s-Hertogenbosch: Malmberg, 1962); ET: *Man and Sin: A Theological View* (London/Melbourne: Sheed and Ward, 1965).

[39]  See Wolfgang W. Müller, "Was kann an der Theologie neu sein? Der Beitrag der Dominikaner zur 'nouvelle théologie'," *Zeitschrift für Kirchengeschichte* 110 (1999), 86–104, at 103. He has suggested that suggested that the *prêtres-ouvriers* phenomenon represents a pastoral expression of "*nouvelle théologie*".

[40]  Étienne Fouilloux, "La 'nouvelle théologie' française vue d'Espagne (1948–1951)," *Revue d'histoire de l'Église de France* 90 (2004), 279–93.

[41]  Bruno Forte, "Le prospettive della ricera teologica," *Il Concilio Vaticano II. Recezione e attualità alla luce del Giubileo*, ed. Rino Fisichella (Milan: San Paolo, 2000), 419–29, at 423.

[42]  Dries Bosschaert, *Joys and Hopes of Louvain Theologians: The Genesis of a Louvain Christian Anthropology and Its Diverse Reception in* Gaudium et spes *(1942–1965)*, unpublished dissertation (KU Leuven, 2017).

[43]  See Gilles Routhier, Philippe Roy, and Karim Schelkens, eds., *La theologie catholique au milieu du XXeme siècle: Entre Renouveau et intransigeance* (Brepols: Turnhout, 2011). Schillebeeckx is referred to on several occasions in this collection.

during the Second Vatican Council as *periti* (Congar, de Lubac, Daniélou) or as a personal advisor to one of the Council fathers or Bishop conferences (Chenu, Féret, Schillebeeckx),[44] and many of them played a role in bringing the "anthropological turn" that came along with theological ressourcement, into the conciliar aula.[45] Generally speaking, one might argue that the Second Vatican Council turned the negative connotations associated with *nouvelle théologie* into positive ones which transformed into a broad acceptance of the movement's principles within Catholicism. Later, this was reflected by the fact that several of its protagonists were made cardinals: Daniélou in 1969, de Lubac in 1983, Congar—sadly too late—in 1994, and Urs von Balthasar in 1988. Then again, this was never the case for the Belgian native Edward Schillebeeckx.

# III. Schillebeeckx as a complex recipient of *nouvelle théologie*

## Paris and Louvain: Hotspots of theological renewal

When seeking the crossroads between the German-speaking kerygmatic theology, or *Verkündigungstheologie*, and the French-speaking *nouvelle théologie*, Belgium occupies a central position. Not only did the three spoken languages (French, Dutch, and German) create opportunities for exchange, they were also home to two places where the above portrayed renewals were launched in the 1930s: Leuven, where Charlier elaborated his vision and where Draguet was among those dismissed in 1942; and Le Saulchoir, the study house of Dominicans like Congar, Chenu, and Féret, which had been located in Belgium until 1937 when it moved to Étiolles on the outskirts of Paris. A glance at his biography reveals that Schillebeeckx had ties

---

44 For those among them who were faced with Roman sanctions, the Council did imply a rehabilitation, albeit without apology or explicit reinstatement Cf. Yves Congar, *Journal d'un théologien 1946–1956* (Paris: Cerf, 2001). Interesting studies on the role and impact of the French theologians and *nouvelle theologie* at Vatican II include: Michael Quisinsky, "Aggiornamento – aber wie? Die Konzilstheologen Henri de Lubac SJ und Yves Congar OP zwischen nouvelle théologie und Konzilsrezeption," *Freiburger Zeitschrift für Philosophie und Theologie* 58 (2011), 5–33; Hans Boersma, "Néoplatonisme belgo-français': 'Nouvelle théologie' and the Search for a Sacramental Ontology," *Louvain Studies* 32 (2007), 333–60; Hans Boersma, *Nouvelle Théologie and Sacramental Ontology: A Return to Mystery* (Oxford: Oxford University Press, 2009); Brian Daley, "The Nouvelle Théologie and the Patristic Revival: Sources, Symbols and the Science of Theology," *International Journal of Systematic Theology* 7 (2005), 362–82; Jean-Claude Petit, "La compréhenssion de la théologie dans la théologie française au XXe siècle: Pour une théologie qui réponde à nos nécessités: la nouvelle théologie," *Laval théologique et philosophique* 48 (1992), 415–31; Michael Quisinsky, *Geschichtlicher Glaube in einer geschichtlichen Welt: Der Beitrag von M.-D. Chenu, Y. Congar und H.-M. Féret zum II. Vaticanum, Dogma und Geschichte* (Berlin: LIT, 2007); Michael Quisinsky, "The 'Interference' Between Nouvelle Théologie and Catholic Practice in Church and Society," *Ephemerides Theologicae Lovanienses* 90 (2014), 71–98.

45 For reference to this "anthropological turn," see Hans-Joachim Sander's commentary on *Gaudium et spes*: Hans-Joachim Sander, "Theologischer Kommentar zur Pastoralkonstitution über die Kirche in der Welt von heute. Gaudium et spes," *Herders Theologischer Kommentar zum Zweiten Vatikanischen Konzil*, ed. Peter Hünermann and Bernd Jochen Hilberath (Freiburg im Breisgau: Herder, 2005), 605.

with both places in the preconciliar era. In what follows we will focus on the way in which his early thoughts were developed within the double horizon of ressourcement theology and of the rising efforts to construct a Christian humanism.

Born in Antwerp on November 12, 1914, Schillebeeckx entered the noviciate of the Dominican Order in Ghent at the age of twenty. His entrance in 1934 was followed by the traditional three years of studies in philosophy, which he did in the Leuven study house of the order. In 1938 Schillebeeckx did his compulsory military service in the Belgian army, where he seemingly had plenty of time to read philosophical and theological books.[46] Then, after a short stay in Leuven, he was again called to military service due to the outbreak of the Second World War. However, his military career was a brief one: he already returned to the study of theology in Leuven in by the middle of 1940 after the capitulation of the Belgian government, where he obtained his lectorate and was ordained a priest in the next year. In 1943, he defended his thesis in Leuven and was appointed as a lecturer at the study house before he even obtained a doctorate. Once the war was over, the young Dominican friar pursued doctoral studies; he moved to Paris, and became a student at Le Saulchoir. For two years, he attended lectures there, as well as at other institutes in Paris. At the Sorbonne he attended classes of Chenu on the *Renaissance et évangelisation au temps des Sommes*, and at Le Saulchoir he would listen to Congar lecturing on Karl Barth. Well trained in French *nouvelle théologie*, he was called back to Leuven in 1947, where Schillebeeckx himself began to teach dogmatic theology. The ties with the Dominicans in Paris were still strong, since he was working on his doctoral dissertation for Le Saulchoir. In 1952 it appeared as a book, entitled *De sacramentele heilseconomie*.[47]

It will hardly come as a surprise that in this work, as Fergus Kerr puts it, "the historical-contextualist approach to Thomas Aquinas, characteristic of Chenu, and the trawling through patristic and medieval scholastic literature as practiced by Congar, are very evident—while the interest in phenomenological philosophy already indicates the conditions for Schillebeeckx to develop his own distinctive approach."[48] This approach is often explicitly connected to the influence of the Le Saulchoir, but there were in fact other factors which also played a role. In the 1950s Schillebeeckx's academic career advanced, and in 1956 he was appointed as professor at the Higher Institute for Religious Studies, of the Catholic University of Leuven. He was not there for long however, and in the autumn of 1957 he left Belgium to become professor in Dogmatics at the Catholic University of Nijmegen, where he started giving his first lectures in January 1958. It is, however, quite relevant to take a closer look at the Leuven Institute. The Institute where Schillebeeckx was hired was established in the pivotal year of 1942, by the Leuven Faculty of Theology.[49] Two pioneers were behind the launching of this autonomous institute: the biblical scholar Lucien Cerfaux and the philosopher Albert Dondeyne, who was himself well versed in

---

[46] Borgman, *Edward Schillebeeckx*, 48.

[47] Edward Schillebeeckx, *De sacramentele heilseconomie: Theologische bezinning op S. Thomas' sacramentenleer in het licht van de traditie en van de hedendaagse sacramentenproblematiek* (Antwerp/Bilthoven: 't Groeit/H. Nelissen, 1952).

[48] Fergus Kerr, *Twentieth-Century Catholic Theologians* (Malden, MA: Blackwell, 2007), 54.

[49] See Lieve Gevers, "Vijfig jaar Hoger Instituut voor Godsdienstwetenschappen: 1942–1992," *Hoger Instituut voor Godsdienstwetenschappen: Faculteit der Godgeleerdheid KU Leuven, 1942–1992. Rondom catechese en godsdienstonderricht*, ed. Mathijs Lamberigts, Lieve Gevers, and Bart Pattyn, Documenta Libraria 13 (Leuven: Peeters, 1992), 3–58.

the Leuven phenomenological school. These founders had gained the support of the vice-rector and later cardinal Léon-Joseph Suenens.[50] Since the theological faculty was at that time a clerical training center, the Institute positioned itself differently: it was made responsible for the religious formation of students who belonged to faculties other than Theology. This implied that teaching there ought to connect theological themes with the interests of lay students and that the Institute was less bound to ecclesiastical control than a traditional faculty. To make its courses available for a broader public, the series *Bibliothèque de l'Institut Supérieur des Sciences Religieuses* was set up in 1945, and would publish many of the lectures given at this institute until the mid-1950s, when it was reformed. As Dries Bosschaert has rightly pointed out, the Institute and its series became fertile ground for new forms of theology focusing on Christian anthropology: "Here 'Christian humanism' (Charles Moeller), 'theology of earthly realities' (especially Gustave Thils), 'theology of history' (*idem*), 'theology of the laity' (especially Gerard Philips), or contemporary philosophy (especially [Franz] Grégoire) were developed."[51] In fact, the Institute's aim was similar, albeit with different points of emphasis, to the basic principles of Chenu's Saulchoir: it was open to the articulation of lived faith in an intellectually responsible way. Through the influence of Dondeyne it cultivated a strong interest in the development of a contemporary brand of Christian humanism and in the articulation of faith through using phenomenological insights. The interest in the human person in relation to the world that typified the Leuven Institute was further developed at the Faculty's Professor of Moral Theology, Louis Janssens, who took up that chair in 1947.[52] All of them, including Schillebeeckx who had received his theological training precisely in the period between 1938 and 1952, could not escape the "new theology" of France

---

50  Léon-Joseph Suenens (1904–1996) was a Belgian archbishop and Cardinal. For Suenens's personal recollections, see Léon-Joseph Suenens, *Souvenirs et espérances* (Paris: Fayard, 1991); Léon-Joseph Suenens, *Les imprévus de Dieu* (Paris: Fayard, 1993); Léon-Joseph Suenens, *L.J. Cardinal Suenens: Mémoires sur le Concile Vatican II*, ed. Werner Van Laer, Instrumenta Theologica 38 (Leuven: Peeters, 2015). Regarding his role at Vatican II, see Leo Declerck and Eddy Louchez, eds., *Inventaire des papiers conciliaires du Cardinal L.-J. Suenens*, Cahiers de la Revue théologique de Louvain 31 (Louvain-la-Neuve/Leuven: UCL Faculté de Théologie/Peeters, 1988); Mathijs Lamberigts and Leo Declerck, "The Role of Cardinal Léon-Joseph Suenens at Vatican II," *The Belgian Contribution to the Second Vatican Council: International Research Conference at Mechelen, Leuven, and Louvain-la-Neuve (September 12–16, 2005)*, ed. Doris Donnelly, Joseph Famerée, Mathijs Lamberigts and Karim Schelkens, BETL 216 (Leuven: Peeters, 2008), 61–217.
51  Bosschaert, *Joys and Hopes of Louvain Theologians*, 57.
52  Louis Janssens was Professor of Moral Theology at Leuven. He studied at the Major Seminary of Mechelen (Malines) and in 1934 was ordained a priest. He then studied theology in Leuven and obtained his doctorate with a thesis titled *La filiation divine par grâce d'après Cyrille d'Alexandrie*. In 1942 he was appointed as a professor at the Faculty of Theology. In 1978 he received emeritus status. His most well-known work was Louis Janssens, *Personne et société: Théories actuelles et essai doctrinal*, Dissertationes ad gradum magistri in Facultate Theologica vel in Facultate Iuris Canonici consequendum conscriptae series II 32 (Gembloux: Duculot, 1939). For more information see Roger Burggraeve, "Le personnalisme holistique du professeur Louis Janssens," *Ephemerides Theologicae Lovanienses* 78 (2002), 267–76; and Jan Jans, *Some Remarks on the Work of Professor Emeritus Louis Janssens, Personalist Morals: Essays in Honor of Professor Louis Janssens*, ed. Joseph A. Selling, BETL 83 (Leuven: Peeters, 1988); Johan De Tavernier, "The Historical Roots of Personalism: From Renouvier's Le Personnalisme, Mounier's Manifeste au service du personnalisme and Maritain's Humanisme intégral to Janssens' Personne et Société," *Ethical Perspectives* 16 (2009), 361–92.

and Belgium. He did not go and study at the Angelicum in Rome, but rather he had received his training in Leuven and Le Saulchoir. As a result, he had direct contact with both the Belgian and French protagonists of renewal. In our next and final part, we would like to illustrate how this filtered through in his theological writings.

# IV. The theological imprint of *nouvelle théologie* and Christian anthropology

To portray Schillebeeckx as both an inheritor of *nouvelle théologie* and of the Leuven school of Christian humanists helps avoid mistaking him for a full member of the movement. Nevertheless, the similarities are at times striking, and Schillebeeckx's early writings display a combination of both backgrounds. In perhaps a rather general way, Schillebeeckx had a strong aversion to neoscholasticism. Already during his student years this caused him to switch from dogmatics to exegesis, in order to study the sources of faith. One of Schillebeeckx's biographers has pointed to "his discontent with speculative theology" as the origin of a two-year study of biblical exegesis,[53] and later, in his "theological testament," Schillebeeckx noted that he had "no positive memories of the rather old-fashioned Leuven theologate of the Dominicans."[54] At this point, there is a third factor of influence to consider. While he thought of most of his early training as irrelevant, he was deeply influenced by one confrere, and would keep on stressing this: Dominicus De Petter was one of the rare figures who had been able to combine modern philosophy with classic metaphysics. He considered the then-dominant form of theology as static, impersonal, non-historical, and immovable. Theology at the time was, in fact, purely based on the interpretation of Thomism by the magisterium, consolidated in a tradition of theological handbooks, or "manuals." As a student, Schillebeeckx reacted against the speculative manualist system, when writing a thesis on *The Sinful Past History of Christianity Following Saint Paul*.[55]

It was in this year, 1942, in which Rome reacted to what was happening in the Dominican Order: two teachers of Schillebeeckx at the Leuven Dominican house were under scrutiny by the magisterium. In February the *Essai sur le problème théologique* of Louis Charlier was placed on the Index of Forbidden Books, along with Chenu's programmatic book on Le Saulchoir, and the publications of Leuven University professor René Draguet. Later that year, the superiors of the Dominican Order removed De Petter from his responsibilities as master of studies in the Leuven study house on account of the aforementioned article on implicit intuition. Although this occurred in the midst of the *nouvelle theologie* condemnations, De Petter's case was slightly different.[56] The renewal of theological discourse was felt in several religious orders in Belgium

---

[53] John Bowden, *Edward Schillebeeckx: Portrait of a Theologian* (London: SCM, 1983), 28.

[54] Edward Schillebeeckx, *Theologisch testament: Notarieel nog niet verleden*, 2nd ed. (Baarn: Nelissen, 1995), 25.

[55] Edward Schillebeeckx, *De zondige voorgeschiedenis van het christendom volgens Sint Paulus*, unpublished thesis (Louvain, 1942).

[56] Cf. Bosschaert, "Dominicus De Petter O.P., a Forgotten Victim of the Crisis Caused by the Nouvelle Théologie?," *Ephemerides Theologicae Lovanienses* 93/94 (2017), 633–56.

who had study houses near the Catholic University of Leuven. With the Dominicans, it had been De Petter who had constructed the foundations of a Catholic philosophy and metaphysics open to the importance of human experience, and this connected well with the interest of others in Leuven for Christian anthropology. The loss of his position as *regens studii* did not, however, prevent him from influencing students such as Schillebeeckx and the Belgian Dominican, Jan Hendrik Walgrave (1911–1986).[57] The former of whom discovered in De Petter's thought the possibility of connecting theoretical insights with lived reality. This was a possibility that Schillebeeckx believed could make the Christian faith relevant again. In addition, Schillebeeckx had, based on the theology of Chenu, found a new path toward establishing a theology that was responsive to everyday life. Walgrave was appointed to a position at the Dominican study house in 1943, and he became just as important to Schillebeeckx. In 1957 Walgrave also started teaching at the Higher Institute for Religious Studies, and he ranked among the strongest proponents of a Christian humanism in the Belgian province of the Dominican Order. As Bosschaert observes:

> Walgrave's book, *Op menselijke grondslag. Christelijke verantwoording van de cultuur,* testified to a broad humanist formation and the will to establish from a Christian perspective an ideal view of the human person and its relationship with culture. Moreover, under the pseudonym *Humanus*, he advocated in the journal *Kultuurleven* for a renewal of culture based upon an increased humanist consciousness.[58]

Walgrave had hoped that his humanism would "be able to bridge the gap between a disincarnated way of being Christian and a world without Christianity."[59]

That said, Schillebeeckx picked up various strands of theological thought in the years just before and during the Second World War. These influences would ring through his work in the preconciliar era. In what follows, we will enumerate some examples. Let us begin with a brief look at the inaugural lecture delivered by Schillebeeckx on September 26, 1943, as a professor in Dogmatics at the Dominican study house in Leuven. The search for a philosophy that was engaged with the actual life of people was perhaps best expressed in this lecture, which pleaded in favor of a strong relationship between theology and life.[60] The unpublished address is entitled "Towards a Theology of Life?" There, Schillebeeckx first reacted against the non-scientific way in which kerygmatic theology tried to connect life and theology. Next, he rejected the drastic separation of theology and life, as promoted by Georg Koepgen in his 1939 book *The Gnosis of Christianity*.[61] Rather, Schillebeeckx put forward his own vision in contrast to these two

---

[57] For more information on Walgrave see Georges De Schrijver, "De theoloog Walgrave," *Selected Writings. Thematische Geschriften. Thomas Aquinas, J.H. Newman, Theologia Fundamentalis by Jan H. Walgrave*, ed. Georges de Schrijver and James Kelly, BETL 57 (Leuven: Peeters, 1982), xi–xxvi; Hans Kothuis and Ron Rolheiser, "Jan Hendrik Walgrave," *Louvain Studies* 8 (1981), 219–26.

[58] Bosschaert, *Joys and Hopes of Louvain Theologians*, 58. See Jan Hendrik Walgrave, *Op menselijke grondslag: Christelijke verantwoording van de cultuur* (Antwerp: Sheed and Ward, 1951); second edition: Jan Hendrik Walgrave, *Op menselijke grondslag: Grond-pijlers voor een christelijk humanisme* (Antwerp: 't Groeit, 1955); Jan Hendrik Walgrave, "Humanisme en christelijk humanisme, de groei van de idee," *Kultuurleven* 15 (1948), 293–300.

[59] De Schrijver, "De theoloog Walgrave," xii.

[60] This inaugural lecture can be found in the Schillebeeckx Archives: *Arch.* 358.

[61] Georg Koepgen, *Die Gnosis des Christentums* (Trier: Spee, 1978).

currents. In his biography, Erik Borgman discusses this as follows: "It was very important for him that faith was not just an existential experience, as the kerygmatic theologians emphasized, or an unconditional submission to the absolute mystery, as it was for Koepgen. Faith was also a form of real, albeit diffuse, knowledge of God."[62] One page prior, Borgman makes it clear that Schillebeeckx's address advocated for a theology which was both scientific and closely associated with a living faith, and he stated that:

> Although he did not spell this out, here at the same time he indicated that the dominant scholastic theology which exclusively occupied itself with the statements defined by the magisterium as "truths of faith", did not meet the demand for a scholarly theology as seen by Thomas Aquinas, the one who by its own account was *the* philosophical and theological authority.[63]

This, of course, is very close to the critical voice of the French Dominicans.

Four days after Schillebeeckx's inaugural address, Pope Pius XII promulgated *Divinu afflante Spiritu*. In this encyclical the door was carefully opened for the implementation of the historical-critical method into biblical research, especially exegesis. This was a milestone in the history of the attitude of the magisterium toward historical criticism. The encyclical is also important in light of Schillebeeckx's own attention to the Bible. Undoubtedly he felt confirmed in his conviction of the great value of a historical approach, such as the one present in the *nouvelle théologie* and defended by Chenu. The need for ressourcement (and the interest in both tradition and the Scriptures) can be felt strongly here, and, later, in his "theological testament," Schillebeeckx wrote:

> Under the guidance of Chenu I read St Thomas from a historical perspective and not just literally, in the context of the philosophy of the time. At Le Saulchoir I learned to tackle problems from a historical perspective. In my courses, in succession, I went through the Old and New Testaments, the teaching of the Fathers, of St Thomas and the post-Tridentine era. I was convinced that faith and reflection on the faith should be in close contact with the tradition.[64]

Together with Chenu, Féret, and Congar, he felt himself to be among the promoters of a historical *ressourcement*. Half a century later, he would state that his feeling for history developed a great deal while he was in Paris. Schillebeeckx could not but take notice of the polemic concerning the *nouvelle théologie*, especially after 1942. Following Schillebeeckx, his interest in historically based renewal "can be traced quite easily" in the book that he published in 1952, *De sacramentele*

---

[62]  Erik Borgman, *Edward Schillebeeckx: A Theologian in His History* (London: Continuum, 2003), 65.

[63]  Ibid., 64.

[64]  Edward Schillebeeckx, *I Am a Happy Theologian: Conversations with Francesco Strazzari* (London: SCM, 1994), 8. Similar information is provided in Schillebeeckx's *Theologisch testament*: "Under the guidance of Chenu I studied the twelfth century and Thomas from a historical point of view, in the context of his time. Also at Le Saulchoir all theology was seen in a perspective of historical development. Later, in my own lectures, I tried to clarify historically all tracts, from the Old Testament to the twentieth century, which was, in fact, unfeasible. I am, however, convinced of the fact that faith, history and theology have to be considered in close connection to each other." Schillebeeckx, *Theologisch testament*, 28. Our translation.

*heilseconomie*, in which he "began with Thomas Aquinas and went back from him to the Church Fathers and then forward to the problems of today."[65]

The Christian humanist influence had certainly not escaped him, nor did the interest in the training of lay people that was also present in Leuven. This is at best felt in a 1949 article in the "journal for spiritual life," *Tijdschrift voor Geestelijk Leven*, where he wrote that:

> The Catholic community of the laity should acquire a deeper responsibility for their vocation and be more competently prepared to take up their Christian task in the world. That they may be conscious of their calling to the very summit of the life of prayer and an intense sacramental life so that they might in turn fully engage in a world-conquering, earthly realization, *ut adveniat Regnum Dei*, so that the Kingdom of God might come. May Thomas More, the sainted lay-humanist, serve as their example![66]

We mention this passage because it makes clear that by the beginning of the 1950s, Schillebeeckx had integrated various schools: Le Saulchoir's historical ressourcement, Leuven's Christian humanism, and De Petter's emphasis on a metaphysically grounded ethos. His grounding in the latter also resulted in Schillebeeckx being at times closer to the French Dominicans, and at other times to his Leuven colleagues, of whom he could be quite critical. This threefold legacy characterized his attitude before the Council, and remained a part of him, even after he moved to Nijmegen, where he would eventually become one of the key theologians of his age. These influences can be traced in his writings from the preconciliar decade. For instance, it is striking that in a three-volume Dutch theological dictionary (1952–1958) all of the contributions relating to key-themes of *nouvelle théologie* are authored or co-authored by Schillebeeckx. This includes keywords such as: "Development of Dogma," "History," "*Humani generis*," and "Theology."[67] Even the term "*nouvelle théologie*" is laid out in the dictionary by Schillebeeckx,[68] wherein he writes that: "most of the time *nouvelle théologie* is connected with the admonitions of *Humani generis* against modernizing theological tendencies, at least so far they would deny or minimize speculative thought in theology."[69] In his contribution on the "Development of Dogma," Schillebeeckx extensively discussed the aforementioned book by Charlier and the series of articles by Draguet, just as he did in the lemma "Theology."

---

[65] Schillebeeckx, *God Is New Each Moment*, 15.

[66] Edward Schillebeeckx "Theologische grondslagen van de lekenspiritualiteit," *TGL* 5 (1949), 146–66, at 166: "Dat de katholieke lekengemeenschap een inniger roepingsverantwoordelijkheid zou verwerven en deskundiger dan voorheen zou opgewassen zijn voor haar christelijke wereldtaak. Dat zij zich geroepen wete tot de hoogste toppen van gebedsleven en van intens sacramenteel leven om zich dan weer ten volle uit te engageren in een stout wereldveroverende, aardse verwezenlijking *ut adveniat Regnum Dei*, opdat 'Gods rijk kome.'"

[67] Henricus Schillebeeckx, *Theol. Woordenboek*, s.v. "Dogma-ontwikkeling," (Maaseik/Roermond: J.J. Romen & Zonen, 1952–8), cols. 1087–106; "Geschiedenis," cols. 1838–40; "*Humani generis*," cols. 2300–02; "Theologie," cols. 4485–542.

[68] Schillebeeckx, *Theol. Woordenboek*, s.v, "*Nouvelle théologie*," cols. 3519–20. For general background on the importance of sacramental thought in the preconciliar writings of Schillebeeckx, see Chapter Seven in this volume by Leo Kenis and Joris Geldhof.

[69] Schillebeeckx, "*Nouvelle théologie*," col. 3520.

From the beginning of his first full academic year at Nijmegen, in October 1958, Schillebeeckx taught two courses, namely, Fundamental Dogmatics and History of Theology. Because of his activities during the Council the latter soon was dropped. Nonetheless, Schillebeeckx was convinced that History of Theology has its rightful place within Dogmatics. This is evident in the way he treated themes like "Christ" and "grace." Only after Schillebeeckx had collected all of the basic elements from the Bible and tradition, he could penetrate into the subject matter, in search of a synthesis. Thus, the nature of the preliminary research was biblical-theological and theological-historical. Yet he never became merely a "historical theologian"; he always also maintained an openness for phenomenology, inherited from his years in Leuven, as well as the metaphysics inherited from De Petter, which were dear to him. When, in 1961, Dondeyne published his famous book *Faith and World* (*Geloof en wereld*), Schillebeeckx was more than simply positive about it. In fact, he argued in an article, which described Dondeyne as a *maître à penser*, that the book was ground-breaking and would become crucial in the events leading up to the Second Vatican Council. Schillebeeckx congratulated Dondeyne for what he dubbed a "beacon of light" on the eve of the Second Vatican Council.[70] And yet, the formation by De Petter again left its traces. "Although his review was generally laudatory, Schillebeeckx remarked that Dondeyne's emphasis on *Ethos*" was a rather weak attempt to connect Christianity to the modern world.[71] It gave up the metaphysical foundation that was always required, or as Schillebeeckx put it:

> It is precisely this *theistic* moment, understood as a person's *rock-bottom position* in the world [...] and for that reason also as the *basis* for an actual religious relationship to God, that I find lacking in the work of professor Dondeyne. And it is precisely this *natural moment*—the highpoint of temporal capacity and the low point or basis of the capacity that is only by grace, or of theological devotion—that seems to me to be the real connection between the temporal and the religious.[72]

As for Schillebeeckx, he was already actively involved in helping to steer the conciliar expectations. In 1960, the Dutch episcopate entrusted him with the task of drafting their pastoral letter, entitled "The Dutch Bishops on the Council."[73] Although this text would ultimately become a problem for Schillebeeckx, as it would prevent him from becoming a conciliar *peritus*,

---

[70] Edward Schillebeeckx, "Ter school bij prof. A. Dondeyne," *TvT* 2 (1962), 78–83, at 83.

[71] Bosschaert, *Joys and Hopes of Louvain Theologians*, 105.

[72] Text translated by Bosschaert from Schillebeeckx, "Ter school bij prof. A. Dondeyne," 82: "Juist dit *theïstische* moment als *dieptepunt* van de mens-in-de-wereld (men zou ook kunnen zeggen als hoogtepunt) en daarom tevens als *basis* van de feitelijke religieuze verhouding tot God mis ik bij prof. Dondeyne. En juist dit *natuurlijke moment* – hoogtepunt van het binnenwereldlijke kunnen en laagtepunt of basis van het slechts-ingenade-kunnen of van de theologale godsdienstigheid – lijkt mij de eigenlijke bindingsfactor tussen het binnenwereldlijke en het religieuze." Cited in Bosschaert, *Joys and Hopes of Louvain Theologians*, 105.

[73] Nederlandse Bisschoppenconferentie, "De bisschoppen van Nederland over het concilie," *Katholiek Archief* 16 (1961), 369–84. On this document, and further on Schillebeeckx at Vatican II, see Erik Borgman, "Introduction: Living Contact with Human Reality Gave Them This Openness – Schillebeeckx on the Second Vatican Council," *The Council Notes of Edward Schillebeeckx, 1962–1963*, ed. Karim Schelkens, Instrumenta Theologica 34 (Peeters: Leuven, 2011), xv–xxiii.

it also echoed all of the theological strands we have examined so far: it called for an historically grounded renewal, and it aimed at rereading tradition in order to rethink the role of the laity and more strongly involve them in the life of the church.

# Conclusion

Just before the opening of the Second Vatican Council, Schillebeeckx's attention turned to establishing a real connection between the temporal and religious elements of reality. To the extent that Schillebeeckx used historical sources from both scripture and tradition, he did present himself as a ressourcement theologian. However, his emphasis was broader than that, and his attention to church structures, to the theology of ministry, and the role of the laity in a modern world was becoming more and more pronounced. In that sense, he was less of an inheritor of *nouvelle théologie* than his colleague, the Dutch Jesuit Piet Schoonenberg. In 1964 Schoonenberg became Schillebeeckx's *collega proximus* at Nijmegen, although the two professors never really worked together amicably. As his later career would make clear, Schillebeeckx never lost an interest in metaphysical debates, and he always remained a speculative theologian. In this regard, he stayed close to one his own teachers in the Dominican Order, De Petter. Finally, Schillebeeckx's attention for phenomenological discourse and the strong emphasis on Christian anthropology seem to mark him out an inheritor of the Leuven school as well. All three of these exceedingly important currents in twentieth-century Catholic theology helped to shape Schillebeeckx and what he became in his later career, but they were also instrumental in the discussions prior to and during the Second Vatican Council. Schillebeeckx is, therefore, a theologian of the Council in several respects, and certainly also a theologian of his time and context.

# Chapter 5

# Schillebeeckx on Dominican Spirituality

Erik Borgman and Anton Milh

Anyone who wishes to understand the work of Edward Schillebeeckx must also consider that Schillebeeckx was first and foremost a Dominican. The Dominican Order, which celebrated its eighth centenary in 2016, was Schillebeeckx's home. The Dominican tradition was the ground in which his theology was rooted, and Dominican spirituality was the soil that permitted it to grow. At the same time, Schillebeeckx, through his life and work, helped shape the order in the twentieth century. At various points in his life, Schillebeeckx reflected explicitly on Dominican spirituality and identity, and this reflection resulted in a series of lectures and publications. The best known of these is an article he published in the 1970s, in which he presented the Dominican tradition as being fundamentally a critical and subversive tradition. The English translation of this text can still be found on the official website of the Dominican Order.[1]

Schillebeeckx's publications on Dominican spirituality were written in three distinct periods: in the early 1950s, the mid-1970s, and around the turn of the twenty-first century. It is hardly necessary to point out that society, the church, and the Dominican Order underwent—and themselves initiated—great transformations during this half-century. Schillebeeckx himself also changed, as did the audience for whom he wrote. His texts from the 1950s were written as master of students for the Flemish friars. In his articles from the 1970s, he addressed the Dominican family as a prominent theologian and professor at the Catholic University of Nijmegen. And he wrote his last texts as a professor emeritus for a wider interested public. The fact that his thinking and writing on Dominican spirituality and identity evolved over time is consistent with what Schillebeeckx regarded as an essential Dominican characteristic. For him, the Dominican tradition is a story that is never complete or finished, but that always continues to develop as new generations add their own chapters to it.

Our current contribution offers a chronological overview of Schillebeeckx's thinking on Dominican spirituality. It links this thinking with the sources that Schillebeeckx used, the style he availed of, and the historical context in which these texts were written; all this viewed in the light of his own biography. We will identify the shifts that took place in Schillebeeckx's thinking and reflect critically on the points of view he adopted. Our chapter will begin with a description of Schillebeeckx's first steps in the Order. In the conclusion we will consider to what extent Schillebeeckx's vision is consistent with, or deviates from, other visions of Dominican spirituality.

---

This chapter has been translated by Brian Heffernan.

[1] Edward Schillebeeckx, "Dominican Spirituality," op.org. http://www.op.org/sites/www.op.org/files/public/documents/fichier/schillebeeckx_dominicanspirit.pdf (accessed October 10, 2018).

# I. "St. Dominic's white habit would not look amiss on you": Schillebeeckx as a young Dominican

Edward Schillebeeckx was admitted to the Dominican Order as a novice in Ghent on September 20, 1934. He was not yet twenty years old at the time, but he had known for a while that he wanted to become a religious priest. His decision to join the Order of Preachers came about not through personal contact with Dominicans, but by reading about Saint Dominic. Afterward, he explained that two elements from Dominic's life had appealed to him in particular. The first was a synergy of "two poles" which he had discerned, "the world of God, the religious, and the world of men, with their secular problems." And second, Dominic impressed him as a "mild and fascinating personality [...] a man who had—and who transmitted—inspiration and was unconcerned by precise rules."[2] This last trait, Schillebeeckx thought, contrasted with his experience of the Jesuits, since he had attended the Jesuit college in Turnhout for his secondary education. The rigidity that prevailed at the Jesuit college ensured that he never felt completely at home there, and this inspired him to look for other possibilities. In May 1933, he wrote a letter to the Dominicans asking whether he could enter the order, and a few days later he received a reply, from the then superior of the Dominican friary in Ghent, Willem Mannes Matthijs (1892–1972). Matthijs wrote that Schillebeeckx's letter had given him the impression "that St. Dominic's white habit would not look amiss on you."[3]

In the friary, Schillebeeckx received the name of Henricus, after the famous Rhineland mystic and Dominican Henry Suso (1295–1366). He signed his publications with his religious name up until the 1960s, when he switched back to his baptismal name.[4] Schillebeeckx began his noviciate with eighteen others: ten French-speakers and eight Dutch-speakers.[5] The noviciate of the single Belgian Dominican province had been split in 1923: from that point on, the French-speakers were initiated into the order in La Sarte near Huy, and the Dutch-speakers in Ghent. In 1929, philosophical studies were also divided along linguistic lines, so that friars from the two parts of the country only met one another for the first time when they came to Leuven for their

---

[2] Joos Florquin, *Ten huize van ... 13* (Leuven/Bruges: Davidsfonds/Orion/Desclée De Brouwer, 1977), 324. Cf. Erik Borgman, *Edward Schillebeeckx: A Theologian in His History*, trans. John Bowden (London: Continuum, 2003), 29–34. According to Schillebeeckx himself, it was mainly a book by the French Dominican Humbert Clérissac (1864–1914) that made a great impression: Humbert Clérissac, *L'esprit de Saint Dominique* (Saint-Maximin: Éditions de La Vie Spirituelle, 1924); ET: *The Spirit of Saint Dominic: A Retreat for Dominicans*, repr. (Providence, RI: Cluny Media, 2015).

[3] Letter dated May 16, 1933, quoted in Edward Schillebeeckx, *Theologisch testament: Notarieel nog niet verleden*, 2nd ed. (Baarn: Nelissen, 1995), 194–95. The letter is also reprinted in English in: Edward Schillebeeckx, *I Am a Happy Theologian: Conversations with Francesco Strazzari*, trans. John Bowden (London: SCM Press, 1994), 86–88. Cf. Borgman, *Edward Schillebeeckx*, 35.

[4] Ted Schoof, *Preface, Bibliography 1936–1996 of Edward Schillebeeckx O.P.*, ed. Ted Schoof and Jan van de Westelaken (Baarn: Nelissen, 1997), 9–12, at 9.

[5] For an overview of Schillebeeckx's noviciate year, see Ambrosius Maria Bogaerts and Leopold Jozef Van Nueten, *Dominikanen in België 1835–1958. Aanvulling tot 1990*, Bouwstoffen voor de geschiedenis der Dominikanen in de Nederlanden (Leuven: Dominikaans Archief, 1990), 108–11. For the organization of the Dominican religious formation in the first half of the twentieth century, see Ambrosius Maria Bogaerts, *Dominikanen in België 1835–1958* (Brussels: Dominikaans Archief, 1969), 188–89 and Claude Sélis, *Histoire des dominicains de Belgique-Sud* (Brussels, 2015), 23–5.

theological studies. It is worth pointing out that one of Schillebeeckx's Walloon classmates was Jérôme Jean Hamer (1916–1996). In the late 1970s, Hamer, then a cardinal and the secretary of the Congregation for the Doctrine of the Faith, was involved in the investigation into Schillebeeckx's orthodoxy.[6]

There were several confreres during his formation who influenced Schillebeeckx, both intellectually and spiritually. First among them was the philosopher Dominicus Joannes De Petter (1905–1971), who greatly influenced Schillebeeckx both as a professor and as his spiritual director.[7] In a later interview, Schillebeeckx recounted that, after his own father, it had been De Petter who had "taught [me] to trust God. He had a touching faith in grace that was infectious and left you no room to become obsessive. For him, God and man were never in competition. He really drove that home for all of us."[8] This dovetailed with the orientation toward the divine and the human that Schillebeeckx had found in Dominic. In Leuven, the Dominican commitment to the "secular pole" took concrete shape in Laurentius Julius Perquy (1870–1946), pioneer of the Belgian Catholic Worker movement.[9] Friars like De Petter and Perquy confirmed Schillebeeckx in his Dominican calling: "I recognised in those two friaries (Ghent and Leuven) what I had learned about Dominic and his order from books."[10]

Unlike philosophy in Ghent, Schillebeeckx initially strongly disliked the theology lectures that he attended in Leuven from 1939 onward. According to his later judgment, they mainly taught a "drab," "abstract and scholastic" Thomism.[11] Exceptions to this rule were the lectures by Raymundus Josephus Martin (1878–1949) and Ludovicus Antonius Charlier (1898–1981). But Charlier was banned from teaching in 1942 and his book *Essai sur le problème théologique* (1938) was placed on the Index of Forbidden Books.[12] De Petter also had to resign as regent of studies at this time after suspicions of heterodoxy were raised. Thus as a theology student Schillebeeckx experienced the tail end of the modernist crisis, and this strongly affected him: "The things that most appealed to me as a theology student at the time were disowned by Rome. That was a great blow!"[13]

Schillebeeckx was ordained a priest in 1941 and he completed his theology studies two years later. As he had been chosen to become a professor of theology, he was sent to Le Saulchoir, the French Dominicans' house of studies in Étiolles near Paris, in the summer of 1945 to begin doctoral studies. There he encountered his confreres Yves Congar (1904–1995), Henri-Marie

---

[6]  See Ted Mark Schoof, ed., *The Schillebeeckx Case: Official Exchange of Letters and Documents in the Investigation of Fr. Edward Schillebeeckx, O.P. by the Sacred Congregation for the Doctrine of the Faith, 1976–1980*, trans. Matthew J. O'Connell (New York: Paulist Press, 1984), 137.

[7]  Cf. Chapter 3 by Dries Bosschaert and Stephan van Erp on De Petter in this volume.

[8]  Florquin, *Ten huize van*, 327.

[9]  On Perquy, see Anton Milh, "Opleiden tot 'katholieken van de daad'. De dominicanen en de Sociale School van Heverlee-Leuven," *Predikbroeders in woord en daad. Dominicanen in Vlaanderen in de twintigste eeuw*, ed. Mathijs Lamberigts, Mark De Caluwe and Anton Milh (Antwerp: Halewijn, 2016), 39–63.

[10]  Florquin, *Ten huize van*, 326.

[11]  Ibid., 327.

[12]  On the difficulties that Charlier's work encountered, see Jürgen Mettepenningen, *Nouvelle Théologie – New Theology: Inheritor of Modernism, Precursor of Vatican II* (London: T&T Clark, 2010), 61–9 and Jürgen Mettepenningen, "L'Essai de Louis Charlier (1938). Une contribution à la nouvelle théologie," *Revue théologique de Louvain* 39 (2008), 211–32.

[13]  Florquin, *Ten huize van*, 327. Cf. Borgman, *Edward Schillebeeckx*, 51–4.

Féret (1904–1992), and Marie-Dominique Chenu (1895–1990). The latter, who had had to resign as regent of Le Saulchoir in 1942, and whose book *Une école de théologie: Le Saulchoir* (1937) had been put on the Index together with Charlier's, was to have great influence on Schillebeeckx.[14] The Parisian curriculum was a little too light for Schillebeeckx's taste, and he frequented other institutions of higher education to supplement it. Thus he attended lectures by the philosophers Étienne Gilson (1884–1978) and Jean Wahl (1888–1974). In Saint-Jacques, the great Dominican friary in Paris, he met Albert Camus (1913–1960), who was a regular visitor there to debate with the friars on philosophical subjects.[15] He also encountered the worker priests of Paris, who were attempting to bridge the divide that had emerged between the church and the working class by living and working together with them. This project held strong attractions for Schillebeeckx; his experiences in Paris truly opened his mind to the world.[16]

In 1946, Schillebeeckx was appointed professor of dogmatics at the Leuven house of studies, as well as Master—supervisor and coach—of the Dutch-speaking Dominican theology students.[17] The French-speaking theology students had been moved to La Sarte in 1941, so that the entire formation program of the French-speaking Dominicans was now located there. In 1948, the philosophy course for the Dutch-speaking students was moved from Ghent to Leuven, so that from that moment on the whole of their formation took place there.[18] As a consequence of this change, Schillebeeckx became master of the philosophy students as well as the theology students, a position he would occupy until 1957.

As Master, he wanted to be the "eldest among brothers," who supported the students in their quest for an adapted form of Dominican life with great openness to the world. It was his aim, he later explained, to "humanize" the religious life, but "without diminishing its theological or religious depth."[19] Some friars apparently regarded Schillebeeckx's approach as "too innovative." In the wake of the 1950 encyclical *Humani generis*, which had condemned the tendency to be guided excessively by "modern conditions and requirements" as "imprudent eirenism,"[20] they successfully petitioned the 1954 provincial chapter to denounce his policy.[21] However, Ludovicus

---

[14]  A good historical overview of Chenu's difficulties with the Magisterium can be found in Étienne Fouilloux, "L'affaire Chenu 1937–1943," *Revue des Sciences philosophiques et théologiques* 98 (2014), 261–352.

[15]  Florquin, *Ten huize van*, 328–29.

[16]  Cf. Borgman, *Edward Schillebeeckx*, 111–17.

[17]  The *magister fratrum studentium* was responsible for ensuring the religious observance of the students, and for forming them in the Dominican life and in Dominican spirituality, and was the personal spiritual director of some of the students. He reported to the *regens studium*, who could be regarded as the rector of the Dominican house of studies. Cf. the descriptions in *Constitutiones Fratrum S. Ordinis Praedicatorum* (Rome: Domus Generalitia, 1954), 234–35, art. 642. Schillebeeckx was master of the students under the regents Mannes Matthijs (1941–1948), Paulus Julius Van Overbeke (1900–1985, regent 1948–1954), and Ceslaus Florent Van den Eynde (1903–1991, regent 1955–1958). Cf. Bogaerts and Van Nueten, *Dominikanen*, 189.

[18]  Bogaerts and Van Nueten, *Dominikanen*, 189.

[19]  Schillebeeckx, *Theologisch testament*, 29–30. Our translation.

[20]  Pius XII, *Humani generis* (August 12, 1950) 12, http://w2.vatican.va/content/pius-xii/en/encyclicals/documents/hf_p-xii_enc_12081950_humani-generis.html.

[21]  Not a trace of this can be found in the official acts of the chapter, however; see *Acta capituli provincialis Provinciae Sanctae Rosae in Belgio diebus 10 maii anni 1954 et sequentibus in conventu ad B.M.V. Immaculate Conceptam Lovaniensi celebrati* (Brussels, 1954).

Arthur Camerlynck (1912–1985), who was elected provincial superior at this chapter, defended Schillebeeckx's approach and received backing for this from the Master General, Manuel Suárez Fernández (1895–1954). Schillebeeckx was kept in his post, but was asked to keep greater distance from the students and to foster more frequent contact with the older friars in order to avoid division or estrangement between the older and younger groups. Calmness returned to the Leuven friary and the whole affair taught the Flemish Dominicans to accept "a certain pluralism or at least a tension" in the religious life, as Schillebeeckx later described it.[22] He himself retained positive memories of this period as master of the students: "together with the young, we were looking for a new spirituality that would still be Dominican, something democratic ahead of its time—if we remember 1968!"[23]

# II. Religious spirituality: The 1940s

Schillebeeckx's first texts on Dominican spirituality date from the early 1950s, but he had laid the foundations for what he wrote there in a number of earlier texts on the religious life and on "religious spirituality," or the particular spirituality of the religious orders. Thus he published an article on "*Kloosterleven en heiligheid*" ("Religious Life and Holiness") in the Dominican apologetic journal *Ons geloof* ("Our Faith") in 1945.[24] It dealt with two questions: whether the religious life offered the best way to achieve Christian perfection, and whether married life as a whole—as an extension of the solemnization of marriage—had a sacramental value, just like the life of the religious was the fulfillment of the vows taken at solemn profession. Schillebeeckx answered the first question in line with the prevailing views at the time by contending that religious—through the vows of obedience, poverty, and chastity, and through community life— were equipped with means that are more "effective" to achieve perfection than those of other forms of life. He immediately qualified this statement, however, by stressing the importance of a good interior disposition in experiencing the things that the religious professed in their vows. This disposition, he believed, could just as easily exist with someone who had a family, and was therefore in no way a prerogative of the religious. In his answer to the second question, Schillebeeckx outlined the "exceptional position" of religious life. He emphasized the willingness to make sacrifices out of love for God in such a way that this sacrificing gift of self became the core of life. In so doing, he described religious life as "the church's compass needle," because it issues forth a call to all the faithful to keep their eyes fixed mainly on God.

The questions that Schillebeeckx addressed in this article express the desire that many of the faithful had in those days for a spirituality adapted to the lay state. Some years later, Schillebeeckx devised the theological foundations for such a spirituality,[25] just as he focused on the spirituality of the diocesan clergy.[26] In his later theology of marriage, he developed the idea that it was not

---

[22] Schillebeeckx, *Theologisch testament*, 31.
[23] Florquin, *Ten huize van*, 332; cf. Borgman, *Edward Schillebeeckx*, 117–18.
[24] Schillebeeckx, "Kloosterleven en heiligheid," *Ons geloof* 27 (1945), 483–86.
[25] Edward Schillebeeckx, "Theologische grondslagen van de lekenspiritualiteit," *TGL* 5 (1949), 146–66.
[26] Edward Schillebeeckx, "Diocesane spiritualiteit," *Kultuurleven* 19 (1952), 144–53; Edward Schillebeeckx, "Literatuur over klooster-, priester- en lekeleven," *TGL* 9 (1953), 695–98.

the valid contracting of marriage before a minister of the church that gave it its sacramental character, but the lived married life as a service to the Kingdom of God, just as for the religious it was not merely saying of the words of profession, but actually living out the three vows that expressed their special connection with God.[27]

## Articles on spirituality

A number of further articles on religious spirituality appeared in the newly founded *Tijdschrift voor Geestelijk Leven* ("Journal for the Spiritual Life"). This had been founded in 1945 on the initiative of Schillebeeckx's confrere Stephanus Gerardus Axters (1901–1977), a specialist in the history of spirituality in the Low Countries.[28] Inspired by the French Dominicans' journal *La Vie Spirituelle*, the aim of *Tijdschrift voor Geestelijk Leven* was to connect spirituality and dogmatics with one another.[29] Axters had sought Schillebeeckx's assistance as well that of Bavo Michaël Van Hulse (1908–1950), a colleague at the Leuven theologate, as the journal's dogmatics specialists. For reasons that remain unclear, Axters's own active involvement in the journal quickly ended. The chief editorship passed to Van Hulse in 1946, and, after his premature death, Schillebeeckx took over. He remained editor in chief until 1964.[30]

In the very first issue of *Tijdschrift voor Geestelijk Leven*, Schillebeeckx published an article entitled "*Schepselbesef als grondslag van ons geestelijk leven*" ("The Consciousness of Being Creatures as the Foundation of Our Spiritual Life").[31] This article outlined the thematic profile of the new journal, but anyone acquainted with Schillebeeckx's later theology will be struck by how important it clearly was in determining the direction of his own thought.[32] In the article, Schillebeeckx looked for the theological basis of spirituality, and found this in the qualification of the relationship between God and man as that between Creator and creature. Closely following Thomas Aquinas, Schillebeeckx argued that the love that God is within himself cannot be other than communicative. God created man, not in the first place on account of man—because God has no need of man—but out of a love for himself which turned outward. This grace-filled stream of love that lies at the origin of man also determines his essential orientation. Human existence is fundamentally and intrinsically oriented toward God; Schillebeeckx would later consistently call this "theologal." This implies on the one hand a form of heteronomy: humans are dependent on God. But this very heteronomy also encompasses the highest form of autonomy, because it is

---

27 Edward Schillebeeckx, *Het huwelijk, aardse werkelijkheid en heilsmysterie*, vol. 1 (Bilthoven: Nelissen, 1963). ET: *Marriage: Secular Reality and Saving Mystery* (London: Sheed & Ward, 1965); cf. Borgman, *Edward Schillebeeckx*, 176–82.
28 On Axters, see Rob Faesen and Anton Milh, "Axters (Gerardus), Stephanus," *Dictionnaire d'histoire et de géographie ecclésiastiques 189b-190* (Turnhout: Brepols, 2018), 903–07.
29 On *La Vie Spirituelle*, cf. Étienne Fouilloux, with Tangi Cavalin and Nathalie Viet-Depaule, *Les Éditions dominicaines du Cerf, 1918–1965* (Rennes: Presses Universitaires de Rennes, 2018), 13–29.
30 On *Tijdschrift voor Geestelijk Leven* in this early period, see P. Hoogeveen, "De beginjaren van TGL (1945–1950)," *TGL* 65 (2009), 13–26, at 14–18; Sander Vloebergs, "Groeien naar een verankerde spiritualiteit. Over het Tijdschrift voor Geestelijk Leven," *Predikbroeders*, ed. Mathijs Lamberigts, Mark De Caluwe, Anton Milh, 195–214, at 197–99; Borgman, *Edward Schillebeeckx*, 99–100.
31 Schillebeeckx, "Schepselbesef als grondslag van ons geestelijk leven," *TGL* 1 (1945), 15–43.
32 Borgman, *Edward Schillebeeckx*, 100–03.

humanity's intrinsic orientation toward God which allows people to strive for the good through their own initiative. From this, it follows that the spiritual life must be rooted in the world, because God had created humanity within the world, and had revealed Himself within the world:

> the spiritual life is nothing other than being quiet, listening, and obeying; loyally carrying out [...] what God inspires us to do through the circumstances of life [...]; nothing other than, having taken cognizance of the circumstances of each moment of life, honestly obeying our sincere conscience.[33]

This is the case because our conscience directs us to the good, which ultimately is God himself.

This definition of the spiritual life, Schillebeeckx believed, did not exclude traditional devotions. But it was necessary for instance when praying the rosary to transcend the level of "droning on, wearily or leisurely" with the Our Fathers and Hail Marys, so as to meditate upon "the salvific reality in Christ" together with the mother of Jesus. In this way, it was possible to formulate the same answer that Mary had once given the angel according to Scripture, *fiat voluntas tua*, "May your will be done." In this act of free surrender, the paradoxical unity of heteronomy and autonomy reached its most articulate form.[34]

There were two further contributions by Schillebeeckx in *Tijdschrift voor Geestelijk Leven* in 1947–1948, both based on lectures he had given as Master of students. At the start of the first article, on "*De ascetische toeleg van de kloosterling*" ("The Ascetic Diligence of the Religious"), Schillebeeckx returned to what he had written in *Ons geloof*.[35] He characterized religious life as a special form of Christian life which is focused on bringing divine love to fulfillment within humanity through specific means. In addition to the good things in which every person may rejoice, there is also the consciousness that human existence is burdened by sinfulness. Asceticism is the means of dealing with this sinfulness, and ultimately overcoming it. This means that asceticism is not an end in itself, and is therefore not good in and of itself. Schillebeeckx stressed that, in asceticism, God is always graciously at work within us, but "in and through a free human and psychological activity."[36] It is entirely grace, and entirely free choice.

According to Schillebeeckx, asceticism consisted of two movements. The first is to accept oneself "as a specific, individually determined given," including both virtue and vice. This does not mean acquiescing to one's negative side, but it does imply subjecting oneself to a thorough self-examination without reticence or fear.[37] In order to accept what one finds with joy, it is necessary to ask for God's grace: "In this way the acceptance becomes surrender and trust, and even encompasses the hope of renewal and transformation of the 'old man' that we are."[38] This is already a first step in the second movement of asceticism, which consists of "reorientation." In this second movement, the person turns toward God's perfect love and attempts to become more receptive to it. Asceticism is therefore a positive and creative work, the transforming

---

[33] Schillebeeckx, "Schepselbesef," 41.

[34] Edward Schillebeeckx, "Rozenkrans bidden in nuchtere werkelijkheid," *De Bazuin* 33 (1949–1950), 1, 4–6.

[35] Edward Schillebeeckx, "De ascetische toeleg van de kloosterling," *TGL* 3 (1947), 302–20. All translations are our own.

[36] Ibid., 304–05.

[37] Ibid., 308–10.

[38] Ibid., 311.

of the experienced deficiency into openness to divine love. It is not "killing, pinching, and wrenching, which inevitably lead to spiritual poverty and emptiness."[39] The most important form of asceticism, Schillebeeckx wrote, was the faithful fulfillment of one's ordinary daily tasks, and not—as the stereotype would have it—in extraordinary penitential practices, which he treated with great circumspection. The purpose of the ascetical aspect of religious vows is not to destroy human nature, but to orient humanity toward God. He believed that the orientation toward God (the "mystical" dimension) should be both the goal and foundation of asceticism. This once again clarifies the paradoxical unity of heteronomy and autonomy that we have pointed to: "the urge to decide for oneself, the core of human nobility, is not frustrated, but is brought to fullness in the freedom of the children of God. This is so because a human being can only be himself, *person and freely deciding being*, in and through total dependence on God."[40]

The subject of Schillebeeckx's second contribution, in the 1947–1948 issue of the *Tijdschrift voor Geestelijk Leven*, on "*Kloosterlijke gehoorzaamheid en zedelijke persoonlijkheid*" ("Religious Obedience and Moral Personality") must be understood against his Dominican background.[41] In the Dominican formula of profession, the friar vows obedience to God, to the Virgin Mary, to Saint Dominic, and to the Master of the Order and his representatives and successors.[42] The *Constitutions* of the order call obedience the "*principalius et essentialius religioni*" among the three vows, the foundation and essence of the religious life, because it implies the human gift of self to God. The other two vows, those of chastity and poverty, are therefore included within obedience.[43] Schillebeeckx regarded the gift of self to God, and thus humanity's self-denial, as "the deepest core of the religious life."[44] By denying ourselves, we are able to do Christ's will. Schillebeeckx's view on obedience in this article is hierarchical: we can know Christ's will by listening to the magisterium of the church, to which the religious superiors also belong. The divine will is revealed to us in the form of very concrete superiors. This is why the name of the person who is Master at the time is included in the profession formula. Although this might evoke a certain resistance, it is essentially the expression of the principle of the incarnation: God speaks through human beings and in human history.

In this article, Schillebeeckx distinguishes between external and internal obedience, and thus between obedience as a vow and as a virtue. The paradox, he believes, is that the church asks religious to take a vow of absolute obedience, but rarely invokes this absolute obedience. The church has even imposed all kinds of restrictions on the possibility of invoking it. This leads Schillebeeckx to the conclusion that the emphasis in the church is on obedience arising from inner conviction: obedience that need not be enforced by the superior. In his view, what is important

---

[39] Ibid., 314.
[40] Ibid., 319.
[41] Edward Schillebeeckx, "Kloosterlijke gehoorzaamheid en zedelijke persoonlijkheid," *TGL* 4 (1948), 321–42. All translations are the our own. Schillebeeckx developed the theological foundation of religious obedience further in Edward Schillebeeckx, "De kloosterlijke gehoorzaamheid. Theologische beschouwingen," *De Kloosterling* 29 (1958), Supplement: Verslag van het congres der actieve vrouwelijke religieuzen, 28–30 mei 1958, 19–32.
[42] For the formula of profession in the *Constitutions* drawn up in 1932 at the request of Master Stanislas Martin Gillet (1875–1951), see 62, art. 155 §1 and 2. For the new *Constitutions*, see art. 199.
[43] *Constitutiones*, 204, art. 542.
[44] Schillebeeckx, "Kloosterlijke gehoorzaamheid en zedelijke persoonlijkheid," 321.

is "that […], under the watchful eye of the Superiors and with the inner willingness to make sacrifices, we must be able also to direct and summon our radical gift of self to God *personally ourselves*, through a personal, mature judgement of conscience, according to the demands of the specific circumstances of life."[45] The religious who on the one hand possesses "the virtuous, Christian attitude of obedient love," and who on the other hand is "personally, morally mature," will achieve a harmonious balance in his or her religious life.[46] But this condition can be attained only through self-denial for the love of God, which enables one to penetrate into the mystery of Christ himself, whose love for his Father was so great that he was obedient to him in everything.

In a 1949 article for *Biekorf* ("Beehive"), an internal magazine for Dominican students in Leuven, Schillebeeckx directed his attention to the meaning of Christian hope from a Dominican perspective.[47] He interpreted hope as the possibility of enduring the tension between "already" and "not yet" that is characteristic of the coming of God's Kingdom, and that can be felt in the life of every Christian. Being a Christian means enduring this tension, in the knowledge that we are unable to reach the salvation to which God has destined us on our own, but also that nothing can separate us from that salvation if God does not wish this. Summarizing, Schillebeeckx contended:

> God is intent on our good; He has no wish to make things agonisingly difficult for us. But we are weak, and we stray constantly. What saves us again and again is hope […]: confessing our own weakness and trusting in God's saving omnipotence. […] *Deus providebit*![48]

God will provide! According to Schillebeeckx, Dominicans try to make of this hope the building block of their spiritual lives. Christian hope inspires man to surrender to God's grace, which then becomes active in the person. By expressing one's hope in Christ in prayer, Christian life acquires a particular Christ-oriented dynamic. He concluded his article as follows:

> The ultimate fulfilment of meaning […] is the realisation of God's goodness *within* creation. […] May it become true […] there, where *we* in our turn must fulfil this commission [to be hopeful]: Mirabilis Deus … in fratris nostris Studentibus! *Our hope* is its assurance![49]

God's greatness becomes visible in the hope from which the student brothers live.

## III. "Ad vos, o Juvenes": The 1950s

A series of four short articles that appeared in the 1952–1953 issue of *Dominikaans Leven* ("Dominican Life"), the journal for the various branches of the order in Flanders, was the hinge that linked Schillebeeckx's publications on religious spirituality in the second half of the 1940s

---

[45] Ibid., 333.
[46] Ibid., 342.
[47] Edward Schillebeeckx, "Vos qui vocati estis sancti," *Biekorf* 32 (1949), 2–13. All translations are our own.
[48] Ibid., 9.
[49] Ibid., 13.

and his first great essay on Dominican spirituality in 1954. The subjects that it broached are clearly reminiscent of what he had written about religious spirituality in the 1940s.

In the first article, with the provocative title *"Hebben wij het beste deel gekozen?"* ("Have We Chosen the Better Part?"), he briefly recapitulated his view of religious life as a life in obedience, but this time without using this terminology. The religious had indeed chosen the better part, Schillebeeckx argued, because their choice was a choice for God in Himself. The professed religious practices self-denial in order to give full weight to God, and—through the religious vows—offers his life up to God. The movement toward God which the religious makes out of love cannot but "lead across the borders of our own life back towards the people we left," and thus result in the apostolate.[50] The Dominican attitude to the apostolate was the subject of further reflection in *"God krijgen en God doorgeven"* ("Receiving God and Passing God On"), a free translation of Thomas Aquinas's dictum *contemplari et contemplata aliis tradere.*[51] For Schillebeeckx, this phrase, which has become an adage of the Order of Preachers, summarized the Dominican relationship between prayer and the apostolate. Prayer, in which the personal relationship with God takes shape, is the source of the apostolate, in which this God is proclaimed. Traditional religious customs, including the communal recitation of the divine office in choir, create a structure that promotes prayerfulness, from which the apostolate can therefore emerge. The structure of the religious life is not, therefore, an ill-fitting harness, but a tailor-made suit that safeguards the prayerful core of the apostolic life.[52]

In the following article, Schillebeeckx addressed the "Dominican audacity" that characterized the attitude of Dominican priests to the apostolate. Through this apostolate, they shared in the work of redemption in which Christ first came to partake through the Father, and this

> is testimony to an incredible audacity, which [...] [is] a form of trust in God: from now on, this young man will commit himself totally to the Kingdom of God, which grows and expands according to other laws than those human reckoning can measure. We are entering a Mystery here, we are subsumed in the divine possibilities of redemption.[53]

A leap of faith thus takes place in and through prayer, so as to commit oneself through the gift of self to God's work of redemption. In *"Het dominikaanse evenwicht"* ("The Dominican Balance"), which concluded the series in *Dominikaans Leven*, Schillebeeckx discussed the spirit of Dominic, which defined the anthropology of his followers. This spirit foregrounded self-denial, but without any destruction of the person's individuality. On the contrary, grace worked to effect a "divine exaltation, transcending ourselves, of that which we are as human beings."[54] By surrendering to the "God of grace," the Dominican becomes "fully human," because the good

---

[50] Edward Schillebeeckx, "Hebben wij het beste deel gekozen?," *Dominikaans Leven* 9 (1952–1953), 2, 8–10.

[51] Thomas Aquinas, *ST* IIIa, q. 40 a. 1 ad 2 and a. 2 ad 3; cf. Marie-Dominique Chenu, *St. Thomas d'Aquin et la théologie*, Maîtres spirituels 17 (Paris: Éditions du Seuil, 1958), 58–65.

[52] Edward Schillebeeckx, "Contemplata aliis tradere: God krijgen en God doorgeven," *Dominikaans Leven* 9 (1952–1953), 6, 7–9.

[53] Edward Schillebeeckx, "Dominikaanse durf: Nooit op schorvrije voeten!," *Dominikaans Leven* 9 (1952–1953), 3, 7–10, at 8.

[54] Edward Schillebeeckx, "Het dominikaanse evenwicht," *Dominikaans Leven* 9 (1952–1953), 5, 5–7, at 6.

aspects of his humanity are perfected through grace, and he is "fully child of God," because he makes himself entirely dependent on God.[55]

Schillebeeckx developed a new, synthetic view of Dominican spirituality in a mimeographed booklet of seventy-four pages under the title *Dominicaanse spiritualiteit* ("Dominican Spirituality"), which appeared around Christmas 1954 as a special edition of the student magazine *Biekorf*.[56] Schillebeeckx dedicated it to the Dominican students ("*Ad vos, o Juvenes*") for whose care he was still responsible despite his difficulties at the chapter, "in the hope of better days" ("*in spe meliorum dierum*"). Schillebeeckx's somber mood was due to events that had taken place earlier that year: the Vatican had ordered the worker priests in France to cease their activities. Among the Vatican's many fears in the context of the Cold War was that these priests were becoming too similar to Communists with regard to both their activities and in their ideas and ideals, and thus ran the risk of infiltration. Moreover, the priests' far-reaching identification with the workers and the decision to share their life was regarded as in conflict with their dignity as representatives of the church. They were to be priests, first and foremost. The ban—lifted by Pope Paul VI after the Second Vatican Council—affected the three Dominican provinces in France and was a heavy blow to Marie-Dominique Chenu and his allies Yves Congar and Henri-Marie Féret, who had attempted to create a theological basis for the project of the worker-priests.[57] This affair saddened Schillebeeckx, not just because confreres he admired had (once again) been condemned, but also because he regarded the project of the worker-priests as one that reflected the spirit of St. Dominic. In their work, he saw how the apostolate of St. Dominic's poor preachers could take shape in his own time.[58]

In his essay, Schillebeeckx wanted to draw the outline of a Dominican spirituality that derived its specificity from "its own tonalities of the experience of God."[59] A first problem was that of the sources, or rather the lack thereof. Whereas the Benedictines have Benedict's *Rule* to fall back on, and the Jesuits the *Spiritual Exercises* of Ignatius, the Dominicans had to face the fact that their founder had left almost no writings. Schillebeeckx was convinced, however, that Dominic had endowed his order with "a spirit, a leaven," that had been handed down through the generations

---

[55]  Ibid., 7; cf. Stephan van Erp, "Fraterniteit in evenwicht: Edward Schillebeeckx over de genadige verscheidenheid van het dominicaanse leven," *Het habijt weer uit de kast: Botsing of ontmoeting tussen generaties in dominicaans perspectief*, ed. Stephan van Erp and Anton Milh (Leuven: Dominicanen, 2016), 67–80, at 75. (French translation: *Identité et visibilité: Conflits de générations chez les dominicains*, Toulouse: Domuni Press, 2019).

[56]  Edward Schillebeeckx, "Dominicaanse spiritualiteit," *Biekorf* (1954), special issue.

[57]  On the worker-priests, see Émile Poulat, *Les prêtres-ouvriers: Naissance et fin* (Paris: Cerf, 1999); François Leprieur, *Quand Rome condamne: Dominicains et prêtres-ouvriers*, Terre humaine (Paris: Plon/Cerf, 1989); François Leprieur, "Do the baptised have rights? The Worker-Priest Crisis," *New Blackfriars* 80 (1999), 384–96; Charles Suaud, *Prêtres et ouvriers: Une double fidélité mise à l'épreuve, 1944–1969* (Paris: Karthala, 2004); Guillaume Cuchet, "Nouvelles perspectives historiographiques sur les prêtres-ouvriers (1943–1954)," *Vingtième Siècle* 87 (2005), 177–87; Yann Raison du Cleuziou, *De la contemplation à la contestation: La politisation des dominicains de la province de France (Années 1940–1970)* (Paris: Belin, 2016), esp. 74–82.

[58]  Cf. Borgman, *Edward Schillebeeckx*, 117–21, and Borgman, "Openheid voor de sporen van de God van heil. Edward Schillebeeckx over dominicaanse identiteit," *Ons rakelings nabij: gedaanteveranderingen van God en geloof*, ed. Manuela Kalsky, André Lascaris, Leo Oosterveen, Inez van der Spek, 2nd ed. (Nijmegen/Zoetermeer: DSTS/Meinema, 2005), 58–72, at 62–3.

[59]  Schillebeeckx, "Dominicaanse spiritualiteit (1954)," 8.

and that could be uncovered through study of the life of Dominic and Dominican saints, of the Dominican *Constitutions*, and the history of the order.[60] For Schillebeeckx, Dominican spirituality was essentially a historical spirituality, which is also evident from the attention he gave to the historical research of the origins of the order that was then underway.[61] According to Schillebeeckx, Dominic's initial intuition had been further developed by the generations that followed him.[62] Every new generation of Dominicans had to live up to the challenge of "giving shape in [its] own time to the original ideal of the Order in all its integrity and in its uniqueness," in other words to "reactivate" the ideal of Saint Dominic and experience it in each generation's own context, and thus to transmit it again to the following generation.[63]

In the first part of his essay, Schillebeeckx went in search of the "unique Dominican qualification of the religious ideal of piety" in a narrow sense, that is, the Dominican approach to asceticism and mysticism.[64] Schillebeeckx used "piety" and "spiritual life" as interchangeable concepts. He did not, therefore, equate "piety" with mere devotional practices, as is often the case today. In Stephanus Axters's broad definition, which undoubtedly influenced Schillebeeckx's thinking, piety was "every experience of the human relationship of dependency towards God."[65] It must be noted that "experience" here does not mean "experience" as in "to have an experience," but something like "becoming conscious of." Following Axters's definition, Schillebeeckx formulated a first characteristic of Dominican spirituality: the recognition that every movement in human life is an initiative of God. The first principle in the spiritual life is not man, but God, who gives us the spiritual life as a form of grace. "Origin, force, perseverance, and fulfilment of the spiritual life: it is all *God's grace*," he wrote.[66] For this reason it was fruitless for a person to strive for self-fulfillment, but one must renounce oneself so that God's grace could work within the person. The grace of God has an "intrinsic efficacy"; that is, it works in and of itself and does not require human completion.[67]

---

[60] Ibid., 12–13.

[61] Schillebeeckx was familiar with the work of his Belgian confreres Raymundus Michael Creytens (1911–1997) and Gerard Gilles Meersseman (1903–1988), who helped found the order's Historical Institute in Rome. He also knew the French historical school well, which includes such scholars as Pierre Mandonnet (1858–1936), Hyancinthe Petitot (1880–1934) and Marie-Humbert Vicaire (1906–1993). Similarly, he was acquainted with the work of the German historians of the order Heinrich Denifle (1844–1905) and Heribert Christian Scheeben (1891–1968). It does not appear that Schillebeeckx knew the English Dominican Bede Jarrett's (1881–1934) biography of Dominic: *Life of St. Dominic* (London: Burns, Oates & Washbourne, 1924). Nor does he refer anywhere to two works on Dominican spirituality that had been published by the Belgian Dominicans more than twenty-five years before: Edgar Janssens, *La Spiritualité Dominicaine*, Études religieuses 105 (Brussels/Ghent: Ed. Soc. d'Études religieuses/Veritas, 1924), and Marie-Martin Rousseau, *La Spiritualité Dominicaine*, Études religieuses 197 (Liège: La pensée catholique, 1928).

[62] Schillebeeckx, "Dominicaanse spiritualiteit (1954)," 13.

[63] Ibid., 9–10.

[64] Ibid.

[65] Stephanus Axters, *Geschiedenis van de vroomheid in de Nederlanden*, vol. 1: *De vroomheid tot rond het jaar 1300* (Antwerp: De Sikkel, 1950), xv. Our translation. See also Axters's broad definition a few years previously, in Axters, *Geschiedenis van de Nederlandsche vroomheid*, [1947], s.l., p. 1: "Piety is understood to mean any experience of any religious confession."

[66] Schillebeeckx, "Dominicaanse spiritualiteit (1954)," 15.

[67] Ibid., 17.

The attitude of openness to grace that Schillebeeckx believed every Dominican should have arose, he thought, from two other typically Dominican traits: the awareness of being a creature, and the theologal orientation of life. We have already seen how Schillebeeckx developed the awareness of being created. The "theologal life" meant a life in faith, hope, and love as orientation toward God, again founded on the consciousness that these virtues were gifts in grace of the Holy Spirit and could not be achieved through human striving. This idea was derived from Ambroise Gardeil (1859–1931), a French Dominican who Chenu regarded as the great example of the kind of theology that he himself had embodied at Le Saulchoir, and who had written a book on *Les dons du Saint-Esprit dans les saints dominicains* ("The Gifts of the Holy Spirit in the Dominican Saints") in 1903.[68] Humanity has to cooperate with these awesome gifts of grace in the spiritual and theologal life, but Schillebeeckx interpreted this cooperation primarily as "a profound docility to God's work of grace."[69]

The humble position that Dominicans assigned to humanity's own activity in the spiritual life resulted in a "quiet-serene, boundless and unconditional trusting in and crediting of God's grace," and thus in a "joy and peace," which Schillebeeckx also discerned in the lives of a number of great Dominican saints.[70] Dominican asceticism was not dolorism, or an attitude of forcing oneself to lead a virtuous life. Its purpose was to develop an inner disposition to receive God's grace within oneself: "being theologally up-lifted in God implies being ascetically unshackled from oneself and everything earthly."[71]

In addition to the strong qualification of human activity in the spiritual life, the emphasis on the working of God's grace had a second effect for Dominicans, according to Schillebeeckx: "the resolute refusal to see a divide between the ordinary life of grace and the mystical life."[72] Although *de facto* the spiritual lives of only very few Christians develop into a mystical life, this is what they are called to *de iure*. This mystical aspect is potentially present in the spiritual life of every Christian, which implies a positive anthropology. This image of the mystic as an advanced believer means that it makes sense to read mystical texts to intensify and deepen the spiritual life (something Schillebeeckx continued to do throughout his life).[73] This notion revealed Schillebeeckx's debt to the French Dominicans André-Marie Meynard (1824–1904) and Réginald Garrigou-Lagrange (1877–1964). One of the latter's articles clearly inspired Schillebeeckx's grounding of the Dominican spiritual life in divine grace.[74]

---

[68] Mettepenningen has described Gardeil as the standard-bearer of a "third way" in the theology of his time (between modernism and antimodernism), and thus as a precursor of *nouvelle théologie*; see his article: "The 'Third Way' of the Modernist Crisis, Precursor of Nouvelle Théologie: Ambroise Gardeil, O.P., and Léonce de Grandmaison, S.J.," *Theological Studies* 75 (2014), 774–94, at 780–82 and 792–94.

[69] Schillebeeckx, "Dominicaanse spiritualiteit (1954)," 19.

[70] Ibid.

[71] Ibid., 21. Schillebeeckx refers here to a quotation—"to go out from oneself and to go into God"—by the Rhineland mystic and Dominican Johannes Tauler (ca. 1300–1361), but this obviously also alludes to the concept of *Gelassenheit* developed by Meister Eckhart (1260–1328).

[72] Schillebeeckx, "Dominicaanse spiritualiteit (1954)," 22.

[73] Cf. Edward Schillebeeckx, "De weg van de mystiek," *TGL* 42 (1986), 352–68, at 355–58; Edward Schillebeeckx, "Foreword," *Poetry of Hadewijch*, trans. Marieke J.E.H.T. van Baest, Studies in Spirituality, Supplement 3 (Leuven: Peeters Press, 1998), 3.

[74] See Réginald Garrigou-Lagrange, "Le caractère et les principes de la spiritualité dominicaine," *La Vie Spirituelle* 4 (1921), 372–81.

The concrete Dominican life takes shape through a number of means—the regular observance of the rule and the Constitutions, study, and liturgical practice including the divine office—to this fundamental spiritual attitude of living with and through God's grace. There is therefore an essential coherence between the Dominican form of life (*forma vitae*) and its "inner shaping principle," to use the words of the American Dominican, Romanus Cessario.[75] Schillebeeckx especially highlighted the particular devotion that Dominicans had for Christ's sacred humanity. This devotion is both adoration and participation, because in Christ's humanity, human beings participate in God's salvation.[76] At the end of his article, he called the working of God's grace in Christ's humanity the core of Dominican spirituality.[77] According to Schillebeeckx, this persistent Christ-centeredness explained why Dominicans—generally—refused to be distracted by particular devotions. As we have seen, devotion to Mary, which was promoted by the order through the apostolate of the rosary, had to be understood in the context of what was an essentially Christ-centered Dominican spirituality: standing beside Mary to penetrate more deeply to the mystery of the Incarnation.[78]

One special sign of the typically Dominican focus on humanity was, Schillebeeckx argued, the so-called principle of dispensation as it appears in the *Constitutions*. This principle stipulates that a Dominican can be dispensed from one or more religious observances or liturgical obligations if he is humanly incapable of observing it, or because his time is occupied by preaching, or by the study which supports preaching.[79] Schillebeeckx himself had been dispensed from the strict (monastic) fast that was then still observed in the order because it was physically too heavy for him.[80] He had at the time much appreciated the "flexibility" of his superiors, but also stressed "the efficiency of Dominic's apostolic sense" that was reflected in the principle of dispensation: the order was founded to preach, and the other aspects of the Dominican life had to be subordinated to this. "To want to abolish this *law* because of possible, and, given human frailty, frequent actual abuse, would be to strike the genius of Father Dominic in the face, and it would also be to forsake a typically Dominican trait of purposeful efficiency," Schillebeeckx wrote.[81] Another element from the Dominican *Constitutions* that he believed was a defining feature of Dominican spirituality was the democratic structure of the order at all levels: in the governance of friaries, provinces, and of the worldwide order. He also mentioned the fact that observance

---

[75] Romanus Cessario, "The Grace St. Dominic Brings to the World: A Fresh Look at Dominican Spirituality," *Logos* 15 (2012), 84–100, at 85.

[76] Schillebeeckx, "Dominicaanse spiritualiteit (1954)," 30–1.

[77] Ibid., 61.

[78] Ibid., 32. For Schillebeeckx's view of Mary, see Edward Schillebeeckx, *Maria, Christus' mooiste wonderschepping: Religieuze grondlijnen van het Maria-mysterie* (Antwerp: Apostolaat van de Rozenkrans, 1954). A reprinted edition appeared the following year under the title *Maria, Moeder van de verlossing. Religieuze grondlijnen van het Maria-mysterie*. Also see Chapter 21 of this volume by Julia Feder.

[79] See *Constitutiones*, 35–36, art. 67–72. The principle of dispensation was present in Dominican legislation from a very early stage (certainly from the chapter of Bologna in 1220) and is in its broadness an original feature of the order. Cf. Antoninus Henricus Thomas, *De oudste constituties van de dominicanen: voorgeschiedenis, tekst, bronnen, ontstaan en ontwikkeling (1215–1237)*, Bibliothèque de la Revue d'histoire ecclésiastique 42 (Leuven: Universiteitsbibliotheek, 1965), 135, 252–53.

[80] Schillebeeckx, *Theologisch testament*, 23; Schillebeeckx, *I Am a Happy Theologian*, 7.

[81] Schillebeeckx, "Dominicaanse spiritualiteit (1954)," 37.

of the *Constitutions* was not obligatory under pain of sin. It was better to develop the virtue needed to observe the *Constitutions* through grace than to enforce its observance. According to Schillebeeckx, the freedom involved in this, just as the concomitant "integral humanity" and "radiant joy," was characteristic of Dominican life.[82]

The Dominican Order was founded with the purpose of preaching to "save souls." This created a special form of life, a mixture of the silent, contemplative life of the monks on the one hand, and the active, apostolic life, with all the various challenges that its context poses, on the other. The order's clear purpose ensured that the apostolate had highest priority, but contemplation remained the source of this apostolate. There was no apostolate (*présence au monde*) without contemplation (*présence à Dieu*). The faith, hope, and love that the Dominican nourishes through his own relationship with God (*contemplari*) could be shared with others only on the basis of this relationship (*contemplata aliis tradere*). Dominicans had to study humanity and the world precisely to ensure that this communicative movement of proclamation would be adjusted to the circumstances. The importance of this is based on a deep awareness of the Incarnation: it is in *this* world that God became human, and this means that something of the divine truth (*veritas*) can be found in this world. God's grace is efficaciously present in the world. Therefore, Schillebeeckx wrote, the Dominican should listen "in dialogical presence to the contemporary world […] the language of truth that, furtively perhaps, deformed and caught up in a web of untruth, but still resounds from the occurrences of the time."[83] Study, so characteristic of the Dominican Order, is thus certainly not limited to the study of theology, but also includes the profane sciences. This eventually led Schillebeeckx to the following definition of Dominican spirituality: "the spiritual attitude to life of those who, with a theologal sense for God, and with human openness, approach the occurrences of their contemporary life and of the world '*ad salutem animarum.*'"[84]

# IV. Thread and cross-thread: The 1970s

In the mid-1970s, Schillebeeckx once again published a series of short articles on Dominican spirituality in *Dominikaans Leven*. The style is clearly different from that of his texts from the 1940s and 1950s: less Thomistic, lighter, and more comprehensible. Many elements from his previous writings returned, but he described them differently this time and structured his argument in a new manner. Publication in *Dominikaans Leven* meant that his audience consisted of the Dominican friars and sisters in Flanders, as well as sympathetic outsiders. There was no longer any real Dominican lay movement (the former third order) to speak of in Flanders, and Schillebeeckx's use of the term "Dominican family" is due to the situation in the Netherlands, to which he had become accustomed: the friars were seen there as just one of several branches of a wider movement, which also encompassed the contemplative and active sisters and laypeople who were connected to and involved in various ways with the order.[85]

---

[82] Ibid., 37–41.

[83] Ibid., 50.

[84] Ibid., 54.

[85] Schillebeeckx had called for a proper place for laypeople within the Dominican Order as early as 1960, in the journal of the Dutch Third Order. See Edward Schillebeeckx, "Derde Orde 'nieuwe stijl'," *Zwart op Wit* 30 (1960), 113–28.

The context in which Schillebeeckx's articles appeared had changed fundamentally compared to twenty years previous. The Second Vatican Council had brought the rehabilitation of many persons, movements, and ideas that had been condemned in the decades before the Council, like Chenu, Congar, and the movement of the worker priests. The 1970s can, moreover, be described as the heyday of liberation theology, which greatly influenced Schillebeeckx's thinking.[86] In 1968, the Latin American episcopal conference (CELAM) in Medellín, Colombia, had articulated the "preferential option for the poor," which was put into practice in many Christian base-communities and in the resistance of Christians to structures that perpetuated poverty and violence. In the wake of these developments, Schillebeeckx's work acquired an explicitly political dimension.[87]

In 1958, Schillebeeckx was appointed professor of dogmatics at the Faculty of Theology of the Catholic University of Nijmegen. Shortly afterward, preparations for the Second Vatican Council began, which Schillebeeckx attended as advisor to the Dutch bishops. Almost immediately after the closure of the Council, its reception strongly divided Dutch Catholics. Schillebeeckx, who was regarded as the theological mouthpiece of the episcopate, was intensively involved in these debates. In the years following the Council he published a great number of articles and volumes of contributions, culminating in his 1974 book *Jezus, het verhaal van een levende* (*Jesus: An Experiment in Christology*). This book definitively established his name as an important and creative, but also controversial, theologian.

The events he witnessed in the Netherlands in the post-conciliar period inspired him in 1967 to write a contribution on the religious life for the *Tijdschrift voor Theologie* ("Journal of Theology"), which he himself had helped found six years earlier. The opening sentence was striking: "If I wished to be unkind—or perhaps I should say optimistic?—I would say that a sign has been posted on the front doors of all religious houses in 1967 that says, 'closed due to renovation.' There is no use trying to deny the malaise."[88] In this article, Schillebeeckx asked whether the religious life should adapt to the world or to the Gospel. According to the Council's decree on the renewal of the religious life, *Perfectae Caritatis,* Christ should be the measure of the "up-to-date renewal of the religious life," but according to Schillebeeckx it did not follow that there was no need to adapt to contemporary times and the modern world. On the contrary, Schillebeeckx called for a "confrontation" with these, but in a way that would not degenerate into either radical rejection or unconditional embrace. As always, his goal was to achieve a dynamic balance between tradition and situation, so that life in the contemporary world would become part of tradition. Schillebeeckx's publications on Dominican spirituality in the mid-1970s must be read against this background of crisis and of a certain despair regarding the future of the religious life in the Low Countries.

The contributions in *Dominikaans Leven* were based on a lecture. Schillebeeckx subsequently joined them together into a single text, which can still be found in many places, particularly in

---

[86] See Erik Borgman, "Theology as the Art of Liberation: Edward Schillebeeckx's Response to the Theologies of the EATWOT," *Exchange* 32 (2003), 98–108.

[87] Cf. Borgman, *Openheid*, 63–64. On Schillebeeckx at the Council, see Borgman, *Edward Schillebeeckx*, 283–365 and Chapter Eight by Stephan van Erp in this volume.

[88] Edward Schillebeeckx, "Het nieuwe mens- en Godsbeeld in conflict met het religieuze leven," *TvT* 7 (1967), 1.

its English translation.[89] His take on the Dominican tradition in this text is that it is "a story," a concept that also occupied an important place in his theological work. According to Schillebeeckx, the human experience of reality has a narrative structure; someone who has experienced something special wants to share this with others as a story. Experiences that reveal a new facet of reality, or shed new light on a forgotten facet, are understood against the background of a particular narrative tradition that is both its gathering place and its critical agency. By adding new elements of experience to a tradition, this tradition becomes a "living" one.[90] Schillebeeckx reminded his readers that he had at one point linked his own life, his own story, with "the story of the order." The image he used for this is that of the weaving of a fabric: thread and cross-thread, warp and weft together form a new whole. The thread of Schillebeeckx's personal story was "crossed" with the cross-thread of the Dominican story, thus creating something new. In Schillebeeckx's words, the Dominicans constituted "a story-telling community" of its own: "Stories of the Dominican Order keep us together as Dominicans. Without stories we would lose our memories, fail to find our own place in the present and remain without hope or expectation for the future."[91] The life story of each Dominican is therefore *a part*, but also *just a small part* of the great narrative of the Dominican Order in past, present, and future. It makes an essential contribution to this narrative, which also places the individual life story in a broader perspective, and thus criticizes its one-sided aspects.

Schillebeeckx drew four conclusions from this view of Dominican tradition and spirituality as a story of thread and cross-thread. The first was that no definition can be given: the story continues as long as people feel called to add another chapter to the Dominican narrative. All these chapters of Dominican history reflect the "tone" that Dominic and his first companions set, and this Dominican "basic story" in turn reflects the story that stands at its origins: the story of Jesus himself.[92] This brings Schillebeeckx to a second conclusion: Dominican spirituality is only "valid" and authentic if it "takes up the story of Jesus and brings it up to date in its own way."[93] Schillebeeckx then refers to the Council's call to recalibrate the consecrated life according to the model of Christ. He calls the various religious institutes "modulations" of the greater ecclesial story, with mutual critical involvement. Third, this Dominican spirituality, as a modulation of the ecclesial calling to imitate Jesus, must always keep Dominic's original inspiration in mind, which "has constantly provided new height and direction to many in the best moments of the history of the Order."[94] His fourth conclusion was related to this: history is not the same thing as spirituality, and it is therefore necessary to continually reshape Dominican tradition in changing contexts.

According to Schillebeeckx, Dominican spirituality was also characterized by its "subversive" nature. Dominic adopted elements from existing traditions, but gave them a new meaning by reforming them or by adding new elements. Thus the Dominican religious life is a mixture of the more monastic life of the Norbertines and Cistercians, as well as the itinerant existence of the

---

[89]  For the full text see: Edward Schillebeeckx, "Dominican Spirituality," *God Among Us: The Gospel Proclaimed*, trans. John Bowden (New York: Crossroad, 1983), 232–48.

[90]  See also Mary Catherine Hilkert, "Experience and Revelation," *The Praxis of the Reign of God: An Introduction to the Theology of Edward Schillebeeckx*, ed. Mary Catherine Hilkert and Robert J. Schreiter, 2nd ed. (New York: Fordham University Press, 2002), 59–77, at 66.

[91]  Schillebeeckx, "Dominican Spirituality," 232.

[92]  Ibid., 233.

[93]  Ibid.

[94]  Ibid., 234.

medieval *Wanderprediger*. And though Dominic appropriated the life of the evangelical poverty movements with their criticism of the established church, he combatted their heretical, dualistic doctrines. Schillebeeckx concluded therefore that Dominican spirituality:

> on the basis of admonitory and critical reflection on the heritage left behind by the past religious tradition, takes up critically and positively the cross-thread provided by whatever new religious possibilities for the future keep emerging among us. Therefore it can never be a *material* repetition of what our Dominican forebears have themselves done admirably. Nor, however, can it be an *uncritical* acceptance of whatever "new movements" (in the mystical or political sense) are now evident in our midst.[95]

New generations of Dominicans had to go in search of their own cross-thread in order to shape the Dominican life of the current era, and in doing so they had to be open both to the good that had been handed down—*omnia autem probate, quod bonum est tenete*—and to the "signs of the times," according to the Council's call to interpret these "in the light of the Gospel." Schillebeeckx himself already proposed the first outlines of this "cross-thread": he suspected that the emphasis in contemporary Dominican life would have to be on *présence au monde*, "the critical solidarity with the human world."[96] In his *Theologisch testament* ("Theological Quests") he reiterated the importance of this function of the religious life to critique the church and society: this clearly reflected the influence of liberation theology, but also the approach of Schillebeeckx's colleague and friend Johann Baptist Metz.[97]

# V. Theology and spirituality: Around the turn of the new millennium

Although Schillebeeckx retired in 1983, he continued to publish and speak in the following decade, and thus continued to affect both the ecclesiastical situation in the Netherlands and international theology. He did not move back to Belgium; he had become acculturated to the Dutch context to

---

[95] Ibid., 238.

[96] Donald J. Goergen, "Spirituality," *The Praxis of the Reign of God: An Introduction to the Theology of Edward Schillebeeckx*, ed. Mary Catherine Hilkert and Robert J. Schreiter, 2nd ed. (New York: Fordham University Press, 2002), 117: "*Présence au monde* is the grace of understanding deeply one's own times and the capacity to respond accordingly." In the third part of Schillebeeckx's article (241–44) he briefly repeated a number of aspects from his 1954 essay: the theologal orientation of Dominican life, its attention for Jesus's humanity, and the principle of dispensation; and he emphasized his thesis of Dominican spirituality as a "subversive story" that always involves changes in course or direction. See p. 244: "A change of course is therefore part of the essence of the Dominican charisma." See Borgman, "Openheid," 65–67 for Schillebeeckx's take on Dominican spirituality against the background of evolutions in the Dutch ecclesiastical landscape of the 1970s.

[97] Cf. Schillebeeckx, *Theologisch testament*, 123–25 and 136–37; ET: "Theological Quests," *Essays, CW* vol. 11 (London: Bloomsbury T&T Clark, 2014), 151–53, 160–61.

such an extent that he remained there for the rest of his life. The period from the end of the 1970s onward was not an easy one for Schillebeeckx, as is clear primarily from the "Introduction" to his book *Church: The Human Story of God* (1989).[98] He regarded the ecclesiastical climate under Pope John Paul II as stifling and felt that everything he had worked for after the Second Vatican Council was being undone. In 2000—Schillebeeckx turned eighty-six that year—he published an article on the sacraments, which, as the subtitle reveals, he viewed as the "*Ritualisering van religieuze momenten in het alledaagse leven*," the ritualization of religious elements in daily life.[99] He announced that he wanted to revisit his dissertation, *De sacramentele heilseconomie* ("The Sacramental Economy of Salvation"), which was his first substantial study published in 1953, from this perspective. He proposed using the approach that had been developed in Ritual Studies. But this plan was not to be: a few years before his death in 2009 he felt compelled to conclude that he could no longer muster the concentration required for such a project.

Around the turn of the century, Schillebeeckx gave two lectures on Dominican spirituality, the texts of which have been preserved: in 2000 at an open day in the Dominican friary in Berg en Dal near Nijmegen, where he lived during the last period of his life, and in 2003 at the annual convention of the Flemish Dominican family in Kortenberg near Leuven.[100] In 2000, Schillebeeckx's starting point was the mural painting of Dominic that Henri Mattisse (1869–1954) had made in the famous *chapelle du Rosaire* in Vence in the south of France.[101] Mattisse had painted only Dominic's outline, without any facial expression or even features. Schillebeeckx regarded this stylized image as an invitation to the viewer to give his or her own interpretation: "*you decide for yourself what I mean to you!*"[102] For him, Dominic was first and foremost a person who, with great freedom, was able to bring various contradictions into harmony within himself. Thus he was at once "rational"—as the organizer of an order—and "theologal"—oriented toward God, and in this sense mystical. He had a charisma that enthused people, and yet dealt with issues in a calm and considered way. In Schillebeeckx's view, Dominic propagated what Thomas would later articulate in the adage *contemplari et contemplata aliis tradere*, a mixed way of life involving both prayer and the apostolate.

Schillebeeckx even more emphatically highlighted the political interpretation of this apostolate, which had already been present in his publications in the 1970s. He argued that the "resting point" of Dominic's contemplation did not lie in monastic contemplation, but with "the people, [...] on the basis of Jesus' proclamation of the Kingdom of God *as* good news for all people."[103] The world in which God is active and in which God wants to establish God's Kingdom is none

---

[98] Edward Schillebeeckx, *Church, CW* vol. 10 (London: Bloomsbury T&T Clark, 2014).

[99] Edward Schillebeeckx, "Naar een herontdekking van de christelijke sacramenten: Ritualisering van religieuze momenten in het alledaagse leven," *TvT* 40 (2000), 164–87. ET: Edward Schillebeeckx, "Towards a Rediscovery of the Christian Sacraments," *Essays, CW* vol. 11 (London: Bloomsbury T&T Clark, 2014), 183–210.

[100] Edward Schillebeeckx, "Dominicaanse spiritualiteit," *Dominicaans Leven* 57 (2000), 4, 5–10.

[101] On the way in which the interior of this chapel was inspired by the Dominican tradition, see Gabrielle Langdon, "'A Spiritual Space': Matisse's Chapel of the Dominicans at Vence," *Zeitschrift für Kunstgeschichte* 51 (1988), 542–73; Marie-Thérèse Pulvenis de Séligny, *Matisse: Vence – La chapelle du Rosaire* (Paris: Éditions du Cerf, 2013).

[102] Schillebeeckx, "Dominicaanse spiritualiteit (2000)," 5.

[103] Ibid., 7.

other than this world, including the people who live there, something Schillebeeckx expressed in his famous dictum *extra mundum nulla salus,* there is no salvation outside the world.[104] To stand in this world, with the people, brings us closer to God, so that the principles of *présence au monde* and *présence à Dieu* no longer conflict with each other, but, on the contrary, belong to one and the same movement of man toward God. In a homily in 1985, Schillebeeckx already characterized Dominic as one of the "true saints"; someone who cannot tell if they have greater love for God or for people, "because they can no longer distinguish between the two, so much are they 'of God,' who is a *God of men and women.*"[105] For Christians, and particularly for Dominicans, what was important was to

> be attentive to what is at stake here and now […] in the world, and to respond to that in fidelity to the faith, because then we are closest *ourselves* to God's active presence. […] [I]n the here and now we can catch glimpses of the grace of the Kingdom of God which never ceases to break through in our history.[106]

Schillebeeckx described the unique feature of the Dominican identity as a "quest," in which one attempts to find God in everyday life—not only in the positive things, but also, even especially, in the negative, contrastive experiences that inspire resistance within us to that which we know should not exist.[107] He understood "Dominican identity […] as openness to what presents itself, and acting on the basis of this."[108] According to Schillebeeckx, the dynamic of *présence au monde, présence à Dieu* also offered perspectives for Dominican life in the Western context. He called for small communities that would not be turned in on themselves, but would, out of their prayer, reach out to people, and would also be receptive to the opposite movement, willing to receive people from outside who wish to have some experience of their prayerful atmosphere.

Schillebeeckx himself regarded the speech he gave in 2003 at the annual convention of the Dominican family in Flanders as "a kind of farewell, a testament for his Flemish confreres."[109] The full title of his lecture was: "Theological challenges for Dominicans—from the current ecclesiastical situation, from socio-cultural world problems, and from concrete multicultural and multireligious societies (especially in Europe, and particularly in Flanders and the

---

[104] Schillebeeckx developed this thought primarily in his book *Church*; cf. Robert J. Schreiter, "Schillebeeckx and Theology in the Twenty-First Century," *Edward Schillebeeckx and Contemporary Theology*, ed. Lieven Boeve, Frederiek Depoortere, Stephan van Erp (London: T&T Clark, 2010), 253–55; and the analysis of Schillebeeckx's book by P. Conway, "The Human Story of God: The Spirituality of Edward Schillebeeckx," *Doctrine and Life* 41 (1991), 523–30, at 524–25: "If history is truly God's gift […] then the process of liberation in history is the very stuff of revelation."

[105] Edward Schillebeeckx, *For the Sake of the Gospel*, trans. John Bowden (London: SCM, 1989), 122. Original version: Edward Schillebeeckx, "Domingo de Guzman: Stichter van de beweging 'de dominicaanse familie'," *Om het behoud van het evangelie. Evangelie verhalen, deel II* (Baarn, Nelissen, 1988), 143.

[106] Schillebeeckx, "Dominicaanse spiritualiteit (2000)," 8–9.

[107] Cf. Kathleen McManus, "Suffering in the Theology of Edward Schillebeeckx," *Theological Studies* 60 (1999), 476–91.

[108] Borgman, "Openheid," 68.

[109] Bernard De Cock, "Leren van conflicten. Over polarisatie binnen een dominicaanse gemeenschap," *Het habijt weer uit de kast: Botsing of ontmoeting tussen generaties in dominicaans perspectief*, ed. Stephan van Erp and Anton Milh (Leuven: Dominicanen, 2016), 27.

Netherlands)."[110] The starting point for his talk was the personal experience of Jesus of Nazareth. This consisted on the one hand in a *"theologal* relationship of trust with the living God [...] [the] absolute freedom-*for-the-good* for people in our world," and on the other in negative contrast experiences occurring in everyday life: the suffering of specific individuals.[111] The tension between these two extremes resulted in Jesus's proclamation of the Kingdom of God, which is essentially "a kingdom of *people* who make the decision to live in *God's living space*," in the awareness that such a Kingdom can only be partially realized by human beings here on earth.[112] In imitation of Jesus, Dominicans were required—through contemplation, study, encounters with people, etc.—to discover where some aspect of God's Kingdom was already present, but also where this Kingdom was still painfully absent. As "border workers," they had to seek out these places and proclaim the Kingdom of God there in word and deed.[113]

The greater part of Schillebeeckx's speech was devoted to an in-depth analysis of the two fundamental dimensions of Dominican life: the theologal dimension of the orientation toward God, and the resulting socio-political-ethical dimension. In his discussion of the theologal, faith dimension, he focused on the *kabood*—the glory of God—which relates "to visible phenomena that, symbolically but really, enable people to experience God's presence (which cannot be experienced)."[114] After the destruction of the Temple, in a time of exile, the Prophet Ezekiel proclaimed that the glory of God could be found "in people who do justice and foster charity" (orthopraxy).[115] People therefore carry the possibility within themselves of becoming bearers of God's glory. For Schillebeeckx, Jesus was God's *kabood* made flesh.

This idea of *kabood* influenced the second part of Schillebeeckx's talk, in which he described the church as *sacramentum mundi*. Schillebeeckx defined the church as "a religious community which, as a reference to God, stands at the service of people who live in a 'finite-autonomous' world, which is a threatened and vulnerable world."[116] The church mediates the glory of God to the extent that the church makes God present among the people in word, deed, and sacrament.

---

[110] Edward Schillebeeckx, *Theologische uitdagingen voor dominicanen*, 2003 (unpublished). An adapted version of this text was published as "Christelijke identiteit, uitdagend en uitgedaagd. Over de rakelingse nabijheid van de onervaarbare God," ed. Manuela Kalsky et al., *Ons rakelings nabij*, 13–32. All page references refer to the original, unpublished version. Translations are our own.

[111] Schillebeeckx, *Theologische uitdagingen voor dominicanen*, 4–5.

[112] Ibid., 5.

[113] This term refers to the description of the order's mission from the general chapter of the Dominicans in 1986 in Ávila, Spain. There, the mission of the order was called a mission to the frontiers ("misión de fronteras"), the frontiers between life and death, between humanity and inhumanity, of Christianity, of the religious experience, and of the church. See *Acta capituli generalis diffinitorum Ordinis Praedicatorum Abulensis in Conventu S. Thomae Aquinatis a die 7 ad diem 27 augusti MCMLXXXVI sub fr. Damiano Byrne Sacrae Theologiae professore totiusque eiusdem Ordinis magistro celebrati* (Rome, Curia Generalitia, 1986), 16–20.

[114] Schillebeeckx, *Theologische uitdagingen voor dominicanen*, 22. According to Schillebeeckx, *Kabood* is also useful as a concept in interreligious dialogue, because it is grounded in the fundamental impossibility of knowing or experiencing God, which prevents him from being "locked up" in any religious tradition. In his text, Schillebeeckx also stressed that dialogue with the adherents of other faiths is one of the core tasks of the order.

[115] Schillebeeckx, *Theologische uitdagingen voor dominicanen*, 23. It is not entirely clear which passage from Ezekiel Schillebeeckx has in mind here, but Ezek 11:19–20 is one of the possibilities.

[116] Schillebeeckx, *Theologische uitdagingen voor dominicanen*, 26.

This is closely related to the twin concepts of *présence à Dieu* and *présence au monde* which he had used in his work in the 1970s to designate the Dominican mission.

In his epilogue, Schillebeeckx offered his confreres three specific pieces of advice. The first was a call to be totally flexible, "starting from today," and to abolish the divisions between the first, second, and third orders (friars, contemplative nuns, apostolic sisters, and laypeople). The order should "be open to different forms of temporary affiliation."[117] This amounted to a radicalization of the expansion of ways of belonging to the order, which he had advocated as early as the 1970s (also because he expressed the hope that women would be admitted to the priesthood in the future). Second, Dominican preaching should remain focused on the salvation of people. The force of the Dominican life was situated in "Christian humanity and humane Christianity" and remaining true to this, he believed, would open possibilities for new vocations. Third, he called on the order to support older friars "to their dying day," but he also exhorted these older confreres not to retire from their commitment to the apostolate.[118]

# Conclusion

The carefully delineated description of Dominican spirituality that Schillebeeckx gave in 1954 had evolved by 2003 into the recognition that it was a "fluid, historical identity," which could never be definitively described since each new generation was called to add its own contribution. What does recur in his writings from the three main periods we have analyzed—the 1950s, the 1970s, and the 2000s—are the twin concepts of *présence au monde* and *présence à Dieu*. The proposition *présence au monde est présence à Dieu* (presence in the world is presence to God) came from the French Dominican Henri-Dominique Lacordaire (1802–1861), and was used in the 1950s by the worker priests to defend their methodology. Schillebeeckx made this proposition his own. He gave *présence au monde* an increasingly overt political interpretation. This was related to Schillebeeckx's approach to Dominican spirituality as a "subversive story"; respectful of historical tradition, but, above all, critical of the church, the order, and the society of his time. This criticism was grounded in Schillebeeckx's theological vision. The Kingdom of God has already appeared in this world, but its full manifestation still lies in the future. People, Christians, Dominicans, have the task to seek and strengthen God's graceful activity in this world, and to remove any obstacles that obstruct the manifestation of the Kingdom of God.[119] In the service of God, who according to Schillebeeckx is essentially a God of human beings, a *Deus humanissimus*, people must strive for true and ever more inclusive humanity.[120] We need not do this on our own

---

[117] Ibid., 29.

[118] Ibid., 29–30.

[119] Cf. Goergen, "Spirituality," 129–30.

[120] Viewed in this light, Emmanuel Sena Avonyo's recent work is interesting: *La spiritualité dominicaine de la compassion et de la miséricorde: Aux sources de la spiritualité dominicaine* (Paris: Parole et Silence, 2018). On p. 48, he argues as follows: "notre hypothèse est qu'il existe une spiritualité dominicaine de la compassion et de la miséricorde qu'on pourrait qualifier de 'spiritualité dominicaine fondamentale'." According to Avonyo, Dominican spirituality always departs from the needs of individuals, and wishes to offer them a way of salvation in word and deed.

or on the basis of our own merit: our primary task is to allow God's grace to work within us. It is this receptive, mystical attitude to God's grace with its political consequences that Schillebeeckx characterized as typically Dominican.[121] Mary Catherine Hilkert has rightly observed that not only are Schillebeeckx's writings on spirituality infused with a "grace-optimism," but that this is also the core of his theological work.[122] It is surely also this aspect of his theology and spirituality that has had the most impact.[123] Anyone who wishes to penetrate to the core of Schillebeeckx's theology will therefore do well to familiarize themselves with his view of Dominican spirituality, and to regard his work as an expression of this.

---

[121] His focus on grace, for instance in the life of virtue, is a feature that distinguishes Schillebeeckx from other thinkers on Dominican spirituality—like Romanus Cessario—who has considerably less to say about this subject (see, for instance, Cessario, "The Grace St. Dominic Brings to the World," 95–98).

[122] Mary Catherine Hilkert, "'Grace-Optimism': The Spirituality at the Heart of Schillebeeckx's Theology," *Spirituality Today* 44 (1991), 220–39. Cf. Erik Borgman, "Theologie met spiritueel gehalte, spiritualiteit met een theologische explicatie: Over de blijvende actualiteit van de theologie van Schillebeeckx," *TGL* 65 (2009), 29–39, 31: "Spirituality [...] for him is the inside of theology, as theology is the theoretical and scholarly reflection on this experience." Our translation.

[123] See especially the work of Erik Borgman, particularly his *Dominican Spirituality: An Exploration* (London, Continuum, 2000); and Erik Borgman, *Leven van wat komt: Een katholiek uitzicht op de samenleving* (Utrecht: Meinema, 2017). The joy that results from the life of grace was also typically Dominican according to Schillebeeckx, but it does not seem that Paul Murray made much use of Schillebeeckx's writings on Dominican spirituality for his popular book Paul Murray, O.P., *The New Wine of Dominican Spirituality. A Drink Called Happiness* (London: Bloomsbury, 2006).

# Chapter 6

# Schillebeeckx's Phenomenology of Experience and Resurrection Faith

Anthony J. Godzieba

Edward Schillebeeckx's treatment of Christ's resurrection in his *Jesus: An Experiment in Christology,* while controversial, remains a potent hermeneutical reflection on the original Easter experience as well as on resurrection faith today.[1] By closely examining Schillebeeckx's theory in its original existential-phenomenological context, I wish to highlight here its continuing explanatory force regarding the origin and meaning of belief in the resurrection of Jesus.

Four questions posed by the theologian William Loewe regarding the New Testament evidence for the Resurrection can help us clarify what is at stake for theological reflection. The first question, "what are the data?" lays the groundwork in terms of the textual evidence. The second is "why are the data the way they are?" The third is "the modern historical question, so oblique to the gospel writers' concerns but unavoidable in our cultural situation," namely, "why are there any data at all? That is, what happened to kick off this whole business of belief in Jesus' resurrection?" Finally, there is what we might call the "so what?" question: "what difference does it make if Jesus was raised from the dead?"[2] It is worth noting that these questions cover the temporal gamut of past, present, and future: the first question deals with the textual evidence as we encounter it now; the second and third probe the "world behind the text," inquiring into the experiences that gave rise to the existence and the form of the textual witness as it has come down to us; the fourth question is a pointedly hermeneutical one that attempts to discern the "world in front of" the text, the evidence's "applicative" moment—how the texts provoke new possibilities for present and future Christian existence that transform the lives of believers and bring them into deeper participation in divine life.

This concern for the structure and origins of experience is appropriate to the discipline of Christology because the Christian tradition is best viewed as a "history of effects," a

---

A version of this chapter originally appeared in *Finding Salvation in Christ: Essays on Christ and Soteriology in Honor of William Loewe,* ed. Christopher Denny and Christopher McMahon (Eugene, OR: Wipf and Stock, 2011), 73–106. It has been newly revised for this volume.

[1]  Edward Schillebeeckx, *Jesus, CW* vol. 6 (London: Bloomsbury T&T Clark, 2014), 289–610 [321–650]. Dutch original: *Jezus, het verhaal van een levende* (Bloemendaal: H. Nelissen, 1974).

[2]  William P. Loewe, *The College Student's Introduction to Christology* (Collegeville, MN: Liturgical Press, 1996), 98.

*Wirkungsgeschichte* (to use Hans-Georg Gadamer's term).[3] That is, the tradition, as an ensemble of practices and reflections, functions as the ongoing, developing reception and realization of the salvific truth of Jesus Christ that was first experienced by Jesus's disciples in their personal encounters with him. As Schillebeeckx puts it, "this astonishing and overwhelming encounter with the man Jesus became the starting-point for the New Testament view of salvation. To put it plainly, 'grace' has to be expressed in terms of encounter and experience; it can never be isolated from the specific encounter which brought about liberation."[4] In light of Christianity's foundational, incarnational, and sacramental commitments, it makes no sense to separate the historical event of Jesus of Nazareth—the initial contextualized impulse of the Christian tradition—from the tradition itself, as did the earliest "quest for the historical Jesus" in turning this into a methodological principle. It is one of the necessary tasks of Christological reflection to probe, as deeply as possible, the events and experiences that have provided the initial impetus for both the tradition and our present activity of belief. Walter Kasper, for example, emphasizes this need for a genetic analysis when he takes up the key issue of the continuation of Jesus's "cause" after his crucifixion and the after-effects of the events that constitute the Paschal Mystery.

> There was continuity after Good Friday; indeed in some senses it was then that movement really began [...] The powerful historical dynamism of this revival can only be made comprehensible, even in purely historical terms, by positing a sort of "initial ignition." Religious, psychological, political and social elements in the situation, as it was at the time, can be cited in explanation. Yet, seen from the point of view of historical circumstances, Jesus' "cause" has very slender chances of surviving. Jesus' end on the cross was not only his private failure but a public catastrophe for his "mission," and its religious discrediting. The renewal must therefore be seen as strong enough not only to "explain" the unnatural dynamism of early Christianity, but to "come to terms with" that problem of the cross.[5]

The search for this "initial ignition" of the development and spread of belief in Jesus as the Christ leads most Christologies to the Gospels' resurrection accounts, and especially to the post-resurrection appearance narratives rather than the empty-tomb narratives. Schillebeeckx is no exception. In the appearance accounts, he maintains, we should look for what provoked the radical change in the disciples, as they turned from seeing their hopes

---

[3]  See Hans-Georg Gadamer, *Wahrheit und Methode: Grundzüge einer philosophischen Hermeneutik,* Gesammelte Werke, vol. 1, Hermeneutik I (Tübingen: Mohr Siebeck, 1990), 305–12; ET: Hans-Georg Gadamer, *Truth and Method,* 2nd rev. ed. trans. rev. Joel Weinsheimer and Donald G. Marshall (New York: Continuum, 2004), 300–07. For the Christian tradition interpreted as a *Wirkungsgeschichte,* see Anthony J. Godzieba, "Method and Interpretation: The New Testament's Heretical Hermeneutic (Prelude and Fugue)," *The Heythrop Journal* 36 (1995), 286–306; Godzieba, "'[...] And Followed Him on the Way' (Mark 10:52): Unity, Diversity, Discipleship," *Beyond Dogmatism and Innocence: Hermeneutics, Critique, and Catholic Theology,* ed. Anthony J. Godzieba and Bradford E. Hinze (Collegeville, MN: Liturgical Press, 2017), 228–54.

[4]  Edward Schillebeeckx, *Christ, CW* vol. 7 (London: Bloomsbury T&T Clark, 2014), 3 [19]; Dutch original: *Gerechtigheid en liefde: Genade en bevrijding,* 2nd ed. (Bloemendaal: H. Nelissen, 1982).

[5]  Walter Kasper, *Jesus the Christ,* trans. V. Green (New York: Paulist, 1977), 124.

dashed in the catastrophe of the crucifixion to confidently proclaiming Jesus's resurrection and the continuation of Jesus's cause.

Schillebeeckx's original argument in the first edition of *Jesus* was that the disciples did indeed have a real encounter with Jesus, resulting in their experience of grace and forgiveness for having forsaken Jesus at the hour of his death. This earlier argument grounds the appearance tradition in the conversion experience of Peter who subsequently reunited the remaining disciples, who in turn had had their own conversion experiences. These experiences of forgiveness, coupled with the disciples' memory of Jesus's life and praxis, "became the matrix of faith in Jesus as the risen one. All of a sudden they 'saw' it."[6] The disciples subsequently expressed their experience of conversion and their real encounter with Jesus, the catalyst of this conversion, in terms of a "'vision' model" meant to convey the historical reality of "an event prompted by grace, a divine, saving initiative." This was their testimony to the fact that "a dead man does not offer forgiveness" but rather the living Jesus.[7]

> The objective, sovereignly free initiative of Jesus that led them to Christological faith, independently of any belief on the part of Peter and his companions, is a gracious act of Christ, which in respect of its enlightening impact is clearly revelational – not a human construct but revelation via a disclosure experience, verbalized later in the appearances model. What it signifies is not a model but a living reality. Understood thus, the ground of Christian belief is indubitably Jesus of Nazareth's earthly offer of salvation, renewed after his death, now experienced and enunciated by Peter and the twelve.[8]

Criticisms were leveled at this argument by Schillebeeckx's theological colleagues as well as by the Vatican's Congregation for the Doctrine of the Faith (CDF). Schillebeeckx subsequently made clarifications and substantive additions to the third Dutch edition of *Jesus*, and his important discussions of "experience" in both the 1977 *Christ* and the 1978 *Interim Report* formed part of his ongoing response to these various critiques.[9] It is precisely in this amplification (indeed the fine-tuning) of his earlier argument that Schillebeeckx tackles the decisive philosophical issues surrounding the issues of experience, objectivity, and "the real," along with their theological import. In the remainder of this chapter, I want to examine one slice of this material, namely,

---

[6]  Schillebeeckx, *Jesus*, 358 [391].

[7]  Ibid., 357–58 [390–91].

[8]  Ibid., 357–58 [391].

[9]  For the additions, see Edward Schillebeeckx, *Jezus, het verhaal van een levende*, 3rd ed. (Bloemendaal: Nelissen, 1975), 528a–e; Schillebeeckx, *Jesus*, 605–10 [644–50]. See also Edward Schillebeeckx, *IR, CW* vol. 8 (London: Bloomsbury T&T Clark, 2014), 3–16 [3–19]; Dutch original: Edward Schillebeeckx, *Tussentijds verhaal over twee Jezusboeken* (Bloemendaal: H. Nelissen, 1978). For a translation of documents relating to the CDF's investigation of Schillebeeckx, along with Schillebeeckx's responses, see *The Schillebeeckx Case: Official Exchange of Letters and Documents in the Investigation of Fr. Edward Schillebeeckx, O.P. by the Sacred Congregation for the Doctrine of the Faith, 1976–1980*, ed. Ted Schoof, trans. Matthew J. O'Connell (Ramsey, NJ: Paulist, 1984). See also the commentary by Herwi Rikhof, "Of Shadows and Substance: Analysis and Evaluation of the Documents in the Schillebeeckx Case," *Authority in the Church and the Schillebeeckx Case*, ed. Leonard Swidler and Piet F. Fransen (New York: Crossroad, 1982), 244–67.

Schillebeeckx's theory of experience, by sketching out its crucial phenomenological background and the impact this theory has on his theology of revelation and his treatment of the Easter appearances. In doing so, I want to make the case that his phenomenological approach to the appearance narratives, as a sophisticated sorting out of the notions of "objective" and "subjective" in a theological setting, fundamentally advances our ability to articulate the objectivity that structures the New Testament accounts while also accounting for the disciples' experience of faith steeped in first-century AD Palestinian Jewish eschatology.

# I. "Experience" and its phenomenological context

Schillebeeckx summarizes his basic view of revelation this way: "God's revelation follows the path of human experiences. Obviously, revelation—the sheer initiative of God's free love of men—surpasses every human experience; in other words, it does not proceed from subjective human experience and thought; but it can only be perceived in and through human experiences. Apart from any experience, there is no revelation either."[10] The claim is not new; it is a common starting point for Roman Catholic theology after the Second Vatican Council. But whereas a more transcendental position such as Karl Rahner's considered God's self-disclosure in revelation as the fulfillment of the possibilities of human ontological structures (reworked from the *existentialia,* the existential structures of Martin Heidegger's *Being and Time*), Schillebeeckx professed to see revelation both rooted in and contrasting with experience: "Divine revelation is the opposite of a human product or project, but this opposition in no way bars revelation from including human projects and experiences, and therefore in no way suggests that revelation should fall outside our experience."[11] But if I am rooted in my experience, how do I appropriate these new elements of "contrast"? If my experience is transcended, how can I know at all?[12]

For Schillebeeckx, experience means "learning through 'direct' contact with people and things," and what is perceived is simultaneously integrated into our field of experiences: "In this way they become the framework within which we interpret new experiences, while at the same time this already given framework of interpretation is exposed to criticism and corrected, changed or renewed by new experiences. Experience is gained in a dialectical fashion: through an interplay between perception and thought, thought and perception."[13] This dialectical framework that guides integration of new experiences is the element of interpretation. It opens up the person to "contrast experiences" that confound our expectations and yet can be appropriated within this expanding framework.[14] Experience and interpretation thus occur simultaneously: "we experience in the act of interpreting, without being able to draw a neat distinction between the element of experience and the element of interpretation."[15] By means of this interpretative dimension, the

---

[10]   Schillebeeckx, *IR*, 10 [11].
[11]   Ibid.
[12]   This is akin to Kant's noumenon/phenomenon problem, to which Schillebeeckx alludes (*Christ*, 41–42 [56]).
[13]   Schillebeeckx, *Christ*, 17 [31–32] (my emphasis).
[14]   Schillebeeckx, *IR*, 11–12 [13].
[15]   Schillebeeckx, *Christ*, 19 [33].

person can admit experiences that transcend the fund of experiences already present. In this way, Schillebeeckx grounds his theory of revelation in a basic epistemological structure of human subjectivity.

Although he is sparing with his references, it can be shown that the main influences on Schillebeeckx's view of experience are those philosophical analyses that come out of phenomenology, specifically those of Heidegger and Maurice Merleau-Ponty (who are not cited in either *Christ* or the *Interim Report*), and Gadamer (whose lengthy section on experience in *Truth and Method* is cited[16]). In fact, his position has much in common with the existential phenomenology popularized in the 1960s by the Dutch philosopher William (Wim) Luijpen, among others.[17] If Schillebeeckx's argument is to have its full impact, we must make his presuppositions clear.

If phenomenology is truly the unspoken presupposition to his fundamental notion of experience, then we should also emphasize that Schillebeeckx employs a method which, in its philosophical manifestation, critiques the subject-object distinction and seeks to surpass metaphysical dualism. This is especially important in the contemporary context. Over the past quarter-century Western theologians have become almost painfully aware of how modern theology's indebtedness to both the post-medieval rationalist heritage (coming after nominalism) and modern metaphysics (the Suarezian influence that was destabilized only with Heidegger) has caused what Joseph O'Leary terms a "lack of fit" between the Christian experience of God and the rationalist-metaphysical categories that promised a comprehensive explanation of that experience. This mismatch stifled theology's ability to carry out its task as *fides quaerens intellectum* and take into account the transformation in being provoked by the unprecedented givenness of God in the Incarnation (and, by extension, the relationality that we now regard as central to any theology of the Trinity). As O'Leary puts it, "There is a complex topology of the world of faith that can never be fitted into the horizons of metaphysical theology, which rather act as a screen against it. A creative retrieval of the tradition today works toward a clearing of the fundamental horizons of faith, and subordinates the quest for metaphysical intelligibility to this prior openness."[18]

It is precisely a retrieval of the original experience of the Easter revelation-event that Schillebeeckx attempts by employing a phenomenological theory of experience to analyze the testimony passed down to us in the New Testament. Rather than "raid" phenomenology for its insights, he seems to follow the insights of phenomenological analysis to their conclusions and uses them to craft a responsive and responsible fundamental theology, convinced that these insights truly illuminate the character of what it means to be human in the grip of grace. And so, in my view, Schillebeeckx not only uses phenomenology, he *proceeds phenomenologically in doing theology,* and specifically in his discussion of the post-Resurrection appearance narratives. The result, I want to argue, is a more adequate treatment of the issues of objectivity, subjectivity,

---

16 Ibid., 30, n. 17 [855, n. 17].

17 E.g., see William Luijpen, *Existential Phenomenology*, trans. Henry J. Koren (Pittsburgh, PA: Duquesne University Press, 1969). Schillebeeckx cites other works by Luijpen (as Luypen) in *Christ*, 26 [41].

18 Joseph Stephen O'Leary, *Religious Pluralism and Christian Truth* (Edinburgh: Edinburgh University Press, 1996), x. See also O'Leary's comment that theology today "must be phenomenological," that is, "theology must constantly question back to the primary level of faith, the original concrete contours of the revelation-event, the 'matter itself' that is apprehended by a contemplative thinking" (ibid., ix).

and corporeality in the appearance narratives than can be derived from other analyses of the Resurrection.

To test this thesis, we will go on to probe the phenomenological background to Schillebeeckx's theory of experience and its application to resurrection faith. My discussion focuses on specific aspects of the works of Merleau-Ponty, Gadamer, and Heidegger that have clear echoes in Schillebeeckx's own discussion.

## Maurice Merleau-Ponty

Merleau-Ponty's original project sought to work out a phenomenological analysis of the encounter between the subject and the world by using Edmund Husserl's "phenomenological reduction," the suspension of the "natural attitude" of belief in the reality of things in order to achieve a transcendental point of view from which to reflect "on the intentions at work in the natural attitude and on the objective correlates of those intentions."[19] He attempted to correct Husserl's idealistic bias (phenomenology as the search for "pure essences") by investigating perception, thereby building a phenomenology from the ground up. This project was stimulated by Heidegger's "existential analytic" of Dasein (Being-in-the-world) in *Being and Time*.[20] Merleau-Ponty's conclusion is that there is no radical separation of the human subject and the world. Rather, there is an effective involvement of subject and world—the human person is an incarnate spirit, and through the interaction of the person (through the modes of the body-subject [perception] and the *cogito* [thought]) and the world, the true human world we inhabit, a "world of meaning," is disclosed, indeed built up. Within that ambiguous region of openness the "text" of the human world is composed, the network of meanings around me and connected to me is constituted in my everyday involvement with my world.[21] Regarding perception, he says that "normal functioning must be understood as a process of integration in which the text of the external world is not so much copied, as composed."[22] Merleau-Ponty subsequently widened his

---

[19]  Richard Cobb-Stevens, "The Beginnings of Phenomenology: Husserl and His Predecessors," *Continental Philosophy in the 20th Century*, ed. Richard Kearney, Routledge History of Philosophy vol. 8 (New York: Routledge, 1994), 5–37, at 19. For Husserl's own (complex) explanation of his "discovery", see his 1907 lectures *The Idea of Phenomenology*, trans. William P. Alston and George Nakhnikian (The Hague: Nijhoff, 1970); Husserl, *Ideas Pertaining to a Pure Phenomenology and to a Phenomenological Philosophy, First Book: General Introduction to a Pure Phenomenology*, trans. F. Kersten, Edmund Husserl: Collected Works vol. 2 (The Hague: Nijhoff, 1983 [Ger. orig., 1913]), 131–43 (§§56–62). See also Dermot Moran, *Introduction to Phenomenology* (New York: Routledge, 2006), 124–63.

[20]  See Martin Heidegger, *Sein und Zeit* (1927) (Tübingen: Niemeyer, 1953); ET: *Being and Time*, trans. John Macquarrie and Edward Robinson (New York: Harper and Row, 1962), esp. Part One, Division One.

[21]  See Maurice Merleau-Ponty, *Phenomenology of Perception*, trans. Colin Smith (London: Routledge and Kegan Paul, 1962), 453: "To be born is both to be born of the world and to be born into the world. The world is already constituted, but also never completely constituted; in the first case we are acted upon, in the second we are open to an infinite number of possibilities. But this analysis is still abstract, for we exist in both ways *at once*."

[22]  Ibid., 9.

field of phenomenological investigation beyond the analysis of behavior and perception, and attempted to develop an ontology which would not only account for the nature of perception but would also include politics and art, and would eventually put him in touch with the source of the "perceived world," namely, "brute or wild Being,"[23] Being which is seen in terms of *Gestalt,* as the ground/background of the world and man.[24]

A text from this later stage, entitled "The Metaphysical in Man" (July 1947), contains a passage which sums up much of his investigation of human experience.

> It is our very difference, the uniqueness of our experience, which attests to our strange ability to enter into others and re-enact their deeds [...] From the moment I recognize that my experience, precisely insofar as it is my own, makes me accessible to what is not myself, that I am sensitive to the world and to others, all the beings which objective thought placed at a distance draw singularly nearer to me. Or, conversely, I recognize my affinity with them; I am nothing but an ability to echo them, to understand them, to respond to them. My life seems absolutely individual and absolutely universal to me.[25]

My openness is now interpreted even more precisely: my experience is the horizon against which universal structures appear, but universality appears only through my immersion in a world where I am in contact with individual persons and things. There is no "metaphysical consciousness" (i.e., consciousness of the being-structures of "world" precisely as being-for-me) without objects of experience.[26] Consciousness only gets "filled out," as it were, only grasps meaning in its very openness to "what is not myself." It is thus radically situated and tied to experience; and it never drifts off to some pure realm of abstract universals through which I might know others and the world. The retreat to some detached knowledge of essences in order to know—a retreat which realism and Cartesianism both undertake—is a false step.

> All knowledge of man by man, far from being pure contemplation, is the taking up by each, *as best he can,* of the acts of others, reactivating from ambiguous signs an experience which is not his own, appropriating a structure [...] of which he forms no distinct concept but which he puts together as an experienced pianist deciphers an unknown piece of music: without himself grasping the motives of each gesture or each operation, without being able to bring to the surface of consciousness all the sediment of knowledge which he is using at that moment. Here we no longer have the positing of an object, but rather we have communication with a way of being.[27]

---

23  Maurice Merleau-Ponty, *The Visible and the Invisible,* trans. Alphonso Lingis (Evanston: Northwestern University Press, 1968), 170.
24  Ibid., 170, 227–28.
25  In Maurice Merleau-Ponty, *Sense and Non-Sense,* trans. Hubert Dreyfus and Patricia Allen Dreyfus (Evanston, IL: Northwestern University Press, 1964), 83–98, at 94.
26  See ibid., 94: "This world, other people, human history, truth, culture [...] [indeed,] metaphysical consciousness has no other objects than those of experience."
27  Ibid., 93.

All my knowledge comes from lived experience which, like the playing of the pianist, ferrets out and discloses the meaning as I am involved in experiencing, and never apart from that involvement. But that involvement precisely does not close me off, but opens me to the other, to things, and to the totality of meanings we call "world." The totality and its structure only get known by means of my involvement with what is "not my own." Meanings are not constituted by consciousness fabricating them on its own, but by consciousness' interaction with the "stuff" of the world, primarily through the body, and then through the *cogito.* My immersion in the world through perception already automatically ensures that from the start my existence is double-edged: it is *absolutely individual* because of my own perspective, rooted in the perceived world by my body. At the same time it is *absolutely universal,* since the interplay between my subjectivity and the world opens me to the *whole world.* This accessibility through my standpoint to what is not myself—to the world and to others—serves to ground my appropriation of meaning or structure. Even though consciousness accomplishes constitution of meaning, it can do so only along the lines of the direction or hint provided by the world that is "found ahead of us, in the thing where our perception places us, in the dialogue into which our experience of other people throws us by means of a movement not all of whose sources are known to us."[28]

Thus it is not only sense perception which is a product of the dialogue between subjectivity and world but also every level of human existence that is dependent on human experience. Meaning is essentially a blending of foreground and background: human experience is the horizon against which the *sens* of the world appears. My experience is both perspectival and open, individual yet universal. Because of my radical situatedness, the "absolute standpoint" is impossible.

> [If] I have understood that truth and value can be for us nothing but the result of the verifications or evaluations which we make in contact with the world [...] that even these notions lose all meaning outside of human perspectives, then the world recovers its texture [...] and knowledge and action, true and false, good and evil have something unquestionable about them precisely because I do not claim to find in them absolute evidence.[29]

Merleau-Ponty thus insists on the contextual situatedness of human existence: all knowledge is founded on experience, and indeed every human act is rooted in the structure of present experience. In the course of his refutation of the absolute standpoint, Merleau-Ponty also implicitly refutes subjectivism by showing that the very workings of experience necessarily include the world, "the other," what is not-myself, alongside subjectivity. This phenomenological analysis of experience reveals experience's double edge (individuality/universality) and also asserts its primacy, points which are crucial to Schillebeeckx's own analysis of experience.

## Hans-Georg Gadamer

Gadamer's analysis of experience can be seen as supplying what is lacking in Merleau-Ponty, namely, a more critical examination of the concept of experience as it relates to thought. The

---

28    Ibid.
29    Ibid., 95.

concept of experience is, for Gadamer, "one of the most obscure we have."[30] That obscurity is not cleared up by the prevailing notions of experience governed by the scientific model, which aims for certainty and strips experience of its historicality in order to objectify it, make it verifiable by anyone, and assure its universality.[31] This reveals a bias akin to the bias of the absolute standpoint criticized by Merleau-Ponty. The authentic character of experience becomes obscured when it is defined not in terms of its own characteristics but in terms of the supposed "result," an absolute that is pre-supposed and is known "absolutely." In its true character, experience is neither a straight-line process nor does it lead consciousness away from its historical rootedness. Rather, experience is a process involving starts, stops, and reversals. It is, paradoxically, a process of negation which leads to development. Even the everyday use of the word manifests this paradoxical character:

> We use the word "experience" in two different senses: the experiences that conform to our expectation and confirm it and the new experiences that occur to us. This latter—"experience" in the genuine sense—is always negative. If a new experience of an object occurs to us, this means that hitherto we have not seen the thing correctly and now know it better. Thus the negativity of experience has a curiously productive meaning. It is not simply that we see through a deception and hence make a correction, but we acquire a comprehensive knowledge.[32]

The negation that we experience is our expectations being confounded, even shattered: this object is *not* as I expected, this situation is *not* as I predicted. My thinking has a certain "fit", and the clash with the world forces thinking to adjust its "fit," to expand in order to comprehend.[33] Consciousness does not control meaning; rather, constitution of meaning takes place when our previous appropriation of meaning and the expectations that have thereby been generated are in turn shattered by an unexpected twist in the manifestation of being. Experience thus leads to a deeper understanding of the world and being, but this occurs only in the process of experiencing, in historical consciousness. The clash between expectation and novelty leads Gadamer to term experience "dialectical." After an experience, nothing remains the same: "In view of the experience that we have of another object, both things change—our knowledge and its object. We know better now, and that means that the object itself 'does not pass the test.' The new object contains the truth about the old one."[34]

Gadamer credits Hegel with revealing the fundamentally dialectical character of experience and asserting its historicity. But, contrary to Hegel's assertion that the primary direction of experience is inward, Gadamer contends that experience's dialectical character first thrusts me outward: by its very nature it forces me to come to grips with the non-I that surpasses my expectations. Once that object/situation/concept is dealt with—that is, once consciousness

---

[30] Gadamer, *Truth and Method*, 346.
[31] See ibid., 347.
[32] Ibid., 353.
[33] To "see the thing correctly" should be taken here in the sense of encounter between Dasein and the world that Heidegger works out in §44 of *Being and Time* (256–73): through Dasein's encounter with things, things are freed in their being – they show themselves from themselves in the clearing opened up by Dasein.
[34] Gadamer, *Truth and Method*, 354.

expands in order to comprehend—the process is repeated, endlessly. Experience, like Husserl's intentionality, always implies both subject and object poles of the encounter (or, in Husserl's more exacting terms, *noesis* and *noema*). Like intentionality, it is a dynamism which constantly drives subjectivity outward. On this point, Gadamer should be quoted in full:

> The truth of experience always implies an orientation toward new experience. That is why a person who is called experienced has become so not only *through* experiences but is also open *to* new experiences. The consummation of his experience, the perfection that we call "being experienced," does not consist in the fact that someone already knows everything and knows better than anyone else. Rather, the experienced person proves to be, on the contrary, someone who is radically undogmatic; who, because of the many experiences he has had and the knowledge he has drawn from them, is particularly well equipped to have new experiences and to learn from them. The dialectic of experience has its proper fulfillment not in definitive knowledge but in the openness to experience that is made possible by experience itself.[35]

There is nothing here that can get boiled down to a predictable and repeatable objectivity, since experience by its very nature confounds predictability.

Besides uncovering the primordial openness of experience to new experiences, Gadamer's phenomenological analysis reveals something still deeper, a fundamental structure of human existence itself. By always including "a qualitatively new element," experience "inevitably involves many disappointments of one's expectations and only thus is experience acquired."[36] Experience also encompasses pain and disillusionment. These descriptions hint at the reality of human limitation and the essential role that the shattering of expectations plays in every experience. "Only through negative instances do we acquire new experiences [...] Every experience worthy of the name thwarts an expectation. Thus the historical nature of man essentially implies a fundamental negativity that emerges in the relation between experience and insight."[37] We are continually brought up short by our own finitude, by the limits of the power of reason, and by "the limited degree to which the future is still open to expectation and planning [...] Genuine experience is experience of one's own historicity."[38] Thus openness to new experiences is at once a spectrum of infinite possibilities and the cause of suffering. In every experience the totality of existence comes into play; it causes me disappointment, yet at the same time it engenders hope by remaining open to new experiences which break the predictability and deception which enslave consciousness.

Schillebeeckx specifically cites this section of *Truth and Method,* and it is easy to see the main outline of his theory of experience in Gadamer's argument: the historical nature of consciousness, the absolute dependence of consciousness on present experience, the limitation of my perspective, and experience's radical openness to new experiences. While Schillebeeckx goes his own way in crafting a theology of revelation, it is instructive to see how far he is willing to follow Gadamer in formulating his theological appropriation of Gadamer's analysis.

---

[35]  Ibid., 355.
[36]  Ibid., 356.
[37]  Ibid.
[38]  Ibid., 357.

# Martin Heidegger

Even though both Merleau-Ponty's and Gadamer's arguments presuppose Heidegger's work, Heidegger is considered last here because his overall philosophical project was a consideration of the meaning of Being rather than a consideration of the structure of consciousness and experience. His analysis of human experience (the "existential analytic" in *Being and Time*) provides a wider focus for a theory of experience and, when appropriated, a theology of revelation, and expands the narrower concerns of Merleau-Ponty and Gadamer. Heidegger's contributions to the discussion are numerous. Here we will deal only with three of the most basic points.

*Truth*—The basic ontological structure of the person is *to be in the world*. Thus human existence (Dasein) is radically historical and temporal. Dasein works out its being-in-the-world as "care," a circumspective orientation toward the world. In being-toward-the-world, Dasein frees entities to be what they are, providing a "clearing" for beings to be disclosed as *phenomena*. This process of *disclosure* is the primordial meaning of "truth," *a-lētheia* (un-covering, re-vealing, "bringing out of darkness [*lēthē*]"). "Truth" is primarily an *event of manifestation*. Only derivatively can the word be applied to what is traditionally referred to as *adequatio*, the agreement between the knowing subject and the known object; any such assertion of agreement is a confirmation of the prior event of "dis-closure" in the encounter between the person and the world in experience.[39] In other words, meaning—the Being-structure of the world and the complex of intertwined meanings which make up "world"—is dependent upon Dasein, the "clearing" that it provides through its circumspective "care," and its act of constitution.[40] There is no independent "world" without Dasein, since "world" is a network or structure of referential meanings both revealed and constituted in the encounter between person and entities. Without the clearing provided by Dasein's experience, there "is" no Being, since the disclosure of the truth of beings and Being is radically dependent for its constitution on the interplay of person and world in experience.[41] But this does not mean that truth is "left to the subject's discretion," because in the experience of dis-closure the person comes "face to face with the entities themselves"—that is, the uncovering of ontological structures is a cooperative venture between the person and entities in the encounter.[42] Entities reveal a sense of Being which does not originate with Dasein.

*Pre-understanding (Vorgriff)*—"Every inquiry is a seeking. Every seeking gets guided beforehand by what is sought."[43] Every approach to an encounter, every action of disclosure and understanding, is already guided by a *Vorgriff*, a pre-conceptual understanding or "fore-

---

[39] "Being-true as Being-uncovered is in turn ontologically possible only on the basis of Being-in-the-World. This latter phenomenon, which we have known as a basic state of Dasein, is the *foundation* for the primordial phenomenon of truth" (*Being and Time*, 261).

[40] "Of course, only as long as Dasein *is* (that is, only as long as an understanding of Being is ontically possible), 'is there' [*gibt es*] Being. When Dasein does not exist, 'independence' 'is' not either, nor 'is' the 'in-itself'" (ibid., 255). Heidegger famously revised the meaning of *"es gibt"* in his later writings; see, e.g., his *Letter on Humanism*, trans. Frank A. Capuzzi and J. Glenn Gray, in *Basic Writings*, ed. David Farrell Krell, rev. ed. (San Francisco: HarperCollins, 1993), 217–65, esp. at 238.

[41] Heidegger, *Being and Time*, 269: "*'There is' truth only in so far as Dasein is and so long as Dasein is*. Entities are uncovered only *when* Dasein *is*; and only as long as Dasein *is*, are they disclosed [...] Before there was any Dasein, there was no truth; nor will there be any after Dasein is no more."

[42] Ibid., 270.

[43] Ibid., 44.

structure" of understanding.[44] For example, the question of the meaning of Being is ontologically prior to all other questions because Dasein is the being for whom Being is an issue. To ask the question means that understanding is incomplete. But Dasein must already have some pre-understanding of Being, or else the question would never have been known in order to have been posed.[45] We somehow "see beforehand," dimly, the goal of the inquiry; it guides the direction of the inquiry and the direction of the progressive understanding. Heidegger terms this development of understanding "interpretation" (*Auslegung*), the articulation and realization of the possibilities grasped by understanding—in other words, the "laying out" (*auslegen*) of the elements of pre-understanding engendered in the earlier stage of the experiential encounter.[46] The *Vorgriff* is not a product of consciousness, but rather the product of the interplay between person and world; once gained, it sets up definite directions for interpretation. While interpretation can either disclose an entity/situation (act positively in revealing its meaning) or close it off (work against what we are interpreting), it is the *Vorgriff* that guides the process and somehow sets standards as to whether a particular interpretation is "revelatory" or successful. But this guiding act of the pre-understanding only comes into play in the experience itself; there is no *Vorgriff* outside experience. The situation set up by the *Vorgriff* is a circular one: "all interpretation [...] operates in the fore-structure [...] Any interpretation which is to contribute understanding, must already have understood what is to be interpreted."[47] This is the hermeneutic circle, the fundamental nature of understanding.

*"Aletheiology" of Being*—This earlier focus on the existential analytic of Dasein as the most appropriate way to get at the meaning of Being gives way in Heidegger's later works to a concentration on Being itself as it manifests itself as language, as art, as history, and as temporality. His main concern is the retrieval of the original experience of Being which can be discerned in the pre-Socratic Greek philosophers but which has fallen into oblivion and been covered over in the subsequent history of philosophy by a thinking that is "calculative"—that is, it treats Being as an object (thus leading to an objectifying metaphysics) and represents "it" as *ousia, idea,* substance, will-to-power, and so on, all of which representations have kept the original experience of Being hidden from view.[48]

What Heidegger advocates instead is "meditative" thinking, a non-representational thinking that thinks Being from "within" the experience of Being as presencing. He finds three words key to his retrieval of the original Greek experience: *physis* (not "nature" but "blossoming forth into presencing"), *alētheia* ("dis-closure," as discussed above), and *logos* (originally

---

[44]   Ibid., 191.

[45]   Ibid., 40.

[46]   Ibid., 190–91: "In interpreting, we do not, so to speak, throw a 'signification' over some naked thing which is present-at-hand, we do not stick a value on it; but when something within-the-world is encountered as such, the thing in question already has an involvement which is disclosed in our understanding of the world, and this involvement is one which gets laid out by the interpretation [*durch die Auslegung herausgelegt wird*]." Cf. Martin Heidegger, *Sein und Zeit*, 12th ed. (Tübingen: Niemeyer, 1972), 150.

[47]   Heidegger, *Being and Time*, 194.

[48]   For the difference between "calculative" and "meditative" thought, see Heidegger's *Gelassenheit* (Pfullingen: Neske, 1959); ET: *Discourse on Thinking*, trans. John M. Anderson and E. Hans Freund (New York: Harper and Row, 1966).

not "word" but "laying-together-in-collectedness").[49] The original experience of Being is the experience of presencing and withdrawing—Being coming to presence as *physis* but at the same time withdrawing into *lēthē*, hiddenness. As Being comes to presence as beings, Being in its true character hides behind beings. The true experience of Being, therefore, and the structure of the whole of reality is presence/absence, *alētheia/lēthē*, a movement which is the root of the experience behind the philosophical fragments of Anaximander, Heraclitus, and Parmenides. Heidegger calls this relationship between Being and beings the "ontological difference," a keystone of his later thought. He explains it this way:

> The Being of beings means Being which is beings. The "is" here speaks transitively, in transition. Being here becomes present in the manner of a transition to beings. But Being does not leave its own place and go over to beings, as though beings were first without Being and could be approached by Being subsequently. Being transits (that), comes unconcealingly over (that) [*Sein geht über (das) hin, kommt entbergend über (das)*] which arrives as something of itself unconcealed only by that coming-over [*Überkommnis*]. Arrival means: to keep concealed in unconcealedness—to abide present in this keeping—to be a being [...] Being in the sense of unconcealing overwhelming [*der entbergenden Überkommnis*] and beings in the sense of arrival that keeps itself concealed, are present, and thus differentiated, by virtue of the Same, the differentiation [*dem Unter-schied*].[50]

Being, in coming over to/as beings, renders itself manifest—beings thus arrive in presence. However, in this very coming-over Being itself is concealed—beings announce the arrival of Being, but Being manifests itself only through beings, never as Being. Thus the arrival-into-unconcealment (*alētheia*) is simultaneous with the withdrawal-into-unconcealment (*lēthē*). Being is the source of this transition to and fro and of the difference (*Unterschied*, the "cutting") between Being and beings which separates them and in the separating (dif-ferring) holds them together. Thus Being's basic structure is presencing-and-absencing ("aletheiological") and never pure presence. This structure is manifested differently in different epochs: Being sends itself (*schicken*) as history (*Geschichte*) and as temporality.

While Heidegger focuses on ontological questions rather than "experience" *per se*, the three "moments" of his project that we have discussed nevertheless serve an important function for our topic. They demonstrate that the primacy of experience has an ontological basis, that the encounter within experience between subjectivity and the world is the primary mode of knowing, that the subject-object distinction fostered by specifically modern approaches to reason is derivative, and that all meaning is radically human in the sense that, without the experience that thrusts human subjectivity outward, there is no meaning, no disclosure of truth. This confirms in a phenomenological (and even more radical) way the basic scholastic principle of knowledge

---

[49]  See Heidegger, *Being and Time*, §44, 256–73; Martin Heidegger, "The Anaximander Fragment," "Logos (Heraclitus, Fragment B 50)," and "Aletheia (Heraclitus, Fragment B 16)," *Early Greek Thinking*, trans. David Farrell Krell and Frank A. Capuzzi (New York: Harper and Row, 1975), 13–78, 102–23.

[50]  Martin Heidegger, *Identity and Difference* [bilingual edition], trans. Joan Stambaugh (New York: Harper and Row, 1969), 64–65 (English), 132 (German).

elaborated in various ways by Thomas Aquinas: *Cognitum autem est in cognoscente secundum modum cognoscentis* ("whatever is known is known according to the mode of the knower").[51] Here, however, there are never absolute meanings, only meanings which are engendered in the event of disclosure which is properly present in experience. The insistence of Merleau-Ponty and Gadamer on the primacy of experience and on the *a priori* openness of experience to what is new and unprecedented thus finds ontological legitimation in Heidegger.

# II. Schillebeeckx's concept of experience

Schillebeeckx's insistence on experience as the starting point for his theological reflection on revelation is incomprehensible without this phenomenological background. The "authority" with which he invests experiences, and the transcendent element of revelation which he sees being mediated through human experiences, would not be credible outside a phenomenological framework, since this account of consciousness and subjectivity gives full weight to experience. If Schillebeeckx were employing a realist epistemology, his theology would have the tendency to ground revelation in rational certainty and his characterization of salvation would wind up in some version of extrinsicism akin to that of Neo-scholasticism.[52] He repudiates this position, however: "The experience of ourselves and the world cannot be completely analyzed in terms of a difference between objective and subjective. Therefore "to find salvation in Jesus's is not *either* a subjective experience *or* an objective fact."[53] On the other hand, he also rejects the view of experience that can be characterized as purely affective. The problem with these alternatives is that they are extremes: realism uses experience only as a launching point that points toward the goal of absolute essences, while any emphasis on experience as a set of emotional states—undoubtedly an essential element of experience—tends to rob experience of "the particular cognitive, critical and productive force" that he believes are its crucial elements.[54]

Schillebeeckx's position echoes Gadamer's description of dialectical experience. Experience is "direct contact with people and things" that touches off a dialectical process:

> The discoveries about reality that we have already made and put into words open up new perspectives: they direct perception in our experience to something particular [...] In this way they become the framework within which we interpret

---

[51] Thomas Aquinas, *ST* Ia, q. 12, a. 4, resp., in *Summa theologiae*, vol. 3 [Ia. 12–13]: *Knowing and Naming God*, trans. Herbert McCabe (Cambridge: Cambridge University Press, 2006), 14–15. See also *ST* Ia, q. 75, a. 5, resp.: *Manifestum est enim quod omne quod recipitur in aliquo recipitur in eo per modum recipientis* ("Obviously the way anything is received depends on how the receiver is fitted to receive it") (vol. 11, *Man*, trans. Timothy Suttor, 22–23). The scholastic dictum *quidquid recipitur per modum recipientis recipitur* goes back at least to Boethius' *Consolation of Philosophy*, Book V, chap. 4.

[52] For a discussion of Neo-scholastic extrinsicism, see Francis Schüssler Fiorenza, *Foundational Theology: Jesus and the Church* (New York: Crossroad, 1984), 266–75; Anthony J. Godzieba, *Bernhard Welte's Fundamental Theological Approach to Christology*, American University Studies, Series VII, vol. 160 (New York/Bern: Peter Lang, 1994), 18–34.

[53] Schillebeeckx, *Christ*, 17 [32].

[54] Ibid., 13 [29].

new experiences, while at the same time this already given framework of interpretation is exposed to criticism and corrected, changed or renewed by new experiences. Experience is gained in a dialectical fashion: through an interplay between perception and thought, thought and perception.[55]

While calling experience the "ability to assimilate perceptions," Schillebeeckx in fact treats experience in a wider way. Reality is "discovered" and frameworks are altered in many ways, not only sensibly. In this context he raises more trenchantly the problem of objectivity.

> Our real experiences are neither purely objective nor purely subjective. On the one hand, they are not purely subjective; for we cannot simply make something out of something at our whim. At least partially, there is something which is "given," which we cannot completely manipulate or change; in experience we have an offer of reality. On the other hand, it is not purely objective; for the experience is filled out and colored by the reminiscences and sensibilities, concepts and longings of the person who has the experience. Thus the irreducible elements of our experiences form a totality which already contains interpretation.[56]

A phenomenological viewpoint holds that meanings are constituted—that is, in Merleau-Ponty's terms, that knowledge comes from lived experience, the intersection of subjectivity and world. In Schillebeeckx's terms, that constitution includes the intersection of past experiences ("reminiscences and sensibilities") with the present, where the past functions as an interpretive framework that both structures what is new but also is "corrected, changed or renewed" by what is new. But that constitution of meaning is driven by a prior moment of disclosure, a grappling with reality that is "given" and that resists our expectations. There are two aspects to note. First, Schillebeeckx rejects the realist *adequatio* foundation of truth in favor of the Heideggerian formulation: reality is disclosed through experience. Second, Schillebeeckx agrees with Merleau-Ponty and Gadamer as to what is revealed in experience: the not-I, what is different, alien—what shatters my expectations.

> The permanent resistance of reality to our rational inventions forces us to constantly new and untried models of thought. Truth comes near to us by the alienation and disorientation of what we have already achieved and planned. This shatters the so-called normativeness or the dogmatism of the factual, of what is "simply given." The hermeneutical principle for the disclosure of reality is not the self-evident, but the scandal, the stumbling block of the refractoriness of reality.[57]

A number of phenomenological insights are at work here in this argument. First of all, Schillebeeckx assumes both Merleau-Ponty's and Gadamer's analyses of experience that make appropriation of the not-I, openness to what is not part of my subjectivity, part of the nature of experience. Then, there is the assumption of truth as the event of *alētheia*: since disclosure is the primary meaning of truth, the assumption is that disclosures are never at an end, that truth is always operative in constituting meaning, and thus we are "constantly" working out interpretations.

---

[55]  Ibid., 17 [31–32].
[56]  Ibid., 19 [33].
[57]  Ibid., 20 [35].

Finally, this resistance of reality to experience and expectation is the source of the contrast of "negativity." Gadamer's remarks should be recalled: in experience I feel the sting of my own finitude and painfully learn that I am radically historical. A comparison of two passages is instructive:

Gadamer:

> Experience [...] inevitably involves many disappointments of one's expectations and only thus is experience acquired [...] Only through negative instances do we acquire new experiences [...] Every experience worthy of the name thwarts an expectation. Thus the historical nature of man essentially implies a fundamental negativity that emerges in the relation between experience and insight [...] [Aeschylus witnesses to this with his phrase "learning through suffering."] He refers to the reason why this is so. What a man has to learn through suffering is not this or that particular thing, but insight into the limitations of humanity, into the absoluteness of the barrier that separates man from the divine. It is ultimately a religious insight—the kind of insight that gave birth to Greek tragedy.[58]

Schillebeeckx:

> The "negativity" which makes us revise earlier insights as a result of the resistance offered by reality is productive; it has a quite special positive significance as a "revelation of reality," even though it may be dialectically negative and critical. People learn from failures—where their projects are blocked and they make a new attempt, in sensitive reverence for the resistance and thus for the orientation of reality.
>
> This demonstrates that human experience is *finite,* that man is not lord of reality, for all his plans, though without them experiences would be impossible.[59]

Both thinkers attempt to articulate what happens at the limit of human experience and the productive force such experiences of negativity and "shattering" have. And both thinkers eventually resort to metaphors suggesting that experience has a fundamentally "religious" structure that is disclosed whenever we encounter what exceeds the limits of expectation.

The real point in showing these parallels is not to demonstrate that Schillebeeckx is beholden to philosophical analyses of human experience, but to show how he uses such a phenomenological framework creatively in a theological context to get at the intrinsic relationship between revelation and experience. By combining the accumulative nature of experience (already implying a thrust outward from subjectivity) with its concomitant critical negativity, Schillebeeckx makes the case for the essential "gift" nature of reality and the fact that reality *exceeds* our experience and our expectations but nonetheless can be encountered only *through* our experience.

> Reality is always more than and different from what we imagine it to be. From a negative, critical point of view this is because of our experience that man cannot ground the possibilities of his own existence [...] This raises the *question* whether he may not and cannot experience reality, to the degree to which it escapes human planning, as a *gift* which frees man from the impossible attempt to find his basis in himself, and makes it possible for him to think and plan endlessly, although

---

[58] Gadamer, *Truth and Method*, 356–57.
[59] Schillebeeckx, *Christ*, 21 [35].

this reality which is independent of him is for its part the basis and source of responsible human action in reason, freedom, and planning.[60]

What differentiates Schillebeeckx's position from a transcendental argument such as Karl Rahner's is that he does not find the divine-human point of intersection *within* experience but sees it *as* experience. Every human experience, and thus humanity's historical nature, is shot through with the frustration of finitude. The person's very historical situatedness is the point of contact with God. This assertion is the basis for Schillebeeckx's entire Christology: that Jesus is the humanity of God, God's pledge to give a saving contrast to present experiences of evil, God's aligning himself on the side of the suffering. For Rahner, the process of divinization is relatively smooth: God supplies the condition for the possibility of existence and fills those needs that the person feels when the person experiences limitation in relatively rare limit-situations. In Schillebeeckx's analysis, limit-situations are constantly present: my constant flow of experiences confronts me with my finitude and hence with suffering in some form. In every situation I feel the ache of frustration as I experience limitless possibilities given to me as well as my inability to match them with limitless response.[61] In every experience, I realize that I am not in control, that my reason is not capable of accounting for every aspect of reality. "Man is not master of reality, but only its steward. From this it emerges in turn that this talk of God and his revelation is indissolubly bound up with our interpretative experience, as believers, of the reality of man and the world."[62]

Schillebeeckx's concept of interpretation, the guiding element that is part of every experience, looks much like Heidegger's *Vorgriff* as read through Gadamer. Interpretation is previous experience which has sedimented in consciousness and thereby becomes a guiding framework that influences the structure of future experiences.[63] However, Schillebeeckx again goes further than his models:

> Interpretative identification is already an intrinsic element of the experience itself, first unarticulated, subsequently as conscious reflection. However, there are interpretative elements in our experiences which find their basis and source directly in what is experienced, as content of a conscious and so somewhat clear experience, and there are also interpretative elements which are handed to us from elsewhere, outside at least this experience, even though this distinction is never clearly maintained.[64]

If I read him correctly here, this is an attempt to account phenomenologically for the directionality which is given to experience by what is experienced—a directionality first grasped pre-conceptually, then articulated. Merleau-Ponty makes the same point in asserting the universal aspect of experience when he argues that understanding picks up a "hint" from the world as to

---

[60] Ibid., 32–33 [47].

[61] While Schillebeeckx does not cite Maurice Blondel, his analysis demonstrates a close affinity with Blondel's "method of immanence". See Maurice Blondel, *The Letter on Apologetics*, in *The Letter on Apologetics and History and Dogma*, trans. Alexander Dru and Illtyd Trethowan (Grand Rapids: Eerdmans, 1994).

[62] Schillebeeckx, *Christ*, 42 [56].

[63] See ibid., 17 [31].

[64] Schillebeeckx, *IR*, 11 [13].

what direction to follow in the constitution of meaning.[65] The content of experience is never totally divorced from the subject, and yet Schillebeeckx can avoid the charge of subjectivism because of his emphasis on the givenness of "the real": "Reality constantly directs our planning and reflection like a hidden magnet [...] Experience is supported and constrained by a permanent reference to the inexhaustibility of the real."[66] Schillebeeckx is certainly committed to the meaning-constituting action of the interplay between experience and interpretation, and committed as well to highlighting the resistance of reality which always confronts us with its "refractoriness" and opacity. But the constitution of meaning is not rudderless; rather, it is anchored in the fundamental givenness and "resistance" of reality that directs experience's constituting operations toward an authentic-though-always-inadequate grasp of the world of our experience. In fact, Schillebeeckx's appropriation of the aletheiological structure serves as the foundation for his theory of revelation.

For the believer, the very existence of humanity and the world is a symbol or a manifestation of the divine, but always in such a way that there is a necessary identity between the revelation and the concealment of the divine. For when confronted with any manifestation of the divine, God's essential reserve is always experienced: God can never be reduced to one of the forms in which God is manifested. Reality continues to surprise us.[67]

# III. A phenomenology of the Easter appearance narratives

How does this phenomenological theory of experience play out when employed in the discussion of the Gospels' post-resurrection appearance narratives? Schillebeeckx employs it to retrieve, as far as it is possible at this historical distance, the original experiences that were the catalyst for those narratives and the precise linguistic form that they take. In other words, he is after a particular moment in the transforming experience of grace that Jesus's disciples had in their encounter with their Lord and that eventually gave rise to the New Testament's message of salvation for all.[68]

Elsewhere I have characterized this as a "strong" theory of the Resurrection that is found in an argument where many might least expect it (precisely because of the criticism raised against Schillebeeckx's earlier formulation of this theory). By a "strong theory," I mean that does three things: [1] affirms the Resurrection as an event which happens both to Jesus himself and to his disciples; [2] sees the empty-tomb narratives and the appearance narratives as interlocking evidence not to be separated; and [3] affirms the true bodily resurrection of Jesus, the

---

[65]  Merleau-Ponty, *Sense and Non-Sense*, 93: "The germ of universality or the 'natural light' without which there could be no knowledge is to be found ahead of is, in the thing where our perception places us."

[66]  Schillebeeckx, *Christ*, 21 [35–36].

[67]  Ibid., 41 [55].

[68]  Schillebeeckx, *IR*, 64 [75]: "The resurrection as a non-empirical event of and with Jesus himself after his death is as such trans-historical, but the belief in Jesus' resurrection is a[n] event of and in our history, and as such, in principle, accessible to a historic genetic analysis". Cf. also ibid., 9 [10].

eschatological transformation of his corporeal identity.[69] With his employment of a specifically phenomenological theory of experience, I believe that Schillebeeckx has provided such a theory, allowing his theology of the Resurrection to respond to critical questions about the role of objectivity in a much more adequate way.

I believe that one can prescind from Schillebeeckx's specific starting point, the narrative of conversion occasioned by the forgiveness experienced by Peter and the other disciples. This is the aspect of Schillebeeckx's retrieval on which many commentators have focused. But the quite speculative nature of this particular reconstructed narrative derails an adequate evaluation of his theology and shunts the critics too quickly into a judgment that the "subjective" aspects of the retrieval overwhelm the "objective." Schillebeeckx, in fact, strongly argues for the equal force of both, and did so even before his revisions (which, in fact, add much-needed precision to his argument).[70]

The more central affirmation of the fundamental structure of the Resurrection experience of both Jesus and the disciples can be retrieved from Schillebeeckx's revised argument if we keep his phenomenological epistemology in mind. Here are two passages to illustrate this.

> From the analysis of the Easter experience it is clear *that the objective and subjective aspects of the apostolic belief in the resurrection cannot be separated.* Without a religious experience it is not possible to speak meaningfully about Jesus' resurrection [...] While not identical with it, Jesus' resurrection—that is, what happened to him personally after his death—is inseparable from the disciples' Easter experience or religious experience [...] But besides the subjective aspect it is equally clear (according to Christian religious belief) that *no Easter experience of renewed life was possible without the personal resurrection of Jesus—in the sense that Jesus' personal-bodily resurrection [Jezus' persoonlijk-lichamelijke verrijzenis] [...] "preceded" any religious experience.*[71]

> I am more concerned with a theological clarification for modern people, through which it becomes understandable why the first Christians seized on the model of Old Testament appearances of God and angels in order to express their Easter experience. *In addition, I will also admit that this need not even be a pure model, but can also imply a historical event.*[72]

These are key passages illustrating Schillebeeckx's hermeneutic retrieval of the disciples' experience and his attempt to clarify its fundamental structure. In this retrieval there are two key phenomenological elements wound tightly together, dealing with the "subjective" and "objective"

---

[69] See Anthony J. Godzieba, "Bodies and Persons, Resurrected and Postmodern: Towards a Relational Eschatology," *Theology and Conversation: Toward a Relational Theology*, ed. Jacques Haers and Peter De Mey, BETL 172 (Leuven: Peeters, 2003), 211–25, at 215.

[70] See, e.g., Schillebeeckx, *Jesus*, 358 [391], and especially Schillebeeckx, *IR*, 68 [79]: "The aim of my book is precisely to emphasize both the objective and the subjective aspect of resurrection faith over against all objective and subjective one-sidedness, and in such a way that the 'object' – Jesus' personal and corporeal resurrection and exaltation to God's side – and the 'subject' – the faith experience which in scripture is expressed in the story of the appearances – cannot be separated."

[71] Schillebeeckx, *Jesus*, 606–07 [645] (*Jezus*, 528b); my emphasis.

[72] Schillebeeckx, *IR*, 69, n. 43 [147, n. 43]; my emphasis.

elements of the constitution of Easter faith.[73] First, there is the emphasis on the meaning-giving role played by "faith-motivated" human subjectivity: truth as an event of manifestation needs the mediation of experience, interpretation, and constitution in order for it to be disclosed in a humanly graspable way (the phenomenological version of *quidquid recipitur per modum recipientis recipitur*). This is the insight behind Schillebeeckx's claim that "the resurrection of Jesus [...] is inseparable from the [...] faith-motivated experience of the disciples" without it being made identical with or reduced to that faith-motivated experience. Schillebeeckx makes it clear that this experience would never have occurred without the non-I catalyst, the "objective" element of the disciples' experience that directed their constitution of the evidence in the direction of the claim that Jesus is personally alive: "He is risen." Schillebeeckx, in a somewhat clumsy expression, emphasizes the objective element—the risen Jesus's transformed corporeality—by saying that Easter faith is impossible without being preceded by "Jezus' persoonlijk-lichamelijke verrijzenis" ("Jesus' personal-bodily resurrection"). This clumsiness, though, is performatively productive: it signals the inadequacies of language for dealing with an eschatological event that nonetheless crosses over into materiality and history, akin to Merleau-Ponty's analogue for the act of knowing, the pianist "who deciphers an unknown piece of music: without himself grasping the motives of each gesture or each operation, without being able to bring to the surface of consciousness all the sediment of knowledge which he is using at that moment."[74]

The structure of the experience that Schillebeeckx retrieves is composed of two aspects. There is (for lack of better terminology) the "subjective" aspect: the disciples' Judaism and their immersion in the traditions of Second Temple Judaism and its prevailing eschatological mind-set;[75] their fundamentally holistic understanding of person;[76] and their memories of Jesus, including his Kingdom proclamations, his parables, his lifestyle, and his horrific death. These function as the disciples' already-appropriated fund of culturally and religiously situated expectations—an interpretive framework—within which they will understand any act of God which touches their experience.

There is also the non-negotiable "objective" aspect (what I would term the "non-I catalyst") that serves to shatter the disciples' expectations and take their understanding of Jewish eschatology, personhood, and Jesus himself in an unexpected direction. This objective aspect is (to use Kasper's phrase) the "initial ignition" that forces the disciples in the midst of their

---

[73]   What Schillebeeckx also demonstrates is the inadequacy of the traditional post-Cartesian understandings of "subjective" and "objective" in dealing with the Resurrection.

[74]   Merleau-Ponty, *Sense and Non-Sense*, 93.

[75]   On the pervasive eschatological background, see James D.G. Dunn, *Christianity in the Making*, vol. 1: *Jesus Remembered* (Grand Rapids, MI: Eerdmans, 2003), 393–406; John P. Meier, *A Marginal Jew: Rethinking the Historical Jesus*, vol 2: *Mentor, Message, and Miracles*, The Anchor Bible Reference Library (New York, Anchor/Doubleday, 1994), 237–70; John Riches, *The World of Jesus: First-Century Judaism in Crisis*, Understanding Jesus Today (Cambridge: Cambridge University Press, 1990), 87–107; E.P. Sanders, *Judaism: Practice and Belief, 63 BCE–66 CE* (London: SCM, 1992), 279–303; N.T. Wright, *Christian Origins and the Question of God*, vol. 3: *The Resurrection of the Son of God* (Minneapolis: Fortress, 2003), 85–206.

[76]   Cf. John L. McKenzie, "Aspects of Old Testament Thought," *The New Jerome Biblical Commentary*, ed. Raymond E. Brown, Joseph A. Fitzmyer, and Roland E. Murphy (Englewood Cliffs, NJ: Prentice-Hall, 1990), 1284–315; Hans Walter Wolff, *Anthropology of the Old Testament* (Philadelphia: Fortress, 1974).

constitution of this experience to stretch all the categories of Second Temple Judaism in which they have been steeped to fit a new, unprecedented experience. The fact that the gospel narratives (as well as Paul in 1 Corinthians) consciously choose the language of vision and body for their testimony, that they "misuse" apocalyptic language (e.g., alongside the belief that *all* will rise at the end of time, they make the claim that *one* has risen before all),[77] that Jesus is both frighteningly unfamiliar and eventually recognized as "good old Jesus" (e.g., Luke 24:36–49; John 21:1–14), forces one to ask what kind of an experience it would have to be that would act as a catalyst for *this particular kind* of consistent testimony *in this particular form,* rather than, say, the language of the martyred prophet or that the cause or the memory of Jesus continues. This is the quintessential phenomenological question. And the answer is that this experience must be one that can *only* be constituted and expressed in this way, that is, an experience of the "real" that is given/disclosed and that gives "direction" or hints for interpretation, for which only the language of person, vision, body, unfamiliarity, familiarity, and "Jesus" is relatively appropriate. It is the experience of the "body as a symbol" of Jesus's self,[78] the self consistent in its identity throughout the transformation. That self's corporeality, which bore the developed constitution of Jesus's self-identity through his human actions, still communicates his unified individuality and provokes continued relationships with his disciples, so much so that the narratives insist that *only* corporeal and visual language are up to the task of conveying the reality and the personal unity of Jesus experienced within his continued relationships with his disciples. The disciples' experience of the risen Jesus is indeed a constituted experience of a personal relationship with him occurring within their history and ours.[79] But that constitution of meaning has resulted from the interpretive interplay of Second Temple Jewish anthropological and eschatological expectations challenged (and in some cases shattered) by the clues of the transformed personal reality and unity of Jesus that, according to the textual evidence, can be knit together in a meaningful way (as the intentional object of the disciples' experience) only when one takes the visual and corporeal clues seriously. It is the implicit judgment of the tradition as transmitted in the gospels' appearance narratives that any talk of "the martyred prophet," "remembering the impact of Jesus' teaching," or other Jewish apocalyptic expectations is simply not adequate to the task.

What is important is that the New Testament texts witness to a crucial *experienced difference,* one that quite obviously provokes a shattering of expectations. At the root of the Easter experience is not simply the familiar Jesus (which would not be an "experience" but simply repetition of already sedimented interpreted experiences) but an identity which has been transformed: he frightens some, goes unrecognized by others, appears in a room with locked doors. So the narratives want to have it both ways—unfamiliar presence *and* good old Jesus—in order to communicate that this is indeed Jesus who is encountered, but somehow different from the pre-Easter Jesus. The narratives, across the various gospel traditions, assume that only the use and the conscious misuse of the language of corporeality can get a handle on this experience. This must make us pause and ask: what kind of experience is this? What kind of bodiliness is this?

---

[77]  See Schillebeeckx, *Jesus*, 362 [395–96].

[78]  Sandra Schneiders, "The Resurrection of Jesus and Christian Spirituality," *Christian Resources of Hope*, ed. Maureen Junker-Kenny (Collegeville: Liturgical Press, 1995), 81–114, at 97.

[79]  As Schillebeeckx insists, the Easter experience "can also imply a historical event." See Schillebeeckx, *IR*, 69, n. 43 [147, n. 43].

How can corporeality support such a transformation, the ultimate possibility promised to those who commit themselves to the values of the Kingdom of God? Again, these are quintessential phenomenological questions about the experiences behind the textual expressions, questions that any theological exploration of the Easter experience must ask.

One seriously misreads Schillebeeckx's analysis of Easter faith if one downplays the "objective" aspect, as many commentators have. Such a reading would force the events surrounding Easter into an order that contradicts the New Testament evidence. To overemphasize the subjective or "visionary" aspect is to say that God the Father has an effect on the disciples who in turn have an effect on the way that Jesus is perceived. The New Testament, on the other hand, insists that "the Easter event is primarily what God did with Jesus, not something that God did with the disciples. What he did with the disciples was only secondary."[80] Schillebeeckx subscribes to this latter order of events wholeheartedly. His strong emphasis on the non-I catalyst of resurrection faith, along with his strong insistence on the equal force exerted both by the objective element (what the Father did for Jesus himself) that shatters expectations and by the constituting and the interpretive subjective element, combine so as to account for the claim of the reality of the Resurrection without resorting to an impossible realist epistemology.

One would also miss the full force of Schillebeeckx's analysis if one did not notice that, under the "pressure" of the Resurrection experience, he implicitly judges as inadequate the use of the traditional modern (i.e., post-Cartesian) definitions of "objectivity" and "subjectivity" to deal with the reality of revelation in general and the Resurrection in particular. This is the crux of the matter. Schillebeeckx, for his part, redefines these terms in the direction of a phenomenological epistemology of constituted knowing that is capacious enough to acknowledge both the participation of subjectivity in knowing reality and also that "reality is always more than and different from what we imagine it to be."[81] The "objective" can be accessed only through the constitution of meaning effected by from the point of view of subjectivity, while the experience gained by subjectivity can only truly be "experience" when it encounters the new, the different, the unprecedented—when its comfortable expectations are shattered by the non-I element of experience. From the negativity and limitation under which subjectivity labors, Schillebeeckx draws two positive results. The first is an anthropological insight: reality can thus be experienced "as a *gift* which frees man from the impossible attempt to find his basis in himself."[82] The second is the aletheiological insight applied to God: "When confronted with any manifestation of the divine, God's essential reserve is always experienced; God can never be reduced to one of the forms in which he is manifested. Reality continues to surprise us."[83] Schillebeeckx's analysis of Easter faith—his strong theology of the Resurrection—guarantees that we will see the reality of Christ's resurrection, along with the resurrection faith that it continually provokes, as perhaps the biggest surprise of all.

---

[80]   Reginald H. Fuller and Pheme Perkins, *Who Is This Christ? Gospel Christology and Contemporary Faith* (Philadelphia: Fortress, 1983), 36.
[81]   Schillebeeckx, *Christ*, 32 [47].
[82]   Ibid., 33 [47].
[83]   Ibid., 41 [55].

# PART II

# The Second Vatican Council
# and Its Aftermath

# Chapter 7

# The World and History as Sacrament

## Schillebeeckx on the Eve of the Second Vatican Council

### Joris Geldhof and Leo Kenis

On January 25, 1959, Pope John XXIII solemnly announced the convocation of a general and ecumenical council. In the same year, Edward Schillebeeckx published his famous study, *Christ the Sacrament of the Encounter with God* (*Christus sacrament van de Godsontmoeting*).[1] It was a revised and expanded version of the less felicitously named book *The Encounter with Christ as the Sacrament of the Encounter with God* (*De Christusontmoeting als sacrament van de Godsontmoeting*), which he had published two years previously.[2] In his foreword, dated February 10, 1959, Schillebeeckx explained that, after publishing the first edition, he had felt obliged to make serious changes to the language, style, and structure of this work. He was keen to avoid specialist jargon, but also made the following theologically pertinent remark: "To a greater degree than was the case in the first edition, the sacraments are placed in a wider ecclesial perspective. For this reason, too, we were obliged to situate the mystery of the church more clearly."[3] Schillebeeckx evidently wanted to highlight more emphatically the sacramental character of the church.

Schillebeeckx's theology in the 1950s was deeply imbued with a sacramental view of reality; this had in fact been evident since the publication of his masterly 1952 study *De sacramentele heilseconomie* (*The Sacramental Economy of Salvation*), a book rarely thoroughly studied, let alone widely received, in which the author addressed the contemporary situation of sacramental theology on the basis of a sustained reflection on Thomas Aquinas.[4] "In line with the old '*sacramentum est in genere signi*'" Schillebeeckx regarded the sacraments "as Christ's cultic symbolic activity in and through his church community; as the characteristic cultic acts, therefore,

---

This chapter has been translated by Brian Heffernan.

[1] Edward Schillebeeckx, *Christus sacrament van de Godsontmoeting* (Bilthoven: H. Nelissen, 1959). ET: Edward Schillebeeckx, *Christ the Sacrament*, CW vol. 1 (London: Bloomsbury T&T Clark, 2014).

[2] Edward Schillebeeckx, *De Christusontmoeting als sacrament van de Godsontmoeting: Theologische begrijpelijkheid van het heilsfeit der sacramenten* (Antwerp/Bilthoven: 't Groeit/H. Nelissen, 1957).

[3] Schillebeeckx, *Christus sacrament*, 5. Our translation. This "forward to the third printing" (which is also the revised, second edition with the simplified title) was not included in the English translations of the text.

[4] Henricus Edward Schillebeeckx, *De sacramentele heilseconomie: Theologische bezinning op S. Thomas' sacramentenleer in het licht van de traditie en van de hedendaagse sacramentsproblematiek* (Antwerp/Bilthoven: 't Groeit/H. Nelissen, 1952). All translations are our own.

of the Church seen as a cultic community in which Christ accomplishes a salvific, transcendent mystery."[5] This means that the sacraments are not an extra-temporal, much less eternally identical, given, but they "have a historical form, in which however a mystery is accomplished."[6] It is this fundamental perspective on sacramental theology which would subsequently determine his view of the world and of history. The one thing Schillebeeckx was absolutely determined to avoid was a partitioning of reality: God reveals himself as salvation *within* the world and within history, and God does this in a sacramental way. In short, history and mystery are intimately interwoven with each other.

A similar emphasis can be discerned in the inaugural lecture which Schillebeeckx gave in 1958 upon taking up his position as professor of dogmatic theology at the Catholic University of Nijmegen. The title of this lecture was *The Search for the Living God* (*Op zoek naar de levende God*).[7] The God of whom he speaks cannot be found outside the course of history, which itself is made transparent to the divine mystery and to revelation. Schillebeeckx concluded his lecture with the following consideration, which again demonstrates a sacramental view that admits of no division of reality into separate spheres:

> Thus the incarnation of the Son in its Old Testament pre-history, in its historic fulfillment, and in its ecclesial form as a mystery is the specific *locus theologicus* which allows us to reach out hopefully towards the intertrinitarian divine mystery that has given itself as the content of all our lives.[8]

This current chapter explores Schillebeeckx's sacramental view of the world and of history. We will develop the hypothesis that his intellectual, theological, and ecclesiastical activities in the late 1950s and early 1960s must be interpreted from this sacramental perspective. We will first examine a number of building blocks of what might be called Schillebeeckx's sacramental world view, before looking more closely at the historical events in which Schillebeeckx was involved very closely on the eve of the Second Vatican Council. We will discuss the reactions to the announcement of the Council, the vota of the University of Nijmegen, and the role that Schillebeeckx played as the author of the letter which the Dutch episcopate addressed to the faithful. We will end with a conclusion that draws out a number of threads that are present in Schillebeeckx's sacramental thought. Schillebeeckx came to expound upon such issues as the place of laypeople in the church, the unity between hierarchy and people, the importance of unity among the world episcopate, the theological (i.e., not just church political) significance of a council, etc.; not despite his explorations in sacramental theology, but precisely because of this thorough and sustained study.

---

[5]  Ibid., vi.

[6]  Ibid.

[7]  Published in Edward Schillebeeckx, *God en mens*, Theologische peilingen 2 (Bilthoven: Nelissen, 1965), 20–35. ET: "The Search for the Living God," *Essays, CW* vol. 11 (London: Bloomsbury, 2014), 35–50.

[8]  Schillebeeckx "The Search for the Living God," *Essays*, 50.

# I. Elementary building blocks of Schillebeeckx's sacramental world view

One of the most important concepts in Schillebeeckx's contribution to the twentieth-century renewal of the theology of the sacraments, a renewal of which he and such figures as Karl Rahner may count as protagonists, is that of encounter. It was no coincidence that this concept featured prominently in several titles of works he wrote in the 1950s.[9] The concept of encounter is important from the perspective of theology and the history of ideas for at least three reasons. First, it made it possible to overcome the alienation that had arisen between the church's sacramental "system" and people's concrete life situations. The discourse on the sacraments that prevailed in church and theology was no longer consistent with many people's sense of the times. The concept of "encounter" tapped into a new existential equivalent of the sacramental offer of salvation, the objectivity of which had previously been emphasized in a mechanistic and causalistic way. Second, this concept respected the elusive character of the experience and revelation of God. An encounter cannot be reduced to an object or a product; it can never be the object of possession, only of memory. Precisely this link between encounter and memory provided great potential for theological reflection on the hermeneutics of tradition, liturgy, and Christology. Third, the concept of encounter also made it possible to do full justice to the personal character of God and Christ. Moreover, the notion included the potential for a meaningful and fruitful parallel between theology and the phenomenology of encounter.

These reasons are revealing for Schillebeeckx's concern not to divide reality into mutually distinct fields that are essentially unconnected. The experiences of people must always be related to the sacraments of the church and vice versa: the church has the duty to offer the salvation it mediates to people in a manner that is comprehensible and that can be experienced. Neither "party" benefits from alienation. At the same time, Schillebeeckx realized that there was a real danger that the two "parties" would not stay "partners," and that they would systematically drift apart. He expressly thematized secularization on several occasions, but always so as to show deep confidence that secularization was unable to affect the core of the Christian faith. He even regarded secularization as an overall gain.[10] Schillebeeckx assumed that every human being has an ineradicable capacity to be addressed by God: "The impossibility of our accounting for our existence ourselves, and the fundamental experience of our wholly contingent presence in this world, brings us face to face with the invisible but real mystery of a personal Giver whose heart is greater than his gifts which surround us and of which we ourselves form part."[11]

This passage contains a key word: *mystery*. It might be argued that for Schillebeeckx, the glue that held together the poles of church and faith on the one hand, and world and history on the other, is "mystery" or "sacrament." He defines "sacrament" as "a divine bestowal of salvation

---

[9]   Lambert Leijssen, *With the Silent Glimmer of God's Spirit: A Postmodern Look at the Sacraments*, trans. Marie Baird (New York: Paulist Press, 2006), 11–15.

[10]  Schillebeeckx, "The Search for the Living God," *Essays*, 37: secularization is "a plus rather than a minus factor." The Dutch text calls it an "*aanwinst*," or a "positive gain." See Schillebeeckx, *God en mens*, 22.

[11]  Schillebeeckx, "The Search for the Living God," *Essays*, 38.

in an outwardly perceptible form which makes the bestowal manifest; a bestowal of salvation in historical visibility."[12] There is no doubt that for this definition of a sacrament, Schillebeeckx was indebted to Dom Odo Casel's influential theology of mysteries. Casel's great contribution was twofold. On the one hand, his detailed philological research had contributed to the insight that the concepts of mystery (*mysterium*) and sacrament (*sacramentum*) had practically been synonyms in the patristic era and in the works of the Fathers. On the other, he drew out the consequences of this insight for theological reflection. It was no longer a matter simply of defending the legitimacy of the seven rituals officially regarded as sacraments by the church's hierarchy since the Middle Ages against its deniers. Instead, what was at stake was to understand and explain how revelation, salvation, and grace are mediated through the liturgy of the church. The theology and liturgy of the early church contained undiscovered treasures that helped to unfold and develop the richness of this intuition in many directions.

In *De sacramentele heilseconomie*, Schillebeeckx had given some attention to Casel's theology and to the so-called School of Maria Laach.[13] Schillebeeckx in a certain sense adopted Casel's basic intuition, and he can be regarded as someone who developed the *Mysterienlehre* further in the important period between the publication of the encyclicals *Mystici Corporis* and *Mediator Dei* in the 1940s and the Second Vatican Council. At the same time, Schillebeeckx was well aware of the controversial nature of Casel's theory of mysteries and he prudently distanced himself from, and criticized authors who, in their excitement, simply dropped the old interpretative frameworks wholesale without giving a thought to tradition, including scholasticism. After much reflection, Schillebeeckx embraced the view that the official magisterium of the church, in particular Pope Pius XII's encyclical *Mediator Dei*, did not in fact condemn, but cautiously confirmed, the *Mysterienlehre*. This approval was conditional upon a rejection of vagueness in the interpretation of the Christian mysteries, and upon the acceptance of a clear link with the sacraments and their visible significatory form.

In any case, this reference to Casel and his doctrine of mysteries is crucially important to understand Schillebeeckx's sacramental world view. He thought there was a fundamental interconnectedness between the supernatural (the divine) and the natural (the world, humankind, and history); an interconnectedness that can aptly be called *mysterious*, and therefore *sacramental*. Moreover, the objective and subjective dimensions of the encounter and dialogue between God and humans meet each other in mystery and sacrament. Schillebeeckx contended that the Greek notion of *mustèrion* indicated:

> the sacrament is a saving act performed by God in the history of the world [...]: the sacramental appearance of the redemptive mystery of Christ, of which the sacraments are the veiled mystery celebration. On the contrary, *sacramentum*, in its Roman meaning, points to humans' active life response to the divine act of salvation: their subjective commitment, their free entry into the redemptive history of salvation. But this subjective commitment too is fully encompassed by the *mustèrion* of the divine act.[14]

---

[12] Schillebeeckx, *Christ the Sacrament*, 10 [15].
[13] Schillebeeckx, *De sacramentele heilseconomie*, 214ff.
[14] Ibid., 662.

In this way, sacrament or mystery must be interpreted as the "intersection of divine and human commitment," enlisted in the great, world-encompassing dynamic of the incarnation of God and the deification of the human.[15] What the remainder of this chapter will show is that this sacramental view of the church, the world, and of history was the fundamental theological driving force behind all of Schillebeeckx's endeavors on the eve of the Second Vatican Council.

# II. Edward Schillebeeckx and the preparations for the Second Vatican Council

## Responses to the Announcement of the Council

Schillebeeckx had been working in the Netherlands for a year when the Council was announced.[16] He had settled in Nijmegen in January 1958, and had since begun giving lectures. He was beginning to acquire prominence in the Netherlands through his lectures and publications in magazines. He was one of the first to comment on the announcement of the Council with a theologically substantive response.[17] He published an article on "The Grace of a General Council" in *De Bazuin* on 7 February 1959.[18] Here, he went straight to the key issue by describing the significance of the Council from the perspective of the history of dogma. History shows, he contended, that newly formulated dogmas can cause the faith to "stiffen" in the newly discovered direction, thus obscuring complementary truths of the faith, and necessitating the restoration of equilibrium in the vision of the faith. This was the case, for instance, with the reception of the First Vatican Council's dogma of papal infallibility. However valuable this definition had been, in due course it was necessary that it should be placed again within the totality of the truth of the faith, by connecting it to the authority of the episcopal office, because "the interactive relationship between the pope and the bishops is essential."[19] The "fullness of the apostolic office" belonged to the college of bishops not just by law, but through ordination.

Schillebeeckx was able to demonstrate how opportune the Council that had been announced was, precisely in view of this correction, because the unity of the entire episcopate in union with the pope came to its full effect specifically in a general council. In addition, a church meeting that brought together bishops from all corners of the world had an added value over and above the

---

15 Ibid., 663.

16 What follows is extensively treated by Erik Borgman, *Edward Schillebeeckx: A Theologian in His History*, trans. John Bowden (London/New York: Continuum, 2003), 283–321. Borgman describes this period with special attention for the development of Schillebeeckx's "project of the theology of culture."

17 For what follows, see J.Y.H.A. Jacobs, *Met het oog op een andere kerk: Katholiek Nederland en de voorbereiding van het Tweede Vaticaans Oecumenisch Concilie 1959–1962* (Baarn: H. Nelissen, 1986), 13–24 (on Schillebeeckx, see 20–22).

18 Edward Schillebeeckx, "De genade van een Algemeen Concilie," *De Bazuin* 42, no. 18 (February 7, 1959), 4–6. Reprinted in Edward Schillebeeckx, *Het Tweede Vaticaans Concilie* (Tielt/The Hague: Lannoo, 1964), 10–18 (citations taken from the latter).

19 Schillebeeckx, "De genade van een Algemeen Concilie," 11–12.

personal exercise of authority by the pope. The mutual exchanges of bishops from very different local churches, nourished by their own experiences and concerns, and assisted by theologians of various schools, would ensure that the result of their consultations would be richer and more nuanced than the thoughts of one person. In addition, this great variety in backgrounds could help to come to an understanding of the ecumenical problem, and could inspire the central authority of the church to adopt greater openness toward the decentralized authority of the diocesan bishops. All this made "a healthy pluralism possible even within the Una Sancta."[20] Schillebeeckx resisted any opposition between the worldwide college of bishops and the Roman curia, and emphasized that a general council sought consensus through mutual consultations, under the guidance of the Spirit. As such, it was an act of the entire faith community, which also meant that the voice of "intellectual laypersons" deserved to be heard.

# The vota of Nijmegen University

While Schillebeeckx's swift response initiated reflection on the problems and opportunities of the coming Council, the Dutch church leadership was more reticent and hesitant in commenting on the pope's initiative. This did not change until the autumn of 1959, after the *commissio antepraeparatoria* set up in May 1959 invited bishops and institutions of learning in the Catholic world to submit their wishes and recommendations for the council.[21] The Dutch bishops responded by engaging in consultation, assisted by theological advisors recruited almost exclusively among their seminary professors. Two Dutch Catholic institutions of learning were also approached: the Catholic University of Nijmegen, and the Canisianum, the Dutch Jesuit faculty of theology. The drafting of the Nijmegen vota took place in a special Senate committee consisting of representatives of all the faculties; the theological faculty was represented by the biblical scholar Jan van der Ploeg.[22] After Schillebeeckx had collaborated in the drafting of the theological faculty's recommendations, he also became involved in the activities of the Senate committee. Thus he participated in the committee's consultations and was a member of its editorial committee. The text of the vota was sent to Rome on April 19, 1960.[23]

This relatively short text, divided into four sections, consisted of sixteen vota, which merit attention because they contain a number of pertinent suggestions for various aspects of the life of the church. Laying the foundations for the proposals to follow, the first section expressed the hope that the mystery of the church would be developed on the basis of the biblical concept of the Kingdom of God, so as to highlight the pneumatic and sacramental character of the church. The text then continued with proposals relating to the hierarchical layers of the church community and their mutual interaction (the pope and the college of bishops; bishops, priests, and deacons; the exclusion of women from the ministry; the position of the laity). With respect to the church's position in the world, the text proposed that the secular state should no longer be approached on the basis of the anti-religious connotations stemming from the nineteenth century, and that

---

[20] Ibid., 15.
[21] Jacobs, *Met het oog op een andere kerk*, 25–60.
[22] Ibid., 62–68.
[23] They are published in *Acta et documenta concilio oecumenico Vaticano II apparando*, Ser. I, vol. IV, Pars II (Rome: Typis polyglottis Vaticanis, 1961), 473–80.

concepts such as Christian tolerance and freedom of conscience should be re-evaluated. The text also contained pleas for freedom of academic research, for the willingness to acknowledge that there were elements of truth in opinions and systems previously condemned by the church, and for the inclusion of modern social sciences in priestly formation programs. With regard to pastoral ministry, it proposed reforms of the liturgy (active participation, use of the vernacular, concelebration, communion under both kinds, adaptation to local cultures), and of missionary activity (integration of religious studies and anthropology into missionary studies, greater attention to Eastern Christianity). Finally, in the field of canon law, the text proposed a reform of the Index of Forbidden Books, and for canon law to be more broadly grounded in natural law.

The Nijmegen vota, founded on an innovative vision of the church, not only formulated a series of intra-ecclesial changes, but also a number of urgent corrections of the way Catholicism positioned itself in modern society, the latter perhaps originating from the contributions of non-theologians. There are no indications that these vota were actually used during the Council.[24] But the drafting of the vota had a different, indirect consequence. During its meetings, the Senate committee decided to propose to the bishops that a Nijmegen professor should go with them to Rome as their conciliar advisor. When the rector of the university delivered the text of the vota to Cardinal Alfrink on April 27, he directly addressed this request to the archbishop, adding that the university considered Edward Schillebeeckx suitable for this role. Two years later, the Dutch bishops accepted this proposal.

## III. Schillebeeckx and the pastoral letter

While the vota were being drafted, Schillebeeckx reflected on the future Council in a second article, published in *Elseviers Weekblad*.[25] He began by reminding his readers that any expectations for the ecumenical sense of a "council of reunification" were perhaps unrealistic.[26] The future Council would be a reform council, focused on renewal within the church, which did not rule out ecumenical openness, but could in fact prepare the ground for later rapprochement. Schillebeeckx also provided a condensed exposé on the significance of a general council in the history of salvation—a passage which many *Elsevier* readers must have found impenetrable. In a council, the apostolic kerygma, in connection with and determined by the historical mystery of Christ, rendered the living, exalted Lord present. The teaching church was the "actualisation of the apostolic kerygma," and an ecumenical council was the tangible, concentrated form of this direction illuminated by the Spirit.[27] It needed to connect with the "general ecclesial sense of the faith," which renews the apostolic faith amid the ever-changing conditions of life. Schillebeeckx

---

[24]  Cf. Borgman, *Edward Schillebeeckx*, 308.

[25]  Edward Schillebeeckx, "Het komend concilie van de R.-K. Kerk," *Elseviers Weekblad* (February 20, 1960). Included in Schillebeeckx, *Het Tweede Vaticaans Concilie*, 19–26 (citations taken from the latter).

[26]  In his first article, Schillebeeckx had only briefly mentioned the reunification of Christians. In a later issue of *De Bazuin*, Jan Willebrands discussed upon this topic specifically: J.G.W. Willebrands, "Het Concilie voor de eenheid," *De Bazuin* 42, no. 19 (February 14, 1959), 4–5.

[27]  Schillebeeckx, "Het komend concilie van de R.-K. Kerk," 21.

again underlined the necessity of restoring papal infallibility to its place within the encompassing context of the totality of the faith. Papal infallibility was based in part on the infallibility of the worldwide college of bishops, which itself rested on the infallible, living faith of the entire faith community. Thus the whole church, "laity and authority" were involved in the Council, which could be called a "sacrament of illumination by the Spirit of Christ."[28]

Schillebeeckx's language was more down to earth when he spoke about his specific expectations for the coming Council. He recalled that this Spirit-led gathering of the world's bishops would ultimately produce human results, which would be subject to the laws of sociology, the human condition, and the operation of a "collective consciousness." At the dogmatic level, the Council would not go beyond the point of current "mainstream theology," meaning the theology of the interwar years that was still dominant in ecclesiastical circles. The Council would not change this situation, but would at best prevent insights in the faith from being "expressed in less fortunate formulations."[29] Pastoral ministry and the liturgy offered better chances for real renewal. Schillebeeckx thought that the Council would draw a number of broad outlines, which would be tested during a decade-long trial period, and would then be assessed and institutionally incorporated in the church by a new council.

This contribution to *Elseviers Weekblad* was the last article about the Council that Schillebeeckx published under his own name in the years prior to its opening.[30] His expectations appear realistic as far as the specific chances for reform were concerned, but in his theological vision he simultaneously made proposals for ecclesiological renewal. His contribution to the preparations for the Council became much more significant when he was asked to participate in an initiative by the Dutch episcopate to set the dynamic of the Council in motion among the faithful.

In order to prepare for the Council, the Dutch bishops had decided to issue a pastoral letter to point out its significance to the faithful and to encourage them to share in the experience of this unique church event.[31] They set up a committee to draft the text, consisting of Edward Schillebeeckx and his colleagues Frans Haarsma (Utrecht) and Jan Groot (Haarlem). Schillebeeckx was responsible for editing the text. After thorough discussion and correction of the text, which included incorporating a number of suggestions by Cardinal Alfrink, the pastoral letter, dated December 24, 1960, was approved and signed by all the bishops. It was published a fortnight later under the title of "The Bishops of the Netherlands on the Council"

---

[28] Ibid., 23.

[29] Ibid., 25.

[30] In July 1960 he published "Het komende concilie als opdracht van de gelovigen," *TGL* 16 (1960), 365–76. This article is a compilation of parts from the previous articles "De genade van een Algemeen Concilie," and "Het komend concilie van de R.-K. Kerk." He did not publish a "new" article on the subject until October 1962 in *De Bazuin*, just a few days before the opening of the Council (for details, see the contribution by Stephan van Erp in Chapter Eight of this volume).

[31] On this issue, see Jacobs, *Met het oog op een andere kerk*, 83–92; Borgman, *Edward Schillebeeckx*, 316–20; Ton H. M. van Schaik, *Alfrink: Een biografie*, KDC Bronnen en Studies 33 (Amsterdam: Anthos, 1997), 300–02, 316–17; Jan Grootaers, *Actes et acteurs à Vatican II*, BETL 139 (Leuven: Leuven University Press and Peeters, 1998), 534–35, 539–41; and Schillebeeckx's own report in Edward Schillebeeckx, *Theologisch testament: Notarieel nog niet verleden*, 2nd ed. (Baarn: Nelissen, 1995), 43, 48.

("*De Bisschoppen van Nederland over het Concilie*"), together with a shorter letter that was read to the faithful on Sunday, January 8, 1961.[32]

The letter was an extensive, clearly argued text. It can be largely ascribed to Schillebeeckx, who was certainly responsible for its central argument about the "dogmatic structure of an ecumenical council."[33] In this text, the church was represented once again as the visible form of the Kingdom of God in the world, albeit "still in a sacramental way, clad in signs," and this form was present as much in every believer as in the ministers of the church.[34] The significance of the Council was expressly explained in terms of the faith community's sense of the faith (*sensus fidei*). It is the church community's collective sense of the faith which, guided by the light of faith, and following a "gradual process of fermentation," can develop an understanding of the faith that is "factually infallible" and can be confirmed as such by the worldwide college of bishops in communion with the pope.[35] Schillebeeckx repeated his conviction in this letter that "the infallibility of the papal office must not be isolated from the totality of the faith."[36] Within this process of growing awareness of the faith, an ecumenical council is a special manifestation of the sense of the faith, a "concentration of the Holy Spirit's operation of grace."[37] It would therefore naturally be in agreement with the church's sense of the faith, and even "with the public opinion that prevails among the faithful concerning the new problems of life."[38] In sum, all the actors in the conciliar decision-making process were brought together in a single movement:

> Thus the conciliar statements and arrangements are the mighty result of the cooperation of the active faith of the entire faith community, of the Pope, the bishops, the priests, and the laity, with the judgement of the hierarchy, led by the Spirit, to probe, specify, and correct everything.[39]

The implications of this vision for the Council's agenda were then treated in relation to various contemporary problems, such as the adaptation of pastoral ministry to the new circumstances of the time, active participation in the liturgy, Catholic moral teaching, ecumenism and spirituality, the demands of Christian charity, the challenges of technology and atheistic and agnostic philosophies. The bishops focused particularly on the problem of ecumenism, and they

---

[32] "De Bisschoppen van Nederland over het concilie" appeared separately as a brochure and was later published as: Nederlandse Bisschoppenconferentie, "De bisschoppen van Nederland over het concilie," *Katholiek Archief* 16 (1961), 369–84. We quote from the latter. Schillebeeckx also included the letter in the very first issue of *Tijdschrift voor Theologie: TvT* 1 (1961), 71–90. It therefore served as a programmatic statement for the new journal in the Dutch context. According to Maarten van den Bos, the letter was included mostly to fill space in the first issue, but even if this is the case, the decision to include it remains a telling indication of its relevance at the time. See Maarten van den Bos, "De waarheid duidelijk aan het licht brengen: De theologische cultuur van seculier Nederland: een geschiedenis en een uitdaging," *TvT* 54 (2014), 170.

[33] "De Bisschoppen van Nederland over het concilie," 370–79 (some sentences correspond literally with parts from the articles by Schillebeeckx mentioned above).

[34] Ibid., 372.

[35] Ibid., 375.

[36] Ibid., 376.

[37] Ibid., 378.

[38] Ibid.

[39] Ibid.

recognized the right of the faithful to criticize, as long as their criticism was competent and free from bitterness or rancor. In a postscript, the bishops thanked the persons who had cooperated in the drafting of the letter, mentioning only Edward Schillebeeckx by name.

The Dutch bishops' letter became known internationally through translations into English, French, German, Polish, and Spanish. But problems arose when an Italian translation was published in the spring of 1962. Objections were raised in certain Roman circles against allegedly heterodox opinions in the text (particularly in respect of papal infallibility),[40] and the publication was pulled from shops after a few months.[41] Cardinal Alfrink was able to clear up various misunderstandings during a private audience with the pope, for instance by pointing to a number of inaccuracies in the translation, after which the case seemed closed. But the incident gave the renown which the letter had earned the Dutch bishops, and indeed the whole Dutch church, an ambiguous character. For many Catholics, it opened a new, realistic, and true to life perspective that caused expectations for the coming Council to soar, but in other ecclesiastical circles, it discredited the Dutch bishops. Schillebeeckx, too, the only editor to be mentioned by name in the letter, shared in this ambiguity. After this incident, he later recalled, the Roman authorities began to monitor him.[42] Shortly afterward he was turned down as an official *peritus* for the Council, without explanation, and despite lobbying by the Dutch episcopate.[43]

In the meantime, the Dutch bishops once again sought Schillebeeckx's advice when they were composing a response to the theological preparatory committee's first draft texts (the so-called "Series Prima").[44] At the initiative of Bishop Bekkers of 's-Hertogenbosch, Schillebeeckx, with the assistance of his colleagues Luchesius Smits and Jan van Laarhoven, was asked to write a "counter-reflection" on the schemata. More than two thousand copies of this long text, translated into Latin and English, were disseminated among the bishops at the Council. It was extremely critical of five of the seven schemata. For many Council Fathers, their reading of Schillebeeckx's critical comments was a first introduction to a new theological approach that rejected the unhistorical and conceptualist aspects of the classical theology with which they were familiar. In this way Schillebeeckx took his first steps toward becoming active at the Council.

---

[40] This included people in the Holy Office, in the Theological Commission (dominated by the Curia at that time), and theologians of the Lateranum. See Jan van Laarhoven, "In medio Ecclesiae ... : Alfrink op het Tweede Vaticaans Concilie," *Alfrink en de Kerk 1951–1976* (Baarn: Amboboeken, 1976), 26; Erik Borgman, "Introduction: Living Contact with Human Reality Gave Them This Openness – Schillebeeckx on the Second Vatican Council," *The Council Notes of Edward Schillebeeckx 1962–1963* ed. Karim Schelkens, Instrumenta Theologica 34 (Leuven: Peeters, 2011), xvii–xviii. On p. xviii (including n. 8), Borgman refers to "secret papers of an investigation into the orthodoxy of the brochure" from the Holy Office.

[41] See the report on this issue: "Herderlijk schrijven van Nederlandse Bisschoppen over Concilie in Italië uit de handel genomen," *Katholiek Archief* 17 (1962), 625–28.

[42] See Schillebeeckx, *Theologisch testament*, 43.

[43] Schillebeeckx has speculated that the request was refused by Cardinal Alfredo Ottaviani, prefect for the Holy Office, because of Schillebeeckx's contribution to the Dutch pastoral letter. Schillebeeckx, *Theologisch testament*, 48.

[44] Jacobs, *Met het oog op een andere kerk*, 99–107, 141–67. Schillebeeckx was not among the twenty-seven Dutchmen chosen for the preparatory commissions for the Council.

# Conclusion

In a number of concise articles published around 1960, Edward Schillebeeckx succeeded in sharply articulating the significance and objectives of the Council. The theological inspiration for his interpretations doubtless came from his thoroughgoing research and reflection in the field of sacramental theology. It is the notion of the sacrament, understood as mystery, that makes it possible to think synthetically and systematically, that is, in such a way that everything is held together, that the separate parts of the whole are considered in their consistency, and that divergence and difference are not turned into absolutes. Schillebeeckx wrote in the foreword of the first edition of *Christ the Sacrament of the Encounter with God* that "every aspect of theology [must] continually be re-thought from a 'panoramic view' of the whole of Christ's temporal economy of salvation as a revelation in mystery of the redemptive Trinity."[45] It was this perspective that enabled him to become the theological mouthpiece of the Dutch bishops. It reveals him as both traditional and innovative, a builder of bridges between hierarchy and laity, an interpreter of the truths of the faith that have been handed down as much as of contemporary critical consciousness; in short, he was—in the best sense of the term—a team player. Because of his deeply sacramental view of the world and of history, Schillebeeckx was ideally placed to stand at the crossroads of culture and faith, to engage in meaningful conversation with all passers-by.

Schillebeeckx's publications on the eve of the Council provide a snapshot of a turn in his theology. Erik Borgman has pointed out that Schillebeeckx broadened his theological vision in these years, and that important themes in his later theology can already be discerned in the texts discussed here.[46] We have discerned impetuses for the broadening and actualization of his initial insights, particularly for the development of his ecclesiology—especially in the direction of his vision of the church as the "sacrament of the world."[47] This also applies to how he envisioned the relationship between the pope and the bishops, the grounding of ministry in the wider faith community, the diversity and plurality of the one church. It is true that the influence of Schillebeeckx's relatively few and difficult articles on public opinion was limited compared to theologians such as Hans Küng and Yves Congar.[48] But his influence was unexpectedly widened when the Dutch bishops decided to enlist his services as their advisor in their preparations for the Council. This is where Schillebeeckx's role in the renewal of the Dutch church began. His input from the preparatory phase onward in the Dutch church's commitment to the Vatican Council can be viewed as a model of cooperation between church leaders and their theologians; a cooperation which benefited both parties, but which, in retrospect, has remained an exception rather than the rule in the Catholic church.

---

[45] Schillebeeckx, *Christus sacrament*, 7. Our translation.

[46] Borgman, *Edward Schillebeeckx*, 306, 318.

[47] On the development of this ecclesiology see Daniel Speed Thompson, *The Language of Dissent: Edward Schillebeeckx on the Crisis of Authority in the Catholic Church* (Notre Dame, IN: University of Notre Dame Press, 2003), 73–145.

[48] See, e.g., the surveys in Jared Wicks, *Doing Theology* (New York/Mahwah, NJ: Paulist Press, 2009), 187–223; Giuseppe Alberigo and Joseph A. Komonchak, eds., *History of Vatican II*, vol. I (Maryknoll, NY/Leuven: Orbis/Peeters, 1995), 33–44, 357–88.

# Chapter 8

# "Sign and Precursor of God's Grace for All"

## *Schillebeeckx's Ecclesiology During the Second Vatican Council*

Stephan van Erp

When Edward Schillebeeckx was asked for his opinion on the Second Vatican Council later on in his life, he confessed that he had had to restrain himself with regard to his views and evaluations at the time of the Council. He considered the Council to be "a compromise council" that had many flaws due to the balance of power and the pluralism of the episcopate present at the time.[1] Moreover, he also believed it to be a "liberal council," meaning a council that bore the marks of Western liberalism, the achievements of the Enlightenment, and the French Revolution. According to Schillebeeckx, the church used the Council to "catch up" with these, which made it rather less than progressive. On the contrary even, for soon after the Council had ended, 1968 saw the next revolution among students and intellectuals that turned against the consequences of liberal society which had proved to be detrimental for certain groups. It meant that the Council had been behind the times and, Schillebeeckx believed, it had also failed to offer something really new in a theological sense. It had mainly affirmed what his own generation of theologians had already asserted earlier.[2] Unfortunately, the Council had led to an increased polarization, which had already been apparent among the bishops during the Council, but which later also began to affect the faithful with detrimental results for both sides of the argument.

This rather less enthusiastic analysis from the 1990s is consistent with Schillebeeckx's assessment shortly after the Council. Even at that time, he warned of a "post-vatican catholicism [*sic*]," comparable to the ossification of the church after the Council of Trent (1545–1563), which produced a "post-Tridentine roman catholicism [*sic*]."[3] He warned against integralism, or a strong reaction against the modernizations the Council had accepted. He quickly added that any such integralist reaction could also be the result of the attitude of the "progressives" who, he believed, "may neglect the value of obedience as a form of loyal self-surrender."[4] Yet another danger lurked in

---

This chapter has been translated by Huub Stegeman.

[1] Edward Schillebeeckx, *Theologisch testament: Notarieel nog niet verleden*, 2nd ed. (Baarn: Nelissen, 1995), 41.

[2] Ibid., 42.

[3] Eduard [*sic*] Schillebeeckx, *The Real Achievement of Vatican II*, trans. H.J.J. Vaughan (New York: Herder and Herder, 1967), 83.

[4] Ibid., 87.

the term "pastoral council," he believed, for it could lead to deemphasizing the dogmatic implications of the views of the Council. According to Schillebeeckx, the Second Vatican Council should also be judged on its doctrinal merits, and its modernizations should in no way be qualified dogmatically.

This warning against any form of complacency after the Council is in sharp contrast to the enthusiasm with which Schillebeeckx had devoted himself to making a properly substantive contribution on the eve of the Council, or the great trust he had had in its successful conclusion after the first session. In this chapter, I will discuss his theological contribution to the Council as the advisor to the Dutch bishops and as an academic theologian. Other chapters in this volume address his role during the preparations for the Council and his involvement in the post-conciliar developments of Dutch Catholicism. I will limit myself to the literature he produced during, and on occasion shortly before or after, the Second Vatican Council. From a thematic point of view, I will focus on the relation between church and world and in particular on his comments on *Gaudium et spes*, when this document was still in its development phase as "Schema XIII." I will begin by providing a survey of primary and secondary literature concerning Schillebeeckx during the Second Vatican Council. Next, I will outline his position vis-à-vis the different camps within the world episcopate and the church in general, and I will offer some critical nuances to an all too positive reading of Schillebeeckx's involvement with the church of his time. Finally, I will describe the fundamental outlines of his ecclesiology and his idea of the church as sacrament of the world, which can be considered one of the most fundamental aspects of his theology.

# I. "One of the greats, but never officially an expert"

Schillebeeckx would accompany the bishops to Rome as their advisor during the four sessions of the Council. This was important for his own theology because in Rome he came into contact with representatives of the so-called "new theology," with whom he would found the journal *Concilium* in 1963.[5] It is well known that he never officially became a *peritus* at the Council, probably because he was the main author of a pastoral letter of the Dutch bishops, which was deemed too progressive by Rome.[6] Still, the Council recognized him as "one of the greats," as Ted Schoof put it, also because of his enormous capacity for work which enabled him to give twenty-three lectures for bishops and other interested parties, even before the first decisive vote on the schema on the sources of revelation, *De fontibus revelationis*.[7] In Rome he would have frequent meetings with *periti*, write lectures for the bishops, give lectures, and write a great number of texts and commentaries, many of which were published in various languages.

---

[5]   The first issue of *Concilium*, published in 1965, contained an editorial by Karl Rahner and Edward Schillebeeckx, and articles by Schillebeeckx, Yves Congar, Joseph Ratzinger, Michael Novak, Rudolf Schnackenburg, Jacques Dupont, and Boniface Willems.

[6]   Published both as a pastoral letter and in the first volume of *Tijdschrift voor Theologie*: "De Bisschoppen van Nederland over het Concilie," *TvT* 1 (1961), 71–90.

[7]   Cf. Ted Schoof, "E. Schillebeeckx: 25 Years in Nijmegen, I," *Theology Digest* 37, no. 4 (1990), 313–32; Ted Schoof, "E. Schillebeeckx: 25 Years in Nijmegen, II," *Theology Digest* 38, no. 1 (1991), 31–44; Erik Borgman, *Edward Schillebeeckx: A Theologian in His History*, trans. John Bowden (London/New York: Continuum, 2003), 320–28.

# Primary literature

Schillebeeckx has amply documented his own opinions for and about the Council. Shortly before and then during the Council, he wrote seven popular articles (and a response to readers' letters) for the weekly *De Bazuin*, in which he kept the readers updated on the topics discussed and the political developments at the Council.[8] These texts have been compiled and published in English as *The Real Achievement of Vatican II*.[9] In the publications of the Nederlandse Documentatie Centrum Concilie (Do-C), he published nine theological discussions of fundamental questions addressed at the Second Vatican Council, such as the ideas of truth and revelation, the position of the laity in the people of God, situational ethics, the relation between church and world, priesthood and celibacy, the Eucharist, and marriage.[10] Many of these texts were also published in English, German, and French by the Do-C. He contributed to *Tijdschrift voor Geestelijk Leven*, a journal for spiritual life, in the form of articles on ministry and religious life, the sacrament of marriage, and an extensive discussion of *Dei verbum*.[11]

Toward the end of the Council and immediately afterward, he published theological material in articles for *Tijdschrift voor Theologie*, and many of these would later be collected in the five-volume *Theological Soundings* series (*Theologische peilingen*). He also published texts not directly related to the debates at the Council, as well as texts that were the direct result of his work as an advisor to the bishops. These include articles on secularization, including two

---

8  Edward Schillebeeckx, "Hoop en bezorgdheid. Op de vooravond van een concilie," *De Bazuin* 46, no. 1 (October 6, 1962), 1–2; Edward Schillebeeckx, "Indrukken over een strijd der geesten: Vaticanum II," *De Bazuin* 46, no. 13 (January 5, 1963), 1, 4–5; Edward Schillebeeckx, "Misverstanden op het concilie," *De Bazuin* 46, no. 15 (January 19, 1963), 1–5; Edward Schillebeeckx, "Paus Johannes en het tweede vaticanum," *De Bazuin* 46, no. 37 (June 29, 1963): 1–5; Edward Schillebeeckx, "De stem van Elckerlyc over het concilie," *De Bazuin* 46, no. 23 (March 16, 1963), 1–3; Edward Schillebeeckx, "Verwachte grote lijnen van het concilie," *De Bazuin* 47, no. 2 (October 12, 1963), 1–2; Edward Schillebeeckx, "Wederwoord," *De Bazuin* 46, no. 25 (March 30, 1963), 5; Edward Schillebeeckx, "De waarheid over de laatste concilieweek," *De Bazuin* 48, no. 12 (December 23, 1964), 4–6.

9  Schillebeeckx, *The Real Achievement of Vatican II*. Dutch original: Edward Schillebeeckx, *Het Tweede Vaticaans Concilie* (Tielt/The Hague: Lannoo, 1964).

10  Edward Schillebeeckx, "De heilsopenbaring en haar `overlevering," *Do-C. Documentatie Centrum Concilie* 1, no. 37 (1962); Edward Schillebeeckx, "Het waarheidsbegrip en aanverwante problemen," *Do-C. Documentatie Centrum Concilie* 1, no. 10 (1962), 11; Edward Schillebeeckx, "De leken in het volk van God," *Do-C. Documentatie Centrum Concilie* 2, no. 85 (1963); Edward Schillebeeckx, "De situatie-ethiek," *Do-C. Documentatie Centrum Concilie* 2 (1963), nr. 50, 51; Edward Schillebeeckx, "Kerk en wereld," *Do-C. Documentatie Centrum Concilie* 3, no. 142a (1964); Edward Schillebeeckx, "Priesterschap en celibaat," *Do-C. Documentatie Centrum Concilie* 3, no. 111 (1964); Edward Schillebeeckx, "Balans van het concilie," *Do-C. Documentatie Centrum Concilie* 4, no. 234 (1965); Edward Schillebeeckx, "Transsubstantiation, transfinalisation, transsignification," *Do-C. Documentatie Centrum Concilie* 4, no. 233 (1965); Edward Schillebeeckx, "De wisselende visies der christenen op het huwelijk," *Do-C. Documentatie Centrum Concilie* 4, no. 225 (1965)225a.

11  Edward Schillebeeckx, "Bezinning en apostolaat in het leven der seculiere en reguliere priesters," *TGL* 19 (1963), 307–29; Edward Schillebeeckx, "Het moderne huwelijkstype: Een genadekans," *TGL* 19 (1963), 221–33; Edward Schillebeeckx, "De ascese van het zoeken naar God," *TGL* 20 (1964), 149–58; Edward Schillebeeckx, "Theologische bezinning op de geestelijke begeleiding," *TGL* 20 (1964), 513–27; Edward Schillebeeckx, "De gods-openbaring en de heilige boeken volgens het tweede vaticaans concilie," *TGL* 21 (1965), 461–77.

extensive articles on Anglican bishop, John A.T. Robinson's bestseller, *Honest to God* (1963), and a fundamental philosophical consideration of the non-conceptual element of the human intellect in the act of faith according to Thomas Aquinas. The articles which he composed that directly connected to the Council or which resulted from discussions about Council documents dealt with ecclesiological and liturgical themes such as the relation between church and world, celibacy and the priesthood, and the Eucharist.[12]

As if this was not enough for such a relatively short period of a little over three years, he also wrote for other periodicals, like *Kultuurleven*, and many of his texts were then published in translation.[13] The final year of the Council saw the publication of the first issue of *Concilium*, the international journal he founded together with Yves Congar and Karl Rahner, and which was meant for reflections on the outcomes of the Second Vatican Council. In the first volumes of this journal, he would publish several articles relating to the Council, among which was an "In memoriam" for Bishop Wilhelmus Bekkers in 1966.[14]

Finally, Schillebeeckx's diaries are an important source of information for what went on behind the scenes at the Council. They contain his often unredacted and rough, spontaneous commentaries on the events in Rome.[15] These diaries were published only in 2011 and show him to be rather more critical than was apparent from his earlier, more cautious publications between 1962 and 1965. At the time, he had been cautious in his public comments, he would later say, in order to defend the Council against its critics.[16] He took notes during the first and second sessions, which are mainly atmospheric descriptions and often show his amazement or sometimes even frustration at the course of events. There are no dairy entries for the third and fourth sessions.

After the Council, Schillebeeckx would also write a commentary on Schema XIII in Paul Brand's *Vaticanum 2*-series, which has largely been translated.[17] He had also taken it upon himself to edit the Dutch publication of a collection of commentaries on the constitutions of the Council, to which he himself contributed a commentary on the laity.[18]

---

12. See Edward Schillebeeckx, "Kerk en Wereld: de betekenis van 'Schema 13'," *TvT* 4 (1964), 386–400; Edward Schillebeeckx, "Christus' tegenwoordigheid in de Eucharistie," *TvT* 5 (1965), 136–72; Edward Schillebeeckx, "Het celibaat van de priester," *TvT* 5 (1965), 296–329.

13. For a comprehensive overview of the available translations, see *Bibliography 1936–1996 of Edward Schillebeeckx O.P.*, complied by T. Schoof and J. van de Westelaken (Baarn: Nelissen 1997).

14. Edward Schillebeeckx, "The Church and Mankind," *Concilium* vol. 1 (1965), 69–101; Karl Rahner and Edward Schillebeeckx, "General Introduction," *Concilium* vol. 1 (1965), 1–4; Edward Schillebeeckx, "The Tridentine Decree on Justification," *Concilium* vol. 5 (1965), 176–79.

15. Edward Schillebeeckx, *The Council Notes of Edward Schillebeeckx 1962–1963: Critically Annotated Bilingual Edition*, ed. Karim Schelkens, Instrumenta Theologica 34 (Leuven: Peeters, 2011).

16. Schillebeeckx, *Theologisch testament*, 41.

17. *Vaticanum 2*, ed. Katholiek archief (1. Kerk en oecumene; 2. De kerk in de wereld van deze tijd; 3. De missionerende kerk; 4. De kerk en het Joodse volk), Hilversum 1967–1968. In volume 2 of this series, Schillebeeckx published his "Christelijk geloof en aardse toekomstverwachting," 78–109. ET: Edward Schillebeeckx, "Christian Faith and Man's Expectation for the Future on Earth," *The Mission of the Church*, trans. N.D. Smith (New York: Seabury Press, 1973), 51–89.

18. Edward Schillebeeckx, "The Typological Definition of the Christian Layman According to Vatican II," *The Mission of the Church*, trans. N.D. Smith (New York: Seabury Press, 1973), 90–116.

# Secondary literature

Compared to the volume of primary literature, there is relatively little secondary literature on Schillebeeckx and the Second Vatican Council. Schillebeeckx hardly features in Peter Hünermann's standard work, *Herders Theologischer Kommentar zum zweiten Vatikanischen Konzil.*[19] The five-volume history of the Council, edited by Giuseppe Alberigo, does pay more attention to Schillebeeckx.[20] A collection of personal accounts and experiences from the Second Vatican Council does consistently mention him as one of the most influential commentators during the Council.[21] A recent text, published in commemoration of the one hundredth anniversary of his birth, explicitly addresses Schillebeeckx's influence during the Council and the way in which the Council continued to influence his work.[22] Erik Borgman has done a great deal of preliminary work in his biography of Schillebeeckx, in particular regarding the build-up to the Council, the spirit of the times, its reception in the Netherlands, and the figure of John XXIII. In his introduction to the publication of Schillebeeckx's Council dairies, Borgman addresses how Schillebeeckx viewed the ponderous and sensitive discussion on episcopal collegiality and the way in which changing views on this issue found their expression in the Council's decisions.[23] In a collection of articles on the occasion of Schillebeeckx's retirement, Gustavo Gutiérrez examines his vision on the church as it developed both during and after the Council.[24] The American theologian Susan Ross addresses the same issue in her chapter on church and sacraments in a book of introductory articles on Schillebeeckx's theology.[25] German pastoral theologian Christian Bauer considers whether there really was such a thing as a "Chenu-Schillebeeckx school" of thought during the Council, as Henri de Lubac had claimed.[26] Bauer concludes that, in Schillebeeckx's efforts in support of the drafts of *Gaudium et spes* he paid explicit attention to the concept of "world." Schillebeeckx was therefore more focused on the sacred than Chenu. Chenu tended to comment mainly on *Lumen gentium*, but in doing so he emphasized the secular character of the church. Bauer claims that, if there ever

---

[19] Peter Hünermann and Bernd Jochen Hilberath, eds., *Herders Theologischer Kommentar zum zweiten Vatikanischen Konzil*, 5 vols. (Freiburg/Basel/Vienna: Herder, 2004).

[20] Giuseppe Alberigo and Joseph A. Komonchak, eds., *History of Vatican II*, 5 vols. (Maryknoll, NY/ Leuven: Orbis/Peeters, 2010).

[21] William Madges and Michael J. Daley, eds., *Vatican II: Fifty Personal Stories* (Maryknoll, NY: Orbis, 2012).

[22] Maarten van den Bos and Stephan van Erp, *Een gelukkige theoloog: Honderd jaar Edward Schillebeeckx/A Happy Theologian: A Hundred Years of Edward Schillebeeckx* (Nijmegen: Valkhof Pers, 2014), 13–16, 51–4.

[23] Erik Borgman, "Introduction: Living Contact with Human Reality Gave Them This Openness: Schillebeeckx on the Second Vatican Council," *Council Notes*, xv–xiii.

[24] Gustavo Gutiérrez, "Twee perspectieven op de kerk: Sacrament van de wereld – keuze voor de armen," *Meedenken met Edward Schillebeeckx*, ed. Herman Häring, Ted Schoof, and Ad Willems (Baarn: H. Nelissen, 1983), 221–45.

[25] Susan Ross, "Church and Sacraments," *The Praxis of the Reign of God: An Introduction to the Theology of Edward Schillebeeckx*, ed. Mary Catherine Hilkert and Robert J. Schreiter, 2nd ed. (New York: Fordham University Press, 2002), 133–48.

[26] Christian Bauer, "Heiligkeit des Profanen: Spuren der „école Chenu-Schillebeeckx" (H. de Lubac) auf dem Zweiten Vatikanum," *Edward Schillebeeckx: Impulse für Theologien im 21. Jahrhundert/ Impetus Towards Theologies in the 21st Century*, ed. Thomas Eggensperger, Ulrich Engel, and Angel F. Méndez Montoya (Ostfildern: Grünewald, 2012), 67–83.

was a "secularization" of the church during the Second Vatican Council, this development was influenced by Chenu, and not by Schillebeeckx.

Judging by the amount of material on Schillebeeckx in the reception studies of the Second Vatican Council, it is tempting to think that his influence must have been much more extensive than what is recorded in the later histories of the Council. However, despite the fact that his role in the Council's reception has so far remained mostly implicit, primary literature seems to suggest that his actual theological contribution to the Council appears to have been bigger than the later reception studies seem to admit. His contribution is obvious in the preparations for the 1959 *Letter of the Dutch Bishops* and the discussions on the church in the Netherlands, shortly after the Council.[27] Even so, Schillebeeckx's contribution to the Council's vision of church and world should also not be forgotten, in particular his reflections on the relation between church and world as it is articulated in *Gaudium et spes*.[28]

## Heeding the attainable: A plea against polarization

A week before the start of the first session of the Council, Schillebeeckx wrote about his concerns and his expectations in *De Bazuin*.[29] He was primarily worried about the discord among the bishops, which carries the risk that the Council could actually worsen the polarization within the church, as he expected it would. Schillebeeckx himself has always been considered to be on the side of the "progressives." This was generally believed at the time and is still the popular conception. The short biographical outline on the back cover of the recently published *Collected Works* states: "Edward Schillebeeckx was an internationally known theologian and one of the leading progressives at the Second Vatican Council."[30] That is, however, a very one-sided and persistent characterization which has been damaging to the reception of Schillebeeckx's theology and which, incidentally, has a completely different connotation in 2018 than it had in 1962. Today, Schillebeeckx would likely not be considered a "progressive" because of his emphasis on the unity of the church, the non-negotiable norm of the tradition, and his plea for a dogmatic approach. If he were asked to answer contemporary questionnaires from sociologists, he would probably be categorized as someone who is very closely involved with the church, and who is orthodox and traditional in his beliefs. Even in 1962 he could not really be qualified as the "progressive" he was, and still is, usually considered to be. He was, however, clearly an advocate of the theological renewal that slowly gained traction at the Council. A nuanced description of his position at the time is essential for a proper understanding of his vision on the church he developed during the Council.

---

[27] The latter topic is discussed by Erik Borgman and Thijs Caspers in Chapter Eleven of this volume.

[28] Daniel Minch has pointed explicitly to the influence of *Gaudium et spes* on Schillebeeckx's reflections on theological anthropology and the relation between "church" and "world." See Daniel Minch, "Eschatology and Theology of Hope: The Impact of Gaudium et spes on the Thought of Edward Schillebeeckx," *The Heythrop Journal* 59 (2018), 273–85.

[29] Schillebeeckx, "Hoop en bezorgdheid," 1–2.

[30] Edward Schillebeeckx, *The Collected Works of Edward Schillebeeckx*, ed. Ted Schoof and Carl Sterkens, 11 vols. (London: Bloomsbury T&T Clark, 2014).

# II. Beyond essentialism and existentialism

Even before the Council had commenced, Schillebeeckx warned against too much emphasis on the spirit of the times. He also firmly believed that personal opinions should not determine the Council's agenda, and instead the spirit of the times should be "heard in the light of God's Word, in order to discern the '*vox dei*' in it and get rid of what could be the product of the voice of the historical weakness of humanity."[31] This was, incidentally, an appeal to both the conservative and the progressive camps, and Schillebeeckx believed that the Council would already be a success if the church would manifest itself as one that listened to all the different voices. His article "Hoop en bezorgdheid" ("Hope and Concern") ended with a appeal to (mainly Catholic) journalists to keep an eye on what was attainable and not focus too much on the disappointment he believed would also follow. This was inspired by his concern for possible disenchantment concerning the Council among the ordinary believers in the Netherlands, who might not always be able to grasp the complexities and the challenges of a worldwide church, let alone the complex power politics that controlled that church.

During the first session of the Council in the autumn of 1962, his fears would prove not entirely unfounded. Although he was mostly enthusiastic when he wrote about a "moral unanimity" among the bishops that called for an official confirmation in the form of a council, he did go on to write two extensive articles on the "struggle of minds" and the "misunderstandings at the council." In those, he wrote that he found it difficult to characterize the fault line that ran through world's episcopate, and was astounded to have to conclude that he sometimes was "more in sympathy with the thinking of Christian, non-catholic [*sic*], 'observers' than with the view of one's own brethren on the other side of the dividing-line."[32] He characterized the two sides of the fault line as "essentialist" on the one hand, and "existentialist" on the other. He believed that the essentialists were attempting to capture the abstract concepts of faith and human life in the most exact wording possible. Schillebeeckx hastened to add that he too abhorred vagueness and preferred a precise, if sometimes abstract, wording of faith. But any formulation of faith must also take into account its historicity, rather than denying the historical dimension, valuing the "essence" over the complexity and the inconstancy of the world.[33]

During the first session, Holy Scripture and revelation were the main topics of discussion. The "essentialist" bishops suffered a defeat when Pope John XXIII, in a departure from the usual procedure after a close and confusing vote, had the schema on revelation removed from consideration and charged a new "mixed commission" with writing a new one on November 21, 1962.[34] Schillebeeckx saw this as a moral victory, but he also warned against the idea that anything would be allowed from now on, and he cautioned against progressive arrogance: "If anyone could cause the Council to fail, I believe it would be the 'existentialists' themselves, in as far as they overdo it on the home front, and would now believe that all their wild ideas

---

[31]  Edward Schillebeeckx, "Hoop en bezorgdheid," 2.

[32]  Edward Schillebeeckx, "The Second Vatican Council," *Vatican II: A Struggle of Minds and Other Essays*, trans. M. H. Gill and Son Limited (Dublin: M. H. Gill and Son Limited, 1963), 9.

[33]  Ibid., 10–11.

[34]  There was no two-thirds majority for the dismissal of the schema on revelation, and for a moment it seemed that a minority of 37 percent would decide. Papal intervention stopped this from happening. See Schillebeeckx, *Council Notes*, 60.

have been given free reign."[35] The "moderns," as he called them on other occasions, might want to broadcast their grievances, but Schillebeeckx counseled calm and told them that the same conscience that compelled them to loudly voice their criticism might also help them to remain quiet, in order for the world episcopate to be able to work.

In his next article, published in *De Bazuin* two weeks later, Schillebeeckx addressed the misconceptions at the Council. Again, the struggle between "the open wing" and "the closed wing" formed his starting point. In his opinion, the open wing had justly scored a victory, but there was still a danger that the conservatives would get their way because of their emphasis on "the truth," a topic largely neglected by the progressives. This became clear during the discussions on ecumenism, during which, he believed, the open wing sometimes seemed to suggest that ecumenism was merely a form of "eirenism," keeping silent about Catholic truths in order not to offend believers of other denominations. The conservative council fathers' strong reaction against such a concept of ecumenism was therefore justified. He did, however, share the open wing's resistance against independent schema on Mary. Not so much because it would alienate other churches from the Council, but because it would lead to an unfortunate shift in focus in dogmatics, as no treatise on Christ had been prepared. Without a corresponding schema on Christ, this would place too much emphasis on Mary, even though such a Marian schema would affirm Christ as the only redeemer.[36]

## Truth in an open tradition

Right from the beginning, Schillebeeckx insisted on the correct understanding of the concept "pastoral" in the designation "Pastoral Council," particularly after the conservative wing's Sebastiaan Tromp, S.J. had claimed that an emphasis on the truth is the pre-eminent pastoral duty.[37] Discussions in Rome seem to have developed in such a way that the conservatives had claimed the word "truth," and in doing so had mainly emphasized its purity, whereas the progressives prided themselves on a pastoral and existential approach. In what may have been too much of a technical discourse for the readership of *De Bazuin*, Schillebeeckx argued for a concept of truth that should be essentially historical and therefore could not be expressed in supra-temporal language. This was a critique of both the essentialist static concept of truth and the exaggerated existential approach that proclaims the insight of its own age to be the truth. Neither past language nor current language will ever exhaustively mediate the truth: "the Church's own language is the ever-changing language of the people, only cast in the idiom of the one revelation and also, as a negative norm, in the language of the Bible."[38]

So on the one hand, Schillebeeckx held a traditional point of view on the truth of faith as a truth that is forever regulated by Scripture and revelation. On the other hand, he also warned against merely repeating Tridentine traditionalism. Although he did consider the pronouncements

---

[35]   Schillebeeckx, "Indrukken over een strijd der geesten," 5.
[36]   Schillebeeckx, "The Second Vatican Council," 22. Later, in 1964, Pope Paul VI would call Mary the "Mother of the Church," and Schillebeeckx considered this to be a solemn rehabilitation after Mary's marginalization in *Lumen gentium*: Schillebeeckx, "De waarheid over de laatste concilieweek," 6.
[37]   See *Council Notes*: second session, pp. 36–7, 67–8.
[38]   Ibid., 25–6.

of earlier councils to be normative, he also claimed that issues that had been ignored in earlier times or were simply not discussed might reveal the truth to a larger extent when this implicit aspect of the truth was finally expressed. So he believed that an open concept of tradition was needed in the church in order to prevent something similar to the original definition of heresy: continuously repeating only part of the truth, separate from the context in which it found its expression. Instead, Schillebeeckx's aim was not "the maintenance of what at one time has been dogmatically stated, but an increasingly shaded integration of what has been defined in the balanced totality of the faith."[39]

## The Church, laity, and the collegiality of the episcopate

In all his considerations, Schillebeeckx never lost sight of the consequences of the results of the Council for the entire church, in particular for the ordinary faithful. Any misunderstanding between the different sides and any form of division among the bishops would spread among all the faithful after the Council, and could be a negative impact, he believed. He published a separate article on this issue in *De Bazuin*, in response to an article by the British author and catholic convert Evelyn Waugh in *The Spectator*:[40] Waugh concluded that the Council Fathers had promised to listen more closely to the laity, but he feared that this would mean that a small powerful minority would force them to take decisions that had little to do with the wishes of the majority of the faithful. Democratic innovations, such as less emphasis on hierarchical order or the celebration of the liturgy in the vernacular, were not at all what the normal churchgoers wanted, Waugh believed. Schillebeeckx responded to this in his article "De stem van Elckerlyc over het concilie," wherein he took Waugh's criticism extremely seriously. He recognized that many believers would have trouble accepting the liturgical changes, and he believed the church should also offer room for those who would prefer to stick to the old ways. This called for a pastoral, moderate approach, he believed: "Sometimes I get the impression that we have exchanged the moving respect for the fragile mystery of newly discovered aspects of the truth that allow us to breathe more freely, for the noise of firecrackers that just give people a fright."[41] Schillebeeckx did realize that the new theology would be dangerous if it did not pay attention to ordinary believers, "the '*anawim*' of the Gospel," but he warned against their conservative intellectual advocates, people like Waugh, who in his opinion did not belong to the normal believers at all, but abused mediocrity of others to stop innovations in the church.

During the third session of the Council, in the so-called "black week," there was a major confrontation between the two sides after they had initially tried to deemphasize the major differences between the factions. Paul VI, who in the meantime had taken office after the death of John XXIII on June 3, 1963, had written a memorandum explaining the Dogmatic Constitution on the Church, *Lumen gentium*, and many believed that in doing so, he had gone against the spirit of the Council. Moreover, shortly before the third session, on August 6, 1964, he published

---

[39] Ibid., 31–32.
[40] Evelyn Waugh, "The Same Again, Please," *The Spectator* (November 23, 1962), 11.
[41] Edward Schillebeeckx, "De stem van Elckerlyc over het concilie," 2.

the encyclical *Ecclesiam suam*, which was also regarded as a form of papal interference.[42] This encyclical explicitly dealt with the relation between the church and a changing world, and, despite its declared intention not to disturb the proceedings at the Council, it nevertheless dealt explicitly with the relation between the Second Vatican Council and the First Vatican Council, and especially with the ways in which the church could deal with contemporary challenges. Schillebeeckx amazed both friends and enemies by claiming that it made no difference for the content of *Lumen gentium*, and that Paul VI's interventions were not all that different from those of the Council Fathers. What was at stake here was the collegial relation between the pope and the bishops. Paul VI's explanatory note left no doubt about how he saw his own position as pope—he is not just one bishop among many, but apart from being the main shepherd of the church, he is also the head of the college of bishops. Paul VI emphatically regarded himself as the "head of the college" when he made nineteen corrections in the Decree on Ecumenism. Again, Schillebeeckx took a lenient view of this.[43] He said that the corrections were "futilities," and the things that non-Catholics might find offensive are "unintentional."[44] Some of the more progressive *Bazuin*-readers were fiercely critical of this, which also caused him to write a response. This discussion again shows all the more clearly that, although he himself belonged to the "open-wing" at the Council, he also cared deeply for the unity of the church and the conciliar and the collegiate process needed to achieve that unity.[45]

# III. *"Pusillus Grex"*: The church as the sacrament of a world to come

The unity of the church is more than the provisional success arising from temporary compromise. If the Council was, as Schillebeeckx saw it, a "compromise council," this meant no guarantee for the unity of the church. On the contrary, in his opinion, the need for a compromise signaled internal division and division between churches. After all, that division is inconsistent with what the church should ideally be: the visible sacrament of divine salvation in the world.

Various Council documents speak of the church as a "sacrament": sign and instrument of divine salvation.[46] During a lecture at an international conference of theologians in Rome in 1966,

---

[42] Cf. Mathijs Lamberigts and Leo Kenis, "Het tweede Vaticaans concilie (1962–1965): een *casus belli?*," *Vaticanum II: geschiedenis of inspiratie? Theologische opstellen over het tweede Vaticaans concilie*, ed. Mathijs Lamberigts and Leo Kenis (Antwerp: Halewijn, 2013), 9–30, 18–19.

[43] See Council Notes, second session: pp. 38–43, 69–72.

[44] Edward Schillebeeckx, "De waarheid over de laatste concilieweek," 6.

[45] CF. Borgman, *Edward Schillebeeckx*, 336–37. Cf. Johann Baptist Metz, "Kirchlichkeit in offensiver Treue zum Konzil," *Mensen maken de kerk. Verslag van het symposion rond de 75e verjaardag van Edward Schillebeeckx*, ed. Huub ter Haar (Baarn: Nelissen, 1989), 13–26.

[46] See: *Lumen gentium* (November 21, 1964) 1, 9, 48, http://www.vatican.va/archive/hist_councils/ ii_vatican_council/documents/vat-ii_const_19641121_lumen-gentium_en.html; *Gaudium et spes* (December 7, 1965) 45 (hereafter cited in text as *GS*), http://www.vatican.va/archive/hist_councils/ ii_vatican_council/documents/vat-ii_const_19651207_gaudium-et-spes_en.html; *Sacrosanctum Concilium* (December 4, 1963) 5, http://www.vatican.va/archive/hist_councils/ii_vatican_council/ documents/vat-ii_const_19631204_sacrosanctum-concilium_en.html.

Schillebeeckx refers to a passage from the Decree on Missionary Activity, *Ad gentes*, to explain what the Council Fathers mean by "sacrament": "Missionary activity is nothing else and nothing less than an epiphany, or a manifesting of God's decree, and its fulfillment in the world and in world history, in the course of which God, by means of mission, manifestly works out the history of salvation."[47] The church is the *revelation* and the *fulfillment* of salvation in the world, Schillebeeckx concludes. In fact, the word "sacrament" does not even feature in this decree, but he reformulates its idea of mission as an image for the church with the help of a quotation from *Gaudium et spes*: "[In Christ] the Church is 'the universal sacrament of salvation,' simultaneously manifesting and exercising the mystery of God's love (*GS 45*)." The church can therefore be regarded as the visible instrument of salvation, and Schillebeeckx adds: "it is not without shadows."[48] That addition has received little attention in the reception of Schillebeeckx's work. Others usually link his interpretation of "*sacramentum mundi*" with either the church's universality, or with the world as a place in which God is present, but not with a call on the church to reform.

According to Schillebeeckx, it was mainly because of John XXIII that the issue of "church and world" had become one of the priorities of the Second Vatican Council.[49] The unique dynamics of the Council and the reactions to it from outside the churches were a reason to merely be concerned with issues within and between churches, but also to the relation between church and world.[50] Schillebeeckx's own interest in that relation had been at least partially stimulated by John A.T. Robinson's *Honest to God*, which he had reviewed rather critically in *Tijdschrift voor Theologie*.[51] In his critique of Robinson, he argued against what he perceived as an identification of a belief in God with "solidarity," which would leave Christ and the church as little more than functional forms of that solidarity. In his opinion, the church was not an expression of the solidarity experienced and practiced in the world, but a condition for belief in God which occurs in the community. It means God's grace is not activated by or found in solidarity, but instead, the *solidarity* is experienced as a *sacramental sign* of God's love. Solidarity can be beneficial for the church, he believes, but it does not constitute the church. Christ is the condition for solidarity, instead of solidarity constituting the church on its own. That is the essence of his criticism of Robinson. He does understand the so-called "Robinson-tendency"—a tendency to horizontalize—in so far as it is a critique of the tendency of others to merely identify the church with the seven sacraments, its doctrine, or its leadership. However, he criticizes the emancipation of solidarity as a separate sacrament, detached from Christ and the church.

---

47  *Ad gentes* (December 7, 1965) 9, http://www.vatican.va/archive/hist_councils/ii_vatican_council/documents/vat-ii_decree_19651207_ad-gentes_en.html. This lecture has been republished as Edward Schillebeeckx, "The Church, the 'Sacrament of the World,'" *The Mission of the Church*, trans. N.D. Smith (New York: Seabury Press, 1973), 43–50, at 44–5.
48  See *Mission of the Church*, 9, 44–5.
49  See *Council Notes*, Appendix/Annex.
50  Edward Schillebeeckx, "Paus Johannes en het tweede vaticanum," 4.
51  Edward Schillebeeckx, "Evangelische zuiverheid en menselijke waarachtigheid," *TvT* 3(1963), 283–325; Edward Schillebeeckx, "Herinterpretatie van het geloof in het licht van de seculariteit. Honest to Robinson," *TvT* 4 (1964), 109–50. ET: Edward Schillebeeckx, "Life in God and Life in the World," *God and Man*, trans. Edward Fitzgerald and Peter Tomlinson, Theological Soundings (New York: Sheed and Ward, 1969), 85–209.

Apart from a critique of an all too existential and non-incarnational concept of solidarity, Schillebeeckx's idea of the relation between church and world is also a critique of an eschatological dualism in which the church would be responsible only for a post-historical future. Instead, the church is very much part of the world and has its own task and function in it. To be able to truly understand that task and that function, a sound understanding of the world is needed. In Schillebeeckx's way of thinking, "World" is theological concept that may refer to a secular reality with its own autonomous structure and laws, but only to the extent that God's Spirit in Christ reveals itself in it, and it is an "objective expression of the life of grace."[52] The Incarnation is the revelation of God's love which, according to Schillebeeckx, keeps all of human history safe. That security exists prior to people being confronted with the church, he believes, but the church is the visible sign and fulfillment of that safety. So on the one hand, his ecclesiology is a confirmation of the fact that God's salvation has become manifest in the church of Christ and is observed as a devotion. On the other hand, this also shows that what is revealed in the church will always and forever be present in human reality: the merciful reality that is God. Another term Schillebeeckx uses for the merciful act is "implicit Christianity." For him, this is,

> a distinctive, non-sacral, but sanctified expression of man's [*sic*] living community with the living God. The church, as the institution of salvation with her communal confession of faith, her worship and her sacraments, is the "set aside," sacral expression of this implicit Christianity.[53]

This concept of an implicit Christianity should, according to Schillebeeckx, lead to the recognition that the hierarchy of the church does not have exclusive authority in secular reality. The Incarnational foundation of salvation in the world and the experiences of people in the present day have of Christ and his message are signs of Christ's presence of the present. That is why the church's task is not primarily to preach the gospel to the world. Instead, the preaching of the church should be regarded as the result of the embodiment of Christ's presence in the world.[54] As Schillebeeckx would later put it: orthopraxis comes before orthodoxy. The church can be called "sacrament of the world," because it discerns the effect of Christ as a sacrament in the world and embodies it. In the end, the "theologal life" of all of humanity is the foundation of the unity of church and world. It is only on this basis that Schillebeeckx can say that at the heart of *Gaudium et spes* there is humanity "with [its] transcendental, absolute destiny, though living in an earthly history with its own plans for the future."[55] This is how Schillebeeckx demonstrates that the autonomy of the world is not a contradiction with the promise of the Kingdom of God.

---

[52] Edward Schillebeeckx, "Church and World," *WC, CW* vol. 4 (London: Bloomsbury T&T Clark, 2014), 75 [99].

[53] Ibid., 77 [101].

[54] Erik Borgman, "Edward Schillebeeckx's Reflections on the Sacraments and the Future of Catholic Theology," *Concilium* 2012/1 [Sacramentalizing Human History: In Honour of Edward Schillebeeckx], 13–24, 20–22.

[55] Schillebeeckx, *The Real Achievement of Vatican II*, 70.

# Conclusion

Schillebeeckx concludes his commentaries on the Second Vatican Council with a reference to Luke 12:32: "*Pusillus grex*, a small flock, but a sign and the forerunner of God's all-embracing mercy."[56] He expresses the hope that the church will overcome its inner divisions in the near future. He is not talking about the polarization between the conservative and progressive wings, which had only intensified after the Council. Instead, he means the gulf between the leaders of the church and the believers, and that between church and world. The Council may have discovered salvation in the world, and the church as the light of the nations, it had also "laid bare a deep disorder of spiritual communication between the centre and the periphery of the Catholic Church."[57] Although he did consider the Council to be a first step toward mending the troubled relations, he believed the real work had yet to begin. The Second Vatican Council was a starting point and should certainly not be regarded as the new status quo. The ecclesiology of the Council had far-reaching consequences for his own theology. The theological hermeneutics he would develop shortly after the Council was characterized by a constant re-reading of the authoritative texts of tradition by the community of the faithful in the light of the signs of the time, and vice versa. His theology of experience, the historical-critical method he that developed, and his ecclesiology of orthopraxis all bear the hallmark of the task that the Council had set for itself and for the world: to become "sign and the forerunner of God's all-embracing mercy" as God's people.[58]

---

[56]  Ibid., 90.
[57]  Ibid., 89.
[58]  Ibid., 90.

# Chapter 9

# In Search of a Catholic Use of Hermeneutics

*Schillebeeckx's Turn to Experience*

Daniel Minch

While Edward Schillebeeckx is perhaps most remembered for his contributions to Christology, even his explicitly Christological works contain much more. Each of his bestselling Christological volumes is a work of fundamental theology, touching on method, ecclesiology, political theology, and the very possibility of human experience of revelation and grace. At the core of his mature thought is a general hermeneutical methodology that acts as a structure for sustained theological reflection. Schillebeeckx became a thoroughly hermeneutical thinker, and any discussion of his legacy must include ample attention to hermeneutics, despite the daunting nature of even knowing where to begin. The most important question for this chapter is "why" it is that Schillebeeckx engaged with hermeneutics in the first place. What was it that pushed him to take the subject on and integrate it so thoroughly into his work, to the point that he appears to have taught one or more courses on the subject every year from 1966 until 1982? We need to also determine if Schillebeeckx was captivated by the zeitgeist of the times, or if he was using contemporary breakthroughs in philosophy for a theological purpose? The main event that stands between the "early" and "late" Schillebeeckx is, of course, the Second Vatican Council. We must, as Schillebeeckx did with Thomas Aquinas, also read him in his context, and so the Council will have a role to play in our estimation of Schillebeeckx's turn to hermeneutics.

In the preceding decades of Schillebeeckx scholarship, there have been several attempts to analyze his relationship to hermeneutics.[1] Erik Borgman and Philip Kennedy privilege continuity in Schillebeeckx's thought, in terms of both the content of his work and the trajectory of Schillebeeckx's development based on his Thomistic foundations. William Portier has presented a "two-stage" model, wherein Schillebeeckx's integration of critical theory marks a significant change in his work—a turn away from Heidegger and toward critical praxis that includes a

---

[1] The best and most important of these are: Philip Kennedy, *Deus Humanissimus: The Knowability of God in the Theology of Edward Schillebeeckx* (Fribourg: University Press Fribourg Switzerland, 1993); Erik Borgman, "Van cultuurtheologie naar theologie als onderdeel van de cultuur," *TvT* 34 (1994), 335–60; Steven M. Rodenborn, *Hope in Action: Subversive Eschatology in the Theology of Edward Schillebeeckx and Johann Baptist Metz* (Minneapolis, MN: Fortress Press, 2014); Daniel Speed Thompson, *The Language of Dissent: Edward Schillebeeckx on the Crisis of Authority in the Catholic Church* (Notre Dame, IN: University of Notre Dame Press, 2003).

shift from the continuity of tradition to the primacy of present experience.[2] Steven Rodenborn has presented a more nuanced form of this model with a "before-after" structure based on his encounter with critical theory, and especially the work of Jürgen Habermas within the period of 1967–1973.[3] I have taken a mixed approach, arguing for change driven by an underlying continuity.[4] Schillebeeckx's fundamental theological concerns about the meaning and relevance of fundamental Christian dogmas precipitated his integration of both hermeneutics and critical theory. The interrelation of eschatology, creation theology, and theological anthropology is incredibly important for understanding Schillebeeckx at any stage in his career. It is the turn to hermeneutics, in light of these dogmatic considerations, that led him to his "mature" theology which became so influential in the 1970s and 1980s. In this chapter, I have looked primarily at the evolution of Schillebeeckx's courses on hermeneutics from the 1960s and 1970s, not in an exhaustive manner, since this would be a nearly impossible task (partially because of the fragmentary nature of the extant syllabi, and the sheer volume of course notes and unofficial student notes in his archives), but in order to understand the general arc of his development and which significant moments punctuated this development.

I will proceed by looking at the early indications of Schillebeeckx's attention to the hermeneutic problem rooted in major ecclesial events in the 1960s that were extremely formative for the situation of Dutch Catholicism: the Second Vatican Council and debates around the Eucharist in the mid-1960s. I will then move to his early courses on hermeneutics from 1966 to 1971, which precede the appearance of volume five of *Theological Soundings* (*Theologische peilingen*) in 1972, published in English as *The Understanding of Faith: Interpretation and Criticism* in 1974. The hermeneutical method he developed in this period, although still incomplete, is visible in this volume and it acts as the foundation for what would follow. I will look specifically at the sources and structures of his courses in order to get a sense of how his thought on the subject developed. I will also frame this within a wider thematic continuity, beginning with his concern for the communication of Christian faith during the Second Vatican Council. As Lieven Boeve has written, Schillebeeckx's goal in his post-conciliar work was "the construction of a plausible and relevant theology within a modern context proceeding from a critical dialogue with this context."[5] The development of Schillebeeckx's theological hermeneutics is essentially a "critical dialogue" with the context, but it begins from the perspective of the church and theology.

---

[2]   William Portier, "Schillebeeckx' Dialogue with Critical Theory," *The Ecumenist* 21 (1983), 20–7; William Portier, "Edward Schillebeeckx as Critical Theorist: The Impact of Neo-Marxist Social Thought on His Recent Theology," *The Thomist* 48, no. 3 (1984), 341–67.

[3]   Rodenborn, *Hope in Action*, 115–65. Rodenborn's careful, detailed work on this period, as well as the comparison to Metz is very illuminating.

[4]   Daniel Minch, "Eschatology and Theology of Hope: The Impact of Gaudium et Spes on the Thought of Edward Schillebeeckx," *The Heythrop Journal* 59 (2018), 273–85; Daniel Minch, *Eschatological Hermeneutics: The Theological Core of Experience and Our Hope for Salvation*, T&T Clark Studies in Edward Schillebeeckx (New York: T&T Clark, 2018).

[5]   Lieven Boeve, "Experience According to Edward Schillebeeckx: The Driving Force of Faith and Theology," *Divinising Experience: Essays in the History of Religious Experience from Origen to Ricoeur*, ed. Lieven Boeve and Laurence P. Hemming (Leuven: Peeters Press, 2004), 200.

# I. The hermeneutic problem and modern Christian faith

It is now well known that Schillebeeckx was involved in the preparations of the Dutch bishops for the Council, and that this kept him from being appointed an official *peritus* during the Council itself.[6] His work in that period was essentially about the questions that were discussed at the Second Vatican Council and the Dutch Pastoral Council: liturgy, ministry and authority, the laity in the church, and the sacraments.[7] What seems clear is that in the aftermath of the Council he had to reflect on the documents it had produced and how these should be meaningfully interpreted within a rapidly changing culture. In 1963, Schillebeeckx described the different factions at the Council: the so-called "open wing" or the majority, and the "closed wing" representing an essentialist minority.[8] He attempted to correct a certain misconception about the meaning of the Second Vatican Council as a "pastoral" council. John XXIII had wanted the Council to be "pastoral" rather than purely "doctrinal."

## The Second Vatican Council and the interpretation of truth

Sebastiaan Tromp, S.J. of the Gregorian University and secretary of the Doctrinal Commission publicly opined that "pastoral" really meant to communicate the truth. Here Schillebeeckx agrees, broadly speaking, but *how* is the truth to be given and interpreted? He writes that to give "contemporary expression to a truth does not mean that we can first strip the truth of all human conceptions and association, so that we can then, as it were, look it straight in the face and, after that, dress it up in its 'new look' attire."[9] An essentialist interpretation of truth, however, especially in terms of the neoscholasticism of the day defended by the "closed wing," identified certain formulations as "the only means whereby the truth remains true" with the consequence that all other expressions are classified as "pastoral" and logically, less true than the "pure" scholastic proposition. Schillebeeckx points out that such a position implies that there is a way to separate expression from the content of what is said such that one formulation gives the essential "core" of the truth, while others are necessarily degraded regardless of context. Further, some formulations would thereby become transhistorical, not by virtue of how we understand them, but simply in and of themselves.

"There is never a moment," Schillebeeckx writes, "not even a fraction of a second, in which we see the 'naked' truth."[10] He moves on to the problem of language in mediating truth, in particular

---

6   John O'Malley, *What Happened at Vatican II* (Cambridge, MA: Belknap Press of Harvard University Press, 2008), 120, 145; Erik Borgman, *Edward Schillebeeckx: A Theologian in His History*, trans. John Bowden (London/New York: Continuum, 2003), 316–19, 320–21.

7   Borgman, "Van cultuurtheologie naar theologie als onderdeel van de cultuur," 342.

8   Edward Schillebeeckx, "The Second Vatican Council," *Vatican II: A Struggle of Minds and Other Essays*, trans. M. H. Gill and Son Limited (Dublin: M. H. Gill and Son Limited, 1963), 16–17. This section of the essay was originally published as: Edward Schillebeeckx, "Misverstanden op het concilie," *De Bazuin* (January 19, 1963).

9   Schillebeeckx, "The Second Vatican Council," 23.

10  Ibid. Funnily, Schillebeeckx wrote in his Council Diary of the American use of Latin: "[Cardinals] Spellman and McIntyre proclaim that Latin is the *only* liturgical language, but pronounce it in such an Americanised fashion that no one understands them: the worse one's spoken Latin the more one

the use of Latin at the Council, which was both positive and negative. As a "common language" understood and variously spoken by all at the Council, it was a blessing. Its merits were hardly absolute, however, since as a "dead language" it "no longer develops spontaneously."[11] Even so, some (especially in the conservative minority) favored Latin as the best way of expressing "unchanging truth" precisely because of its "finished" character, which also carries worrying implication that truth is known and quantified in doctrines expressed in the past and repeated in the present. Schillebeeckx argues that the expression of truth must actually have a progressive character, "if the fullness of truth is to be allowed the free scope it is due," and in order to safeguard continuity between understanding in the past and in the present.[12] He does not think that "newness offers safeguards because it is new," but he also points out that this is equally true for what is "old." Rather, what is important is coming to a new understanding of what was rightly understood and expressed in ages past since, "each new understanding of the truth leaves the old understanding essentially untouched."[13]

In other words, coming to a new understanding of truth in the present does not negate the authenticity or veracity of formulations of it in the past. Here, he has solidly expressed the principle of the development of doctrine in the hope that the Council will deal with the truths of the Catholic faith in a way that is understandable and suitable for the context, instead of merely repeating or reaffirming what was said at Vatican I or at Trent, as some had expected that the Council would. This one article gives us some insight into Schillebeeckx's very early "hermeneutical" considerations from before he had begun a serious engagement with hermeneutic philosophy.[14]

## Interpreting the Eucharist

The communication and preservation of meaning in terms of religious content was a core element of Schillebeeckx's theology in the 1960s, just as it had been in his earlier dissertation on the sacraments. The Second Vatican Council was itself, as John XXIII stated in his opening address, a council dedicated to the investigation and promotion of Catholic doctrine according to the demands

---

is inclined to favour it. It is a '*status symbol*' of priest-'intellectuals' as opposed to the 'idiots'!! *Also among many South Americans.*" See Edward Schillebeeckx, *The Council Notes of Edward Schillebeeckx 1962–1963* ed. Karim Schelkens, Instrumenta Theologica 34 (Leuven: Peeters, 2011), 13 [Dutch: 53].

[11] Schillebeeckx, "The Second Vatican Council," 27.

[12] Ibid.

[13] Ibid., 28.

[14] He was, however, already using the term "hermeneutics" "in his reflections on the history of marriage" in the mid-1960s. He was teaching a course on marriage from 1963 to 1965 (Arch. 414, 823), and published *Marriage: Human Reality and Saving Mystery* in 1963. A second volume on human sexuality never appeared, although it appears he had prepared it through his lectures on marriage. The title was to be: *Metabletica van de christelijke sexualiteit* (Arch. 821). See Ted Schoof, "E. Schillebeeckx: 25 Years in Nijmegen, I," *Theology Digest* 37, no. 4 (1990), 326, 330–31, n. 19.

of the times.[15] Thus the whole of the Catholic world was, in different ways, directly engaged in the task of hermeneutics. The Dutch controversy over the Eucharist is an interesting example of this, and one in which Schillebeeckx became intimately involved. He had lectured on the theology of the Eucharist in his first full academic year at Nijmegen in 1958–1959 based on his earlier sacraments courses from Leuven.[16] He was a recognized expert on sacramental theology given his doctoral dissertation and the short book published in 1957, *De Christusonmoeting als sacrament van de Godsontmoeting*, which was expanded in 1959 into *Christ the Sacrament of the Encounter with God*.[17] After the third session of the Council, a debate over the meaning and place of the Eucharist flared up in the Dutch church prompted, in part, by the ongoing reform of the liturgy. This push for reform reached a crucial turning point with the promulgation of *Sacrosanctum Concilium* in 1963.

One of the primary figures in the Eucharist debate was Schillebeeckx's colleague in Nijmegen, Piet Schoonenberg, S.J. who was appointed as professor for dogmatics in 1964. Schoonenberg had been involved in debates on real presence and Eucharist since 1959.[18] He argued that Eucharistic presence begins first and foremost from Christ's *"presence in the community celebrating the Eucharist"* and through this celebration the bread and wine become signs of the self-giving presence of Christ.[19] The Eucharistic elements remain what they are in terms of their physical and chemical properties, but their very being is indelibly altered by the Eucharistic celebration where Christ makes himself present. In light of contemporary philosophical and scientific understanding, "transubstantiation" can be thought in terms of "a transfinalization or transsignification."[20] Other theologians in the Netherlands joined the conversation, attempting to locate the Eucharist within its properly liturgical context, within contemporary thought, and in a world which no longer thinks in terms of Aristotelian "substances" and "accidents."[21] In order to head off criticism from Rome and calm critical voices from conservative circles, the Dutch bishops published a pastoral letter in May of 1965 affirming the traditional, Tridentine dogmas, while also allowing for theological discussion and advancement.[22] Just before the start of the fourth session of the Council, Paul VI published his encyclical *Mysterium fidei*, which more or less ended the debate and created a tense situation with the Dutch bishops who had wanted

---

[15] Pope John XXIII, *Gaudet Mater Ecclesia* (October 11, 1962) 6, https://w2.vatican.va/content/john-xxiii/la/speeches/1962/documents/hf_j-xxiii_spe_19621011_opening-council.html: "oportet ut haec doctrina certa et immutabilis, cui fidele obsequium est praestandum, ea ratione pervestigetur et exponatur, quam tempora postulant nostra."

[16] See Borgman, *Edward Schillebeeckx*, 456, n. 209. See also Arch. 554, 3091, 3119.

[17] Schoof, "E. Schillebeeckx: 25 Years in Nijmegen, I," 320. Edward Schillebeeckx, *De Christusontmoeting als sacrament van de Godsontmoeting* (Antwerp/Bilthoven: 't Groeit/H. Nelissen, 1957); Edward Schillebeeckx, *Christ the Sacrament of the Encounter of God*, trans. Paul Barrett and Lawrence Bright, *CW* 1 (London: Bloomsbury, 2014).

[18] Piet Schoonenberg, "De tegenwoordigheid van Christus," *Verbum* 26 (1959), 148–57; Piet Schoonenberg, "Eucharistische tegenwoordigheid," *Verbum* 26 (1959), 194–205.

[19] Piet Schoonenberg, "Tegenwoordigheid," *Verbum* 31 (1964), 413. My translation. Emphasis original. See also, Luchesius Smits O.F.M.Cap., *Actuele vragen rondom de transsubstantiatie en de tegenwoordigheid des heren in de eucharistie* (Roermond: Romen, 1965).

[20] Ibid., 415.

[21] For a contemporary summary of the debate, see "Fragen der Theologie und des religösen Lebens: Diskussion um die Realpräsenz," *Herder Korrespondenz* 19 (1965), 517–20.

[22] Pastoral letter published in: *Ephemerides Theologicae Louvanienses* 41 (1965), 690–94.

to avoid premature intervention by the hierarchy in order to allow the debate to progress and mature.[23]

Schillebeeckx's first major article on the Eucharist was actually written in 1965 before the appearance of *Mysterium fidei*, and which forms the first part of a short book he published in 1967 on the subject.[24] This debate occurred at when the Eucharist was being returned to its liturgical context. I have argued that his book, *The Eucharist*, is essentially a hermeneutical exercise which deals with the contemporary interpretation of the Eucharistic dogmas of the Council of Trent.[25] The point of his work on the subject, and indeed of the efforts of other theologians, is "to safeguard the authentic doctrine" of Eucharistic change, but "in such a way that the people of God, especially the clergy, form more and more in a non-scholastic mentality, might live it in a more authentic fashion."[26] In a modern context, however, the theologian is placed in a new ethical situation wherein theology is addressed to the masses, and not just to a learned few in ecclesial and academic circles. Theologians, Schillebeeckx writes, are people whose faith is "a faith-in-historicity" and who were tasked with making the faith understandable to the wider public.[27] This aligns with Thomas's assertion that in order to assent to the propositions of faith, one must to a certain degree understand their content.[28] With explicit reference to Rudolph Bultmann, Schillebeeckx explains that it is our preunderstanding (*Vorverständnis*) that allows us to recognize what we find in revelation as meaningful. This also applies to worship in the liturgy. Something that is meaningful has the potential to have an impact on the existential situation of a human being in the world, affecting every aspect of our being human. Revelation "presents itself as *full of meaning* because it is *full of being*."[29] So he seeks to interpret the Eucharistic dogmas of Trent in light of contemporary preunderstanding because while the dogmas contain meaning, they must be interpreted in such a way that this meaning becomes comprehensible for modern people.

For this task, Schillebeeckx proceeds historically. The first part of the book is devoted to an investigation of the Tridentine formulations on the Eucharist, including the *Acta* of the Council.[30] One of the main problems is whether or not we need to hold to an Aristotelian view of physics in order to continue to affirm transubstantiation since Aristotelian "natural philosophy" no longer forms our understanding of what a "substance" is. Schillebeeckx shows that although the Council Fathers of Trent used scholastic terminology and the philosophical beliefs that went with that

---

[23] Borgman, *Edward Schillebeeckx*, 338–39, 457, n. 222.

[24] Edward Schillebeeckx, "Christus' tegenwoordigheid in de eucharistie," *TvT* 5 (1965), 136–72; Edward Schillebeeckx, *Christus' tegenwoordigheid in de eucharistie* (Antwerp: Patmos, 1967); Edward Schillebeeckx, *The Eucharist*, trans. N.D. Smith (London/New York: Burns & Oates, 2005).

[25] Daniel Minch, "Language, Structure, and Sacrament: Reconsidering the Eucharistic Theology of Edward Schillebeeckx," *Approaching the Threshold of Mystery: Liturgical Worlds and Theological Spaces*, ed. Joris Geldhof, Daniel Minch, and Trevor Maine, Theologie der Liturgie 10 (Regensburg: Friedrich Pustet, 2015), 98–119.

[26] Edward Schillebeeckx, "Transubstantiation, Transfinalization, Transignification," *Worship* 40, no. 6 (1966), 325.

[27] Schillebeeckx, *Christus' tegenwoordigheid in de eucharistie*, 1967, 11. My translation.

[28] Ibid., 12–13. Cf. Thomas Aquinas, *ST* II-II, a.8, q.8, ad.2.

[29] Schillebeeckx, *The Eucharist*, 18–19. Emphasis original.

[30] Ibid., 29–53.

terminology, there are different levels in the dogmas themselves.[31] "Transubstantiation" worked in the sixteenth century because it fit the context and "most fittingly" expressed the reality of Eucharistic change, but this was also in continuity with earlier formulations of this change on the level of reality or ontology.[32] The wording of the dogma was and remains essential to the content of what it says. It was certainly "thought out in Aristotelian categories, but the strictly Aristotelian content of these categories was not included in what the dogma intended to say."[33] The expression of Eucharistic change therefore included, at the level of preunderstanding, both "philosophical" and "ordinary" meanings of the language.

Schillebeeckx distinguishes between three levels in the dogma: faith, ontology, and natural philosophy. The first two levels are historically attested in the longer tradition of the church, and he regards them as essential to the meaning of the dogma. The third element, however, depends on a view of cosmology and the natural world that we no longer share and which we experience either as a historical category or as "non-sense"—it no longer makes sense to speak of "substances" as they did in the sixteenth century. To continue to hold to the "natural" level in Eucharistic change would actually betray the first two by making it a physio-chemical change in the elements such that the bread is no longer "bread" in a scientific sense. We would cease to think sacramentally and only think in terms of a naïve realism, separate from the liturgical context.[34]

Schillebeeckx's conclusion is that in the reaction against Eucharistic materialism, Schoonenberg and others have legitimately emphasized the "interpersonal relationship between Christ and us ... in which Christ gives himself to man [*sic*] by means of bread and wine."[35] Insofar as the terms "transfinalization" and "transignification" indicate a change in purpose and significance, they also denote a change in the very reality of the elements themselves, although not in a physio-chemical sense. He wants to show that these terms are not out of step with *Mysterium fidei* as long as they are not understood extrinsically, or "with a *purely* phenomenological interpretation without metaphysical density."[36] From the perspective of hermeneutics, it is clear that Schillebeeckx is already working with a sophisticated, but not explicitly developed, understanding of the problem. He sees a "crisis of meaning" in this debate and the need to do justice to the content of Christian faith by explaining it in such a way that it is meaningful to contemporary people. This is challenging, both for "modern" people who must struggle to understand concepts coming from the past, and for ecclesial authorities who are still thinking in terms of a neoscholastic synthesis that seems to explain everything as long as the presuppositions of that world view are not challenged. With the growing disconnect between "modern" and "scholastic" worldviews, hermeneutical mediation becomes essential, particularly for how human beings could understand their own existential situation in relation to God.

---

[31] Ibid., 72–6. In particular, he shows that the Fathers used "species" and "accident" interchangeably in preparatory documents, while "species" ended up in the final draft of Canon 2 (the *substance* is changed, while the *species* remains).

[32] Ibid., 72–3.

[33] Ibid., 102.

[34] Schillebeeckx, "Transubstantiation, Transfinalization, Transignification," 334.

[35] Ibid., 337. He also thought that Schoonenberg and Smits had not been careful enough in their reinterpretations of the doctrine. Unfortunately, Paul VI's intervention effectively halted the discussion before the theology was able to advance further. See Borgman, *Edward Schillebeeckx*, 342–45.

[36] Schillebeeckx, *The Eucharist*, 150. Emphasis original.

# Secular meaning and the world

One of the most important overriding themes of Schillebeeckx's theology is the presence of salvation in the world and the necessary interrelation of divine and human reality. This is also essential to his adoption of hermeneutics. We have seen that he was preoccupied with the transmission of the truth of the faith in contemporary society in a way that is understandable for that society. In this vein, he was extremely critical of any dualism between "church" and "world," especially in the debates during the Second Vatican Council. In an important article originally written in September 1964, Schillebeeckx directly addressed the meaning of "Schema XIII," or the draft version of *Gaudium et spes*.[37] Just after the opening of the third session of the Council, Schillebeeckx declared that "the secular meaning of the Second Vatican Council stands or falls on the outcome of Schema 13."[38] That is to say, the meaning of the Council for the world depends on what attitude the document will take toward the "modern" and "secular" reality, which is no longer under the control of a hegemonic Christian (and Eurocentric) culture. He goes on to question the traditional problem of "nature and supernature" as a theological starting point, especially in terms of the betterment of the world at large. Ultimately, the church/world relation is a question of the eschatological salvation of humanity. We now recognize, however, that eschatological salvation also includes partial salvation "here and now." This turn away from an individualized and overly spiritualized concept of salvation is not universally accepted, and in fact some advocate strengthening the division between "nature" and "grace," "church" and "world."[39]

Schillebeeckx, on the other hand, sees nature as the *object* of grace.[40] Nature and history are meaningful on their own, by virtue of being created. In 1964, Schillebeeckx called for Schema XIII to illustrate the church's self-understanding as an *eschatological* community of salvation— that is a community embedded in history and not yet fully identical with the Rule of God. The development of the schema should therefore follow the course set by *Dei verbum*: "just as there is a development of dogma in the church's tradition, so too can the church's attitude towards the world evolve recognisably in the course of history."[41] This implies that just as the church has contributed to the betterment of the world in various ways in the past, it can also learn from non-ecclesial realities and cooperate with them in the humanization of the world. The world does not need to be "sacralized" or divested of its profane significance and made dependent for all meaning on the institutional church. Rather, the world must be sanctified, or made holy by achieving the original dignity invested by God through creation, which is an eschatological process in which the church plays an indispensible role.[42]

---

[37] The published version came a few months after it was originally given as a speech on September 16, 1964, at the opening of the new Dutch Documentation Center in Rome.

[38] Schillebeeckx, "Kerk en Wereld: de betekenis van 'Schema 13'," *TvT* 4 (1964), 387. This sentence is left out of the English translation, Edward Schillebeeckx, "Church and World," *WC, CW* 4 (London: Bloomsbury, 2014), 73–87 [96–114].

[39] Ibid., 74 [97].

[40] Edward Schillebeeckx, "Faith Functioning in Human Self-Understanding," *The Word in History: The St. Xavier Symposium*, ed. T. Patrick Burke (New York: Sheed and Ward, 1966), 43.

[41] Schillebeeckx, "Church and World," *WC*, 84–5 [112].

[42] Ibid., 84 [111].

This address on the relevance of Schema XIII (eventually *Gaudium et spes*) is foundational for Schillebeeckx's turn to experience and, moving forward, his full implementation of hermeneutics. It is indicative of a move away from his early search for a "theology of culture," and toward a *theology within culture*. That is, by seeing creation and humanity, in which the church appears, as eschatologically oriented toward the coming future, present experience becomes a *locus theologicus*. Schillebeeckx saw Christians trying to formulate a way of living out their religious faith in their everyday lives in a context where the traditional formulations of faith (like the language used to describe Eucharistic change) "clashed" with the existential experience of people in society. Without understanding the content of the faith, how could people be expected to recognize the truth contained in it? And further, how could the church expect to say anything to "the world" at large if it understands neither the needs of people nor their language? This includes humanity's "illumination" of its own existence, including human efforts, plans, and expectations for a better, more human future. As Schillebeeckx points out: "A church in monologue with herself is not a partner. If she does not listen to the world, she will disregard as much human knowledge, influenced by anonymous grace, as there are people outside her institutional boundaries or outside the hierarchy."[43]

Two years later, in the spring of 1966, Schillebeeckx made his first trip to the United States for a conference called "The Theological Task Confronting the Church Today," held at St. Xavier College in Chicago.[44] Here, again he addressed the transmission of meaning through tradition based on a framework that combined both experiential elements and a more "metaphysical" background in line with his previous reliance on the epistemological model inherited from his teacher, Dominicus De Petter, O.P.[45] De Petter's model of "implicit intuition" aimed to bridge the gap between subject and object, and between perception and reality based on neo-Thomist and Husserlian foundations. He reacted against the modern dualism between subjective knowledge and the things-in-themselves which made it impossible to know or experience objective reality as such. Knowing an object in experience always presupposes the wholeness of reality which already encompasses both subject and object. The prior unity of being is expressed in the formation of knowledge in concepts, albeit in a way that does not exhaust the fullness of reality itself. It is not a separate reality in the intellect, but a condition of possibility realized in each intellectual act of judgment.[46]

At the St. Xavier symposium, Schillebeeckx was still working within his teacher's epistemological framework while mediating the "church-world" dialectic through an appeal to human experience. He begins by using rather traditional language in terms of "nature" and "supernature," but he claims that "nature" as a concept is related to revelation and not necessarily to an Aristotelian definition.[47] Revelation *presupposes* the free response of nature, which he

---

[43] Ibid., 79 [105].

[44] Among the other speakers were Yves Congar, Jean Daniélou, Henri de Lubac, George Lindbeck, Johann Baptist Metz, Karl Rahner, and Alexander Schmemann. See T. Patrick Burke, "Introduction," *The Word in History: The St. Xavier Symposium*, ed. T. Patrick Burke (New York: Sheed and Ward, 1966), vii–xi.

[45] See Borgman, *Edward Schillebeeckx*, 38–51.

[46] Stephan van Erp, "Implicit Faith: Philosophical Theology After Schillebeeckx," *Edward Schillebeeckx and Contemporary Theology*, ed. Lieven Boeve, Frederiek Depoortere, and Stephan van Erp (London: T&T Clark, 2010), 214–15.

[47] Schillebeeckx, "Faith Functioning in Human Self-Understanding," 42.

presents along Thomistic lines—nature and grace are not in competition with one another: "The human person is the subject presupposed in and by grace itself."[48] By being an embodied, historical entity, the human person exists in an intersubjective relation with others in the world and is therefore not a self-enclosed, monadic unit or consciousness. Human beings become themselves through contact with others in the world, and therefore through self-consciousness or self-understanding. This relates the reception of grace by nature because "human consciousness— the intrinsic condition for the possibility of revelation—is a self-awareness which is reached in and through the awareness of fellowmen [*sic*] in the world."[49] Such self-understanding acts a "pre-reflexive or unthematic self-understanding" which grounds and enables all reflection and experience.[50] As historical, humans remain limited in their ability to express reality, even absolute meaning given in revelation which "can only be explicated in categorial forms."[51]

Schillebeeckx connects knowledge via categories to a transcendental foundation "constituted by the implicit transcendental relation to God" which is experienced in each moment, but cannot be exhaustively named and therefore remains a religious mystery.[52] The ultimate ground of being, God, calls humanity to self-understanding. This self-understanding is formed in the unthematic "background" of experience, but revelation sharpens that self-understanding by making it explicitly religious in the offer of grace and salvation. Once salvation is explicitly part of human self-understanding, then God is actively shaping "anthropology" through "theology," or reflection on the revelation of Godself in history. Here, Schillebeeckx is using De Petter's framework but he gives it a more existential and historical interpretation. He affirms that the unthematic presence of God is made explicit in experience and can be sharpened through reflection. Thus, "theological Dogmatics must keep pace with man's [*sic*] historically conditioned self-understanding."[53] As in his Conciliar writings, Schillebeeckx is concerned with the transmission of the Christian faith in history and this involves being attuned to the expression of truth and humanity's ability to know and understand such truth. He goes on to cite Thomas's dictum that the act of faith does not terminate in the linguistic expression, but in the reality that is aimed at. In other words, our concepts that give expression to the "unthematic" *theologal*, or intersubjective, relationship with God are always approximate.[54] Even so, those concepts are based on a real implicit relationship that can be truly but inadequately expressed.[55]

I find this article illuminating in mapping Schillebeeckx's theological development because of his focus on self-understanding and clear concern for the core problem of hermeneutics: the interpretation of meaning. He continues by discussing the interpretation of the dogmas of Trent, pointing out, just as in his work on the Eucharist, that we in the present cannot simply bracket out our modern presuppositions in the work of interpretation.[56] Each new era entails a new effort

---

[48] Ibid., 43.
[49] Ibid., 43–4.
[50] Ibid., 44.
[51] Ibid., 51.
[52] Ibid.
[53] Ibid., 53.
[54] Edward Schillebeeckx, *God and Man*, trans. Edward Fitzgerald and Peter Tomlinson, Theological Soundings (New York: Sheed and Ward, 1969), 161, n. 4. In this note he explains the context and meaning of "theologal" (*theologaal*) as "intersubjectivity with God."
[55] Schillebeeckx, "Faith Functioning in Human Self-Understanding," 54.
[56] Cf. Schillebeeckx, *The Eucharist*, 20–21.

at interpreting the collective past, emphasizing the necessary recognition of human historicity. Mere "material repetition" of propositions in a new context can be dangerous because it does not take seriously the particularities of either the past or present.[57] Echoing his language from 1963, he states that we cannot "'dress' and 'undress' a dogma with the ease with which children play with dolls."[58] This is directly related to human self-understanding, or *anthropology*, since the postulation of "pure meaning" also assumes that all anthropological assertions are merely a matter of changing the outward form without affecting the content. If we accept that self-understanding and the expression of meaning are historical and in constant flux, then expressions of meaning would actually become divorced from reality altogether as long as we are only defining "the real" as an infinitely repeatable and objectively knowable "core" that can be expressed in various contingent ways. Here, we see two opposing worldviews: Schillebeeckx's view which takes historicity and creation as a starting point, and an older way of conceiving of "truth" as purely conceptual and ahistorical. Schillebeeckx is laying out a general sketch of the problem of expressing faith in light of contemporary self-understanding, and he does so with an overriding eschatological focus on human salvation. In the next section, we will examine the material evolution of his courses on hermeneutics which will help to shape his response to this problem in the years following the Second Vatican Council.

# II. The definitive turn to hermeneutics

Schillebeeckx's longtime assistant and editorial secretary of *Tijdschrift voor Theologie*, Ted Schoof, has said that Schillebeeckx "from 1966 onwards had to give a new course on [hermeneutics] to all students of the theological faculty," who, in this period, were mostly graduate students.[59] Schoof suggests that it was the requirement to teach the course that compelled Schillebeeckx to delve so deeply into the philosophical hermeneutic debates of the time period. Even so, the "new status of theology in the Church" after the Council would have obliged him to give some attention to it had he not been required to teach the class. We have certainly seen evidence of "the new status of theology" in Schillebeeckx's work up until this point, and it is also attested to in the high-profile theological discussions during the Second Vatican Council on the international stage and also in the Dutch context during the pastoral council. Looking at the list of course notes in Schillebeeckx's personal archive, we find a number of items dating back to the academic year of 1966–1967 when he gave his first lectures on the subject.

## The sources

It is in these years that we see an increase in English and German-language sources in Schillebeeckx's work, in contrast to the overwhelming number of French-language sources as

---

[57] Schillebeeckx, "Faith Functioning in Human Self-Understanding," 56.
[58] Ibid.
[59] Mark Schoof, O.P., "Masters in Israel: VII. The Later Theology of Edward Schillebeeckx," *The Clergy Review* 55, no. 12 (1970), 950.

in his earlier articles. Schillebeeckx had a broad linguistic background, in part thanks to the unique geographic and historical position of Flanders "between" political and linguistic groups. He was aided specifically by his extraordinary mastery of other languages and by his voracious reading habit in general. In this period, he began to study and integrate German literature on phenomenology and hermeneutics, and English literature primarily on linguistic analysis, logical empiricism, and the "new hermeneutics."[60] Certainly he was attuned to French structuralism, which he presented in 1967–1968 as a reaction against existential phenomenology. The earlier course notes are still very much a "sketch" of what is happening in academic discussions almost contemporaneously with the lectures themselves. The sources are, in some cases, just barely published in time to be taught, or even in the case of two chapters from *The Understanding of Faith*, including "Theological Criteria" and "The New Critical Theory," distributed in mimeographed versions preceding actual publication.[61]

Schillebeeckx's starting point is the necessity to mediate between the "older theology," meaning neoscholasticism, and modern understandings of humanity and culture. The Catholic "retreat" into neoscholastic thought and the Catholic cultural bubble in much of the Western world began to break down after the Second World War, forcing a confrontation between different forms of language and different expressions of reality. Certainly, the meaning of faith needed to be explored in a new existential, that is, *lived* situation. By adopting Heideggerian philosophy, Rudolph Bultmann had attempted this in his "kerygmatic" push against Liberal Protestantism.[62] Both Barthian "dialectical theology" and Bultmann's school of "kerygmatic theology" expressed diverging theological reactions against reigning systems of thought from the nineteenth century: Hegelian inspired Liberal Theology and Historicism. As with Barth, Bultmann's method was forged in part by the "crisis mentality" that had formed in Europe, and especially in Germany.[63] This was a crisis of scientific methodologies as well as a crisis of culture, which only accelerated after the First World War.

Catholic scholars came late to these discussions, at least in an official, non-apologetic capacity. Schillebeeckx himself had studied existentialism (in particular Jean-Paul Sartre) and phenomenology quite extensively (Husserl with De Petter and Maurice Merleau-Ponty during his doctoral studies in Paris). Of course, Catholic appropriations of Heidegger and of phenomenology had already existed in various forms (exemplary are Karl Rahner and Bernhard Welte), but theologians after the Council found a new freedom to deal with non-traditional sources and integrate them into the wider matrix of Catholic thought. Schillebeeckx's main

---

[60] Schoof notes the influence of Ian T. Ramsey's work in linguistic analysis (himself influenced by Wittgenstein). Ramsey was the Anglican bishop of Durham from 1966 to 1972. See Ian T. Ramsey, *Religious Language: An Empirical Placing of Theological Language*, The Library of Philosophy and Theology (London: SMC Press, 1957); Ian T. Ramsey, *Models and Mystery. The Whidden Lectures* (London: Oxford University Press, 1964).

[61] This occurs in the course of 1970–1971, although the article version of "Theological Criteria" was published in 1969 as "Het 'rechte geloof', zijn onzekerheden en zijn criteria," *TvT* 9 (1969), 125–49. The latter chapter was published as "Naar een verruiming van de hermeneutiek: de 'nieuwe kritische theorie'," *TvT* 11 (1971): 30–50.

[62] Helmut Peukert, "Bultmann and Heidegger," *Rudolph Bultmann in Catholic Thought*, ed. Thomas F. O'Meara and Donald M. Weisser (New York, NY: Herder and Herder, 1968), 196–221.

[63] Charles R. Bambach, *Heidegger, Dilthey, and the Crisis of Historicism* (Ithaca, NY: Cornell University Press, 1995), 20–54.

sources in this period can be divided into a few main categories. First, there is Bultmann and the "post-Bultmannian" school which represents the "new hermeneutic" in theology. Here, I would also include the "historical school" of Pannenberg and the critiques of Bultmann.[64] Second, there are the hermeneutic philosophers: Heidegger, Gadamer, Paul Ricoeur, Karl-Otto Apel.[65] The third set of sources is somewhat surprising, in the sense that it plays a "covert" role in Schillebeeckx's thought and writing, especially after 1972: Anglo-American linguistic analysis and phenomenological Structuralism including the later Wittgenstein, Ian T. Ramsey, and John Macquarrie.[66] The fourth group of sources represents neo-Marxist social critical theory and the confrontation between ideology critique and hermeneutics, which later took the form of a debate between Gadamer and Jürgen Habermas.[67] By 1968, he was already familiar with the work of Herbert Marcuse and had begun to draw on "negative dialectics" derived from Theodor Adorno.[68] Consonant with the interest in "hope" and utopia as a theme for fundamental theology,

---

[64] Key texts include: Rudolf Bultmann, *New Testament and Mythology and Other Basic Writings*, trans. Schubert M. Ogden (London: SMC Press, 1985); Rudolf Bultmann, *Jesus Christ and Mythology* (London: SCM Press, 1960); Rudolf Bultmann, *Galuben und Verstehen*, 4th ed. vol. 2 (Tübingen: J.C.B. Mohr (Paul Siebeck), 1965); Wolfhart Pannenberg, "Hermeneutik und Universalgeschichte," *Zeitschrift für Theologie und Kirche* 60 (1963), 90–121; James M. Robinson and John B. Cobb Jr., eds., *The New Hermeneutic*, New Frontiers in Theology 2 (New York: Harper & Row, 1964); James M. Robinson and John B. Cobb Jr., eds., *Theology as History*, New Frontiers in Theology 3 (New York: Harper & Row, 1967); Jürgen Moltmann, *Theology of Hope: On the Ground and Implications of a Christian Eschatology*, trans. James W. Leitch (Minneapolis: Fortress Press, 1993).

[65] Key texts include: Hans-Georg Gadamer, *Truth and Method*, trans. Joel Weinsheimer and Donald G. Marshall, 2nd ed. (London/New York: Continuum, 2004); Paul Ricœur, *History and Truth*, trans. Charles A Kelbley, Northwestern University Studies in Phenomenology and Existential Philosophy (Evanston, IL: Northwestern University Press, 1965); Paul Ricœur, *The Conflict of Interpretations*, trans. Don Ihde, Northwestern University Studies in Phenomenology and Existential Philosophy (Evanston, IL: Northwestern University Press, 2007); Karl-Otto Apel, "Heideggers philosophische Radikalisierung der Hermeneutik' und die Frage nach, Sinnkriterium' der Sprache," *Die hermeneutische Frage in der Theologie*, Schriften zum Weltgespräch 3 (Wien/Freiburg: Herder, 1968), 86–153.

[66] See Ludwig Wittgenstein, *Philosophische Untersuchungen/Philosophical Investigations*, trans. G.E.M. Anscombe, P.M.S. Hacker, and Joachim Schulte, Revised 4th edition (Chichester, West Sussex/Malden, MA: Wiley-Blackwell, 2009); Norman Malcom, "Wittgenstein's Philosophical Investigations," *The Philosophical Review* 63, no. 4 (1954), 530–59; Ramsey, *Models and Mystery*; Ramsey, *Religious Langauge*; John Macquarrie, *God-Talk: An Examination of the Langauge and Logic of Theology* (London: SMC Press, 1967); John L. Austin, *How to Do Things with Words: The William James Lectures Delivered at Harvard University in 1955*, ed. James O. Urmson and Marina Sbisà, 2nd ed. (Cambridge, MA: Harvard University Press, 2009). Also, Roman Jakobson's work would become very influential.

[67] *Hermeneutik und Ideologiekritik*, Theorie-Diskussion (Frankfurt am Main: Suhrkamp, 1971); Albrecht Wellmer, *Kritische Gesellschaftstheorie und Positivismus* (Frankfurt am Main: Suhrkamp, 1969); Kennedy, *Deus Humanissimus*, 195–200.

[68] Schoof, "E. Schillebeeckx: 25 Years in Nijmegen, I," 326; Herbert Marcuse, *One-Dimensional Man: Studies in the Ideology of Advanced Industrial Society*, Routledge Classics Philosophy (London: Routledge, 2007); Theodor W. Adorno, *Negative Dialectics*, trans. E.B. Ashton (New York: Continuum, 1983).

Schillebeeckx also gave attention to Ernst Bloch's philosophy of the future already in his courses in 1966.[69]

I find it difficult to separate Schillebeeckx's use of different sources into distinct "stages." Rather, we find a still-evolving system of thought that has its roots in dogmatic considerations. Further, in 1968 alone he published ten new articles in journals or periodicals (not counting numerous translations of previous articles or introductions), and about the same number in the following year. That is to say that things were moving very quickly and an attempt to make clear divisions in his thought gives the false impression of a static periods of contemplation or systematic progression. This is obviously not the case, which is especially clear when one looks at how drastically the organizational structure of hermeneutics syllabus changes from year-to-year, even when much of the same material is preserved.

# The Early hermeneutics courses

Here, I will briefly examine the structure and the content of Schillebeeckx's early teaching on hermeneutics in the period from roughly 1966 to 1971.[70] This is an important period because it comes after the closure of the Council when theologians are now both "free" from the burden of preparing commentaries and documents, and also tasked with working out the implications of receiving the teachings of the Second Vatican Council and implementing them in full. Perhaps this is part of the reason that Schillebeeckx refers so often to Trent and to the formation and meaning of Tridentine dogmas in the mid-1960s—history provides a model for reception, but this is necessarily a historical task. He began to give courses to the graduate students in general hermeneutics in 1966. These were primarily focused on philosophical and literary hermeneutics stemming from the debate around Bultmann and the "new hermeneutics" which "seeks to expose the ontological structures of the theological understanding of reality as a totality."[71] This includes discussion of Heidegger, Gadamer, and Ricoeur and the ontological implications of hermeneutic interpretation.

The syllabus expanded considerably in the next year, where the course from 1966 to 1967 was framed as "Part I" and was presupposed for the students taking Part II. Required literature included Schillebeeckx's new article on hermeneutics, "Toward a Catholic Use of Hermeneutics," as well

---

[69] Schoof, "E. Schillebeeckx: 25 Years in Nijmegen, I," 326; Ernst Bloch, *The Principle of Hope*, trans. Neville Plaice, Stephen Plaice, and Paul Knight, 3 vols. (Oxford: Basil Blackwell, 1986).

[70] For this, I rely on Schoof's articles as well as mimeographed copies of his syllabi from the Nijmegen theology faculty's student organization, Alcuin. These are currently part of Schillebeeckx's personal archive (Archive number: 656) at the Catholic Documentation Center (KDC) in Nijmegen, but they have not yet been categorized and included in the official catalogue. From the uncategorized syllabi, I utilize: Hermeneutics 1967–1968 (Wednesday afternoons, 2 versions); Hermeneutic Theory 1968–1969 (Monday mornings); Hermeneutics 1969–1970 (Wednesday afternoons); Hermeneutics 1970–1971 (likely Wednesday afternoons). I will also refer to the typed course notes included in this group: World and Church 1967–1968 (Wednesday mornings), by student A. Jongerius.

[71] Schillebeeckx, "Towards a Catholic Use of Hermeneutics," *GFM, CW* vol. 3 (London: Bloomsbury T&T Clark, 2014), 2 [4].

as an article by his colleague Bas van Iersel on Bultmann and exegesis.[72] In Part I, the basic hermeneutic problem was laid out including: the hermeneutic circle and the "new hermeneutics" with attention to Bultmann's view of history; the "old solution" to the problem including the "essential core" meaning and "mode of expression"; the problem of present interpretation of the past and the future horizons and critiques of Bultmann and Hans-Georg Gadamer; and the problem of the identity of faith in the interpretation of the Bible, tradition, and magisterium. Part II, taught in 1967–1968, was more explicitly about the function of hermeneutics for Catholic thought. This was organized as follows:

## Section I: Two fundamental problems

Chapter 1: Jesus and the biblical kerygma (including Bultmann, form criticism, the new quest for the historical Jesus, "theology of history" with reference to Pannenberg, and Bloch's *The Principle of Hope*)

Chapter 2: Speaking about God (religious language, patristic and high medieval language for God, secular interpretation of faith concepts)

## Section II: Attempts to approach a solution

Chapter 1: The authority of the Bible and the magisterium in the church (authority of Scripture and inspiration, magisterial interpretation and the Holy Spirit, authority of the community of faith and *sensus fidelium*, scientific "authority" from exegesis and theology at the service of the church and magisterium)

Chapter 2: Revelation, self-understanding, and understanding of faith (existential phenomenology, analysis of experience and criticism, the correlation method and Paul Tillich, historicity and the understanding of being, self-understanding and revelation, Jesus as the normative revelation of God)

Chapter 3: The identity of faith in the process of interpretation (the development of dogma, biblical concepts of faith and contemporary interpretation, the hermeneutic work of the church led by the magisterium, socio-political implications of the gospel, orthodoxy and plurality, the meaning of the *symbolum fidei*)

---

72  Original Dutch version: Edward Schillebeeckx, "Naar een katholiek gebruik van de hermeneutiek," *Geloof bij kenterend getij: Peilingen in een seculariserend christendom*, ed. Hendrik van der Linde and H.A.M. Fiolet (Roermond: J.J. Romen & Zonen, 1967), 78–116; Bas van Iersel, "Ontmythologiserende Schriftuitleg?," *Geloof bij kenterend getij: Peilingen in een seculariserend christendom*, ed. Hendrik van der Linde and H.A.M. Fiolet (Roermond: J.J. Romen & Zonen, 1967), 136–84. Students were also given the choice of reading one of the following books: Heinz Zahrnt, *Die Sache mit Gott: Die protestantische Theologie im 20. Jahrhundert* (Munich: Piper, 1967); or John Charles Cooper, *The Roots of the Radical Theology* (Philadelphia: Westminster Press, 1967).

In the following year (1968–1969, Monday mornings) most of this material was retained but sections of Part II were reorganized over a four-part course that now included significant material on linguistic analysis and the tension with literary hermeneutics due to the rising scholarly interest in the later Wittgenstein.[73] In the introduction to Part II of this course, Schillebeeckx presents the problem that necessitates a theological consideration of linguistic analysis. Modern culture functions on an experiential "Verification Principle" which creates difficulties for religious language such that "the modern human being no longer understands religious language."[74] This problem is formulated in three stages: first, modern people do not understand religious language; second, if religious language is unintelligible then it is unverifiable; and third, people *can understand* religious language but this takes special effort, specifically a call for a "new language." He affirms that "the history of dogma appears correctly as a process of continuous linguistic change (e.g., from Jewish to Hellenistic [language]). To cling to a given language against this development actually gives rise to formal heresy." Simple repetition of a dogmatic proposition, when it is not intelligible, risks distorting or losing the meaning of the dogma and therefore falling into a kind of "formal heresy." He then explores linguistic analysis as a possible "more scientific" way of understanding language because it provides a way of making the meaning of dogmatic propositions and religious speech intelligible for modern people.[75]

As Schillebeeckx's thought in this area continued to evolve, he changed tactics for the academic year of 1969–1970. Schoof tells us that in this year "he explicitly treated specific questions raised by various specialized groups" from among the students on Wednesday afternoons.[76] This is clear because the content of the course is decidedly more "theological" and less theoretical. It was broken up into five chapters: the relation of exegesis and dogmatics; the canon; the Holy Scriptures and the sacred books of other religions; ethics ("biblical ethos and modern ethics" and "ethics as hermeneutic starting point for dogmatics"); and hermeneutics in connection with pastoral theology. The mimeographed typescript includes parts of the first two chapters. He identifies a "pathological hermeneutical circle" in the interpretation of the Bible when it acts as the sole norm *and* criteria for theology. Theology becomes merely the interpretation of the specific Christian faith-tradition—revelation in the scriptures is treated as an *a priori* which then is used by theologians to interpret the same scriptures. This implies that there is no authority in the church itself as a community, but it must be based on the "external" authority of the Bible. We accept the Bible "because the church affirms the scriptures, and the scriptures further affirm the authority of the church, which is based on the bible." He identifies this as a problem in the work of Ernst Fuchs, Barth, Bultmann, and Gerhard Ebeling.

Schillebeeckx wants to locate "authority" not in an external source, but in the appeal that the *meaning* of the Bible and tradition has for a human person—the meaning must be existentially meaningful for me. At the core of this question of authority is Jesus as God's decisive work of salvation in history, but he can only be understood as such when his life is seen as authoritative

---

[73] Cf. Schoof, "E. Schillebeeckx: 25 Years in Nijmegen, I," 326–27.

[74] Ramsey, *Religious Langauge*, 12.: "According to the 'Verification Principle' we must exclude from language all propositions which cannot, at any rate, be verified by sense experience – what is seen, heard, touched, tasted and smelt."

[75] He sees this as an "ideology free" method, but not as a form of neo-positivism or a "pure" formal method because it is, in practice, impossible to perfectly separate method and content.

[76] Schoof, "E. Schillebeeckx: 25 Years in Nijmegen, I," 327.

for the ultimate meaning of human life. By historicizing Jesus's life, and by seeing "religious authority" in terms of existential meaning, Schillebeeckx wants to avoid circularity. Contact with Jesus through the scriptures or tradition is also a direct appeal to a person and an offer of ultimate meaning within a given life situation. This existential appeal is continued and reactualized in experience which can be interpreted and mediated to others. Such a faith affirmation is not empirically verifiable, as it relies on human experience of the authority of faith, but it can be made rationally understandable and acceptable. Because faith responses are experiential, there is always a certain pluralism involved, as seen in the theological pluralism of the Bible itself. It is the Christ Event that ultimately sets the boundaries of that legitimate pluralism.

Schillebeeckx goes on to classify two contemporary trends in hermeneutics. First, there is "pure hermeneutics" which deals with the Bible in a circular fashion as described above. This type has been practiced since the beginning of Christianity, and now includes the phenomenological hermeneutics of Bultmann, Fuchs, Ebeling, and Gadamer. Such a method, however, is not critical enough of its own foundations. Second, there is "critical hermeneutics," exemplified by Pannenberg, which places all "external" authority (external to the experiencing subject) under scrutiny. According to Schillebeeckx Pannenberg looks to a Hegelian view of history. In this course, we see Schillebeeckx dealing with two familiar themes but in more critical ways: the transmission of meaning through tradition, and the place of human self-understanding in that transmission. As he says, "the human being exists on the basis of self-understanding and understanding of reality." The human affirmation of "creation faith" (*scheppingsgeloof*) brings the Logos into focus as the source of creation, and from this perspective human deeds can be seen in light of God's deeds. When God is the subject of human speech, we are not today dealing with a "secular interpretation" of religion, but rather a human and secular interpretation of human words and deeds "wherein God's characteristic acts are made manifest in a special way." What these very dense paragraphs are pointing at, which I hope he explained at greater length in class, is that hermeneutics of tradition seeks to reactualize a relationship between God and humanity in each new context. Here, the content of revelation helps to form human perception of reality, but revelation can only reach humanity in and through that contextual reality of which it becomes an integral part. Revelation, he tells us, "correlates with human self-understanding. The interpretive answers [to revelation] belong to the core of revelation itself. Revelation is therefore only given in the human answer to reality." Revelation is definitively given in the person of Jesus and we can identify God's decisive salvific in history in Jesus's life, revealing the ultimate meaning of human life. This, coupled with the normative function of Jesus for the contemporary interpretation of faith, logically leads to the question of who Jesus was and what we can know about him; precisely the questions addressed by Schillebeeckx's first *Jesus* book.[77]

---

[77] As Schoof puts it, can "the universal nature and transcendence of Jesus also be maintained in the modern age? This points toward the book, [*Jesus:*] *An Experiment in Christology*." Ibid., 328.

# Critical theory

The course of 1970–1971 is a significant step in Schillebeeckx's teaching on hermeneutics. This course was divided into two parts, with Part I dealing with "theory" and Part II with practical, or pragmatic rules of thumb for theological interpretation based on the theoretical work from Part I. The syllabus gives no outline for Part II, but Part I is structured in three chapters, each of which represents part of the hermeneutic problem. The first chapter is a presentation of hermeneutic theory and the possibility of "objective" interpretation over-against the subjective aspect found in "the new hermeneutics." The chapter was to include two practical exercises based on contemporary interpretations of examples from the Old Testament and New Testament. Chapter 2 is based on Schillebeeckx's own work on ideology critique and critical theory which would later be published in *The Understanding of Faith* in 1972.[78] Chapter 3 continued with linguistic analysis and what this field can potentially contribute to a "non-arbitrary" theological hermeneutics. Most significant here are: first, Schillebeeckx's primary reference point for hermeneutical interpretation is the meaning of the Bible; second, this marks a more complete integration of critical theory in his work, including a lengthy dialogue with Habermas (and the Gadamer-Habermas debate), as well as material on the first-generation members of the Frankfurt School of social critical theory including Adorno, Max Horkheimer, and Marcuse, as well as Bloch insofar as he can be considered part of the Frankfurt School.[79] Bloch had been on Schillebeeckx's radar starting around 1965–1966, in conjunction with Moltmann, Metz, and Pannenberg. Interestingly, critical theory is first seen in Schillebeeckx's lectures on eschatology, which began again in 1967 after a hiatus for lectures on marriage in 1962.[80]

Based on some very extensive typewritten notes on the course "World and Church" ("*Wereld en Kerk*") from 1967 to 1968 by student A. Jongerius, we can more clearly see how Schillebeeckx approached critical theory. This course gave a theological account of secularization, beginning with American "death of God" theology and moving to historical-theological accounts of secularization based on Thomas Aquinas and Albert Magnus, Robert Bellarmine, the Reformation, and Kant (followed by a break in classes for Schillebeeckx's first American lecture tour). In addition to a lengthy section on hermeneutics (including the work of Barth, Bultmann, Tillich, Ebeling, Pannenberg, and Moltmann), we can here find the earliest expression of "negative contrast experience" worked out in terms of eschatological hope and stemming from a political-ethical consideration of *Gaudium et spes* (pp. 15–20). Ultimately, *Gaudium et spes* tells us that in "scanning the signs of the times" we are expected to deal with contemporary problems in the light of the gospel and human experience (p. 15). Based on the ethical imperative of negative contrast experiences, Christian eschatological faith must have a socio-political critical function (p. 18), which he links to a hermeneutics of the Rule of God. The Rule of God can never be identified with what already exists, but it can must be worked out

---

[78] An additional source was the 1969 German translation of: Peter Berger and Thomas Luckmann, *The Social Construction of Reality: A Treatise in the Sociology of Knowledge* (Garden City, NY: Anchor Books, 1966).

[79] See Edward Schillebeeckx, "The New Critical Theory," *UF, CW* vol. 5 (London: Bloomsbury T&T Clark, 2014), 90–95 [103–09].

[80] Schoof, "E. Schillebeeckx: 25 Years in Nijmegen, I," 323, 328.

within history itself and not above or outside of historical reality—history must be made into a history of salvation (p. 20).

This shows a clear link with the "theory-praxis" mediation central to critical theory. From here, Schillebeeckx comes to another key concept that had not yet been fully worked out in print—the "new image of God" wherein God's transcendence is identified with the coming future.[81] The "new image of God" also implies a "new image of humanity," or a new theological anthropology that comprises modern self-understanding. The modern human being is oriented toward the future and intent on reshaping the world through human initiative. Based on his reading of *Gaudium et spes*, God reveals humanity to itself through revelation (*GS* 22, 38, 40, 41), placing human self-understanding (anthropology) in a reciprocal relationship with our images of God (theology).[82] Thus, at this early stage, eschatological faith in the transcendent future, identified with salvation coming from God, is explicitly connected to hermeneutics through critical negativity in order to determine the meaning and content of orthopraxis. He builds this based in part on an evaluation of the "death of God" theologies current in the moment, but his creative reading of these authors yields a much more durable and interesting set of insights than the original thinkers themselves offer.[83] Further, we can clearly see that hermeneutics is a nexus-point for fundamental and dogmatic theology as a grounding principle for ongoing evaluation and expression of human experience, including faith experience.[84]

# Conclusion

The content and context of Schillebeeckx's work changed dramatically during the 1960s, thanks in part to his own inclinations and interests, and also because of the irresistible influence of outside factors, such as the Second Vatican Council and the changes it helped to bring about. It is, however, impossible to entirely separate one from the other. It is interesting to see how rapidly his focus shifted from the work on sacraments to questions of method as the needs of the church changed. In order to properly address "traditional" topics like the sacraments, eschatological salvation, and the relation of the church to the world, new language was required to be able to meaningfully express the content of Christian faith to contemporary people. "For a very long time," Schillebeeckx writes, "catholic [*sic*] theologians looked for a purely metaphysically orientated 'natural theology,' which tried to attribute meaning to God before [God] began to

---

[81]   The first attempt at this future-oriented "new image of God" was already in print as Edward Schillebeeckx, "Het nieuwe mens- en Godsbeeld in conflict met het religieuze leven," *TvT* 7 (1967), 1–27. His more well-known synthesis of eschatology and secularization theory appeared in early 1968 as "Het nieuwe Godsbeeld, secularisatie en politiek," *TvT* 8 (1968), 44–65. In English as Edward Schillebeeckx, "The New Image of God," *GFM, CW* vol. 3 (London: Bloomsbury T&T Clark, 2014), 101–25 [169–203].

[82]   Minch, "Eschatology and Theology of Hope," 279–80.

[83]   See Thomas J.J. Altizer and William Hamilton, eds., *Radical Theology and the Death of God* (Indianapolis/New York/Kansas City: Bobbs-Merrill Company, 1966).

[84]   In the typescript we find the note: "the [act of] being-human has a fundamentally dialogical character" (p. 4).

speak." Such a theology was a failure having proved itself to be unintelligible, "precisely because of its rigid and abstractly metaphysical standpoint."[85]

In order to be *credible*, Christian faith must be *intelligible*, although as "faith" it can never be made purely *rational*. Taking a key point from linguistic analysis, meaning logically precedes truth.[86] Only a statement that we experience as meaningful can prove to be true or false. Ultimately, this is intimately related to contemporary belief in Jesus. Despite widespread "secularization" and large drops in church attendance during this time period, especially in the Netherlands, Jesus seemed to be everywhere in different forms: scholarly books, popular media, films including *The Greatest Story Ever Told* (1965) and Pasolini's *The Gospel According to St. Matthew* (1964), and eventually the countercultural Jesus Movement in the United States in the early 1970s. The church teaches that Jesus is the source of salvation, God's decisive salvific act in history. It is therefore unsurprising that Schillebeeckx's courses focused explicitly on "salvation in Jesus coming from God" and considerations of who Jesus is and how we can meaningfully interpret him—this is the core of his Christological project.[87]

---

[85] Schillebeeckx, "Correlation Between Human Question and Christian Answer," *UF, CW* vol. 5 (London: Bloomsbury T&T Clark, 2014), 77 [88].

[86] Ibid.

[87] Ted Schoof, "E. Schillebeeckx: 25 Years in Nijmegen, II," *Theology Digest* 38 (1991), 32.

# Chapter 10

# Interpretation and Interrelation of Tradition and Situation

## *Schillebeeckx's Later Theological Hermeneutics*

### Daniel Minch

"A modern theologian," Edward Schillebeeckx wrote in 1967, "may feel *secure* as a believer and yet *hesitant* as a theologian—in this, he is respecting the mystery."[1] In 1972, a number of articles were collected into volume 5 of *Theological Soundings* (*Theologische peilingen*) and published as *The Understanding of Faith* (English: 1974).[2] Here, he explored the task of "modern theology" more deeply in order to try and locate a firm starting point for speaking about Christian faith in a modern, rapidly secularizing context. To carry out the hermeneutical task of faithfully reinterpreting Christian truth claims, it became necessary for him to engage deeply with both methods of interpretation and thinkers who sharply criticized traditions of experience and their language as inherently oppressive. Ultimately, Schillebeeckx came to believe that his former metaphysical presuppositions could no longer be easily assumed or universalized. This sent him in search of a new point of contact for expressing human self-understanding in relation to God.

In this chapter, I will proceed by first looking at Schillebeeckx's foundational insights into the task and principles of theological hermeneutics. For this task, I will point to key methodological texts written by Schillebeeckx, including elements of his Christology. The most important of these come from *The Understanding of Faith* and the 1968 publication *God the Future of Man*.[3] I will examine the interface of critical theory and hermeneutics in his work, which led to the development of negative contrast experience. This section will also include Schillebeeckx's use of linguistic analysis for assessing the possibility of universal human meaning. This will lead to an assessment of how hermeneutics serves as a "structure" for human subjectivity, rather than merely as a method. This structure is ultimately oriented toward the eschatological future. In the final section of this chapter, I will examine Schillebeeckx's valedictory lecture, "Theological Interpretation of

---

[1] Schillebeeckx, "Towards a Catholic Use of Hermeneutics," *GFM, CW* vol. 3 (London: Bloomsbury T&T Clark, 2014), 13 [19].

[2] Edward Schillebeeckx, *Geloofsverstaan: Interpretatie en kritiek*, Theologische peilingen 5 (Bloemendaal: Nelissen, 1972).

[3] *God the Future of Man* was the published result of his 1967 lecture tour of the United States, and interestingly it appeared first in English and was never made available in Dutch as a "book," although each of the chapters were published as articles in 1967–1968. The first chapter of *God the Future of Man*, "Towards a Catholic Use of Hermeneutics" from 1967, was used as the first chapter of the Dutch version of *The Understanding of Faith*.

Faith 1983," in order to explore his concept of the "proportional norm" of continuity as well as his later thoughts on the interrelation of "tradition" and "situation." This chapter will elucidate the intrinsic connection between salvation and hermeneutics for Schillebeeckx's work, such that it is accurate to call it an "eschatological hermeneutics" of human existence.

# I. Developing a Catholic use of hermeneutics

Edward Schillebeeckx's first major article on hermeneutics lays out the contours of the "hermeneutic problem" based on the contingency of human life. The "rediscovery of man's true historicity as a creature of time," as he writes in 1969, places humanity on course toward the future but only on the basis of an awareness of the past.[4] But it also throws into question how we perceive and mediate meaning in light of that historicity. No "concepts," even transcendental ones, can be entirely isolated from the contemporary existential situation. Material repetition is no guarantee of orthodoxy and can even become a serious danger. The meaning of words, as co-constituted by the context, changes over time, so what is an appropriate and faithful expression of truth in one era may become misleading in another era. The meaning of an utterance within the horizon of the past, as a historical entity, remains valid, but the point is about how it can become meaningful *for us*. Formulations like those of Chalcedon and Trent continue to be meaningful as expressions of the truth of faith for us, but not automatically, independent of context or the question of meaning.

The "old solution" to the hermeneutical problem involves the metaphor of the essential "kernel" and "husk" or the mode of expression. The traditional Catholic way of phrasing this was to draw a distinction between "the 'essential dogmatic affirmation' (the *id quod*) and its 'mode of expression' (the *modus cum quo*)."[5] Schillebeeckx points out that this model implies a more "objective" historical view of what is "essential" and what is contingent. He denies, however, that an earlier formulation of the faith is "the pure content of faith"; rather, it is a *faithful interpretation* of the faith for the era in which it was created. During periods of transition between different paradigms or interpretations, we run into distinct problems and disjunctions between older and newer expressions. His present context was such a time of transition, which, in the wake of the Second Vatican Council and rising secularization in Europe, is quite clear.

## The "new" hermeneutical problem

Schillebeeckx's engagement with modern hermeneutic philosophy was theologically determined from the beginning. Schillebeeckx acknowledges that Catholic theology has actually been involved with this problem for a long time under the category of "development of dogma"; however, his earliest explicit reflections on hermeneutics came in response to difficulties raised by Rudolph Bultmann.[6] The modern discussion of "the hermeneutic problem" descends from

---

[4]   Edward Schillebeeckx, "The Interpretation of the Future," *UF, CW* vol. 5 (London: Bloomsbury, 2014), 3 [4].
[5]   Schillebeeckx, "Catholic Use of Hermeneutics," *GFM*, 6–7 [10–12].
[6]   Ibid., 3–4 [5–7].

Friedrich Schleiermacher, who inaugurated the study of "general hermeneutics" as the art or science of interpretation.[7] This gives rise to what we know as "the hermeneutic circle"—the interrelation of "whole" and "part" in the recognition of meaning in a text, or the relation between the reader and the text. The hermeneutic circle has become central to any study of literature or literary theory and remains one of the main philosophical starting points for any theory of history.[8] The great historians and biblical scholars of the nineteenth century derived their work in part from the "general" hermeneutical principles or laws given by Schleiermacher. This led from Romantic hermeneutics to the development of "historicist" methodologies.

Martin Heidegger brought about a new development in the search for the universal structure of understanding by locating it in the realm of fundamental ontology rather than merely at the level of epistemology.[9] Understanding is not a "function" performed by human beings, but co-constitutive of human being-in-the-world in the first place. Here, hermeneutics becomes "a fundamental theory of how understanding emerges in human existence," not as an attribute of subjectivity, but in the very existence of the subject within the world in which it is always already included.[10] Hermeneutics is not fundamentally about an epistemological attribute of human consciousness, but it is a question of how human beings are and become themselves in the world and in history. This understanding of "ontological" hermeneutics builds on Schillebeeckx's earlier reading of Heidegger in relation to transcendence and "the secular." Human transcendence has a horizontal dimension that constitutes a historically situated self-transcendence: "Emerging from a particular past, [the human being] is continually finding himself [*sic*] in a particular situation from which he projects a new future."[11] Humanity is constituted as self-transcending freedom, but within a historical and temporal context. The orientation of the self-transcending human subject *from* the past *within* the present and *toward* the future constitutes the existential situation and the starting point for theological hermeneutics. With this in mind, Schillebeeckx's earliest published considerations on hermeneutics begin with Bultmann, who was greatly influenced by the early Heidegger.[12] He then continued to expand his work through reading Heidegger, Paul Ricoeur, and Hans-Georg Gadamer.[13] Both Gadamer and Ricoeur had a lasting effect on Schillebeeckx's theology, although Gadamer appears more prominently in citations from this period.

Schillebeeckx's first efforts present a standard version of "the hermeneutic circle": understanding occurs in a "circular" movement between the question–answer structure of

---

[7]  Richard E. Palmer, *Hermeneutics: Interpretation Theory in Schleiermacher, Dilthey, Heidegger, and Gadamer*, Northwestern University Studies in Phenomenology and Existential Philosophy (Evanston, IL: Northwestern University Press, 1988), 84–97.

[8]  Paul H. Fry, *Theory of Literature*, The Open Yale Courses Series (New Haven, CT: Yale University Press, 2012), 27–38.

[9]  Palmer, *Hermeneutics*, 130–32.

[10]  Ibid., 137.

[11]  Edward Schillebeeckx, *God and Man*, trans. Edward Fitzgerald and Peter Tomlinson, Theological Soundings (New York: Sheed and Ward, 1969), 162.

[12]  Helmut Peukert, "Bultmann and Heidegger," *Rudolph Bultmann in Catholic Thought*, ed. Thomas F. O'Meara and Donald M. Weisser (New York, NY: Herder and Herder, 1968), 196–221.

[13]  Mark Schoof, O.P., "Masters in Israel: VII. The Later Theology of Edward Schillebeeckx," *The Clergy Review* 55, no. 12 (1970), 952–55. Schillebeeckx was involved in awarding an honorary doctorate to Paul Ricoeur in 1968. See his address on the occasion: Edward Schillebeeckx, "Le philosophe Paul Ricœur, docteur en théologie," *Christianisme social* 76 (1968), 639–45.

preunderstanding. Each "question" arises out of an earlier preunderstanding of the world and presupposes an answer. Another way of presenting this is the problem of "parts" and "whole": we know reality, especially as objectified in a text, through the parts that give us a sense and expectation of the meaning of the whole, which is either confirmed or altered through taking on more "parts."[14] In Bultmann's analysis, this "develops into a circle between self-understanding (man's [*sic*] understanding of his own existence) and the understanding of faith," which gives rise to the "existential" interpretation of Christian faith and the New Testament.[15] It is the existential existence of the human subject in relation to the given datum of revelation as God's Word *for me* in the interiority of human experience and of the conscience.[16] Bultmann draws a distinction between "what is said" (*das Gesagte*) and "what is intended" (*das Gemeinte*) in the biblical texts, which allows him to apply his method of "demythologization" to the texts in order to separate its intention from mythological language used by a past culture.[17] Protestant scholars like Bultmann were particularly concerned with the interpretation of the Bible for modern people, following the Reformation principle of *sola scriptura* and Karl Barth's emphasis on the radical otherness and uniqueness of God's Word as encountered in the Bible.[18] For Catholic theology, however, hermeneutics inevitably involves tradition, doctrine, and magisterium. Theologians must search for appropriate expressions of the faith in their contexts, while the magisterium acts as "the judge of our *hermeneia* or interpretation of faith and the Bible."[19] Given this responsibility of theologians, he outlines some hermeneutic principles for Catholic interpretation.

## Distanciation: The pastness of the past

The first major principle for hermeneutic interpretation is the hermeneutic function of distanciation, or the "gap" between the past and the present. The hermeneutic task is not merely bridging a void or a gap between the author and the present through a kind of re-experiencing or transposition, as Schleiermacher contended. Following Gadamer, the intervening history between past event and the present interpretation is what forms the background for our present horizon of understanding. Human consciousness is a historically effected consciousness, or one formed by the "history of effects" (*Wirkungsgeschichte*) that constitutes the historical distance between the horizon of the past and that of the present.[20] An event in the past produces effects that continue in time. These effects cannot be ignored in historical interpretation by simply transposing my consciousness into a "pure past" since that past has produced the present. Understanding is therefore not merely

---

14  Schillebeeckx, "Catholic Use of Hermeneutics," *GFM*, 4–5 [7–8].

15  Ibid., 5 [9].

16  Thomas F. O'Meara, "Bultmann and Tomorrow's Theology," *Rudolph Bultmann in Catholic Thought*, ed. Thomas F. O'Meara and Donald M. Weisser (New York, NY: Herder and Herder, 1968), 222–49.

17  Rudolf Bultmann, "New Testament and Mythology: The Problem of Demythologizing the New Testament Proclamation," *New Testament and Mythology and Other Basic Writings*, trans. Schubert M. Ogden (London: SMC Press, 1985), 10–15.

18  See Schillebeeckx, "Correlation Between Human Question and Christian Answer," *UF, CW* vol. 5 (London: Bloomsbury T&T Clark, 2014), 76–77 [87–88].

19  Schillebeeckx, "Catholic Use of Hermeneutics," *GFM*, 12 [17–18].

20  Hans-Georg Gadamer, *Truth and Method*, trans. Joel Weinsheimer and Donald G. Marshall, 2nd ed. (London/New York: Continuum, 2004), 301.

a subjective act transcending historicity but is rather a participation in *"an event of tradition,"* which is a continual mediation of the past and present.[21] Whereas Schleiermacher focuses on understanding the mind and motivations of an author, Gadamer concentrates on the text itself. Although an author produces a text, the author cannot control how the text is received or interpreted. Ricoeur takes this a step further, saying that the distance of a text and the interpreter, whether in temporal, cultural, or linguistic terms, "is not only what understanding must conquer, but it is also its condition."[22] Distanciation is necessary for interpretation, since understanding only occurs through some kind of confrontation with otherness—there is a "polarity of familiarity and strangeness."[23]

The space between the horizons of past and present is "filled by the continuity of tradition."[24] Gadamer appeals to the authority of tradition as providing the "pre-understanding" necessary for interpretation via linguistic tools, symbols, and images, which allow people to communicate, discern, and ultimately to understand anything at all. The pre-understanding imparted by tradition is not static, but always exists in a state of hermeneutic flux. We understand the "whole" of a situation based on a prior expectation of meaning. We then interpret the "parts" that arise in experience in light of our pre-understanding. The future is already present in understanding as implied in the "expectation" of experiences to come.[25] Understanding occurs in the fusion of the past and present horizons in the act of judgment. The "fusion of horizons" is performed in understanding and reveals the interconnectedness of the past and present, and thereby also a continuity between the two.[26] This continuity is not necessarily an easy continuity. How we see past events must change as we move forward in time, since the accumulation of events inevitably changes our self-understanding and understanding of reality, which has a reciprocal influence on how we will then reinterpret events. We do not understand the New Testament in the same way as the Council Fathers of Trent because our place in the history of effects gives us a different form of self-understanding.

When we attempt to understand an event, we are implicitly asking a question about its meaning. The question is not the product of a purely "scientific" or objective consciousness, but arises out of our pre-understanding, and is historically situated. It comes from the point of view of the interpreter who stands in a specific historical tradition. The meaning and "concepts of a historical past" are gained, therefore, "in such a way that they also include our own comprehension of them."[27] There is no transcendent point beyond history that provides objective access to the "whole": "Historical objectivity is the truth of the past *in the light of the present* and not simply a reconstruction of the past in its unrepeatable factuality."[28] Thus, Schillebeeckx's particular understanding of human historicity is consonant with the Gadamerian rejection of positivist and historicist notions of the "objectivity" of history. The present, in other words, is not an absolute or end-moment; neither is it a "storm free zone" that is somehow superior. It is always a present

---

[21]  Ibid., 291.
[22]  Paul Ricœur, "The Hermeneutical Function of Distanciation," *Philosophy Today* 17, no. 2 (1973), 133.
[23]  Gadamer, *Truth and Method*, 295.
[24]  Schillebeeckx, "Catholic Use of Hermeneutics," *GFM*, 15 [21].
[25]  Gadamer, *Truth and Method*, 305–6.
[26]  Ibid., 305.
[27]  Ibid., 367.
[28]  Schillebeeckx, "Catholic Use of Hermeneutics," *GFM*, 17 [24]. Emphasis original.

*in history on the way to a future*. By coming out of a particular past, the act of understanding presupposes both a *question* about meaning and *answers* based on the expectation of meaning.

# Prejudices and authority

Tradition shapes pre-understanding and thereby partially determines how the process of understanding operates. The formation of the "question" of meaning itself arises in a historical situation and is therefore historically conditioned. Certainly, this also means that the interpreter must submit to the authority of the text to a certain extent. The text determines what we can get from it in terms of valid meaning.[29] Tradition lays claim to authority, and this authority "has power over our attitudes and behavior."[30] Here, Gadamer introduces the role of "prejudices," which are produced by the interpretive framework that arises out of a tradition.[31] Prejudices are not exclusively negative; they play a positive role in interpretation and understanding by providing a baseline for our expectations of the world, literally as "pre-judgments" of what the world is like. These are then either confirmed or corrected through experience. The interpreter can never eliminate presuppositions entirely. By bringing something into speech, we do not merely express a prior "non-linguistic" intuition or understanding, but are actually engaged in the act of understanding itself.[32] Language has an ontological function and an original relation to human becoming in the world since it is instrumental to human self-understanding. Understanding is, in fact, interpretation, "and all interpretation takes place in the medium of a language that allows the object to come into words."[33]

In keeping with the "linguistic turn" in existential philosophy, Schillebeeckx refers to the "ontological aspect of language," which precedes logical and structuralist analysis.[34] Language is the medium through which human beings experience the world, while tradition is likewise made up of linguistic components. To be "experienced in" a tradition is to have access to a language that must always be "translated" in the confrontation with contemporary experience. Language is never static or frozen; it is always in a state of flux, constantly being renewed and actualized through use in the present. So the past, as tradition, has authority, but it never appears as an "objective" meaning of history that could be viewed, as it were, from "outside" of history. Hence, meaning is always also linguistic and appears through the fusion of horizons.

In his early reflections on hermeneutics, Schillebeeckx goes on to criticize "the new hermeneutics" from an eschatological perspective. His criticisms are aimed at Bultmann (and his followers), but also at Gadamer. First, Bultmann still presupposes a form of the "kernel" and "husk" solution to the hermeneutic problem, but he locates the solution in the subjective rather than in the objective side of the equation. For Bultmann, the truth of the gospel is encountered

---

[29] Ibid., 16–17 [26].
[30] Gadamer, *Truth and Method*, 281.
[31] Ibid., 272–73.
[32] Ibid., 399.
[33] Ibid., 390.
[34] Schillebeeckx, "Linguistic Criteria," *UF, CW* vol. 5 (London: Bloomsbury T&T Clark, 2014), 24 [37–38].

in subjective existential experience rather than in "objective" doctrinal formulations. The distinction between "what is said" and "what is intended" assumes that the author never actually says what is meant or means what is said, and the "comfortable consequence of this for the interpreter is that he can insert his own meanings into the text."[35] Second, Bultmann's use of hermeneutics is not radical enough, because "what is intended" is not always fully or consciously manifest in "what is said."[36] Meaning arises from the text irrespective of the author's intentions. Third, Schillebeeckx argues that the perspective of the new hermeneutic thinkers is "ultimately one-sided because they question only those human existential possibilities *that have already been brought to expression*."[37] By emphasizing the dynamic between the past and present so strongly, these thinkers neglect the possibilities presented by the future, which is essential for a biblical perspective on reality. They forget that which is "new and completely *unprecedented*" as it appears in reality, because of either a reliance on the existential attitude of the individual (Bultmann) or the *de facto* authority afforded to tradition in experience (Gadamer).[38] He credits Wolfhart Pannenberg and Jürgen Moltmann for trying to correct this problem, and Moltmann in particular for pointing to a biblical understanding of history in terms of God's promise.[39] This eschatological view of history has essential consequences for our relation to dogma—dogmas are themselves oriented toward the coming future, implying an "openness to the future and to new historical realizations."[40] This helps account for the lack of objectivity in language due to its historical nature. There is no "explicitly fixed *representation* of truth," which is different from claiming that there is no content of faith at all, or that we do not have access to it.[41]

Anticipating his integration of critical theory into an overall hermeneutical framework, Schillebeeckx points toward the need for a hermeneutics of praxis.[42] He credits Gadamer's emphasis on the importance of legal hermeneutics for this insight. The performative aspect of legal hermeneutics—the need to *apply* the text of the law in the present—points to the dialectical unity of theory and praxis. This unity appears in the faithful application of the gospel in pursuit of the Rule of God, thus professing and practicing Christian faith and thereby making that faith true. This is an essentially ecclesial task, because the reality of faith can only be revealed to the world through dialogue with the church, and specifically "by the Church as *sacramentum mundi*."[43] Ultimately, however, the "object of faith is God, who in Christ is the *future* of humanity."[44]

---

[35]  Schillebeeckx, "Theological Criteria," *UF, CW* vol. 5 (London: Bloomsbury T&T Clark, 2014), 51 [57].
[36]  Schillebeeckx, "Catholic Use of Hermeneutics," *GFM*, 22 [32].
[37]  Ibid., 24 [35]. Emphasis original.
[38]  Ibid.
[39]  Jürgen Moltmann, *Theology of Hope: On the Ground and Implications of a Christian Eschatology*, trans. James W. Leitch (Minneapolis: Fortress Press, 1993), 95–138.
[40]  Schillebeeckx, "Catholic Use of Hermeneutics," *GFM*, 24 [36].
[41]  Ibid., 27 [40].
[42]  Gadamer, *Truth and Method*, 321–36, 398–99. See Schillebeeckx, "Catholic Use of Hermeneutics," *GFM*, 25 [37].
[43]  Schillebeeckx, "Catholic Use of Hermeneutics," *GFM*, 29 [43].
[44]  Ibid., 25 [28]. Translation amended.

# II. Critical theory and questioning language

The use of new philosophical sources in Catholic theology clearly accelerated after the Second Vatican Council, especially as theologians searched for the proper ways to implement reforms and effectively communicate the faith in a rapidly changing situation. One of the main problems faced by theology was the estrangement between "theory," the content of (especially neoscholastic) theology, and "praxis," the everyday experiences of Christians in society.[45] This perceived gap was precisely the problem that the worker priest movement set out to tackle in the 1940s' France and Belgium. After the Second Vatican Council, some theologians began to use tools provided by the neo-Marxist critical theory more broadly.[46] Marx's famed eleventh thesis on Feuerbach became programmatic: rather than merely interpret the world (philosophically or theologically), the goal should be to change the world.[47] The rediscovery by the Second Vatican Council of biblical theology as a starting point for systematic theology and the rise of a new "political theology" also fueled a turn toward social engagement, rather than a theology based on private piety and reflection. The use of Marxist theory gained global importance thanks especially to Latin American liberation theology, which eventually drew the ire of Joseph Ratzinger and the Congregation for the Doctrine of the Faith. Schillebeeckx's attempt to meaningfully engage with critical praxis within a hermeneutic framework holds a significant place in this history.[48]

## Two approaches: Negative contrast, positive meaning

Schillebeeckx's four major essays on hermeneutics and critical theory, forming chapters 4–7 of *The Understanding of Faith,* were all originally published in *Tijdschrift voor Theologie* during 1969–1971. It is significant that the so-called "Gadamer-Habermas debate" also occurred around this time. Habermas questioned the "universality" of hermeneutic experience and of hermeneutic

---

[45] Gregory Baum, "The Impact of Marxist Ideas on Christian Theology," *The Twentieth Century: A Theological Overview*, ed. Gregory Baum (Maryknoll, NY: Orbis, 1999), 179–81.

[46] Several authors have pointed to the influence of the Belgian Marcel Xhaufflaire's work on Schillebeeckx in his turn to critical theory. Xhaufflaire was part of a short-lived movement of radical Catholicism in Germany and the Benelux countries known as "critical" Catholicism, "contestation" theology, or the Tegenspraak Collective. See Steven M. Rodenborn, *Hope in Action: Subversive Eschatology in the Theology of Edward Schillebeeckx and Johann Baptist Metz* (Minneapolis, MN: Fortress Press, 2014), 136–41; Dennis Rochford, "The Appropriation of Hermeneutics in the Theological Works of Edward Schillebeeckx : An Historical Textual Evaluation of the Theological Project to Bridge Christian Faith with Modern Culture" (Dissertation, Katholieke Universiteit Leuven, 1995), 4.12–4.16. For a partial summary of Tegenspraak's history, see Karl Derksen, "Theologie – praxis – context: Fasen op een weg," *Meedenken met Edward Schillebeeckx*, ed. Herman Häring, Ted Schoof, and Ad Willems (Baarn: H. Nelissen, 1983), 115–29.

[47] Baum, "The Impact of Marxist Ideas on Christian Theology," 182. Schillebeeckx, "Theological Criteria," *UF*, 53 [59], 59 [66]; Edward Schillebeeckx, "The New Critical Theory and Theological Hermeneutics," *UF, CW* vol. 5 (London: Bloomsbury T&T Clark, 2014), 109 [124].

[48] See Chapter 26 in this volume by Michael E. Lee.

structures.[49] His concern was that, by raising hermeneutics above the general level of the particular sciences and by giving priority to tradition in the formation of pre-understanding, the critical role of science and reflection is negated.[50] To some extent, he misreads Gadamer, placing more emphasis on the automatic authority of tradition than Gadamer in fact does, but his critique of inherited language and linguistic structures is important. Habermas's Marxist perspective shows that "[l]anguage is *also* a medium of domination and social power; it serves to legitimate relations of organized force," making language ideological insofar as it replicates and confirms oppressive power structures.[51] Habermas is correct in this, although his solution involves a radicalization of the Enlightenment ideal of "reflection" in unmasking prejudices, such that this reflection can break up prejudices and transcend tradition entirely.

Ultimately, Schillebeeckx does not accept all of Habermas's critiques of hermeneutics, but he does acknowledge that Gadamer has an implicit faith in the trustworthiness of the tradition as a communicator of meaning. Following Habermas, hermeneutic interpretation is only realized *theoretically* or based on the interpretation of meaning in the present. This "practical" critique is essential for Christian faith because its realization is always eschatologically contingent: "although the object of faith has indeed been realized, in Christ, it has only been realised as our promise and our future."[52] Hermeneutics must *also* have a practical-critical intention so that the past can be approached critically and creatively as "action in faith" or as critical praxis. As a critical observation, this does not introduce a major problem for his hermeneutical framework, which is already oriented toward the future thanks to his underlying eschatological concerns. However, there is a problem in terms of making any "God-talk," or theological content, meaningfully available to contemporary people.

## Linguistic criteria for talking about God

Modern "correlation theology," with which Schillebeeckx has been associated, attempts to assign universal significance to "God" as the answer to human questions about meaning. The assumption is that God is relevant for human life, and even if only vaguely, "secular" questions can and actually must ultimately be answered "theologically." Schillebeeckx points to two major problems with this assumption, both of which concern intelligibility. First, there is the problem of mediation, where transcendent revelation is expressed in human words and "God" becomes the highest possible being in thought.[53] Second, there is the problem of making a "category error" in speaking about God between different language games: "God, an essentially religious reality,

---

[49] *Hermeneutik und Ideologiekritik*, Theorie-Diskussion (Frankfurt am Main: Suhrkamp, 1971); Jürgen Habermas, "A Review of Gadamer's Truth and Method," *The Hermeneutic Tradition: From Ast to Ricoeur*, ed. Gayle L. Ormiston and Alan D. Schrift (Albany, NY: SUNY Press, 1990), 213–44; Hans-Georg Gadamer, "The Universality of the Hermeneutic Problem," *The Hermeneutic Tradition: From Ast to Ricoeur*, ed. Gayle L. Ormiston and Alan D. Schrift (Albany, NY: SUNY Press, 1990), 147–58.

[50] Habermas, "A Review of Gadamer's Truth and Method," 237–39.

[51] Ibid., 239.

[52] Schillebeeckx, "Theological Criteria," *UF*, 53 [59].

[53] Schillebeeckx, "Correlation," *UF*, 74 [84–85]. This would lead to "silence" about God, as proposed by the Death of God theologians, which he rejects. The experience of God necessitates speaking about God, even if in an apophatic way.

can therefore not be the answer to a non-religious question."[54] He follows the later Wittgenstein's concept of "language games," although not without some critical distance.[55] Schillebeeckx is asking how God can be relevant for modern people without their having to accept both the religious language game and alienating traditional formulations of the faith. From the perspectives of both philosophical linguistic analysis and Christian faith, it matters whether or not God functions in a properly theistic way that respects the givenness of creation and the transcendence of God. If God is merely the answer to any question, regardless of the language game, then this God is merely a stop-gap solution to explain the world as it is, negating the gratuity of creation, the divinity of God, and the credibility of Christian faith claims.[56] Faith should not be an unintelligible decision or a claim to a purely exclusive realm of meaning within human language.

Schillebeeckx is looking for a way to bridge the "universality gap" between human language and Christian experience, or a kind of "natural theology" that can address different language games and still point to the same reality. This is possible because Schillebeeckx categorizes *interpretation*—the actualization of meaning from the past in the language of the present—as the "language game of human history."[57] Meaning is always presupposed in interpretation because it is praxically realized in history. The ability to continually realize meaning based on the interrelation of language games through meaningful interpretation draws a "bridge" between linguistic analysis and hermeneutics. Thus, "the meaning of one language game is interpreted in another language game and, in this case, not according to the norms of meaning and meaninglessness which are specific to one language game, but in real diachronic communication."[58] If theology is seen as part of the religious "language game," it is also a part of the wider "language game of human history" that is hermeneutic interpretation.

As Philip Kennedy writes, "if language is a form of life, then praxis (human history) may be regarded as a wider criterion of meaning (than a purely theoretical interpretation) of faith."[59] Although faith does not find its justification, or its truth content, in reason, the occurrence of revelation in human history makes it accessible for reason in a certain way. The most important gain from Schillebeeckx's studies in this area is that linguistic analysis does not assume that texts are meaningful. That a text is meaningful must first be proven based on logic, or internal analysis of the text itself. Even logic, however, is still subject to the conditions of perspective and historicity, since these elements change the meaning of what is said and how logic can be applied.[60] This leads Schillebeeckx to a key insight: "Propositions can be meaningful or meaningless, but only meaningful propositions can be true or untrue."[61] A meaningless statement cannot be judged to

---

54  Ibid., 75 [86].
55  Schillebeeckx, "Linguistic Criteria," *UF*, 39 [43]. See Ludwig Wittgenstein, *Philosophische Untersuchungen/ Philosophical Investigations*, trans. G.E.M. Anscombe, P.M.S. Hacker, and Joachim Schulte, Revised 4th edition (Chichester, West Sussex/ Malden, MA: Wiley-Blackwell, 2009); Norman Malcom, "Wittgenstein's Philosophical Investigations," *The Philosophical Review* 63, no. 4 (1954), 530–59.
56  Schillebeeckx, "Correlation," *UF*, 79 [90].
57  Schillebeeckx, "Linguistic Criteria," *UF*, 39 [43].
58  Ibid., 40 [44].
59  Philip Kennedy, *Deus Humanissimus: The Knowability of God in the Theology of Edward Schillebeeckx* (Fribourg: University Press Fribourg Switzerland, 1993), 194.
60  Schillebeeckx, "Linguistic Criteria," *UF*, 30–31 [33].
61  Ibid., 31 [34].

be true or untrue, and so meaning needs to be assessed prior to questions of truth. The "truth" and "meaning" of theological statements need to be treated differently, and a theological statement must be intelligible before it can be assessed according to the specific criteria for truth. Literalist readings of the Bible and material repetition of statements from the past are ruled out in advance. The only choice is, in fact, to embark on a path of critical interpretation in search of Christian meaning, which is embedded within the wider field of human history through which we come to self-understanding. This is a hermeneutic process.

This excursus on linguistic analysis is important because it points to the centrality of critical theory for theological hermeneutics. In order for religious language to be meaningful, even when it is "updated" or translated, then the realization of meaning must already be possible. The potential for hermeneutic interpretation, whether conceived of as translation, the radical constitution of meaning by the context, or even the "old" kernel/husk solution, assumes a universal horizon for the realization of meaning in history. This speaks to the ontological foundation of language and understanding in general, and so a universal pre-understanding of meaning is a kind of "metaphysical" assumption. Schillebeeckx proceeds to build the case for a universally accessible pre-understanding of meaning along two fronts: negative dialectics and positive affirmations of meaning in experience.

# Negative dialectics

Schillebeeckx's use of "negative dialectics," taken over from the work of Theodor Adorno, is one of the most famous and often misused aspects of his theological legacy.[62] He reworked this concept into his own theological category of "negative contrast experience." Here, I will not explore the ethical considerations, or the ontological-epistemological foundations of negative contrast experiences.[63] Instead, I will stick to the role of contrast experience in the hermeneutic mediation of meaning. "Critical negativity" forms the "universal pre-understanding of all positive views of man [*sic*]," based on the observation that "resistance to inhumane situations reveals, if only indirectly, at least an obscure consciousness of what must be confessed positively by human integrity."[64] In short, an experience of negative contrast is the automatic human recoil from unmerited suffering, or the reaction against being subjected to suffering because the experience

---

[62] Important sources include: Lieven Boeve, "Experience According to Edward Schillebeeckx: The Driving Force of Faith and Theology," *Divinising Experience: Essays in the History of Religious Experience from Origen to Ricoeur*, ed. Lieven Boeve and Laurence P. Hemming (Leuven: Peeters Press, 2004), 199–225; Bernadette Schwarz-Boenneke, "Die Widerständigkeit der Wirklichkeit als erstes Moment des Erfahrens," *Edward Schillebeeckx: Impulse für Theologien im 21. Jahrhundert/ Impetus Towards Theologies in the 21st Century*, ed. Thomas Eggensperger, Ulrich Engel, and Angel F. Méndez Montoya (Ostfildern: Grünewald, 2012), 94–109; Mary Catherine Hilkert, O.P., "The Threatened Humanum as Imago Dei: Anthropology and Christian Ethics," *Edward Schillebeeckx and Contemporary Theology*, ed. Lieven Boeve, Frederiek Depoortere, and Stephan van Erp (London: T&T Clark, 2010), 127–41; Kathleen Anne McManus, *Unbroken Communion: The Place and Meaning of Suffering in the Theology of Edward Schillebeeckx* (Lanham, MD: Rowman & Littlefield Publishers, 2003).

[63] I have done this extensively in: Daniel Minch, *Eschatological Hermeneutics: The Theological Core of Experience and Our Hope for Salvation*, T&T Clark Studies in Edward Schillebeeckx (New York: T&T Clark, 2018), 99–113, 121–52.

[64] Schillebeeckx, "Correlation," *UF*, 80 [92].

is identified *as suffering* and as *negative*. This reveals both a prior, more fundamental expectation of goodness and well-being:

> the absence of what things ought to be like. Thus "what should be here and now" is to a certain extent, though incipiently and still vaguely, already perceived. Protest is possible only where there is hope. A negative experience would not be a contrast-experience, nor could it excite protest, if it did not somehow contain an element of positive hope in the real possibility of a better future.[65]

Suffering points to a universal pre-understanding of positive meaning, but only implicitly. This is one of the most important gains from critical theory: "It is not really in the first place knowledge, but a praxis which is motivated by hope and within which an element of knowledge can be formulated."[66] There is no one universally valid, positive view of what humanity is or can be. The *humanum*, the fullness of humanity, cannot be theoretically interpreted, deduced from transcendental categories, or assembled from historically contingent experience. The irreducible pluralism of human life calls into question any absolutization of one pre-understanding of humanity. Such a pre-understanding would necessarily be historical, contingent, and subject to ideological pressures in its language and the worldview that it imparts. This is consistent both with Schillebeeckx's eschatological orientation toward the future and with his convictions about theological anthropology following the Second Vatican Council: there is no universally valid, positive "Christian" view of humanity because what humanity is and will become remain a mystery determined in the ongoing historical interaction between God and creation.[67] Humanity is not the "universal subject" of history, and as such cannot be theorized in a totalizing way from within history itself.[68] This does not preclude provisional and limited attempts at realizing human meaning, but self-realization is given in hermeneutic interpretation itself, and is therefore a fact of human existence.

## Positive experiences of meaning and salvation

Despite the lack of a universal anthropology and the recognition of negativity in suffering, there are positive experiences in human history, both collective and individual. There is also the universal *possibility* of meaning that grounds all negative experiences, which are experienced as meaninglessness, or non-sense. Negativity breaks into human experience against an expectation of goodness and "sense." As such, it is impossible to theoretically project the meaning of the whole of history.[69] The existence of so much negativity subverts all attempts to interpret it away or to make it fit a predetermined utopian pattern, as if it was all in service of a universally thinkable and achievable image of the *humanum*. Without meaningfulness, critical negativity

---

[65] Edward Schillebeeckx, "The Church as the Sacrament of Dialogue," *GFM, CW* vol. 3 (London: Bloomsbury T&T Clark, 2014), 83 [136].

[66] Schillebeeckx, "Correlation," *UF*, 80 [92].

[67] Edward Schillebeeckx, "Christian Faith and Man's Expectation for the Future on Earth," *The Mission of the Church*, trans. N.D. Smith (New York: Seabury Press, 1973), 51–89.

[68] Schillebeeckx, "Correlation," *UF*, 80 [93]. God is the universal subject of history, but this can only be recognized in faith.

[69] Edward Schillebeeckx, *Christ, CW* vol. 7 (London: Bloomsbury T&T Clark, 2014), 718 [725].

would also be impossible. The full meaning of an individual human life is assembled out of particular instantiations over a lifetime of partial meaning which cohere with and reciprocally shape that person's self-understanding. Self-understanding arises from the interaction of pre-understanding and experience, placing the hermeneutic circle at the center of this process of becoming a "self." In fact, the continued praxical act of being in history shows that people decide implicitly that life is meaningful—either positively or negatively, we assume a wholeness of "meaning" in action, assigning reasons to what occurs and acting according to our beliefs. So, in praxis, individual instantiations of partial, historical meaning reveal an assumption and implicit question about "ultimate" or final meaning.[70] We can theorize and expect a total meaning of history in both individual and cosmic terms, but we can never exhaustively know or control it.

The universal expectation of meaning is not an *a priori* assumption, but only arises after critical reflection on relative experiences of suffering and "salvation" in human life. These are not yet given a religious character, as we are still not within the language game of faith. Rather, the point is that we can speak meaningfully about an "ultimate" meaning of human life and history as an intelligible human reality. Schillebeeckx does not suggest that, in the "question-answer" correlation of interpretation, we can automatically give a Christian answer to the human question about meaning. Rather, what he shows is that the answer that we anticipate to the question of the meaning of human life will always be inadequate, which throws the question itself into a new light for consideration. Humanity does not possess a fully transcendent freedom to theoretically determine these elements ahead of time. Rather, we have a "situated freedom," which allows us to realize possibilities based on the contingencies of history.[71] This is a hermeneutical freedom, because it arises from self-understanding shaped by tradition. Freedom embedded in finitude reveals to us that there is something "extra" in reality, something not determined by humanity and our history.[72] At this point, the human expectation that life "must have meaning" can be met with a specific Christian affirmation in faith that it "will have meaning," and therefore revelation builds on a universally human, "secular" foundation.[73]

## Unity of theory and praxis

Schillebeeckx ultimately rejects the "hermeneutics of the humanities" as the sole way of understanding Christian experience in the modern world. His integration of linguistic theory and critical theory added to his overall hermeneutic worldview, but they did not come to replace it; he neither reduces the Christian message to logic, nor rejects the richness of tradition wholesale. What he makes clear in his *Jesus* volumes is that the "beginning of the Christian tradition is ... not a doctrine but rather a history of experience."[74] Experience is always also interpretation, where interpretation occurs in light of received tradition. As interpreted experience, it is not, therefore, "a neutral, previously given structure, which can afterwards be directed towards the saving mystery

---

[70] Schillebeeckx, "Correlation," *UF*, 84 [96].
[71] Schillebeeckx, "The New Critical Theory and Theological Hermeneutics," *UF*, 111 [126].
[72] Schillebeeckx, "Correlation," *UF*, 87 [100].
[73] Ibid., 86 [98].
[74] Edward Schillebeeckx, *IR, CW* vol. 8 (London: Bloomsbury T&T Clark, 2014), 7 [7].

of Christ."[75] Tradition is not a preexisting unity that is automatically meaningful in every new moment and context. Rather, it is better to view the hermeneutic process as an "understanding of tradition *against* tradition."[76] If "theory" is identified with the relative continuity of past tradition understood in the present, then praxis is the application of that tradition in view of a redeemed future for humanity. This opens the way for our active responsibility for the future, guided by critical negativity as that which shows us what is essentially life-denying. Even so, critical theory cannot itself become an ideological rejection of tradition. We must maintain a tension between theoretical and practical reason. Christianity has a "logos tradition" in terms of "theory" or the hermeneutic quest for meaning.[77] But it also has an "anti-logos tradition," identified with liberating praxis, and above all with the crucifixion and resurrection of Jesus wherein "God reveals himself as wielding power over history, albeit not in the form of sovereignty but of the helplessness of the servant whom he raises up and sustains."[78]

The development of a critical theological hermeneutics has major consequences for Schillebeeckx's overall theological framework. Humanity does not fully know what it is to be human, and as we have seen, we have a difficult time anticipating either a purely "human" answer or an explicitly "Christian" answer to questions of ultimate meaning. Ontological hermeneutics provides the insight that we become "human" through self-understanding, which is inherited from the past through historical mediation of tradition. When self-understanding changes in a substantial way, then this alters what it means to be "human." We see this already in the 1967 essay, "The New Image of God, Secularization and Man's Future on Earth."[79] As a result of secularization and the gradual realization of human technological ability to shape the world based around human needs, we are now increasingly oriented toward "planning" the future through applied praxis.[80] Our concept of transcendence likewise becomes orientated toward the future rather than expressing an idealized or eternalized past that must be continued or reinstated.[81] Our understanding of "self" and "world" is necessarily altered, which has reciprocal effects on our image of God who is identified with transcendence. In continuity with the tradition of Christian *experience*, the present is the site of our "actual relationship with God" and is therefore "the hermeneutic principle for the interpretation of religious expectations of the future, but also the principle which links the future of this earth with the transcendent *eschaton*."[82] We can only really *anticipate* what this future will be based on our expectations arising out of past tradition and the fragments of sense and meaninglessness (suffering) experienced and critically taken up in the present. The lack of a universal positively defined concept of the *humanum* shatters any reasonable expectation that we can logically or dogmatically bring about a predefined utopian

---

[75] Schillebeeckx, "Theological Criteria," *UF*, 54 [60].

[76] Schillebeeckx, "The New Critical Theory and Theological Hermeneutics," *UF*, 115 [131]. Emphasis original.

[77] Schillebeeckx, "The New Critical Theory," *UF*, 92 [105].

[78] Schillebeeckx, "Theological Interpretation of Faith 1983," *Essays, CW* vol. 11 (London: Bloomsbury T&T Clark, 2014), 67.

[79] Edward Schillebeeckx, "The New Image of God," *GFM, CW* vol. 3 (London: Bloomsbury T&T Clark, 2014), 101–25 [169–203].

[80] Schillebeeckx, "The New Image of God," *GFM, CW* vol. 3 (London: Bloomsbury T&T Clark, 2014), 103–04 [172–73].

[81] Schillebeeckx, "The Interpretation of the Future," *UF*, 4 [4–5].

[82] Ibid., 9 [10].

ideal. To do so would be to enact an ideological program without regard for its historicity and its inability to meaningfully encompass the fullness of reality. This was one of the main problems that Schillebeeckx found in older forms of dogmatic theology, including that of his mentor Dominicus De Petter: "they tried to attribute meaning to God before [God] began to speak."[83]

# III. Metaphysics and hermeneutics

In 1974, Schillebeeckx published *Jesus: An Experiment in Christology* to the surprise of many in Flanders and the Netherlands who had been familiar with him as a sacramental theologian and then as an important voice in fundamental theology and theological method.[84] He never lost his concern for "dogmatic" topics, exemplified by his continued exploration of meaning and salvation. "Salvation" is in some ways the main topic of the first two *Jesus* books and *Interim Report*, but from his perspective there can be no talk of soteriology, or eschatology as *final salvation*, without Christology since it is in Jesus Christ that we encounter salvation coming from God.

> The ultimate fulfillment of man [*sic*] at the end of time, which all men are seeking but cannot formulate and can only partly realise, is the universal pre-understanding of the *humanum* that is promised to us in Christ. Eschatology and christology [*sic*] coincide essentially here.[85]

He goes on to say that, based on the New Testament, "soteriology is the way to christology [*sic*]."[86] This kind of language is already clearly visible in his 1969–1970 lectures on hermeneutics.[87] His investigations of the "historical Jesus" are meant to make Jesus and his message meaningful for modern people. He wants to avoid Bultmann's devaluation of the "historical Jesus" in favor of the Christ of faith encountered in existential experience. It matters very much who Jesus was for the plausibility of the Christian kerygma, but at the same time, we cannot interpret Jesus apart from his religious significance both now and for the first disciples.[88] Given the distance between Jesus and the texts of the New Testament, not to mention the New Testament and the secularizing context of the 1970s, a hermeneutic method is necessary to appropriately deal with the vast amount of historical-critical data.

## Eschatology and hermeneutics as structure

In Schillebeeckx's Christology, he clearly uses hermeneutics as a "method," but it also serves as a "structure"—it forms the ontological structure of human subjectivity. We have already addressed the ontological function of language and the linguisticality of being; human subjects become themselves through the interplay of interpretation and understanding in experience. Traditions,

---

83 Schillebeeckx, "Correlation," *UF*, 77 [88].
84 Edward Schillebeeckx, *Jesus, CW* vol. 6 (London: Bloomsbury T&T Clark, 2014).
85 Schillebeeckx, "Correlation," *UF*, 86 [98].
86 Schillebeeckx, *IR*, 10 [12].
87 Ted Schoof, "E. Schillebeeckx: 25 Years in Nijmegen, I," *Theology Digest* 37 (1990), 327.
88 Schillebeeckx, *Jesus*, 50–51 [70].

made up of linguistic elements, form the background for pre-understanding. The actualization of pre-understanding is a performative act, or a matter of historical praxis that places the subject in contact with reality mediated by language. In this experience, the subject comes up against its own essential limitations and those of language. In this linguistic framework, all experience is necessarily interpreted experience, and "[n]aively trusting in so-called immediate experiences seems to [Schillebeeckx], therefore, to be a form of neo-empiricism."[89] There are three basic elements of Schillebeeckx's theory of experience. First, there is the *interpretandum*, the so-called "lived element" of experience.[90] This is the contact with alterity (what is not identical with the self). Second, there are the *interpretaments*, or the "concrete images, concepts and narratives," which give expression to the *interpretandum*.[91] These are linguistic elements of expression and form the precondition for expression.

The network of *interpretaments* that human beings use is all held within an all-encompassing "theory," interpretive framework, or a model that arises from, and also contains, the linguistic elements of interpretation.[92] Schillebeeckx makes a distinction between "theory" and "model." Because all experience is interpreted experience, he gives priority to theories and models over experience in the sense that without theoretical understanding, there could be no experience. Models are a combination of narrative and practical elements forming a framework for interpreting the world. These are unfinished, and therefore open to include more and different elements, and they are based on underlying prejudices about the world and how it works. From these, we develop specific "theories" and expression, which become the "*interpretaments*."[93]

An appeal, therefore, to "pure" experience is really a kind of empiricism—it reduces all meaningful experience to something "direct" or "unmediated," which Schillebeeckx contends does not exist. There is no "religious" experience as such, but only that which comes out of a specific tradition—Islamic, Christian, Jewish, or otherwise.[94] Models can and do change throughout history, and cannot therefore be absolutized. A heliocentric view of the universe changes our anthropology—our historically situated self-understanding—and by extension shapes the modern image of God. Models help us interpret and express what occurred in "the history of Jesus' life and which through this model is being put into words. This thinking-in-models is important because it enables us to make a conscious distinction between the substance of faith and the model in which the faith is put into words."[95]

Apart from the model and the interpretive elements is the "lived element of experience" or the "*interpretandum*"—that which must be interpreted. This "objective" element has its own *direction of interpretation* and it exerts a force on us.[96] It is not merely a free-floating datum that can be twisted one way or another with equal validity. Such a pure objectivity would actually make it impossible to learn anything from the object, calling us to merely *observe* it without

---

89  Schillebeeckx, *IR*, 15 [18].
90  Boeve, "Experience According to Edward Schillebeeckx," 202–03.
91  Ibid., 207. These terms are explained in Schillebeeckx, *Jesus*, 645 [746].
92  Boeve, "Experience According to Edward Schillebeeckx," 207.
93  Edward Schillebeeckx, "The Role of History in What Is Called the New Paradigm," *Paradigm Change in Theology: A* Symposium *for the Future*, ed. Hans Küng and David Tracy, trans. Margaret Kohl (Edinburgh: T&T Clark, 1989), 308–09.
94  Schillebeeckx, *IR*, 5–6 [6].
95  Schillebeeckx, "The Role of History," 308–09.
96  Schillebeeckx, *Church*, 37–38 [38].

interpretation. We cannot do anything with it, and we cannot be changed by it, or spoken to by it; otherwise, we cease to be "objective." This can never be the case, since all experience is linguistic and, by definition, a form of interpretation. Hence what Schillebeeckx says about the Christian experience of Jesus: "We must view him in this way, because this is how he is."[97] Reality exerts a critical force on understanding because "[r]eality is always different from and more than had been thought."[98]

Every experience, no matter how mundane or repetitive, is in some aspect different, and so adds to and reshapes our expectation horizon and our theoretical framework. Our narrative historicity changes through each experience. The negative aspect is milder, and when our expectation horizon "cracks" under the weight of reality, the "suffering" we experience is not pronounced; it cannot be named as suffering in the same way as that of unmerited suffering of victims of violence and oppression. Still, the break in our understanding, fleeting though it may be, produces an essential "negative" moment and a contrast with what was expected. The hermeneutical character of experience is the very core of the experiencing human subject, moving from the anticipated "whole," and the whole of the subject's self-understanding, to elements or fragments that do not entirely confirm that whole. The whole changes in light of the parts, and new breaks occur with every experience, only to be reconstituted in the process of interpretation.

All experience searches for continuity in the overwhelming face of difference. When this continuity is frustrated, the "pain" of the break in our interpretive horizon throws us back upon ourselves, and our expectation of meaning is thwarted in favor of a confrontation with an otherness that does not yet have a meaningful place within the whole of our narrative historicity. All experience is essentially *contrastive*, and, as Mary Catherine Hilkert says, "we learn by way of discovery."[99] Understanding involves a moment of "loss of self," or of the realization of a break in our interpretive horizon that helps constitute the boundaries of the self.[100] The heart of experience, its "engine" so to speak, is the radical finitude of the creature. That creatures are finite, bound up inside their "absolute limit" that constitutes them as an entity separate from others, is what allows for the movement of experience.[101] Without this, there would be no alterity, no mediation, and no interpretation, only pure "presence." Radical contingency and historicity rule out pure presence either as immanence or as transcendence. There is a back-and-forth between discovery and concealment, but it is not necessarily "circular" insofar as it includes transcendence toward the future.

According to Schillebeeckx, modern consciousness is oriented toward the future, rather than toward the past. Today, we look to build the future through technology and mastery of the world. This is not always a good thing, but it is a recognition of the "secularity" of creation itself as "not-God," as a gift from God with its own laws and processes that, as "for-itself," can become what it will be in history. And yet, eschatological salvation, experienced partially in the present, always arrives in the God-who-is-to-come, or God the future of humanity. At the deeper structural level, this reveals the *eschatological* nature of human subjectivity. The hermeneutic circle is a

---

[97] Schillebeeckx, *IR*, 10 [11].

[98] Schillebeeckx, *Christ*, 20 [35].

[99] Hilkert, "Experience and Revelation," 63.

[100] Hans-Georg Gadamer, "On the Problem of Self-Understanding," *Philosophical Hermeneutics*, trans. David E. Linge (Berkeley, CA: University of California Press, 2008), 51.

[101] Schillebeeckx, *Church*, 75–78 [77–80].

mediation between the self produced out of the past and the self as it exists in the present, but there is never a "pure" present capable of being grasped. Every moment is a new experience of an "outside" or of alterity. Thus, the "circle" is only an apparent circle.[102] A "vicious" circle entails that a specific statement leads to an opposing statement, and vice versa, but this is not what occurs in experience. There is a forward advance, since new experiences, even ones that fundamentally alter the content and makeup of the prior interpretive framework, will be integrated into a new "whole," leading to a new and different self-understanding. The subject, in becoming itself, is always becoming different but in an essential hermeneutic continuity with the past. Instead of being caught in a circle of "past" and "present," the hermeneutic structure of the subject empowers that subject to go beyond itself, self-transcending into the future. It does this on the basis of an anticipation of the future forming a third, "expectation horizon" for the fusion of horizons.

The anticipation of the future is nothing less than the anticipation of total meaning; the meaning of the "whole." At the level of purely human meaning, this is the postulated meaning of human life based on the previous expectation and experience of partial meaning, which is narratively directed toward a larger, future expectation. Today, we expect that this meaning will be realized specifically by technical manipulation of the present to bring about the desired and expected future. Thus, the temporal orientation toward the future brought out by secularization makes apparent what was already structurally implicit in human subjectivity: "Man's [*sic*] future-building freedom thus essentially presupposes an open eschatology, an expectation of the future, a will towards the future which, in itself, slips into the ambiguity of all history making freedom."[103]

The total meaning of history cannot be exhaustively named or grasped because "[a]s long as history is still in a process of developing, it still does not possess any totality in itself and its totality of meaning can only be given in anticipation."[104] Human meaning has an anticipatory structure, and the specifically Christian form that this takes is *eschatological*. What has been accomplished in Jesus in history provides only a partial glimpse of salvation, which although decidedly present is also still being reconciled with the continuing history of suffering and sin.[105] Humanity is given to itself as hermeneutical, but it is created by God as eschatological—fundamentally oriented toward future final salvation based on the saving deeds of God already present in the past. What remains is for this salvific meaning to be reached through critical orthopraxis, and finally through God's ultimate presence at the *eschaton*:

> Eschatology is the expression of the belief that history is in God's hands, that the history of the world can reach its fulfillment in Christ who embodies God's promise … eschatology expresses the belief that the true faithful can and must bend this history into the salvation of all.[106]

---

[102] Edward Schillebeeckx, *Collegedictaat hermeneutiek 1978–1979*, ed. Frank G. Bosman (Nijmegen: Stichting Edward Schillebeeckx, 2004), 107–08.

[103] Schillebeeckx, "The Interpretation of the Future," *UF*, 3 [4].

[104] Schillebeeckx, *IR*, 88 [101].

[105] Ibid., 89 [101].

[106] Schillebeeckx, "The Interpretation of the Future," *UF*, 9 [11].

# IV. Theological understanding of faith—tradition and situation

By the time of Schillebeeckx's retirement in 1983, the hermeneutic question had changed to a certain degree. He places less emphasis on the continuity of interpretation—the "same" message being said differently—and gives more attention to fundamental ways of interpreting reality, within which the Christian identity is performed. It is only from *within* the Christian experience of reality that we can begin to consider how that experience has been and remains historically consistent.[107] In a rapidly secularizing Western Europe, it was increasingly important to define "tradition" and "situation," as well as the relation between them. In the 1970s, and especially in *Interim Report*, he referred to his method as a mutually critical correlation between tradition and situation. In his valedictory lecture of 1983, he redefines this position in order to clarify misinterpretations of the "correlation." "Correlation theology" is often criticized for assigning a normative status either to "tradition" as defined by a specific reading of that tradition (a hermeneutic key through which the rest of a complex history is read) or to the "situation." Modern theologians like Schillebeeckx, Metz, Karl Rahner, and others have been criticized for adapting the Christian message too closely to modern culture and thereby making the "situation" normative.[108] This presupposes that the two "poles" really exist as separate entities, and that is what Schillebeeckx sets out to correct. In fact, he heavily criticizes Hans Küng for holding to only one "source" for theology—the Bible and the early church—which is separate from the situation. This turns the present into a "theology-free zone" where an objective message from the past is applied to the present. So the idealization of "tradition" is not an exclusively "conservative" problem for theology.[109]

To theologize adequately, two elements are necessary. First, a theological proposition needs to be "justifiable in terms of the theologian's religious tradition."[110] This means that all theologians essentially are engaged in a process of interpretation, which is actually necessitated by tradition. Tradition itself needs norms and criteria for interpretation, i.e., method. No method can be perfect, or even entirely innocent and free of interest. Second, a theological proposition needs to be "justifiable in terms of an analysis and interpretation of the 'current situation.' Otherwise one creates a short circuit between experiential and thought categories from the past and present."[111]

"Situation," as Schillebeeckx uses it, is not a univocal concept that can ever be exhaustively known and explained: "*No theory* can encompass 'the situation' in its entirety."[112] It includes

---

[107] Edward Schillebeeckx, *Church, CW* vol. 10 (London: Bloomsbury T&T Clark, 2014), 35–40 [36–40], 77–80 [79–83]; cf. Schillebeeckx, "Catholic Use of Hermeneutics," *GFM*, 15 [22–23].

[108] Lieven Boeve, *God Interrupts History: Theology in a Time of Upheaval* (New York: Continuum, 2007), 30–37. Cf. James K.A. Smith, *Who's Afraid of Postmodernism? Taking Derrida, Lyotard, and Foucault to Church*, The Church and Postmodern Culture (Grand Rapids, MI: Baker Academic, 2006), 123–27; Tracey Rowland, *Catholic Theology*, Doing Theology (New York: Bloomsbury, 2017), 143–55.

[109] Schillebeeckx, "Theological Interpretation of Faith 1983," *Essays*, 59. Küng absolutizes the earliest church communities, while Joseph Ratzinger famously gives preference to Hellenistic Christianity as the normative form of "tradition."

[110] Schillebeeckx, "Theological Interpretation of Faith 1983," *Essays*, 60.

[111] Ibid.

[112] Ibid., 56. Emphasis original.

such a plurality of interlocking realities that it cannot be scientifically anticipated in an absolute way. Further, the "present situation" also includes a substantial relationship with the past, and the future, and as such is never a "pure present." Humanity's temporal existence includes a kind of transcendence of time, but this is only a relative transcendence, making us "reach beyond experienced time into both the past and the future."[113] The *Wirkungsgeschichte* extending from past events to the present rules out any easy identification of a "situation" separate from its past or from the coming future. Further, the complex hermeneutical-eschatological nature of human subjectivity also rules out a separate or even a stable notion of "situation" as "the present" in exclusion to other temporal horizons. The intricate nature of the Christian situation also points to it as a *locus theologicus* and a site of God's saving activity. The reactualization and active "handing-on" of tradition occur in understanding. Each moment is an active part of tradition, meaning that the subjective aspect of faith and the objective "tradition" that is being interpreted belong essentially to one another. As Schillebeeckx puts it: "Christian *awareness of meaning* is always achieved in creative *attribution of meaning* or in producing new meaning or 're-reading' the religious tradition in terms of a new situation."[114]

The gospel imparts meaning, implying that it also carries meaning. All great traditions, religious or otherwise, impart meaning historically through mediation. The disclosure of meaning occurs in and through traditions of experience. A religious tradition, in particular, "opens up a horizon of possible experience also for modern people. This is not primarily a disclosure of theoretical meaning, but in the first place a narrative revelation of meaning."[115] The disclosure of meaning does not occur in a value-free or objective way, but as a narrative, or a story rather than as a "metaphysical" superstructure added onto reality from above. The narrative of tradition is itself plural: the biblical narratives include the theology of the "author" within the text. Thus, the play between theory and praxis (as actualization of meaning in text) is already present in the Bible, which in no way presents us with a pure "word" or an objective datum of revelation. If the "situation" is a complex whole, then tradition is equally complex, hence the length of Schillebeeckx's first two *Jesus* volumes, and their painstaking reconstruction of the various historical layers of tradition. All of these layers are part of the one narrative that aims at the transformation, liberation, and salvation of human beings.[116]

## Correlation and proportional norm of faith

The "correlation" method that Schillebeeckx follows is necessarily complex. Correlation is a metaphor that basically means "*interrelationship* in a very general sense."[117] It carries a range of possibilities with it, including a harmonious "correlation" as is usually meant in the familiar critiques of correlation theology, but it can and should also entail some measure of conflict and resistance. Otherwise, there would be nothing "critical" in the correlation, and elements of ideology could not be criticized and removed from the tradition. Given that this is really

---

[113] Schillebeeckx, "The Interpretation of the Future," *UF*, 3 [4].
[114] Schillebeeckx, "Theological Interpretation of Faith 1983," *Essays*, 64. Emphasis original.
[115] Ibid., 54.
[116] Ibid., 55.
[117] Ibid., 57. Emphasis added.

an "interrelationship," it would be better if Schillebeeckx's model were called a theology of *critical interrelation* of tradition and situation. Although "correlation" is a misleading metaphor, and he continues to use it, Schillebeeckx attempts to qualify it, saying that it is better to speak of "an encounter of cultures."[118] Even when understood metaphorically, he is very aware that "correlation" can end up absolutizing the "modern context" as an ultimate norm. For example, although we often speak of "the biblical era," this is really a construct from our contemporary perspective.

The truth of the gospel, its identity of meaning, does not "lie at the level of the Bible and past religious tradition *as such*, hence is not to be found in a material replication of the past."[119] At the same time, it cannot be found in the present situation *as such*, no matter our political stance on the goodness or fallenness of Modernity. Rather, Christian identity "is only to be found at the level of a *corresponding relation between the original message* (tradition) and the constantly changing *situation*, then and now."[120] For Schillebeeckx, this is the definition of the *analogia fidei*. The "analogy of faith" exists in the relationship between the tradition and situation—it is how we in the present understand and interpret "the message" that reaches us through a history of effects, and therefore not independent of its historical baggage *from within the present*. This makes the *analogia fidei* an existential category, pertaining to fundamental Christian self-understanding. As constituted by self-understanding, human beings are hermeneutically related to human becoming in history. The analogy of faith opens up an essential dimension of theological anthropology. All statements about humanity are also statements about God; although theology is not the same as anthropology, anthropology reveals who we are to be in relation to the creator.[121] Following *Gaudium et spes*, "God reveals himself by revealing man [*sic*] to himself."[122]

This brings us to the essence of Christian continuity for Schillebeeckx's hermeneutics: continuity of meaning does not consist in corresponding *terms*, but in corresponding *relations* between terms.[123] This is significant because [1] it affirms that linguistic expression of meaning through "terms" is always necessary; [2] a pure translation model of hermeneutics, the correspondence of terms, is inadequate because it assumes an "original" or objective meaning present in one linguistic formulation that can be expressed merely through explanation in different words (a revised version of the "kernel/husk" model); and [3] proportional *relation* between terms allows for the complexities of different contexts in which terminology is used to be seen as essential to meaning. He expresses this proportional equality as an equation where the relation between message (Jesus's message, the New Testament message, the Patristic religious interpretation, etc.) and context (the various historical contexts in which the message is given) must be preserved over time. Christian identity is not "a matter of *equality* but of *proportional equality*."[124] The relation is between the *interpretation* of religious content and the *context* in which that interpretation occurs. Interpretations of religious content, or "religious substance,"

---

[118] Ibid., 58.

[119] Schillebeeckx, "Theological Interpretation of Faith 1983," *Essays*, 62.

[120] Ibid. Emphasis original.

[121] Schillebeeckx, "Christian Faith and Man's Expectation for the Future on Earth," 54; Schillebeeckx, *Christ*, 42 [56].

[122] Schillebeeckx, *Christ*, 31 [45–46].

[123] Schillebeeckx, "Theological Interpretation of Faith 1983," *Essays*, 62.

[124] Ibid., 63; Schillebeeckx, *Church*, 41 [42].

are diverse across different periods of time, and within different contexts. We should not think of this diversity as pernicious or contradictory, but it also cannot be "harmonized" or distilled into an easily discernable objective content. Consequently, we cannot think of the "evolution" of dogma as merely the expanding explanation of a "kernel" that was previously known explicitly or implicitly. Ultimately, this is because "revelation" in the strict sense of the term is not "propositional content" that has to be accepted or rejected. It is the person of Jesus Christ who invites us into a loving relationship with a personal God, and it is this *relationship* that must be maintained in a constant way throughout space and time.

One problem with the way Schillebeeckx presents hermeneutic continuity and interpretation is that the "equation" model tends to break down in its use of identifiable time periods that have "clear borders." For example, the first message/context complex is "Jesus' message/Jesus' socio-historical context," but that context is itself ambiguous. When did it end? How is it distinct from the "New Testament socio-historical context"? Both are included in the period of the early Roman Empire, or what is often called "Second Temple Judaism," but even these are ambiguous. Jesus's context did not disappear, exactly, when he was executed. Identifying a beginning or end to the New Testament sociohistorical context in contrast to the Patristic one becomes even more difficult since the New Testament texts were written over such a long period of time and in a wide geographic range. Further, there is also the question of the history of effects, and how this plays into the continuity between two proportional relations. Does the pre-Vatican II synthesis include all of the proportional relations of prior centuries, which is then recontextualized after the Council for a post-conciliar interpretation of faith in Modernity? I wonder if Schillebeeckx meant this model as more of a heuristic way of presenting continuity rather than as a technical paradigm to follow methodologically. Certainly, it is only meant to represent *authentic* interpretations of faith in a context, which accounts for continuity, but it becomes difficult to account for discontinuity, which he rightly says is often necessary in order to maintain the authenticity of the gospel message. The Second Vatican Council was an example of this "faithful discontinuity," precisely because it productively recovered elements of tradition from the past that had been lost or marginalized, thereby restoring a greater continuity.[125]

# Conclusion

Continuity is certainly present throughout the several decades of development of Schillebeeckx's theological synthesis, and this is at least partially due to his particular Thomistic background. The hermeneutical problem—the mediation of meaning in history—became extremely important thanks to the rapid pace of societal change in Western Europe after the war and due to the reforms of the Second Vatican Council. Schillebeeckx's early Thomistic orientation certainly provides a key to understanding how and why he was so uniquely positioned to construct a new hermeneutic synthesis out of a Christian engagement with contemporary philosophical insights. After all, the act of faith does not terminate in the linguistic expression, but in the reality of faith itself. In

---

[125] Schillebeeckx, "Theological Interpretation of Faith 1983," *Essays*, 67; Schillebeeckx, "The New Critical Theory and Theological Hermeneutics," *UF*, 114–15 [130–31].

a rapidly changing world, it was the common question of the "meaning" of faith that inspired Schillebeeckx to take up the problem. In this chapter, we have seen how he integrated modern philosophical hermeneutics in order to better mediate the content of faith. We have followed his further integration of critical theory, built on the realization that there must always be a critical element in faith—orthopraxis—in order to realize orthodoxy. This also led to the development of "negative contrast experiences," which has become an integral part of his theological legacy. All of these developments were in fact motivated by an overriding concern for the mediation of Christian faith in service of realizing salvation in and through history. This eschatological consideration became integral to his hermeneutic synthesis—the human orientation toward the coming future is, in Christian faith, also an orientation toward the God who is our future. Thus, his hermeneutic model of human subjectivity is an "eschatological hermeneutics" of experience built on our anticipation of future meaning. In the Christian tradition, this anticipation is of the present-yet-absent Rule of God, toward which we must always strive. Finally, this chapter has attempted to clarify some elements of Schillebeeckx's method, including the structure of experience as hermeneutical-eschatological, and his use of a critical correlation of tradition and situation. Schillebeeckx's thought is highly nuanced, and although some ambiguities remain with his model of a "proportional norm" for the gospel and historical context, his understanding of theology as a *critical interrelation* of meaning and temporal horizons remains important. I believe that, with Schillebeeckx's hermeneutics as a foundation, there remains much more work to be done in terms of developing contemporary theological understandings of temporality and salvation history within the present global economic and political reality. Schillebeeckx's work can be used as a fruitful starting point, but as he himself acknowledged, "only as a starting point," since we are now dealing with a new situation and must—in continuity with the tradition of faith—make our own way.[126]

---

[126] Edward Schillebeeckx, "Letter From Edward Schillebeeckx to the Participants in the Symposium 'Theology for the 21st Century: The Enduring Relevance of Edward Schillebeeckx for Contemporary Theology,'" *Edward Schillebeeckx and Contemporary Theology*, ed. Lieven Boeve, Frederiek Depoortere, and Stephan van Erp (London: T&T Clark, 2010), xiv.

# Chapter 11

# At the Service of Faith as a Quest

*Schillebeeckx During the Post-Conciliar Years*

Erik Borgman and Thijs Caspers

Edward Schillebeeckx was the leading theologian in the Netherlands in the period immediately following the Second Vatican Council (1962–1965).[1] He was a celebrity, even for people not directly involved in church and theology. This was primarily due to the fact that Schillebeeckx was almost constantly in the news, appearing frequently as a commentator to discuss current developments in the Catholic Church on television and in the press. He had been the advisor of the Dutch bishops during the Council, and they continued to avail of his services afterward. This was one of the reasons why Schillebeeckx was widely regarded not only as a protagonist but also as a main instigator of developments within the Dutch church that were receiving considerable international coverage. Just like France in the immediate postwar years, in the immediate post-conciliar years the Netherlands was viewed as a laboratory where experiments were being conducted and a battle was being waged over the shape of the church of the future. However, the way that Dutch Catholics experienced their faith and the changing place of the Roman Catholic Church in the Dutch society were not merely, or not even primarily, the result of new theological views. We will begin this chapter therefore with a brief characterization of the Dutch situation prior to the Council. We will then go on to discuss the position of the Dutch church within a rapidly modernizing society and Schillebeeckx's position in the church during the post-conciliar period. Finally, we will examine the controversy over the new Dutch Catechism from 1966, especially Schillebeeckx's role in this important moment in the history of the Catholic Church in the Netherlands.

## I. On the eve of the council

In the years directly following the Second World War, the primary focus in the Netherlands, in both church and society, was on restoring the prewar situation. Plans were being proposed

---

This chapter has been translated by Brian Heffernan.

[1]  For more background to this chapter, see Erik Borgman, *Edward Schillebeeckx: A Theologian in His History*, trans. John Bowden (London/New York: Continuum, 2003), 283–365, esp. 320–65.

immediately after the war for the renewal of social and political life, which had been strongly segregated along religious and ideological lines. The phenomenon of "pillarisation" (*verzuiling*) caused Catholics, Protestants, and socialists to live almost their entire lives in tightly knit social networks that were strongly isolated from one another. These ideological "pillars" encompassed all aspects of life, from cradle to grave (including education, unions, hospitals, social and sporting organizations, news and entertainment media, and even political parties)—even though these networks had already lost much of their influence by the 1950s.[2] The Dutch bishops' policy in the 1950s was focused strongly on preserving and strengthening Catholic unity. In retrospect, it seems that despite their best intentions, this policy actually expedited the loss of a coherent and unifying Catholic identity. The emphasis on unity obscured the purpose of this unity and gave the impression that the primary function of the Catholic message was to preserve the power of the church in society and the authority of its hierarchy over the thoughts and actions of lay Catholics.

Moreover, the emphasis placed on unity was itself a sign of the fact that this unity was apparently coming under pressure. There were many causes for this, including rapid industrialization, increasing urbanization, and growing mobility, all of which undermined traditional relationships. The rise of the mass media made it impossible for people within the various "pillars" to remain ideologically isolated. Moreover, the mutual dialogue that had arisen across the boundaries of these pillars during the German occupation in the Second World War had led many among the elites to doubt the desirability of continuing the segregation. New expectations and new ideals for people's lives began to develop, thanks in part to the first stirrings of a consumer society. Instead of duty and obedience to fixed norms, people began to think in terms of self-development and personal authenticity. Catholic intellectuals, comprising priests as well as a broadly expanded group of highly educated laypeople (this latter category the result of the successes of the Catholic educational system), increasingly regarded it as problematic that the church's hierarchy was proposing views that clashed directly with ideas and insights acquired outside of the church, and that this was done not on the basis of arguments but was based exclusively on the alleged authority of their own tradition.

When the Dutch bishops admonished their coreligionists in their pastoral letter *De katholiek in het openbare leven van deze tijd* ("Catholics in Contemporary Public Life") in 1954 to preserve their unity, both among themselves and with their bishops as leaders, many believed they were engaging in a hopeless rearguard action. In this document, which has gone down in Dutch history as the *Mandement*, they banned Catholics from membership of the socialist trade union NVV and the socialist broadcasting society VARA, and they strongly advised Catholics against joining the *Partij van de Arbeid* ("Labour Party"), the socialist party that had come to espouse the goal of *doorbraak* or "breakthrough" to the Protestant and Catholic parts of society after the war.[3] The

---

2    For a synthetic description of the developments, see Kees Schuyt and Ed Taverne, *1950: Welvaart in zwart-wit*, Nederlandse Cultuur in Europese Context (The Hague: Sdu, 2000). For an overview of developments within Dutch Catholicism after the Second World War, see Erik Borgman and Marit Monteiro, "Katholicisme," *Handboek religie in Nederland: perspectief, overzicht, debat*, ed. Erik Borgman, Marjo Buitelaar, Yme Kuiper, Robert Jozef Johanna Maria Plum, and Meerten Berend ter Borg (Zoetermeer: Meinema, 2008), 86–121.

3    "*Mandement*" in Dutch is a technical term for a solemn message of the Roman Catholic bishops of a Church Province, giving directions regarding contemporary questions.

bishops' almost exclusive insistence in their letter on maintaining and, where necessary, restoring unity had precisely the opposite effect. It strengthened the consciousness, already growing among the social and ecclesial Catholic cadre, that developments in society necessitated fundamental changes in the church's attitude to the world.[4]

When in 1959, Pope John XXIII unexpectedly announced the convocation of a general council, declaring that the up-to-date renewal of the church—*aggiornamento*—would be the central item on the agenda of what would become the Second Vatican Council, many opinion leaders in the Dutch Catholic community therefore regarded this as an invitation to finally introduce modern culture's important achievements into the church. Schillebeeckx's actions must be seen against this background. His aim was to be at the service of the renewal of the church and theology in the context of changing circumstances; he came to see the necessity of this renewal very clearly during the Council. However, the circumstances proved to be less propitious for this purpose than they had initially seemed to be, and this rendered Schillebeeckx's own specific contribution partially invisible.

## Dutch Catholics in the mid-1960s

In the early 1960s, the Dutch economy experienced exponential growth, in part due to the discovery and exploitation of a large natural gas field in Slochteren, Groningen. Individual prosperity also increased. Television sets, refrigerators, and passenger cars came within the means of increasing numbers of people, and this fundamentally changed their daily lives. The introduction of the contraceptive pill in 1963 clearly brought to light the changing conceptions of marriage, sexuality, and reproduction that had developed over the previous period. These and similar developments gave the Dutch the feeling that they were being parachuted into an entirely new era, just as was the case with the people of many other nations in the industrialized West. Traditional religious patterns of thought and life no longer seemed appropriate to this new situation.

It seems to be that this was even more the case for Dutch Catholics than for their compatriots from other groups in society. As a socially disadvantaged group, Catholics in the Netherlands had long fought for an equal place in society. Once they had achieved this, and society began to rapidly change, many of the leading voices among them looked with amazement and incomprehension at the patterns of behavior and thought that had been common in their own community only very recently. The Catholic alienation vis-à-vis Catholicism's own history was expressed in almost canonical form in a book published in 1963 by the publicist Michel van der Plas: *Uit het rijke Roomsche Leven* ("*[Scenes] from the Rich Roman Life*"). The title was derived from that of a photo feature in the first Catholic popular magazine of the Netherlands, *De Katholieke Illustratie* ("The Catholic Illustration"), which recorded all kinds of facts and trivia from Catholic life.[5] According to van der Plas, this feature, which he regarded as paradigmatic for Catholic culture, constantly

---

[4]   For the first impulses in this direction, see Hanneke Westhoff, *Geestelijke bevrijders: Nederlandse katholieken en hun beweging voor geestelijke volksgezondheid in de twintigste eeuw*, Bronnen en studies Katholiek Documentatie Centrum Nijmegen 30 (Nijmegen: Valkhof 1996).

[5]   Tijn Hottinga, *De Katholieke Illustratie: De verkochte bruid. Honderd jaar tijdschriftgeschiedenis* (Baarn: Tirion, 2000); cf. also Leonard Jentjens, *Van strijdorgaan tot familieblad: De tijdschriftjournalistiek van de Katholieke Illustratie 1867–1968* (Amsterdam: Cramwinckel, 1995).

implied that it was "a never to be sufficiently esteemed privilege to be a Catholic," and that this meant leading a "life filled with blessings, that was in fact far exalted above the existence of those unfortunate non-Catholics."[6] In his eponymous book, van der Plas collected facts, photographs, and quotations from articles and advertisements from the interwar years, all of which testified to a Catholicism whose introversion and narrow mindedness, he believed, seemed all but incredible to his contemporary readers. His bestselling pictorial book was a call to finally settle scores with this past. This attitude was not unique to Dutch Catholics, although it was particularly prevalent among them. The year 1964 saw the publication of two comparable books about Protestant culture, and another one about the socialists followed suit in 1965.[7] By the mid-1960s, opinion leaders in the Netherlands were collectively pushing for a rupture with the forms and ideas of their forebears.

In all Western countries, social relations were radically restructured during these years. One aspect specific to the Netherlands was that the belief that radical change was necessary arose not only, or even primarily, from the masses but also from the managerial and intellectual elites.[8] Thus, barely half a decade after the *Mandement*, the Dutch bishops and the higher clergy encouraged their faithful to accept and even to actively condone the adaptation of the Catholic Church to modern circumstances, although it must also be said that the faithful appear to have wholeheartedly accepted this invitation. The view that change in the Catholic Church in the Netherlands did not come from below, as a spontaneous expression of the collective will of the faithful, the so-called *sensus fidelium*, but was strongly pushed, stimulated, and led by members of the elite, was long the preserve of critical conservative Catholics.[9] More recently, however, this view has been put in its rightful place in Catholic historiography.[10] In the post-conciliar period itself, however, the dominant perception was that the preparations for the Council and the Conciliar discussions themselves had set in motion a "delayed revolution." After the conviction had grown in the second half of the 1950s that the existing structures and the principles upon which they were based were no longer sufficient, the Council seemed to offer opportunities to effect changes in Catholicism. Such changes were necessary to ensure "the proper functioning of the church as an institute in a modern, urbanised, and populous society."[11]

---

6   Michel van der Plas, ed., *Uit het rijke Roomsche Leven: Een documentatie over de jaren 1925–1935* (Utrecht: Ambo, 1963), 9–21, quotations at 9 and 21.

7   See Ben van Kaam, *Parade der mannenbroeders: Protestants leven in Nederland, 1918–1938* (Wageningen: Zomer en Keuning, 1964); A.C. de Gooyer, *Het beeld der vad'ren: Een documentaire over het leven van het protestants-christelijke volksdeel* (Utrecht: Ambo, 1964); Igor Cornelissen, ed., *De taaie rooie rakkers: Een documentaire over het socialisme tussen de twee wereldoorlogen* (Utrecht: Ambo, 1965). Cf. also H.J.L. Vonhoff, *De zindelijke burgerheren: Een halve eeuw liberalen* (Baarn: Hollandia, 1965).

8   James C. Kennedy, *Nieuw Babylon in aanbouw: Nederland in de jaren zestig* (Amsterdam: Boom, 1995), 46–48.

9   See particularly Jan Bots, "Die Niederlände," *Handbuch der Kirchengeschichte*, vol. VII: *Die Weltkirche im 20. Jahrhundert* (Freiburg/Basel/Vienna: Herder 1979), 467–574; Jan Bots, *Zestig jaar katholicisme in Nederland*, De Rots vol. 11, 7–8 (Venlo, 1981).

10   Maarten van Den Bos, *Verlangen naar vernieuwing: Nederlands katholicisme 1953–2003* (Amsterdam: Wereldbibliotheek, 2012); see also Jos Palm, *Moederkerk: De ondergang van Roomsch Nederland* (Amsterdam: Contact, 2012).

11   Walter Goddijn, *De beheerste kerk: Uitgestelde revolutie in rooms-katholiek Nederland* (Amsterdam: Elsevier, 1973), 16.

Less than a year after the closure of the Second Vatican Council on December 8, 1965, the Pastoral Council for the Dutch Church Province was opened in Noordwijkerhout, on November 27, 1965. Its aim was to apply the Council's decisions to Catholic life in the Netherlands, but it was set up as "the common consultation of all the faithful of the entire Dutch church province" about the "self-realisation of the people of God according to the requirements of the gospel, the Second Vatican Council's new insights, and the needs of our time."[12] Partially as a result of this, discussion groups were established throughout the Dutch church, which stimulated Catholics to reflect on their faith and on contemporary developments within the church. The unchallenged premise of these reflections was that faith, church, and theology needed to change to reflect the social and cultural changes. There was much less awareness of the fact that these latter developments were not unproblematic themselves, and that faith, church, and theology might be well-advised to keep some distance from them, or even attempt to influence or criticize these developments. Conservative groups that retained the strongly anti-modern attitudes that the Roman Catholic Church had adopted in the wake of the First Vatican Council (1869–1870) were relatively small in the Netherlands, and the voice they expressed in their own publicity organs hardly penetrated the national media and the public sphere. On the other side of the spectrum, there were groups of young religious who sought to reshape the religious life as a radical and prophetic imitation of Christ and who looked to contemporary radical political and social movements for inspiration. Their influence also remained limited, not least because many of them eventually left the religious life, and often also the church.

## Aggiornamento as modernization

The idea that revolutionary modernization was required was by far the most dominant strand of thought in the Dutch Catholic community in the 1960s. This placed Schillebeeckx's theological project in a difficult position. Schillebeeckx also believed that church and theology had to be changed radically in response to the contemporary situation. He found confirmation of this view in the emphasis which the Pastoral Constitution on the Church in the Modern World, *Gaudium et spes,* placed on reading the "signs of the times," an expression largely coined by his confrere Marie-Dominique Chenu (1895–1990).[13] However, Schillebeeckx had consistently opposed any superficial interpretation of this process of *aggiornamento* that Pope John XXIII had set in motion. According to Schillebeeckx, it was not a matter of adapting to the spirit of the times, as if this should somehow be regarded as the norm. Looking back retrospectively at the time of the closing of the Council, he concluded that it was important for the church to raise

---

12  "Nota over de voorbereidingsgeschiedenis," *Katholiek Archief* 21 (1966), 1221–32, at 1221.
13  See Marie-Dominique Chenu, *Peuple de Dieu dans le monde* (Paris: Édition du Cerf, 1966). See especially pp. 11–34, "Une constitution pastorale de l'Église," and pp. 35–55, "Les signes du temps." For background information, see Giuseppe Alberigo, "Un concile à la dimension du monde: Marie-Dominique Chenu à Vatican II d'après son journal," *Marie-Dominique Chenu: Moyen-Âge et modernité*, ed. Joseph Dore and Jacques Fantino (Paris: Cerf, 1997), 155–72; Giovanni Turbanti, "Il ruolo del P. D. Chenu nell'ellaboratione della constituzione *Gaudium et spes*," *Marie-Dominique Chenu: Moyen-Âge et modernité*, ed. Joseph Dore and Jacques Fantino (Paris: Cerf, 1997), 173–209.

an evangelically purer form of religion peculiar to the church, so that Christ's church can make her legitimate dogmatic claims really true in the eyes of all. This raises the problem of the religious *aggiornamento* of the entire church, both in depth and breadth.[14]

According to Schillebeeckx, *Gaudium et spes* was ultimately the Council's most important document. He believed that it testified to a

> "secular" spirit [new to church documents], borne by faith in God, the creator, who is also our undeserved salvation (so that the entire concrete reality in which we live comes to us like a grace in the ordinary everyday things, in the face of our fellow man [*sic*] and in the great aspirations of humanity today).[15]

This spirit, he believed, ought to penetrate to the faithful.[16] This was the aim of his activities in the post-conciliar church and in post-conciliar theology.

Yet Schillebeeckx's position was usually interpreted in terms of the campaign of modernization that was already ongoing in the Dutch Catholic church in the second half of the 1960s. It was almost impossible in those days to escape being pigeonholed either as a "progressive" or as a "conservative." Moreover, the image had arisen already during the preparations for the Council that the Dutch church was fundamentally open to contemporary developments and had to contend therefore with a Roman hierarchy that seemingly lacked courage, was endowed with a reprehensible attachment to outmoded structures and ideas, and was determined to retain its power whatever the cost and therefore dedicated to sabotaging necessary and salutary change. Initially, the Dutch shared the wider confidence that Pope John XXIII would be able to keep the Council on the right track. But from the Dutch perspective, the actions of Pope Paul VI, who acceded to the papacy on June 21, 1963, were ambiguous from the start. This was exacerbated by the fact that the Council's Theological Commission added an explanatory note to the Dogmatic Constitution on the Church *Lumen gentium*, which had been adopted with a very large majority (November 21, 1964), to mitigate any potentially radical implications of the text for the power of the church's hierarchy, and that a footnote was inserted into the Pastoral Constitution on the Church in the Modern World *Gaudium et spes* (December 8, 1965) that appeared to limit the authority of the document. Both measures were clearly taken to assuage the conservative minority, and both caused a storm of indignation. In 1965, shortly before the official closing of the Council, Paul VI published the encyclical *Mysterium fidei* on the Eucharist, which was clearly a response to recent theological reflections on that subject by Dutch theologians in the context of the practical renewal of the liturgy that had been occurring in the Netherlands ever since the promulgation of *Sacrosanctum Concilium*, the Conciliar constitution on the liturgy.[17] Schillebeeckx responded

---

[14] Edward Schillebeeckx, "Reflections on the Final Results of the Council," *The Real Achievement of Vatican II*, trans. H.J.J. Vaughan (New York: Herder and Herder, 1967), 67; Edward Schillebeeckx, "Bezinning op het eindresultaat van Vaticanum II," *Oecumene* 5 (1966): 12–23; reprinted as "Bezinning op het eindresultaat van het concilie," *Het Tweede Vaticaans Concilie*, II (Tielt/Den Haag: Lannoo, 1966), 58–84.

[15] Schillebeeckx, "Reflections on the Final Results of the Council," 78.

[16] Ibid. 78–79.

[17] The pope had previously told the Dutch bishops of his concerns about developments in the Dutch church.

by trying to explain that the pope's concerns were legitimate, but that his interpretation of the discussion that was taking place in the Netherlands on this subject was mistaken.[18]

The conservative image of Paul VI was confirmed for many Dutch Catholics in the post-conciliar years by his refusal to allow discussion on the decoupling of the priesthood and celibacy, a cause that had been warmly supported in the Netherlands. This was reinforced even more by the publication of the encyclical *Humanae vitae* in 1968. This document, sweeping aside the objections of the majority of the drafting committee, reiterated the traditional Catholic doctrine that "artificial birth control" was intrinsically evil. The negative image of Paul VI was consolidated definitively when he appointed Jo Gijsen as bishop of Roermond in 1970 and Ad Simonis as bishop of Rotterdam in 1972. These appointments of clearly profiled conservatives ignored the shortlists drawn up in the dioceses themselves and seemed like deliberate attempts to frustrate the transition toward a more democratic, less hierarchical, and clerical church.

Although Schillebeeckx was a major presence in the post-conciliar Dutch church, this situation in fact left little space for his own specific theological contribution. This was perhaps most clearly evident in his futile plea at the Dutch Pastoral Council not to precipitate the process of adapting the church to contemporary society, but to ground reflections in what he called a "fundamental document" that would formulate a vision on the place of faith in a secularized world. His proposal was that a text should first be drawn up that would "explain *comprehensibly* and *transparently* why the world had radically changed, and why this posed a challenge for the church, which is thereby invited to take up a 'changed' position in the world of the faith."[19] His plea, articulated repeatedly during the preparations for the sessions of the Pastoral Council and on one final occasion publicly on the eve of the start of the sessions in 1967, went unheeded. The Franciscan priest and sociologist Walter Goddijn, who had been charged by the Dutch bishops to organize the Pastoral Council and attend to its development, focused instead on modernization of the church with a view to improving its service to Dutch society. This was reflected in the pragmatic "working formula," which was approved by the bishops on July 18, 1967. This document offered no opportunities for developing a fundamental view of the faith and of theology in relation to contemporary society and culture, as Schillebeeckx had advocated.

# II. Schillebeeckx's double position

The strong focus on adaptation of the church made Schillebeeckx's position in the Netherlands after the Council ambiguous. He had returned from Rome hoping to be able to truly tackle the problems that he had identified in the early 1960s. The 1963 book *Honest to God* by the Anglican

---

[18] Edward Schillebeeckx, "Transubstantiation, Transfinalization, Transignification," *Worship* 40, no. 6 (1966), 324–38. Schillebeeckx developed his own theological vision in the articles: Edward Schillebeeckx, "Christus' tegenwoordigheid in de eucharistie," *TvT* 5 (1965), 136–72; Edward Schillebeeckx, "De eucharistische wijze van Christus' werkelijke tegenwoordigheid," *TvT* 6 (1966), 359–94; edited versions of which he published in the book, Edward Schillebeeckx, *The Eucharist*, trans. N.D. Smith (London/New York: Burns & Oates, 2005).

[19] Edward Schillebeeckx, "Pastoraal Concilie: óók theologisch beluisteren van Nederlandse situatie. Op zoek naar een fundamenteel document," *Kosmos + Oecumene* 1 (1967), 181–92.

bishop of Woolwich, John A.T. Robinson, played an important role in his analysis of these problems. This book demonstrated convincingly that there was a fundamental chasm between the lives of contemporary people and the vision of the faith upheld by traditional Christianity. The book had a tremendous impact across the Western world, and the Netherlands was no exception. This can be illustrated by an anecdote about the British Dominican and theologian Cornelius Ernst (1924–1977), who came to the Netherlands to give a lecture in 1963. Some technical malfunction caused a blackout, which did not however affect one illuminated sign for an adjacent shoe shop called Robinson, which shone as the only light illuminating the darkness; Ernst declared that this was characteristic of the attitude in the Netherlands. His remark received wide recognition.[20] For many, including many in the Netherlands, the response to the situation that Robinson had identified was to translate the gospel into secular terms. Robinson himself argued for this, in keeping with Rudolf Bultmann's "demythologisation" program and Dietrich Bonhoeffer's plea for a "religionless Christianity."[21]

Schillebeeckx's response, on the other hand, was fundamentally different. He wrote quite extensively about Robinson's book on two occasions, both in the journal he had founded shortly after coming to Nijmegen. The first issue of *Tijdschrift voor Theologie* appeared in 1961, and the journal developed over the following years into a forum that showcased post-conciliar theological renewal in the Netherlands and Flanders. Building on his pre-conciliar work, but adopting a new tone, Schillebeeckx responded to Robinson by observing a hidden presence in the secularized world, a presence of God which, he believed, could and should be articulated: "A veiled *hope* seems to sustain and strengthen in sprit of certain signs of despair on all sides and a sense of the absurd in the history of the world."[22] In line with the document that would eventually become *Gaudium et spes*, but which was called "Schema XIII" during the Council, the church should, according to Schillebeeckx,

> seize hold of this concealed hope and invite the world to its explicit expectation: "If you knew the gift of God" (Jn 4:10) from with you, world, are unconsciously living! If only you recognised God's gift![23]

He believed that this had in fact been done in *Gaudium et spes*, and he hoped that the "fundamental document" he was advocating for prior to the Pastoral Council would do the same for the Dutch situation. He was in dialogue with theologians from other parts of the world, and Schillebeeckx wrote article upon article with what he called an "almost feverish sense of urgency" to develop—

---

[20] The lecture, which contains no direct reference to Robinson, was published as "Words Facts and God," in Cornelius Ernst, *Multiple Echo: Explorations in Theology*, ed. Fergus Kerr and Timothy Radcliffe (London: Darton, Longman and Todd, 1979), 13–27, and is dated there as "St. Thomas's day 1963." At that time, before the post-conciliar reform of the calendar of saints, the feast of Thomas Aquinas was on March 7. This anecdote was told to Erik Borgman by Ted Schoof.

[21] John A.T. Robinson, *Honest to God* (London: SCM Press, 1963).

[22] Edward Schillebeeckx, "Church and World," *WC, CW* vol. 4 (London: Bloomsbury T&T Clark, 2014), 86 [113]. See also his "Evangelische zuiverheid en menselijke waarachtigheid," *TvT* 3 (1963), 283–325; and his "Herinterpretatie van het geloof in het licht van de seculariteit: Honest to Robinson," *TvT* 4 (1964), 109–50. Reprinted in *God en mens*, Theologische Peilingen 2 (Bilthoven: Nelissen, 1965), 115–49 and 66–115. ET: Edward Schillebeeckx, *God and Man*, trans. Edward Fitzgerald and Peter Tomlinson, Theological Soundings (New York: Sheed and Ward, 1969), 160–209, 85–160.

[23] Edward Schillebeeckx, "Church and World," *WC*, 86 [113].

in confrontation with current discussions and intellectual developments—a theological approach that would reveal the coherence between the world's hidden hope and Christianity's explicit expectation.[24] Many of his dialogue partners were theologians that he already knew personally thanks to the Council and with whom he corresponded in the context of the international theological journal *Concilium*, which he had helped found.

These endeavors ultimately bore fruit, albeit in an unexpected manner. Around 1970, Schillebeeckx came to the conclusion that he should focus on speaking about Jesus and his message in such a way that contemporary people would again be able to experience and become conscious of his presence among them and that he should do this through a confrontation with recent research on the "historical Jesus." In 1974, he published the results of this confrontation: *Jesus: An Experiment in Christology* (*Jezus, het verhaal van een levende*), which established his name as an important internationally recognized and innovative theologian, both inside and outside of the Roman Catholic Church.[25] In 1978, his first *Jesus* book was followed by *Christ: The Christian Experience in the Modern World* (*Gerechtigheid en liefde: Genade en bevrijding;* published as *Christ: the Experience of Jesus as Lord* in the United States), in which Schillebeeckx explicitly linked the confession of Jesus Christ with what he regarded as contemporary experiences of hope and grace.[26]

At the same time, however, Schillebeeckx's work after the Council had taken on a radically different aspect. The Dutch Catholic comedian Fons Jansen said in one of his theatre shows *De lachende kerk* ("The laughing church") in 1962 that whenever the Dutch bishops were at a loss as to what to do with a particular theological question, they put it out on the street. Then, according to Jansen, "the Schillebeeckx would come on Fridays." In Dutch, Schillebeeckx's name alliterates with the word *schillenboer*, "waste food collector," who used to come and empty the waste food bins in many Dutch neighborhoods at the time and sell it to farmers to feed their animals.[27] After the Council, Schillebeeckx continued to act as a troubleshooter for the Dutch bishops, and this above all else determined the image that the wider public had of him—even up to today. This forced him to deal with problems that were perhaps less urgent from the perspective of his own theological vision, but which were controversial from the perspective of church politics. It is to a large degree because of this role that he increasingly became seen as a spokesperson for the "progressive" wing.

Two other important developments also contributed to the "progressive" image. First, it became clear in 1968 that the Congregation for the Doctrine of the Faith (until 1965 the Supreme Sacred Congregation of the Holy Office) had launched an investigation into Schillebeeckx's orthodoxy. It is still not entirely clear what the precise focus of this investigation was, and after explanations made by Karl Rahner, who was appointed Schillebeeckx's advocate, the case was

---

24    See Edward Schillebeeckx, "The New Image of God," *GFM, CW* vol. 3 (London: Bloomsbury T&T Clark, 2014), 101 [169].

25    Edward Schillebeeckx, *Jezus, het verhaal van een levende* (Bloemendaal: Nelissen, 1974). ET: Edward Schillebeeckx, *Jesus, CW* vol. 6 (London: Bloomsbury T&T Clark, 2014).

26    Edward Schillebeeckx, *Gerechtigheid en liefde: Genade en bevrijding* (Bloemendaal: Nelissen, 1977). ET: Edward Schillebeeckx, *Christ, CW* vol. 7 (London: Bloomsbury T&T Clark, 2014).

27    Maarten van den Bos and Stephan van Erp, *Een gelukkige theoloog: Honderd jaar Edward Schillebeeckx/A Happy Theologian: A Hundred Years of Edward Schillebeeckx* (Nijmegen: Valkhof, 2014), 9.

dropped without further consequences.[28] The investigation was in fact a belated result of the conflict that had arisen about a pastoral letter published by the Dutch bishops about the Council in 1961.[29] In this letter, they expounded a vision of the authority of the pope, the bishops, and the laity within the church, which anticipated what the Council Fathers would say in *Lumen gentium*. In 1961 however, the letter proved highly controversial and was translated into several languages, including in Italian, but this version was withdrawn from the bookshops after pressure from within the Curia. Schillebeeckx had drafted the letter in collaboration with the dogmatic theologians Jan Groot of the major seminary of Warmond and Frans Haarsma of the major seminary of Rijsenburg. However, it was Schillebeeckx who was the main author of the text. Even the style was recognizably his, and the Dutch bishops explicitly thanked him in a postscript to the text. From that moment on, Schillebeeckx became a controversial theologian in the Roman Catholic Church, and consequently he could not be appointed as an official *peritus* at the Second Vatican Council but went instead as an advisor to the Dutch bishops. This reputation also ensured that he and Bernard Cardinal Alfrink, the archbishop of Utrecht, were already viewed as representatives of the progressive Dutch church when they arrived in Rome for the Council's first session in 1962. The Congregation for the Doctrine of the Faith's 1968 investigation again made Schillebeeckx appear in the public mind as a protagonist of progressive Dutch Catholicism, which was forced to defend itself against Roman forces of obscurantism.

Moreover, opponents of the developments that had begun in the Netherlands during the Council were starting to make themselves heard, albeit at a modest scale. They made an explicit stand on the basis of the tradition of the church and necessary fidelity to this tradition. Schillebeeckx felt compelled to defend the inevitability of change and the importance of renewal against their attacks. This, too, placed him in the progressive camp in the context of the clash between progressives and conservatives in the Roman Catholic Church. This impression was confirmed at the international level by the fact that *Concilium* was increasingly being regarded as a mouthpiece of the progressive voice within worldwide Catholicism. In 1972, Joseph Ratzinger, then a professor at the University of Regensburg, and the Swiss theologian, Hans Urs von Balthasar (1905–1998), took the initiative to found the international Catholic journal *Communio* as an opposing voice. But Schillebeeckx's own focus was on creating and retaining scope for the developments that he believed the church had to undergo, not in order to conform itself to the spirit of the time, but to be able to authentically bear witness to God's grace in the contemporary world. He felt ill at ease with polarized relations within the church, but at the same time he was a welcome guest at organizations that had a progressive profile within that polarized situation in the Roman Catholic Church of the 1970s and 1980s. In 1979, he authored the main article in a book entitled *Basis en ambt* ("Base and Ministry") by the *Basisbeweging van Kritische Groepen en Gemeenten in Nederland* ("Grassroots Movement of Critical Groups and Communities in the Netherlands"), which supported the view that ministers should come from the local faith communities. Among other things, he defended the legitimacy, in emergency situations, of practices that were illicit

---

[28] For a reconstruction, see Richard Auwerda, *Dossier Schillebeeckx: Theoloog in de kerk der conflicten* (Bilthoven: Nelissen, 1969), 56–96.

[29] Nederlandse Bisschoppenconferentie, "De bisschoppen van Nederland over het concilie," *Katholiek Archief* 16 (1961), 369–84; cf. for the content, Jan Jacobs, *Met het oog op een andere kerk: Katholiek Nederland en de voorbereiding van het Tweede Vaticaans Oecumenisch Concilie 1959–1962* (Baarn: Nelissen, 1986), 88–92.

according to canon law, but that were defensible on the basis of faith, theology, and the pastoral situation.[30] In 1985, Schillebeeckx addressed a demonstration organized on the eve of Pope John Paul II's visit to the Netherlands to protest the official program of this visit and show "the other face of the church" in the Netherlands.[31] This demonstration would lead to the foundation of the *Acht Mei Beweging* ("8th of May Movement"), which became the standard-bearer of the progressive wing of Dutch Catholicism until its dissolution in 2003.

## III. "Confrontation" surrounding *The Dutch Catechism*

Although the symbolism was seemingly not intentional, it was both telling and significant that ten months after the closing of the Council, on October 4, 1966, the Dutch bishops presented a "new catechism for adults."[32] They had commissioned this new 600-page book, whose primary aim was to not rehash language used in the church in the past, but to be relevant in the present day.[33] It was its express purpose, "as much as possible to reflect and contain what has grown within the church, especially at the Council, in the field of insight, reflection, and clarification over the last decade."[34] This was highly innovative for a catechism.

> The whole message, the whole of the faith remains the same, but the approach, the light in which the faith is seen, is new. Everything that lives has both to remain itself and to renew itself. The message of Christ is a living thing, and hence this new type of catechism tries to present the faith of our fathers in a form suitable to the present day.[35]

---

[30] Edward Schillebeeckx, "Basis en ambt: Ambt in dienst van nieuwe gemeentevorming," *Basis en Ambt. Ambt in dienst van nieuwe gemeentevorming* (Bloemendaal: Nelissen, 1979), 43–90. An edited version of this article was included in idem, *Kerkelijk ambt: Voorgangers in de gemeente van Jezus Christus* (Bloemendaal: Nelissen, 1980), which itself was published in redacted form as *Pleidooi voor mensen in de kerk: Christelijke identiteit en ambten in de kerk* (Baarn: Nelissen, 1985). The same arguments appear in the brochure *Kerk en ambt: Onderweg naar een kerk met toekomst*, published by the Dutch Dominican province in 2007.

[31] Printed in *Archief van de Kerken* 40 (1985), 659–70; ET: Edward Schillebeeckx, "You and I have the Right to Be There," *For the Sake of the Gospel*, trans. John Bowden (London: SCM, 1989), 151–59.

[32] A long history preceded the publication of *De nieuwe katechismus*, a history that began long before the Council. See Paul Cooreman, "De ontstaansgeschiedenis van de Nieuwe Katechismus," *Geloof leren geloven: Twintig jaar "De nieuwe katechismus,"* ed. Jan van Lier and Jan Simons (Nijmegen: Hoger katechetisch instituut, 1987), 15–48. Cf. also Paul Cooreman, *De Noord-Nederlandse R.K. schoolkatechese in het spanningsveld tussen theologie en pedagogiek: Een studie van een proces van identiteitsbepaling tussen 1907 en 1966* (Dissertation, Katholieke Universiteit Leuven, 1974), 389–466.

[33] *De nieuwe katechismus: Geloofsverkondiging voor volwassenen* (Antwerp/'s-Hertogenbosch/Maaseik: Paul Brand/L.C.G. Malmberg/J.J. Romen en Zonen, 1966).

[34] "Herderlijk schrijven van de bisschoppen van Nederland over de nieuwe katechismus," dated September 8, 1966, and read in churches on October 9. Published in *Het dossier van de Nederlandse katechismus* (Utrecht: Bruna, 1968), 67–69.

[35] Kevin Smyth, trans., *A New Catechism: Catholic Faith for Adults* (New York: Herder and Herder, 1972), VII.

Thus, Cardinal Alfrink emphatically presented the book as a "safe guide" for the faithful.

"*The New Catechism* begins with the human being in his quest for God. It ends with God in his quest for man. Its starting point is human life, and it points out how the question about God arises there," according to the press release for the launch of the book by the *Hoger Katechetisch Instituut* ("Higher Catechetical Institute"), which was officially responsible for the text.[36] Commentators also regarded its emphasis on human life in all its concreteness as the Dutch Catechism's characteristic feature.[37] The book thus reflected a theological development that had fully come to the fore during the Council. From the 1930s onward, many Catholic theologians, despite various and sometimes significant differences, had begun to regard their discipline as a reflection on the lived experiences of the faithful with their faith in their everyday lives. According to many, the conciliar constitution on revelation, *Dei verbum*, had approved this notion by affirming that insight in the content of the faith grows "through the contemplation and study made by believers" and "through a penetrating understanding of the spiritual realities which they experience."[38] The tradition of the church is not primarily handed down in the teachings of the Magisterium, but first and foremost in the lived faith of the faithful. At the launch of the Dutch Catechism, the Higher Catechical Institute expressed the hope that the book would "be an invitation to dialogue, to a conversation about concrete human life, and within this to a conversation about great human life questions,"[39] thus contributing to the further development of Catholic tradition.

The Dutch Catechism was the occasion for countless conversations in many different places about the content and meaning of the Catholic faith. The text was read in innumerable discussion groups, where many Dutch Catholics appropriated its perspective in the second half of the 1960s. But it also led to a confrontation. On November 22, 1966, the Catholic daily newspaper *De Tijd* carried a report about an anonymous letter to the pope—beginning with the formula "Prostrate at the feet of Your Holiness, we write"—which complained that much of what "many Catholic writers and speakers, both from the laity and from the regular and secular clergy" were propounding was not in accord with Catholic doctrine. This had caused "great scandal," which was "increasing from day to day" and was "inflicting suffering ... and great sadness upon very many of the faithful." The newly published *Nieuwe katechismus*, "written at the behest of the bishops," was the main target of the criticism.[40] The following day, Schillebeeckx wrote a response in which he recounted that he had had the sensation, while browsing through a few old Catholic catechisms, of being confronted with a "textbook ... about some strange religion or other," a voice from a world in which he "was unable to recognise the contemporary Catholic life of faith." He concluded from this that any catechism was "naturally" bound by the limitations of

---

[36] "Documentatie voor de pers," *Witboek over de nieuwe katechismus*, ed. Willem Bless (Baarn: Ambo, 1969), 14–25, at 18.

[37] See, for instance, Gottfried Bitter, "Leben suchen und Leben erproben: Der Holländische Katechismus als Zeugnis einer 'Theologie des Volkes,'" *Theologie des Volkes*, ed. Adolf Exeler and Norbert Mette (Mainz: Matthias-Grünewald, 1978), 63–75.

[38] *Dei verbum* (November 18, 1965) 8, http://www.vatican.va/archive/hist_councils/ii_vatican_council/documents/vat-ii_const_19651118_dei-verbum_en.html.

[39] "Documentatie voor de pers," 17.

[40] "Brief van de 'confrontatiegroep' aan de heilige Vader," *De Tijd* (November 22, 1966); included in *Het dossier van de Nederlandse katechismus*, 70–71.

its time.[41] It was however precisely this notion that was an outrageous innovation in the eyes of the complainants. In their eyes, catechisms should convey the unchangeable teaching of the church, so as to protect the faithful against error. Only then, they believed, could a catechism truly be called a "safe guide."

The anonymous complaint against the Dutch catechism had a prior history. A stenciled bulletin had appeared under the title *Confrontatie* ("Confrontation") on November 1, 1964, which reported on an initiative taken by Catholics who were deeply concerned by the situation in the Dutch church at the time. Jan Bongaarts from Tegelen and Jules Thywissen from Venlo wrote that a "loose circle ... of priests and laypeople, men and women" had spontaneously emerged who by and large agreed that the "Catholic revival which had so painstakingly been set in motion after the war" had been "corrupted and blown off course" by recent developments, which were supported by the bishops. They called themselves "Confrontation," because they, as they explained, "were seeking a confrontation with those who have a different opinion on these very important issues."[42] The bulletin mentioned that possibilities were being investigated for publishing a journal in the same spirit. *Confrontatie* did indeed appear as a journal from June 1965 onward, and it ran until 1994.

The journal's official aim was formulated as "the defence of orthodoxy in faith and morals" and the "practice of prudence in implementing renewal."[43] Writing in a personal capacity however, Bongaarts, one of the instigators, declared forthrightly that *Confrontatie* was a "combative journal" directed against what he regarded as "cryptogamous heretics" among the opinion leaders of the Catholic elite, both priests and laypeople.[44] At a dialogue meeting organized at the behest of Cardinal Alfrink, Bongaarts, on behalf of *Confrontatie*, diagnosed the Dutch church as suffering from "a liberal movement that is quite dominant, or that, wherever it is not, paralyses large sectors of the church province, or causes it to function ambiguously or incorrectly." He called this movement a "hybrid," "partly Catholic, partly Protestant, partly humanist, preaching a pragmatic faith and a pragmatic morality, attuned to so-called real life."[45] It was mainly this lack of order and clarity that *Confrontatie* appeared to object to. The turn toward the modern world and acceptance of internal pluralism in the church were regarded by opinion leaders among the clergy and among articulate Catholic laypeople as an opportunity to turn the Catholic Church once more into a relevant factor in contemporary society. For the constituency to which *Confrontatie* catered, however, it stood for a betrayal of the mission of preserving the church from modern confusion and to orient itself only to God as the certain and unchangeable truth.

The petition to the pope concerning the Dutch Catechism had "*not* come from *Confrontatie*," the journal assured its readers.[46] But there were significant similarities, also observed by contemporary commentators, between the content of the petition and the comments that a "leading theologian" had made on the Dutch situation in an interview with the journal. In a later issue, the journal called Schillebeeckx's response to the petition a "philippic against a

---

[41] "Nieuwe bloei van integralisme: Rome-brief gevaarlijk," *De Volkskrant* (November 23, 1966); included in *Het dossier van de Nederlandse katechismus*, 72–75, at 72.

[42] Jan Bongaarts and Jules Thywissen, "Confrontatie," *Confrontatie* 1 (1964), 2–3.

[43] "Confrontatie," *Confrontatie* 4 (1965), 2–3.

[44] Jan Bongaarts, "Status quo, reveil of anarchie," *Confrontatie* 4 (1965), 3–4.

[45] "Verslag van de contact-bijeenkomst met 'Confrontatie', 20 mei 1968," *Katholiek Archief* 23 (1968), 1102–14, at 1113.

[46] "Petitie aan de Paus," *Confrontatie* 17 (1966), 3.

leading theologian."[47] There is little doubt that Schillebeeckx's confrere Jan van der Ploeg, who was the linchpin of *Confrontatie*, had written the petition in a personal capacity. The striking vehemence of Schillebeeckx's response was partly due to his irritation at the activities of his then fellow member of the Dominican priory in Nijmegen and colleague at the Catholic University of Nijmegen. In his view, van der Ploeg was sabotaging the Dutch episcopate's careful policies that fostered unity and openness, and he was casting aspersions on and obstructing Schillebeeckx's own work as a theologian. The latter was done in a fashion that Schillebeeckx regarded as defamatory and irresponsible, with insinuations and anonymous complaints. Van der Ploeg in fact later admitted that he had also been a driving force behind the complaint that led to the first inquiry into Schillebeeckx's orthodoxy in 1968.[48]

## Faith understood as a quest

Schillebeeckx believed that the petition to the pope targeted more than simply the text of the Dutch Catechism. He was very eager to show his understanding for those of the faithful "whose experience of the faith and whose thinking is still marked by what I might call the atmosphere of the old catechisms" and who now "have and even cultivate the feeling that they are confronted with a new, but heretical catechism." Moreover, he believed many legitimate criticisms could be made of *De nieuwe katechismus*: "it is possible to make critical comments almost on every page … [e]specially on [the sections on] morality, which, I think, lack social commitment." In fact, the specifics of the Dutch Catechism's content and approach were rather far removed from Schillebeeckx's own theological priorities.[49] The book's *auctor intellectualis* was the Dutch Jesuit theologian Piet Schoonenberg (1911–1999), who had been a colleague of Schillebeeckx's in Nijmegen since 1964. *De nieuwe katechismus* adhered to an evolutionary view of the world and of the history of the human mind and of religion, one inspired by the views of the French Jesuit and paleontologist, Pierre Teilhard de Chardin (1881–1955), who had been controversial in the 1950s. Schillebeeckx had little affinity with this way of thinking. In line with the work of Chenu, whom he regarded as his mentor, he focused instead on the relationship of concrete human history to faith and theology. Moreover, as early as the 1960s, he linked the meaning of the faith not only to existential but also, emphatically, to societal and social questions.

Despite its shortcomings however, he regarded the Dutch Catechism as "precisely the catechism that the Netherlands needs in the following five years." His identification with this book was strong enough to agree to travel to Gazzada in Italy in 1967 with Schoonenberg

---

[47] For the criticisms of the anonymous "leading theologian," see "Theologische kritiek op katechismus," *Confrontatie* 15–16 (1966), 34–43. For the designation of Schillebeeckx's response to the petition as a "philippic against a prominent theologian," see *Confrontatie* 36 (1968), 18.

[48] Tensions rose between van der Ploeg and Schillebeeckx, both of whom were members of the same Dominican priory, and in 1970 this led to the departure of the former. See Marit Monteiro, *Gods predikers: Dominicanen in Nederland (1795–2000)* (Hilversum: Verloren, 2008), 696–97. Cf. also Auwerda, *Dossier Schillebeeckx*, 40–48.

[49] For the Dutch catechism's content and approach, see Erik Borgman, "God en mens op zoek naar elkaar: Karakterisering van de inhoud," *Geloof leren geloven: Twintig jaar "De nieuwe katechismus,"* ed. Jan van Lier and Jan Simons (Nijmegen: Hoger katechetisch instituut, 1987), 49–54.

and his fellow Jesuit, Wim Bless, to defend *De nieuwe katechismus* in a meeting with three theologians appointed by the Holy See. An investigation had been launched into the orthodoxy of the catechism in response to the petition addressed to the pope in the previous year.[50] The decisive factor for Schillebeeckx was that the Dutch catechism did not treat the faith as a set of truths and rules, but as a living mystery, which the text implied "in a very careful, tentative formulation."[51] In a "contact meeting" with people from *Confrontatie* in 1968 at which he was present, Schillebeeckx explained that he had hoped that the Dutch Catechism would indeed become a safe guide for the post-conciliar period because the book "could have caught what was happening in the quest of faith."[52] This was obviously something that he believed was critically important.

It is quite tragic for Schillebeeckx that, in spite of himself, he became a factor in the polarization of the post-conciliar period, which was the very thing that hampered this process of catching what was happening in the search for faith. As early as 1952, he had written in the preface to his first major book, *De Sacramentele heilseconomie* ("The Sacramental Economy of Salvation"), that true theology is not alienated from life because "it emerges from the life of faith itself, and in turn feeds the life of faith."[53] This is what he tried to foster throughout his own lifetime. Before the Council, his main concern was to demonstrate that concepts that appeared in the theology of the time as abstract concepts, alienated from reality, in fact were, and could once more become, the expression of living faith in a living God. In this sense, the title of his 1958 inaugural lecture for his professorship in Nijmegen, "In Search of the Living God," provides a good summary of the nature of his work up to that point.[54] After the Council, his efforts were concentrated mainly on showing that the faith is a light that reveals the present as the place where God's future has been and is being proclaimed. The formula that he eventually found to express this was *extra mundum nulla salus*—there is no salvation outside the world.[55] But this occurred in a context in which many people believed either that theology and the faith should simply be made to conform to contemporary culture or that culture should be subjected to a particular, allegedly unchangeable manifestation of faith and of theology. The impasse to which this led pained him, although he regarded the latter aspect as more stifling than the former.

Schillebeeckx was well able to understand that people were having difficulty with the traditional formulas of the faith. He believed that theology would be able to integrate the secularized view

---

50  Cf. for this, see *Il dossier del Catechismo Olandese* (Milan: Mondadori, 1968). For a substantive analysis, see Erik Borgman, "De discussie met Rome," *Geloof leren geloven: Twintig jaar "De nieuwe katechismus,"* ed. Jan van Lier and Jan Simons (Nijmegen: Hoger katechetisch instituut, 1987), 96–102.

51  Schillebeeckx, "Nieuwe bloei van integralisme," 72–73.

52  "Verslag van de contact-bijeenkomst met 'Confrontatie,'" 1111.

53  Henricus Edward Schillebeeckx, *De sacramentele heilseconomie. Theologische bezinning op S. Thomas' sacramentenleer in het licht van de traditie en van de hedendaagse sacramentsproblematiek* (Antwerp/Bilthoven: 't Groeit/H. Nelissen, 1952), v.

54  Edward Schillebeeckx, "The Search for the Living God," *Essays, CW* vol. 11 (London: Bloomsbury T&T Clark, 2014), 35–50.

55  To my knowledge, this happened for the first time in Edward Schillebeeckx, "Spreken over God in een context van bevrijding," *TGL* 40 (1984), 7–24, esp. 18–24. According to a footnote, this article was based on a lecture given by Schillebeeckx in 1983. It is a major theme in Edward Schillebeeckx, *Church, CW* vol. 10 (London: Bloomsbury T&T Clark, 2014).

of the world and thus remove their objections. He could not imagine that secularization would cause all sensibility to any religious perspective on reality to all but disappear. It saddened him that the church that he so ardently wished to serve offered him so little space to further develop his reflections on the insights that he had obtained partly due to the Council. This not only gave him a sense that the church failed to appreciate him, but also led to doubt whether his theological work ultimately had any meaning. After his death in 2009, a note was found among his papers that probably dates back to 1980 and which has since become identified as the "drawer text" due to the place where it was found. Probably written in preparation for a speech to fellow theologians, it said that, despite the resistance he had encountered, doing theology had become something he was "existentially unable to do without," and that he would continue to do it, if need be in defiance of ecclesiastical condemnation.[56] When he wrote this, he was waiting for the outcome of the investigation launched by the Roman Congregation for the Doctrine of the Faith into the orthodoxy of his book, *Jesus: An Experiment in Christology* (1974). The reflection that he wrote after finally received the ruling (which incidentally did not contain any condemnation) shows that the encounters in Rome and his inability to make his interrogators understand what he was trying to do, caused him great sadness.[57]

It is striking that the "drawer text" mentions none of the issues that had been the object of the Roman investigation. This note bears out that the crucial issue for him was to continue reflecting on the relationship between the salvation that comes from God and takes shape in the world, on the one hand, and the ecclesial and faithful awareness of this salvation and its theological conceptualization, on the other hand. There is no use speculating what else Schillebeeckx might have done in this field had he not suffered so much on account of the ecclesiological winter that set in—he believed—under Pope John Paul II and Joseph Ratzinger as prefect of the Congregation for the Doctrine of the Faith. The impressive number of texts that he wrote despite these circumstances suggests that a new generation should continue where he left off, particularly because in the meantime situations have materialized in the world and in the church that are wholly different from and unforeseen by his generation.[58] It was never Schillebeeckx's intention to form a school of students and followers. But this has not prevented his works from continuing to influence theologians. Luckily, and hopefully, this influence will continue.

---

[56] This remarkable text, discovered by Ted Schoof among Schillebeeckx's papers, will be published in the not too distant future.

[57] Edward Schillebeeckx, "Theologische overpeinzing achteraf," *TvT* 20 (1980), 422–26. Cf. for these documents on the case, see Ted Mark Schoof, ed., *The Schillebeeckx Case: Official Exchange of Letters and Documents in the Investigation of Fr. Edward Schillebeeckx, O.P. by the Sacred Congregation for the Doctrine of the Faith, 1976–1980*, trans. Matthew J. O'Connell (New York: Paulist Press, 1984).

[58] See, for example, the attempt to write the "fundamental document" for the contemporary Dutch situation and for modern society which Schillebeeckx so passionately argued for in 1967 prior to the Pastoral Council, but which was never written, in Erik Borgman, *Leven van wat komt: Een katholiek uitzicht op de samenleving* (Utrecht: Meinema, 2017).

# Chapter 12

# "A Conductor Who Is Playing the Violin Part"

## Schillebeeckx and Historical-Critical Exegesis

### Laura Tack

"Take your Bible and take your newspaper, and read both. But interpret newspapers from your Bible."[1] This often-quoted advice by Karl Barth could as well have served as a motto for Edward Schillebeeckx's theological project. Few Catholic systematic theologians have given the biblical corpus such a prominent place in their theology as he did; even less have recognized the critical potential of the biblical narratives for present-day Christian experience. In his first *Jesus* book from 1974, Schillebeeckx fully embraced the historical-critical approach to exegesis in order to develop his own critical *prolegomena* toward a contemporary Christology.

In order to explain Schillebeeckx's methodological option for historical-criticism, this article starts off by succinctly showing that Schillebeeckx has always had a particular preference for including biblical revelation in his theological reasoning. The second part is devoted to Schillebeeckx's methodological rationale behind the inclusion of historical-critical exegesis in his *Jesus* books. It successively treats Schillebeeckx's own understanding of historical-critical exegesis, his treatment of prejudice in the exegetical works, and his navigation between myth and historical truth.

Schillebeeckx's particular interest in historical-critical exegesis, however, cannot be understood without taking into account the broader hermeneutical context of his work. By relying on historical-criticism, Schillebeeckx not only aspires to bring the stories of the New Testament in relation with contemporary Christianity, but also resolves to bring exegesis and theology in a mutually enriching dialogue. In his response to the exegete Piet Schoonenberg, he explains the methodological endeavor by comparing this dialogue to the situation of an orchestra. "When theology has come to a dead end," he writes, "it is inevitable for the 'conductor' to also play the violin part from time to time, to blend into the orchestra in order to see where its pressure points are."[2] In other words, according to Schillebeeckx, it is the theologian's task to conduct the orchestra, in which historical-critical exegesis plays the prestigious violin part. The following article attempts to investigate how Schillebeeckx is both the conductor and the first violinist in the orchestra of his Christological project.

---

[1] "Barth in Retirement," *Time Magazine*, May 31, 1963. http://content.time.com/time/subscriber/article/0,33009,896838,00.html.

[2] Edward Schillebeeckx, "Schoonenberg en de exegese," *TvT* 16 (1976), 44–54, 54.

# I. Schillebeeckx and the Bible: A constant in his work

Schillebeeckx's early works have, perhaps undeservedly,[3] been characterized as bearing the stamp of the early-twentieth-century neo-Thomistic theology. Already in these first works, however, biblical analysis discreetly introduces fresh insights. In his 1952 dissertation on the sacramental theology of Thomas Aquinas, for instance, Schillebeeckx includes a section on the sacrament as *"mustèrion,"* which consists of a succinct study of Old and New Testament passages.[4] The first chapter of *Christ the Sacrament of the Encounter with God* (*Christus sacrament van de godsontmoeting* [1959]), which deals with the Christological foundation of the sacraments, is based on continuous references to biblical passages.[5] However, one cannot quite yet consider this chapter as a dress rehearsal for the exegetically informed Christology of his first *Jesus* book since it lacks references to contemporary exegetical literature and is not yet equipped with the clear-cut methodological reflection that characterizes his later trilogy.

Nonetheless, the seeds of the later methodological awareness are already present in the writings of the 'early' Schillebeeckx. His 1958 article on Holy Scripture in the Dutch theological dictionary, *Theologisch woordenboek*, is the first to contain a reflection on the place of the Bible in revelation and theology.[6] His 1962 article entitled *Exegese, Dogmatik und Dogmenentwicklung*[7] presents a more extensive discussion on the complex relationship between theologians and exegetes, a concern that was already voiced in an earlier study on Mariology.[8]

Schillebeeckx's particular interest in the place of Scripture in the revelatory process grew during the course of the Second Vatican Council. In 1965 he published an article in which he explains the Council's understanding of revelation and Scripture to a broader public.[9] The first volume of his "Theological Soundings" series, *Revelation and Theology* (*Openbaring en theologie*), first published in 1964, is fully devoted to the relationship between revelation and theology. The first part of the volume contains a fundamental reflection on the Bible as segment of the revelation. In the second part, which deals with the faithful response to the revelation, Schillebeeckx incorporates his 1962 article on dogmatics and exegesis, which shows its central role for his own thought process.[10] Although the second volume of the same series from 1965,

---

[3]  Stephan van Erp, "Tussen traditie en situatie. Edward Schillebeeckx voor een volgende generatie," *TvT* 50 (2010), 6–26, 11–12.

[4]  Henricus Schillebeeckx, *De sacramentele heilseconomie: Theologische bezinning op S. Thomas' sacramentenleer in het licht van de traditie en van de hedendaagse sacramentsproblematiek* (Antwerp/ Bilthoven: 't Groeit/H. Nelissen, 1952), 35–48.

[5]  Edward Henricus Schillebeeckx, *De Christusontmoeting als sacrament van de Godsontmoeting: Theologische begrijpelijkheid van het heilsfeit der sacramenten* (Antwerpen/Bilthoven: 't Groeit/H. Nelissen, 1959), 13–33.

[6]  Henricus Schillebeeckx, *Theol. Woordenboek*, s.v. "Schrift, H." (Roermond/Maaseik: J.J. Romen & Zonen, 1958), cols. 4294–99.

[7]  Eduard Schillebeeckx OP, "Exegese, Dogmatik und Dogmenentwicklung," *Exegese und Dogmatik*, ed. H. Vorgrimler (Mainz: Matthias Grünewald, 1962), 91–114.

[8]  Edward Schillebeeckx, "Verschillend standpunt van exegese en dogmatiek," *Maria in het boodschapsverhaal: Verslagboek der zestiende Mariale dagen 1959* (Tongerlo, 1960), 53–74.

[9]  Edward Schillebeeckx, "De godsopenbaring en de heilige boeken volgens het tweede vaticaans concilie," *TGL* 21 (1965), 461–77.

[10]  Edward Schillebeeckx, "The Bible and Theology," *RT, CW* vol. 2 (London: Bloomsbury T&T Clark, 2014), 119–37 [I 184–214].

*God and Man* (*God en Mens*), has a different line of approach, it nonetheless contains an early discussion with biblical scholarship. The fourth chapter of this volume begins with a critical evaluation of *Honest to God* (1963), the controversial work by the Cambridge New Testament scholar and Anglican Bishop John A.T. Robinson.[11] Robinson suggested emptying faith of its biblical and allegedly mythological language by replacing it with modern terminology in order to make faith understandable in a secularized world. Contrary to Robinson's plea, Schillebeeckx remarks that it is impossible to "peel off" these biblical expressions so as to reach the "*nuda vox Dei*," since it is impossible to talk about the divine reality without a certain conceptional representation.[12] Schillebeeckx's concern with biblical expressions and conceptualizations also shines through the third volume of this series on *World and Church* (*Wereld en Kerk*) in 1966, wherein he develops a biblical anthropology in the third chapter.[13]

Schillebeeckx's preoccupation with the privileged place of Scripture in the revelation process, which emerged by the end of the 1950s and matured during the 1960s, culminated in 1974 in the publication of *Jesus: An Experiment in Christology* (*Jezus, het verhaal van een levende*).[14] In 1972 he already voiced his trust in the historical-critical exegesis as the most adequate way to fully grasp the New Testament testimony of the historically unique Jesus-event.[15] In the first volume of his trilogy, he substantiates this claim by incorporating numerous historical-exegetical studies on the gospels. Historical-criticism remains the framework in which he presents the New Testament theology of grace in the second volume of his trilogy *Christ: The Christian Experience in the Modern World* (*Gerechtigheid en liefde: Genade en bevrijding*) from 1977.[16] The biblical basis of ecclesiology and soteriology also shimmers through to the surface of the third chapter of *Church: The Human Story of God* (*Mensen als verhaal van God*), the final volume of his trilogy published in 1989.[17]

The gospel narrative continues to hold a prominent place in his later publications, *Evangelie verhalen* (1983), *Om het behoud van het evangelie* (1989), and, more recently, *Verhalen van een levende: Theologische preken* (2015).[18] These are collections of his sermons in which Schillebeeckx reveals himself not only as a theologian who incorporates gospel narratives on a systematic level, but also as a narrator who evokes the gospel message in an ever-fresh way to his present-day audience.

---

[11] Edward Schillebeeckx, *God and Man*, trans. Edward Fitzgerald and Peter Tomlinson, Theological Soundings (New York: Sheed and Ward, 1969), 140–54.

[12] Ibid., 142–43.

[13] Edward Schillebeeckx, "Man and His Bodily World," *WC, CW* vol. 4 (London: Bloomsbury T&T Clark, 2014), 177–86 [230–43].

[14] Edward Schillebeeckx, *Jezus, het verhaal van een levende* (Bloemendaal: Nelissen, 1974); ET: Edward Schillebeeckx, *Jesus, CW* vol. 6 (London: Bloomsbury T&T Clark, 2014).

[15] Edward Schillebeeckx, "De toegang tot Jezus van Nazareth," *TvT* 12 (1972), 28–59.

[16] Edward Schillebeeckx, *Gerechtigheid en liefde: Genade en bevrijding* (Bloemendaal: Nelissen, 1977); ET: Edward Schillebeeckx, *Christ, CW* vol. 7 (London: Bloomsbury T&T Clark, 2014).

[17] Edward Schillebeeckx, *Mensen als verhaal van God* (Baarn: Nelissen, 1989); ET: Edward Schillebeeckx, *Church, CW* vol. 10 (London: Bloomsbury T&T Clark, 2014).

[18] Edward Schillebeeckx, *Evangelie verhalen* (Baarn: Nelissen, 1982); Edward Schillebeeckx, *Om het behoud van het evangelie. Evangelie verhalen II* (Baarn: Nelissen, 1989); Edward Schillebeeckx, *Verhalen van een levende: Theologische preken van Edward Schillebeeckx*, ed. Hadewych Snijdewind (Nijmegen: Valkhof, 2014).

# II. Historical-criticism and Schillebeeckx's theological project

According to Hermann Häring, the publication of the first *Jesus* book in 1974, in which Schillebeeckx consistently reflects on Jesus Christ from a historical perspective, marked a turning point in his thought.[19] As will be demonstrated below, this development goes hand in hand with the incorporation of historical-critical exegesis in his work. Schillebeeckx, however, did not blindly follow historical-criticism as such, but always maintained a critical distance by integrating it in a broader hermeneutical framework. His ceaseless interest in the New Testament Jesus of Nazareth is nonetheless remarkable and continues to surface, even in a later article published in 2002.[20]

It is not my intention to critically evaluate Schillebeeckx's dependence on historical-critical exegesis to deal with particular problems. This would lead us too far and has already been amply covered in a substantial number of critical articles and reviews by both systematic theologians and biblical scholars following the book's original publication in 1974.[21] I want to focus instead on Schillebeeckx's own meta-reflection on the place of historical-criticism within his theological project.

## Historical-criticism: A tentative definition

To comprehend the way in which Schillebeeckx relates to historical-critical exegesis, it is necessary to first define what historical-criticism is. I will follow the description by George Aichele, Peter Miscall, and Richard Walsh in their 2009 article addressing the ever-growing abyss between historical-critical and postmodern interpretations of the Bible.[22] The possible disadvantage of taking this definition as our starting point is that we are basing ourselves on an understanding of historical-critical exegesis with which Schillebeeckx's contemporaries in

---

[19] Hermann Häring, "God – 'puur verrassing': Edward Schillebeeckx' doorbraak naar een narratieve theologie," *TvT* 45 (2005), 15.

[20] Edward Schillebeeckx, "De vroeg-christelijke receptie van Jezus bezien vanuit het heden: Een kritisch model voor christelijk geloven nu," *TvT* 42 (2002), 390–400.

[21] Albert Descamps and Piet Schoonenberg, for instance, commented at the time on Schillebeeckx's position with regard to the Q-community, his alleged neglect of John in favor of the synoptics, and his interpretation of the story of the empty tomb. Albert L. Descamps, "Compte Rendu. Edward Schillebeeckx, Jezus. Het verhaal van een levende, 1974," *Revue théologique de Louvain* 6 (1975), 212–23. Piet Schoonenberg, "Schillebeeckx en de exegese," *TvT* 15 (1975), 255–68. Also, Joseph Ramisch gives a critical appraisal of his exegetical work. Joseph Ramisch, "The Debate Concerning the 'Historical Jesus' in the Christology of Schillebeeckx," *Semeia* 30 (1984), 29–48 (especially pp. 44–45). Next to voicing some general concerns with Schillebeeckx's theological intent, the Classics scholar and Catholic convert Cornelia de Vogel also included some marginal notes on Schillebeeckx's integration of Hellenistic parallels. Cornelia J. de Vogel, *De grondslag van onze zekerheid: Over de problemen van de Kerk heden. Een bijdrage tot reële theologische discussie* (Assen/Amsterdam: Van Gorcum, 1977), 144–52.

[22] George Aichele, Peter Miscall, and Richard Walsh, "An Elephant in the Room: Historical-Critical and Postmodern Interpretations of the Bible," *Journal of Biblical Literature* 128 (2009), 383–404.

the field of biblical studies would most likely not have identified with, since the postmodern diversity in biblical approaches was not yet so forcefully present at that time. Yet, the description by Aichele and his colleagues has the advantage that it situates historical-criticism in a broader hermeneutical field containing other approaches to the biblical text. Historical-criticism remains the most important, but not the only player in this field. This comes in handy for our understanding of historical-criticism in Schillebeeckx's broader theological framework.

First, as Aichele and his colleagues point out, it is reductive to speak of historical-criticism as a clear-cut *method* that has remained invariable in different contexts and over different periods of time. It is, on the contrary, "not a single, scientific method, repeatable in different laboratories."[23] It is better to speak of it as an *approach*.

Second, historical-criticism functions as an *umbrella term* to characterize the diversity of methodologies that belong to it.

> Historical criticism [...] comprises the congeries of well-known methods such as source criticism, form criticism, grammatical studies, and archaeology, and it attempts to combine them in ways that will produce assured and agreed-on interpretations of the biblical text, whether these be understood as the author's intention, the understanding of the original audiences, or reference to actual historical events.[24]

The common denominator of the methodologies associated with historical-criticism is their *focus on the original historical context*, be it the authorial intent, the way in which the biblical message was originally received, or the retrieval of the historical events underlying the biblical text. This focus on the historical 'object' as such implies that, according to the historical-critical approach, biblical scholars are supposed to be wholly objective and to not let their scientific judgment be clouded by their own presuppositions. This would be the only way to reach the "agreed-on interpretations" that historical-criticism aims at. The mere willingness of the approach to be scientifically objective, however, does not automatically entail that historical-criticism as an approach would be without prejudice. According to Emmanuel Nathan, "its presuppositions [are] that truth is acquired by means of objective methods."[25] The great prejudice that underlies historical-criticism is, therefore, its "prejudice against prejudice."[26]

Third, since Schillebeeckx critically engages with historical-critical exegesis in a trilogy that aims to retrieve the significance of the historical Jesus of Nazareth for present-day Christians, it is important to also take into account the following remarks by Aichele and his colleagues. Although "historical Jesus research" operates according to the standards of objectivity in historiography, "it would not be too extreme to describe much of this research as markedly Christian or, at least, fundamentally religious."[27] Notwithstanding the results of the different quests into the historical Jesus that have often been looked upon as revolutionary in view of doctrinal authority, the fact that Jesus of Nazareth has at all attracted the interest of historical-critical exegetes has much

---

[23]  Ibid., 396.

[24]  Ibid., 384.

[25]  Emmanuel Nathan, "Truth and Prejudice: A Theological Reflection on Biblical Exegesis," *Ephemerides Theologicae Lovanienses* 83 (2007), 281–318 (at 282).

[26]  Ibid., 290.

[27]  Aichele, "An Elephant in the Room," 392.

more to do with the central role of Jesus in their own religious life than with their objective standards. Even the tendency to strip off the mythological language describing Jesus in the New Testament in order to call forth the "bare" historical Jesus often results in the creation of yet another modernized Christ-myth that is the spitting image of the critical exegete that created it.[28] Just like fictional characters in contemporary novels, these images of Jesus often play the role of the critical and modern individual that rebels against the repressive establishment.[29]

This description of the historical-critical approach to the Bible puts forward three questions that we need to keep in mind when discussing the influence of historical-criticism on Schillebeeckx's work. [1] What kind of historical-critical approach does Schillebeeckx prefer and why? [2] Is Schillebeeckx aware of the presuppositions that might be involved in the exegetical studies he includes, and how does he deal with these theological prejudices? [3] Where does Schillebeeckx situate himself on the spectrum between myth and historical truth? What kind of historical Jesus does Schillebeeckx present, and how is his Jesus fundamentally religious?

Before we answer these questions, it is important to give the floor to Schillebeeckx himself and read how he motivated the necessity of integrating historical-critical exegesis in his first *Jesus* book. In an introductory "Note on exegesis and theology," he writes the following. Since his reasoning is rather comprehensive, we opt to reproduce it unimpaired.

> If the New Testament incorporates the first, constitutive impulse of the movement centred on Jesus in a potent testimony of faith, consciously guided and governed by what had been achieved through God's saving activity in Jesus of Nazareth, then theological reflection of any sort inevitably hinges on understanding this New Testament. Here, in human language, in words and images deriving from the social, cultural and religious idiom of the time, Christians expressed their belief in the decisive, God-given salvation-in-Jesus which they had experienced. In such circumstances, to dispense with a scientific approach to the bible using all the methods of modern literary criticism would simply be to flout what is usually referred to as the "Word of God"—which in any case only reaches us through the words of religious people. If a believing community [...] wants to recover precisely what those affirmations of human faith signified at that time, it cannot do without literary criticism in its approach to the New Testament [...]— unless it is prepared to ignore a fundamental belief, namely that the church itself, whether local congregation or governing authority, falls under God's judgement and lordship, being subject to the norm presented by the person and activity of Jesus of Nazareth, whom it acknowledges as "the Christ, the only begotten Son, our Lord."[30]

Schillebeeckx clearly voices the conviction that one does not respect the biblical text if one does not study it in its historical context, adopting modern literary critical methods. This conviction is not new for Schillebeeckx. In his 1958 article for *Theologisch woordenboek*, he had already

---

28  Ibid., 389–96.
29  Ibid., 393.
30  Schillebeeckx, *Jesus*, 18–19 [36].

articulated a similar concern.[31] What is new, however, is the realization of his own, religious motivation for opting for a historically based approach to the New Testament. His concentration on the historical Jesus is not so much motivated by a modern scientific intent to access the objective historical facts, as it is driven by a religious constellation in which the church itself has radically turned to a historical person, Jesus of Nazareth, who is confessed as the Christ.

## Historical-criticism according to Schillebeeckx

We begin by describing *what kind* of historical-critical exegesis Schillebeeckx incorporates. It is clear that Schillebeeckx, when it comes to historical-criticism, does not believe in "exploiting one particular method alone" and takes into consideration diverse methodological implementations and results.[32] This awareness underlies "Section 2" of the first, methodological part in *Jesus: An Experiment in Christology*, which not only contains references to redaction criticism, form criticism, and tradition criticism, but also includes a discussion on the Q-hypothesis. Moreover, the first part of the book provides the substructure for the mainly exegetical study in the second and third parts, wherein Schillebeeckx engages in a dialogue with the authoritative historical-critical exegetes of his time. Given the *Forschungsgeschichtliche* context at that given moment, it is not surprising that a substantial number of his exegetical conversation partners came from the German-speaking world (Ferdinand Hahn, Odil Steck, Klaus Berger, etc.). This elicited a reproach from the Congregation for the Doctrine of the Faith that Schillebeeckx had aligned himself too closely with Liberal Protestant exegetes.[33]

One can only admire Schillebeeckx's rare ability to synthesize such an amount of exegetical literature in his *Jesus* books. It even seems to have been an impossible task, as Albert Descamps remarks laconically at the end of his elaborate review of the first book: "*la tâche était impossible, parce que démesurée.*"[34] Schillebeeckx himself tries to curtail the immensity of the task at hand by choosing to only discuss the exegetical conclusions that also have a significant systematic-theological impact, but even then, the amount of work must have been considerable.[35]

In the first volume of his trilogy, the dependence on historical-critical exegesis was mainly concerned with historical-Jesus research. This methodological focus shifts in *Christ: The Christian Experience in the Modern World*, since he no longer deals with the "historical person" of Jesus but with "the New Testament elaboration of what Christians experienced in their encounter

---

[31] "De religieuze heilsbetekenis en de goddelijke inhoud van de openbaring worden in de H.S. immers uitgedrukt op een eigentijdse, joodse, oosterse wijze, en zijn in hun uitdrukking mede geconditioneerd door de opvattingen en de denkwijze van de gewijde schrijvers, die in een bepaald milieu stonden, door de tijdgeest, door thematische bedoelingen van waaruit de heilsgebeurtenissen en het woord van Christus worden beluisterd, enz." Schillebeeckx, "Schrift, H.," col. 4298.

[32] Schillebeeckx, *Jesus*, 20 [38]; Schillebeeckx, *Jezus, het verhaal van een levende*, 30.

[33] "Mais il est difficile de nier que vous trouvez de préférence (pas toujours certes) votre inspiration du côté de l'aile radicale des chercheurs protestants." Franjo Seper, "Questions au sujet du livre 'Jezus: het verhaal van een levende', adressées par la Congrégation pour la Doctrine de la Foi au Révérend Père Edward Schillebeeckx, O.P. [20th of October 1976]," *De zaak Schillebeeckx: Officiële stukken*, ed. Ted Schoof (Bloemendaal: Nelissen, 1980), 20.

[34] Descamps, "Compte Rendu," 223.

[35] Schillebeeckx, "Schoonenberg en de exegese," 47.

with Jesus the Lord."[36] This entails a priority of literary approaches to the biblical texts over historiography. These literary approaches are, however, fully embedded in a historical-critical perspective. Schillebeeckx's intention is to understand how these texts were written within their original context, for their original audience.[37]

Our answer to the second part of the question—namely, *why* did he choose that particular kind of historical-critical exegesis?—has to be slightly longer. As mentioned above, Schillebeeckx consciously opts for historical-criticism because of theological reasons. But there is more to say about this theologically conscious option. First, according to Schillebeeckx, historical-critical exegesis occupies the front rank when it comes to gaining access to the earthly Jesus. In his 1972 article, he discussed both the perturbing and positive aspects of historical-critical exegesis, which, especially in the nineteenth century, had been the cradle of many anti-dogmatic tendencies. Without denying this problematic aspect, Schillebeeckx eventually stresses the necessity of the approach "precisely because of the Christian faith."[38]

The privileged position of historical-criticism is closely related to the privileged place that the Scriptures have in revelation, which Schillebeeckx has already stressed in his other works. The New Testament is "irreplaceable" because of its unique access point to the Christian movement that arose in the wake of the Jesus-event, which is, for Schillebeeckx, the one and nonrecurrent historical event that is normative for theology.[39]

In *Interim Report on the Books Jesus & Christ* (*Tussentijds verhaal over twee Jezusboeken* [1978]), Schillebeeckx writes that, by reading these privileged testimonies to the Jesus-event with the help of historical-critical exegesis, he "cherished the hope that it would then become possible to catch a glimpse of what in Jesus must have been the source of both the positive and negative shock for his contemporaries."[40] This brings us to the second point. Schillebeeckx's preference for historical-criticism is indeed ideological-critically motivated. The historical focus is first and foremost the touchstone of his theological project because, as he writes, "without exegesis all theologizing will be up in the air."[41] Schillebeeckx already reflected on this in his 1962 article on exegesis and dogmatics, in which he pointed out that the "Christian exegesis and biblical theology also possess a critical function with respect to the contemporary arguments of theological dogmatics."[42] In addition to this, it is primarily the historical Jesus who exercises a "corrective function" with regard to Schillebeeckx's Christology.[43] This point was already present in his 1962 article in which he emphasized the never-ending critical potential of the original Jesus-event that has to be brought under attention by the exegete.[44] In 1972, Schillebeeckx added

---

[36] Schillebeeckx, *Christ*, 6 [22]; Schillebeeckx, *Gerechtigheid en liefde*, 20.

[37] Schillebeeckx, *Christ*, 7–9 [23–25].

[38] My translation. Edward Schillebeeckx, "De toegang tot Jezus van Nazaret," *TvT* 12 (1972), 28–60 (at 29–30): "juist omwille van het christelijke geloof." The article has largely been included in the first chapter of the first section of part I of *Jezus, het verhaal van een levende* (pp. 35–61).

[39] Schillebeeckx, *Jesus*, 40 [58–59]; Schillebeeckx, "De toegang tot Jezus van Nazaret,"47.

[40] Schillebeeckx, *IR, CW* vol. 8 (London: Bloomsbury T&T Clark, 2014), 26 [31]. Translation of Edward Schillebeeckx, *Tussentijds verhaal over twee Jezusboeken* (Bloemendaal: Nelissen, 1978), 39.

[41] Schillebeeckx, *Jesus*, 20 [38]; Schillebeeckx, *Jezus, het verhaal van een levende*, 30.

[42] Schillebeeckx, "Exegese, Dogmatik," 96: "christliche Exegese und die Bibeltheologie haben auch eine kritische Funktion gegenüber den heutigen Thesen der theologischen Dogmatik."

[43] Ramisch, "The Debate," 47.

[44] Schillebeeckx, "Exegese, Dogmatik," 113–14.

a substantial part on the critical potential of the *memoria Jesu*, which prevents present-day theologians from randomly reading their own needs and demands into the persona of Jesus.[45]

The importance of the remembrance of Jesus is related to a third point. Historical-criticism also serves the critical-hermeneutical confrontation of the Christian past with the Christian present, which is one of the central topics of the article by Schillebeeckx from 2002.[46] This point leads us already in the direction of Schillebeeckx's hermeneutics, which we cannot discuss in detail in this contribution, but which is nonetheless important in order to understand how Schillebeeckx relates to historical-criticism.

## Schillebeeckx on historical-critical exegesis and prejudice

Schillebeeckx consciously opts for historical-critical exegesis. He is, however, equally conscious about the possible presuppositions that might be silently present in the exegetical studies themselves. His willingness to integrate the results of historical-critical research into his own Christological thinking process consequently goes hand in hand with a critical distance toward historical-criticism. Schillebeeckx admits this in the methodological introduction to his first *Jesus* book, where he grappled with the lack of scholarly consensus on certain exegetical matters. It is striking, however, that he does not ascribe this lack of consensus to an inaccurate or faulty application of the historical-critical method as such but to the variety of prejudices held by the biblical scholars themselves. He deems it to be the theologian's principal task to recognize and evaluate these prejudices.[47]

Even in those cases in which a consensus reigns among exegetes, one has to investigate the prejudices potentially underlying those positions.[48] That is precisely the reason why Schillebeeckx does not want to be overly reliant on "global exegetical studies." In the guise of summaries of certain exegetical topics, they, in reality, often reflect the presuppositions of the compiler and reduce the theological diversity of the New Testament. Schillebeeckx prefers the "detailed studies" instead, which have a bigger chance of critically challenging his own assumptions.[49] Or as New Testament scholar and Schillebeeckx's colleague in Nijmegen, Bas van Iersel, remarked, "as a theologian" Schillebeeckx likes "to enter the jungle of the detailed exegetical studies by himself."[50] But even in the midst of the exegetical jungle, Schillebeeckx retains the necessary distance toward the exegetical research results. He even quotes Yves Congar in order to accentuate this point: "I respect and I constantly examine the science of exegetes, but I reject their magisterium."[51]

According to some of his critics, Schillebeeckx's unwillingness to uncritically submit to historical-critical exegesis makes him blind to the prejudice in his own theological venture.

---

[45] Schillebeeckx, "De toegang," 44.
[46] Schillebeeckx, "De vroeg-christelijke receptie," 394.
[47] Schillebeeckx, *Jesus*, 19 [37].
[48] Ibid.
[49] Ibid., 20 [38].
[50] Bas van Iersel, "Onontbeerlijk prolegomena tot een verhaal over Jezus," *Kosmos en Oekumene* 8 (1974), 174–79, at 175.
[51] Schillebeeckx, *Jesus*, 22 [40]. Quoting Yves Congar: "*Je respecte et j'intérroge sans cesse la science des exégètes, mais je récuse leur magistère.*"

Descamps, for instance, reproaches the theologian Schillebeeckx to subordinate the exegetical results to a *"christologie pré-établi,"* and he continues, alluding to the above-mentioned quote by Congar, that "[Schillebeeckx] is certainly right to reject, as a theologian, the magisterium of the exegetes. One wonders, however, if exegesis has not been submitted here to the magisterium of the theologian."[52] Piet Schoonenberg seems to want to make a similar point when he asks Schillebeeckx if he, in his rejection of global exegetical studies, has not in fact written exactly such a global study with his first *Jesus* book.[53] Schillebeeckx answers this critique by slightly nodding to Schoonenberg and even whimsically adding that, in the case that he had written such a global study, at least his has the advantage of having integrated more recent exegetical literature than the previous studies that existed before the publication of his own *Jesus* book.[54]

Both remarks hint at the existence of some kind of *a priori* Christology that appears to regulate Schillebeeckx's selection of the exegetical results. To evaluate the pertinence of these remarks, it is necessary to answer the third question that was mentioned above: What kind of historical Jesus does Schillebeeckx present, and how is his image of the historical Jesus fundamentally religious?

# III. Historical truth and myth in Schillebeeckx's reconstruction of the historical Jesus

The setup of Schillebeeckx's first *Jesus* book demonstrates that he deems it possible to access the "historical Jesus" with the help of the New Testament texts. The nature of this venture shows Schillebeeckx's affinity with the proponents of the so-called 'New Quest' into the historical Jesus.[55] Contrary to Rudolf Bultmann, who starts from the unbridgeable fissure between the Jesus of history and the Christ of the church, Schillebeeckx aligns himself with Ernst Käsemann. According to Schillebeeckx, Käsemann rightly relativizes the radicalism of this fissure between "Jesus" and "Christ."[56] Instead, Schillebeeckx stresses the continuity between the two: "The four gospels are undeniably [...] overlaid with the evangelists' own theology; but nonetheless they are thought to contain sufficient basic information about Jesus and recollections of him, with respect to his message, his attitude to life and his conduct as a whole."[57]

---

[52] Descamps, "Compte Rendu," 215–16. "[Schillebeeckx] a certes raison de récuser, comme théologien, le magistère des exégètes; on se demandera toutefois si l'exégèse n'a pas été soumise ici au magistère du théologien."

[53] Schoonenberg, "Schillebeeckx en de exegese," 267.

[54] Schillebeeckx, "Schoonenberg en de exegese," 48.

[55] As has already been stated by Schoonenberg, "Schillebeeckx en de exegese," 256; Reginald H. Fuller, *"The Historical Jesus: Some Outstanding Issues," Thomist* 48 (1984), 368–82 (at 375); Ramisch, "The Debate," 32. Also, in this case, however, Schillebeeckx keeps some critical distance when he writes that there are still some "liberal residues" to be found in the works of "the so-called proponents of the 'New Quest,'" who are still "looking for a 'phantom,' a sort of Jesus of Nazarath 'an sich.'" My translation. Schillebeeckx, "De toegang," 56; Schillebeeckx, *Jesus,* 50–51 [69–70].

[56] Schillebeeckx, *Jesus,* 51–52 [71].

[57] Ibid., 52 [72].

Schillebeeckx agrees with Bultmann, however, when he maintains that the soteriological reality of faith cannot be proven historically:

> In any case a historian as such cannot demonstrate that in Jesus God conducted a truly salvific activity. He cannot objectively establish it as a salvific fact. Whether before or after Jesus' death, that requires a religious decision based on events centered on Jesus, which are certainly identifiable but remain historically ambiguous, hence cannot be considered rationally cogent.[58]

Schillebeeckx, therefore, values Bultmann's distinction between a historical perspective and a faith perspective. In his 2002 article he repeats this point, stating that the question into the truth of Christianity cannot be answered by merely gathering historical knowledge of Christianity's origins.[59] He nonetheless maintains that a radical division between these two perspectives leads to the construction of "a kerygma-without-Jesus."[60] Here we reach the heart of Schillebeeckx's methodological decision to embrace historical-criticism, which is deeply ideologically critically motivated. If the core of Christianity were a kerygma without a historical foundation, Christianity would revolve around an idea, instead of a historical person; thus, he writes:

> In that way Christianity loses its universal purport and forfeits the right to continue speaking of God's ultimate saving activity in history: one would let the world be regulated by an *Ideengeschichte*. Ideas so often let us down or end up functioning as ideologies. I can only believe and put my trust in persons [...]. That is why for me the Christian faith entails not only the personal, living presence of the glorified Jesus, but also a link with his life on earth; for it is precisely that earthly life that was acknowledged and empowered by God through the resurrection. For me, therefore, a Christianity or kerygma minus the historical Jesus of Nazareth is ultimately vacuous—not Christianity at all, in fact. If the very heart of the Christian faith consists in an affirmation in faith of God's saving activity in history—decisively accomplished in the life history of Jesus of Nazareth—for the liberation of human beings [...], then the personal history of this Jesus cannot be lost sight of, nor can our talk about it in the language of faith degenerate into ideology.[61]

Schillebeeckx's own historical Jesus research is thus clearly religiously motivated, and yet the religious image of the historical Jesus that he presents in his first *Jesus* book has been considered to be reductionist by several critics. In its 1976 document on Schillebeeckx, the Congregation for the Doctrine of the Faith reproaches him for "a reduction of the texts to an undeniable kernel."[62]

---

[58] Ibid., 54 [74]. Cf. Schillebeeckx, *Tussentijds verhaal*, 35–37.
[59] Schillebeeckx, "De vroeg-christelijke receptie," 393.
[60] Schillebeeckx, *Jesus*, 56 [75].
[61] Ibid.
[62] Ted Mark Schoof, ed., *The Schillebeeckx Case: Official Exchange of Letters and Documents in the Investigation of Fr. Edward Schillebeeckx*, O.P. *by the Sacred Congregation for the Doctrine of the Faith, 1976–1980*, trans. Matthew J. O'Connell (New York: Paulist Press, 1984), 20. Original text: Franjo Seper, "Questions au sujet du livre," 21: "une *réduction* des textes à un noyau dur."

Similar remarks have been made by William Vandermarck and Cornelia De Vogel.[63] The latter perhaps chooses the fiercest formulation for her criticism when she writes: "It is 'the Gospel according to Edw. Schillebeeckx,' not the Gospel of the Church."[64] It is furthermore surprising that de Vogel, as a convert to Roman-Catholicism, chooses in her arduous criticism to give preference to the Liberal Protestant Bultmann and his option for the Christ of the church, rejecting the historical Jesus. As a consequence, she reproaches Schillebeeckx because he "gives preference to the historical Jesus—and places it in opposition to the Christ of the Church and the Christological dogma."[65] This last quote brings the criticism to Schillebeeckx's alleged reductionism to a head.

This reprimand, however, appears to be unjust based on three arguments. [1] Schillebeeckx himself is critical of any attempt to empty the biblical language, as was evident from his reception of Robinson's work. [2] Schillebeeckx by no means intends to give priority to a historically reconstructed Jesus-image over the Jesus of faith. In his response to the Congregation for the Doctrine of the Faith,[66] as well as in *Interim Report*, he stresses the distinction between "the 'Jesus of history,' i.e., Jesus himself living in Palestine in contact with his contemporaries, and the 'historical Jesus,' in the sense of the abstract result of a historical-critical investigation" and clearly emphasizes that "[i]t is not the historical image of Jesus, but the living Jesus of history who stands at the beginning and is the source, norm and criterion of what the first Christians interpretatively experienced in him."[67] Schillebeeckx's interest in contemporary historical-Jesus research is precisely faith-based and driven by his willingness to show to his present-day readers that Jesus actually lived and that his life is historically verifiable. [3] As is evident from his discussion with Schoonenberg, Schillebeeckx is fully aware of the relativity and open-endedness of each historical and systematic-theological construction, including his own.[68] He would, therefore, be the first to admit that any historical reconstruction necessarily entails a certain reduction. Besides, in the first methodological part of *Jesus*, Schillebeeckx already mentioned the possibility that the scholar's faith can influence the historical reconstruction.[69]

Once again, we have shown Schillebeeckx's religious point of view on the historical Jesus. Contrary to a strict historical-critical approach to exegesis, moreover, Schillebeeckx does not want to completely exclude faith from his exegetical venture. According to him, even the impulse of modern historical Jesus research is already driven by faith. One studies the historical Jesus precisely because of Jesus's significance for the present-day communities of faith.[70] Indeed, it is

---

[63] William Vandermarck, "Bijbelonderzoek, analogie en theologie," *Bijdragen* 35 (1974), 391: "Wanneer de gelovige in de werkelijkheid méér ziet dan de wetenschappelijke observering erin kan achterhalen, waarom zou hij dan de omvang en de dimensie van die werkelijkheid laten inperken door de wetenschappelijke observering, d.i. zich door de historisch-kritische methode laten voorschrijven hoe men Gods Woord, Jezus van Nazareth, moet verstaan?".

[64] de Vogel, *De grondslag*, 187. My translation. "Het is 'het Evangelie volgens Edw. Schillebeeckx', niet het Evangelie van de Kerk, die door haar eenstemmig belijden de grondslag is van onze zekerheid."

[65] Ibid., 184. My translation. "Schillebeeckx kiest de historische Jezus – en stelt deze *tegenover* de Christus van de Kerk en van het christologisch dogma."

[66] Schoof, *The Schillebeeckx Case*, 48–49. Original: *Réponses de E. Schillebeeckx O.P. au questionnaire n. 46/66 lui adressé par la Congrégation pour la Doctrine de la Foi* [April 13, 1977], *De zaak Schillebeeckx*, 60–1.

[67] Schillebeeckx, *IR*, 29 [33]; Schillebeeckx, *Tussentijds verhaal*, 42.

[68] Schillebeeckx, "Schoonenberg en de exegese," 44–5.

[69] Schillebeeckx, *Jesus*, 54–55 [73–5].

[70] Ibid., 50 [69–70]; Schillebeeckx, "De toegang," 56.

because the "Jesus of history" became the "Jesus of faith" that historical-critical Jesus research is interesting from a faith perspective.[71]

Still, the relationship between historiography and religious faith is complicated, as Schillebeeckx indicates in his 2002 article. Here, he first discusses the complexity on the level of the New Testament. Indeed, the New Testament offers theologically diverse perspectives on the Jesus-event, but that does not make its subject matter a mere myth. The New Testament has to be read as a variety of faith testimonies that find their foundation in the experience with the living Jesus.[72] Also, the New Testament finds itself within the hermeneutical circle, moving between situation and interpretation: "Without Jesus there would never have been a Christ and without Christ no Jesus."[73] He consequently discusses this complexity on the level of faith. In the first place, faith has to do with trust in God, but faith also means relating oneself to God as he is mediated to us by the interpreted experiences of the Jesus-event.[74] This interpretation of the Jesus-event occurs usually in the form of stories, which brings us to the final part of this chapter.

## The priority of the story

The story is the place where the historical event and its interpretation intersect, and it is the story that has priority for Schillebeeckx:

> when, after all its analyses and interpretations, reason is no longer able to articulate theoretically what is left to be said, it is obliged to express its elusive "surplus reality" in stories and parables. Hence an argumentative Christology should also end up as a story about Jesus, a narrative Christology, and not as an all-encompassing, theoretical "Christological system."[75]

The story that Schillebeeckx wants to tell draws its vigor from the past. The unique and historical Jesus-event, as recounted by its first witnesses in the New Testament, is its driving force. Schillebeeckx even remarks that history itself is constructed by stories.[76] However, he wants to bring these narrative testimonies into the present and retell the story for a present-day audience.

This is precisely why Schillebeeckx thinks that exegesis and systematic theology have to depend on each other. Exegesis investigates how the story sounded in the original historical context, while systematic theology deals with the way that the story is told in the subsequent centuries. Both exegesis and systematic theology are interrelated with each other as in a hermeneutical circle. On the one hand, the orientation of systematic theology toward exegesis has to go deeper than the search for "*dicta probantia*" for its proper hypotheses. Systematic theology has to be open to the critical challenge presented by exegesis through constant remembrance of the interpreted experiences of the original Jesus-event.[77] On the other hand, the orientation of

---

[71] Schillebeeckx, *IR*, 27 [32].
[72] Schillebeeckx, "De vroeg-christelijke receptie," 391.
[73] Ibid., 392.
[74] Ibid., 393.
[75] Schillebeeckx, *Jesus*, 59 [79].
[76] Schillebeeckx, *IR*, 28 [32].
[77] Schillebeeckx, "Exegese, Dogmatik," 96, 114.

exegesis on systematic theology implies that the exegete is more than a philological crafts(wo) man who operates outside the boundaries of the church.[78] In his first *Jesus* book, Schillebeeckx even uses the term "theological exegesis." Such a "theological exegesis sets out to discover the theological dimension in the actual historical phenomenon of early Christianity; this is where the truth question first arises, not just in the bible's 'topicality' for us today."[79] As such, the theologian navigates between the historical truth and religious truth that intersect in the New Testament stories about Jesus.

# Conclusion

Schillebeeckx's interest in historical-critical exegesis is genuinely historically motivated and fits well with the particular attention for the Bible in his works. At the same time, Schillebeeckx maintains a critical distance toward historical-criticism as such, especially its prejudices and its relationship to religious truth and faith. Schillebeeckx aligns himself with the historical-critical exegetical works of his time to get to the heart of the Christological matter: the historical event of an encounter with Jesus of Nazareth. Consequently, his attention for historical-criticism cannot be considered apart from his Christological project, which is itself rooted in faith and aimed at telling the story of the living Jesus to its present-day readers. In this regard, Schillebeeckx moves in a hermeneutical circle going from the "*fides quaerens intellectum historicum*" towards the "*intellectus historicus quaerens fidem*" and vice versa.[80] Schillebeeckx's main concern is the critical-hermeneutical confrontation of present-day believers in their own historical situatedness with the historical Jesus-event as it was interpreted in the New Testament.[81] This confrontation with the Jesus of history is from the beginning onward oriented toward the present and the future. As Schillebeeckx writes in his Prologue to his *Christ* book: "The account of the actual life of Christians in the world in which they live is a fifth gospel; it also belongs at the heart of Christology."[82]

---

[78] Ibid., 101–02.
[79] Schillebeeckx, *Jesus*, 21 [39]. This reflection on theological exegesis is not a new insight, but was already prepared in Schillebeeckx's article in the theological dictionary.
[80] Schillebeeckx, *IR*, 29 [34].
[81] Schillebeeckx, "Schoonenberg en de exegese," 44: "Een van de historiciteit ontdane theologie, zou voor in de tijd levende mensen irrelevant worden en dan ook geen voorlopige mijlpaal kunnen zijn op hun pelgrimage naar een grotere toekomst."
[82] Schillebeeckx, *Christ*, 2 [18].

# Chapter 13

# The Schillebeeckx Case

*Three Acts and an Open Ending*

Leo Kenis and Lieven Boeve

Beginning in the early 1960s, the theological activities of Edward Schillebeeckx met with a growing response from the public, both inside and outside of church life. An increasing number of Christians recognized Schillebeeckx as a theologian who was able to express their experiences in a rapidly changing world and context. Schillebeeckx, in his speaking and his writing, came to be seen as someone who offered them the opportunity to come to a new and meaningful understanding of their faith. However, he also elicited feelings of uncertainty and distrust among other believers, especially those who were afraid that certain forms of "renewal" would ultimately undermine their traditional certainties and practices. Thus, as the mouthpiece and promoter of church renewal in a rapidly secularizing Western Europe, Schillebeeckx unintentionally became involved in the polarization process that divided the Catholic Church of the Netherlands. Moreover, since the beginning of the Second Vatican Council, he was distrusted by central authorities of the church. Figures in Rome began to investigate his orthodoxy, and these inquiries continued in fits and starts during the decades that followed. So intense was the focus on his work that the "Schillebeeckx case" eventually threatened to turn into an "endless story."[1] The notoriety engendered by the investigations also had the effect of making Schillebeeckx even more famous—he became a symbol of reform gone too far for some, and a martyr of unjust ecclesial persecution and outdated processes for others. In our account of this story, we will concentrate on the essential facts of the case, sketch the specific ecclesiastical and historical context of the investigations, and, finally, we will give a brief historical-theological assessment of the case against Edward Schillebeeckx, which played out in three acts. This affair began with a short but crucial prelude, and it ended without a true finale, leaving the story, for better or for worse, open-ended.

---

[1] See Ad Willems, "Die endlose Geschichte des Edward Schillebeeckx," *Katholische Kirche – wohin? Wider den Verrat am Konzil*, ed. Norbert Greinacher and Hans Küng, Serie Piper 488 (Munich and Zürich: Piper, 1986), 411–23; ET: Ad Willems, "The Endless Case of Edward Schillebeeckx," *The Church in Anguish: Has the Vatican Betrayed Vatican II?*, ed. Hans Küng and Leonard Swidler (San Francisco: Harper & Row, 1987), 212–22.

# I. Prelude to conflict (1961–1962)

The problematic relationship between Edward Schillebeeckx and the Roman authorities cannot be separated from his position in the Catholic Church of the Netherlands, and particularly his connection with the Dutch episcopate. After his appointment as professor of theology in Nijmegen in 1958, Schillebeeckx was soon engaged as theological adviser to the Dutch bishops in the governance of their church. One of the results of this cooperation was a pastoral letter, wherein the Dutch bishops addressed their faithful to inform them about the coming ecumenical council.[2] The letter, published in January 1961, was actually composed by Edward Schillebeeckx and some colleagues, but at the end of the letter only Schillebeeckx was explicitly thanked by name, implicitly identifying him as its author. In their letter, the bishops formulated a number of key ideas aimed at renewal, for example the church as People of God, the relationship between the hierarchy and the community of believers, and the relation of papal primacy to the world episcopate.

The pastoral letter became internationally known, but in the spring of 1962, when an Italian version was published, criticism was expressed in Roman circles against certain opinions in the text (e.g. on papal infallibility).[3] The Archbishop of Utrecht, Bernard Alfrink, had to intervene in order to avoid a conflict with Rome. This incident brought the Dutch bishops and their church into question with a number of Catholics, particularly in higher ecclesiastical circles.[4] Edward Schillebeeckx, mentioned by name as a main contributor to the letter, shared in this ambiguity. He would come to believe that it was from this incident onward that Roman authorities began to monitor him and his activities.[5] The implications of their mistrust soon became clear when he was refused as official *peritus* at the Council.[6] Later on, his activities, especially as an adviser to the Dutch bishops at the Council, sharpened his ambivalent reputation in the Curia. Internationally, for friend and adversary alike, Edward Schillebeeckx became a sort of symbol for the Dutch Church and its struggle for renewal. Some years after the Council, church leaders in Rome who saw in this renewal a threat to Catholic faith decided to intervene directly in the ecclesial affairs in the Netherlands, and Edward Schillebeeckx became one of their first targets.

---

[2]  The full text was published separately as a brochure and reprinted as Nederlandse Bisschoppenconferentie, "De Bisschoppen van Nederland over het Concilie," *Katholiek Archief* 16 (1961), 369–84. An English translation appeared in *The Furrow* 12 (1961), 365–81. See also Chapter 7 on Edward Schillebeeckx and the preparation for the Second Vatican Council in this volume.

[3]  Jan van Laarhoven mentions the Holy Office, the Theological Commission, and theologians from the Lateranum around the journal *Divinitas*. Jan van Laarhoven, "In medio Ecclesiae … : Alfrink op het Tweede Vaticaans Concilie," *Alfrink en de Kerk 1951–1976: Historische en theologische essays, aangeboden aan kardinaal Alfrink bij zijn zilveren bisschopsjubileum* (Baarn: Amboboeken, 1976), 12–33, at 26.

[4]  Ibid., 22.

[5]  See Edward Schillebeeckx, *Theologisch testament: Notarieel nog niet verleden*, 2nd ed. (Baarn: Nelissen, 1995), 43.

[6]  Schillebeeckx thought that the request was rejected by Cardinal Ottaviani because of his contribution to the pastoral letter. Ibid., 48.

# II. The first case: On various theological issues (1968)

The first investigation into the work of Schillebeeckx became publicly known on September 24, 1968, when the French journalist Henri Fesquet announced in the newspaper *Le Monde* that the Congregation for the Doctrine of the Faith (the recently renamed Supreme Sacred Congregation of the Holy Office) had initiated "a sort of process" against Edward Schillebeeckx, without the knowledge of the persons concerned.[7] The Congregation had likely started the dossier after receiving complaints from Schillebeeckx's fellow Dominican and academic colleague Jan van der Ploeg.[8] The charges referred to various opinions taken from Schillebeeckx's publications and also contained all kinds of information (even press clippings) taken from his successful lecture tour of the United States in November–December of 1967.

The examination of Schillebeeckx's work was entrusted to three theologians who were active in Rome: the Belgian Jesuit Eduard Dhanis and the Dominicans Benedictus Lemeer and Mario Luigi Ciappi. They were expected to investigate various parts of Schillebeeckx's theology, such as his concept of revelation, his views on the natural knowledge of God and on the relation between church and world, his opinions on the Eucharist and transubstantiation, and on priestly celibacy. Cardinal Franjo Seper, the newly named successor of Alfredo Ottaviani as prefect of the Congregation for the Doctrine of the Faith, had appointed Karl Rahner a *relator pro auctore*—or Schillebeeckx's "defendant," a newly created function in these procedures. Rahner, who was a professor in Münster at that time, had become friends with Schillebeeckx as co-editor of the journal *Concilium* that was founded in 1965 with the purpose of giving theological support to church reforms begun at the Second Vatican Council.[9] The announcement of the inquiry into Schillebeeckx's work provoked much protest among Catholics.[10] The procedures of the process employed by the Congregation were sharply criticized, and Cardinal Alfrink clearly expressed his confidence that there was nothing blameworthy about his theologian.

On October 7, two weeks after the announcement of the inquiry, the consulters of the Congregation for the Doctrine of the Faith came together to discuss the matter with Rahner. He convincingly refuted the objections against Schillebeeckx's theology and did not refrain

---

[7] Extensive and detailed information in Richard Auwerda, *Dossier Schillebeeckx: Theoloog in de kerk der conflicten* (Bilthoven: Nelissen, 1969), esp. 56–110; "Verwikkelingen rondom prof. mag. dr E. Schillebeeckx," *Katholiek Archief* 23 (1968), 1010–18, 1048–55. See also Schillebeeckx, *Theologisch testament*, 59–60.

[8] On this, see Auwerda, *Dossier Schillebeeckx*, 61–63; Marit Monteiro, *Gods Predikers: Dominicanen in Nederland (1795–2000)* (Hilversum: Verloren, 2008), 698.

[9] Along with Rahner and Schillebeeckx, some of the Catholic theologians committed to renewal were also involved in the journal, such as Hans Küng, Roger Aubert, Yves Congar, Marie-Dominic Chenu, Gerard Philips, and Johann Baptist Metz. See Hadewych Snijdewind, "Genèse et organisation de la revue internationale de théologie Concilium," *Cristianesimo nella Storia* 21 (2000), 645–74; Paul Brand and Hermann Häring, "Aggiornamento als wissenschaftliches Projekt: Über Anfänge und Programmatik der Internationalen Zeitschrift für Theologie 'Concilium'," *Hans Küng: Neue Horizonte des Glaubens und Denkens: Ein Arbeitsbuch*, ed. Hermann Häring and Karl-Josef Kuschel (Munich and Zürich: Piper, 1993), 779–94.

[10] There is a broad survey of reactions in Auwerda, *Dossier Schillebeeckx*, 67–96, with a collection of press reports and personal expressions of support; further *Katholiek Archief* 23 (1968), 1011–18, 1048–55.

from denouncing the way in which the accusation had been set up.[11] Then, the formal process fizzled out, and the persons involved received no official communication on the outcome of the investigation. Rome gave the impression that it wanted to minimize the affair altogether. Eventually, on June 29, 1969, the case was officially dismissed by a decision made by Pope Paul VI and Msgr. Pierre-Paul Philippe, secretary of the Congregation for the Doctrine of the Faith.[12]

The "first Schillebeeckx case" took place amidst the very tense situation in which the Dutch Catholic Church found itself in the late 1960s.[13] The church in the Netherlands had become a kind of pioneer in church reform, up to that moment still under the guidance of its unanimous episcopate. This striving for a renewed church life was manifest in the famous "Nederlands Pastoraal Concilie" (Dutch Pastoral Council, 1966–1972), in which a large group of the faithful, with their bishops, attempted to realize the ideas of the Second Vatican Council in the local church community. This experiment drew attention from all over the world, but it was also viewed in a very negative way, particularly in Roman circles. Equally, suspicion about the Dutch Church was overtly visible in the examination and subsequent doctrinal correction of the *Nieuwe Katechismus*, the so-called "Dutch Catechism," published in 1966 with the approval of the episcopate, in which a present-day faith instruction for adult believers was presented.

These kinds of reforms in the life of the church were not welcomed by all people, even in the Netherlands, and precipitated an internal polarization in most church communities of the western world. Moreover, the tension affected the relationship between the magisterium and theologians, especially those who aimed at renewing theology in the spirit of the Council, and had, to that purpose, assembled around the journal *Concilium*. The *Concilium* theologians, often led by the initiative of Hans Küng, published critical statements, for example, with regard to the procedure (or lack thereof) in investigations of the work of theologians.[14] On December 16, 1968, in a declaration entitled "For the Freedom of Theology," they made concrete proposals to develop more just and transparent procedures in cases against theologians.[15] Rome reacted to the critique with irritation, but actually complied with some of the suggestions.[16] In the "*Nova agendi ratio in doctrinarum examine*," issued on January 15, 1971, some improvements were introduced in the procedure for investigations by the Congregation for the Doctrine of the Faith.[17]

---

[11]  Auwerda, *Dossier Schillebeeckx*, 98.

[12]  The official notice in the Italian newspaper *Il Messaggero*, June 29, 1969; mentioned in *Katholiek Archief* 24 (1969), 699.

[13]  For a general outline of this situation (with additional bibliographical references), see Chapter Eleven by Erik Borgman and Thijs Caspers in this volume.

[14]  See Küng's own report in his memoirs: Hans Küng, *Disputed Truth: Memoirs* (New York: Continuum, 2008), 45–8.

[15]  An English version of the declaration can be found in Hans Küng, *Reforming the Church Today: Keeping Hope Alive* (New York: Crossroad, 1990), 177–80; see also *Katholiek Archief* 24 (1969), 8–10; Auwerda, *Dossier Schillebeeckx*, 104–07.

[16]  See the anonymous answer in *L'Osservatore Romano*, January 4, 1969, translated into Dutch in *Katholiek Archief* 24 (1969), 136–37. *Katholiek Archief* 24 also includes the reply by the general secretary of *Concilium*, January 9, 1969, on pp. 208–09.

[17]  *AAS* 63 (1971), 234–36; ET: *Origins* 1 (1972), 648, and on http://www.doctrinafidei.va/documents/rc_con_cfaith_doc_19710115_ratio-agendi_en.html.

# III. The second case: On Jesus and Christology (1979)

Meanwhile, Edward Schillebeeckx had earned a growing reputation in the world of Catholic theology. His international fame reached a peak halfway in the 1970s, with the publication of his major work, *Jesus: An Experiment in Christology*, the first of his three "*Jesus* books," that appeared in 1974.[18] However, a few years after publication, the Congregation for the Doctrine of the Faith started an inquiry into the book.[19] This time the Congregation likely reacted to concrete accusations by the Dutch classical scholar and convert to Catholicism, Cornelia de Vogel, who was supported in her critique, once again, by Van der Ploeg.[20] On this investigation, which would take more than five years, we are very well informed by the extensive documentation, published by Dr. Ted Schoof, Schillebeeckx's "right-hand man" in Nijmegen and the editorial secretary for the journal *Tijdschrift voor Theologie* at the time.[21]

The Congregation made the first move in October 1976. It presented Schillebeeckx with a questionnaire, which required explanations to various unclear and disputable opinions from his first *Jesus* book.[22] The critical questions were related to three problem areas. First, a number of methodological questions were raised concerning Schillebeeckx's adoption of the historical-critical method (including his preference for certain exegetical currents, his "reductionist" exegetical method, and his use of hermeneutics), his view on the historical Jesus as the norm and criterion of every Christological interpretation, and the relation between Jesus and the first interpretative responses to Jesus's life and work. The second series of questions dealt with research on the historical Jesus: Jesus as a human person, as eschatological prophet and servant of Yahweh, his relation to the Father, and his resurrection. Finally, the questionnaire added a number of remarks on systematic (dogmatic) issues, particularly on Schillebeeckx's view on the Incarnation, the Trinity, the virginal conception of Jesus, and the church.

In April 1977, Schillebeeckx sent his answers to Rome.[23] He expressed his reply to the questions in a pertinent style, sometimes pointedly, but also rather candidly—in sharp contrast to some of the questions, which, in fact, had the character of accusations. He discussed the methodological issues most extensively because he realized that divergent opinions on this level

---

18  Edward Schillebeeckx, *Jesus, CW* vol. 6 (London: Bloomsbury T&T Clark, 2014).
19  On this second inquiry, see Peter Hebblethwaite, *The New Inquisition?: The Case of Edward Schillebeeckx and Hans Küng* (San Francisco: Harper & Row, 1980); "Kwestie Schillebeeckx," *Archief van de Kerken* 35 (1980), 649–74; *De zaak Schillebeeckx: Reflecties en reacties*, special issue no. 4 of *TvT* 20 (1980), 339–426 (esp. Edward Schillebeeckx, "Theologische overpeinzing achteraf," 422–26); Schillebeeckx's own account in *Theologisch testament*, 60–3.
20  See Paul Luykx, *Cornelia de Vogel: leven en bekering* (Hilversum: Uitgeverij Verloren, 2004), 150–55.
21  *De zaak Schillebeeckx: officiële stukken*, ed. Ted Schoof (Bloemendaal: H. Nelissen, 1980) contains the original French texts with Dutch translations; ET: *The Schillebeeckx Case: Official Exchange of Letters and Documents in the Investigation of Fr. Edward Schillebeeckx, O.P. by the Sacred Congregation for the Doctrine of the Faith, 1976–1980*, ed. Ted Mark Schoof, trans. Matthew J. O'Connell (New York: Paulist Press, 1984). An extensive analysis of the dossier was made by Herwi Rikhof, "De zaak Schillebeeckx: Eindfase: Inhoudelijke balans van de stukken," *TvT* 22 (1982), 376–409; abridged English version: Herwi Rikhof, "Of Shadows and Substance: Analysis and Evaluation of the Documents in the Schillebeeckx Case," *Journal of Ecumenical Studies* 19 (1982), 244–67.
22  *The Schillebeeckx Case*, 18–39; *De zaak Schillebeeckx*, 18–52.
23  *The Schillebeeckx Case*, 46–67; *De zaak Schillebeeckx*, 56–91.

threatened to create unnecessary misunderstandings and disagreements over content. He observed one such misunderstanding in the fact that his interrogators tended to equate his historical reading of the figure of Jesus—being the starting point for the understanding of faith in Christ—with ontological propositions, and this identification inevitably, but erroneously, gave rise to their critiques of his statements as dogmatically insufficient.

On July 6, 1978, Schillebeeckx received a new document from the Congregation, which proved to be a quite critical "*appréciation*" of his answers.[24] The very elaborate text, written by one anonymous author, scarcely pursued the methodological issues that were essential for Schillebeeckx, but concentrated mainly on Christological questions. In large part, the "appreciation," or evaluation, was not much more than a repetition and reinforcement of the critical position presented by the questionnaire. The text hinted at a number of serious shortcomings that needed correction.

On December 13, 14, and 15, 1979, the so-called "colloquium" took place in Rome.[25] Schillebeeckx was not allowed to be accompanied during the meetings by his Nijmegen colleague, Prof. Bas van Iersel, who was there to advise and assist Schillebeeckx.[26] As a "compromise," Van Iersel was allowed to wait in an adjacent room and could be consulted in private, and he could enter the examination room during the coffee break.[27] Schillebeeckx's "discussion partners," as he learned only now, were Msgr. Albert Descamps, a biblical exegete and former rector of the Catholic University of Louvain, the Belgian Jesuit Jean Galot, and the Dominican Albert Patfoort. Alberto Bovone, Undersecretary of the Congregation, presided over the meetings. From the protocol of the meetings, we can observe that the tenor of the discussion was for the most part in line with the tendency of the previous, written texts. Although the Dutch text of his book would be discussed, the actual "conversation" took place in French.[28] Later, Schillebeeckx explained that, whereas with Descamps he could discuss detailed exegetical questions, the confrontation with Patfoort, and especially with Galot, remained a "dialogue of the deaf," precisely because Schillebeeckx's dialogue partners were unable or unwilling to comprehend the hermeneutical principles underlying his theology.[29] The "conversation" in Rome made clear what was already implicitly present in the previous texts: the subject of discussion was gradually reduced to the demand for Schillebeeckx's viewpoints to conform to the formulas prescribed by the magisterium.[30] Prior to the conversation, Schillebeeckx had officially protested

---

[24]  *The Schillebeeckx Case*, 75–107; *De zaak Schillebeeckx*, 96–149.

[25]  *The Schillebeeckx Case*, 109–34; *De zaak Schillebeeckx*, 151–85.

[26]  Later on, Bas van Iersel published very critical reflections on (church-) juridical aspects of the case: Bas van Iersel, "De onderzoeksprocedure van de congregatie voor de geloofsleer: Persoonlijke kanttekeningen bij de regeling en de feitelijke gang van zaken," *TvT* 20 (1980), 3–25; abridged German version: Bas van Iersel, "Wie fair war das Kolloquium mit Schillebeeckx?," *Orientierung* 44 (1980), 42–5.

[27]  Hebblethwaite, *The New Inquisition?*, 62–63.

[28]  Ibid., 62–3.

[29]  Later on, Schillebeeckx asserted that hermeneutics was under suspicion and a kind of "magisterial fundamentalism" had creeped in again. Schillebeeckx, "Theologische overpeinzing achteraf," 425.

[30]  Rikhof shows how, in the colloquy, attention moved away from questions of method and content toward the question of the theologian's obedience to the magisterium of the church. Rikhof, "De zaak Schillebeeckx," 381–82, 405–06; Rikhof, "Of Shadows and Substance," 246, 267.

against some procedures, especially against the presence among the questioners of Jean Galot, who had previously publicly opposed Schillebeeckx's Christology.[31]

After the minutes of the colloquy were signed, on November 25, 1980, Schillebeeckx received a short letter from Msgr. Seper, representing the conclusions of the cardinals of the Congregation, and approved by the pope (now also with some references to the recently published *Christ: The Christian Experience in the Modern World* and *Interim Report on the Books Jesus and Christ*, which appeared in 1977 and 1978, respectively).[32] According to the Prefect, Schillebeeckx's answers had given clarifications and rectified some of the issues, but certain ambiguities remained, particularly concerning Jesus's virginal conception, the validity of faith for theology in its entirety, the resurrection, and Christology. In addition, other questions had arisen, among others, regarding Schillebeeckx's view on the relation of revelation and experience, which might require more explanation. This statement by Prefect Seper was documented by a *"Note annexe,"* which was published in *L'Osservatore Romano* half a year later, on June 26, 1981.[33] Schillebeeckx had refused to make this note public because he found that it did not correctly represent his actual opinions.[34] Schillebeeckx had already sent some documents including a recent article to the Congregation as his "clarification" of the remaining issues, but this apparently did not suffice for the members of the Congregation who seemed to want a public "clarification," and so published the "Note" as a response.[35]

It is important to emphasize that this investigation—the most significant of the three Schillebeeckx inquiries—did not end in a real condemnation.[36] But once again, the whole affair raised an enormous commotion in the Catholic world, far above that of the first case of 1968. The Schillebeeckx case was hot news in the media and elicited a wave of sympathy for Schillebeeckx from many Catholics (and other people) worldwide, as well as indignation about the treatment of

---

[31] On December 4, 1979, on the Vatican radio, Galot had practically called Schillebeeckx a "heretic," and the incident was problematic enough that the director of Vatican Radio apologized to Schillebeeckx. See Hebblethwaite, *The New Inquisition?*, 64.

[32] Full English version in *The Schillebeeckx Case*, 141–50 (*De zaak Schillebeeckx*, 189–90 only includes a summary); also in *Origins* 10 (1980–81), 523–25, and on http://www.doctrinafidei.va/documents/ rc_con_cfaith_doc_19801120_schillebeeckx_en.html. See Edward Schillebeeckx, *Gerechtigheid en liefde: Genade en bevrijding* (Bloemendaal: Nelissen, 1977); Edward Schillebeeckx, *Tussentijds verhaal over twee Jezusboeken* (Bloemendaal: Nelissen, 1978); ET: Edward Schillebeeckx, *Christ*, CW vol. 7 (London: Bloomsbury T&T Clark, 2014); Edward Schillebeeckx, *IR*, CW vol. 8 (London: Bloomsbury T&T Clark, 2014).

[33] Published in Rikhof, "De zaak Schillebeeckx," 406–09 (original French text); English version in *The Schillebeeckx Case*, 145–49 ("Attached Note").

[34] Rikhof shows that in the "Note," Schillebeeckx's opinions expressed in the colloquy and in later documents were rendered incorrectly, and some of Schillebeeckx's explanations were unjustly interpreted as retractions or "concessions." This explains Schillebeeckx's refusal to publish the "Note" himself, since he clearly felt it was inaccurate. Rikhof, "De zaak Schillebeeckx," 388–406; "Of Shadows and Substance," 248–67.

[35] *The Schillebeeckx Case*, 154–55. The publication of this document by the Congregation can be seen either as wanting to close the matter officially, despite the "Note" expressly saying the case still needed clearing up, or as retaliation either for Schillebeeckx's unwillingness to publish the "Note" itself (or an official "clarification") or for the mounting bad press that the case had brought on the Congregation.

[36] Schillebeeckx, *Theologisch testament*, 63: "geen enkele veroordeling of berisping," Schillebeeckx concluded: no condemnation, no admonition.

his case by the Holy See.[37] Numerous associations and faculties of theology praised the scholarly qualities and integrity of their colleague. For example, the Theological Faculty of the Catholic University of Leuven issued a motion in support of their honorary doctor on October 30, 1979.[38] Most spectacular was the action of Amsterdam theology students, who gathered 60,000 signatures protesting the procedure against Schillebeeckx and delivered them to the Vatican.[39] Furthermore, Dutch Archbishop Johannes Willebrands, the successor in Utrecht to Alfrink, made a statement in favor of Schillebeeckx. Thus, Willebrands took a firm position on the issue, which was a signal not only to the faithful who sympathized with Schillebeeckx but also to those Catholics who rejected the kind of renewal they associated with the Nijmegen professor. In the past decade, the Catholic Church in the Netherlands had become extremely polarized, particularly by some sharply contested appointments of new bishops by Rome. In fact, Willebrands and his colleagues were, at that very moment, preparing the extraordinary synod for the Dutch church, which was scheduled to open in January 1980. The express purpose of the synod was to find solutions for the crisis in their divided church. In addition, the climax of the Schillebeeckx case coincided with the decisive step taken in the Roman process against another famous theologian, Hans Küng. On December 18, three days after the Schillebeeckx colloquy, a final verdict sealed the fate of the Tübingen professor, when the Congregation for the Doctrine of the Faith decided that Küng could no longer be considered a Catholic theologian and that his *missio canonica* was withdrawn.

# IV. The third case: On church ministry (1984)

The third investigation into Edward Schillebeeckx's work shows that he was not only occupied with theological theory, but put himself, as a theologian, at the service of practical ecclesiastical action, a commitment that was actually inherent to his concept of theology.[40] Around the turn of the 1970s–1980s, he was involved in discussions about the office of ministry in the church, especially the need to adapt it to the new pastoral situation. He did this in direct consultation with, and for the benefit of, critical base communities that were active in the Dutch Catholic Church.[41] Schillebeeckx elaborated his vision in the book *Ministry: Leadership in the Community of Jesus Christ (Kerkelijk ambt)*, published in 1980. Here, he suggested that in order to relieve the actual crisis in ministry caused by a shortage of priests, in situations of pastoral necessity, non-priests

---

[37] See Ted Schoof, "Getuigen in de 'zaak Schillebeeckx': Theologische lijnen in de publieke en persoonlijke reacties," *TvT* 20 (1980), 402–21.

[38] *Archief van de Kerken* 35 (1980), 668.

[39] Hebblethwaite, *The New Inquisition?*, 28–29.

[40] On this, see "Derde kwestie Schillebeeckx," *Archief van de Kerken* 40 (1985), 131–42; with an opinion by Bas van Iersel (see col. 136–41), originally published in *NRC Handelsblad* (January 15, 1985); German translation included in "Schillebeeckx – der dritte 'Fall'," *Orientierung* 49 (1985), 19–22, at 20–22: "Zugespitzter Konflikt: Rom und Schillebeeckx." See also, Schillebeeckx, *Theologisch testament*, 63–65.

[41] See Edward Schillebeeckx, *Basis en Ambt: Ambt in dienst van nieuwe gemeentevorming* (Bloemendaal: Nelissen, 1979), particularly the study (with the same title), "Basis en ambt: Ambt in dienst van nieuwe gemeentevorming," 43–90. He wrote this book in cooperation with the base movement of critical groups and congregations in the Netherlands.

were appointed as "extraordinary ministers" of the Eucharist.[42] Soon, the Congregation for the Doctrine of the Faith started a third investigation against this work.

This time, the Congregation first submitted a number of questions to the Master General of the Dominican Order, Vincent de Couesnongle, who charged a commission of Dutch-speaking Dominican theologians to examine the book. Their final judgment was unanimously positive, and Schillebeeckx himself replied to some critiques in an article.[43] Yet, on October 27, 1982, he received a letter from Cardinal Joseph Ratzinger, the new Prefect of the Congregation, in which some of Schillebeeckx's opinions were declared incompatible with Catholic doctrine. Schillebeeckx explained his viewpoint in an answer dated November 20, 1982 (complemented by a second letter on July 30, 1983). He held on to his proposal to appoint "extraordinary ministers" to consecrate the Eucharist and argued that such a measure was an open question, theologically, historically, and canonically.

On June 13, 1984, however, Ratzinger informed Schillebeeckx again that his opinion was irreconcilable with the doctrine of the church.[44] Moreover, the Prefect now referred to a brief, entitled *Sacerdotium ministeriale*, that had been published in the meantime by his Congregation on August 6, 1983.[45] In this text, it was stated that according to an inner logic based on magisterial documents of the church, the "extraordinary" option, as suggested by Schillebeeckx, had to be excluded. Ratzinger made it clear that, with this letter, "*le dernier mot*," the last word, on the issue had been spoken.[46]

On July 24, 1984, Schillebeeckx, accompanied by Damian Byrne, the new Master General of the Dominicans, had a short meeting with Ratzinger in Rome. Here, Schillebeeckx informed the Prefect that he had taken into account the critical remarks of the Congregation. He had a new book that was forthcoming, which no longer mentioned the "extraordinary ministers" and, in his opinion, contained nothing contrary to the prescriptions of *Sacerdotium ministeriale*.[47] The book mentioned was entitled *The Church With a Human Face: A New and Expanded Theology of Ministry* (Dutch title: *Pleidooi voor mensen in de kerk*, literally translated as "a plea for people in the church") and was published some months later.[48]

In the beginning of 1985, however, Schillebeeckx again felt forced to react, when on January 11, *L'Osservatore Romano* published the letter of the Congregation from June 13, 1984, and

---

[42] Edward Schillebeeckx, *Kerkelijk ambt: Voorgangers in de gemeente van Jezus Christus* (Bloemendaal: Nelissen, 1980); includes a revised and extended version of the study mentioned in the previous note, pp. 13ff. Second edition in 1981; ET: *Ministry: Leadership in the Community of Jesus Christ* (New York: Crossroad, 1981).

[43] Edward Schillebeeckx, "De sociale context van de verschuivingen in het kerkelijk ambt," *TvT* 22 (1982), 24–59 (especially the historical parts of this article were further developed in *Pleidooi voor mensen in de kerk*, see below, n. 48).

[44] *AAS* 77 (1985), 994–97; ET: *Origins* 14 (1984–85), 523–25, and on http://www.doctrinafidei.va/ documents/rc_con_cfaith_doc_19840613_schillebeeckx_en.html. The letter was made public in *L'Osservatore Romano* of January 11, 1985 (see below).

[45] *AAS* 75 (1983), 1101–09; ET: *Origins* 13 (1983–84), 231–33.

[46] See Schillebeeckx, *Theologisch testament*, 64; Edward Schillebeeckx, *I Am a Happy Theologian: Conversations with Francesco Strazzari*, trans. John Bowden (London: SCM Press, 1994), 37–39.

[47] Schillebeeckx confirmed this answer to the letter of the Congregation in a letter, dated October 5, 1984.

[48] Edward Schillebeeckx, *Pleidooi voor mensen in de kerk: Christelijke identiteit en ambten in de kerk* (Baarn: Nelissen, 1985). ET: Edward Schillebeeckx, *CHF, CW* vol. 9 (London: Bloomsbury T&T Clark, 2014).

rumors were spread that Schillebeeckx had withdrawn his opinion. On January 22, he held a press conference in Nijmegen and declared that in his new book he did not recant his vision, but rather radicalized it.[49] He emphasized that it was nothing less than an ecclesiological requirement to give, in urgent cases, an official recognition, through imposition of hands, to animators of communities of believers, such as pastoral workers.

Eventually, almost two years later, on September 15, 1986, the Congregation for the Doctrine of the Faith published a *Notificatio*, which declared that, on important points such as the apostolic succession by sacramental ordination, Schillebeeckx continued to hold opinions that remained "out of harmony with the teaching of the Church."[50] With this notification, the third Schillebeeckx case was closed. Later, Schillebeeckx expressed serious objections to the procedure of the Congregation (particularly the use of *Sacerdotium ministeriale*) and doubts concerning the validity of the *Notificatio*.[51]

The conflict on this issue, in which Schillebeeckx had engaged in efforts to give shape to a more evangelical and vigorous form of faith-experience in a changed society, must have brought him to recognize the increasing powerlessness of the faithful and their theologians when faced with the unwillingness of the hierarchy to lend any institutional support to new ways of being church. Eventually, this feeling of disappointment led him to the conclusion, as far as his work as a theologian was concerned, that, in the given circumstances, "it was better to investigate the heart of the gospel and the Christian message."[52]

# V. Longstanding effects of "the Schillebeeckx case"

In drawing some conclusions from the three Schillebeeckx inquiries, it may be useful to keep in mind, as a final assessment of the facts, that Schillebeeckx was never explicitly condemned by the Holy See. After the second investigation, Schillebeeckx himself remarked: "Are my books, now, orthodox? I'm not condemned, that's all."[53] But this situation—not being condemned—is, obviously, of little comfort. Inevitably, the continual lack of confidence exhibited by church authorities could not but have a chilling effect on his work as a theologian, even though it did not seem to affect the growing recognition of his position as one of the leading theologians of his time.[54]

---

[49] Dutch text in *TvT* 25 (1985), 180–81; see also *Archief van de Kerken* 40 (1985), 141–42.

[50] *AAS* 79 (1987), 221–23; ET: *Origins* 16 (1986–87), 344 and on http://www.doctrinafidei.va/documents/rc_con_cfaith_doc_19860915_libro-schillebeeckx_en.html.

[51] In the French translation of *Pleidooi voor mensen in de kerk*: Edward Schillebeeckx, *Plaidoyer pour le peuple de Dieu: Histoire et théologie des ministères dans l'Église*, Théologies (Paris: Éditions du Cerf, 1987), 299–304: "Épilogue: La 'Notification' du cardinal J. Ratzinger."

[52] Edward Schillebeeckx, *Church, CW* vol. 10 (London: Bloomsbury T&T Clark, 2014), xxi [xiii]; translation amended: we have corrected "religion" to "message," as in the original: Edward Schillebeeckx, *Mensen als verhaal van God* (Baarn: Nelissen, 1989), 5.

[53] Schillebeeckx, "Theologische overpeinzing achteraf," 426: "Zijn mijn boeken nu orthodox? Ik ben niet veroordeeld, dat is alles."

[54] Schillebeeckx also observed that, after some time, he gradually became less intimidated by the actions against his works. See Schillebeeckx, *Theologisch testament*, 65.

The vicissitudes of Edward Schillebeeckx's position can be placed in the larger context of the post-Conciliar evolution of the relation between Catholic theologians and the Roman magisterium. In this matter, Schillebeeckx did not stand alone. Following the dynamics of the Second Vatican Council and the prominent role theologians played in the preparation and editorial process of its documents, many theologians considered it their responsibility to continue their efforts for the renewal of Catholic faith, and they showed a new self-confidence as a group within the church. They expressed this self-awareness in various common statements, also with regard to the freedom of theological research and the duty of the magisterium to guarantee such freedom.[55] Shortly after the Council, this claim to the freedom of theology, as well as the renewal of theology itself, provoked opposition within the church and suspicion among church authorities. By the end of the 1970s, the tensions escalated in various inquiries into the orthodoxy of suspect theologians, soon leading to condemnations of theologians such as Hans Küng and Jacques Pohier (who, in the "dramatic" year 1979, were both sanctioned almost simultaneously with the investigation of Schillebeeckx). When we consider this development and survey the decades that followed, we cannot but conclude that the end of the pontificate of Paul VI marked the suspension of a relatively benevolent policy of the Roman authorities with regard to their theologians. Henceforth, that flexibility was put aside for, again, a hardline under the new pope, John Paul II and his prefect Joseph Ratzinger.

In the final decades of the twentieth century, theology seemed, again, to be perceived as a potential threat to the unity and integrity of the church. This resulted in several attempts by ecclesiastical authorities to more explicitly define the place and task of theologians in the church. The Instruction *Donum veritatis,* "On the Ecclesial Vocation of the Theologian," published by the Congregation for the Doctrine of the Faith on May 24, 1990, is particularly significant here. *Donum veritatis* accentuated the subservience of theology to the magisterium.[56] It appeared as a reaction to the so-called Cologne Declaration (*Kölner Erklärung*) of January 6, 1989, wherein 163 theologians pleaded for more freedom for theologians and a more critical-constructive role for theology in the church. Furthermore, the Congregation brought about structural and individual measures to ensure the loyalty of theologians to the magisterium. The best example hereof is the "Formula to be used for the profession of faith and for the oath of fidelity to assume an office to be exercised in the name of the Church," issued on January 9, 1989,[57] and integrated in the Code of Canon Law on May 18, 1998, by the motu proprio *Ad tuendam fidem.*[58]

---

55 We should regard the outspokenness of both the "*Concilium*" as well as the "*Communio*" theologians as part of this same trend. They were united in their convictions about the importance of theology for the life of the church. See our comments on the *Communio* theologians and the church hierarchy vis-à-vis the earlier *Concilium* group below.

56 *AAS* 72 (1990), 1550–70; ET: *Origins* 20 (1990), 117–26 and on http://www.vatican.va/roman_curia/congregations/cfaith/documents/rc_con_cfaith_doc_19900524_theologian-vocation_en.html.

57 *AAS* 81 (1989), 104–07; ET: http://www.vatican.va/roman_curia/congregations/cfaith/documents/rc_con_cfaith_doc_1998_professio-fidei_en.html.

58 *AAS* 90 (1998), 457–61; ET: http://www.vatican.va/holy_father/john_paul_ii/motu_proprio/documents/hf_jp-ii_motu-proprio_30061998_ad-tuendam-fidem_en.html.

Correlative to this juridical procedure of anchoring the obedience of theologians to church authority was the growing list of numerous notifications issued against theologians and their work.[59] The list is a clear indication of the continuity in the policy of the Congregation for the Doctrine of the Faith during the final decades of the past and the beginning of the present century. In 1997, the procedure of investigations was further specified with new regulations,[60] which basically introduced two changes: the local ordinary of the theologian became involved in the process as an intermediary, and the theologian was allowed to select his advisor.[61] In general, however, the continuous stream of processes, inquiries, and notifications were indicative of the successful efforts of the Congregation to control the development of Catholic theology. An interesting signal of this could already be seen in the third case against Edward Schillebeeckx—more precisely in the claim, expressed by Joseph Ratzinger, that with regard to the issue of the "extraordinary ministry" of the Eucharist, the letter *Ministerium sacerdotale* (issued by his Congregation) had spoken "the final word."[62]

The list of investigations can be extended with many other similar measures and examinations by doctrinal commissions of episcopal conferences and local bishops. Taking this into account, the problem of the relationship between church authorities and their theologians can be enlarged and chronologically connected with measures from previous periods. Bradford Hinze suggests engaging in such a large research topic by starting from a "hermeneutics of lamentations," which focuses on the experiences and testimonies of targeted theologians, and uses these as a source to investigate "contrasting narratives." These narratives can, in his view, be directly considered as a development of Schillebeeckx's hermeneutics of negative contrast experience.[63] Such a perspective might create a more realistic image of the relationship between the Catholic Church and its theologians and as such contribute toward overcoming

---

[59] Notifications (in addition to those already mentioned) appeared on the work of, among others, Leonardo Boff, Charles E. Curran, André Guindon, Tissa Balasuriya, Anthony De Mello, Reinhard Messner, Jacques Dupuis, Marciano Vidal, Roger Haight, and Jon Sobrino. See the list in Bradford E. Hinze, "A Decade of Disciplining Theologians," *When the Magisterium Intervenes: The Magisterium and Theologians in Today's Church*, ed. Richard R. Gaillardetz (Collegeville, MN: Liturgical Press, 2012), 3–39, at 12–13. See also the full list of notifications: http://www.vatican.va/roman_curia/congregations/cfaith/doc_dottrinali_index.htm.

[60] *Agendi ratio in doctrinarum examine*, May 30, 1997, in *AAS* 89 (1997), 830–35; ET: *Origins* 27 (1997), 221–24 and on http://www.doctrinafidei.va/documents/rc_con_cfaith_doc_19970629_ratio-agendi_en.html.

[61] See the "explanatory note," in *Origins* 27 (1997), 223–24, and Hinze, "A Decade of Disciplining Theologians," 9–12.

[62] On this, see also: Giuseppe Ruggieri, "La politica dottrinale della curia romana nel postconcilio," *Cristianesimo nella Storia* 21 (2000), 103–31, at 121.

[63] Hinze, "A Decade of Disciplining Theologians," 31–32. A quick catalogue of such testimony is already the most revealing (and can be easily retrieved from Schillebeeckx's experiences). Hinze lists ten particular laments: anonymous accusers and critics; the scourge of secrecy, torturous isolation; unfair interpretations; contested doctrines frozen in time; the same people act as accusers, investigators, prosecutors, and judges; a failure to communicate; interrogation masked as dialogue; defamation of character; failure to trust the community of theologians and the faithful People of God as a whole; creating a culture of surveillance, policing, control, and intimidation (33–37).

the ecclesial impasse, occasioned by the unwillingness to productively integrate loyal dissent into the life of the church.[64]

Finally, the tension between theology and the magisterium, as exemplified by the Schillebeeckx case, is to be considered in light of the broader discussion on the significance of the Second Vatican Council. Some claim that at the Second Vatican Council, the church had sought too much of a dialogue with the modern context—so much so that it threatened to put the integrity of the Christian faith and the church at risk. Already at the Council itself, during the discussions on the text of *Gaudium et spes*, such criticism was ventured even by theologians belonging to the majority.[65] After the Council, their reservation led to the foundation, as early as 1972, of the periodical *Communio* by Hans Urs von Balthasar, Joseph Ratzinger, and others, as an alternative to the aforementioned *Concilium*. It is no accident that the more prominent members of the editorial board of *Communio* have often been chosen for important positions in the hierarchy of the church, whereas theologians belonging to the *Concilium* group have almost never been considered for such posts. The latter have been criticized most often precisely because of their openness to the context, and their attempts to theologize from the lessons they learned from that context; for dialogue puts identity at risk—but it also preserves tradition as a living-tradition. Recently, Pope Francis has taken a very different attitude when compared with that of his predecessor by advancing a critical-dialogical attitude to the world—in line with Vatican II—and in so doing making more room for theologians fostering that same dialogue. This is a perspective which would have also filled Edward Schillebeeckx with joy and hope.

---

[64] For Edward Schillebeeckx's view on the problematic relationship between the magisterium and the theologians, and particularly on theological dissent, see Daniel Speed Thompson, *The Language of Dissent: Edward Schillebeeckx on the Crisis of Authority in the Catholic Church* (Notre Dame, IN: University of Notre Dame Press, 2003), 147–62. Schillebeeckx himself wrote an important article on the topic: Edward Schillebeeckx, "The Magisterium and Ideology," *Authority in the Church*, ed. Piet F. Fransen, Annua Nuntia Lovaniensia 26 (Leuven: Leuven University Press, 1983), 5–17; also published in *Journal of Ecumenical Studies* 19 (1982), 5–17.

[65] On this, see Massimo Faggioli, *Vatican II: The Battle for Meaning* (New York/Mahwah, NJ: Paulist Press, 2012), 50–53, 66–90.

# PART III

# Theological Themes

# Chapter 14

# Schillebeeckx on God

Philip Kennedy

God is not a thing in the world that can be encountered and measured precisely. Because God is not able to be met, counted, or quantified in any way, no theologian has ever succeeded in describing God. Edward Schillebeeckx is acutely aware in all of his publications and homilies that human beings do not possess divine concepts of the Divine. They only articulate human concepts of God. Their attempts to do so will share all human limitations of being incomplete, imprecise, perspectival, and blinkered. For Schillebeeckx, theology is a mere stammering. It is like a ceaseless wrestling match in which an ever-elusive opponent proves incapable of being subdued. Like all other theologies, everything Schillebeeckx says about God is a mere form of human stuttering.[1] It is an incomplete discourse struggling to elucidate what Christians, and other believers, mean when they profess, "We believe in God." The God in whom people believe is always a *Deus absconditus*—an absconding God—who escapes each and every human attempt neatly to define God.

The topic of God is peppered throughout Schillebeeckx's multifarious writings. He never attempts arrogantly to define God, but he is always at pains to help people understand what might be entailed in professing faith in God. To that end, he uses a large variety of names and terms for God, but always underscoring what God is not—a measurable entity like any observable thing.

# I. The twin pillars of Schillebeeckx's theology

If a simile could be engaged at this point, Schillebeeckx's theology is like a large bridge: it is a massive, complex structure resting on two huge foundational pillars or piers—just like the twin piers supporting London Bridge. The pillars undergirding the entire edifice of Schillebeeckx's theology are [1] belief in God the Creator and [2] belief in Jesus Christ as the condensation of all that is good in creation. These foundational pillars also happen to form the structure of the opening statements of classical Christian creeds, such as the Apostles' Creed, the Athanasian Creed, and the Niceno-Constantinopolitan Creed. For Schillebeeckx, Jesus was and is a human manifestation in history of what God might be like. He regards Jesus as a parable, cipher,

---

[1]   Edward Schillebeeckx, *Church, CW* vol. 10 (London: Bloomsbury T&T Clark, 2014), xxiii [xv].

sacrament, prophet, and incarnation of God. In Schillebeeckx's terms, "The story of God is told in the story of Jesus."[2]

The twin creedal bases of Schillebeeckx's theology find expression in the titles of two successive chapters of his book, *God Among Us: The Gospel Proclaimed*: "I believe in God, Creator of Heaven and Earth" and "I Believe in the Man Jesus: The Christ, the Only Beloved Son, Our Lord." Hence, the first fundamental way Schillebeeckx understands God is as the Creator of all there is. His second cardinal way is to regard Jesus as the unique and only Son of God, who is nonetheless a man. Schillebeeckx's elemental comprehension of both God and Jesus Christ is thereby perfectly creedal, orthodox, and traditional.

Yet Schillebeeckx also talks about both God and Jesus Christ in strikingly innovative ways that are informed by his sustained study of biblical exegesis, coupled with his familiarity with a broad range of philosophies, ancient and modern. Schillebeeckx is a theologian who is very well acquainted with the past 300-year history of modern Higher Biblical Criticism. In that, he is unusual among dogmatic and many systematic theologians.

## Those without hope

Always to be remembered when reading Schillebeeckx is that the contents of the Christian creeds are not personally problematical for him. He accepts them and he believes them, even as he engages modern hermeneutics to interpret them. While his own faith was life-long and profound, he has consistently been motivated in his publications to help people who are losing their faith, angry with the church, confused about what to believe, or entirely bereft of religious convictions.

Whenever Schillebeeckx inscribes the beginnings of his books with an epigraph, it is well worth paying close attention to what he says. It is not inconsequential that he was a Dominican friar for his entire adult life. Since the Middle Ages, the Dominicans have been driven to maintain what is called in Latin a *cura animarum*—a "care of souls." They are not an Order of Professors, but a band of preachers and pastors trying to help others. Schillebeeckx often manifests this pastoral disposition in his epigraphs. He begins his greatest book, *Jesus, the Story of Someone Alive*, conventionally translated as *Jesus: An Experiment in Christology*, with an epigraph taken from the First Letter of Paul to the Thessalonians: "That you may not grieve as others do who have no hope" (1 Thess 4:13). This text clearly evinces that Schillebeeckx is writing to help people so that they are not left bereft of hope. With the book *Jesus*, he is not trying to solve an abstruse Christological and conceptual conundrum. He is striving to bridge a gap he perceives between academic theology and people raising critical questions and doubts about traditional formulations of Christian beliefs. Many of such questions relate to how God is to be considered in relation to the first-century Galilean Israelite, Jesus.

---

[2]  Edward Schillebeeckx, *God Among Us: The Gospel Proclaimed*, trans. John Bowden (New York: Crossroad, 1983), 31.

# The nature of God

Undertaking a brisk synoptic overview of Schillebeeckx's many writings readily reveals the arresting variety of ways in which he understands and talks about God. Here is a sampling: God is a Loud Cry;[3] "a familiar friend";[4] "the one who was and is to come";[5] and an "absolute freedom" who is "eternally young."[6] God is "a Living God";[7] who is "new each moment" and "a constant source of new possibilities";[8] "a reality which evades the exact sciences";[9] "a constant surprise";[10] "concerned for humankind";[11] "the source of pure positivity" and "more human than any human being";[12] immutable, uncreated, eternal, absolute freedom, and permanently new;[13] "liberating love in Jesus Christ for whatever is not God."[14] Moreover, "God's own most being, in absolute freedom, is love of man [people] which achieves their redemption."[15] God is thus "the God of salvation"[16] and an "inner-divine" and economic Trinity.[17] Above all, God is "the Creator and Father of Jesus Christ."[18]

# Creation

The Christian theology of creation and belief in God as the Creator are foundational for every type of Christian theology. All Christian beliefs are related to, and stem from, the personal and collective trust that the Living God is the Creator of all there is. Such faith in God as the Creator is one of the only major tenets of Christian faith over which there has never been a large schism between denominations. It unifies all of the roughly 38,000 contemporary Christian denominations.[19]

---

3   Ibid., 73.
4   Schillebeeckx, *Church*, xxvi [xviii].
5   Schillebeeckx, *God Among Us*, 7. Schillebeeckx, *Church*, 4 [4]; Edward Schillebeeckx, "Secularization and Christian Belief in God," *GFM, CW* vol. 3 (London: Bloomsbury T&T Clark, 2014), 50 [81].
6   Schillebeeckx, *Church*, 98–99, 127 [101, 129]; Edward Schillebeeckx, *God Is New Each Moment*, trans. David Smith (Edinburgh: T&T Clark, 1983), 29.
7   Edward Schillebeeckx, *God and Man*, trans. Edward Fitzgerald and Peter Tomlinson, Theological Soundings (New York: Sheed and Ward, 1969), 38; Edward Schillebeeckx, "Revelation, Scripture, Tradition and Teaching Authority," *RT, CW* vol. 2 (London: Bloomsbury T&T Clark, 2014), 4 [I 5].
8   Schillebeeckx, 99 [101]; Schillebeeckx, *God Is New Each Moment*, 29.
9   Schillebeeckx, *God and Man*, 19.
10  Schillebeeckx, *Church*, 121 [122].
11  Ibid., 4 [4], 113 [114], 120 [122].
12  Edward Schillebeeckx, *Jesus in our Western Culture: Mysticism, Ethics and Politics*, trans. John Bowden (London: SMC Press, 1987), 62; Schillebeeckx, *God Among Us*, 61.
13  Schillebeeckx, *God Among Us*, 104.
14  Ibid., 105.
15  Ibid., 104.
16  Schillebeeckx, "Revelation, Scripture, Tradition and Teaching Authority," *RT*, 4 [I 4]; Schillebeeckx, "The Non-Conceptual Intellectual Element in the Act of Faith: A Reaction," *RT, CW* vol. 2 (London: Bloomsbury T&T Clark, 2014), 249 [46].
17  Schillebeeckx, *Church*, 99 [101].
18  Ibid.
19  See Martin Marty, *The Christian World: A Global History* (New York, NY: Modern Library, 2007), p. 4; and David B. Barrett, George T. Kurian, and Todd M. Johnson, eds, *World Christian Encyclopedia: A Comparative Survey of Churches and Religions in the Modern World*, 2nd ed., 2 vols. (Oxford and New York: Oxford University Press, 2001).

In Schillebeeckx's body of theological writings, belief in God as the Creator does not serve as either a cosmology or a cosmogony. It does not seek to compete with empirical sciences to account for the dimensions of the universe, or the origins of the observable world. It is primarily a way of understanding God or, rather, comprehending what God is *not*.

To speak of the world and all there is in it as God's creation is first and foremost to make an observation about God. Similarly, the first two creation stories in the Book of Genesis are not primarily focused on ancient cosmologies. What they say about the material genesis of the world is factually mistaken. Their authors cannot be blamed for assuming the now-defunct Mesopotamian cosmology of their time, but their stories are not fundamentally scientific cosmologies or biologies. They are discourses about God and God's relation with humanity and Israel.[20] To profess that God is the Creator affirms a basic ontological distinction between God and all that God creates. Daniel Migliore explains this ontological distinction very succinctly: "By calling God the 'creator' and everything that constitutes the world 'creatures,' Christian faith affirms *the radical otherness, transcendence, and lordship of God*."[21]

# II. Essence and existence

The ontological divergence obtaining between God and all things stems from a difference between essence and existence. A host of theologians, including Schillebeeckx, assume this distinction when speaking about God. A differentiation between essence and existence is made by the Islamic theologian, Avicenna; the Jewish theologian, Moses Maimonides (1138–1204); the Doctor of the Church, St. Thomas Aquinas; the Protestant theologian, Paul Tillich; and the contemporary philosopher-theologian, John Caputo.

Maimonides, in his major work, *The Guide for the Perplexed*, has this to say about essence and existence:

> It is known that existence is an accident appertaining to all things, and therefore an element superadded to their essence. This must evidently be the case as regard everything the existence of which is due to some cause; it existence is an element superadded to its essence. But as regards a being whose existence is not due to any cause—God alone is that being, for His existence, as we have said, is absolute —existence and essence are perfectly identical; He is not a substance to which existence is joined as an accident, as an additional element.[22]

What is meant by such a way of speaking? Quite simply, yet profoundly, with regard to all things, even mental things like ideas, a differentiation can be made between the essence of a thing and

---

[20] See Mark S. Smith, *The Priestly Vision of Genesis 1* (Minneapolis, MN: Fortress Press, 2010); and Günther Weber, *I Believe, I Doubt: Notes on Christian Experience*, trans. John Bowden (London: SCM Press, 1998), 62–65.

[21] Daniel L. Migliore, *Faith Seeking Understanding: An Introduction to Christian Theology*, 3rd ed (Grand Rapids, MI: Eerdmans, 2014), 103–04.

[22] Moses Maimonides, *The Guide for the Perplexed*, trans. M. Friedländer (New York: Dover Publications, 2016; original written in Arabic in 1190), Chapter LVII, p. 80.

its existence. For example, the essence of a unicorn is to be a horse-like animal with a large horn protruding from its forehead. Do unicorns exist? Not in so far as can be known. Even so, with the concept of a unicorn a distinction can still be made between its essence and existence. No such divergence obtains in God. This is because God's essence *is* existence itself. God is not a being, but Being itself; not a life, but Life itself; not a loving person, but Love itself.

Thomas Aquinas notes a clear dissimilitude between essence and existence in his *Compendium of Theology*: "in God, there is pure actuality, not potentiality and actuality. Therefore, he is his essence. It is further necessary that God's essence is nothing but his existing."[23] In short, because God is the Creator, God is not a thing that exists and which can be counted along with other things. This explains why Schillebeeckx is always careful not to speak of God as if God were a locatable, measurable, countable, and observable reality, for "He, the living God, knows that his immeasurable, all-embracing, matter-of-course presence is impenetrable obscurity for his creatures."[24]

Because God is not an entity like a creature, the British philosopher John Hick speaks of God as "transcategorical," that is, "beyond the range of our human concepts or mental categories."[25] Speaking of God as transcategorical is simply a way of chiming with Christian theological tradition which affirms that God will always remain unknowable by people in their history because God is neither *cogitable* (able to be gasped by the mind) by human beings nor *cognizable*, that is, *perceptible, recognizable*, or unmistakably *identifiable*. Such is the case, because God is spatially, experientially, temporally, epistemologically, and ontologically *transcendent* to humanity.

Paul Tillich recognizes as much when he says, "God is no object for us as subjects. He is always that which precedes this division." Tillich dismisses those who try to prove or disprove that *a* Supreme Being, God, exists. God can never be grammatically identified with an indefinite article. God is not *A* anything. God is not a being, but Being itself. This is why John Caputo explains that "The debate between theists and atheists is futile. It proves nothing because they are arguing about nothing, literally. Tillich's claim is that there is nothing there; there is no 'there' there, no Supreme Being to prove or disprove."[26]

All of which leads to the conclusion that only God is Absolute. Everything pertaining to human experience is not. It is finite, contingent, limited, mortal, variable, perspectival, and utterly constrained by historical and cultural context.

## Finitude

Human limitation, or finitude, is the crux and starting point of Schillebeeckx's way of talking about God. In his theology, creation is regarded as a free divine act that establishes a divergence between God and all that is a non-godly—creation. Everything that is not divine is finite, yet the finitude that results from God's act of creation is not a mistake or flaw, but the intrinsic basis from

---

[23] Thomas Aquinas, *Compendium of Theology*, trans. Richard J. Regan (Oxford: Oxford University Press, 2009), I, 11, p. 23.

[24] Schillebeeckx, *God and Man*, 11.

[25] John Hick, *Who or What Is God? And Other Investigations* (London: SCM Press., 2008), 5.

[26] John Caputo, *The Folly of God: A Theology of the Unconditional* (Salem, OR: Polebridge Press, 2016), 11.

which a distinction between God and non-godly creatures can be made in the first place. Here Schillebeeckx chimes with the Book of Genesis: that which God creates is not merely good, but "very good" (Gen 1:31).

To speak of finitude, immanence, or contingency is simply to designate human beings' experiences of their daily limitations and sense of mortality. For humans are not sovereign over either themselves or their universe. They cannot control what will transpire in their lives and their world. In addition, they do not find in themselves a necessary reason or explanation for, or the absolute cause of, their existence. They cannot find within their isolated selves a justification for why they exist.[27] The cause of their existence lies elsewhere—in God.

Throughout his adult life, Schillebeeckx was at pains to study what is entailed in human finitude. In the seventeenth century, Baruch Spinoza was the first notable philosopher to enunciate a systematic philosophy of radical this-worldly immanence. According to Spinoza's philosophy of immanence, existence in the world is

> the only actual being, and the unique source of ethical value and political authority. All being is this-worldly and there is nothing beyond it, neither a personal creator-God who imposes His divine will on man, nor supernatural powers or values of any kind. The laws of morality and politics, too, end even religion, stem from this world by the natural power of reason; and recognizing this is the prelude and precondition for human emancipation.[28]

Spinoza's philosophy of immanence is a direct nullification of Christian belief in a transcendent Creator. It asserts that limited, historical, finite human existence in history is the only existence there is, for there are neither supernatural potencies, a personal Creator-God, nor values existent separately from and beyond the earthly, profane existence in which people find themselves. It is also a view that finds expression in a large variety of modern and postmodern thinkers, including Hegel, Marx, Nietzsche, Sartre, and Derrida.

Finitude is the plinth of all of these philosophers' view of the world. It is also the pivot of the way Schillebeeckx speaks of God. While philosophers of immanence defer to finitude as a basis for debunking belief in God, Schillebeeckx refers to it precisely in order to account for faith in God.

He engaged with philosophies of immanence while he was studying in Paris as a young man. He undertook doctoral studies in France between 1946 and 1947. In Paris, he came across a book by Jean-Paul Sartre that was a particularly astute philosophical analysis and robust recognition of finitude, or this-worldly existence. The book is called *L'être et le néant* (*Being and Nothingness*). Schillebeeckx studied this text intensively under the direction of Louis Lavelle. It had been published in Paris in 1943, shortly before Schillebeeckx arrived there. Four decades after Schillebeeckx read this tract he was still able to observe: "No one has analysed this radical finitude of being human in this contingent world better than an agnostic who was originally in fact a militant atheist, Jean-Paul Sartre."[29]

---

[27] Schillebeeckx, *Church*, 76 [78].
[28] Yirmiyahu Yovel, *Spinoza and Other Heretics: The Adventures of Immanence* (Princeton, NJ: Princeton University Press, 1989), ix.
[29] Schillebeeckx, *Church*, 76 [78].

A significant result of Schillebeeckx's engagement with Sartre's account of human finitude is that he concurred entirely with Sartre's perception that human existence is radically and inescapably finite. It was clear, for Schillebeeckx, that both believers and atheists share exactly the same pre-linguistic awareness of being utterly circumscribed and constrained by finitude.

Where Schillebeeckx clearly diverges from Sartre and atheists of his kind is in his stance that the human experience of finitude is the intrinsic *source* of belief in God as the Creator, and not the confirmation that there is no God. For Schillebeeckx, all human beings experience a pre-linguistic awareness of being limited and contingent in situations in which they feel nakedly vulnerable—situations, in particular, when they feel sick, diseased, or threatened by death. While believers and atheists share exactly the same perception of finitude, that *differ* in their *interpretations* of an awareness of their radical contingency.

In Schillebeeckx's theology, finitude is simply another term for "secularity"—that which is not God. The secular, in his view, is not flawed, bad, smutty, or mistaken. It is simply not God. More than that, the secular in itself accrues a direct reference or pointer to its source, that which is sacred, not secular—a divine Creator:

> For the believer, non-divine finitude is precisely the place where the infinite and the finite come most closely into contact. From this close contact of the secular and the transcendent, the infinite and the finite, there arises, as mystics say, the spark of the soul; there all religion takes fire.[30]

## The soldier's moral dilemma

For atheistic philosophers of immanence, the source of moral value and ethical norms lies within humans themselves and not with a transcendent Creator. In Schillebeeckx's book, *Jesus in Our Western Culture*, he tells a story about a young soldier facing a moral dilemma. The story illustrates very well the way Schillebeeckx relies on human experiences of finitude and constraint as a springboard for distinguishing between God and humanity, and as a way of illustrating that God is the ultimate origin or of moral value and goodness. Schillebeeckx narrates the story in this way:

> Suppose that a young soldier in a dictatorship is told on penalty of death to shoot dead an innocent hostage, purely and simply because the hostage is, for example, a Jew, a Communist or a Christian. The soldier refuses to carry out the order on grounds of conscience. He is certain that he himself will be shot along with his hostage (who in any case will be shot by someone else). In this refusal the soldier recognizes in the humiliated bewilderment of the hostage an unexpressed and perhaps inexpressible moral summons which he experiences as a demand. The other makes a demand on his freedom: he finds it ethically impossible to kill him and therefore refuses to carry out the order.[31]

---

[30]  Ibid., 231 [234]. See *Church*, 75 [77], for Schillebeeckx's examples of human experiences of radical finitude.

[31]  Schillebeeckx, *Jesus in Our Western Culture*, 58.

From the vantage point of a philosopher of immanence, the soldier's response to the order to kill an innocent hostage may be regarded as heroic, but it is nothing more. It is an entirely futile gesture, made in the full awareness that by refusing to comply with the command, both the young soldier and the hostage will be killed.

Why not just follow the order to kill and spare at least one life? Because of what Schillebeeckx calls "an unexpressed and perhaps inexpressible moral summons," which the soldier experiences as a demand made of him. The soldier has perceived that this-worldly existence might not be the sum total of reality. He senses an Ultimate Goodness, God, who is the source of human goodness. The soldier's bravery is a victory of goodness over nihilism. Finitude is related directly to Infinity. The soldier's gesture is grounded in a hope that his death and that of the hostage will not end in oblivion. The ground of his hope is none other than God. Schillebeeckx is fond of referring to this story of the young soldier.[32]

## Negative contrast experiences

The story of the heroic young soldier illustrates what is the most significant concept in the theology of Schillebeeckx that he formulated between 1966 and the end of his life. The concept is that of a negative contrast experience. During the late 1960s, he became convinced that classical Christian and dogmatic nomenclature were not well understood among his contemporaries in Western Europe and the English-speaking world, which he first encountered in 1966 during a trip to the United States. His conviction is clear in a declaration such as the following in his book, *God the Future of Man*: "It is clear that Christian revelation in its traditional form has ceased to provide any valid answer to the questions about God asked by the majority of people today."[33]

In the midst of what Schillebeeckx perceived as a profound and pervasive crisis of faith among his contemporaries, he searched fervidly for a new theological language that would help him talk about God, Jesus Christ, and the significance of Christian faith in the decades following two devastatingly destructive World Wars. He eventually came to the conclusion that he should rely on language and concepts all humans share, thereby potentially enhancing the prospect of mutual understanding among very different people. He decided that his new theological language should be couched in terms of human experience. In particular, he brought to the center of his new theological language what each and every human experiences at some stage—an intense experience of suffering and negativity. He coined the term, negative contrast experience, to designate the awfulness of suffering all humans undergo.

Such an experience is *negative* because it entails suffering. It is *contrastive* because it is the opposite of happiness, health, goodness, and positivity. A negative experience of pain, torture, or humiliation stands in sharp contrast to its opposite—liberation, freedom, salvation, or bliss. When Schillebeeckx turned his attention to developing a new narrative Christology in the 1970s, he engaged the notion of a negative contrast experience to interpret the crucifixion of Jesus. In relation to God, this notion is yet another way of illustrating how an experience of finitude forms the ground for an awareness of God as the complete opposite of limitation.

---

[32] See ibid., 60; Schillebeeckx, *God Is New Each Moment*, 53; Schillebeeckx, *Church*, 110–12 [112].
[33] Edward Schillebeeckx, "Secularization and Christian Belief in God," *GFM, CW* vol. 3 (London: Bloomsbury T&T Clark, 2014), 31 [53].

# Schillebeeckx's relational ontology

Even though human limitation clearly demarcates God from human beings in Schillebeeckx's theology, he is always at pains to point out that any awareness among humans of separation from God rests entirely with them. They can only speak of what *they* perceive as their inability to find or encounter God, because God is not like them and cannot be located in their world. All of which is to say that humans cannot speak for God. Undergirding everything Schillebeeckx says about God is a recognition of an ontological relation, rather than separation, between God and humanity. While finitude is an acute self-awareness among humans, they are in no position to declare what God may or may not be able to accomplish in relation to them.

In Schillebeeckx's first major work to attract international attention, *Christ the Sacrament of the Encounter with God*, he says this: "Man cannot sever himself from God, because God will not let him go."[34] Human contingency, the consciousness that humans do not find within themselves an explanation for why they exist, establishes an ontological boundary between creatures and their Creator. Even so, the boundary is part of *their* experience and does not in any way constrain God. Idolatry is a human attempt to remove such a boundary and to aspire to being divine.

Abjuring such an attempt, Schillebeeckx acknowledges the goodness of human finitude, but emphasizes over and again that people, not God, are circumscribed by their contingency. In Schillebeeckx's theology, a recognition of an ontological relation or link between God and humanity undergirds any talk of a boundary between God and people. For God, no such boundary exists because, as Schillebeeckx says, "God is concerned to be our God in our humanity and for our humanity, in and with our finitude."[35]

The recognition of a relational ontology between the Creator and creature is the intellectual core of Schillebeeckx's entire theological output. It is the Rosetta Stone for anyone trying to grasp the fundamental features and structure of his theological thought. For Schillebeeckx, humans can know God particularly through the medium of a divine creation. In other words, a human being is always ontologically related to God who is their Creator. A human being's relation to God is not in any way a heteronomous feature added on to human nature. It is *part* of that nature.

Schillebeeckx will not acknowledge that there is such a thing as a purely isolated and independent human nature. On the contrary, *God includes the human I*.[36] Humans cannot sever themselves from God, so to speak: "Man cannot sever himself from God, because God will not let him go."[37] For Schillebeeckx, "In the end, the pure subject becomes the empty subject. The autonomous subject is no longer in a position to be related to itself in any other way than as to an object."[38] Otherwise expressed, "From a Christian point of view the world and human beings are utterly different from God, but within the presence of the creator God."[39] Very early in Schillebeeckx's career, he observed that, "Our whole life is lived within the vast sphere of

---

[34] Edward Schillebeeckx, *Christ the Sacrament, CW* vol. 1 (London: Bloomsbury T&T Clark, 2014), 6 [7–8].

[35] Edward Schillebeeckx, *IR, CW* vol. 8 (London: Bloomsbury T&T Clark, 2014), 101 [115].

[36] Schillebeeckx, *Church*, 98 [100].

[37] Schillebeeckx, *Christ the Sacrament*, 6 [7–8]; Edward Schillebeeckx, "The Ecclesial Life of Religious Man," *WC, CW* vol. 4 (London: Bloomsbury T&T Clark, 2014), 110 [141].

[38] Schillebeeckx, *Church*, 65 [67].

[39] Schillebeeckx, *IR*, 100–01 [114].

the personal God who embraces us."[40] That embrace is another way of designating a relational ontology obtaining between the Creator and creatures.

# III. Christ as concentrated creation

Linked to the relational ontology assumed in all of Schillebeeckx's speech about God is the second foundational pillar of his theology—belief in Jesus Christ. In sum, Schillebeeckx regards creation as *an act* of God that [a] constitutes human beings in their contingency; and [b] reveals the nature of God as the One who constitutes the salvation and happiness of human beings. Creation is thus inextricably linked to soteriology in Schillebeeckx's works. Creation and salvation are mutually explicative: through the divine act of creation God constitutes the ultimate salvation of human beings.

When in 1957 Schillebeeckx moved from Leuven to Nijmegen to accede to a chair in dogmatic theology and the history of theology, he delivered an inaugural lecture soon after arriving. In that lecture, he stated that theology is ultimately concerned with the intelligibility of God *as salvation*. He also declared that the only way to understand God, as constituting salvation for humans, is through the human *history* of salvation.[41]

If beliefs in God as Creator and in Jesus Christ are the twin primordial foci of Schillebeeckx's entire theological output, the second focus forms a link or mediation between the first and humanity. For Schillebeeckx, Jesus Christ is the visibility (sacrament) of an invisible and anonymous God. As Schillebeeckx declares in his book, *World and Church*, "Only Christ can do away with the anonymity of God."[42]

Schillebeeckx explains the link between God and Christ by designating Christology as "concentrated creation." By that phrase he means that, in Jesus Christ, Christians perceive a manifestation of what God wills Creation to be.[43] For Schillebeeckx, Christology makes "belief in creation more precise, gives it specific content, in terms of our human history and the historical appearance of Jesus of Nazareth in it."[44] In Jesus, Christians perceive that God, the creator, the one in whom they trust, "*is* liberating love for humanity."[45]

## Classical Christology and Schillebeeckx's Christology

Above, Schillebeeckx's book, *Jesus: The Story of Someone Alive*, was described as his greatest work. This is partly because it is one of the first non-metaphysical Christologies to be published in the twentieth century. Another such work is Hans Küng's tome, *On Being a Christian*, published in German in 1974. Schillebeeckx's book was published in the same year.

---

40  Schillebeeckx, *God and Man*, 9.
41  Edward Schillebeeckx, *Op zoek naar de levende God* (Utrect/Nijmegen: Dekker en van de Vegt, 1958), 19.
42  Edward Schillebeeckx, "Priest and Layman in a Secular World," *WC, CW* vol. 4 (London: Bloomsbury T&T Clark, 2014), 26 [33].
43  Schillebeeckx, *IR*, 111 [128].
44  Ibid., 111 [127].
45  Ibid., 112 [128]. Emphasis original.

Classical Christologies, typified by the dogmatic formulas of the episcopal councils Nicaea and Chalcedon, attempt to achieve what cannot be done. They seek to identify, ontologically, that which is particular—the man Jesus—with that which is absolute—God. By "absolute" in this context is meant that which is infinite and unconstrained by human history, as well as by time and space. The mistake of such Christology is to focus overly on specifying a divine nature in Christ, instead of concentrating on the focus of his life—the kingdom of God. Focusing on the primary preoccupation of Jesus's life, on what he said and did, and by relating *dogmatics* to Higher Biblical Criticism, constitutes the substantial worth of Schillebeeckx's book, *Jesus*.

While the historical finitude of Jesus cannot be identical to God, no one can speak in such absolute terms as to say that God is not seen or revealed, even partially, in Jesus. With *Jesus: The Story of Someone Alive*, Schillebeeckx develops a narrative Christology as a complement to classical Christologies. The elemental guiding assumption of the work is that *action is revelatory of identity*. By telling the story of Jesus, of his life, words, deeds, and death, it is possible to achieve a glimpse of his identity. As with classical Christologies, Schillebeeckx seeks to specify the identity and universal significance of Jesus the Christ, but unlike dogmatic approaches, he does so in a story-telling way, rather than with a conceptually defining manner.

In Schillebeeckx's narrative Christology, developed in many publications beginning most notably in 1974, Schillebeeckx talks about Jesus and his actions in relation to the kingdom of God, which he specifies in these terms: "The kingdom of God is the presence of God among men and women, affirmed or made welcome, active and encouraging, a presence which is made concrete above all in just and peaceful relation among individuals and people."[46]

Some of Schillebeeckx's most rhetorically persuasive prose is captured when he speaks about God, Jesus, and the kingdom of God. Here is a case in point:

> It is striking above all in Jesus' parables how he relativizes the absolute of the principle of justice. There are parables which have the aim (then as now) of shocking our sense of justice. The one who works form the eleventh hour gets just as much as the one who works from the first hour (Matt. 20:1–17), and from someone who has nothing, even what he has shall be taken away (Matt. 25:9). Jesus wants us to learn from this that the rules for the praxis of the Kingdom of God have nothing to do with the social rules in our societies. *It is an alternative mode of action.* Jesus does not defend immoral or anarchic people, he goes and stands next to them. [...] Jesus reacts sharply against those who uphold the social rules. Strict justice can even include the excommunication of those who have already been cast out. The coming of the Kingdom of God does not know the human logic of precise justice.[47]

By speaking thus, Schillebeeckx does not by any means shun or discount classical Christology. He is simply striving to show that God is revealed to humanity, not in a divine nature, but "through the non-divine aspect of Jesus' humanity."[48] Whatever is divine in the identity and significance of Jesus

---

[46] Edward Schillebeeckx, *For the Sake of the Gospel*, trans. John Bowden (London: SCM, 1989), 117.

[47] Ibid., 106–07. See also Schillebeeckx, *Church*, 134–35 [136]; Schillebeeckx, *Christ*, 640–41 [651].

[48] Schillebeeckx, *For the Sake of the Gospel*, 108.

Christ is refracted in his humanity, and especially in his preferential options to help the stranger, the prisoner, the thirsty, the poor, and the hungry human being. Whatever is divine about Jesus is revealed in his humanity and his actions; not next to, or apart from, his humanity. In Schillebeeckx's terms, Jesus's image of God is moulded by the outcasts mentioned in Matthew 25.[49]

# IV. Schillebeeckx's new concept of God

In the late 1960s, Schillebeeckx began speaking of his "new" concept of God. The newness entailed is related to eschatology. The Marxist philosopher, Ernst Bloch, published his *Das Prinzip Hoffnung* in Berlin between 1954 and 1959. Schillebeeckx acknowledges this work as the first to attempt to conceptualize the primacy of the future for cultures planning for a better future of humankind[50] (see GFM, 180, and 205, n. 4). Schillebeeckx uses this idea of the primacy of the future to challenge traditional ways of God that normally tie God and God's transcendence to the past or present. The novelty involved in Schillebeeckx's "new concept God" rests with the way he links God's transcendence to the future. Thus, *pace* Karl Barth, God is not Wholly Other, but "wholly New."[51] God is "the One who is to come," "the God who is *our* future."[52] Were God Wholly Other, it would be entirely understandable for humans to regard God as wholly irrelevant to their lives.[53]

Schillebeeckx began speaking in this way after he visited the United States and encountered there the American "death of God" theologians. He concluded that classical and time-honoured ways of talking about God were not communicating effectively to Western citizens of the second half of the twentieth century. Hence his formulation of a new notion of God couched in terms of futurity, promise, and constant Newness.

## God in four ways

In the history of Christianity and its theologies, theologians have consistently spoken about God in at least four basic ways. Schillebeeckx, too, refers to God in the same four patterns. They are (1) anthropomorphic images taken from daily life, (2) philosophical or abstract concepts, (3) apophatic terms, and (4) concepts based on introspective subjectivity or individual consciousness. These four styles of God-talk have been present during seven major periods of human civilization which have been (1) Hebraic, (2) Ancient Greek and Roman, (3) Patristic, (4) Medieval, (5) Renaissance/Reformation, (6) Modern, and (7) Postmodern/Contemporary.

1. The popular anthropomorphic images stemmed from different aspects of human living and varied from epoch to epoch depending on varying historical contexts. From family life and human relations the words father, mother, companion, friend, and helper were and are applied to

---

[49] Ibid., 107.
[50] Schillebeeckx, "The New Image of God," *GFM*, 108, 108, n. 4 [180, 205, n. 4].
[51] Ibid., 181 [109].
[52] Ibid.
[53] Schillebeeckx, "Correlation Between Human Question and Christian Answer," *UF, CW* vol. 5 (London: Bloomsbury T&T Clark, 2014), 76–77 [87].

God in each of our seven major periods. From human occupations the titles of shepherd, potter, builder, caretaker, warrior, leader have all been applied to God. From politics God came to be called king, prince, lord, master. From nature the images of wind, spirit, force, and power all came to be used of God. And especially after the Enlightenment, concepts from science came to be used of God, concepts such as evolution and force field.

2. Concurrently with popular daily-life concepts, people have consistently used philosophical categories to talk about God throughout the history of Western civilization. One of the earliest philosophical understandings of God comes from Pythagoras through Plato. Pythagoras sought to understand reality by seeking explanations with mathematical terminology. He concluded that "The ultimate principle of all reality, order, and goodness is to be found in the origin of all numbers, the *One*. God, the originate source of all being, was not dependent upon any other being, and was thus the sole ultimate, without beginning, without change, without parts, existing from all eternity."[54] This fundamentally Greek way of regarding God as the indivisible One became fused among Jews and Christians with the Hebraic view of God as "He Who Is" (Exod 3:14), or as Being.

It is frequently noted that theologians in the early church borrowed Greek philosophical concepts to explain their understanding of God, but it is worth noting that they did so in a very selective way. They could be highly critical of Sceptics and Epicureans, but were content to appropriate Stoic ideas about God's providence. Crucially, they relied on Platonic and neo-Platonic thought to distance their thinking from Greek and Roman mythological language about the Gods. The early Christians' language of One Unchanging God sharply differentiated their faith from their contemporaries who professed an unrestrained polytheism.

So too did their conviction that Jesus Christ was God incarnate. This belief, central to their faith, also created severe intellectual difficulties for them, because if it is said that God became incarnate, then God changed. The attempt to understand how an unchanging God could enter time and history resulted in the emergence of Trinitarian theology.

3. Simultaneously with popular, philosophical, and subjective patterns of God-talk, throughout the seven principal phases of Western civilization, God has also been discussed negatively or apophatically. Apophatic theology draws its distinctiveness from its conviction that human language is entirely inadequate to speak of the unspeakable. In a supreme irony of history, philosophical postmodernism and postmodern theologies both flow from exactly the same conviction.

4. Finally, concurrently with popular and philosophical images for God, concepts stemming from human subjectivity have also always been employed in theology. Another way of saying this is to observe that the human soul has often been regarded as the seedbed for recognizing God. Plotinus and Augustine both thought that God is directly present within the human soul. God is interior to us. And so it is that we find Augustine concluding in his book, *On the Trinity*, that the mystery of the Trinity can be comprehended through an analogy with the human soul. In this view a person's knowledge of himself or herself furnishes knowledge of God, and just as self-awareness, self-knowledge, and self-self-affirmation are all interlinked, so too are the persons of the Trinity, Father, Son, and Spirit.

---

[54] Francis Schlüssler Fiorenza and Gordon D. Kaufman, "God," *Critical Terms for Religious Studies*, ed. Mark C. Taylor (Chicago and London: The University of Chicago Press, 1998), 136–59, at 142.

The four ever-present ways of talking about God in Christian tradition are amply represented in the works of Schillebeeckx. For example, in his works, one can find:

1. Anthropomorphic images taken from daily life: God is the Father Almighty; "I prefer to see God not as an unchangeable and unchanging God, but rather as eternal youth."[55]
2. Philosophical concepts: God is a Pure Positivity and an "Absolute Freedom."
3. Apophatic terms: the apophatic way becomes: "we cannot know God's being";[56] "God is always a mystery";[57] "if you are really in search of God, you must reconcile yourself to living in religious darkness"; the ascesis of a person seeking God lies in "an obstinate refusal to confuse God with any creature whatever: with an experience, with an insight, a feeling, an apostolic work, a book that one writes about God"; "We only have human words for talking about God"; "we do not have a divine language."[58]
4. Concepts based on introspective subjectivity, human experience, or individual consciousness: God is "a familiar friend"; "the God who loves humankind."[59]

# Conclusion

Very little has been said above about Schillebeeckx's understanding of the Christian dogma of the Trinity. That is simply because he never lectured on the Trinity during his long academic and Dominican life, and he never wrote a monograph on the Trinity. In his many and multifaceted publications, he makes references to the Trinity, and he takes belief in the Trinity for granted, but he rarely expounds on the topic at any length. He inclined to the view that treatises devoted to the Trinity were somewhat pretentious in their aspirations conceptually to elaborate who God might be.

The most strikingly original way in which Schillebeeckx speaks of God is to locate a definition of humanity in God, and not in human beings. Hence, his language that God is "more human than any human being";[60] "Through his message and his way of life Jesus redefines in word and deed what being human is and what being God means. And he does this by declaring humanity to be the nature of God";[61] "In the last resort Jesus, too, whom we may name as his [God's] only beloved Son, is a human being like you and me, except he is more human."[62] In Schillebeeckx's theology, Jesus is a paradigm of humanity and a parable of God, whom Schillebeeckx calls in Latin, *Deus humanissimus*—the Most Human God.[63]

---

[55] Schillebeeckx, *God Is New Each Moment*, 29.
[56] Ibid.
[57] Ibid.
[58] Schillebeeckx, *For the Sake of the Gospel*, 86, 88.
[59] Ibid., 25.
[60] Schillebeeckx, *God Among Us*, 61.
[61] Schillebeeckx, *For the Sake of the Gospel*, 48. Cf. Schillebeeckx, *Church*, 142–43 [145].
[62] Schillebeeckx, *For the Sake of the Gospel*, 115.
[63] See Schillebeeckx, *Jesus*, 627 [669].

# Chapter 15

# Schillebeeckx's Praxis of Creation

Martin G. Poulsom

Edward Schillebeeckx's theology of creation is most clearly expressed in four distinct sources from his later work, though these have a significant structural continuity with material from his early writings before the Second Vatican Council. In fact, when read closely, the various sources have a remarkable continuity of expression, even when the more ephemeral threads of his argument are considered. This is even more striking when the texts are compared in Dutch, showing that at least some of the changes seen in English are introduced by the translation process itself. Reading the texts in parallel allows the development of Schillebeeckx's thought to be traced, suggesting that there is an important conjunctural shift in his thinking on creation during this time.

Despite this discontinuity,[1] Schillebeeckx's account of creation remains very much in continuity with the structural elements of classical theism, drawing in particular on Thomas Aquinas.[2] Although Schillebeeckx seeks to help this tradition to engage with contemporary men and women in a language that they can understand, the deepest dimensions of his thought, when articulated, have changed only a little over the course of his work as a theologian, and are not so different from those of his thirteenth-century Dominican brother. One way of helping Schillebeeckx's theology of creation to speak to men and women today—particularly in the context of the search for climate justice and a way of life that is more in harmony with the ecosystem in which we live—is to put his later material on creation into dialogue with Catholic

---

[1]   Discontinuity seems to be the preferred term used in volume 11 of the Collected Works of Edward Schillebeeckx as a translation of the Dutch term "*breuk*," though it is also fair to say that the somewhat more straightforward translation "break" does also appear in the translation. See, for example, Chapter Five ("Discontinuities in Christian Dogmas") and Chapter Six ("Theological Quests") and especially the opening page of Chapter Six, which uses both terms to translate the Dutch word: Edward Schillebeeckx, "Theological Quests," *Essays, CW* vol.11 (London: Bloomsbury T&T Clark, 2014), 111–61, at 111. For the Dutch text, see Edward Schillebeeckx, *Theologisch testament: Notarieel nog niet verleden* (Baarn: Nelissen, 1994), 69.

[2]   Schillebeeckx describes the "structural aspects" of history as having "a timespan of many centuries," resulting in "enduring structures of human thought." These change very slowly, and are not synchronous with the "conjunctural aspects of our thinking," which other writers have called paradigms. As a result, he says, "basic structures survive even the most radical revolutions," forming what he calls "the structural depth elements of human thought." It is this understanding of the structural and conjunctural that is operative in this chapter. See Edward Schillebeeckx, *Jesus, CW* vol. 6 (London: Bloomsbury T&T Clark, 2014), 539–41 [577–78]. Also see Martin Poulsom, "New Resonances in Classic Motifs: Finding Schillebeeckx's Theology in Translation," *Louvain Studies* 38 (2014), 370–81, especially 371–75.

Social Tradition. Such a dialogue can be mutually enriching, leading to a further development of a "Schillebeeckian" understanding of creation, which can make a contribution to twenty-first-century debates on the place of humanity in the created order, in dialogue with Pope Francis's writing on care for our common home.[3]

In this chapter, the term "creation faith,"[4] found in the 1983 collection of sermons, lectures, and primarily "pastoral" articles entitled *God Among Us: The Gospel Proclaimed* is preferred to the expression "belief in creation," which is used more frequently in the other English sources as a translation of the Dutch term "*scheppingsgeloof*."[5] It is also employed more often than "theology of creation," for similar reasons, although other Schillebeeckx scholars also translate *scheppingsgeloof* more literally as "creation faith." Debates about belief in creation, which often take place in the wider context of discussing the relation between science and religion, tend to privilege *what* it is that people of faith believe, often as opposed to what their scientist counterparts believe. This results in a debate that leans very strongly in a propositional direction, as if a tradition of faith can be adequately summed up in a list of claims, which can then be compared with scientific claims about the origin of the universe. Describing and assessing an author's theology of creation often results in a similar emphasis on conceptual content, especially when— as is the case with Schillebeeckx—the writer in question is a systematic theologian. Neither of these ways of describing the subject matter is incorrect, as such. However, what both can easily neglect is that faith—and, as a result theology—cannot be exhausted by a consideration of the ideas that it propounds. Systematic theology, of course, contains many important concepts, and Schillebeeckx's theology of creation does include important ideas, which merit attention. However, in order to be faithful to the way that he works, it is just as important to stress that faith is not only held, but it is also lived. As William J. Hill tellingly observes, Christian faith, for Schillebeeckx, "is more a matter of orthopraxis than orthodoxy; it is more a matter of living out the truths and values of the gospel than of illuminating them theoretically."[6]

---

[3]  See Martin G. Poulsom, *The Dialectics of Creation: Creation and the Creator in Edward Schillebeeckx and David Burrell* (London: Bloomsbury T&T Clark, 2014), 11; Francis, *On Care for Our Common Home: Laudato Si'* (May 24, 2015) (hereafter cited in text as *LS*), http://w2.vatican.va/content/francesco/en/encyclicals/documents/papa-francesco_20150524_enciclica-laudato-si.html.

[4]  Edward Schillebeeckx, *God Among Us: The Gospel Proclaimed*, trans. John Bowden (London: SCM Press, 1983), 91–102 (see, for example, 92, 94, and 96).

[5]  For the parallel citations to those mentioned above, see Edward Schillebeeckx, *IR, CW* vol. 8 (London: Bloomsbury T&T Clark, 2014), 99, 102, 103 [113, 116, 118]; and Edward Schillebeeckx, *Church, CW* vol. 10 (London: Bloomsbury T&T Clark, 2014), which does not contain the material in which the first citation is found, but does contain the other two at pp. 227, 229 [229, 231]. In the respective Dutch sources, the references are Edward Schillebeeckx, *Evangelie verhalen* (Baarn: Nelissen, 1982), 92, 95, 96; Edward Schillebeeckx, *Tussentijds verhaal over twee Jesusboeken* (Bloemendaal: Nelissen, 1978), 129, 132, 134; and Edward Schillebeeckx, *Mensen als verhaal van God* (Nelissen: Baarn, 1989), 247, 249.

[6]  William J. Hill, "A Theology in Transition," *The Praxis of the Reign of God: An Introduction to the Theology of Edward Schillebeeckx*, ed. Mary Catherine Hilkert and Robert J. Schreiter, 2nd ed. (New York: Fordham University Press, 2002), 1–18, at 3.

# I. The sources

Philip Kennedy has identified three major sources for Schillebeeckx's creation faith, which he describes as "singularly succinct expositions" which follow "exactly the same line of argument."[7] The publications that he uses are Chapter Six of *Interim Report on the Books Jesus and Christ* (entitled "Kingdom of God: Creation and Salvation"), Chapter Sixteen of *God Among Us* ("I Believe in God, Creator of Heaven and Earth"), and Chapter Five of *Church: The Human Story of God* ("By Way of an Epilogue").[8] Kennedy's comment on the argument that these sources pursue fits well with his proposal that there is continuity underlying the discontinuities in Schillebeeckx's theological development,[9] and with that voiced here that the texts have common conjunctural and structural themes. The title of Chapter Six of *Interim Report* in particular makes it clear that, for Schillebeeckx, creation is not an isolated topic in theology and that it must be explicitly linked to salvation. As a result, it is important to add the chapters that follow immediately in both *Interim Report* (entitled "I Believe in Jesus of Nazareth") and *God Among Us* ("I Believe in the Man Jesus: the Christ, the Only Beloved Son, Our Lord"). Doing so introduces the fourth source, an article published in English in 1980 ("I Believe in Jesus of Nazareth: the Christ, the Son of God, the Lord"). This text follows the *God Among Us* content very closely indeed, making the same structural connection between creation and salvation in Christ that is made throughout the material, though it contains a different concluding section.[10]

Shedding clear light on the misunderstandings that can distort belief in creation, both in the lives of Christians and in the minds of those who enter into dialogue with them, can be a helpful way of clearing the ground for a more kataphatic presentation of creation faith. These two strategies interweave in Schillebeeckx's account, but it is beneficial to gather them together as distinct threads of argument, partly because doing so also reveals the underlying motivations that direct his account.

## Misunderstanding creation

Kennedy accurately describes Schillebeeckx as a "markedly anti-dualist" thinker, and the way that he introduces the subject of creation in *Interim Report* makes this very clear.[11] He observes that faith in creation and in Jesus as the Christ are linked in the Creed, stressing that: "Creation and salvation, therefore, shed light on each [other], mutually and essentially." Because the two beliefs are so closely interrelated, any "alienating vision of creation" will "distort the Christian

---

7  Philip Kennedy, *Schillebeeckx* (Collegeville, MN: Liturgical Press, 1993), 82.

8  Philip Kennedy, "God and Creation," *The Praxis of the Reign of God: An Introduction to the Theology of Edward Schillebeeckx*, ed. Mary Catherine Hilkert and Robert J. Schreiter, 2nd ed. (New York: Fordham University Press, 2002), 37–58, at 42.

9  See Philip Kennedy, "Continuity Underlying Discontinuity: Schillebeeckx's Philosophical Background," *New Blackfriars* 70 (1989), 264–77.

10  Edward Schillebeeckx, "I Believe in Jesus of Nazareth: The Christ, the Son of God, the Lord," trans. by Gerard Sloyan, *Journal of Ecumenical Studies* 17 (1980), 18–32. It is interesting to note that where *God Among Us* uses the expression "creation faith" in this chapter, "I Believe in Jesus of Nazareth" has "faith in creation," keeping the helpful focus on faith, rather than belief, that was noted earlier.

11  Kennedy, *Schillebeeckx*, 93.

vision of Jesus, or even make it impossible."[12] As a result, "creation faith is only liberating […] if we understand creation neither dualistically nor as an emanation."[13] In *God Among Us*, which reads as a slightly re-edited version of the *Interim Report* material, he says that *"dualism* arose from the offense caused by the suffering, evil and injustice in our world."[14] A dualistic misconception of the world, like genuinely liberating Christian faith, opposes all these things, but dualism does so absolutely,[15] seeing the finite world as flawed: "In that case, finitude is not the normal condition of creatures, but is traced back to a fault in creation or to a mysterious primal sin." Whether the current state of affairs arose because of a Fall in Eden, leading to the created world becoming a place of corruption and decay, or because of a heavenly rebellion, resulting in banishment into materiality, dualism "denies that God, when creating, willed the world precisely as world, and men and women precisely as human beings."[16] Instead, in a dualistic "view the created world is a kind of compromise between God and some power of darkness."[17] Dualism avers that the compromise will not last and that this first stage of the story of God's dealings with creation will be superseded "in an unexpected and terrible future which, given the terrible mess in which we live, is imminent."[18] Thus, it also drives a wedge between creation and salvation, and its distortion of creation faith leads to a misunderstanding of salvation.

If dualism arises from a sense that the world should not be the way it is, then emanation, for Schillebeeckx, could be seen as the flip side of the coin. It derives, he says, "from a concern to safeguard God's transcendence." In this portrayal, emanationism shares some of dualism's preconceptions, holding that "God is so great and so exalted that it is beneath his dignity to meddle directly with creatures and to compromise himself" by doing so. Alluding to the Gnostic creation myths condemned by the early church, he says that in emanation, God "entrusts creation to a representative, a principal viceroy of a somewhat lower order," which Gnostics called the demiurge.[19] One result of this misunderstanding is that God is not both creator and saviour, but becomes the one who intervenes to rescue men and women from the exile of materiality, separating creation and salvation in a way that is similar to dualism. Another problem that Schillebeeckx observes with the emanationist scheme is that the "flowing forth of things from God is seen above all as a necessary process."[20] This is a good example of a structural element of Schillebeeckx's thinking, in continuity with Thomas Aquinas. Thomas encountered emanation principally in the

---

[12] Schillebeeckx, *IR*, 98 [111].

[13] Ibid., 98 [111–12]; parallel in *God Among Us*, 91.

[14] Schillebeeckx, *God Among Us*, 91; parallel in *IR*, 98 [112], which translates the Dutch word *ergernis* found in both sources as "scandal." See Schillebeeckx, *Evangelie verhalen*, 91; parallel in Schillebeeckx, *Tussentijds verhaal*, 128.

[15] Dualism says an absolute "No!" to the situation of suffering, evil, and injustice in which men and women find themselves. Schillebeeckx admits that "our history of suffering" is a significant challenge to faith in a liberating God. Genuine Christian faith, however, neither shies away from this challenge nor treats it as absolute, responding "And nonetheless!" See Schillebeeckx, *IR*, 98 [111].

[16] Schillebeeckx, *IR*, 98 [112]; parallel in Schillebeeckx, *God Among Us*, 91.

[17] Schillebeeckx, *God Among Us*, 91–92; parallel in Schillebeeckx, *IR*, 99 [112].

[18] Schillebeeckx, *IR*, 98–99 [112]; parallel in Schillebeeckx, *God Among Us*, 91.

[19] Schillebeeckx, *IR*, 99 [112]; parallel in Schillebeeckx, *God Among Us*, 92. See Robert Haardt, "Gnosis," *Sacramentum Mundi: An Encyclopedia of Theology*, ed. Karl Rahner, with Cornelius Ernst and Kevin Smyth, vol. 2 (London, Burns & Oates, 1968), 374–81, at 375.

[20] Schillebeeckx, *IR*, 99 [112]; parallel in Schillebeeckx, *GAU*, 92.

writings of eleventh-century Muslim scholar, Ibn Sina. However, Ibn Sina's writings were later opposed, amongst others, by al-Ghazali. In the philosophical account of creation presented by Ibn Sina and other Muslim philosophers, Ghazali finds an incoherence with the Muslim belief that Allah creates the world freely. This is because the model used in the philosophical emanation scheme—that of the logical deduction of premises from a first principle—implied that the One would have to create of necessity. It also meant, as David Burrell points out, that "the First in such a scheme could not adequately be distinguished from the premises that follow from it."[21] Paradoxically, the desire to safeguard God's transcendence, which lies at the heart of the emanationist misunderstanding of creation, elides the very distinction that it seeks to secure, resulting in a view of the "world and men [as] degradations of God—divinity reduced in rank."[22]

Straight after his treatment of emanationism in *Interim Report*, Schillebeeckx begins his consideration of the misunderstanding of creation as an explanation.[23] He first avers that creatures are "there without any explanation or foundation in themselves or in anything else in this world, nature or history."[24] This means that neo-Darwinian evolutionary theory does not offer a rival explanation for the origin of life on earth to that found in Genesis[25] and that the search for a Grand Unified Theory in physics, if successful, would not lead to a situation in which there was "nothing for a creator to do."[26] In structural continuity with Aquinas once more, Schillebeeckx's position is that unaided human reason is not able to provide a definitive and complete answer to the question about the origin of the world.[27] Picking up on his presentation of emanationism as implying the necessity of creation, he adds that "belief in the creating God cannot be an explanation either, [... because] the creature has no prior necessity at all and does not find any explanation in any connection with this world," even that of creation. Schillebeeckx begins the parallel material in *Church* with this misunderstanding, perhaps because debates about science and religion became more common over the course of the decade that the later sources span. In material that is only

---

21   David B. Burrell, *Faith and Freedom: An Interfaith Perspective* (Oxford: Blackwell, 2004), 113–26, at 115; also see David B. Burrell, *Freedom and Creation in Three Traditions* (Notre Dame: University of Notre Dame Press, 1993), 13–14, 53.

22   Schillebeeckx, *IR*, 99 [112]; parallel in Schillebeeckx, *God Among Us*, 92.

23   Strangely, only the first sentence of this paragraph is found in *God Among Us*, despite the fact that, when the Dutch texts are compared, the material is present in both *Tussentijds verhaal* and *Evangelie verhalen*. (Compare Schillebeeckx, *IR*, 99 [113] and *God Among Us*, 92, with *Tussentijds verhaal*, 129 and *Evangelie verhalen*, 92.)

24   Schillebeeckx, *IR*, 99 [113].

25   See, for example, the suggestion that religious beliefs are cultural memes, which operate analogously to genes, in Richard Dawkins, *The Selfish Gene*, rev. ed. (Oxford: Oxford University Press, 1989), 189–201.

26   See Schillebeeckx, *Church*, 227 [229], which adds a comment about "the natural sciences and anthropology" to material taken from the earlier sources about creation as an explanation (cf. Schillebeeckx, *IR*, 102 [116]; parallel in Schillebeeckx, *God Among Us*, 94). For the quote, see Carl Sagan, "Introduction," *A Brief History of Time: From the Big Bang to Black Holes*, Stephen W. Hawking (London: Bantam Press, 1988), x.

27   Aquinas argues that philosophy is not able to solve the problem of whether the universe is eternal or begins with time, because creation is not a change, but is—philosophically, at least—the causing of existence. Such an understanding is compatible with an eternal universe, or one that begins with time. See William E. Carroll, "Creation and Science in the Middle Ages," *New Blackfriars* 88 (2007), 678–89 (at 686–89).

found in *Church*, he uses an arresting image to portray the idea that God is an explanation of the way things are in the world, because from this perspective, "human beings and our whole world [become] a puppet-show in which God alone holds the strings in his hands behind the screen: human history as a large-scale Muppet show!"[28] If this is the way things are, "then any attempt to change them would indeed be blasphemous. In that case our sole duty would be to fit in with the predetermined and preconceived universe."[29] Postulating an inevitable "progressive evolutionary progress to an ideal state," rather than a plan set in place at the origin of the universe, he says, "makes little difference to the pattern of explanation used." In both cases: "Historicity is then reduced either to a genetic development of a preprogrammed plan or to a process which takes place by the logic of development."[30] But humanity is not helpless in the face of history—indeed, for Schillebeeckx, men and women have a crucial role to play in making the world a better place.

Although he does so only briefly in the creation parallels, Schillebeeckx also presents pantheism as a misunderstanding of creation. The brevity of his treatment may well be influenced by the agreement of most theologians that Christianity is not a pantheistic tradition of faith even if, as has been shown above, some forms of emanationism can tend in a pantheistic direction.[31] It may also be because the comments he makes almost seem to be an aside during his discussion of God's absolute presence, which will be examined later. Pantheism, he says, compromises God's presence in the world, as Christianity understands and experiences it. If God's presence were to mean that everything other than God "were in some way to be explained as an illusion or as part of the actual definition of God, then God would not seem to have sufficient active presence to bring autonomous, [non-divine] beings into existence."[32] The transcendence of God, which dualism and emanationism both overstress, is nevertheless an essential aspect of creation faith, which cannot be dispensed with. An exclusively immanent God is just as much of a distortion of creation as a God who is solely transcendent.

# II. Schillebeeckx's creation faith

How God's transcendence and immanence interact is a key component of creation faith, and Schillebeeckx is resolutely theistic in his presentation of the relation between creation and its creator. Christian belief in creation is, for him, not found at the mid-point of a continuum between dualism, at one extreme, and pantheism at the other. Such a conceptualization presents

---

[28] Schillebeeckx, *Church*, 227 [230].

[29] Schillebeeckx, *God Among Us*, 94; parallels in Schillebeeckx, *IR*, 102 [116], Schillebeeckx, *Church* 227–28 [230].

[30] Schillebeeckx, *Church*, 228 [230]; parallels in Schillebeeckx, *IR*, 102 [116–17], Schillebeeckx, *God Among Us*, 95.

[31] See the overview offered by Ismael Quiles, in "Pantheism," *Sacramentum Mundi: An Encyclopedia of Theology*, ed. Karl Rahner, with Cornelius Ernst and Kevin Smyth, vol. 2 (London, Burns & Oates, 1968), 335–36.

[32] Schillebeeckx, *God Among Us*, 93; parallel in Schillebeeckx, *IR*, 100 [114]. The term "non-divine" in square brackets (found in the 2014 translation of *Interim Report*) is preferred to the translation "non-godly" found in both of the earlier translations to avoid the misunderstanding that it might be taken to imply sinfulness. This is not what Schillebeeckx means—he is speaking of creation as being other than God.

transcendence and immanence as poles that need to be held in balance, because they pull in opposite directions: transcendence pulls God away from the world, whereas immanence pulls God closer to the world. For Schillebeeckx, God's transcendence and immanence are mutually co-constitutive, such that each one helps us to understand the other.[33] The dialectic between them is not polar, but relational, enabling an account of creation faith to be fashioned in which they exist in direct proportion to each other, not inverse proportion.[34] Thus, the more transcendent God is, the more immanent God is. This perspective on transcendence and immanence finds its underpinning in the structure of creation faith that Schillebeeckx espouses, offering an understanding of the ontological distinction that is both insightful and persuasive.

Schillebeeckx secures God's transcendence by noting that there is an important distinction to be drawn between the creator and everything that God creates: "If God is creator, then he does indeed create the non-divine [*het niet-goddelijke*], that which is wholly other than himself, in other words, finite things. Creatures are not copies of God."[35] Creation faith helps us to understand that God is infinite, whereas creatures are finite. This is not merely a state of affairs that needs to be taken into account in our thinking about God and the world. Echoing the first chapter of Genesis, Schillebeeckx stresses that it "is good that man is just man, the world just the world" and that "God's blessing rests precisely on this."[36] Creatures are not copies, replicas, or degradations of God; therefore, the absolute limit that our finitude places on us is not a problem, but a blessing. This means that we "may and must simply be human beings in a living world which is simply the world [...] To want to transcend finitude is megalomania or arrogance which alienates people from themselves, from the world and from nature."[37] Another way of putting the basic insight is to say that if "God is Creator, then the creature is indeed not-God [*niet-God*], other than God."[38] However, the way that the world is not-God is not the same as the way that God is not-world. The relation "other than" is not identical in both directions. Once again, this is a theistic structure of thinking, in continuity with Aquinas, even though the ephemeral shape of the argument is somewhat different.

Aquinas does not use the category of distinction to articulate the connection between God and the world—the term "ontological distinction," though often traced back to Aquinas, is actually a

---

[33] Cf. the presentation of the interplay between theory and practice in Schillebeeckx in Martin Poulsom, "The Place of Praxis in the Theology of Edward Schillebeeckx," *Keeping Faith in Practice: Aspects of Catholic Pastoral Theology*, ed. James Sweeney, Gemma Simmonds and David Lonsdale (London: SCM Press, 2010), 131–42, at 136.

[34] Schillebeeckx pursues what Kathryn Tanner has called a "non-contrastive" account of God's transcendence, a strategy that she recommends in *God and Creation: Tyranny or Empowerment?* (Oxford: Blackwell, 1988), 45.

[35] Schillebeeckx, *IR*, 100 [113]; parallel in Schillebeeckx, *God Among Us*, 92. In the Dutch sources, the material is identical, apart from one word—the term "*kopieën*" in *Tussentijds verhaal* has been changed in *Evangelie verhalen* to "*repliek*," accurately translated in *God Among Us* as "replicas." See Schillebeeckx, *Tussentijds verhaal*, 129; Schillebeeckx, *Evangelie verhalen*, 93.

[36] Schillebeeckx, *IR*, 99 [113]; parallel in Schillebeeckx, *God Among Us*, 93. In Dutch, the parallel is exact (see Schillebeeckx, *Tussentijds verhaal*, 129; Schillebeeckx, *Evangelie verhalen*, 92).

[37] Schillebeeckx, *God Among Us*, 93; parallel in Schillebeeckx, *IR*, 100 [114]. The term "megalomania" is not found in the Dutch text of *Tussentijds verhaal* (p. 130), but is in the 2014 translation of *IR*, rather than "arrogance," which is found in both Dutch sources. *Evangelie verhalen* (p. 93) adds the term megalomania when it edits the *Tussentijds verhaal* text.

[38] Schillebeeckx, *IR*, 100 [114]; parallel in Schillebeeckx, *God Among Us*, 93.

product of modernity. Interestingly, however, the philosophical structure of a distinction can be shown to be similar to that of a relation, the term that Aquinas himself uses.[39] The first important feature of both is that statements about them have a directional quality—thinking about the distinction between God and the world proceeds in the opposite direction to thinking about the distinction between the world and God.[40] This means that, for the theist, the ontological distinction between the world and God does not imply an ontological distinction between God and the world. If the distinction were ontological in both directions, then God and the world would be completely separate, and God would not be able to act in the world.[41] Once the shift to Aquinas's terminology is made, the implications of this directional sensitivity become even clearer. Aquinas speaks of real relations and notional relations,[42] and Burrell points out that the real relation of creation establishes a causal dependence in the creature that is absolute.[43] The very existence of the creature, and every aspect of its existence, is absolutely dependent on God, at every moment of its existence. God, however, is not dependent on creatures for anything. As Robert Sokolowski expresses it:

> God could and would be God even if there were no world. [...] The most fundamental thing we come to in Christianity, the distinction between the world and God, is appreciated as not being the most fundamental thing at all, because one of the terms of the distinction, God, is more fundamental than the distinction itself.[44]

God is not subject to the ontological distinction, because it is, in fact, produced by God's creative action. There is more ephemeral variation when Schillebeeckx is considered, because he does not use the technical philosophical language of distinction or relation explicitly. He speaks of the ontological distinction as an "unsurpassable boundary (on our side) between the finite and the infinite."[45] In this quote from *Church*, the last of the creation parallels to be published, Schillebeeckx changes the order of "the infinite and the finite" in this expression from that found in the earlier texts, as a result of which the directionality of the "between" statement becomes clearer, helping the reader to understand what he means by speaking of the boundary as being only "on our side."[46] In God, the distinction is not unsurpassable, which means that the utterly transcendent God can, at the same time, be completely immanent. As Schillebeeckx puts it in 1958, "I am myself in dependence on God: the more I am God's, the more I become myself."[47]

---

[39] See, for example, Thomas Aquinas, *ST* Ia, q. 13, a. 7.

[40] Cf. Poulsom, *Dialectics of Creation*, 29–31.

[41] Interestingly, this is an accusation not infrequently leveled against classical theism by panentheists, suggesting that the theistic account of the ontological distinction is not self-evident, and perhaps needs elucidation at a length that is not possible in this chapter.

[42] David B. Burrell, *Aquinas: God and Action* (London: Routledge, 1979), 84–87.

[43] Burrell, *Aquinas: God and Action*, 132–34.

[44] Robert Sokolowski, *The God of Faith and Reason: Foundations of Christian Theology*, rev. ed. (Washington, DC: Catholic University of America Press, 1995), 33.

[45] Schillebeeckx, *Church*, 229 [231].

[46] Cf. Schillebeeckx, *IR*, 103 [118], Schillebeeckx, *God Among Us*, 96.

[47] Edward Schillebeeckx, "Dialogue with God and Christian Secularity," *God and Man*, trans. Edward Fitzgerald and Peter Tomlinson (London: Sheed and Ward, 1969), 210–33, at 215.

In addition to the concept of finitude, Schillebeeckx often uses the philosophical notion of contingency to speak of creation. In an expression that sounds somewhat similar to the one cited earlier about creatures being finite, he says: "From a Christian perspective, the world and man are totally other than God, but within the presence of the creator God. [...] God remains in and with the contingent, the other-than-God."[48] Contingency, for Schillebeeckx, is the kataphatic equivalent of his apophatic insistence that creation is not necessary. If creation is not-God, "then it could be otherwise," which is the definition of contingency—if something is contingent, it could be other than it, in fact, has turned out to be. How it is now is not necessary.[49] There is also a deeper level of contingency, which implies that, because they are not necessary, contingent things "could just as well not have been there" at all.[50] Contingency, perhaps even more than finitude, stresses that God does not have to create in order to be God. As Sokolowski observes, if this is the case "the world is there through an incomparable generosity."[51]

Although Schillebeeckx does not use the category of relation in the way that Aquinas does, his thinking is nevertheless strongly relational. Kennedy stresses this element of his thought, noting that, for Schillebeeckx, "creatures exist *in relation* to divine being."[52] Elsewhere, he describes Schillebeeckx's creation faith in terms that are even more reminiscent of Aquinas, maintaining that this "relation *constitutes the creature*."[53] This is not merely an ephemeral preference for terminology, but is a deep, structural element of his thinking, found not only in his creation faith, but throughout his oeuvre. Kennedy designates it a "'relational ontology' or 'ontology of relation,'"[54] which places Schillebeeckx very much in continuity with Aquinas, who avers that God creates "by knowledge and love."[55] Schillebeeckx goes so far as to say that creation "is ultimately the meaning that God has wanted to give to his divine life. He wanted, freely, also to be God for others,"[56] an expression that echoes the way that creation is other than God that was examined above. This recognition that God wants to give life to creatures makes creation faith "good news, which says something about God, and about humanity and the world, in their relation to one another."[57] Similar themes can be found in Schillebeeckx's early work, in which he states that creation is "a divinely transcendent act which does not take place from without, but which from the very essence of all things holds them creatively in its hand."[58] This is a very confident articulation of divine immanence and, as has already been

---

48 Schillebeeckx, *God Among Us*, 93; parallel in *IR*, 100–01 [114–15].
49 My translation of Schillebeeckx, *Tussentijds verhaal*, 130 (exact parallel, *Evangelie verhalen*, 93). Cf. Schillebeeckx, *IR*, 100 [114]; parallel in Schillebeeckx, *God Among Us*, 93, which both render the Dutch term *anders* as "different."
50 Schillebeeckx, *IR*, 99 [113]. This is in the material that is absent from *God Among Us*, 92, though it is present in the Dutch text: Schillebeeckx, *Evangelie verhalen*, 92.
51 Sokolowski, *The God of Faith and Reason*, 34.
52 Kennedy, *Schillebeeckx*, 89.
53 Philip Kennedy, *Deus Humanissimus: The Knowability of God in the Theology of Edward Schillebeeckx* (Fribourg: University Press Fribourg Switzerland, 1993), 363.
54 Ibid., 106.
55 Burrell, *Aquinas: God and Action*, 87.
56 Schillebeeckx, *Church*, 229 [232].
57 My translation of Schillebeeckx, *Evangelie verhalen*, 91. Cf. Schillebeeckx, *God Among Us*, 91.
58 Edward Schillebeeckx, "Man and His Bodily World," *WC, CW* vol. 4 (London Bloomsbury T&T Clark, 2014), 177–205 [230–68], at 187 [243].

shown, goes hand in hand with an equally robust account of God's transcendence. In spite of all the difficulties and limits that human beings face as a result of their finitude, Schillebeeckx is assured that "we are securely held in the embrace of God."[59] In the creation parallels, he asserts, in a similar way, that "He is 'with us' in all that this finitude entails, both in positive experiences and in failure, suffering and death."[60] This is because, as creator, God "is after all the creator of this entire 'saeculum,' so that there are no eras, no centuries and not even any hours in which he leaves no witness to himself."[61] God is never absent from anything in the world because, if he were, that thing would immediately cease to be, since its existence is dependent on God at every moment.

This means that when Schillebeeckx deals with the autonomy of the creature, he does not speak of independence, separation, or the absence of God—not even in the depths of the most profound suffering that can be experienced: "Finite beings are a blend [*mengsel*] of solitude and presence."[62] This assertion expresses a relational dialectic of distinction and relation, rather than a polar dialectic of presence and absence. The autonomous creature exists in solitude and, as a Dominican, Schillebeeckx holds that it is possible to experience the presence of God in solitude. In fact, the deeper the solitude, the greater the potential for becoming aware of God's presence, for example, in contemplative prayer. As a result of this direct proportion between solitude and presence, he can say that, from "a Christian perspective, the world and man are totally other than God, but within the presence of the creator God."[63] This articulation of God's presence is linked to the relation of creation and, given the complete dependence on God that this relation expresses, it is a presence that is closer to us than that of any other we know. It is an "insight of faith that finitude is not left in its solitude but is [supported] by the absolute presence of the creating God."[64] This emphasis on the presence of God being absolute rather than relative, and never varying—even if it is not always possible for us to detect it —combined with the 2014 translation rendering "*de scheppende God*" as "the creating God" (where the earlier texts translated it as "the creator God") also helps to stress that God is always creating. Creation is not only about initiation. As he puts it, "creation is no one-time event somewhere in the beginning, but [an ongoing] dynamic event. God wants to be the origin, here and now, of

---

[59] Schillebeeckx, "Dialogue with God and Christian Secularity," 233.

[60] Schillebeeckx, *IR*, 117 [134]; parallels in Schillebeeckx, *God Among Us*, 110; Schillebeeckx, "I Believe in Jesus of Nazareth," 25.

[61] Schillebeeckx, *IR*, 105 [119]; parallel in Schillebeeckx, *God Among Us*, 98.

[62] My translation of Schillebeeckx, *Tussentijds verhaal*, 130 (exact parallel in Schillebeeckx, *Evangelie verhalen*, 93). Cf. Schillebeeckx, *IR*, 100 [114]; exact parallel in Schillebeeckx, *God Among Us*, 93, which translate *mengsel* as "mixture."

[63] Schillebeeckx, *God Among Us*, 93; parallel in Schillebeeckx, *IR*, 100–01 [114]. This translation is preferred because the expression "*totaal-andere van God*" is more closely—and more helpfully— translated as "totally other than God" here. Cf. Schillebeeckx, *Evangelie verhalen*, 93; exact parallel in Schillebeeckx, *Tussentijds verhaal*, 130.

[64] Schillebeeckx, *IR*, 106 [121–22], earlier translation of "*gedragen wordt*" as "supported" is preferred to the 2014 translation "borne." Cf. Schillebeeckx, *Tussentijds verhaal*, 138.

the worldliness of the world and of the humanity of man. He wants to be with us, in and with our finite task in the world."[65]

Schillebeeckx speaks of God's absolute presence in *Interim Report* four more times, linking it with Christian creation faith (twice), with our task in the world, and with the "proviso of the creator God."[66] All of these references are found in *God Among Us*, and he adds another in a section about history and human society that is not found in *Interim Report*.[67] After the material about God's absolute presence in human solitude, he adds an example about the treatment of the elderly, which uses the expression twice more, suggesting the importance of this conjunctural element of his thinking. Turning to the last of the creation parallels, written a decade later, it is possible to discern further development. Although only two of the five earlier instances of the terminology are found, both are helpful in tracing the development of Schillebeeckx's thinking at this conjunctural level. The first occurs in the section on humanity's task in the world. He avers, in all three parallels, that the task of transforming the world and overcoming suffering and evil "is our task and our burden" and, at the same time, that it is carried out in God's presence. In *Interim Report* and *God among Us*, he says that we carry it out "within the absolute presence of God."[68] In *Church*, he writes that we do so "within the absolute saving presence of God among us."[69] This shift in language is stressed in the following paragraph, where Schillebeeckx inserts two more examples. After speaking of the contingency of everything that exists, he adds that this contingency "is supported by the absolute saving presence of God," pointing out that the "believer knows that God makes himself present in a saving way in [...] history."[70] Later in the parallel material, speaking explicitly about solitude and presence, he makes similar changes, saying that "finitude is not left in its solitude but is supported by the absolute saving presence of the living God."[71] This development, however, is not a break with what came before. Rather, the later expressions more clearly signal that, for Schillebeeckx, creation and salvation are not two

---

[65] Schillebeeckx, *IR*, 101 [116]. The earlier translation of *"voortdurend"* as "ongoing" is preferred to the 2014 translation "sustained"; parallel in Schillebeeckx, *God Among Us*, 94; cf. Schillebeeckx, *Tussentijds verhaal*, 132; parallel in Schillebeeckx, *Evangelie verhalen*, 94. This preference is expressed for two reasons: the first is that using the expression "sustained" may give the mistaken impression that Schillebeeckx is departing from Aquinas' creation-faith and using a more Bonaventurian schema. Bonaventure restricts creation *ex nihilo* to the beginning of the universe and speaks of God's holding the world in being after this as conservation. See Steven Baldner, "St. Bonaventure on the Temporal Beginning of the World," *The New Scholasticism* 63 (1989), 206–28, at 226–27. The second reason is to distinguish Schillebeeckx from those contemporary theologians who—especially in the context of the science and religion debate—support the use of *creatio continua* in addition to *creatio ex nihilo*. See John Polkinghorne, *Science and Christian Belief: Theological Reflections of a Bottom-Up Thinker* (London: SPCK, 1994), 73–75; Arthur R. Peacocke, "Theology and Science Today," *Cosmos as Creation: Theology and Science in Consonance*, ed. Ted Peters (Nashville: Abingdon Press, 1989), 28–43, at 34.

[66] See Schillebeeckx, *IR*, 100 [114], 107 [122], 103 [118], and 105 [119] respectively; parallel in Schillebeeckx, *God Among Us*, 93, 102, 96, and 98.

[67] Schillebeeckx, *God Among Us*, 98.

[68] Schillebeeckx, *IR*, 103 [118]; parallel in Schillebeeckx, *God Among Us*, 96.

[69] Schillebeeckx, *Church*, 229 [231].

[70] Ibid., 229 [231]; cf. parallels in Schillebeeckx, *IR* 103 [118], and Schillebeeckx, *God Among Us*, 96.

[71] Schillebeeckx, *Church*, 231 [233]; parallels in Schillebeeckx, *IR* 107 [122], Schillebeeckx, *God Among Us*, 102, as cited earlier.

separate events. The God who is creator is the same as the God who saves, and so the relation of creation and the relationship of faith are closely intertwined.

Similar intertwining is also found in what can be called Schillebeeckx's definition of creation, which uses one of his typical structural expressions. Near the start of the parallel material about Christology as concentrated creation, he says:

> Creation is an act of God which, on the one hand, unconditionally gives us our own particular character—finite, not divine, and destined for true humanity. Simultaneously, on the other hand, creation is an act in which God presents himself in selfless love as our God: our salvation and happiness, the supreme content of what it means to be true and good humanly. God creates men and women freely for the salvation and happiness of man himself; however, in the very same act, with the same sovereign freedom, he wills himself to be the deepest meaning of human life, its salvation and happiness.[72]

This definition presents two sides of the coin of creation faith, connecting them using the expression "on the one hand ... on the other hand." Each of these can be seen to represent distinctive threads in his argument, and the way that he connects them shows that they are mutually co-constitutive. On the one hand, God's creative act establishes human beings as autonomous, finite creatures that are other than God, reflecting God's transcendence. On the other hand, creation is also an act in which God makes himself absolutely present to those creatures, immanent within creation in love, inviting them to enter into a relationship with him in faith, which will lead them to full humanity and salvation. The second sentence of the definition strongly recalls his statement from 1958, that "the more I am God's, the more I become myself."[73] The two sides of the coin mutually reinforce one another for Schillebeeckx, in a relational dialectic that intertwines not only the distinction and the relation of creation, but also the mysteries of creation and salvation.[74]

# III. Creation faith *sequela* Schillebeeckx

A significant way that creation faith can be developed *sequela* Schillebeeckx is by investigating the implications of another conjunctural shift in his later work and putting it into dialogue with Catholic Social Tradition.[75] In the second half of the last chapter of *Church*, he considers whether salvation is a purely spiritual reality and begins by reflecting on the way that his work emphasizes justice and peace, and human solidarity.[76] Looking back on how these themes developed, he says: "In the 1950s and above all the 1960s the word 'co-humanity' became a fashionable replacement

---

[72] Schillebeeckx, *IR*, 110 [114]; parallels in Schillebeeckx, *God Among Us*, 104; Schillebeeckx, "I Believe in Jesus of Nazareth," 19.

[73] Schillebeeckx, "Dialogue with God and Christian Secularity," *God and Man*, 215.

[74] For a fuller account of the expression, and how it functions in polar and relational dialectic, see Poulsom, *Dialectics of Creation*, 92–98.

[75] For an account of this way of following another, and of the important distinction between *sequela* and *imitatio*, see Poulsom, *Dialectics of Creation*, 144–45.

[76] Schillebeeckx, *Church*, 232 [234].

in our everyday language for the familiar term love of neighbour."[77] He portrays this as a heady and optimistic time (perhaps somewhat naïve, even), noting that, in the 1970s, a more critical stance emerged, in the face of challenges including "nuclear energy, nuclear armament, the pollution of the environment [and] the exhaustion of our natural resources."[78] He comments: "The contrast with the 1960s could not have been greater."[79] Looking back, it became clear that the previous decade had been "the time of an emphasis on a 'God of human beings'" and that it had become important to emphasize that "*God is not just a God of human beings.*"[80] He is not, however, making a clean break with what went before, replacing one form of solidarity with another. The 2014 translation of *Church* helps here, by adding the expression "an emphasis on," which is not present in the Dutch or in the earlier translation. Schillebeeckx is *not* claiming that *only* human beings mattered in the 1960s. This finesse of the translation also fits well with what he goes on to say: "Or rather, one dimension was forgotten," which he then names, in Dutch, "*de medeschepselijkheid.*" The English translations struggle to articulate this and actually avoid translating the term itself altogether, but, given the structural similarity with *medemenselijkheid* (co-humanity), it seems reasonable to translate it as co-creaturehood.[81]

As he continues his reflection, putting this new emphasis into dialogue with Scripture, he says, three paragraphs later: "Co-creaturehood and co-humanity must go hand in hand."[82] The shift he notes takes place at the same time as a similar shift in Catholic Social Tradition, and placing the two side by side can result in mutually beneficial interaction. The 1960s saw the birth of the idea of integral human development as a way of expressing human solidarity, which can be traced back to Paul VI's encyclical *Populorum progressio*, which opens as follows: "The progressive development of peoples is an object of deep interest and concern to the Church."[83] At the same time, commenting on notions that were prevalent in that period, Paul VI refuses to narrow down the idea of development to just one thing:

> The development We speak of here cannot be restricted to economic growth alone. To be authentic, it must be well rounded; it must foster the development of each man and of the whole man. As an eminent specialist on this question has rightly said: 'We cannot allow economics to be separated from human realities, nor development from the civilization in which it takes place. What counts for us is man—each individual man, each human group, and humanity as a whole' (*PP* 14).'[84]

Twenty years after its publication, John Paul II celebrated the contribution that *Populorum progressio* made to ideas about integral development and human solidarity in his social encyclical

---

[77] Ibid., 233 [235].

[78] Ibid.

[79] Ibid., 233 [235].

[80] Ibid., 234 [236], italics added from Schillebeeckx, *Mensen als verhaal van God*, 253.

[81] See Schillebeeckx, *Mensen als verhaal van God*, 253; cf. the translation in Schillebeeckx, *Church*, 234 [236].

[82] My translation of Schillebeeckx, *Mensen als verhaal van God*, 254; cf. Schillebeeckx, *Church*, 235 [237].

[83] Paul VI, *Populorum progressio* (March 26, 1967) 1 (hereafter cited in text as *PP*), http://w2.vatican.va/content/paul-vi/en/encyclicals/documents/hf_p-vi_enc_26031967_populorum.html.

[84] Quoting Louis-Joseph Lebret, O.P., *Dynamique concrète du développement* (Paris: Economie et Humanisme, Les editions ouvrières, 1961), 28.

*Sollicitudo rei socialis*, and in 2009 Benedict XVI did the same in *Caritas in veritate*, indicating the importance of these themes in Catholic Social Tradition.[85] As the time between the 1960s and the early twenty-first century has elapsed, however, the relation between human solidarity and development, on the one hand, and ecological solidarity, on the other, has become a rather vexed issue.[86] Francis takes a significant step forward with his idea of "integral ecology," proposed in *Laudato Si'*, though it is important first to set the context for what he is doing with reference to his apostolic exhortation *Evangelii gaudium*. There, he presents an image to back up the statement, made very much in continuity with his predecessors, that the "whole is greater than the part, but it is also greater than the sum of its parts."[87] He says that the model he is using here "is not the sphere, which is no greater than its parts, where every point is equidistant from the centre, and there are no differences between them." This image calls to mind the reduction of every issue to one problem, or one interpretative scheme, which was what Paul VI was arguing against. Francis continues: "Instead, it is the polyhedron, which reflects the convergence of all its parts, each of which preserves its distinctiveness (*EG* 236)." In this image, the complexity that arises from multiple perspectives is not interpreted as a problem, but a richness. If those who come together do so in a spirit of solidarity, ready to offer what they have and to learn from others, then the whole picture is not only greater than what emerges out of a consideration from the dominant perspective, but also can be greater even than the sum of the parts that are contributed.

He continues to develop this line of thought in *Laudato Si'*, saying: "Everything is connected. Concern for the environment thus needs to be joined to a sincere love for our fellow human beings and an unwavering commitment to resolving the problems of society (*LS* 91)." Speaking of the global financial crisis and the environmental crisis as he outlines what he means by integral ecology, he stresses that humanity is "faced not with two separate crises [...], but rather with one complex crisis which is both social and environmental. Strategies for a solution demand an integrated approach to combating poverty, restoring dignity to the excluded, and at the same time protecting nature (*LS* 139)." Francis is not saying the same thing as Paul VI here, but he is not saying something completely different either.

When Schillebeeckx responds to critics who accuse him of "a fashionable adaptation to later trends" when he writes about ecological issues in *Church*, he objects that "I was already writing substantially the same thing in 1974 and even in 1960," citing two articles to support his contention.[88] His use of the term "substantially" here is significant, indicating that there is a depth dimension to his thinking that has remained present—not without development—

---

[85]  See John Paul II, *Sollicitudo rei socialis* (December 30, 1987) 32, http://w2.vatican.va/content/john-paul-ii/en/encyclicals/documents/hf_jp-ii_enc_30121987_sollicitudo-rei-socialis.html. Here, the document uses the expression "integral human development." Benedict XVI first makes the link between the two explicitly in *Caritas in veritate* (June 29, 2009) 8, http://w2.vatican.va/content/benedict-xvi/en/encyclicals/documents/hf_ben-xvi_enc_20090629_caritas-in-veritate.html.

[86]  See Martin Poulsom, "The Place of Humanity in Creation," *Faiths in Creation*, The Institute Series 8, ed. Catherine Cowley (London: Heythrop Institute for Religion, Ethics and Public Life, 2008), 25–35.

[87]  Francis, *Evangelii gaudium* (November 24, 2013) 235 (hereafter cited in text as *EG*), http://w2.vatican.va/content/francesco/en/apost_exhortations/documents/papa-francesco_esortazione-ap_20131124_evangelii-gaudium.html.

[88]  Schillebeeckx, *Church*, 237, n. 4 [263, n. 4].

throughout his writing that unifies co-humanity and co-creaturehood. Although the latter term does not become explicit in his writing until *Church*, it is clearly not a break with the value of co-humanity. Schillebeeckx's account of solidarity became more integral as a result of this conjunctural shift, but it might be better described as a conjunctural enrichment—an addition of another facet to the polyhedron of his thinking, at the service of the reign of God. With the benefit of hindsight, he came to recognize that his thinking—and that of others around him—in the 1960s overemphasized human solidarity at the expense of ecological solidarity. However, co-humanity and co-creaturehood can—and should—be mutually co-constitutive. Integral ecology invites us to place the two into direct proportion with each other, such that the greater the co-creaturehood we aim for, the greater the co-humanity we achieve. At its best, it is a non-zero-sum game: the two can exist in a relational dialectic that is greater than the sum of its parts. The conjunctural model of integral ecology offers to theology *sequela* Schillebeeckx the possibility of developing such an integral whole, in a similar way to that in which the model of integral human development helped him to articulate a particular Christian account of praxis on behalf of the *humanum*, in dialogue with critical theory. Thus, creation faith *sequela* Schillebeeckx can play a role in the development of Catholic Social Tradition alongside contributions from magisterial teaching and the way that all the faithful strive to live out this tradition in Catholic Social Practice.[89] Such interplay between these three different perspectives on the tradition of faith can lead to a whole that is both theoretical and practical, a Catholic Social Praxis that can make a decisive contribution to the future of our common home.

---

[89] For a deeper exploration of this proposal, see: Martin G. Poulsom, "Schillebeeckx and the *Sensus Fidelium*," *New Blackfriars* 98 (2017), 203–17.

# Chapter 16

# Schillebeeckx's Sacramental Theology of the Sacraments

Joris Geldhof

There is a specific motivation for the title of this contribution. To call Schillebeeckx's theology of the sacraments sacramental is by no means tautological. On the contrary, it reveals both an intuition and a program. Without a doubt, Schillebeeckx had a strong sense for sacramentality, that is, for signs and symbols of God's presence in the world through the incarnation. When he elaborated his theological visions, it was always on the basis of a peculiar receptivity for God's saving mysteries. The goal of this chapter is to sound out the roots of Schillebeeckx's theology of the sacraments and to demonstrate that it is intrinsically connected with a robust understanding of sacramentality.

Given this purpose, it will be indispensable to attach great weight to his groundbreaking study *De sacramentele heilseconomie* (*The Sacramental Economy of Salvation*), which appeared in 1952 but sadly has not yet been translated into English.[1] In addition, we will deal of course with *Christ the Sacrament of the Encounter with God* and *The Eucharist*, the English translations of which appeared in 1963 and 1968, respectively. It will also be necessary to highlight the ultimate contribution Schillebeeckx delivered to the field of sacramental theology, his renowned 1999 article in which he announced he was working on a new book on the sacraments. So, although his final book never appeared, we can nevertheless say that Schillebeeckx's impressive career can be characterized by an *inclusio*: he ended where he began, with sacramental theology.[2]

In order to demonstrate why and in which respects Schillebeeckx's theology of the sacraments can be rightly called sacramental, the present contribution consists of four parts. First, it is necessary to sketch the fundamental perspective from which Schillebeeckx's theology of the sacraments departs, which is none other than the history of salvation. Second, Schillebeeckx devoted a great amount of attention to liturgy, which was not evident for a Catholic dogmatic theologian in the years between the end of the Second World War and the Second Vatican

---

[1] Henricus Schillebeeckx, *De sacramentele heilseconomie. Theologische bezinning op S. Thomas' sacramentenleer in het licht van de traditie en van de hedendaagse sacramentsproblemaiek* (Antwerp/Bilthoven: 't Groeit/H. Nelissen, 1952). There is, however, a French translation of this book: *L'économie sacramentelle du salut: Réflexion théologique sur la doctrine sacramentaire de saint Thomas, à la lumière de la tradition et de la problématique sacramentelle contemporaine*, Studia Friburgensia 95 (Fribourg: Academic Press, 2004).

[2] For a comparison and discussion of Schillebeeckx's early and late theology of the sacraments, see Joris Geldhof, "The Early and Late Schillebeeckx OP on Rituals, Liturgies, and Sacraments," *Usus Antiquior* 2 (2010), 132–50.

Council. Third, it is crucial to tackle the issue of the Eucharist, since Schillebeeckx significantly contributed to theological thinking about the "source and summit" of the Christian life of faith in the second half of the twentieth century. Fourth, Schillebeeckx's particular concern to keep a strong connection between the celebration of the church's sacraments and the real life of people deserves to be discussed in some detail. I will show that the topics of the three earlier sections culminate in the final one, and that Schillebeeckx's position in sacramental theology can be characterized by a remarkable consistency and commitment.

# I. Sacraments and the economy of salvation

According to Schillebeeckx, the fundamental horizon against which the meaning of the sacraments has to be interpreted and explained is God's revelation to humankind. This revelation has a concrete anchor point in history, which is the incarnation of Christ. However, the incarnation as a singular event makes sense only in the light of the history and the economy of salvation.[3] Sacraments are thus intimately interwoven with the past, present, and future dimensions of God's initiative to redeem humanity. In other words, the theological significance of the sacraments appears only if one takes seriously their soteriological embeddedness. However, soteriology here does not refer to an individual chapter in the whole of Christian doctrines, that is, the explanation for why and how believers, or human beings in general, are saved, but soteriology instead refers to the grand (meta-) narrative of Christian faith: of God creating the world and giving human beings a special calling and privileged position in it; of people distorting the initial order God had envisioned; of the history of God time and again trying to put people on the right track again. It is about God renewing and reaffirming the covenant, finally sending his own Son and the latter's rising from the dead, and of the way to fulfilment which was laid open through the resurrection of Jesus Christ and the coming of the Holy Spirit. Sacraments thus encompass, embody, and express the entirety of the paschal mystery.

The very construction of Schillebeeckx's (early) sacramental theology is permeated by these profound theological intuitions and convictions. Three elements require particular attention in this respect. First, one has to refer to Schillebeeckx's interpretation and appropriation of the rich contents covered by the concept of "mystery." Not only was Schillebeeckx profoundly aware of Odo Casel's groundbreaking theory of *Mysteriengegenwart*,[4] as well as of the controversies in which it was entangled,[5] he also had thoroughly informed himself about the history and the semantics of the Greek word *mustèrion*. He had thereby focused on its use among the Church Fathers and was convinced of the enormous theological potential of contemporary dealings with

---

[3] In this context, reference must be made to a lecture that Schillebeeckx delivered only one year after the publication of *De sacramentele heilseconomie*: "*Theologia* or *Oikonomia?*," *RT, CW* vol. 2 (London: Bloomsbury T&T Clark, 2014), 271–88 [II 79–105].

[4] Odo Casel, *The Mystery of Christian Worship*, Milestones in Catholic Theology (New York: Crossroads, 1999). The original German title of this seminal work, which actually consists of a collection of fine scholarly essays, was *Das christliche Kultmysterium*. It first appeared in 1932 and is widely considered to be one of the most important works by Casel.

[5] Schillebeeckx did not think that Casel's theology was condemned by Pope Pius XII's notorious 1943 encyclical *Mediator Dei* (*MD*). See his excursus in *De sacramentele heilseconomie*, 230–32.

the concept. It is not an exaggeration to say that Schillebeeckx's outspoken enthusiasm for a theology which circles around "mystery"—although he communicates this enthusiasm, typically, quite moderately—has had a lasting impact on his intellectual development.

In *De sacramentele heilseconomie* Schillebeeckx synthesizes the findings of many scholars who had studied the patristic meanings of *mustèrion* in a clear and competent way. Its core meaning is God's "plan of redemption, the *divine economy of salvation* as elaborated in Christ," as well as the "*veiled revelatory form* of this economy," which makes it possible that believers come to know it through words, things, events, and, eventually, rites, feasts, and celebrations.[6] Schillebeeckx underscores that mystery is not so much about God's transcendent essence but about his reaching out to human beings; the fundamental content of mystery is the reality of salvation.[7] In this context he refers to a concise but telling quotation from Gregory Nazianzen, who said that "all the mysteries are there for humans' salvation"; in other words, "they establish a real participation in the salvific power of the Christ mystery."[8] The cultic meaning of the sacraments is inextricably connected with the mystic core of God's revelation and Christian faith.

It was above all the already mentioned German scholar and Benedictine monk of the abbey of Maria Laach, Dom Odo Casel, who was a pioneer in the renewal of sacramental theology in the first half of the twentieth century. He had done that primarily by showing that the concept of *mustèrion* virtually equals the notion of "sacrament." The rediscovery of the rich and multilayered contents of *mustèrion* shed a refreshing light on the prevailing (neo-)scholastic interpretations of the sacraments. It was no doubt a surprising as well as intriguing insight for many theologians at the time.

Schillebeeckx can definitely be counted among the adopters of the *Mysterienlehre* after the Second World War. His overall appreciation of it was very positive. According to him, one of its most notable strengths was that it taught again to see Christianity "as a fact of salvation, a *Heilsgeschichte*; not as a sum of truths, but as truths of salvation which are implied in the historical Christ Event."[9] Schillebeeckx significantly adds that he deplores a "shyness for metaphysics," which he observes in some of the representatives of the *Mysterienlehre*, as a consequence of which there is not always a right balance between the truth value and the factual historical aspects of Christian faith. It is no doubt remarkable that Schillebeeckx insisted so vehemently on metaphysics in his early sacramental theology.

Second, attention must be drawn to the very notion of encounter, which he uses quite prominently and for which he became famous in sacramental theology. Schillebeeckx explains that the encounter between God and the human being constitutes the essence of faith and the Christian religion. In the introduction to *Christ the Sacrament of the Encounter with God* he says: "Religion is above all a saving dialogue between man [*sic*] and the living God. Although man can reach God through creation, he cannot, through his creaturely powers alone, establish any immediate and personal contact with God."[10] This means that the real "encounter" of the

---

6    Schillebeeckx, *De sacramentele heilseconomie*, 61 (italics in the original; all translations from this book are my own).

7    Ibid., 63.

8    Ibid., 87.

9    Ibid., 229.

10   Edward Schillebeeckx, *Christ the Sacrament, CW* vol. 1 (London: Bloomsbury T&T Clark, 2014), 1 [2].

human being with God must be seen especially from the perspective of grace and salvation and, therefore, within the horizon of a broadly understood soteriology. Schillebeeckx even identifies the notion of encounter with salvation and simultaneously suggests an unbreakable connection between revelation and religion: "The act itself of this encounter of God and man, which on earth takes place only in faith, is what we call salvation. On God's part this encounter involves a disclosure of himself by revelation, and on the part of man it involves devotion to God's service—that is religion."[11]

It is indeed this soteriological perspective which for Schillebeeckx determines the Christology implied in the sacraments. "Just as Christ through his risen body acts invisibly in the world, he acts visibly in and through his earthly body, the Church, in such a way that the sacraments are the personal saving acts of Christ realized as institutional acts in the Church."[12] Schillebeeckx again connects the very notion of encounter with human beings' salvation through Christ: "[W]hat takes place in the sacraments is the immediate encounter in mutual availability between the living *Kyrios* and ourselves. The sacraments are this encounter."[13] This identification of sacraments and the encounter with the risen Lord reveals Schillebeeckx's metaphysical realism. The sacraments are not simply signs referring to what God once upon a time did for humans but strong symbols that embody his saving initiative. Sacraments are incarnations of the economy of salvation and set forth its history in the world, inasmuch as the church facilitates them as veritable encounters with God.

Third, Schillebeeckx's determination to shift the focus within sacramental theology to the fruitfulness of the sacraments is worthwhile mentioning in this context. Along with many others, Schillebeeckx observed that for a very long time the emphasis had been placed almost exclusively on the validity of the sacraments. While it remains important to emphasize the "objective" dimension of the sacraments, Schillebeeckx makes a strong case for their "subjective" side as well. In particular, he underscores the freedom of the subject receiving a sacrament. According to him, it is a foundational principle of the church that no one can be forced, against her or his will, to become a member of the church: "An adult must enter into the sacramental economy of salvation as a person: grace must be accepted freely and, therefore, also the sacrament which leads to that grace, must be assented to freely."[14] This personalist dimension is significant, for it makes sure that, through the sacraments, a real connection is made between God and human beings. In other words, "sacrament is a symbolization of Christ's historical work of redemption *inasmuch as it accomplishes itself to this [particular] person.*"[15] The real encounter between Christ and the human person does not occur if one's participation in the liturgy "is not also a

---

[11] Schillebeeckx, *Christ the Sacrament*, 2 [3].

[12] Ibid., 42 [70–71]. It is important to note that the Dutch original of this text has "*ambtsdaden*" and that "*ambt*" actually means "office" or "ministry." This means that the translation "institutional acts," though not wrong, is one-sided and that the word has a broader conceptual content in the original.

[13] Schillebeeckx, *Christ the Sacrament*, 43 [74]. See also the "first general definition" Schillebeeckx gives of a sacrament: "Each sacrament is the personal saving act of the risen Christ himself, but realized in the visible form of an official act of the Church." Ibid., 38 [64]. The translation here has "official act" but the Dutch original is again "*ambtsdaad*" (footnote 12 above). Moreover, this sentence is put in italics in the original Dutch text.

[14] Schillebeeckx, *De sacramentele heilseconomie*, 481.

[15] Ibid., 484. Emphasis original.

personal prayer expressed in the ecclesial symbolic act."[16] There must somehow be a receptivity for God's grace.

Clearly, it is the sacraments' embeddedness in the broader reality of the history of salvation that makes Schillebeeckx so sensitive to the issue of their fruitfulness. The attention and emphasis he lays on this issue are not consequences of seeking possible relevance for the sacraments outside of faith and church. On the contrary, it is precisely because of theological concerns and reasons that Schillebeeckx emphasizes and develops the "human" side of the sacramental economy: "Notwithstanding its strong objectivist approach and perspective of mysteries, [the sacramental economy of salvation] is nonetheless strongly personalist, [it is] the appropriate place of the most tender drama of love between God and the soul and at once the strongest breeding ground for the mystical life."[17] The fruits the sacraments bear are by no means extrinsic to their objective nature: "the religious and personal experience enters entirely *into* the objective shape of sacramentality."[18] Furthermore, "sacramental grace is the grace of redemption itself, since the deepest meaning of the Church's sacraments lies in Christ's act of redemption. This remains a permanent actuality in which we become involved through the sacraments. All turns upon a participation in the grace of Christ."[19]

# II. Sacraments and liturgy

The concreteness that profoundly characterizes Schillebeeckx's theological speculations about the meaning of the sacraments and their anchoring in the economy of salvation is also evident from his take on the liturgy. Schillebeeckx is convinced that there is a mutual relationship between theological interpretations of the sacraments and their concrete liturgical shape. On the one hand, he says, "theological reflection [is] dependent on the contemporary liturgical and sacramental life of the Church," but, on the other hand, liturgy itself is and has always been "dependent on the *theological* state of the ecclesial consciousness of faith at a certain moment."[20] This fundamental standpoint is both reflected upon theoretically and practically applied. In what follows, both these aspects are discussed.

From a theoretical perspective, the relation between liturgy and theology is, for Schillebeeckx, a reciprocal one. Liturgy shapes theology, but theology also shapes liturgy. There are historical examples where the worship practices of Christians have inspired their thinking, but there are also cases showing that theological ideas determined the form and content of liturgical celebrations. It is not an either–or story for Schillebeeckx; rather, it is a permanent interwovenness: "dogma and liturgy are constantly acting and reacting on each other."[21] This reciprocity, however, does not imply an equality or a symmetry. When it matters, it is theology that decides. Referring to the infamous line from Prosper of Aquitaine, Schillebeeckx warns that "one must be careful to

---

[16] Schillebeeckx, *Christ the Sacrament*, 100 [173].
[17] Schillebeeckx, *De sacramentele heilseconomie*, 637.
[18] Ibid., 559.
[19] Schillebeeckx, *Christ the Sacrament*, 130 [223].
[20] Schillebeeckx, *De sacramentele heilseconomie*, 239.
[21] Schillebeeckx, "The Liturgy and Theology," *RT, CW* vol. 2 (London: Bloomsbury T&T Clark, 2014), 159 [243].

emphasise, in affirming the *lex orandi lex credendi*, the primacy of the objective reality of the dogma which is actively experienced in the liturgy."[22] Liturgy is indeed dogma experienced, but doctrines are much more precise in their formulation and therefore to be preferred.[23]

With this standpoint, Schillebeeckx perfectly aligns himself with the official vision of the magisterium. The infamous adage he refers to, *lex orandi lex credendi* (the law of prayer [is] the law of belief), had been touched upon by Pope Pius XII in his 1943 encyclical *Mediator Dei*. The pope warned against an overt enthusiasm for liturgy, because such an attitude could easily run the risk of downplaying doctrine and the magisterial authority that the church exercises in this respect. Pius XII mentions, "the error and fallacious reasoning of those who have claimed that the sacred liturgy is a kind of proving ground for the truths to be held of faith,"[24] and he straightforwardly asserts that "this is not what the Church teaches and enjoins" (*MD* 47). Knowing the original phrase where the adage is based on, he adds that "it is perfectly correct to say, '*Lex credendi legem statuat supplicandi*'—let the rule of belief determine the rule of prayer," thereby actually reversing "the well-known and venerable maxim, '*Legem credendi lex statuat supplicandi*'—let the rule for prayer determine the rule of belief' (*MD* 48).

Schillebeeckx knew this encyclical all too well. He had studied it very carefully and he himself raised the question whether it contained a condemnation of Casel's theory of *Mysteriengegenwart* or not in an excursus in *De sacramentele heilseconomie*. He is convinced and firmly states that the encyclical does not do this in so many words. What the encyclical did do, however, was criticize vague theories about mysteries and mysteriousness, that is, theories that do not (sufficiently) take into account the input and content of God's revelation. Schillebeeckx stresses that it is not clear from the text of the encyclical itself that it has Casel in mind.[25] At the same time, Schillebeeckx shared a deep conviction with the German Benedictine, namely that liturgy can bear God's mystery.

This fundamental conviction led Schillebeeckx to investigate in some more detail the basic constituents of liturgy. Liturgy is for him always a combination of word and deed, of both speech and actions. Moreover, this very observation is one of the central insights that he draws from a close reading of the history of sacramental doctrine. As Augustine famously said, there is a sacrament when the "word" "comes to" the "element": *accedit verbum ad elementum et fit sacramentum*.[26] In the patristic mindset, for a sacrament to happen, one needs specific words and

---

[22]  Schillebeeckx, "The Liturgy and Theology," *RT*, 158 [242–43].

[23]  Ibid., 159 [243]. It is unclear whether this argument can somehow be said to reveal a Hegelian trait of this type of thinking, in that it privileges rational comprehension (*Begriff*) over concrete religious images (*Vorstellungen*). It is also unclear to what extent Schillebeeckx holds on to this idea under the influence of the contemporary (neo-)Thomism prevailing at the time. Finally, it is evident that Schillebeeckx differs in this respect from liturgical theologians' "robust" understanding of liturgy as *prima theologia*, as one finds this example in the work of Alexander Schmemann and Aidan Kavanagh.

[24]  Pius XII, *Mediator Dei* (October 20, 1947) 46 (hereafter cited as *MD*), http://w2.vatican.va/content/pius-xii/en/encyclicals/documents/hf_p-xii_enc_20111947_mediator-dei.html.

[25]  Schillebeeckx, *De sacramentele heilseconomie*, 230–32.

[26]  One finds this quotation is in Augustine's *In Ioannis euangelium tractatus* 80, 30. Augustine is commenting there on the first verses of Chapter 15 of John's Gospel, and he is talking in this passage particularly about baptism. If no (specific) words are spoken, Augustine argues, the water of baptism is nothing special but mere water. Schillebeeckx discusses this iconic passage at some length in *De sacramentele heilseconomie*, 358–63.

actions—*legomena* and *drômena*, as Schillebeeckx would persistently say by using the Greek concepts.[27] He concludes: "So [in both Greek and Latin patristics], a sacrament is a complex whole of words and liturgical actions whereby the word, which is a 'verbum Christi' [word of Christ] becoming a '*verbum fidei*' [word of faith] in the community of the Church, really makes the sacrament into a *sacramentum Christi*."[28]

This double nature of sacraments was to be continuously conceptualized through the Middle Ages as well. Scholastic authors, however, would use a different language to refer to it and actually think and talk in terms of *forma* and *materia*. In the first phase, this would not be done with references to, and intellectual support from Aristotelian hylemorphism, but as soon as Aristotle's philosophy was broadly received among theologians working at the cathedral schools and the universities emerging from them, there would be a harmonizing of the different terminologies and frameworks. The reason that Schillebeeckx attaches so much weight to Thomas Aquinas's theory of the sacraments is that, according to him, he was the first one to actually use "hylemorphism as theological principle of intelligibility."[29]

In line with other theologians favoring a *ressourcement*, a rediscovery of the value of the sources of Christian faith—in particular the Bible and the Church Fathers—Schillebeeckx opined that the scholastic synthesis of matter and form was less rich and comprehensive than the ancient distinction between "words" and "actions," partially because of an increasing alienation from original liturgical settings.[30] Medieval sacramental hylemorphism, Schillebeeckx finds, is contingent and bound to a certain context.[31] Yet Schillebeeckx would hasten to add that, above all, one needs to remind that, after all, the very fact that the double nature of the liturgy continued to determine the thinking about the sacraments is an important, if not the most important, datum of the entire tradition of faith and theology. This datum is for him even absolute and unchangeable.

This historical, and at the same time theological, conclusion explains why Schillebeeckx deals with the liturgy of the sacraments also from a practical point of view. His extensive discussions of liturgical "facts" and developments reveal not only the formidable erudition of a scholar, but also his theological search for the meaning of the sacraments. "In speculative theology it is not about a superstructure onto liturgical facts but about a faith-insight into these facts, in which Christ accomplishes a mystery of salvation. In other words, it is about the internal intelligibility of these facts themselves."[32]

It is interesting to note that Schillebeeckx predominantly focused on the sacraments of Christian initiation (baptism, confirmation, and the Eucharist),[33] and that the way he approaches

---

[27] Schillebeeckx uses this terminology in many of his writings, but a noteworthy illustration of where he does this in an exemplary way is his contribution about the ancient Greek mystery cults to the Dutch theological dictionary: s.v. "Mysteriëncultus," *Theol. Woordenboek*, vol. 3 (Roermond/Maaseik: J.J. Romen & Zonen, 1958), cols. 3392–94.

[28] Schillebeeckx, *De sacramentele heilseconomie*, 364.

[29] Ibid., 374.

[30] Schillebeeckx, *Christ the Sacrament*, 66 [112].

[31] Schillebeeckx, *De sacramentele heilseconomie*, 387; *Christ the Sacrament*, 67 [114].

[32] Schillebeeckx, *De sacramentele heilseconomie*, 393.

[33] These are the sacraments to which he mostly refers to both in *De sacramentele heilseconomie* and in *Christ the Sacrament*. Also worth mentioning is his very well-documented entry on confirmation in *Theol. Woordenboek*, cols. 4840–70.

them corresponds with certain issues for which the Liturgical Movement had special attention. This can be illustrated by the fact that, when discussing liturgical data pertaining to the Eucharist, Schillebeeckx elaborates at some length the question of the epiclesis "versus" the consecration.[34] Instead of trying to formulate a standpoint in favor of either the words of institution (consecration) or the invocation of the Holy Spirit (epiclesis) as the "words" that accompany the transubstantiation of the bread and the wine into the body and blood of Christ, he meticulously surveys the available textual and historical evidence. It must be added that Schillebeeckx was up-to-date when it comes, for example, to editions and commentaries of ancient anaphoras. His state of the art, though now dated, still has some scholarly relevance, but it is primarily because of its theological significance that Schillebeeckx's intellectual tour de force deserves most praise. In a way, what he realizes in *De sacramentele heilseconomie* with liturgical "facts," methodologically anticipates his dealings with exegetical data in his later Jesus books.

# III. The Eucharist

Although Schillebeeckx devoted a separate book to it, one cannot say that the Eucharist has been a central focus of his research and reflections. It is likely that this is largely due to the fact that his first books about the sacraments are concerned with what is classically called the "general" theology of the sacraments—the treatise *de sacramentis in genere*—whereas it is the "particular" theology of the sacraments that deals with individual sacraments. This same observation, however, implies that one cannot discuss Schillebeeckx's discussions of the Eucharist unless one sees them in close relation with his explorations in the theology of the sacraments in general.

As a matter of fact, Schillebeeckx only rarely speaks about the Eucharist in *Christ the Sacrament of the Encounter with God*. On two occasions he finely distinguishes between the sacrament of the Eucharist and the other sacraments because of the fullness of God's sacramental saving grace in the former. Christ is sacramentally present in all the sacraments, but the Eucharist clearly stands out.[35] While still emphasizing Christ's real presence, Schillebeeckx elsewhere utters some beautiful lines about the working of the Eucharist as constitutive of the church as well as beneficial for the individual believer:

> The Eucharist [...] brings about [...] a deepening of the inner belonging to the eucharistic People of God: it is the sacrament of the unity of the Church, the bond of which is love. [...] The individual becomes personally united with Christ in his sacrifice of the Cross to the extent that, by taking part in the Eucharist and especially in receiving Communion, he enters into the sacrificial community of the Church.[36]

An issue which, unsurprisingly, demanded Schillebeeckx's special interest was the much-debated concept of transubstantiation. What fascinated him was that this emphatic notion was originally the result of thorough reflections on the Eucharist which brought about nothing less but a renewal

---

[34] Schillebeeckx, *De sacramentele heilseconomie*, 307ff.
[35] Schillebeeckx, *Christ the Sacrament*, 42 [71]; 56 [96].
[36] Ibid., 127 [217–18].

in medieval theology. This renewal was a reaction against, as well as a solution for problems related to, naïve physicalist interpretations of the Eucharist that were no longer tenable. "All the 'new' theologians [of the 13th century] were in complete agreement about one thing—Christ did not transfer his dwelling from heaven to the altar, and he did not make himself small so as to 'conceal' himself in a mysterious manner in the consecrated hosts."[37] At the same time, it was important for theologians such as Thomas Aquinas and Bonaventure that the metaphysical claims implied in the Eucharist were not discarded but preserved.

The historical observation that transubstantiation was a solution instead of a cause of problems stood in a sharp contrast with the contemporary situation Schillebeeckx was confronted with in the 1960s, when the infamous concept was both seriously misunderstood and virulently despised. In addition, new theories and proposals to get rid of "transubstantiation" had seen the light of day. They attempted to replace the scholastic category of "substance" and came up with alternatives such as "transignification" and "transfinalization."[38] As one rightly expects, Schillebeeckx's dealings with this whole dossier excels in scholarly depth, hermeneutical nuance, and theological breadth. In the first part of his book *The Eucharist*, he painstakingly examines the Tridentine dogma, whereas the second part consists of a subtle endeavor to reinterpret and reformulate it. It seems that his position was to think the real presence and the change of the Eucharistic gifts beyond transubstantiation but not without it.

In the historical part of his study, Schillebeeckx shows himself once more to be a meticulous reader of primary sources. He quotes the texts issued by the Council of Trent as well as different versions of them which preceded the final ones. Schillebeeckx finds interesting material in that redaction process. At one point he is more enthusiastic than elsewhere and reveals his own personal opinion about a proposal of one of the council fathers. He refers to a bishop who "preferred to speak more precisely of a 'sacramental change' (*conversio sacramentalis*), instead of the exuberant but rather meaningless adjectives 'unique and wonderful' in connection with the *conversio*. From the sacramental theological point of view, I personally think that this was one of the best suggestions that was made during these sessions."[39]

According to Schillebeeckx, there were different issues at stake simultaneously. First, there is no doubt that the Council Fathers at Trent and the theologians who assisted them wanted a very strong affirmation of Christ's real and enduring presence in the Eucharist. Second, they also wanted to unambiguously construe the change of the bread and wine into the Body and Blood of Christ in ontological terms. Third, they were of the opinion that this change can best be theorized by relying on concepts from a philosophy of nature that they were (most) familiar with, that is, Aristotelian philosophy. Fourth, there was a vehement "polemical context" against the background of which they were operating and in which they were everything but keen on staying neutral.[40] It is the combination of all these factors that made the council fathers at Trent opt

---

[37] Edward Schillebeeckx, *The Eucharist*, trans. N.D. Smith (London: Burns & Oates, 2005), 13.

[38] Edward Schillebeeckx, "Transubstantiation, Transfinalization, Transignification," *Living Bread, Saving Cup: Readings on the Eucharist*, ed. R. Kevin Seasoltz (Collegeville: Liturgical Press, 1982), 175–89. Originally, this text was a talk Schillebeeckx gave in French during the last session of the Second Vatican Council. It first appeared as Edward Schillebeeckx, "Transubstantiation, Transfinalization, Transignification," *Worship* 40 (1966), 324–38.

[39] Schillebeeckx, *The Eucharist*, 32–33.

[40] Ibid., 48.

for "transubstantiation," however not—as Schillebeeckx subtly notices—without hermeneutical prudence, for they said that this is a "very appropriate" (*aptissime*), not the only one possible, conceptualization.

This state of affairs raises the question for Schillebeeckx "[i]f we, living in the twentieth century, are to discover the genuine content of the Tridentine faith in connection with Christ's presence in the Eucharist, we must also enter intimately into this content of faith, reassessing it and making it actual and present, because we can never really grasp it in its 'pure state.'"[41] In other words, Schillebeeckx tries to trace a fundamental "fact" of faith, which medieval theologians and the Council of Trent expressed in a certain way but which may not be literally repeated for future generations. He wants to stay loyal to the tradition and examine it very carefully. By doing that, he observes that there is continuity between the Church Fathers and Trent but that things were framed differently.[42] Schillebeeckx even claims that one can discern biblical undertones in the concept itself of transubstantiation.

This definitely helps him to further draw fine conceptual distinctions and come to his own personal theological standpoint: "The metaphysical interpretation of transubstantiation must be dissociated from the categories of natural philosophy, while the fundamental realism contained in it must be apparent at the level of sacramental symbolic activity—as a *reality* appearing in a sign."[43] Again, one records here a strong metaphysical realism in Schillebeeckx's sacramental theology. What he wants to preserve is an ontological core or "fact" of faith which can be encapsulated in different intellectual frameworks, but which ought not to be diminished or neglected by them. Correspondingly, he employs this double standard as the key with which to scrutinize and evaluate alternative proposals for "transubstantiation": in spite of their good intentions and their adaptation to a modern consciousness, do they sufficiently respect the metaphysical core implied in the faith as passed on through the church's tradition? Put differently, what is their potential to express the mystery of faith? This makes him conclude that he "cannot personally be satisfied with a *purely* phenomenological interpretation without metaphysical density," because "realism is essential to the Christian faith."[44] All he means by that "is that Christ's eucharistic presence is a *reality*,"[45] not merely a sign, a symbol, or an event. Therefore, "[w]hat is required in any attempt to reinterpret, is an approach to the reality of salvation that is both diffident and reverent without being either timid or opportunist and a severely critical attitude towards one's own thinking. No single formulation can exhaust the faith, but this does not make every expression of faith true, meaningful or in accordance with faith."[46]

---

[41] Ibid., 62–63.
[42] Ibid., 69. This observation of continuity is surely in line with the findings of *De sacramentele heilseconomie*, where he had also concluded that the fundamental realities of faith are the same in the patristic and scholastic ages.
[43] Ibid., 99.
[44] Ibid., 150–51.
[45] Ibid., 155.
[46] Schillebeeckx, *The Eucharist*, 158.

# IV. Sacraments and life

From the very beginning of his theological career, the concrete life situations and the existential experiences of people have been important for Schillebeeckx. The reason why this is the case has not so much to do with a desire for relevance, but rather with his image of God and with his ideas concerning revelation and salvation, and, thus, with an intrinsic theological motivation. God is there *for* human beings and their being well. Clearly, this ties in smoothly with the overall soteriological vision he developed on sacraments and sacramentality which was discussed in the first section of the present contribution.

This fundamental and all-permeating theological vision also explains why Schillebeeckx stresses so much the relevance of the sacraments for people's life in the very last article he wrote.[47] It is probably correct to say that it is precisely because Schillebeeckx had a robust sacramental view on reality as a whole that he could make such a strong case for the inextricable bond between the church's sacramental and liturgical life of faith and people's experiences. Four different aspects may exemplify and at the same time reinforce this observation. In addition, the discussion of these four aspects is meant to show the overall consistency of Schillebeeckx's *sacramental* theology of the sacraments.

First and foremost, reference must be made to Schillebeeckx's *anthropology*. It can be argued that Schillebeeckx's view on the human person is deeply permeated by his sacramental view on reality as a whole. It is the great merit of Jennifer Cooper to have demonstrated this intrinsic connection.[48] Even if Schillebeeckx himself never wrote a substantial work on Christian or theological anthropology, it is clear that his entire work is marked by a specific interpretation of who and what the human person is. Cooper explains:

> Schillebeeckx is developing a sacramental theology that is coherent with the non-dualistic, non-reductive and hence non-competitive relation between the divine and human: this relation—the sacramental relation between personal humanity and divine grace—is creative, salvific, sanctifying, participative and personal.[49]

It does not require a lot of explanation that such an anthropology is profoundly permeated by, occasions, and inspires a radical openness towards culture and society, and that it is precisely because of authentic theological reasons that Christians have a mission to make the world into a better place for all to live. The model for this theological anthropology is Christ himself, the incarnate Son of God, from which everything depends. "In essence, for Schillebeeckx the incarnation that establishes our human existence as *filii in Filio* is the ultimate revelation of the intrinsic relation between humanity's metaphysical and moral significance."[50] Becoming like Christ is what Christians have to try to achieve in their lives, and there is no better way of doing

---

[47] Edward Schillebeeckx, "Towards a Rediscovery of the Christian Sacraments," *Essays, CW* vol. 11 (London: Bloomsbury, 2014), 183–210. Originally, this article was published in Dutch in *Tijdschrift voor Theologie* in 2000.

[48] Jennifer Cooper, *Humanity in the Mystery of God: The Theological Anthropology of Edward Schillebeeckx*, T&T Clark Studies in Systematic Theology (London: T&T Clark, 2009).

[49] Cooper, *Humanity in the Mystery of God*, 158.

[50] Ibid., 162.

this than through the church and the sacraments, which perpetuate Christ's redemptive activity in space and time. "This is precisely what the sacraments are: the face of redemption turned visibly towards us, so that in them we are truly able to encounter the living Christ."[51]

The second aspect underlining the intrinsic bond between sacraments and life is the modest but, upon close inspection, not surprising role *mysticism* plays in Schillebeeckx's sacramental theology. Granted, it is a dimension that is not elaborated to the full, and Schillebeeckx himself is not particularly known for a mystical style of theologizing and writing. Yet, it is striking that his two major early works on sacramental theology contain forays into, or even a separate chapter devoted to, mysticism. His relatively brief but profound reflections about the mystical core of sacramental grace underscore his deep-rooted confidence in God's love and the efficacy with which it is communicated to people so that they can participate in this pervasive, all-embracing reality. The sacraments are there for the fullness of people's lives, no matter what happens and how well developed one's moral and religious virtues are.

God's love goes deeper than one can imagine; it does not just rectify things, but also, and more importantly, prevents certain things from happening and orients lives in ways that go beyond human beings' capacity of comprehension and control. "The sanctifying effect of sacramental grace penetrates too deeply for its operation ever to be fully apparent in our active lives. It is in this gratuitous quality, this absolute generosity, that the mystical aspect of the Redemption reaches its highest point."[52] This mystical essence becomes manifest in the sacraments, where a level can be attained which is situated beyond any concern about their validity. It is the point where their fruitfulness achieves such an intensity that the outward sign and the interiorization of what they accomplish coincide, and where, as a consequence, the way to reconciliation with God is opened. A life permeated by the full meaning of sacramentality participates in the grand dynamics of salvation. "In the liturgical-sacramental celebration of mysteries God's *theophaneia* takes place, as well as the *reditus creaturarum ad Deum*, in accordance with St. Thomas' beautiful quote: '*Venit* autem *in* mundum ... ut per ipsum habeamus *accessum ad* Patrem.'"[53]

Third, it is necessary to point to the connection Schillebeeckx sees between the sacramental life of the church and the ethical and political commitment of its members. There is for him an inherent relation between God's offer of grace and the Christian fight against poverty, injustice, and oppression, for they integrally participate in the work of sanctification culminating in the Christ Event. Again, a Christological emphasis is evident here. Bruce Morrill comments:

> By seeing the resurrection and the founding of the Church as one integral event, Schillebeeckx links the sanctified life of the Church with the life of the Sanctified One. The presence of Jesus in the Spirit makes Jesus the Christ the one who sanctifies the people of God. This people's mission is to the world, a mission of liberation (the reform of societal structures) and redemption (participation in the

---

[51]  Schillebeeckx, *Christ the Sacrament*, 31 [52].

[52]  Ibid., 160 [271].

[53]  Schillebeeckx, *De sacramentele heilseconomie*, 663. The quote is from the *Summa Theologiae: ST* III, q. 40, a. 1. It means: Christ (the Son) "*came in* the world so that we would have *access to* the Father." Italics are in the original; Schillebeeckx wants to underscore the movements of God's *descent* and humanity's *ascent*.

already but not yet fully realized life of the reign of God) in the one history of salvation of all people together.[54]

Finally, a reference to the last article Schillebeeckx wrote is only but appropriate, for it ardently argues against an alienation of the sacraments from ordinary life and for the interweaving of Christian liturgy with rituals marking important moments in people's biographies. For apparent theological reasons, Schillebeeckx finds it indispensable that research results in ritual studies are integrated into reflections about the sacraments; because of God's revelation and the incarnation, theology and anthropology cannot be strangers for each other.

Hence, it comes as no surprise that Schillebeeckx takes rituality very seriously, for "[h]uman life is only possible within rhythms and structures and in socio-cultural contexts. Rites are never purely decorative or some sort of etiquette, even though a ritual system may be given a decorative setting."[55] At stake are, ultimately, the human body and processes of embodiment, without which the sacraments have no sense whatsoever. Schillebeeckx relies on research in ritual studies to claim "that the Christian sacraments as human rituals cannot be inferred directly from religious faith. As noted already, the soil in which ritual as such (and that includes the Christian sacraments) is rooted is human corporeality."[56] This insight, then, opens up an immense potential for further reflections, especially in the fields of pastoral theology, spirituality, and catechesis. But, alas, those applications cannot be the subject of the present contribution.

---

[54] Bruce T. Morrill, "Liturgy, Ethics, Politics: Constructive Inquiry into the Traditional Notion of Participation in Mystery," *Mediating Mysteries, Understanding Liturgies: On Bridging the Gap Between Liturgy and Systematic Theology*, ed. Joris Geldhof, BETL 278 (Leuven: Peeters, 2015), 187–206, 202. It is interesting to note that Morrill's most important source for his interpretation of Schillebeeckx is one of his Jesus books, *Christ*, and that he affirms the idea that Schillebeeckx's entire work is actually permeated by the strong sacramental vision of which his earliest books already testify.

[55] Schillebeeckx, "Rediscovery of the Christian Sacraments," 193.

[56] Ibid., 197.

# Chapter 17

# Openness for God

## *Schillebeeckx's Early Theological Anthropology*

### Mary Catherine Hilkert

There is no single volume of Edward Schillebeeckx's extensive publications which provides a systematic treatment of the theme of theological anthropology. Yet questions of what it means to live a truly human life, what constitutes human flourishing, whether there is a hidden transcendent dimension to human experience, whether there is a future for humankind and the Earth, and whether and how human persons can encounter and speak about the mystery of God have remained central to his theological writings from the time of his earliest essays as was evident in his 1958 inaugural address in Nijmegen, "The Search for the Living God."[1]

Although theological anthropology as a distinct theological topic is a modern phenomenon, the doctrinal topics that it addresses were included in classical treatments of dogmatic theology under diverse theological loci such as revelation and fundamental theology, creation, providence, sin and grace, Christology, soteriology, grace, eschatology, moral theology, sacramental theology, and spirituality.[2] Schillebeeckx addressed many of these central issues in the context of his writing on a broad array of related topics including the Creator/creature relationship; the implications of creatureliness with a particular focus on bodiliness, finitude and freedom and the ethical responsibilities of human persons as "created in the image of God"; original sin and the impact of sin on human freedom and history; questions of why God allows evil, the extent and impact of radical human suffering on human personhood and whether suffering has meaning or can be considered redemptive; the relationship between Christology and anthropology; the relationship

---

[1]  Edward Schillebeeckx, "The Search for the Living God," *God and Man*, trans. Edward Fitzgerald and Peter Tomlinson (London: Sheed and Ward, 1969), 18–40.

[2]  For development of theological anthropology as a discipline, see David H. Kelsey, "Human Being," *Christian Theology: An Introduction to Its Traditions and Tasks*, ed. Peter Hodgson and Robert King (Philadelphia, PA: Fortress Press, 1994) 167–93; Kelsey, *Eccentric Existence: A Theological Anthropology*, vol. 1–2 (Louisville, KY: Westminster John Knox Press, 2009); Edward Farley, "Toward a Contemporary Theology of Human Being," *Images of Man*, ed. J. William Angell and E. Pendleton Banks (Macon, GA: Mercer University Press, 1984), 57–78; Kathryn Tanner, *Jesus, Humanity, Trinity* (Minneapolis, MN: Fortress, 2001); and John Webster, "The Human Person," *The Cambridge Companion to Postmodern Theology*, ed. Kevin J. Vanhoozer (New York: Cambridge University Press, 2003). Roman Catholic theology tended to focus on distinct doctrinal loci related to anthropology, with particular attention to theologies of grace. Note for example that there is no chapter on "theological anthropology," but rather distinct chapters on "Creation," "Sin and Grace," and "Eschatology," in both editions of the volume *Systematic Theology: Roman Catholic Perspectives*, ed. Francis Schüssler Fiorenza and John P. Galvin, 2nd ed. (Minneapolis, MN: Fortress Press, 2011).

of nature and grace; grace (salvation) as described in multiple biblical metaphors; the meaning of religious experience and mysticism; and death and human hope for final salvation in the kingdom of God. In writings on fundamental theology and theological method, Schillebeeckx also addressed the relationship between revelation and human experience, the meaning of religious experience and mysticism, and whether critical examination of human experience, culture, and the "signs of the times" is an appropriate starting point for theological investigation.[3]

Within the broad scope of the field, this chapter will trace key anthropological insights in Schillebeeckx's writings prior to 1967, before turning to the anthropological shift to history, the future, and concrete human experience which he identified in his approach to theology in the final essay in his volume *God the Future of Man*.[4] There Schillebeeckx explains that, although his focus remained theocentric, the cultural shift toward radical secularization in Western Europe and the United States by the mid-1960s led him to conclude that the only human access to the mystery of God was to be found in the creation and history where God had chosen to become manifest and to extend an offer of friendship to humankind. Recognizing that that offer ("revelation-in-reality") is necessarily mediated through human experience and interpretative categories, Schillebeeckx pointed to the necessity of a faith perspective ("revelation-in-word") for a person or community to perceive and respond positively to the offer of saving grace as an encounter with God. As he would state explicitly in his later writings, revelation is located in human experience, but is not identical with it.

A subsequent chapter will consider the further anthropological insights that emerged in the context of Schillebeeckx's Christological trilogy in the 1970s in light of his growing awareness of radical and senseless suffering on a global scale and his concern about misplaced Western confidence in the empirical sciences and technocratic reason as providing the way forward for human progress in a secularized modern world.

In spite of those significant cultural and methodological shifts, central convictions remain in Schillebeeckx's writings about the divine–human relationship. From the time of his early writings on revelation, faith, and the sacramental economy of salvation to his final unfinished project in sacramental theology from an anthropological and historical perspective, Schillebeeckx's passion was to speak a credible word about the mystery of the living God whose absolute creative and saving presence is "bent toward humanity" and toward all of God's beloved creation. Two key anthropological themes explicitly articulated in the final volumes of his Christological trilogy serve as a leitmotif in his earlier work as well: "God's cause is the human cause" and "*extra mundum nulla salus*, there is no salvation outside the world."[5] In his early writings, however, those themes are developed in the context of reflection on the Christian doctrine of the incarnation which provided the linchpin for the related soteriological and anthropological insights to which we now turn.

---

[3]   See Kelsey's discussion of the relationship of these topics to theological anthropology in *Eccentric Existence*, Chapters 1A–2B.

[4]   Edward Schillebeeckx, "The New Image of God," *GFM, CW* vol. 3 (London: Bloomsbury T&T Clark, 2014), 101–25 [169–207].

[5]   Edward Schillebeeckx, *Christ, CW* vol. 7 (London: Bloomsbury T&T Clark, 2014), 627–29 [638–39]; Edward Schillebeeckx, *Church, CW* vol. 10 (London: Bloomsbury T&T Clark, 2014), 12 [12].

# I. Incarnation and early theological anthropology

## Sacramentality and bodiliness

The conviction that it is in and through the humanity of Christ who is God Incarnate that human persons encounter the living God and receive an offer of an ongoing relationship which is both redemptive and transformative (divinizing) is the source and guiding principle of Schillebeeckx's groundbreaking sacramental theology as well as his early writings on revelation and faith. In both cases, the underlying anthropological issue at stake is whether and how human persons can engage in a mutual encounter with the mystery of God.

One of the great achievements of Schillebeeckx's early sacramental theology was his fundamental claim that Jesus is the primordial "sacrament of the encounter with God" precisely because he is both the fullest historical, visible, and bodily expression of God's offer of salvation and, at the same time, the supreme realization of free human response to the offer of divine love. Schillebeeckx addressed the dilemma of how that historical and bodily mediation of salvation remains present in history in dogmatic terms, explaining that the glorified Christ continues to mediate salvation in and through his glorified bodiliness. Since that transformed bodiliness is no longer present in history in an earthly visible way, however, the risen Christ continues to mediate an encounter with God in and through the visible church and its sacraments. Although Schillebeeckx would later raise significant critical question about the extent to which the risen Christ is to be identified with the historical church, in his earlier dogmatic theology, he affirmed that the church and its sacraments "constitute the ongoing earthly extension of the body of the risen and glorified Christ."[6]

## Revelation, faith, and the human capacity for transcendence

Prior to the mid 1960s, Schillebeeckx approached similar questions of the human person's capacity for and invitation to relationship with the mystery of God primarily in his essays on revelation and faith. Initially he discussed the dynamic of God's offer and human response in terms of an epistemological analysis of the human mind's capacity to grasp supernatural truths expressed in dogmatic concepts. Nevertheless, he recognized that the revelation-faith dynamic referred to an interpersonal encounter and offer of friendship which involved more than an intellectual assent to truths which exceeded reason's grasp.

Schillebeeckx was well aware that the Modernist controversy at the beginning of the twentieth century had raised the specter of reducing revelation to human experience. Nevertheless, in a lecture in Ghent in 1954, he turned to Aquinas's writings on faith (in particular the *lumen fidei* and *instinctus fidei*) to argue that the Modernists were right to insist that "more attention should

---

[6] Edward Schillebeeckx, *Christ the Sacrament, CW* vol. 1 (London: Bloomsbury T&T Clark, 2014), 30–32 [50–53]. On this point, he cites Pope Leo the Great: "What was visible in Christ has now passed over into sacraments of the Church." See Sermo LXXIV, 2 (PL, 54, col. 398) as cited in *Christ the Sacrament*, 32 [54].

be given to the inward, subjective, non-conceptual aspect of the act of faith, that is to religious experience."[7] At the same time he defended the necessary role of concepts in the mediation of human experience of the divine. In Schillebeeckx's judgment, Dominic De Petter's claim that a preconceptual, yet intellectual, consciousness of reality is an essential element in all human knowledge was the most adequate way to preserve the distinction between the natural openness of the human mind to grasp reality (and thus as open to receive God's offer of grace) and the graced transformation of the human intellect which made it possible for the human person to be drawn into participation in "God's intimate life."[8]

## Desire for God, experience of grace, and the nature/grace disputes

Although Schillebeeckx embraced De Petter's analysis of the openness in the human person for the divine offer of grace, rather than Joseph Maréchal's account of how the divine offer is located in the dynamism of the transcendental depths of the human spirit as adopted by Karl Rahner, he agreed with Rahner and others that, apart from the language of faith, the offer of grace is indistinguishable from the human experience of self-transcendence. In his words:

> We are addressed, in the divine invitation to faith, by Someone who is the inner, absolute ground of our existence, *interior intima meo,* 'more intimate to me than I to myself' ... God's testimony of himself is experienced *in ourselves* ... [Yet] what we ultimately *experience* is only our human existence that is personally addressed by God and informed by grace—we are associated with God himself only *in faith* ... That is why we cannot, *outside the revelation in Word,* distinguish grace from nature—that is, from human life.[9]

The question of whether it is possible to experience grace *as grace* was one dimension of the larger twentieth-century Catholic disputes about nature and grace. Those disputes were concerned to protect the gratuity of God's Self-offer, but at the same time, not to reduce God's offer of friendship to a divine command with no interior experience of invitation. The distinction, but lack of separation, between nature and grace was fundamental to Schillebeeckx's approach to the disputed notion of what Thomas Aquinas meant by "natural desire for God" as well as to another ongoing concern in his later writings—the question of the relationship between creation and salvation.[10]

Rather than framing the question of the gratuity of grace in the category of "pure nature," a practice that was prevalent since the time of Baius, Schillebeeckx approached the question of the human capacity for encounter with God from the perspective of God's twofold gift of creation and salvation. The two orders form an existential unity according to Schillebeeckx, but he insisted

---

7   Edward Schillebeeckx, "The Concept of 'Truth'," *RT, CW* vol. 2 (London: Bloomsbury T&T Clark, 2014), 192 [II 10].
8   Ibid., 199 [21].
9   Edward Schillebeeckx, "The Non-Conceptual Intellectual Element," *RT, CW* vol. 2 (London: Bloomsbury T&T Clark, 2014), 262 [II 66–7]. Emphasis original.
10  See Edward Schillebeeckx, *Christ,* 503–15 [515–30]; and the chapter "Kingdom of God: Creation and Salvation," in Schillebeeckx, *IR, CW* vol. 8 (London: Bloomsbury T&T Clark, 2014), 93–108 [105–25].

on the importance of the distinction between the human person's dynamic spiritual openness to the absolute (as gift of creation) and God's further invitation to intersubjective communion (gift of salvation/covenant). It is God's graced offer of covenant that transforms the human person's creaturely capacity for self-transcendence to enable the possibility of encounter with God in the mode of mutual friendship. The human person remains a creature but the offer of interpersonal friendship (theologal relationship with the living God, later described as "encounter" with God) makes possible a self-transcendence and fulfillment that exceed created capacities, revealing that the ultimate human vocation is in fact participation in God's own life.

From the time of his earliest writings, Schillebeeckx stressed that the fulfillment of human life—final salvation—is an eschatological reality. He drew on the insight of Aquinas that "grace builds on nature" to emphasize that divinization is the fulfillment of humanization, not an overcoming of finite creaturely existence. In his words:

> The fullness of human life is in fact superhuman—it is divine life in a human subject. And however much we may stress that grace is an *inward* fulfillment of human life, we should all the more place full emphasis on the fact that this life-fulfillment is a transcendent completion of our humanity ... Nonetheless, we do at the same time find, *in* this self-transcendence, the best of ourselves included as an additional gift.[11]

## The human person as a self-that-is-in-the-world and the possibility of religious experience

Even as he emphasized the spiritual dimension of the human person as capable of a transcendence, which includes the possibility of sharing in divine life, Schillebeeckx stressed that human persons are a unique composite unity of matter and spirit. Hence his reminder early on that "[T]he spiritual subject that comes into contact with God in faith is a physical subject and, what is more, its physical nature is *terrestrial*. This means that grace is, in all its aspects and dimensions, entirely bound up with our life in this world."[12]

In his description of a sacramental economy of salvation in which God's offer of grace is made available in and through the created, material, and human world, Schillebeeckx drew on the insights of the phenomenologists F.J.J. Buytendijk and Maurice Merleau-Ponty among others to describe the human person as a self-that-is-in-the-world, neither pure spirit, nor pure self, but a spirit that can only express and reveal itself in bodiliness and worldliness, in particular through going out of oneself in relation to other human persons. For that reason, Schillebeeckx affirmed that it is only through bodily forms of communication that human persons express their deepest spiritual depths and form interpersonal relationships.[13]

---

11  Schillebeeckx, "The Non-Conceptual Intellectual Element," *RT*, 261–62 [II 65].
12  Ibid., 262–63 [II 67].
13  Edward Schillebeeckx, "The Sacraments: An Encounter with God," (1957) in *Christianity Divided: Protestant and Catholic Theological Issues*, ed. Daniel J. Callahan, Heiko A. Oberman, Daniel J. O'Hanlon (New York: Sheed and Ward, 1961), reprinted in *Edward Schillebeeckx, OP*, Theologians Today Series (New York: Sheed and Ward, 1972), 11–52, at 11.

At the same time, as bodily creatures who are co-constituted by spirit, human persons spontaneously search to understand the meaning of human existence. The unique composite unity of body-spirit gives human persons the capacity for self-transcendence, which includes not only the possibility of perceiving a depth-dimension to human experience and reality itself as referring-back-to-God but also the possibility of interpersonal encounter with God.[14]

In terms of religious experience, Schillebeeckx argued that, on the one hand, human existence as bodily and the absolute transcendence of God precluded any direct human experience of God in the sense of a particular and separate human capacity for religious experience or a "special feeling for God." Rather, religious experience is always and necessarily mediated by concrete human experience in the world of history and interpersonal relationships. On the other hand, he affirmed that human awareness of the utter contingency of our existence is a form of pre-reflexive consciousness of the mystery of God as the foundation of everything and thus, by its very nature, is a form of religious self-consciousness. This pre-reflexive self-awareness includes a worldview and an ethical view of life as well as an implicit awareness of something that surpasses human experience. Reframing the nature/grace disputes in terms of those insights, Schillebeeckx distinguished a human "natural affirmation" of God's existence from the grace-transformed interpersonal encounter with God ("theologal communion") available within the horizon of faith that includes both cognition and personal surrender. In Schillebeeckx's words,

> Basing ourselves merely on this world, we cannot, of course, meet God in a genuine interpersonal relationship. But because, by definition, mystery can only be possessed by surrender, man's interpretation of himself in human experience is the root of all religiosity, that is to say, is the human openness which can be raised by the graciousness of God to a God-centered, a "theologal" communion with the living God.[15]

Five important conclusions about the human person as creature as well as recipient of the invitation to share friendship with God, all of which appear in a new key in Schillebeeckx's later writings, follow from this phenomenological analysis.[16] (1) God, as Creator, belongs to the full definition of the human person inasmuch as the human person's contingent existence is sheer gift; the creature remains absolutely dependent on the mystery of God who holds all things in existence; (2) Human existence is a mystery; the promise of the Absolute in history is experienced as openness to the future, a mysterious transcendental horizon of human life as gift; (3) Revelation as invitation to encounter with God is available to human beings only if it is made available through created reality and human experience and perceived by faith; (4) In the

---

[14] Edward Schillebeeckx, "Faith Functioning in Human Self-Understanding," *The Word in History*, The St. Xavier Symposium, ed. T. Patrick Burke (New York: Sheed and Ward, 1966), 41–59, at 47.

[15] Ibid. In a clarifying note, Schillebeeckx states that the word *"theologal"* is a neologism which refers to the communion with the living God. This communion surpasses the "natural" capacities of man and is possible only through the gratuitous self-communication of God. He distinguishes it from the traditional word "supernatural" since the latter refers only to the surpassing of human powers while "theologal" expresses the mutual communion of intersubjectivity of God and the human person. He further distinguishes the term "theologal" from the term "transcendental" which refers to the implicit depth-dimension of "nature." See "Faith Functioning in Human Self-Understanding," p. 59, n. 1.

[16] The insights summarized here are developed further in "Faith Functioning in Human Self-Understanding," 44–53.

history of salvation, which according to Christian faith reaches its fulfillment in Jesus Christ, the implicit religious depth-dimension or transcendental horizon of all human life is transformed into a theologal horizon (God's absolute Self-communication) by the explicit offer not only of human fulfillment but also of participation in God's own life of love; (5) To consciously perceive that offer and surrender explicitly to the mystery of God require the gift of faith, both as interpretative horizon and as surrender to the mystery. At the same time, in his early writings on revelation and faith, Schillebeeckx, like Rahner, was convinced that God's universally active saving will was the basis for believing that that offer was extended to all human persons, whether explicitly recognized or not. As a result, Schillebeeckx affirmed that "[b]y virtue of God's universally active saving will there is no longer a purely natural human life; wherever [human persons] are found, their life is determined by a theologal life-horizon which they have (albeit implicitly) accepted or refused."[17]

# II. The turn to history, the future, and human experience

A significant shift occurred in Schillebeeckx's approach to theological anthropology and the entire theological endeavor in 1967 as he grappled with the implications of the growing cultural shift of (Western) human consciousness toward the concrete world of human history and the future. His concern about the secular emphasis on the possibility and responsibility of human beings to create and control the future by the exercise of rational, scientific, and technological knowledge and free agency was not only that it rendered the language of faith to be meaningless but also that it threatened to reduce human beings "to the level of things—mere material for objective analysis and planning."[18] At the same time, Schillebeeckx judged that the shift to the future and the quest for human progress in Western culture provided the opportunity for a corresponding deeper theological understanding of the living God revealed in the Scriptures, the meaning of human history and freedom, and how the divine–human encounter occurs in history. A response to these new challenges to the very possibility of God-talk required a new focus on fundamental questions of theological anthropology. Those new understandings would emerge, however, only if theologians were to take the "foreign prophecy" (insights coming from contemporary culture, in this case Western culture) seriously and begin theological reflection with a critical analysis of human experience and culture.

## From nature and grace to history and future transcendence

Although he remained critical of the limited horizons, scientific and technological bias, and anthropological hubris of much of the secular culture in Western Europe and the United States at that time, Schillebeeckx also highlighted aspects of the "turn to the future" and emphasis on human agency and possibility that were congruent with the biblical depiction of the living God

---

[17]  Ibid., 53.
[18]  Schillebeeckx, "The New Image of God," *GFM*, 106 [176]. The influence of Adorno and others from the Frankfurt School of critical theorists, including Herbert Marcuse, is evident here. Schillebeeckx cites critical insights from Paul Ricoeur as well.

as always leading God's people into new and uncharted territory and opening up an unknown future. The eschatological symbol of the kingdom of God which constituted the horizon of Israel's messianic hopes and the heart of Jesus's preaching prompted Schillebeeckx to remark that the living God of the biblical and Christian tradition is always "the One who is to come in the very history he [*sic*] nonetheless transcends."[19] The central revelation and confirmation of Christian hope in the God of the promise, he argued, is to be found in the resurrection of Jesus Christ. As Schillebeeckx remarked, "This reality is the most powerful religious symbol of what truly is possible as the future, the future which has *de facto* already commenced in Jesus as the Christ."[20] Because the future is God's future, Schillebeeckx asserted that the Christian leaves the future far more open than does the Marxist. No philosophy of history is adequate to the open promise that God is the future of humankind, the Earth, and the cosmos.

From this new cultural perspective oriented toward history and the future, Schillebeeckx continued to maintain a distinction, but not a separation, between human activity and the graced action of the Holy Spirit, but in the language of history and future transcendence rather than the categories of nature and grace. Recasting his Thomistic convictions that grace is always mediated and that grace transforms nature in historical terms, Schillebeeckx affirmed that God is active in and through human history, but also transcends human history with the promise of a future and final fulfillment of the kingdom of God. That final promise of "a new heaven and a new earth" (Rev. 21) can never be fully realized within the limits of human history; far less can the kingdom of God be identified with any concrete political system or social program.

At the same time, Schillebeeckx affirmed that there is a truth in the modern claim that human persons create history and the future. The gift of grace remains a task entrusted to human beings—a grace-empowered yet free cooperation in the transformation of history that makes God's kingdom manifest in fragmentary ways here and now. Tracing the main lines of a theological anthropology that he would develop in his later Christological project, Schillebeeckx argued that although Christians and all human beings remain finite and sinful, human persons and communities hold the power and the responsibility to change the many ways in which human history, institutions, and structures fall short of the reign of God proclaimed by the prophets and enfleshed in the life, death, and resurrection of Jesus.[21] In a real sense, Schillebeeckx insisted, Christians are empowered by the Spirit to make history a history of salvation and to seek to overcome all that is opposed to salvation. For that reason, Schillebeeckx described the dynamics of sin and grace at work in history precisely as mediated by human freedom:

---

[19]  Ibid., 110 [182–83].

[20]  Ibid., 112 [185].

[21]  Ibid., 109–13 [181–86]. This conviction relies on a twofold conviction about creation and salvation. First, the Creator God empowers human creatures with their own autonomy and agency. Further, in view of sin, the God of Jesus Christ redeems humankind's sinful past and provides the graced power of the Spirit to enable human persons to achieve what is not only beyond the power of their proper nature, but also an undeserved gift of grace which previously had been rejected. In Schillebeeckx's words, "God gives us in Jesus Christ the possibility of making the future–that is, of making everything new and transcending our sinful past and that of all humankind" (p. 109 [181]). Likewise on p. 113 [186], Schillebeeckx refers to "an inward re-creation which makes us 'new creatures' dead to sin, thus radically transforms our commitment to make a world more worthy of man, but at the same time it reduces to only relative value every result which has so far been achieved."

Just as our sinful freedom makes our human history into a history without salvation, so too will God transform this history without salvation into a saving event *in and through* our freedom into which we have been liberated in faith. The believer not only interprets history—[but] above all *changes* it. Anyone who disputes this is clearly forgetting that human freedom is the pivot of the historical event—via human freedom, grace is thus able to change history itself.[22]

## Grace mediated through human praxis and communities of hope

Schillebeeckx's turn to concrete human history and to grace mediated by human freedom involves a further shift of emphasis in his theological anthropology as well as in his Christological writings—the turn from theoretical claims to the concrete practice of the Christian life as the necessary form of verifying the truth of Christian hope for the future. In the face of academic disputes among linguistic analysts about what might constitute a "verification principle"—or even a "principle of falsification"—for Christian faith-claims, Schillebeeckx was forthright in his recognition that Christian faith is not based on what is empirically and objectively verifiable. At the same time, he realized that where genuine concrete Christian witness was lacking (or worse, contradicted) by Christian communities, Christian faith-claims would be dismissed as meaningless, incredible, and sheer ideology. He argued that although Christian faith can never be proven, it can—and must—be verified, even if only indirectly, by the living witness and concrete lives of believing communities that give evidence of the hope within them (1 Pet 3:15).

It was in this sense that Schillebeeckx called for a truly "secular" faith—the turn to human history and life on earth as the arena of salvation—foreshadowing the theme that would become increasingly prominent in his later writings: "*Extra mundum nulla salus.*"[23] In the 1960s, Schillebeeckx took seriously the crisis of faith that resulted for many with the demise of the "God of the gaps"—a *Deus ex machina* who intervened in history or nature at the points where scientific or historical explanations had reached their limits. At the height of the death-of-God movement in the United States, Schillebeeckx was quite willing to agree that "*That* God is dead."[24] But he argued that that construct was a faulty theological understanding of the Creator God who brought creation into existence freely and out of love, and who gave creation its own autonomy and agency even as God's absolute creative and saving presence sustained and empowered God's creatures.

In terms that echoed Thomas Aquinas's non-contrastive explanation of the Creator-creature distinction, Schillebeeckx argued that it is precisely God's utter transcendence that makes

---

[22] Ibid., 112 [185–86].
[23] This was also Schillebeeckx's final message to a group of theologians gathered to celebrate the enduring relevance of his theological work. See "Letter from Edward Schillebeeckx to the Participants in the Symposium," *Edward Schillebeeckx and Contemporary Theology*, ed. Lieven Boeve, Frederiek Depoortere, and Stephan van Erp (London: T&T Clark, 2010), xiv–xv.
[24] Schillebeeckx, "The New Image of God," 116 [191].

possible the divine immanence within creation. In his words: "Apparently absent, he [*sic*] will thus, because of his all-penetrating immediacy, be more intimately close to us."[25] The conviction that God's saving grace penetrated all of creation and human history was the reason for Schillebeeckx's conviction that Christians should turn their attention to the transformation of concrete human history, both resisting all that opposes the salvation preached and embodied by Jesus Christ and making that kingdom of God present in fragmentary, but tangible, ways. Rather than a competition between human efforts on behalf of historical and earthly liberation and God's salvation, Schillebeeckx insisted that the two were profoundly linked. Christian faith empowered and commissioned human efforts on behalf of the future of humankind and God's grace operated precisely through those efforts, even as it exceeded them. As Schillebeeckx described this "paradox of Christianity": "we tread in the footsteps of the God who is to come to us from the future and, in so doing, it is still we who make history."[26]

## The quest for human meaning in a secular age

Even as he reinterpreted Christian faith for believers, Schillebeeckx also engaged the growing challenges of atheistic secularism and the critical perspective of linguistic analysts who denied that religious language held any cognitive meaning for those who didn't share a confessional interpretative framework. He agreed with linguistic analysts that a religious answer could not respond directly to human questions of those who had no framework for speaking of transcendence, raising questions about Paul Tillich's proposed "method of correlation."[27] At the same time, he distanced himself from fideistic claims that revelation is self-authenticating, arguing instead that Christians needed to offer a defense of their hope which was comprehensible, even if not persuasive, to their secular contemporaries, whether humanists, atheists, or both.[28]

He located that defense in a turn to the ultimate question of the meaningfulness of contingent human existence. Schillebeeckx granted that belief in God and religious worship do not solve human problems or offer intellectual answers to why evil exists. Neither does faith, prayer, or worship fulfill a directly functional role in a technocratic society. On the contrary, he suggested that the most basic religious conviction is that human life and creation itself is an utterly gratuitous gift and that there is a transcendent source, goal, and sustaining presence of all that exists. That kind of "creation-faith" is a plausible religious and human conviction which can neither be proved nor disproved. He further argued that belief in a Creator God whose absolute creative saving presence sustains and empowers human history and all of creation, but who does not directly intervene in history, may point to the most authentic form of human existence.

---

25 Ibid., 115 [190].
26 Ibid., 115 [190].
27 Edward Schillebeeckx, "Correlation Between Human Question and Christian Answer," *UF, CW* vol. 5 (London: Bloomsbury T&T Clark, 2014), 74–75 [85]. This essay first appeared in *Tijdschrift voor Theologie* in 1970 and appeared in the Dutch essay collection as Edward Schillebeeckx, *Geloofsverstaan: Interpretatie en kritiek*, Theologische peilingen 5 (Bloemendaal: Nelissen, 1972). Schillebeeckx credited Tillich with the recognition that the religious answer to the human question expanded and reformulated those questions, but he pointed out that the reformulated questions were not universal ones, but rather available only to Christian believers.
28 Ibid., 76–77 [87–88].

Rather than making religious faith irrelevant with this turn to the secular world as the realm of salvation and the essential role of human mediation of that salvation, Schillebeeckx proposed that it may provide the key to genuine human authenticity and fulfillment in an age where human life was viewed increasingly in terms of functionality and productivity. Returning to the nature-grace dilemma in a new key, he wrote:

> We shall […] only be able to worship God properly when we no longer need him in any way to solve or to minimize our existential and social problem. It is only then that God can be worthy of our worship and that *agape* can clearly become happiness as a gift that is purely without necessity, as when a hostess says to a visitor who hands her flowers, although she is happy and grateful, 'it really is not necessary.' Authentic human life seems unthinkable unless we experience complete gratuity. Is this perhaps the authentic correlation between our being [human] and God's grace?[29]

## Turn to the "threatened humanum": Negative contrast experience as starting point

Schillebeeckx's historical "turn to the humanum" as the necessary starting point for all speech about God or the divine–human encounter was not, however, a turn to a classical metaphysical or even Thomistic analysis of human nature or a phenomenological analysis of the constitution of the human person as bodily self-in-a-world. He was increasingly aware that multiple philosophical, linguistic, cultural, and religious frameworks provided distinct and often conflicting analyses of human life. In terms of the larger framework of the meaning of human history, he agreed with Pannenberg and others that the definitive meaning of human history as a whole is not available within the context of unfolding history. Turning his attention to radical suffering and injustice, Schillebeeckx argued, in addition, that there are human events in history (e.g., Auschwitz) that are so complicit with evil as to be utterly incomprehensible and impossible to incorporate into a rational explanation of history.[30] For all of these reasons, the final meaning of human life escapes any definitive or universal rational explanation. Neither believers nor non-believers can fully grasp or explain what constitutes "what it is human desirable" (Paul Ricoeur's term).[31] Nevertheless, he remained convinced that at the core of the multiple and plural religious and philosophical answers to the question of ultimate human meaning—as well as in all practical

---

[29] Ibid., 79 [90].

[30] See the discussion of the problem of "universal history" within Schillebeeckx's discussion of "the history of suffering in search of meaning and liberation" in *Jesus, CW* vol. 6 (London: Bloomsbury T&T Clark, 2014), 575–86 [612–25]. Schillebeeckx explains that it was the turn to history as the arena for testing faith's claims of universal meaning and truth which led him to break with De Petter's "implicit intuition" of total meaning to be found in every particular experience of meaning as an adequate philosophical foundation for faith (p. 580 [618]).

[31] Schillebeeckx, "The New Image of God," *GFM*, 116 [191]. For discussion of whether the universal meaning of history is available within history and the kinds of "historical scraps" of violence, oppression, and evil such as Auschwitz which are utterly without meaning, sense, or reason ("outside the 'logos' which the historian looks for in history"), see Schillebeeckx, *Jesus*, 575–86 [612–25], especially p. 576 [614].

resistance to evil and injustice—there lies an implicit awareness of what it means to be human and a common search "to realise the constantly threatened *humanum*."[32]

In the anthropological move for which he is perhaps best known today, Schillebeeckx's turn to history led him to identify "contrast experiences" (later "negative contrast experience") as the most universal form of human experience and the necessary human pre-understanding for meaningful religious speech. He used the term (borrowed from critical theorist Theodor Adorno) to refer to personal and social experiences of negativity that elicit protest and resistance. In one early description of how negative contrast experiences function, Schillebeeckx described their implicit power to reveal glimpses of what it means to be human and what is required to construct a more human future in the following way:

> [F]uture-making decisions cannot be deduced from revelation; they arise out of negative or "contrast" experiences which evoke the protest "No! It can't go on like this; we won't stand for it any longer!" Such negative experiences make us realize the absence of what things ought to be like. Thus "what should be here and now" is to a certain extent, though incipiently and still vaguely, already perceived. [...] A negative experience would not be a contrast-experience, nor could it excite protest, if it did not somehow contain an element of positive hope in the real possibility of a better future.[33]

This universal and pre-religious experience of a "no" to the world as it is, which is to say, to see it as a world characterized by senseless and radical suffering and systematic injustice and oppression, is the most basic human experience in Schillebeeckx's assessment, at least for "those who don't go through life blindly."[34] Two things are important to note here.

First, the fundamental "no" to the current situation of injustice or dehumanizing suffering would not function as an experience of contrast if there were not also positive experiences of meaning, including experiences of goodness, beauty, love, and joy which formed one's memories and empowered hope that life could be—indeed, should be—different. In a more extended discussion of whether human suffering has theological meaning or can be considered redemptive in *Christ*, Schillebeeckx refers to the scandal of the "barbarous excess of suffering and evil in our history." He continues:

> There is too much *unmerited* and *senseless* suffering. [...] This suffering is the alpha and omega of the whole history of mankind; it is the scarlet thread by which this historical fragment is recognizable as human history: history is an "ecumene of suffering." Because of their historical extent and their historical density, evil and suffering are the dark fleck in our history.[35]

---

32 Schillebeeckx, "Correlation Between Human Question and Christian Answer," *UF*, 80 [91].

33 Schillebeeckx, "The Church as Sacrament of Dialogue," *GFM, CW* vol. 3 (London: Bloomsbury T&T Clark, 2014), 171–84 [118–40], at 83 [136].

34 Schillebeeckx, *Church*, 5 [5].

35 Schillebeeckx, *Christ*, 718 [725]. The reference to history as "an ecumene of suffering" is taken from J.B. Metz in J.B. Metz and J. Moltmann, *Leidensgeschichte. Zwei Meditationen zu Markus 8, 31–38* (Freiburg, 1975), 57 as cited in *Christ*, 718, n. 1 [891, n. 65]. In a similar vein in *Church*, Schillebeeckx laments that "these fragments of goodness, beauty and meaning are constantly contradicted and crushed by evil and hatred, by suffering whether blatant or dull, by the misuse of power and terror" (p. 5 [5]).

There, too, however, he clarifies that experiences of negativity in and of themselves would not give rise to ethical resistance, much less to hope for a different future. The practical and critical force of negative contrast experiences arises from the tension between the two. Schillebeeckx clarifies:

> As *human*, earthly experiences of meaning are always "on the way," they are therefore always threatened by the negative and thus develop a critical and productive force. Thus recollection of positive experiences of meaning and joy refine the concern to track down suffering and strengthens resistance against it. [...] So we have to say that the *critical* practical force does not lie either in the positive or in the negative, but only in their dialectical tension, that is, *in* the experience of contrast in suffering of [those]who receive and give meaning.[36]

Schillebeeckx viewed this pre-religious experience of human indignation that moves one to action on behalf of the *humanum* as a kind of "natural theology" that discloses an openness to a contrasting, but unknown, future that warrants affirmation. That positive hope for a new and different future in turn is nurtured and sustained by previous experiences of meaning and happiness, however fragmentary.[37] Although Schillebeeckx emphasized the dialectical tension inherent in negative contrast experiences, he argued that the open "yes" to the future is even stronger than the "no" to evil since the hope embedded in the positive "yes" is what makes the opposition possible.

A second concern about the universality of this basic human "negative contrast experience" arises as well. Given the extent and destructive power of suffering and evil in a world which is an "ecumene of human suffering," what is the basis for the assumption that all human persons have adequate experiences of meaning and happiness to nurture, let alone sustain, that fundamental human trust that life is meaningful, and reality is trustworthy? Further, Schillebeeckx's caveat that the human response of "no" to evil, injustice, and violations of the *humanum* is universal "*unless we go about [life] blindly; keen only on consumption, bustle, and oblivion ... or power*"(emphasis added) raises a related question about contemporary global culture and its impact on "basic human experience" especially in light of Schillebeeckx's hermeneutical claim that there is no uninterpreted experience. How universal can we expect the supposedly spontaneous human response to evil and the inhumane to be in a globalized culture of commodification, racism, sexism, terrorism, the trafficking of children as well as adults, especially women, for sexual and labor exploitation, war and the proliferation of nuclear weapons, global climate change, forced migration, hatred of the stranger, and ecological devastation?[38]

Although Schillebeeckx borrowed the notions of "critical negativity" and "negative contrast experience" from critical theorists, he did not share their optimism with regard to human reason. He affirmed that human ethics, even ethical heroism, is possible outside the framework of a

---

[36] Schillebeeckx, *Christ*, 814–15, n. 77 [897, n. 158].

[37] See Schillebeeckx, *Church*, 5–6 [5–6] for this discussion.

[38] For discussion of the need to develop further the impact of social conditioning and structural sin on the formation of human, and specifically moral, consciousness and conscience, see Mary Catherine Hilkert, "The Threatened Humanum as *Imago Dei*," *Edward Schillebeeckx and Contemporary Theology*, ed. Lieven Boeve, Frederiek Depoortere, and Stephan van Erp (London: T&T Clark, 2010), 127–41, at 132–33.

religious worldview. Still he averred that if the history of the twentieth century were to be viewed only through the lenses of rationality and power, Schillebeeckx saw little reason to hope that the future would—or could—be different from the present and past. But Schillebeeckx distinguished human optimism rooted in a rational and technocratic culture from Christian hope. For Christian believers who viewed history through the lens of the life, death, and resurrection of Jesus, he insisted, the basis for hope in the future of humankind is rooted not in human creativity and power, but in the power of the living God to raise Jesus from the dead.

## Hope for the *humanum* in Jesus the Christ

For that reason, Schillebeeckx could write at the end of the 1960s that "the humanly impossible is made really possible in Jesus the Christ. The message—which Christianity brings to the secular world is this—humanity is possible."[39] Two decades later, he reaffirmed his confidence that humanity, human ethics, and even heroic ethical martyrdom are possible outside of Christianity or any religious framework. On the basis of autonomous human ethics, one can judge good to be superior to evil and justice to injustice. But the basis for that judgment is unclear and cannot find its grounds in anthropology or history per se since human beings are a source of threat and violence as well as a source of grace for others. Further a postulatory hope, although courageous, offers no hope for the victims of history.[40] Recognizing that believers cannot rationally prove the basis for their hope, Schillebeeckx nevertheless maintained that belief in Jesus as the human face of the divine, and the fullest possible historical revelation of what the reign of God means for human flourishing, transforms the "fundamental muttering of humanity" into a well-founded hope.[41] That claim became the central focus of the Christological trilogy to which Schillebeeckx was to turn in the 1970s. Embedded in that soteriological Christology are the main lines of his later theological anthropology, the focus of the next chapter in this volume. Schillebeeckx's desire to address widespread suffering and injustice on a global scale and the limits of technocratic reason to provide a livable and sustainable future for human communities and the Earth prompted him to retell the story of the human Jesus of Nazareth as the story of God at work in history. His hope was to do so in such a way that both believers and those searching for belief could recognize it as the story of human possibility and flourishing, in spite of the forces of evil and injustice at work in the world precisely so that they might be moved to act on behalf of the *humanum*.

---

[39] Schillebeeckx, "The New Image of God," *GFM*, 117–18 [193].

[40] Schillebeeckx's discussion of autonomous human ethics in relation to Christian ethics takes account of the insights of Kant and Levinas, but offers a critical perspective as well. See *On Christian Faith: The Spiritual, Ethical, and Political Dimensions* (New York: Crossroad, 1987), 55–64.

[41] Schillebeeckx, *Church*, 6 [6].

# Chapter 18

# The Story of Jesus and Human Flourishing

## *Schillebeeckx's Later Soteriological Anthropology*

### Mary Catherine Hilkert

Although Edward Schillebeeckx is known far more for his writings on Christology and soteriology than for his insights in the field of theological anthropology, the goal of his Jesus-project was to give rise to hope and action on behalf of God's beloved creation—humankind and the Earth. His growing awareness of an interconnected and globalized world and his dialogue with liberation theologians led Schillebeeckx to the realization that the human experience of two-thirds of the world's population is fundamentally a struggle to survive in situations of dehumanizing suffering. He began to see that "scarlet thread" of radical and senseless suffering on a global scale as the greatest challenge to belief in a loving Creator God with the power to save humankind. That reality of global suffering and injustice, along with the turn to the empirical sciences and technocratic reason as providing the way forward for human progress in a secularized modern world, provided the context for Schillebeeckx's later writings about the meaning of human life and the possibility of human hope and ethics. What had been implied in his earlier work now became explicit: "Soteriology, Christology, and anthropology cannot be separated; they mutually clarify each other."[1]

Writing in a narrative-practical key, Schillebeeckx explained that anthropology cannot be separated from Christology precisely because the story of Jesus is at once the parable of the living God at work in history and the paradigm of humanity fully alive.[2] Likewise, in the *Christ* volume, Schillebeeckx describes the quest for what Christians refer to as "salvation" as the deepest human longing for a "livable humanum" in spite of worldwide conditions permeated by violence, injustice, and radical and senseless suffering. In the final volume of his trilogy *Church: The Human Story of God*, he emphasizes even more clearly, in the face of growing ecological devastation, that this anthropological goal is possible only amid a flourishing creation.[3]

---

[1]  Edward Schillebeeckx, *IR, CW* vol. 8 (London: Bloomsbury T&T Clark, 2014), 53 [62]. For a more fully developed exploration of Schillebeeckx's early insights in theological anthropology, see Jennifer Cooper, *Humanity in the Mystery of God: The Theological Anthropology of Edward Schillebeeckx* (London: T&T Clark, 2011).

[2]  See Edward Schillebeeckx, *Jesus, CW* vol. 6 (London: Bloomsbury T&T Clark, 2014), 589 [626], and Schillebeeckx, "The 'God of Jesus' and the 'Jesus of God'," *Jesus Christ and Human Freedom, Concilium* vol. 93, ed. Edward Schillebeeckx and Bas van Iersel (New York: Herder and Herder, 1974), 110–26.

[3]  Edward Schillebeeckx, *Church, CW* vol. 10 (London: Bloomsbury T&T Clark, 2014), 231–43 [234–46].

# I. The Christological lens: The human story as the story of God

In his writings in the 1960s, Schillebeeckx pointed to Jesus and specifically the resurrection as God's promise of a human future and a final flourishing beyond human imagination or power. In his 1974 *Jesus* book, Schillebeeckx attempted to trace the source of that faith by reconstructing a plausible historical reconstruction of the life, preaching (in word and action), and death of Jesus as well as the Easter experience of the first disciples. Schillebeeckx hoped to retell the story of Jesus in a way that would disclose the secret and source of that life as radical trust in Abba, the living God, and which would prompt others to "go and do likewise" by engaging in the praxis of the kingdom of God. The soteriological and anthropological intent of Schillebeeckx's Jesus-project is even more evident in the second volume of the trilogy and its original Dutch title: *Gerechtigheid en liefde: Genade en bevrijding* (*Justice and Love: Grace and Liberation*). There, Schillebeeckx traces multiple New Testament expressions of the "salvation coming from God in Jesus" experienced by diverse early Christian communities in order to lay the foundation for the construction of contemporary social and political expressions of that experience of grace which would not only prove faithful to the original apostolic experience of Jesus's offer of the kingdom of God, but also respond to the challenges of their own unique historical and cultural context. Schillebeeckx writes:

> In the end the coming salvation imparted by God, which Jesus proclaimed and for which he lived and died, the reign of God directed to mankind [*sic*], seems to be the person of Jesus Christ himself: the eschatological man, Jesus of Nazareth, who is exalted to sit beside God and, who, of his plentitude, sends us God's Spirit, thus opening up "communication" among human beings. Thus, Jesus of Nazareth in his own person reveals the eschatological face of all mankind and, in so doing, the trinitarian fullness of God's unity … God's cause as the cause of man is personified in the person of Jesus Christ.[4]

Whether speaking of New Testament formulations of the human encounter with God, later theological, doctrinal, or mystical expressions of that experience, or contemporary new attempts to formulate a theology of grace or salvation in new contexts, Schillebeeckx identified the same fundamental dynamic of divine offer and human response at work: "So for believers, *revelation* is an *action of God* as *experienced* by believers and *interpreted* in religious language and therefore expressed in human terms, in the dimension of our utterly human history."[5] Schillebeeckx emphasized that this encounter is initiated by God and that although revelation is mediated through human experience, it cannot be reduced to human experience. Rather, the authoritative element of revelation is to be found not in the interpretative elements or cultural expressions

---

[4] Schillebeeckx, *Jesus,* 629 [669–70].

[5] Edward Schillebeeckx, *Christ, CW* vol. 7 (London: Bloomsbury T&T Clark, 2014), 66 [78]. Although Schillebeeckx does not incorporate an analysis of the theological or doctrinal Christian tradition beyond the New Testament era in this volume, he remarked in *Interim Report* that the same structural elements apply there and that distortions in the history of Christian spirituality can be viewed as failures to do justice to one or more of these New Testament structural elements.

of even the biblical language of grace, but rather the offer that is experienced in and through that human mediation. In Schillebeeckx's words: "*In* our human experiences we can *experience* something that transcends our experience and proclaims itself in that experience as unexpected grace."[6]

## Early Christian experiences of grace: Four structural elements

Schillebeeckx's reading of diverse New Testament theologies of grace yielded a fundamental synthesis of what he identified as four structural elements, which provide the fundamental orientation for later Christian formulations of the experience of human encounter with God in history. The four elements not only resonate with his earlier work, but also highlight in a new way the interconnection of anthropology, soteriology, and Christology.

First, in response to the ultimate human question of the meaning and purpose of human life, and in particular, in response to the anguish of apparent meaninglessness and radical human suffering, Schillebeeckx draws from both Hebrew Scriptures (especially Exodus) and the New Testament to identify the fundamental claim of a truly theological anthropology: "God himself [*sic*] is the guarantor that human life has a positive and significant meaning."[7] Throughout the biblical narratives, God shows Godself to be the source of the gift of life itself, a God "bent toward humanity," and one who sides with the poor, the oppressed, and the outcast. The Creator God is the author of all that is good and the one who opposes evil by standing in solidarity with those who are poor and exploited. Focusing on human hopes and fulfillment, Schillebeeckx describes salvation as "concerned with human wholeness and happiness … [which is the fruit of] an intrinsic mutual relationship involving the solidarity of man with a living God who is concerned with mankind [*sic*]."[8] Throughout the Jewish and Christian Scriptures God shows Godself to side with human beings on the side of life.

Second, from the perspective of diverse New Testament texts, a consistent element of a Christian theology of grace is that the meaning and purpose of human life are most fully revealed in the life, death, and resurrection of Jesus of Nazareth. Jesus is the face of God turned toward God's beloved children, in particular the little ones and those who suffer, the crucified people of every era. If the death of Jesus as execution called into question God's fidelity, power, and promise to be in solidarity with God's beloved (as Schillebeeckx suggests that it did), the resurrection is God's confirmation of all that Jesus preached and of his very person as well as the affirmation that God is love, a love firmly committed to solidarity with humankind and creation. In the face of radical and senseless suffering (a primary concern in Schillebeeckx's later soteriological anthropology), Schillebeeckx reads the complex history of New Testament interpretations of suffering and theologies of the cross as in agreement on one central point: suffering is not redemptive in itself, but only when it is suffering in solidarity with others, suffering for the sake

---

6   Schillebeeckx, *Christ*, 66 [78]. See also p. 622 [632] regarding "interpretative elements which find their foundation and source directly in the experience itself" as distinct from "interpretative elements which are offered from elsewhere."
7   Ibid., 627–29 [638].
8   Ibid., [628] 639.

of the reign of God and in opposition to all that violates that reign, including all violations of God's beloved people.[9]

Third, Christian life and living communities of Christian faith are essential mediations of the history of Jesus as a living tradition, empowered by the Spirit. The story of Jesus cannot be told only in words; transmitting orthodox confessions of faith is not a sufficient way of handing on a "living Christology." Disciples bear witness with their lives even to the point of death, as Jesus did. In terms of anthropology, the conviction that human happiness is to be found in the following of Jesus who enfleshed God's faithful solidarity with humankind, especially those who suffer, requires that Christian disciples and Christian communities write a "fifth gospel" with their lives.[10]

Schillebeeckx's treatment of the necessary ongoing human mediation of the kingdom of God, which Jesus preached is treated in the *Christ* volume in explicitly ecclesiological terms, but in later work, especially the volume *Church: The Human Story of God*, his accent is more on the human mediation of the reign of God, which occurs whenever good is promoted and evil is resisted. Schillebeeckx continued to describe the church's vocation as a call to be "sacrament of salvation in and for the world," but he was far less optimistic about ecclesial fidelity to that mission especially as it had been articulated by the Second Vatican Council. In that volume, he stated clearly that the church (both community and leaders) can fail in that mission and prove to be a stumbling block, rather than a mediation of grace. At the same time, he remained optimistic about signs of new life emerging in local grass-roots communities of faith. Because he distinguished more clearly in his later work between salvation (the experience of grace) and revelation (recognition, confession, and celebration of that grace), he likewise affirmed that the mediation of God's grace is necessarily historical, but not always ecclesial or explicitly religious. Rather, salvation goes forward wherever fragments of the reign of God are enfleshed in human history, as when a glass of water is given to the thirsty.

In his fourth and final structural element of grace, Schillebeeckx turns to the final human experience in every life–death. Just as the death of individuals breaks the thread of their own person historical story, Schillebeeckx remarks that the story of God at work in history, which is most fully enfleshed and disclosed in Jesus, cannot be told fully within the confines of history even when that story is faithfully mediated by communities of his followers. Although God's promise of justice, love, grace and liberation can and must be mediated in concrete historical lives, relationships, and structures, those historical realities remain fragmentary expressions of God's promise of final solidarity and fulfillment. At the same time, the paradox of the biblical promise is that human happiness and liberation and the "new heaven and a new earth" which constitute the final coming of God's kingdom cannot be realized within the confines of human history. Both in the Hebrew Scriptures and in the New Testament, the promise of salvation is mediated historically, but its fulfillment is always in the open-ended mode of God's future. Likewise, a Christian theology of grace in any context needs to include this eschatological proviso. What human life is and can become remains finally a mystery that is beyond human knowledge or imagination. But if that promise is not to be dismissed as sheer illusion, fragmentary realizations

---

9   Ibid., 629–30 [640].
10  See ibid., 2 [18]: "The account of the actual life of Christians in the world in which they live is a fifth gospel; it also belongs at the heart of christology [*sic*]."

of human life as lived in communion with God and in solidarity with others are necessary mediations of that promise.

## The glory of God: Humankind fully alive

Schillebeeckx turned to the constructive task of scrutinizing the signs of the times in his own era and proposing a contemporary theology of grace in social and political terms and with an eye toward a worldwide ethics of liberation in Part Four of the *Christ* volume. That his soteriological concern is at the same time an anthropological one (perhaps even an overly anthropocentric one viewed from a later ecological perspective) is evident from the title of that section "God's Glory and Man's Truth, Well-being, and Happiness," which echoes Irenaeus's *Gloria Dei, Vivens Homo.*

Schillebeeckx's reading of the story of Jesus as clear evidence that "God does not want humankind to suffer" and his exploration of diverse biblical theologies of grace provided the lenses for his own scrutiny of the "signs of the times" in the late twentieth century in both Western Europe and the broader global context.[11] Schillebeeckx identified the multiple and pervasive threats to human well-being, systematic forms of injustice, and challenges to hope around the globe as evidence of the "absence of salvation." That absence took on two distinct but interrelated forms: on the one hand, the dehumanizing and meaningless suffering of two-thirds of the world's population and, on the other hand, the lack of evidence of solidarity among the other one-third, who were focused on preserving power and their own standard of living and who viewed "the other" as a threat.

Schillebeeckx was well aware of the criticism lodged against Western political and liberation theologians who wrote about a preferential option for the poor from positions of relative privilege in contrast to Latin American liberation theologians (and others) who speak from the underside of history and from concrete situations of poverty and oppression. He recognized the truth in their challenge: "our 'liberation' is not your 'freedom.'"[12] Yet, at the same time, he saw theologians in Western Europe and the Northern hemisphere faced with a twofold challenge: (1) to continue to address the real challenges to faith in their own local contexts (including those coming from secular humanism, atheistic Marxism and technocratic rationalism), and at the same time, (2) to address their role in the worldwide crises of injustice, poverty, and oppression. Further, he argued that the call to conversion for those who benefit from unjust systems (whether political or ecclesial) is a summons to repentance, solidarity with those who suffer most from that injustice, and concrete actions to change those systems.[13]

---

[11] For the conviction that God does not want humankind to suffer and its roots in the life, ministry, death, and resurrection of Jesus, see *Christ*, 717–23 [724–30], in particular pp. 722–23 [729–30].

[12] See Schillebeeckx, *Church*, 51–54 [53–55] and *Christ*, 753–59 [758–62]. The text from *Christ* in the *Collected Works* edition reflects the revised and expanded 1982 edition of the Dutch text. For the need for a worldwide ethics as a challenge to all theologians, see *Christ*, 640–41 [651].

[13] Schillebeeckx, *Christ*, 640 [650]. Aside from occasional references to neo-colonialism or racism in his social analysis, Schillebeeckx wrote, for the most part, in abstract terms about those who suffer from exploitation and oppression, "not only from individual human beings but above all from socio-political, economic and bureaucratic systems [and] anonymous forces". For inclusion of the challenge to conversion in ecclesial life, see Edward Schillebeeckx, "The 'Gospel of the Poor' for Prosperous People (Luke 6.17, 20–26)," *God Among Us: The Gospel Proclaimed* (New York: Crossroad, 1983), 175–79.

Schillebeeckx also noted that the globalized world at the end of the twentieth century was marked not only by violence and senseless suffering, but also by plural religious and cultural worldviews, which cannot be harmonized into a single universal agreement on what it means to be human or to create a just world order. In spite of that lack of agreement, the challenge that the international community was facing—and continues to face—is how to establish systems of justice which respect and defend "universal human rights."[14] Accepting a necessary pluralism of theoretical approaches to ultimate human questions, Schillebeeckx argued that the primary challenge facing both believers and non-believers is the immediate ethical one. In a world of radical, senseless, and dehumanizing suffering on both individual and structural levels as well as a rapidly deteriorating environment crisis, the questions facing humankind require practical ethical responses from which further insights about the meaning of what is truly human and how human beings are related to the rest of creation will emerge.

The ethical response which is primary here is the distinctly human one which Schillebeeckx described as emerging from negative contrast experiences. It does not arise from a theoretical universal or rational conviction about human nature, but at the same time, in its resistance to what is inhumane and not worthy of humanity or what violates the well-being of other creatures and the Earth, it includes an impulse toward human well-being, happiness, and hope for the future in right relationship with other creatures and as part of a cosmic community of solidarity.[15]

From the perspective of Christian faith, it is the Creator God who is the source and sustaining power of both the ethics and the hope at work in that action on behalf of the *humanum*. The absolute creative and saving presence of God pervades all of creation, holding it in being and empowering it to achieve its destiny. At the same time, the Creator God has granted a radical autonomy to creation—both to nature itself and to human freedom. Schillebeeckx maintains that explicit faith in God's creative and saving presence as well as remembering and celebrating the story of Jesus provide a critical and productive power which shapes the ethical action of the Christian. Nevertheless, precisely because God has given creation its own autonomy, the responsibility to shape concrete human history and to respond to the ecological crisis in specific times and cultures remains that of humankind.

---

[14] Schillebeeckx identifies these "eternal questions" as "What is [humanity]? How [are human beings] in the last resort to live out his life? For what kind of humanity must [human beings] finally decide?" "What constitutes a good, true, and happy future, a future worth living, and what must we do to secure such a future?" See Schillebeeckx, *Christ*, 649, 661 [658, 670]. Schillebeeckx recognized that the oppression which affects humankind as a whole and international calls for "human rights" in secular terms were not the focus of biblical texts, even the prophetic texts which focused more on fidelity to the covenant. But at the same time he pointed to universal impulses in both Testaments which spoke of God's universal salvific will (1 Tim 2:4) and a vision of the kingdom of God which "envisages a humanity in which there are no more exploiters and nor more exploited humanity, no more individual or structural servitude, and no more slaves." (*Christ*, 641 [651]).

[15] See Edward Schillebeeckx, "Naar een 'definitieve toekomst': belofte en menselijke bemiddeling," in *Toekomst van de religie–Religie van de toekomst?* (Bruges: Uitgeverij Emmaüs, 1972), 37–55 excerpt and translation in Robert J. Schreiter, ed., "Contrast Experiences," *The Schillebeeckx Reader* (New York: Crossroad, 1984), 54–56. For the description of all human beings as "ecological beings" and creation as "a cosmic community in solidarity," see *Church*, 243 [245]. Schillebeeckx is clear that God wills salvation for all creation, but he emphasizes human ethical responsibility as essential mediation of that salvation.

# II. The anthropological constants: Parameters of the human

Although Schillebeeckx rejected the notion that there can be a universal, cross-cultural, interreligious, or theoretical resolution to the ultimate question of "what is humanity?" he nevertheless judged that it was important to try to delineate what he termed "anthropological constants"—enduring human impulses, orientations, spheres of value, which are necessary dimensions of a "true and livable humanity." Each of these aspects of human life which are constitutive aspects of *"personal identity* within *social culture"* must be taken into account in any effort to protect human dignity, to create ethical human norms, to build communities and institutions more worthy of human beings, to promote solidarity among people and nations, and to create a livable world for future generations, other species, and the Earth. Christians flesh out the content of those constants in light of the life, ministry, death, and resurrection of Jesus, but Schillebeeckx viewed the constants themselves not as a unique form of Christian anthropology, but rather as dimensions of human life, which serve as the basis for human ethics, and just societies and world order. After a brief overview of each, the essay will conclude with a return to Schillebeeckx's Jesus-project and how interpretations of these constants from the perspective of Christian faith can contribute specific insights to the common human search for human well-being and flourishing.

## Bodily

The first constitutive dimension of human life which Schillebeeckx identifies is that human persons are bodily and thus uniquely related to nature and the ecological environment. Each person is a unique composite unity of body and spirit or body, mind, and spirit. Human well-being includes bodily safety and well-being and a concern for all dimensions of the human person including psychological, emotional, mental, and social health. Each person's constitution is unique and has its own unique strengths and limitations. Human bodiliness is also a share in the broad ecological network of all creatures that are of the Earth and that share in mortality and finitude. Human integrity includes a recognition of shared creatureliness and kinship with all other living creatures as well as a call to right relationship with all other creatures and with the Earth as our common home. Human awareness of being part of a larger network of nature calls for a recognition of boundaries and limits, not only for human survival, but also for the survival and well-being of other creatures and of the Earth.

At the same time, the interrelationship of human persons with other creatures and with nature provide opportunities for bonds with other creatures, for aesthetic experiences of beauty and awe, and for a sense of joy and respect in communion with nature. Although Schillebeeckx expressed concern about the human propensity to manipulate, instrumentalize, and dominate nature, which is often associated with the modern scientific and industrial revolutions, he also recognized that scientific and technological developments are expressions of creativity and can be sources not only of humanization and positive cultural developments, but also of protecting other species and healing and preventing ecological devastation. The creation of norms for human intervention in nature is the responsibility of human communities, but Schillebeeckx warned against purely technological solutions to human dilemmas or the view that if something is scientifically possible (e.g., nuclear weapons or gene manipulation), then human beings should develop that capacity. Rather human persons and communities are called to develop ethical norms with all six of the anthropological constants in mind as they determine which decisions will protect the full humanity of the most vulnerable members of the human community and best serve the common good of the global human community and the entire community of creation.

In making those decisions, Schillebeeckx's first constant emphasizes that human persons are more than "rational animals." Rather, he wrote, "[The human person] is not only reason, but also temperament; not only reason, but also imagination; not only freedom, but also instinct; not only reason, but also love; and so on."[16] For that reason, he stressed two dimensions of human knowledge and agency—the active knowledge and practical initiatives through which human persons shape the world and their environment, and contemplative knowledge through which human persons are receptive and responsive to initiatives coming from beyond the self, as in contemplation, play, and love. In making concrete decisions in a world of global suffering, Schillebeeckx highlighted the "pathic epistemological power" of negative contrast experiences as providing a unique link between active and contemplative forms of knowledge which is at the core of their practical-critical impact and their power to open up future possibilities. In his words:

> Experiences of suffering come upon people in the form of a negative experience, quite different from the positive enjoyment of contemplative, playful and aesthetic experiences. On the other hand, under the aspect of the experience of *contrast* or critical negativity, the experience of suffering forms a bridge towards possible action which might remove both suffering and its causes.[17]

# Relational

The second and third constants of human existence which need to be considered in ethical decision-making as well as in theological interpretations of salvation are that human personal identity is essentially relational and social. Many theologians who make that claim derive it from trinitarian doctrine and consider it a distinctly theological and specifically Christian reflection on what it means to be created in the image of the trinitarian God revealed by Jesus Christ.[18] Others begin with the biblical creation narratives in the first chapter of Genesis to ground a "revealed anthropology" of personhood as a call to self-gift and a gendered reading of persons-in-communion, which is the dominant relational anthropology in Pope

---

16  Schillebeeckx, *Christ*, 730 [736].
17  Schillebeeckx, *Christ*, 814 [818].
18  See, for example, Christoph Schwöbel and Colin E. Gunton, eds., *Persons Divine and Human* (Edinburgh: T&T Clark, 1991); John D. Zizioulas, *Being as Communion* (Crestwood, New York, 1997); Catherine Mowry LaCugna, *God for Us: The Trinity and Christian Life* (San Francisco: HarperSanFrancisco, 1991); and Stanley Grenz, *The Social God and the Relational Self: A Trinitarian Theology of Imago Dei* (Westminster: John Knox Press, 2001).

John Paul II's theology of the body and subsequent magisterial documents in the Roman Catholic tradition.[19]

Schillebeeckx instead describes the relational character of human personhood in terms which are more broadly accessible and in language shared by philosophers and social scientists. Citing the agreement of multiple existential and phenomenological thinkers, he argues that analysis of human existence reveals that human persons are not isolated individuals who choose whether or not to enter into human relationships and social contracts. On the contrary, human persons are essentially related to others and in fundamental ways authorized and confirmed by others.[20] Humanity is in fact co-humanity; human subjectivity is inter-subjectivity. A truly "livable humanity" and genuine self-realization require self-transcendence in and through loving acceptance of the other in her or his freedom.

Further, the vulnerable other who is in need makes a particular demand on one's freedom. Schillebeeckx agrees with Emmanuel Levinas that this demand is a-symmetrical; the other is not Kant's *alter ego*, but rather someone whose very existence can make demands on me which go beyond the moral demands that I can make on her or him. Challenging the individualism of the Cartesian *ego* and the modern bourgeois notion of freedom (*pour soi*) as expressed by Jean-Paul Sartre, Schillebeeckx sides with Levinas in his claim that the freedom of the other arises out of their transcendence, not out of a conviction that he or she should enjoy the same freedom as one's own. On the contrary, according to Levinas, "[t]he other imposes himself or herself as a demand which dominates my freedom, and therefore as more original than anything that takes place in me."[21] Nevertheless, Schillebeeckx does not find Levinas's ethical claim that the other makes an absolute demand on the self to be adequate precisely because others may be the source not only of an ethical claim, but also of demands of violence and injustice. For that reason, Schillebeeckx endorses Kant's critique that if human beings, rather than universal norms of justice, are the ultimate source of ethics, there is no guarantee that evil will not triumph over good.

# Social

Schillebeeckx's third anthropological constant moves beyond the description of persons as constituted by relationality and intersubjectivity in the sense of the I-Thou relationship of encounter described by Martin Buber. Rather, in concert with Levinas, social psychologists, sociologists, and cultural anthropologists, Schillebeeckx affirmed that human persons are not

---

19  See, for example, Pope John Paul II, *Man and Woman He Created Them: A Theology of the Body* (Boston: Daughters of St. Paul, 2006); *idem.*, "*Mulieris dignitatem*" (Apostolic Letter "On the Dignity and Vocation of Women") *Origins* 18 (1988), and International Theological Commission, "Communion and Stewardship: Human Persons Created in the Image of God," 2004, available online at http://www.vatican.va/roman_curia/congregations/cfaith/cti_documents/rc_con_cfaith_doc_20040723_communion-stewardship_en.html.

20  As corroborating sources, Schillebeeckx cites L. Binswanger, M. Nédoncelle, G. Gusdorf, F. Buytendijk, R. Kwant, and Gabriel Marcel, among others. See Schillebeeckx, *Christ*, 730, n. 5 [892, n. 75].

21  Schillebeeckx's summation of the insight of Emmanuel Levinas, *Totalité et Infini: Essai sur l'extériorité* (The Hague: Nijhoff, 1961), 201, cited in Schillebeeckx, *On Christian Faith: The Spiritual, Ethical and Political Dimensions* (New York: Crossroad, 1987), 57.

only essentially relational in interpersonal terms, but also that the deepest structure of human personality is social.[22] Human persons form—and are formed by—social systems and institutions, including familial, tribal, civic, national, and religious structures, among others. Schillebeeckx stressed that this analysis of the social constitution of the human person goes beyond the modern Western notion of two distinct entities—an individual subject ("I") and society which need to be negotiated in some fashion. He further opposed both the notion that the individual is a sum of social relationships and the notion that society is merely a sum of individual actions. Rather person and society constitute a dialectical polarity. For that reason, Schillebeeckx observed that

> the human ego itself is a social and cultural process, and the so-called inner life is itself a living part of a cultural process [...] From our childhood, even before there is personal consciousness, we human beings are socialized. Becoming a person is acculturation.[23]

The concrete historical systems and structures constructed by human beings in diverse social contexts are necessary to protect the dignity and rights of the most vulnerable members of society, to foster human freedom and well-being, to order common life and support the common good. At the same time, institutions take on a life of their own and all too often give the impression of being unchangeable—rooted in the natural law or metaphysical necessity—rather than historical, contingent, human cultural creations intended to promote human well-being and foster the common good. Schillebeeckx recognized the need for institutions and structures, but he stressed that institutions are created by human beings and can and should be changed not only when they enslave or violate human persons, but also when they fail to foster human freedom and well-being. As developed elsewhere in this collection, this insight applies to ecclesial as well as secular institutions; hence, Schillebeeckx's call for a "church with a human face."

## Contextual

The fourth constant of human existence highlights that human beings exist in concrete historical, geographical, and cultural contexts from which they interpret their contemporary situation, human history, and future options. Human life is an ongoing hermeneutical enterprise precisely because there is no universal standpoint outside of one's concrete social location from which to interpret the meaning of human existence.[24] This constant intersects with the first constant in that there are natural phenomena and events which are threats to human life and well-being, but which human beings have no control over with the final boundary and threat to personal existence being death itself. The natural and social sciences can contribute to human self-understanding, but not resolve the ultimate question of the meaning of historical existence.

---

[22] Schillebeeckx, *Christ*, 731 [737]; Schillebeeckx, *Church*, 45–54 [46–55]. Resources which Schillebeeckx cites include Peter Berger and T. Luckmann, J. Habermas, N. Luhmann, A. Schütz, A. Gehlen, H.-G. Gadamer, and P. Vogler, among others (Schillebeeckx, *Christ*, 732, n. 6 [892, n. 76]).

[23] Schillebeeckx, *Church*, 47 [48].

[24] Here the influence of Hans-Georg Gadamer is evident in Schillebeeckx's understanding of human experience as necessarily *interpreted* experience. Schillebeeckx cites Gadamer's *Truth and Method*, trans. W. Glen-Doepel (London: Sheed and Ward, 1975), 235–74.

Further, there are historical and geographical developments which may not have been necessary developments, but which now place specific demands on human persons, communities, and nations which differ from those of others. Here Schillebeeckx draws attention to the disproportionate distribution of resources needed for basic human survival and well-being across the globe, particularly in the global South. That geographical and political reality places a particular call to solidarity and to global economic reform and divestment on the part of prosperous people and nations. From the perspectives of Latin American Liberation Theology and Catholic Social Teaching, Gustavo Gutiérrez and Pope John Paul II likewise argue that the call to solidarity and an option for the poor are not only matters of Christian ethics, but fundamental human demands in the contemporary globalized world. Political philosopher Martha Nussbaum and economist Amartya Sen concur that poverty is at the root of multiple forms of human deprivation and that the demands of human justice require an ethical response.[25]

## Ethical

This awareness of human solidarity and ethical responsibility in a global context and the search for a code of international human rights are themselves developments which have occurred in history as human beings have questioned what constitutes basic humanity and human responsibility to and for the other. Although Schillebeeckx develops this constant, like each of the others, in secular terms, he notes that reflection on the historical and cultural conditioning of human awareness necessarily includes reflection on the wisdom traditions, including religious traditions, which have served as a stimulus for the search for what constitutes a livable *humanum*, viable human communities, and ethical international norms of justice.

As important as critical reflection is for any understanding of human life and ethics, human history is created by the exercise of human freedom and action, as Schillebeeckx argued in his earlier writings on history and the future. Reflection on what is genuinely human in history is possible only if human persons and communities are active in creating fragmentary expressions of more humane, just and livable communities and societies. For that reason, Schillebeeckx identified the mutual relationship of theory and praxis as the fifth constitutive dimension of human existence.

## Religious

The sixth constant which Schillebeeckx identifies as an enduring human impulse is one not included in the analysis of Nussbaum and Sen, but crucial to Schillebeeckx's reading of what constitutes human integrity as well as his reading of anthropology from the perspective of Christian faith. What he terms the "religious and 'para-religious' consciousness of human

---

[25]  See Gustavo Gutiérrez, "Memory and Prophecy," *The Option for the Poor in Christian Theology*, ed. Daniel G. Groody (Notre Dame, IN: Notre Dame Press, 2007) 17–38; and John Paul II, *Sollicitudo Rei Socialis*, 1987. For Nussbaum and Sen's analysis of a minimum threshold of basic human capabilities which are necessary for survival, and therefore demanded by norms of human justice, see *The Quality of Life* (New York: Oxford University Press, 1993).

persons" refers not to a specific religious faculty, but rather to the human desire to make sense of life—both nature and history—as a meaningful whole. Human persons give evidence of this "utopian element in human consciousness" in both religious and non-religious terms when they express their ultimate vision of what inspires them and what makes life worth living.[26]

In that broad sense, Schillebeeckx argued that faith and hope are constitutive impulses of human existence. Even without any explicit form of religious belief, a truly human life requires some sort of faith that life as a whole holds meaning and that there is hope for the future, including the hope that the future can be different from the past and that human efforts to create a more human world are worthwhile. Without those basic forms of faith and hope, human persons and whole societies lose a sense of their identity, the motivation for action for change, and even the will to live. But the person who has a reason to live can withstand the most desperate of circumstances as the Holocaust survivor and psychotherapist Viktor Frankl maintained in *Man's Search for Meaning*.[27]

In terms of critical reflection on whether life as a whole has a meaning and purpose, the nihilist response is negative. Life is absurd and any kind of practical human heroism or self-sacrifice for the sake of solidarity with the other is incomprehensible. Others embrace a variety of wagers (secular forms of "faith" according to Schillebeeckx) about who or what will determine the final outcome of human history and the cosmos, whether that be attributed to fate, evolution, human beings, or "nature" itself. For the religious believer (here Schillebeeckx speaks in the language of theistic believers who profess faith in a divine Creator), the future of history as a whole and of the cosmos lies in the hands of the living God.

## The dynamic tension between the constants

What Schillebeeckx described as a final, seventh constant of human existence is the insight that all six of the previous enduring aspects of truly human persons and cultures need to be held in dynamic tension with one another as persons and communities make concrete decisions about how to respect the human dignity of every person and to develop and change institutions and societies so that they better serve the common good. Thus, for example, human welfare, social justice and ecological sustainability all need to be considered when making economic and political decisions about international trade agreements or decisions about use of natural resources.

These constants do not offer a formula for ethical solutions when a conflict of competing goods occurs in a world of finite human resources. Rather they identify multiple aspects of human life and justice which need to be considered when making ethical decisions on behalf of the *humanum* and other creatures. Once again, however, Schillebeeckx emphasizes that the necessary starting point for establishing norms or making responsible human decisions is to attend to contemporary negative contrast experiences and the memories of fragments of salvation which engender hope. In the context of religious and cultural pluralism and significant differences of worldviews, truly human norms can be established only through free and rational communication among all those

---

[26] Schillebeeckx, *Christ*, 734 [740].
[27] Viktor Frankl, *Man's Search for Meaning* (Boston, MA: Beacon, 1963). See also William F. Lynch, *Images of Hope* (Baltimore, MD: Helicon, 1965).

impacted by decisions. Recognizing that power dynamics are operative in all human situations and that no political process or party can be identified with the reign of God, Schillebeeckx nevertheless argues that politics cannot be reduced to what is currently possible in given limited and sinful human situations; rather, "politics is the difficult art of making possible what is *necessary* for human salvation."[28]

## The perspective of Christian faith: Anthropological constants as dimensions of salvation

Schillebeeckx sketched these seven constants of what constitutes human wholeness or well-being as a way of pointing to what he termed "the height and breadth and depth of human salvation." He argues in the *Christ* volume that the search for human and creaturely well-being and a worldwide ethic is not only a religious concern, but also a global human concern. In both secular and religious terms, this complex and multi-dimensional reality cannot be identified with any single aspect of well-being such as ecological sustainability, defeat of oppressive political systems, overthrow of an unjust economy, or interpersonal harmony. Schillebeeckx intentionally addressed questions of human integrity and flourishing in terms widely accessible to persons from diverse religious and cultural perspectives.

At the same time, he wrote as a Christian believer and saw Christian faith not only as one language game among others, but also as having a unique critical and productive power rooted in the living God who is the source and goal of all creation and whose grace is the creative and saving power at work in all efforts on behalf of liberation and flourishing. It is noteworthy that his discussion of the anthropological constants is located within the framework of his soteriological Christology. The story of Jesus as the story of human encounter with the living God in history fleshes out dimensions of a specifically Christian theological perspective on the anthropological constants as constitutive dimensions of being human.

# III. Schillebeeckx's contributions and the need for future constructive work

Among Schillebeeckx's contributions to theological anthropology, all of which need to be engaged and developed more fully and from a variety of perspectives today, are the importance of locating anthropology in the larger context of creation, an emphasis on the theological significance of bodiliness, a theology of human finitude and even failure, a theology of original sin in an evolutionary context as that relates to personal and social sin and human responsibility for global suffering, the centrality of forgiveness to human flourishing, the essential connection between ethics and anthropology and the human mediation of grace, and the contemplative dimension of human flourishing.

---

[28] Schillebeeckx, *Christ*, 737 [743].

# Relocating the human in the context of creation

The central implication of the first anthropological constant for Christian faith's reflection on human salvation is clear: salvation is not simply a matter of "salvation of souls," but rather the final flourishing of all aspects of the human person. As noted in *Church: The Human Story of God*, God's promise of salvation includes not only the full flourishing of humankind, but also "a new heavens and a new earth." There, Schillebeeckx emphasizes that human beings share creaturehood not only with other living beings, but also with inorganic and organic creatures. Noting that in the first creation account humans were created on the same day as "the cattle, the creeping things, and the wild beasts," he likewise highlights that God wants a future for all of God's creatures and that the biblical promise reflected by the psalmist is that humans and beasts together will share in God's salvation (Ps 36:7). At the same time, Schillebeeckx continued to affirm a unique ethical and religious role for human creatures as those charged to be guardians of creation and the creatures who have the capacity to offer praise and thanks, roles signified by the designation of human persons as created in the image of God. Whether those claims can and should be maintained today—or whether they continue to perpetuate an outdated anthropocentric worldview—is the cause for lively discussion in the fields of ecological theology and creation theology today.[29] What is not in doubt on either side of that debate is that, whatever else may be true of human persons, they are bodily, earthly animals who share creaturely existence with all other creatures and with the natural environment of which they are a part.

# Bodiliness

The first constant further underlines the theological significance of human bodiliness, a positive contribution of Schillebeeckx's theological anthropology from the time of his early sacramental writings. In terms of anthropology, the constitutive dimension of bodiliness to human personhood reaches a climax in his discussion of death and Christian hope. He soberly admits that physical death of the human body is the definitive end of human personhood as understood within the contours of human history. Yet from the perspective of Christian faith he underlines the language of the apostolic profession of faith as a key metaphor for human flourishing: "I believe in resurrection of the body." Acknowledging that the meaning of that claim was totally beyond his comprehension or imagination, he nevertheless maintained that it is a profession of faith in the power of the living God to do something radically new—to bring about a new mode of existence, which constitutes the person's final fulfillment in God. What that means in terms of corporeal existence beyond death is completely unknown as he emphasized even in the context of preaching on this mystery. But at the same time, he stressed the importance of the language of "resurrection of the body" to emphasize how fundamental corporeality is to human personhood. In a homily on "I Believe in Resurrection of the Body," he remarked:

---

[29]   See, for example, the *Proceedings of the Annual Meeting of the Catholic Theological Society of America*, vol. 72 (Albuquerque, New Mexico, June 8–11, 2017), *passim.* Note especially the sessions on "Creation Faith and the Contemporary Context: New Applications of Edward Schillebeeckx's Theology of Creation" and "Anthropology." Proceedings available online at https://ejournals.bc.edu/ojs/index.php/ctsa/issue/view/977/showToc.

> [T]he physical expression of someone who finds complete personal fulfilment in God, in whom God himself has become completely transcendent in the hallowed human figure, transcends all our earthly capacities for imagination .... But what can human consummation ultimately mean for human beings if it leaves out the corporeality which is so familiar to us? In that case I am no longer "I," and this "I" has not achieved definitive salvation.[30]

Although Schillebeeckx was clear about the centrality of the body to human flourishing both in history and beyond, he did not engage important contemporary debates about what constitutes human bodiliness, the mind-body relationship, the disputed language of "soul" and "spirit," or the significance of bodily differences including sex, sexual orientation, gender, race, and bodily impairments—all of which remain key questions in contemporary theological anthropology.

## Finitude and failure

Schillebeeckx's remarks on finitude and failure from the perspective of creation faith and reflection on Jesus's life and ministry offer further possibilities for Christian anthropology and spirituality. Human persons and communities bear responsibility for efforts to establish a more livable and shared home for humanity and all other inhabitants of their common home, the Earth. In the language of Christian faith, human beings have been entrusted with the task of making the reign of God more of a concrete reality in history. At the same time, human persons remain finite creatures with limited capacities and power. Even the best of human efforts remain fragmentary, marked by creaturely limits and mistakes. From a faith perspective, in contrast to other theologians who speak of finitude as a regrettable aspect of fallen humanity, Schillebeeckx stresses that finitude is a dimension of the blessing of being created, not its failure. In his words, "it is good that man [*sic*] is just man, the world just the world."[31]

The other side of this good news of human persons as creatures is that the Creator is at every moment absolutely present, sustaining and empowering God's creatures with the saving power of divine love. Thus, human persons as finite creatures empowered by God with their own freedom and agency have the responsibility to help shape human history as a history of salvation, while at the same time recognizing that all human efforts will fall short of the final vision of the kingdom of God and a new heaven and a new earth. Salvation in history remains always "already," and "not yet." So integral is finitude to human existence that Schillebeeckx notes that even Jesus's efforts to establish the kingdom of God in his historical context fell short. From a human and historical standpoint, the ending of his life and mission with his execution could be judged a "fiasco."[32]

Schillebeeckx's discussion of failure as a dimension of all human life, including that of Jesus, is a crucial dimension of his theological anthropology on the personal, interpersonal, and social

---

[30] Edward Schillebeeckx, "I Believe in the Resurrection of the Body," *God Among Us: The Gospel Proclaimed* (New York: Crossroad, 1983), 137–38.

[31] Schillebeeckx, *IR*, 99 [113].

[32] Schillebeeckx, *Christ*, 825 [829]. At the same time, Jesus's acceptance of his own finitude and his radical and unconditional trust in the Creator God whom he addressed as *Abba* manifests the unconditional character of his proclamation and practice. (See *Christ*, 790 [794]).

levels. He neither inflates nor ignores the value and necessity of human efforts to contribute to the historical mediation of the reign of God. Yet, those who have embraced the technological incessant demand for progress and activists overwhelmed by the immensity of suffering and desperate needs around the world, including those motivated by a passion for social justice, are also in need of fuller awareness of this theological and spiritual perspective on human finitude and creaturely limits.

## Guilty failure and radical forgiveness

At the same time, Schillebeeckx makes a clear distinction between human efforts which fail because of sheer finitude and those personal, interpersonal, and social failures which are guilty failures, or in the language of faith, the result of personal and social sin. When describing the dynamics of negative contrast experiences, Schillebeeckx did not discuss in any detail the structures of injustice which foster them or the personal and interpersonal misuses of human freedom which most often bring them about.[33] But one of the critical contributions of religious faith to an understanding of human life is the explicit language of sin and guilt to name the multiple ways in which human persons violate one another, create structures which are dehumanizing and threaten the lives of other creatures and species as well as one's human neighbors, and ultimately, in and through one's free actions, reject the living God. Like actions on behalf of life and the *humanum*, these human actions which fail to further the good and to oppose evil have consequences and are historically irrevocable. In and through them human persons contribute to making history a history of sin and suffering rather than a history of salvation.

Forms of personal alienation, interpersonal violations of relationships, and even social oppression can be addressed and changed through human intervention and efforts. But the language of faith addresses a deeper human alienation and participation in guilt which is finally a rejection of God and the offer of grace. Although it calls for recognition and repentance, no human effort can bring about reconciliation with God. The very need for that level of reconciliation is itself recognized in the awareness of God's mercy and forgiveness which is the reason for gratitude rather than terror. Schillebeeckx's approach to human sinfulness and the mystery of iniquity and its relation to suffering is explored more fully elsewhere in this volume. But in the context of Schillebeeckx's discussion of anthropology and soteriology, it is important to note that the mystery of the human person includes human participation in the mystery of iniquity. He ultimately viewed the doctrine of original sin as an optimistic doctrine precisely because it identified human sinfulness neither as finding its source in God who is pure positivity of Love nor as constitutive of the human creature who was created good. Rather, Schillebeeckx turned to Aquinas to identify sin as the original, but not inevitable, initiative of human finite freedom and suggested that this Thomistic insight was

---

[33] He recognizes that there can also be negative contrast experiences which are brought about by natural phenomena which cause immense suffering for humans and other creatures. At the same time, those events often implicate guilty human failure as well, for example, the human responsibility for climate change resulting in destruction of the Great Barrier Reef as well as increasing the devastation of floods in poorer countries such as Bangladesh.

worthy of further development.[34] He did not, however, address the question of how a theology of human culpability for the origins of personal and social sin and radical alienation from God is to be understood in the context of evolutionary biology and current discussions of whether other creatures may have capacities not only for altruism and compassion, but also for ethical agency.

A further contribution of Schillebeeckx's theological anthropology is his emphasis on the Pauline insight that in the face of the overwhelming impact of evil and the sin of the world, "grace abounds still more" in the mode of forgiveness (Rom 5:20). The deepest alienation and cause of human suffering, he suggests, are precisely alienation from God. That radical alienation can be overcome only by a love that is not only free gift, but also forgiving and reconciling—a sheer gift of divine mercy which lies beyond the capacity of human imagination. Hence the importance of the Pauline insight that human beings are the recipients of the forgiveness of sins and the outpouring of God's love "while we were still sinners" (Rom 5:8). Those who participate in that kind of gratuitous and forgiving love abide in God and God in them. In a particular way, human flourishing is to be found in fragmentary ways of restoring broken relationships and furthering reconciliation in a world of injustice and violence.

## Anthropology and ethics

As the Dutch title of Schillebeeckx's *Christ* volume makes clear, if God's free and forgiving love is to be recognized in our day, it needs to be named and enacted not only as love and grace, but also as justice and liberation. The political, ethical, and practical dimensions of Schillebeeckx's anthropology are clear in his consistent return to the fundamental insight that God's saving grace is always mediated in human history via the exercise of human freedom, the bonds of human relationships, and social structures and political activity which fosters the future of human persons, especially the most vulnerable, as well as of other creatures and the Earth. Thus, he argues that the freedom of the children of God is not solely a matter of the liberation of persons from sin and all that binds the human spirit, although that is an essential and often ignored dimension of human freedom, but it also involves interpersonal reconciliation and social liberation. Love is not only a matter of the heart; it involves concern situated for human bodies and for vulnerable creatures and social structures which protect their well-being. Drawing on his theology of creation, he remarks that the sheer gift of God's love and forgiveness is at the same time a charge to human beings to make that grace visible and concrete in human life and historical structures that humanize and demonstrate a concrete care for the rest of creation.[35]

---

[34] Schillebeeckx, *Christ*, 720–22 [728–29]. For Schillebeeckx's discussion of the Christian doctrine of original sin as a hopeful one, see Schillebeeckx, "The New Critical Theory and Theological Hermeneutics," *UF, CW* vol. 5 (London: Bloomsbury T&T Clark, 2014), 130–31 [149–50]. He argues there that the doctrine expresses not only the human need for redemption, but also "the conviction that the human situation not only can, but must be, different in Christ, and that this change takes place in human history." From that perspective, he argued that "the dogma of original sin 'enshrines critical negativity, but does this when within the positive sphere of understanding of the promise, which has then to be constitutively linked to Christian praxis.'"

[35] Schillebeeckx underlines the importance of this ethical action on behalf of the *humanum* and the Earth when he writes, "It is to the human action of doing good that God gives an unexpected future in which his forgiveness plays a major role." (Schillebeeckx, *Christ*, 789 [792–93]).

Although earthly efforts and liberation and humanization are not identical with God's eschatological salvation, they are the necessary fragments of a history of salvation, which the living God will transform and multiply in the final coming of the kingdom of God. The great risk of God as Creator has been to entrust humankind with the historical project of making the history of salvation (the kingdom of God) a concrete reality in every time and culture.[36]

## The contemplative dimension of human life

Ethical activity, as described concretely, for example, in Matthew 25, remains the primary and most dense mediation of God's saving presence. But for the Christian, it is faith in God's absolute creative and saving presence that provides the critical and productive power which inspires and sustains believers to be active on behalf of humankind and the Earth, working to give evidence that God's will for humankind and for all of creation is "life in abundance" (Jn 10:10). Awareness of God's surprising and utterly gratuitous compassion evokes another essential dimension of human life—gratitude which for believers also leads to praise. Schillebeeckx's anthropology has a strong political and ethical accent, but at the same time, he underlines the mystical and contemplative dimension of being human. Recognition that human efforts alone cannot bring about final salvation, but that the good news is that the Creator God is at work in and through those finite efforts and in spite of human failure is what Schillebeeckx describes as "the mystical power of faith"—an awareness of the immediacy of the presence of God which at the same time remains always a form of "mediated immediacy." In Schillebeeckx's reading, experience of God is available only in the darkness of faith, the "hope against hope" that trusts that "despite everything, goodness and mercy have me, all of us, in their grasp."[37] Likewise even profound experiences of joy or overwhelming love can be disclosures of divine love, but in and through the human experience which goes beyond explanation. In that context, prayer can be viewed as the human search for the presence of the transcendent God who remains the mystery that is too immanent to ever be experienced directly. Because God's absolute nearness transcends human experience and categories of expression Schillebeeckx refers to prayer as, on the one hand, the playful search for God—a "game of hide and seek"—and, on the other hand, "not so much meditation as conversion."[38]

Because there is always a dimension of darkness in the experience of the hidden God, the quest of prayer is an ongoing radical act of faith made often in situations of utter impasse where God's presence is perceived only as a "black hole" or "a wall."[39] Nevertheless the contemplative dimension of human life remains the source of creative and prophetic energy for action on behalf

---

[36] In addition to "The New Image of God," in *GFM* see "Kingdom of God: Creation and Salvation," in *IR*, 93–108 [105–24]; "I Believe in God, Creator of Heaven and Earth," *God Among Us*: The Gospel Proclaimed (New York: Crossroad, 1983), 90–102, and "Doubt in God's Omnipotence: 'When Bad Things Happen to Good People,'" *For the Sake of the Gospel* (New York: Crossroad, 1990), 88–102.

[37] Schillebeeckx, *Christ*, 811 [815].

[38] Ibid., 812–13 [816–17].

[39] Schillebeeckx, *Church*, 69 [70]. For a contemporary discussion of impasse in relation to the notion of "dark night" in the mystical writings of John of the Cross, see Constance FitzGerald, OCD, "Impasse and Dark Night," *Living with Apocalypse: Spiritual Resources for Social Compassion*, ed. Tilden Edwards (San Francisco: Harper and Row, 1984).

of the reign of God at the same time that it includes awareness of the limits and failures of human persons and communities. Here, Schillebeeckx returns to his analysis of experiences of human suffering and specifically negative contrast experiences to probe the unique pathic epistemological power which they hold. Experiences of injustice and protest are neither contemplative celebrations of universal reconciliation nor demonstrations of the power of human controlling knowledge and activity. But in an inchoate way they link the two. The protest and resistance which arises amid experiences of injustice and violations of the *humanum* reveal an implicit longing for liberation and happiness and hope of a better future. That contemplative hope gives rise to the ethical action necessary to begin to mediate that future.

# Revisiting Schillebeeckx's sacramental vision: The story of Jesus shapes the human story

Schillebeeckx's conviction that the story of Jesus provides the fullest vision of human flourishing was at the heart of the sacramental project, which he outlined in his final years. As ritual remembrances of the life, death, and resurrection of Jesus, sacramental celebrations form the imagination and ethical visions of human communities of faith in what Christians believe to be God's vision for human life in abundance—the story of Jesus. Precisely because human beings are bodily, historical, and social, Schillebeeckx emphasized the need for bodily, communal, and social sacramental rituals to shape the human imagination in the form of God's vision of humanity and to prompt human action in service of the reign of God. In his view sacramental celebrations as ritual performances of faith have everything to do with life in the world because when the Christian community gathers to remember and celebrate the life, death, and resurrection of Jesus, those gathered also anticipate what human life is meant to be. The community is formed and challenged by the ritual it performs.

These forms of living remembrance of the life, death, and resurrection of Jesus are sources not only of deepening eschatological hope, but also of renewed engagement in the world, including resistance to all that falls short of the vision of human life and of care for the Earth which were at the center of Jesus's preaching of the reign of God. For that reason, sacramental celebrations rooted in the hope of Jesus's resurrection irritate as well as inspire because they serve as the ultimate critique of, and resistance to, any form of violation of human beings or of God's beloved creation. The critical and productive force of Christian faith reaches an intensity and clarity which impels the community to action. Schillebeeckx was aware that the liturgical vision which he described was itself necessarily incarnated in concrete historical and ecclesial communities and forms which fell short of this vision, yet he remained confident that the eschatological vision of God's kingdom transcends the limitations and betrayals of human communities and ministers.[40]

As celebrations of Jesus's vision of the reign of God "distilled to ritual," sacramental celebrations are at the same time a performance of Christian anthropology—a dramatic rehearsal of the final human hope. From the perspective of Christian faith, that eschatological hope can be described only in the language of biblical promises of God's final defeat of evil and therefore the

---

[40]  Edward Schillebeeckx, "Rediscovery of the Christian Sacraments," *Essays, CW* vol. 11 (London: Bloomsbury T&T Clark, 2014), 183–210, esp. 208.

absence of suffering, tears, and pain (Rev 21:4) and in the metaphorical language of "resurrection of the body" as the flourishing of human persons, the coming of the "kingdom of God" as the transformation of human relationships and societies, and a "new heavens and a new earth" symbolizing the inclusion of all creatures, the Earth, and the entire cosmos in communion with the living God.[41] In Schillebeeckx's view, it is those metaphors which provide the best clues to "God's grand dream for the future of humankind [...] living in peace and joy with all their fellow creatures even here on earth."[42]

---

[41] Edward Schillebeeckx "Theological Quests," *Essays, CW* vol. 11 (London: Bloomsbury T&T Clark, 2014), 158–61. See also Edward Schillebeeckx, *On Christian Faith: The Spiritual, Ethical, and Political Dimensions* (New York: Crossroad, 1987) 29–30 (Dutch 1986); Schillebeeckx, *Church*, 130–32 [132–34]. From the perspective of Christian faith he adds a fourth metaphor of the "parousia of Jesus Christ" in which Jesus's normative significance will be evident to all. In *Church*, Schillebeeckx remained open to the notion that newer metaphors might capture the classic significance of these biblical metaphors (p. 132 [134]) another worthy project for contemporary theological anthropology.

[42] Schillebeeckx, "Theological Quests," *Essays*, 158–59.

# Chapter 19

# Christ and Grace

## Christiane Alpers

What does it mean to talk of a graced world at present? Many Western contemporaries, if not discounting the question outright as irrelevant, might associate talk of a graced world with a politically quietist ignorance of injustices, suffering, and pain, reminiscent of Karl Marx's "opium for the people." Instead of calling the world graced, people are expected to act in a morally good way, to make this world into a better place. Somewhat counterintuitively, when seen against this background, the most prominent protagonists of the Roman Catholic Church's theological renewal in the twentieth century all agreed that perceiving the world as graced, far from being a mere intellectual speculation, was of the utmost socio-political importance. When asked what it means that the world is graced, however, different *Ressourcement* theologians provided rather divergent answers, leading to internal disputes within what might otherwise have been conceived as a more homogenous theological movement.

Henri de Lubac's objection to the neoscholastic separation of a theologically neutral world from grace has received much attention, as it has been prominently developed, on the one hand, by Radical Orthodoxy as well as by contemporary heirs of the Second Vatican Council's *Communio* group, and, on the other hand, fiercely criticized by certain neo-Thomists.[1] In order to complement the picture, this chapter highlights Edward Schillebeeckx's particular contribution to the controversy.[2] More specifically, I contest the common view that Schillebeeckx differs from *Ressourcement* theologies as well as from neo-Thomism, due to his supposed wholesale

I would like to thank Josh Furnal for his helpful comments on an earlier draft of this chapter.

[1]   Cf. Thomas J. Bushlack, "The Return of Neo-Scholasticism? Recent Criticisms of Henri de Lubac on Nature and Grace and Their Significance for Moral Theology, Politics, and Law," *Journal of the Society of Christian Ethics* 35 (2015), 83–100; Lawrence Feingold, *The Natural Desire to See God According to St. Thomas Aquinas and His Interpreters*, 2nd ed. (Ave Maria, FL: Sapienta Press, 2004); Reinhard Hütter, "Aquinas on the Natural Desire for the Vision of God: A Relecture of Summa contra Gentiles III, c. 25 après Henri de Lubac," *The Thomist* 73 (2009), 573–79; Steven A. Long, "On the Possibility of a Purely Natural End for Man," *The Thomist* 64 (2000), 211–37; Bernard Mulcahy, *Aquinas's Notion of Pure Nature and the Christian Integralism of Henry de Lubac: Not Everything Is Grace* (New York: Peter Lang, 2011).

[2]   Erik Borgman's *Leven van wat komt: Een katholiek uitzicht op de samenleving* (Utrecht: Meinema, 2017) is presently the most important proposal of the contemporary political relevance of Schillebeeckx's theology of grace, as outlined in this chapter. See also Stephan van Erp, "World and Sacrament: Foundations of the Political Theology of the Church," *Louvain Studies* 39 (2016), 100–18.

adaptation of theology to modern culture.[3] According to my interpretation, Schillebeeckx's approach to modernity should be classified as Christocentric. As such, his approach is not any less theologically responsible than de Lubac's. The differences between them stem from Christological disagreements, most prominently about the way in which eschatological salvation in Christ differs from immanent progress. Far from merely affirming modernity, with its denial of God and concomitant trust in humanity, Schillebeeckx's engagement with secular culture is motivated by a thoroughly theocentric vision of communion with God in a sinful world.

# I. Christological critiques of the separation of nature from Grace

It is beyond dispute that Roman Catholic debates about nature and grace in the twentieth century have been of great importance for remodeling the church's relation to the world, as it has been documented at the Second Vatican Council and hotly debated ever since.[4] Dissatisfied by the authoritarian church of their time, its lack of lay involvement, and its failure to resist the state's totalitarianism, *Ressourcement* theologians did not search for solutions to these ecclesial problems in secular society, as they were convinced that society itself was as deeply entangled in these problems as the church. An authoritarian church, detached from worldly affairs, and a self-sufficient world, with no regard for ecclesial authority were seen as the two sides of the same theological error: the neoscholastic construal of a scheme of two parallel orders: one natural and

---

[3] See Tracey Rowland, *Catholic Theology* (London: Bloomsbury T&T Clark, 2017), 94. Schillebeeckx's theology of grace has been praised by some for providing a significant gateway for contemporary theological engagements with a secular world (Robert J. Schreiter, "Indicators of the Future of Theology in the Works of Edward Schillebeeckx," *Edward Schillebeeckx: Impulse für Theologien im 21. Jahrhundert/Impetus Towards Theologies in the 21st Century*, ed. Thomas Eggensperger, Ulrich Engel and Angel F. Méndez Montoya (Ostfildern: Matthias Grünewaldverlag, 2008), 34; Mary Catherine Hilkert, "'Grace-Optimism': The Spirituality at the Heart of Schillebeeckx's Theology," *Spirituality Today* 43 (1991), 220–39 (available at http://www.spiritualitytoday.org/spir2day/91433hilkert.html); Erik Borgman, *Edward Schillebeeckx: A Theologian in His History*, trans. John Bowden (London/ New York: Continuum, 2003), 57; Philip Kennedy, *Schillebeeckx* (Collegeville, MN: Liturgical Press, 1993), 135; Stephan van Erp, "The Sacrament of the World: Thinking God's Presence Beyond Public Theology," *ET Studies* 6 (2015), 128. Yet, no one has systematically defended Schillebeeckx's understanding of grace against the accusation of being a theologically irresponsible adaptation of theology to secular trends.

[4] Hans Boersma, "Sacramental Ontology: Nature and the Supernatural in the Ecclesiology of Henri de Lubac," *New Blackfriars* 88 (2007), 249; Hans Boersma, "Nature and the Supernatural in *la nouvelle théologie*: The Recovery of a Sacramental Mindset," *New Blackfriars* 93 (2011), 35; Gabriel Flynn, "Introduction: The Twentieth-Century Renaissance in Catholic Theology," *Ressourcement: A Movement for Renewal in Twentieth Century Catholic Theology*, ed. Gabriel Flynn and Paul D. Murray (Oxford: Oxford University Press, 2011), 11–12; Sean Larsen, "The Politics of Desire: Two Readings of Henri de Lubac on Nature and Grace," *Modern Theology* 29 (2013), 279–310.

the other supernatural.[5] This scheme placed human beings squarely within the natural order, elevated into the order of salvation only with the help of the additional gift of God's supernatural grace. Humans, according to this conception, can be fulfilled within this world, and the gift of supernatural salvation is an additional extra, offered by God to those redeemed in Christ.

Viewed from a systematic perspective, the neoscholastic separation of nature and grace was motivated by two complementary anxieties: first, an anxiety not to put constrains on God's limitless freedom by human desires.[6] Supernatural revelation, stemming from God's free decision, was separated from the sphere of nature wherein human beings could perfectly know natural truths about this world by the powers of their intellect. In order to access the supernatural truths about salvation, they relied entirely upon God's revelation, as transmitted by the official church.[7] An implied second "anxiety" concerned the assurance of God's salvation which could be definitively known once supernatural revelation had been clearly separated from the messiness of the natural realm.

Both Edward Schillebeeckx and the first generation of *Ressourcement* theologians rejected this strict separation of nature and the supernatural, and they did so for Christological reasons.[8] Whereas neoscholastics understood the tradition of the church as the guardian of the supernatural truths of faith, preserved in eternally fixed doctrinal systems, *Ressourcement* theologians explored the core Christian conviction that, in Christ, God has become incarnate in history. This rendered the study of contemporary society an integral element to any Christian understanding of the supernatural truths of faith. The free sovereignty of a God who risked entering the messiness of history did not have to be protected from human thoughts by an anxious church. At the same time, if that same God's revelation had been inseparably interwoven with frail human attempts at faithful responses from the start, then the church could not offer any unambiguous proof of God's salvation to an anxious world. Acknowledging the centrality of Christ's Incarnation for any Christian understanding of truth and salvation requires that nature be interpreted not as a self-sustaining sphere but as intricately interwoven with the supernatural.

Having deemed the model of a "self-sustaining" modern secular sphere as theologically problematic, *Ressourcement* theologians did not look at developments in secular society to renew the church. Instead, they re-examined the Christian tradition as an abundant wellspring of riches, of which only some have been emphasized in the actual course of Western history.[9] The solution to contemporary impasses was sought in the Catholic tradition's suppressed undercurrents,

---

[5] Boersma, "Nature and the Supernatural," 36; Edward T. Oakes, *A Theology of Grace in Six Controversies* (Grand Rapid, MI: Eerdmans, 2016), 19; Gerard Loughlin, "Nouvelle Théologie: A Return to Modernism?," *Ressourcement: A Movement for Renewal in Twentieth Century Catholic Theology*, ed. Gabriel Flynn and Paul D. Murray (Oxford: Oxford University Press, 2011), 44–45.

[6] Fergus Kerr, *Twentieth Century Catholic Theologians* (Oxford: Blackwell Publishing, 2007), 73.

[7] Ibid., 1–16.

[8] Stephen J. Duffy, *The Graced Horizon: Nature and Grace in Modern Catholic Thought* (Collegeville, MN: The Liturgical Press), 53.

[9] Henri de Lubac, *Paradoxes of Faith* (San Francisco: Ignatius Press, 1987), 57–58. For a presentation of de Lubac's spiritual exegesis of Scripture and the Church Fathers as a critical alternative to a "historicist" understanding of Christian sources, see Thomas P. Harmon, "Historicism Versus History and Spirit: Henri de Lubac on What We Can Learn from Studying Origen," *Logos: A Journal of Catholic Thought and Culture* 19 (2016), 29–58; David Grumett, "Henri de Lubac: Looking for Books to Read the World," *Ressourcement: A Movement for Renewal in Twentieth Century Catholic Theology*, ed. Gabriel Flynn and Paul D. Murray (Oxford: Oxford University Press, 2011), 236–49.

underneath the pronounced neoscholastic confinement of that same tradition into one reductive stream.[10] *Ressourcement* theologians challenged the church's political quietism under the neoscholastic paradigm by highlighting the paradoxical relationship of nature and grace instead of associating Christianity's particular domain of supernatural grace exclusively with the intra-ecclesial sphere. According to the *Ressourcement* interpretation, laypeople should understand their daily lives within the "natural" sphere and the political challenges of society as pertaining to the realm of salvation, allowing the superabundant reality of the supernatural to complete the redemption of this world from its fallenness.

# II. Modern progress and eschatological redemption

Despite the shared Christocentric corrective to the neoscholastic two-layer scheme, there had been disagreements within the *Ressourcement* movement about how precisely the interwoveness of nature and grace should be conceived. In general, certain theologians focused more on ascent of nature to the supernatural, others more on the descent of the supernatural into nature.[11] As most prominent promoter of the first view, Henri de Lubac asked how nature always already points towards its supernatural salvation. Schillebeeckx regarded nature and supernature as interwoven from the opposite direction. He asked mainly how supernatural grace is sacramentally present in the immanent world.[12]

To overcome the neoscholastic understanding of supernatural grace as something extrinsically superadded to nature, de Lubac reconceived of all humankind as endowed with a natural desire for the supernatural.[13] This natural desire provides the necessary continuity between the secular world and the church, enabling Christianity to offer its supernatural truths of salvation as something meaningful and relevant to a humanity that naturally longs for God.[14] Especially after the Second Vatican Council, de Lubac emphasized the inability of atheism to satisfy humankind's deepest and most far-reaching desires. Far from constituting a satisfactory sphere for human

---

[10] A.N. Williams, "The Future of the Past: The Contemporary Significance of the Nouvelle Théologie," *International Journal of Systematic Theology* 7 (2005), 347–61. For a critical comparison of de Lubac's hermeneutic of continuity and Michel de Certeau's hermeneutic of rupture, when relating the Patristic past to the present, see Brenna Moore, "How to Awaken the Dead: Michel de Certeau, Henri de Lubac, and the Instabilities Between the Past and the Present," *Spiritus: A Journal of Christian Spirituality* 12 (2012), 172–79.

[11] Whereas de Lubac emphasized more the way in which divine grace elevates human beings to unprecedented heights, Marie-Dominique Chenu and Hans Urs von Balthasar focused more on the ways in which nature is always already graced. See, Boersma, "Nature and the Supernatural," 34.

[12] For Schillebeeckx's self-positioning in twentieth century debates about nature and grace, see especially Edward Schillebeeckx, "Arabisch-Neoplatoonse achtergrond van Thomas' opvatting over de ontvankelijkheid van de mens voor de genade," *Bijdragen* 35 (1974), 298–308, and Edward Schillebeeckx, "The Non-Conceptual Intellectual Element," *RT, CW* vol. 2 (London: Bloomsbury T&T Clark, 2014), 239–68 [II 30–75]. For a discussion of the latter see the chapter "Grace as Intersubjective Relationship: The Personalism of Juan Alfaro and Edward Schillebeeckx," Duffy, *The Graced Horizon*, 145–68.

[13] Henri de Lubac, "Duplex Homini Beatitudo," *Communio* 35 (2008), 599–612.

[14] Henri de Lubac, *A Brief Catechesis on Nature and Grace* (San Francisco: Ignatius Press, 1984), 40.

beings to abide in, a purely immanent world is but a vale of tears, echoing back and forth humankind's unheard yearning and groaning. The church must hear these cries and offer Christ as salvation to a world, which otherwise lies in waste.[15] De Lubac associated the church's socio-political relevance with its promise that the whole world's desires will (only) be fulfilled in Christ. This should motivate people to continuously improve the world without ever accepting any rest or final contentment.[16] This "thoroughly Christocentric"[17] vision of redemption had the church follow its calling more faithfully, to be the meeting point of God's descent into the world and humankind's ascent to God, from which God's supernatural grace might radiate into the secular sphere.[18]

Some place de Lubac's Christocentrism against Schillebeeckx's alleged overarching concern to render the church acceptable to a modern society, with a consequent reductive adaptation of the Christian faith to contemporary trends.[19] It is true that, compared to de Lubac, Schillebeeckx conceives of the world somewhat more positively, as always already pervaded by God's grace, due to God's unconditional "yes" to human history in Christ's resurrection.[20] However, this stress on God's descent into history is seldom considered as itself a conviction inspired by the desire to be faithful to the God revealed in Jesus Christ, and more often as the weak capitulation to a secular culture that is confident in its own achievements and can no longer believe in God.[21] Schillebeeckx's understanding of grace is suspected of being infected by a naïve belief in the modern myth of progress, according to which the world's immanent developments provide sufficient grounds for hope, since this development will supposedly fulfil every human dream and aspiration.

Such an adaptation of theology to modern culture is believed to be problematic insofar as it risks losing sight of the church's most distinct ability to serve a world in need.[22] The atheist worldview might have become so powerful that the church could no longer resist it, thereby losing its ability to offer any meaningful alternative to interpret, be, and act in the world. In this case, the church would render itself ultimately superfluous.[23] According to de Lubac, it is

---

[15]  Nicholas J. Healy, "Henri de Lubac on Nature and Grace: A Note on Some Recent Contributions," *Communio* 35 (2008), 564; Aidan Nichols, "Henri de Lubac: Panorama and Proposal," *New Blackfriars* 93 (2012), 18; Francesca A. Murphy, "De Lubac, Grace, Politics and Paradox," *Studies in Christian Ethics* 23 (2010), 429–30.

[16]  Kerr, *Twentieth Century Catholic Theologians*, 75.

[17]  Rowland, *Catholic Theology*, 107. See also Noel O'Sullivan, *Christ and Creation: Christology as the Key to Interpreting the Theology of Creation in the Works of Henri de Lubac* (Bern: Peter Lang, 2009).

[18]  Boersma, "Sacramental Ontology," 243, 262, 270–71; Henri de Lubac, *The Splendor of the Church*, trans. Michael Mason (San Francisco: Ingnatius Press, 1999), 131–33, 142, 152. See also, Henri De Lubac, *Corpus Mysticum: The Eucharist and the Church in the Middle Ages: Historical survey*, trans. Simmonds Gemma, ed. Laurence Paul Hemming and Susan Frank Parsons (London: SCM Press, 2006), 249–51.

[19]  Rowland, *Catholic Theology*, 157–58, 164–65.

[20]  Schillebeeckx is cited on this point by De Lubac in *A Brief Catechesis*, 192. Edward Schillebeeckx, *Le monde et l'Église*, Approches théologiques vol. 3 (Brussels/Paris: Editions du C.E.P., 1967), 145–49. This is the French translation of: Edward Schillebeeckx, "The Sorrow of the Experience of God's Concealment," *WC, CW* vol. 4 (London: Bloomsbury T&T Clark, 2014), 69–72 [91–95].

[21]  Boersma, "Sacramental Ontology," 249–50; Kerr, *Twentieth Century Catholic Theologians*, 77.

[22]  De Lubac, *A Brief Catechesis*, 205, n. 26.

[23]  William Hill, "Schillebeeckx's New Look at Secularity: A Note," *The Thomist* 33 (1969), 164–69.

precisely part of the human fallenness to be unable to see that all developments in the modern world, instead of leading towards and culminating in God's eschatological kingdom, are themselves in vain.[24] The worldly valley is so dark that people cannot even see anymore that their destiny is disproportionately higher, and that, when trusting in immanent progress, they put their hopes in realities that can never satisfy their innermost thirst.[25] Schillebeeckx might betray humankind's loftier aspirations when failing to envision the Kingdom of God as anything more radically different in kind from historical progress.[26] According to de Lubac, Schillebeeckx fails to acknowledge that Christianity's spiritual vision enables people to pierce through appearances and to see everywhere in the visible world a symbol of the invisible.[27] Only through the recognition of the contours of nature's eschatological elevation is the church truly a redemptive sacrament for the world.[28] Contrary to the view that Schillebeeckx unconcerned about faithfulness to the Christian tradition, opportunistically joined the modern rejection of the Church's hierarchical structure and enthusiasm for a natural sphere independent from any supernatural realm,[29] I interpret Schillebeeckx's engagement with the modern world as being motivated by a specific Christocentrism. According to Schillebeeckx, the world's eschatological fulfillment is not any less, but perhaps even more different in kind from natural progress, than de Lubac would have it.

## The Christological depths of finitude

Overall, de Lubac and Schillebeeckx were in fundamental agreement regarding their affirmation that the world is graced as well as in their shared refusal to regard nature as a realm independent from God. Moreover, they both regarded human beings as graced with a particular relation to God in comparison with other creatures.[30] Not dissimilar to de Lubac's reference to the church as providing the light for a world that otherwise does not even know its own innermost desire,

---

[24] Boersma, "Sacramental Ontology," 271.

[25] Henri de Lubac, *Catholicism: Christ and the Common Destiny of Man*, trans. Lancelot C. Sheppard and Elizabeth Englund (San Francisco: Ignatius, 1988), 368. Radical Orthodoxy's founder John Milbank further elaborates the criticism that atheistic humanism's lack of any explicit reference to the supernatural leads to a culture aimed solely at the preservation of humankind's animalistic nature, and that only a culture aimed at supernatural salvation could push humankind to the cultural heights of maximum bodily and spiritual flourishing. See, John Milbank, *The Suspended Middle: Henri de Lubac and the Debate Concerning the Supernatural* (London: SCM Press, 2005), 9, 21.

[26] De Lubac, *A Brief Catechesis*, 228.

[27] Ibid., 214–15.

[28] Ibid., 205, n. 26.

[29] Rowland, *Catholic Theology*, 94, 155–56. For a more positive, but in my estimation equally mistaken evaluation of Schillebeeckx's supposed anthropocentric Soteriology, see Michael Stickelbroeck, *Das Heil des Menschen als Gnade* (Regensburg: Friedrich Pustet, 2014), 21–23.

[30] Henri de Lubac, *The Mystery of the Supernatural*, trans. Rosemary Sheed (New York: Herder and Herder, 1967), 102–16; Edward Schillebeeckx, *Christ, CW* vol. 7 (London: Bloomsbury T&T Clark, 2014), 503–04 [515–16], 508–11 [520–22], 519 [531]; see also Edward Schillebeeckx, "The Tridentine Decree on Justification," *Concilium* 1 (1965), 173–76. One element that distinguished Schillebeeckx from other *Ressourcement* theologians who drew mainly on Patristic texts is that Schillebeeckx mainly examines biblical understandings of grace. Kerr, *Twentieth-Century Catholic Theologians*, 66; Philip Kennedy, "Human Beings as the Story of God: Schillebeeckx's Third Christology," *New Blackfriars* 71 (1990), 120–31.

Schillebeeckx argues that sinful humanity has brought disorder into God's good creation, and therefore needs God's salvific light to recognize the offered graces.[31] However, when turning to the biblical identification of God's salvific light with Jesus Christ, Schillebeeckx adds an important qualification to the logic of de Lubac's argument.

According to Schillebeeckx, human beings can, by the strength of their natural intellect, know that human knowledge remains limited insofar as it cannot surpass the world.[32] Human beings experience this as lack and recognize their need for divine wisdom in order to surpass natural limitations of the human intellect. De Lubac interprets this certain mismatch between the finite world and the human intellect as a wound inscribed in human nature which can never be healed, and which, precisely for that reason, inspires the elevation of this world through human culture,[33] but to let it participate in the intellect's surpassing of this world, effecting the world's continuous transformation.[34] Despite this association of the *human* intellect with this world's elevation to supernatural heights, de Lubac remains theocentric. The tension with the finite world acts as dynamic inspiration to transform the world but only because God guarantees that this process of infinitizing the world is not in vain. God promises to heal the wound of human dissatisfaction with the world at the eschaton.[35]

Schillebeeckx also associates the Incarnation of God in the humanity in Christ with an "opening up to us [of] the deepest possibilities for our own life," and he is therefore as unconcerned as de Lubac with the neoscholastic need to strictly separate theocentrism from anthropocentrism. This is evident when he argues that "*in this* God is expressed. The divine revelation accomplished in Jesus directs us to the mystery of man [*sic*]."[36] Yet, for de Lubac, it is the experience of lack, and of an unsurpassable tension between human life in this world and eschatological salvation which constitutes the fundamental entrance point for assenting to the Christian faith in a salvific God and the engine that motivates people to transform culture. In Schillebeeckx's argument, it is more central that the eschaton has already been initiated in the corporeal life of Jesus Christ.[37] This reverses the relationship between lack and fulfillment: instead of focussing on the feeling of discontent with this finite world and God's supernatural gift of fulfillment, Christian cultural engagement begins with the anticipatory experience of eschatological fulfillment in the present world. This disassociates the human experience of the world as lacking the principle to satisfy human desires from discontent with the world, a denigration of finitude, associating it instead with humanity's short-sightedness.[38] Instead of inspiring the intellect to "infinitize"

---

[31] Schillebeeckx, *Christ*, 511–12 [523].

[32] Ibid., 546–48 [556–57].

[33] De Lubac, *Mystery of the Supernatural*, 102–08; Henri de Lubac, *Vom Erkennen Gottes*, trans. Robert Scherer (Freiburg: Herder, 1949), 106–08.

[34] Henri De Lubac, "The total Meaning of Man and the World," *Communio* 35 (2008), 616–20, 633.

[35] Henri de Lubac, "Duplex Homini Beatitudo," *Communio* 35 (2008), 611.

[36] Schillebeeckx, *Christ*, 64 [76].

[37] Ibid., 547–48 [557].

[38] When confronted with the complaints of his contemporaries concerning God's righteousness, Jesus stresses that God's righteousness indeed differs from their expectations. See, Schillebeeckx, *Christ*, 532–33 [542]. This corresponds to the Thomistic rejection of any faulty desire to become like God, perhaps implied by a person's experience of being as a quantifiable lack See, Tina Beattie, "Deforming God: Why Nothing Really Matters. A Lacanian Reading of Thomas Aquinas," *New Blackfriars* 95 (2014), 229–30.

this world, God saves humanity by reverting the human intellect to the world, allowing it to detect infinite depths within finitude. In this respect, it would be misleading to account for the differences between Schillebeeckx and de Lubac by appealing to the Schillebeeckx's reliance on the "Aristotelian" Thomas Aquinas, and de Lubac's reliance on the "Platonist" Augustine.[39] As Rowan Williams has shown, Augustine's perspective differs from Platonism precisely due to Augustine's commitment to the Christologically motivated search for wisdom within the world.[40] Furthermore, Schillebeeckx also rejects one-sided associations of Aquinas with Aristotelianism. He specifically points to the Neoplatonic aspects of Aquinas's work.[41] Therefore, any easy dualism between Thomist and Augustinian approaches in Schillebeeckx and de Lubac would be inaccurate.

Whereas de Lubac criticizes modern people's forgetfulness of their innermost desire for eschatological salvation, Schillebeeckx doubts that there can be such a straightforward criticism of modern atheists. Here, the anticipatory experience of eschatological fulfilment in the present world is not a general element of human nature, but it is enjoyed only by those whose intellect has been transformed through an encounter with Jesus Christ.[42] By being recreated in Christ, a human being's life, thoughts, psyche, and senses are so transformed that one's outlook is changed.[43] Humans can naturally recognize the need for divine salvation by the strength of their intellect. However, God's surprising offer of salvation in Christ first frustrates and then fulfills in a way that there is no natural transition from human expectation to divine gift.[44] In Christ, God reveals that the world, with its limitations, is good, an insight

---

[39] Cf. David Grumett, "De Lubac, Grace, and the Pure Nature Debate," *Modern Theology* 31 (2015), 123–46).

[40] Rowan Williams, "Wisdom in Person: Augustine's Christology," *On Augustine* (London: Bloomsbury, 2016), 141–54.

[41] Schillebeeckx, "Arabisch-neoplatoonse achtergrond van Thomas' opvatting over de ontvangelijkheid van de mens voor de genade," *Bijdragen: Tijdschrift voor Filosofie en Theologie* 35 (1974), 298–308.

[42] Schillebeeckx, *Christ*, 519–20 [531], 533–34 [543]; Edward Schillebeeckx, *Jesus, CW* vol. 6 (London: Bloomsbury T&T Clark, 2014), 125 [145–46].

[43] Schillebeeckx, *Christ*, 519–20 [531–32]: "Natural and all too-human attitudes" are being transformed through grace.

[44] Ibid., 4 [20]. Here, Schillebeeckx is very close to Karl Rahner's criticism of de Lubac, wherein de Lubac assumes too much continuity between nature and grace. The result is that God will have to offer whatever human beings desire. See, David Schindler, "Introduction to the 1998 Edition," *The Mystery of the Supernatural*, Henri de Lubac (New York: Herder & Herder), xxiii; Duffy, *The Graced Horizon*, 86, 89, 99, 104; Neil Ormerod, "The Nature-Grace Distinction and the Construction of a Systematic Theology," *Theological Studies* 75 (2014), 525–27. In order to better highlight the gratuity of supernatural grace in the sense of its non-necessity from the perspective of nature, Rahner reconceived of de Lubac's natural desire for the supernatural in terms of a supernatural desire for the supernatural, which is nonetheless present in all human beings. See, Karl Rahner, "Nature and Grace," *Theological Investigations*, trans. Kevin Smyth, vol. 4 (London: Darton, Longman & Todd, 1966), 178–82. Schillebeeckx likewise acknowledged the possibility that God's offer of grace might differ from humankind's natural expectations. See, Schillebeeckx, *Christ*, 514–15 [526]. He calls the elevation of humankind into the supernatural sphere a mystery which cannot be proven by reason alone. See Edward Schillebeeckx, "De zin van het mens-zijn van Jesus, de Christus," *TvT* 2 (1962), 157.

that humankind is hardly able to acknowledge by its own strength.[45] Once converted, a person can pierce one level deeper through secular reality. Thus, Schillebeeckx describes the Christian mystic as someone who first undergoes a disintegrating "source experience," in which natural expectations are shattered, resulting in a purge of all certainties and perceptions.[46] After this initial experience, however, the mystic "gets everything back a hundredfold," and receives an "integrating and reconciling mercy with everything."[47] This is why Schillebeeckx associates mysticism with an impetus for dedication to the world, not a flight from the world. While de Lubac expects supernatural grace to elevate humankind out of this miserable vale of tears, Schillebeeckx challenges us to look a bit closer so that we do not prematurely overlook the traces that Christ has already left.

# III. Communion with God as eschatological salvation

Once the centrality of conversion in Schillebeeckx's Christology is acknowledged, it also becomes apparent that he did not identify modern progress with eschatological salvation. Instead, he envisioned eschatological salvation to be something rather different in kind, only to be recognized after conversion in Christ. More precisely, Schillebeeckx associated a human being's reception of supernatural grace, eschatological salvation, with living in friendship with God. In Christ, God offers to humankind the possibility of being taken up into an interpersonal communion with God already in this world.[48] That those accepting God's offer of salvation are enabled to judge the entire world in light of their experience of God[49] does not mean that they would perceive the world as already sanctified in its present state.[50] Far from affirming everything in this world as good, the Christian faith, according to Schillebeeckx, bears witness to the fact that "human life in the world [can be] experienced as an encounter and in this respect as a disclosure of God."[51] This is culturally transformative, as most explicitly evidenced by Schillebeeckx's contention that "prayer—and I think only prayer—gives Christian faith it's [*sic*] most critical and

---

[45]  According to Schillebeeckx, Jesus differs from apocalyptic and eschatological prophets of his day because he focused primarily on God's graciousness towards the world and not merely on God's judgement of the world. Schillebeeckx, *Jesus*, 116–20 [135–40], 123–24 [143–45].

[46]  Edward Schillebeeckx, *Jesus in Our Western Culture: Mysticism, Ethics and Politics*, trans. John Bowden (London: SCM Press, 1986), 68.

[47]  Ibid., 69.

[48]  Schillebeeckx, "De zin van het mens-zijn van Jesus," 130–33. In Christ, people can encounter God immediately, but this immediacy does not exclude worldly mediations, to the disappointment of some loftier expectations.

[49]  Schillebeeckx, *Christ*, 772–74 [775–76]. Schillebeeckx explains that "[*i*]n our human experiences we can *experience* something that transcends our experience and proclaims itself in that experience as unexpected grace." See ibid., 66 [78]. Emphasis original.

[50]  This is de Lubac's criticism in *A Brief Catechesis*, 219.

[51]  Schillebeeckx, *Christ*, 17–18 [32]. In this way, Schillebeeckx also understands the Christian expectation of life after death as grounded in "the *religious* depth of the present." "[L]ife *today*, in fellowship with God," allows one to already "gaze" into this eschatological future. See ibid., 796 [800]. Emphasis original.

productive force."[52] According to Schillebeeckx, it is not political theology but the prayer of the faithful that can change the face of the world.

Prayer is politically transformative insofar as it can influence God's concrete offer of salvation, and thereby the course of history. The gift of an interpersonal communion with God introduces a kind of reciprocity into God's relation of love towards the world.[53] Human prayer is valid before God in that God listens and reacts. In this sense, Schillebeeckx understands salvific grace as an explicit experience of dialogue with God.[54] There is an essential contrast with Hans Urs von Balthasar's more famous lament that theology as prayer has been replaced by a rationalistic theology, which emphasizes the importance of prayer by way of devaluing modernity.[55] For Schillebeeckx, on the other hand, prayer is most distinct from other human attempts at improving the world, inasmuch as it makes any such degradation of alternative ways of life in this world obsolete. Rather than ascribing responsibility for the shortcomings of contemporary culture and politics to clearly identify culprits, Christians are allowed to turn to God in prayer, and ask that the situation will be changed in a direction that is beneficial for everyone. If critics ask how this could make any difference, they may already have lost sight of the unsurpassable precious joy of living in prayerful communion with God.

This celebration of an already present relationship with God as a human being's anticipatory experience of eschatological salvation can lead to an even more radical conception of the difference in kind between innerworldly progress and eschatological salvation than is possible in de Lubac's theology. In Schillebeeckx's view, those who already experience communion with God now might not only be discontented with worldly achievements, but even with their personal desires for such achievements. The identification of salvation with a prayerful relationship to God might result in the human being's realization that one's natural expectations of salvation might have been mistaken, and need to be sacrificed.[56] Eschatological salvation is so radically different from immanent progress that humankind's elevation enables people to embrace an attitude of complete self-denial and openness to others.[57] Primarily, the recipients of grace are

---

52  Ibid., 813 [817]. For the most comprehensive elaboration of this claim, see David Ranson, *Between the "Mysticism of Politics" and the "Politics of Mysticism": Interpreting New Pathways of Holiness within the Roman Catholic Tradition* (Hindmarsh: ATF Theology, 2014).

53  Schillebeeckx, "De zin van het mens-zijn van Jesus," 132–33. Schillebeeckx stresses that theologians should not be preoccupied with protecting the absoluteness of God at the expense of acknowledging God's offer of reciprocity to humankind. This explains how, although Christ is objectively present in the Eucharist, the unbeliever has no access to this level of reality. Although Christ's real presence in the Eucharist does not depend on humankind's acceptance of it, this real presence, as an offer of reciprocity, can only become fully realized when it is accepted. Edward Schillebeeckx, "De eucharistische wijze van Christus' werkelijke tegenwoordigheid," *TvT* 6 (1966), 385–86.

54  Schillebeeckx, *Christ*, 77 [88].

55  Hans Urs von Balthasar, *Explorations in Theology II: Spouse of the Word* (San Francisco: Ignatius Press, 1991), 206; see also Marc Ouellet, "Paradox and/or supernatural existential," *Communio* 18 (1991), 279.

56  Schillebeeckx, "Het dominikaanse evenwicht," *Dominikaans Leven* 9 (1952–1953), 6–7.

57  Schillebeeckx, *Christ*, 520 [532]. Especially in his earlier years, Schillebeeckx stresses that humankind's elevation by supernatural grace is oftentimes a painful experience. Cf. Schillebeeckx, "Het dominikaanse evenwicht," 6–7.

called to serve all of humankind for God's sake.[58] Their communion with God makes them aware that the most fatal lack is not one's personal dissatisfaction with the finite world, but the fact that not all human beings experience a life in communion with God.[59]

## The modern myth of progress as opening to God

This indicates that, despite the stress on the difference in kind, of eschatological salvation, Schillebeeckx did not think that faith in communion with God was politically irrelevant or incommunicable to atheists. Yet, this communication would not begin with a critical accusation or pointing to what atheists unconsciously lack. Christians should not understand themselves as the graciously elected few out of a *"massa damnata,"* endowed with the task of enlightening an otherwise dark world.[60] Since Christians are most distinct from atheists only in the way in which they relate to reality, namely in prayerful communion with God, they are not any better equipped to see how to heal this broken world other than by inviting all people to commune with God.[61] Focussing on God's offer of grace as the only adequate cure for a fallen world's struggles, Schillebeeckx responded to modernity's disinterest in, and disillusionment with, faith in God not by highlighting what atheists lack. Rather, he directed both atheists and the church towards the grace already present within this world. This alone could motivate the world to pause in thankfulness and awe for the Creator, who has promised to heal all that remains wounded.[62] At the same time, it could also lead to a way for the church out of its current impasses, reminding the church that "[p]raying means looking for God. We need to understand that God is a living being who knows how to disappear now and then so that we keep on looking further for him, and how to appear for a moment now and then so that we do not get tired of looking."[63] Schillebeeckx reminded the church of his time that the prayerful Christian is called to look for the reality of salvation within this world, "as long as God is still there."[64]

---

58  Schillebeeckx, *Jesus*, 197 [222–23]; Schillebeeckx, *Christ*, 500–01 [513–14]. Here, Schillebeeckx more explicitly refers to the Christian task to liberate the world from injustice. Whereas de Lubac and von Balthasar present this ascetic embrace of self-denial as the converting event that allows Christians to enter communion with God, Schillebeeckx understands Christian self-denial as a *consequence* of having already been converted in the primarily joyful encounter with Christ. See de Lubac, *Splendor of the Church*, 258, 263; Schillebeeckx, *Christ*, 520 [532]. In this way, Schillebeeckx escapes contemporary criticisms of von Balthasar's understanding of Christianity as essentially kenotic. See Karen Kilby, *Balthasar: A (Very) Critical Introduction* (Grand Rapids, MI: Eerdmans, 2012); Linn Marie Tonstad, *God and Difference: The Trinity, Sexuality, and the Transformation of Finitude* (New York and London: Routledge, 2016).

59  Kathleen Anne McManus, *Unbroken Communion: The Place and Meaning of Suffering in the Theology of Edward Schillebeeckx* (Lanham, MD: Rowman & Littlefield, 2003), 103. Kathleen McManus's claim that "there simply is no other human context for understanding the nature of Christology apart from suffering" is suggestive at this point. The Christian joy in detecting already realized signs of salvation in this world cannot be triumphant as long as the communion with those who do not experience this joy is still broken.

60  Schillebeeckx, *Christ*, 625–27 [636–37].

61  Ibid., 500–01 [513–14].

62  Ibid., 511–12 [523], 547–48 [557].

63  Ibid., 811–12 [816].

64  Ibid., 773–74 [776].

Schillebeeckx's approach to modernity was motivated by the fundamentally theocentric conviction that, when faced with the church's and atheism's unfaithfulness to the God incarnated in Christ, Christians can trust that humankind "cannot abandon 'God,' for the [...] simple reason that God will not abandon man [*sic*] and continues to 'visit' us by routes which we cannot map in advance."[65] Schillebeeckx's more positive attitude towards modernity was motivated by the belief that Christians should sacrifice their wishful dreams of how this world could be redeemed from all remaining sin in order to acknowledge that God's forgiveness is more fundamental than any atheist or ecclesial denial of God.[66] A Christian life should reveal that "it is precisely this sinful world which is an object of God's mercy."[67] That some people no longer believe that their desires can only be satisfied by God should not primarily be seen as an obstacle to the furthering of God's Kingdom, but Christian theologians should pierce through the desires, the pain, and the joys of these people and look for how God is offering them a salvation which the church might not have expected. For, only the rejection of this offer to perceive the world with its limitations, as an invitation to a relationship with God, would mean to abide in sin.[68]

# Conclusion

The repeated criticism that Schillebeeckx's renewal of Christian theology in dialogue with secular thought was motivated by the aspiration to render the church relevant for a modern world is a serious one. The underlying worry, in de Lubac's case, was not any unnuanced conservative rejection of change, symptomatic of an essentialist understanding of the Christian tradition. The danger that de Lubac associated with the adaptation of the Christian faith to modern culture was a loss of the critical distance to the world. Such a critical distance is needed to diagnose societal problems and to cure them. An adaptation to modern culture, in particular, might be symptomatic of modernity's most serious problems, namely its illusionary self-image—perceiving itself as the climax of the progress of the whole world, denigrating other cultures, and unable to receive anything they could offer as valid critique. Yet, this chapter has shown that Schillebeeckx did not fall prey to the modern myth of progress. He did not identify his surrounding culture's developments as salvific because they struck him as perfect, but because he was prepared to discern prayerfully the contours of salvation in the frailty of human projects.[69] Schillebeeckx never lost sight of the most distinct gift Christianity can offer to the world: its invitation to enter a prayerful relationship with God already in this world, despite all its ambiguities, catastrophes, and disasters.

---

[65] Ibid., 11 [28–29].

[66] This contrasts von Balthasar's criticism that any reconciliation between Christianity and modernity fatally avoids the necessary participation in Christ's suffering to redeem a world that sinfully rejects the gospel. Instead of adapting to modern culture, the church should be prepared to suffer in commitment to the scandal of the Gospel which the sinful world refuses to accept. Kerr, *Twentieth-Century Catholic Theologians*, 135; Hans Urs von Balthasar, *Wer ist ein Christ?* (Einsiedeln: Johannesverlag, 1965), 30.

[67] Schillebeeckx, *Christ*, 547–48 [555–57].

[68] Ibid.

[69] Edward Schillebeeckx, "Ons heil: Jezus' leven of Christus de verrezene?," *TvT* 13 (1973), 147.

De Lubac associated Christianity's distinctness with its ability to criticize the modern world's self-complimenting satisfaction with humanly initiated developments. Christianity must remind people that they are inhabited by a desire that can never be fulfilled within this world. The Christian faith's distinct offer to a modern world, as presented by Schillebeeckx, is to remind modern people that their self-congratulatory enjoyment of human abilities contains a depth that can only be experienced and expressed by thankfully addressing the Creator and Redeemer of this world. In order to invite people into the reality of salvation, to enter a prayerful relationship with God, the church must build on that which people already regard as good and enjoyable. In Schillebeeckx's own day, this meant that Christians could regard the secular humanist focus on humankind's intrinsic worth as an occasion to turn to God in gratitude.[70] Christian spirituality anchors this ethical action in the hope of a God who works in and through humanist actions, which motivates people "even if we see how little the face of the earth and mankind [*sic*] is renewed, despite every effort."[71]

To understand the world as graced means, for Schillebeeckx, that each moment can be understood as an invitation to prayer, and that life can be lived in friendship with God. This does not mean that each moment is unambiguously good and that one suffers no more pain. The person living in and from this grace also knows moments of suffering, mourning, and loss. They can, however, live through these moments, trusting that God has not abandoned them and that better times will come.[72] Even if God's presence is hardly felt by such a person, they can trust in God's loving and compassionate embrace. The sole reason that they cannot yet feel it is the disruptive and numbing experience of sin. Primarily, for Schillebeeckx, the church is called to show that this world allows for another way of life than one of complaint and despair.

---

[70] Schillebeeckx, *Jesus in Our Western Culture*, 50.
[71] Schillebeeckx, *Christ*, 501 [514], 551–52 [561].
[72] Ibid., 631 [642]; Schillebeeckx, *Jesus*, 122–23 [142–44].

# Chapter 20

# Resurrection of the Person

Bernard P. Prusak

Tracing Edward Schillebeeckx's theological thinking about resurrection is like watching a flower opening to the morning sun or a butterfly emerging from its cocoon to experience the world in an adventure of flight. In *Christ the Sacrament of the Encounter with God* (the translation of the Dutch 1958 revised second edition), resurrection is summarily presented as the Father's acceptance of Jesus's sacrificial offering up of his life, lived as the expression of his adoration of God.[1] In what follows, we shall see Schillebeeckx discover new and deeper ways of thinking about the resurrection.

## I. Resurrection in *Jesus*: *An Experiment in Christology*

In *Jesus: An Experiment in Christology* (Dutch title literally translated: *Jesus: The Story of One Who Is Alive*), Edward Schillebeeckx proposed that the heart of the disciples' Easter experience was a concrete experience of forgiveness which, on Jesus's initiative, broke in upon and reassembled the disciples who had scattered after the arrest and crucifixion of Jesus.[2] In that regard, he proceeded from a critical analysis of the empty tomb and appearance narratives, and meticulous attention to the developed and structured descriptions of Paul's conversion *experience* of the risen Jesus and his "missioning," in Acts of the Apostles (chapters 9, 22, and 26).[3] In Schillebeeckx's view, the gospel narratives, as products of already established churches, reflect the memory of "something that happened, a historical occurrence that provided a basis for Jesus' disciples to reassemble after his death in the name of Jesus the Christ, the definitive salvation."[4] "Even the earliest, pre-Pauline creedal formulations" Schillebeeckx argued, "are the result of protracted theological reflection and not the immediate articulation of the original experience."[5]

From his analysis, Schillebeeckx concludes that the New Testament narratives point to a salvation-historical event, but they do not specify the concrete historical event in which the

---

[1] Edward Schillebeeckx, *Christ the Sacrament, CW* vol. 1 (London: Bloomsbury T&T Clark, 2014), 16, 23–24 [22–23, 32–33].

[2] Edward Schillebeeckx, *Jesus, CW* vol. 6 (London: Bloomsbury T&T Clark, 2014), 289–363, 477–84, 605–11 [321–97, 518–25 & 644–50].

[3] Ibid., 329–45 [360–79].

[4] Ibid., 353 [386].

[5] Ibid., 358–59 [392].

renewed offer of salvation in Jesus was manifested. That renewed divine offer by the heavenly Jesus was "an act of amazing grace" that made the disciples return to the living, crucified one:

> The objective, sovereignly free initiative of Jesus that led them to Christological faith, independently of any belief on the part of Peter and his companions, is a gracious act of Christ, which in respect of its enlightening impact is clearly revelational—not a human construct but revelation via a disclosure experience, verbalized later in the appearances model.[6]

Through their reflection upon this renewed offer of salvation, which affected a profound experience of conversion, the disciples returned to Jesus in a present fellowship and came to a fuller understanding of his meaning. They experienced Jesus as "one who is alive ... A dead man does not offer forgiveness."[7]

Schillebeeckx maintains that both the very term "resurrection" and the narratives about "appearances" reflect the process of interpretation, wherein the disciples developed the *language*, within a given hermeneutical horizon, to articulate their original experience of conversion.[8] Emphasizing that intermediary historical factors are always involved in occurrences of grace, Schillebeeckx asks "what would a straight appearance of Jesus in the flesh prove? Only *believers* see the one who appears; a faith motivated interpretation enters into the very heart of the event." Thus, in his perspective, we should not insist on grounding faith in

> pseudo-empiricism, thereby raising all sorts of false problems: whether this "Christological mode of seeing" was a sensory seeing of Jesus, whether it was "objective" or "subjective"seeing, a "manifestation" or a "vision" and things of that sort. All such questions are alien to the New Testament.[9]

For Schillebeeckx, "the ground of Christian belief is indubitably Jesus of Nazareth's earthly offer of salvation, renewed after his death, now experienced and enunciated by Peter and the twelve."[10]

In Schillebeeckx's interpretation of the development of the earliest Christian traditions, the events or experiences that gave rise to the earliest testimonies to the faith by Peter and his associates were overlaid by interpretations from Matthean, Lukan, and Johannine theology, and by Paul's personal experiences: "They already contain the core of a reflexive ecclesiology." The original experience that engendered the development of the appearance narratives is "no longer recoverable from the mingling of tradition and redaction."[11] Karl Rahner similarly allowed that:

> we can admit without any qualms that the reports which are presented to us at first glance as historical details of the event of the resurrection or of the appearances [of Jesus] cannot be harmonized completely. Hence they are to be explained as secondary literary and dramatic embellishments of the original experience that

---

6   Ibid., 357 [390].
7   Ibid., 358 [391].
8   Ibid., 359–63 [392–97], also 606–07 [645–46].
9   Schillebeeckx, *Jesus*, 357, n. 15 [710, n. 119].
10  Ibid., 358 [390–91].
11  Ibid., 352 [385].

"Jesus is alive," rather than as descriptions of the experience itself in its original nature.[12]

Schillebeeckx affirms this mixture of ecclesiology and theology in early Christianity, since "[e]arly Christian local churches all had an Easter experience, that is, knew the reality [of Jesus as alive and with God] which other churches explicitly referred to as 'resurrection.'"[13] In that regard, one might compare Acts of the Apostles 3:20–21, where Jesus is identified with the coming messiah, with 2:23–24, which refers to God raising Jesus after being crucified. Churches that espoused an "Easter Christology" articulated *how* God had brought Jesus back from the realm of the dead by *resurrection*. The Jewish notion of God's power to bring the dead back to life was the hermeneutic horizon in which they spoke of the living Jesus after his death, but they did so in a non-apocalyptic way. Jewish literature had never envisioned an individual experiencing the eschatological resurrection before the end time. Early Christians, by contrast, considered Jesus's resurrection to be the dawning of the "final age,"[14] Schillebeeckx claims that "a present (realized) eschatology is not the outcome of a long evolutionary process; it is one of many early Christian eschatologies, even prior to Paul."[15]

Other early creedal trends, such as the *maranatha* or Parousia Christology, believed Jesus was alive and with God, experienced him as the Lord actively present in their community, and expected that he would soon come again (again, see Acts 3:20–21). But they did not consider *how* Jesus had been taken up to God and they did not explicitly proclaim Jesus's *resurrection*. By its proclamation of resurrection, that God had raised Jesus from the dead, Easter Christology articulated "a reality that figured only implicitly in the kerygmatic scheme of other early Christian communities." That likely explains why it became "the governing and canonical kerygma." At its core was Peter's conviction after Jesus's death that "the God of Jesus is a God who identifies with outcasts."[16] Resurrection, therefore, "offered the best way of making explicit an earlier spontaneous experience that initially had not been explicated."[17]

For Schillebeeckx, "each and every Easter experience, in whatever guise, really is the faith-motivated experience and confession of the power of God that has brought the crucified One to life again."[18] From the faith perspective of the early Christian communities, "Jesus' resurrection, the sending of the Holy Spirit, the founding of the church and the Easter experience (expressed as 'appearances') are real aspects of a single great saving event: by his resurrection Jesus is with us in a new way. That is what the appearances seek to express."[19]

In the clarifications added to the third Dutch edition (1975) of *Jesus*, Schillebeeckx insisted that a prior religious experience made it possible to speak meaningfully about Jesus's resurrection. Otherwise, without such a prior experience, it would be like talking about colors when everybody

---

[12] Karl Rahner, *Foundations of Christian Faith: An Introduction to the Idea of Christianity*, trans. William V. Dych (New York: Seabury/Crossroad, 1978), 276.

[13] Schillebeeckx, *Jesus*, 363 [396].

[14] Ibid., 362 [395–96].

[15] Ibid., 397 [434].

[16] Ibid., 363 [396].

[17] Ibid., 362–63 [396].

[18] Edward Schillebeeckx, *Jesus: An Experiment in Christology*, trans. Hubert Hoskins (New York: Crossroad, 1981), 397. Not found in new edition.

[19] Ibid., 363. Not found in original edition.

has been blind from birth. While not identical with it, Jesus's resurrection—that is, what happened to him personally after his death—is inseparable from the disciples' Easter experience, or religious experience: that is to say, from their conversion process, in which they perceived the work of Christ's Spirit.[20]

Schillebeeckx added that "without this Christian faith experience the disciples had no way of gaining insight into Jesus' resurrection."[21]

Schillebeeckx made it clear that, besides the subjective aspect of the disciple's faith experience, Christian belief maintains "that no Easter experience of renewed life was possible without the personal resurrection of Jesus—in the sense that Jesus' personal/bodily resurrection (in terms of logical and ontological priority; here chronological priority is meaningless) 'preceded' any religious experience." Schillebeeckx did not explain what he meant by this compound term, "personal/bodily resurrection." He simply observed that to say

> Jesus himself rose in his own person, then, means not only that he was raised from the dead by the Father [...] but also—and just as essentially—that in the dimension of our history God gives him a community (later called the church); at the same time it means that the Jesus exalted to be with the Father is *with* us, in an altogether new way.[22]

The meaning of "personal/bodily resurrection" is clarified, however, in Schillebeeckx's ensuing discussion of the basis of Jesus's "*Abba* experience," his personal experience of God as father. He then emphasizes that one should not seek the ground of Jesus's original "Abba experience" in anything other than his creaturely human status. Noting that "Jesus transposes the epicenter of his life to God, the Father," Schillebeeckx stresses that union with God never results in any loss of humanness.[23] Intimate union with God in a historical person does not involve two components, humanity *and* divinity, rather it involves "two total 'aspects': real humanity in which 'being of God,' in this case 'being of the Father,' is realized."[24] Schillebeeckx thus says "it would be misleading to say that Jesus, in himself a human person, is 'assimilated' into the Logos, thereby deepening and perfecting his humanity." Jesus should not be "presumed" in advance to be already constituted as a human person that is then assimilated into the Logos. Such prior personhood, separate from his "being of the Father," is nowhere postulated. Hence, Schillebeeckx argues that, "Jesus' human personhood cannot be a presupposition of his constitutive relation to the Father into which he is assimilated. That relation in fact postulates his personhood as the unique individual Jesus."[25]

---

[20] Schillebeeckx, *Jesus*, 606 [645].
[21] Ibid., 606 [645]. Cf. Schillebeeckx, *Jesus*, 645. The old English edition reads: "Apart from this experience of Christian faith the disciples had no organ that could afford them a sight of Jesus' resurrection." This is much closer to the Dutch original which refers to the physical act of "seeing" with an "organ": "Zonder deze christelijke geloofservaring ontbreekt het de leerlingen aan elk orgaan dat het zicht op Jezus' verrijzenis zou kunnen geven." Edward Schillebeeckx, *Jezus, het verhaal van een levende*, 9th ed. (Bloemendaal: Nelissen, 1982), 528b.
[22] Ibid., 606–07 [645–46].
[23] Ibid., 614–15 [655].
[24] Ibid., 615 [655].
[25] Ibid., 615 [656].

Schillebeeckx observed that no one can be considered a human being without personhood. In relation to Jesus's personhood, he explains:

> In religious language we say that the man Jesus is this person *because* of his constitutive relation to the Father, just as—at each person's own level—everyone is this particular person because of his essential relation to the creator God. For Jesus it means that his relation to the Father makes him the Son of God *in his humanity* [...] The man Jesus is this person because that is what makes him the Son of the Father, and without forfeiting any of his humanity—on the contrary, confirming, deepening and perfecting all that positive human perfection, hence *a fortiori* human personhood, entails. So any *anhypostasis*, loss of human personhood, in Jesus, must of course, be rejected; yet this rejection still does not define the exact nature of Jesus' human personhood in his relation to the Father.[26]

Part of Jesus's uniqueness is in his relation to the Father, since "[i]n his humanity Jesus is so intimately 'of the Father' that precisely by virtue of this he is Son of God."[27] In speaking further about Jesus's *Abba* experience, Schillebeeckx writes:

> The Word of God, the Father's self-communication, is the very ground underlying the *Abba* experience. This in fact means something like a "hypostatic identification" without *anhypostasis*: within the human limitations of (psychological and ontological) human personhood this man, Jesus, is identical with the Son, that is, the second person of the trinitarian fullness of divine unity, the second which achieves human self-consciousness and shared humanity in Jesus.[28]

To posit two human persons in one identity involves a contradiction. But a finite human personhood and a divine, infinite personhood united in one identity is not a contradiction.

In responding to the Congregation for the Doctrine of Faith, Schillebeeckx emphasized that in the Dutch original of *Jesus*, he had not called Jesus a human person, but always said that Jesus is "personally human," that the humanity of Jesus is personalist. Jesus is one and the same ("*unus et idem*"), both true God and true man.[29] He therefore proposed "the idea of hypostatic identification, that is, not a union of two persons, one human and one divine, but an identification (which is ontological, of course) of the second Person of the Trinity with a formally spiritual human nature."[30] For Schillebeeckx,

> The constitutive relation to God is intrinsic in the existential and personal core of each creature. Thus, because of the hypostatic identification of that in God whose manifestation in Jesus we call "Son of God," with Jesus' human personhood, the man Jesus has a constitutive (filial) relationship with the Father, a relation that in

---

[26] Ibid., 615–16 [656–57].

[27] Ibid., 617 [658].

[28] Ibid., 625 [666–67].

[29] Ted Mark Schoof, ed., *The Schillebeeckx Case: Official Exchange of Letters and Documents in the Investigation of Fr. Edward Schillebeeckx, O.P. by the Sacred Congregation for the Doctrine of the Faith, 1976–1980*, trans. Matthew J. O'Connell (New York: Paulist Press, 1984), 59.

[30] Ibid., 59–60.

the dynamics of Jesus' human life develops into a deepening, mutual *enhypostasis*, reaching an acme in the resurrection.[31]

In Jesus, the one divine consciousness and absolute freedom of the Word became a humanly conscious center of action and human freedom. Jesus's personhood is not extrinsic to his humanity, but one cannot call him simply a "human person."

The following observations are therefore appropriate. Obviously, the divine person who became human in Jesus was never in need of resurrection, but the resurrection was not simply a matter of bringing Jesus's body back to life. Nor was it simply the raising up of his human nature. What was brought back to life was the human personhood of Jesus. The human personhood of Jesus and the divine, infinite personhood of the Word were one in identity. To speak of Jesus's "personal/bodily resurrection" is to say that the human personhood of Jesus, with its historical individuality fulfilled in a bodily/corporeal way of living and dying was raised, and that his human personhood is now inseparably and eternally identical with the Word. That is the "acme" reached in the resurrection.

The resurrection was God's "amen" to Jesus's person, message, and activity, confirming "that God was constantly with Jesus throughout his life—right up to the human forsakenness of his death on the cross, the moment also of God's silence .... Thus, our faith in the resurrection is itself still a prophecy and a promise to this world—and as such unsheltered and unprotected, defenceless and vulnerable!"[32]

# II. Resurrection in *Christ: The Christian Experience in the Modern World*

In *Jesus*, Schillebeeckx noted that Jesus ever continued to rely on the Father who had sent him. But during his crucifixion, the Father did not intervene:

> Nowhere, indeed, did Jesus see any visible aid from him whose cause he had so much at heart. Historically it can hardly be denied that Jesus was torn by inner conflict between his consciousness of his mission and the utter silence of the one whom he was accustomed to call his Father. At least the historical kernel of the struggle in Gethsemene cannot be argued away.[33]

Schillebeeckx returned to that theme in his second *Jesus* volume: *Christ: The Christian Experience in the Modern World* (Dutch title literally translated: *Justice and Love: Grace and Liberation*). He then rejected, on exegetical grounds, the possibility that Jesus had been abandoned by God. Those who maintain such a view that God abandons Jesus cite the first verse of Psalm 22 which Mark (15:34) and Matthew (27:46) place on Jesus's lips as he is hanging on the cross: "My God, my God, why have you forsaken me?" In response, Schillebeeckx emphasizes that, in its entirety, Psalm 22

---

[31]  Schillebeeckx, *Jesus*, 625 [667].
[32]  Ibid., 604–05 [643].
[33]  Ibid., 284 [317].

expresses the believer's conviction that in situations where God's redemptive help and support cannot actually be experienced, in situations in which men no longer experience any glimmer of hope, in impossible situations, *God nevertheless remains near at hand* and that salvation consists in the fact that man still holds fast to God's invisible hand *in* this dark night of faith.

Adopting an expression from St. John of the Cross, Schillebeeckx notes that it refers to "the true believer who trusts in God knows that he is still held in God's hand, even though there is no help that he can touch or feel, and in utmost emptiness will not let go of this hand."[34]

In his helplessness, Jesus entrusted himself and all his efforts to his *Abba* (Mk 14:36). Nothing would separate him from his *Abba*.[35] This is evident in Schillebeeckx's exegesis of the Gospel of John:

> The Fourth Gospel, sees this very helplessness as the character of divine power, the supremacy of God's success in the life of Jesus which was shattered *by his fellow men*, a success which consisted in the fact that despite this annihilation Jesus did not let go of God .... Jesus was successful by virtue of his living communion with God, which is stronger than death.[36]

Experiencing how much his execution contradicted his proclamation of a God concerned with humanity, and thus his whole way of life, Jesus, in grief, but willingly, *entrusted all his failure to God*. He had to reconcile an evident human experience of failure (being rejected and crucified) with his trust in God. In the Fourth Gospel, the resurrection of Jesus will thus mean:

> a break-through or *manifestation* of a *presence* of God which, though *hidden beforehand*, was nevertheless *real* in and with Jesus—what seems to be failure is in fact nothing of the sort. In that case, the resurrection is a new factor which is nevertheless in line with what was already a living reality on the cross, but in a hidden way, within the contours of earthly contingency: an act of God which will prove to be the deepest source of Jesus' identity.[37]

Schillebeeckx makes clear that Jesus was not made a success by his resurrection. Rather his success was constituted in and through his love on the cross:

> we must see the failure of Jesus and the divine success which is manifested in it as a complex of differences as well as a unity. In my view it should not be presented as though on the one hand, in the dimensions of our *history*, the message and life of Jesus proved a failure because of human misunderstanding and resistance, while on the other hand, on a *supra-historical*, transcendent level, God transformed this fiasco into a divine victory and redemption, at the same time leaving the fiasco as what it really is. In that case we would again be venerating a kind of two-stage dualism. Rather, we have to say that God's transcendent overcoming of human

---

[34] Edward Schillebeeckx, *Christ, CW* vol. 7 (London: Bloomsbury T&T Clark, 2014), 820–21 [824–25].
[35] Schillebeeckx, *Christ*, 795 [799], 820–25 [825–29]; Schillebeeckx, *Jesus*, 600–01 [638].
[36] Schillebeeckx, *Christ*, 821 [825].
[37] Ibid.

failure is historically incorporated in Jesus' never-ceasing love for God and man, during and in the historical moment of his failure on the cross.[38]

In Schillebeeckx's view, only love is redemptive: "Love is taking the side of another person."[39] He observes that in the later parts of the Old Testament, references to the coming resurrection indicate a manifestation of God's yes to a life which is given for a good and just cause.[40] Jesus's death was the price he paid for a lifestyle of care for all who suffered, and "[i]n the resurrection of Jesus it becomes evident what Jesus was before and in his death." The resurrection is the manifest recognition of the permanent validity of what occurred in the crucifixion, namely, "that such an unconditional way of life which through the inexorability of history eventually leads to death … has a permanent value *in and of itself* (for the whole of history), and not just by a subsequent ratification on the part of someone, even if this is on the part of God." Such a crucifixion has definitive value as an intrinsic consequence of radical love. Jesus's ideal way of living with boundless love can "as it were be detached from his person and continue to work as a ferment in our history."[41] God's affirmation of the definitive validity of Jesus's unconditional act of identification with the suffering of others is therefore divine, that is creative: the definitive validity of the person of Jesus himself. Thus, the "[r]esurrection is the continuation of the personal life of Jesus as a man beyond death …. God identifies himself with the person of Jesus, just as Jesus identified himself with God: 'God is love.'"[42]

The resurrection of Jesus is God's yes to the person and the life of Jesus. "God endorses Jesus' filling his death with love for God and man."[43] Jesus is given a renewed and exalted life. Christian communities, a living remembrance of Jesus as the Christ, are part of his total identity.[44] Resurrection faith can empower Christians with "unshakeable freedom, boldness in the face of 'the powers of this world.'"[45] Such a faith opens a new future for humanity and challenges Christians to shape that future, by working to overcome oppression and injustice. The heart of the Christian message of the resurrection of Jesus is that he "summons us to acts of liberation and human healing, to the task of being mutual happiness to one another and not living from illusions and ideologies."[46]

# III. Resurrection in the *Interim Report on the books Jesus and Christ*

Responding to critics in his subsequent *Interim Report*, Schillebeeckx notes that the Belgian exegete Albert Descamps made some pertinent historical observations concerning Schillebeeckx's interpretation of the empty tomb and the appearances. However, Schillebeeckx repeatedly

---

[38]  Ibid., 826 [830].
[39]  Ibid., 829 [834].
[40]  Ibid., 672 [680].
[41]  Ibid., 792 [796].
[42]  Ibid., 793 [796].
[43]  Ibid., 795 [799].
[44]  Schillebeeckx, *Christ*, 798 [802]; Schillebeeckx, *Jesus*, 27–29 [43–45].
[45]  Schillebeeckx, *Christ*, 796 [800].
[46]  Ibid., 840 [845].

argued that he has in no sense reduced Easter Christology, and thus the Christian faith, with his interpretation.[47] Schillebeeckx acknowledges that the resurrection kerygma precedes the filled-out stories of "appearances of Jesus," and that in the New Testament, there is an intrinsic connection between Jesus's resurrection and the Christian Easter experience, expressed in the model of "appearances."[48] This involved "the merging of various original traditions of a divergent kind" that had developed in places where Jesus had been. In some traditions, resurrection was the starting point; in others, the *Maranatha* conviction of "the Coming One" was the point of origin.[49]

Schillebeeckx emphasizes that the aim of his first book, *Jesus,* is precisely to emphasize both the objective and the subjective aspect of resurrection faith over against all objective and subjective one-sidedness, and in such a way that the "object"—Jesus's personal-corporeal resurrection and exaltation to God's side—and the "subject"—the faith experience which in scripture is expressed in the story of the appearances—cannot be separated. Without the Christian faith experience, we lack any sense organ which can give us insight into Jesus's resurrection. But also the other way around: without the personal resurrection of Jesus, there can be no Christian Easter faith experience either. Therefore, the fact that Jesus is risen never exclusively means that he was raised from the dead by God but, at the same time and just as essentially, that God gives him a community or church in the dimension of our history. It means at the same time that the exalted Jesus is actively present among us. This indicates the salvific significance of Jesus's resurrection for us.[50]

Schillebeeckx agrees that it is a historical certainty that shortly after Jesus's death, a few people claimed to have seen Jesus. For him, "[t]here is no reason to question this assertion. There is reason, however, to study critically what they really meant when they said this, for 'revelation' articulated in terms of 'seeing,' is a fundamental biblical datum, and where it occurs one must determine, each time according to the context, precisely what is meant by this 'seeing.'"[51] What "seeing" means, in this context, needs to be examined. He notes that Descamps "gives the visual aspect a historically more precise place than I do within the whole of what I call the conversion process, though [Descamps] admits that the risen Christ 'physically showed himself' in no 'sign' at all—whether this be the empty tomb, the appearances, or a (cognitive) conversion process (my position)."[52] Schillebeeckx affirms that this was precisely the reason why he had "deliberately kept silent about possible visual elements in the conversion process or the Easter experience." Schillebeeckx's own intention "was to free this visual element from the heavy dogmatic significance which some attach to it, namely of being the foundation of the whole of the Christian faith."[53] He now concedes that it would have been better to discuss this visual element

---

[47] Schillebeeckx, *IR, CW* vol. 8 (London: Bloomsbury T&T Clark, 2014), 63 [74]; A. L. Descamps, "Compte Rendu" [Schillebeeckx, *Jezus, het verhaal van een levende*], *Revue Théologique de Louvain* 6 (1975), 213–23, esp. 218, 220, 221.

[48] Schillebeeckx, *IR*, 64 [74].

[49] Ibid., 74 [85].

[50] Ibid., 68 [79].

[51] Ibid., 69, n. 43 [147, n. 43].

[52] Ibid., 71 [82]; Descamps, "Compte Rendu," 221.

[53] Schillebeeckx, *IR*, 71 [82].

in his book and to point out its "historical-psychological value, but at the same time its extremely low dogmatic value."[54] He points out that when he was asked whether he would "deny all visual elements as historical-psychological happenings in what the New Testament calls 'appearances of Jesus,'" he always rejected that as an option, while adding that "*this visual element* cannot be the foundation of Christian (resurrection) faith."[55]

Schillebeeckx admits that the three stories in Acts, in which the conversion of Paul (in Acts 9 and 22) is transformed into the missioning of Paul (Acts 26), made him "search in the direction of 'appearances' as originally more pronounced conversion stories than is clear in the final scriptural redaction."[56] He came to see that "resurrection and the saving presence of Jesus in the midst of his own on earth are one and the same reality with difference aspects, so that *in* the experienced saving presence, Jesus' being risen 'appears': 'shows' itself before the eyes of believers."[57] The all-encompassing cognitive aspect of the Easter experience viewed as a conversion is "the experience of the new (pneumatic or spiritual) presence of the risen Jesus in the regrouped community."[58] He stresses that in his conversion hypothesis, all the initiative originates from the risen Christ, and that "the logical and ontological priority of Jesus' personal and corporeal resurrection to belief in the resurrection is explicitly affirmed."[59] But Schillebeeckx does not further clarify what "personal and corporeal" means. In turning to a discussion of the significance of the empty tomb, he cites Descamps's statement that "a corpse that has disappeared is not a resuscitated body." Schillebeeckx remarks that "this expression, with no mention of the corporeal *person*, is an intolerable dualism."[60] But it expresses what he likewise maintains: that the empty tomb, a very old and persistent tradition, is not the foundation of the Christian resurrection faith.

# IV. Resurrection in *The Church with a Human Face*

In Schillebeeckx's 1985 book on ministry, *The Church with a Human Face*, he declares that only a new action by God can connect Jesus's historical life that ended with his crucifixion with the "Christ of faith" and the confession that he is risen.[61] To the believer, the resurrection makes clear God's judgment on, and relationship to Jesus, and his message, activity, and death. God thereby authenticated the person and the whole way of life of Jesus. In the resurrection, God "puts his seal on it and speaks out against the human judgment" on Jesus. Through and in Christian resurrection faith, the crucified but risen Jesus remains active in our history. His resurrection, sending of the Spirit, the Christian community, and the New Testament witnesses of faith are distinct but also

---

54  Ibid.
55  Ibid., 71, n. 46. [148, n. 46].
56  Ibid., 72 [83].
57  Ibid., 68 [80]. Emphasis is mine.
58  Ibid., 69 [80].
59  Ibid., 72 [83].
60  Ibid., 74–75 [86]. Emphasis is mine.
61  Schillebeeckx, *CHF, CW* vol. 9 (London: Bloomsbury T&T Clark, 2014). Dutch version: Edward Schillebeeckx, *Pleidooi voor mensen in de kerk: Christelijke identiteit en ambten in de kerk* (Baarn: Nelissen, 1985). For the controversy and background to this book, see Chapter Thirteen of this volume by Leo Kenis and Lieven Boeve.

intertwined. Reflecting further on this interrelation, he writes: "One can say that the communities of God which came into being on the basis of the resurrection of Jesus are what is meant *at the deepest level* in the New Testament by the appearances of Jesus. The crucified but risen Jesus appears in the believing, assembled community of the church."[62]

# V. Resurrection in *Church: The Human Story of God*

In his third *Jesus* volume, *Church: The Human Story of God* (1989), Schillebeeckx locates the discussion of the life, death, and resurrection of Jesus within a broad historical context. He affirms that there can be "no salvation outside the world," and undertakes an analysis of the process of liberation in history as the medium and material of divine revelation.[63] He surveys the growing emphasis on human freedom and autonomy, and the theological tensions regarding the relationship between God's omnipotence and human freedom, which lead to the understanding that God has chosen to be affected by the suffering of the world. Schillebeeckx speaks of God's defenselessness, which need not *per se* contradict God's power. "We know from experience that those who make themselves vulnerable can sometimes disarm evil."[64] God makes himself vulnerable by giving freedom and creative space to humans. God has undertaken an adventure full of risks.

God freely determined to be an ally in our suffering and absurdity, and also in the good that we do. On the cross, Jesus shared in the brokenness of our world. It was not God but humans who put him to death: "God was not powerless when Jesus hung on the cross, but he was defenseless and vulnerable as Jesus was vulnerable."[65] Any meaningful statement about the resurrection of Jesus must not trivialize his shameful and defenseless death. In what humans did to him there is only negativity.

"Only when we have seen the defenselessness of the cross can we and may we also look for the significance of Jesus' resurrection."[66] Reprising the themes seen in *The Church with a Human Face*, Schillebeeckx again says that only a new action by God in history, the resurrection, could link Jesus's life and death with the Christ of the church's faith and the confession that he is risen. The resurrection was God's verdict on Jesus, and the way that God's evaluation of Jesus's message, life, and death became clear to believers: "Just as the death of Jesus cannot be detached from his life, so his resurrection cannot be detached from his life and death."[67]

God's relationship to history and human freedom is central in the ensuing section about the kingdom of God as both already and not-yet present. The kingdom of God is described as "the definitive salvation or the radical liberation of humankind into a brotherly and sisterly society and community in which there are no longer any master-servant relationships, in which pain and tears are wiped out and forgotten, and in which 'God will be all in all' (1 Cor.15.28)."[68] Noting,

---

[62] Schillebeeckx, *CHF, CW* vol. 9 (London: Bloomsbury T&T Clark, 2014), 31 [33–34].
[63] Schillebeeckx, *Church, CW* vol. 10 (London: Bloomsbury T&T Clark, 2014), 5–9 [5–9].
[64] Ibid., 87–88 [89–90].
[65] Ibid., 125–26 [126–28].
[66] Ibid., 127 [129].
[67] Ibid., 127–28 [129].
[68] Ibid., 131 [133].

in a parenthesis, that the *individual* is "called *sarx*, body or flesh, in the Bible," Schillebeeckx observes that "in the Christian tradition of faith the achievement of the salvation and happiness of the individual within this perfected society [the kingdom of God] is called 'resurrection of the body,' i.e. of the human person including his or her human corporeality."[69] Identifying the resurrection of the body with "resurrection of the *person* including his or her corporeality," Schillebeeckx explains that corporeality is "the visible orchestration, the personal melody, of a person which others also enjoy." He declares that "this glorified corporeality has nothing to do with the body which is left behind, it has everything to do with the personal corporeality in which I lived on earth."[70]

# VI. Resurrection in "Theological Quests"

In "Theological Quests," the second part of Schillebeeckx's "theological testament" (*Theologisch testament*), published in 1994, he describes the development and deepening of his theological thinking over the years.[71] He speaks of humans as historical beings who are trapped in history, but who likewise want to make history: "Being created by God, 'of God,' they go through life 'with God.' But it can become a journey without, even against God." The fact that human life is contingent—having a beginning and an ending—inevitably raises the question: "Is my death the end of everything? Is there hope, a future beyond the boundary of death?"[72]

Schillebeeckx observes that the Christian tradition developed its response to such questions in the area of theology known as eschatology and then summarizes its perspectives:

> The foundation of the Christian belief in eternal life is not a philosophical creed about the immortality of a spiritual soul within human beings, but their earthly covenant of grace or community with the eternal God, the believer's Godcentred life in the sense of an interpersonal relationship with God, lived in service of others and for the good of future humans. Accordingly the real object of Christian faith in eternal life is not the spiritual immortality of the soul, but the resurrection of the entire person, down to its corporeality; expressed succinctly and elliptically, faith in the resurrection of the body.[73]

He then explains what he intends by "the resurrection of the entire person, down to its corporeality":

> Without any dualism a human being is still a mind-body duality, so achievement of our personal destiny does have a physical component. But from our earthly perspective we cannot concretely visualise what a glorified, "heavenly" body looks like. At any rate it has nothing to do with the rising of a corpse or re-animation:

---

[69] Ibid.

[70] Ibid.

[71] Schillebeeckx, "Theological Quests," *Essays, CW* vol. 11 (London: Bloomsbury T&T Clark, 2014), 111–61. Dutch original: Edward Schillebeeckx, *Theologisch testament: Notarieel nog niet verleden*, 2nd ed. (Baarn: Nelissen, 1995), 69–137.

[72] Schillebeeckx, "Theological Quests," 136.

[73] Ibid.

resurrection is far rather the *visible radiance and bodily expression* of a perfect human person who has been assimilated into God. Thus faith in life beyond death concerns human beings in their mind-body duality.[74]

In a subsequent section, Schillebeeckx reiterates, what he had written five years earlier in *Church: The Human Story of God* concerning the resurrection and the kingdom of God:

> The perfect salvation and joy of the person (what the Bible calls *sarx*, body or flesh) in that perfect community [beyond death] is known in the Christian tradition as the *resurrection of the body*, that is divine affirmation of the human person down to our human corporeality, which is the visible orchestration, the distinctive melody of a person that others can also enjoy (even though the glorified body has nothing to do with the corpse it has left behind, it has everything to do with the person's humanity and hence with her or his personal corporeality [in which she or he lived on earth]).[75]

In the much earlier essay, "Man and His Bodily World," originally given at a symposium at the medical faculty of the Catholic University of Nijmegen in 1959, Schillebeeckx noted that our terms body and soul were unknown to Old Testament writers. They saw the human person "as a self-evident unity. For them, the whole man was body and the whole man [*sic*] was spirit."[76] The *human* body was the whole man. Non-bodily spirit, or soul, was something integral, not added to the body of a *human*. For Schillebeeckx,

> the *humanity* of the body is something of the soul itself, the soul's communication of itself to the body, by means of which man is man. In this way, the human body is the spirit appearing in our world. A corpse is not a human body and really has nothing more to do with the deceased person … Unlike a corpse, the human body is the visible appearance of an I. The humanization of the body is synonymous with man's being as spirit.[77]

# Conclusion

A human is an embodied spirit having consciousness and freedom. Freedom involves openness to possibilities and having to decide. What is ultimately decided over the course of an embodied lifetime is the self, and one's relationship to God. Resurrection of the body refers to the *self* or person, alive beyond death, with the corporeal identity established through all the decisions and actions of an embodied consciousness and freedom within history. What is resurrected beyond death, and taken into union with God, may fittingly be called "the melody" of an individual

---

[74] Ibid.

[75] Ibid., 159.

[76] Edward Schillebeeckx, "Man and His Bodily World," *WC, CW* vol. 4 (London: Bloomsbury T&T Clark, 2014), 177–87 [231–44]. Originally published in Edward Schillebeeckx, *Wereld en kerk*, Theologische peilingen 3 (Bilthoven: Nelissen, 1966), 227–47.

[77] Ibid., 187.

person's life. All the *notes* of our individual melodies are composed within an embodied history, like molecules of ink on a material score. In the transformed mode of existence called bodily resurrection, our corporality may be likened to a melody—encapsulating the whole story of our life and identity—ever playing in union with God, rather than the molecules of the body in which our personal identity, or the notes of our life were composed.

Applying such statements to Jesus, one may say that the resurrected "personalist humanity of Jesus," hypostatically identified with the *Logos*, incorporates the distinctive identity that Jesus established in his corporeal earthly life, in his ministry and his way of dying. The resurrected "personally human mode of being" of Jesus is thus inseparably united with his bodiliness—all that he was and became while embodied and alive within history. Or, to apply Schillebeeckx's metaphor, Jesus's risen corporeality is the visible orchestration, the distinctive personalist melody that he composed during his embodied life, taken up to be eternally *identical* with the Word that became human.

# Chapter 21

# Mary, Model of Eschatological Faith

## Julia Feder

Edward Schillebeeckx has written relatively little on Mary in comparison with his large volume of work on Christology and the church. When he does approach Mariology as a topic, his impulse is to avoid a consideration of Mary in isolation from the broader framework of God's saving work in the world through the person of Jesus Christ. For this reason, a separate chapter on Mary in this volume may seem not only strange, but at crosscurrents with Schillebeeckx's own intuitions. However, a close examination of Schillebeeckx's Mariology can provide us with an opportunity to highlight the synthetic nature of Schillebeeckx's thought overall, lifting up the connections between his descriptions of Mary and his descriptions of eschatological faith and the nature of salvation history. In addition, considering the ways in which Schillebeeckx's thought has significantly influenced contemporary Roman Catholic understandings of Mary—particularly, to the extent that he impacted the Mariological debates as the Second Vatican Council—a close examination of Schillebeeckx's Mariology lays bare the delicate contemporary Catholic balance of avoiding Marian excess while still preserving Marian devotions that uphold the whole human person as graced by God or, if you will, full of grace.

In this chapter, I will analyze the development of Schillebeeckx's thought on Mary and suggest avenues for future development of a contemporary Mariology in line with his mystical-political approach to theology. Over the course of his writing career, he argues that Mary is best understood as our sister in faith. She is one of us, as she strove to be a friend of God and hoped for God as her future. Insofar as she lived in close relationship with the Holy Spirit and, after her death, was assumed into heaven body and soul, she is ahead of us on the way. She serves as our guide for mature, adult faith. I begin the essay with an analysis of Schillebeeckx's 1954 book on Mary titled *Mary, Christ's Most Beautiful Creation*, written as a prompt for priests' homilies during the Marian year. Desiring to provide a stronger historical analysis of the Jewish mother of Jesus, Miriam, and wanting to portray salvation as more eschatological, Schillebeeckx revises the first edition and retitles it *Mary, Mother of the Redemption* in 1955. I detail Schillebeeckx's concerns with the first edition and the changes that he made for subsequent editions of this work. These shifts in Schillebeeckx's thought over the 1950s provide a foundation for the arguments that he will make to bishops at the Second Vatican Council, encouraging them to treat Mary within the document on the church rather than in a separate schema. I review this history, emphasizing Schillebeeckx's role as advisor to the Council Fathers and the anxieties that motivated bishops on both sides of the debate. Next, I examine Schillebeeckx's writings on Mary in the 1990s which sought to construct a pneumatological Mariology as well as to correct earlier statements with a more developed consciousness of feminist concerns. Finally, I offer some suggestions for future development of Schillebeeckx's Mariology in light of contemporary concerns for sexual, racial, and environmental justice.

# I. Mary in the Christian tradition

Scripture provides very little information about Mary, the mother of Jesus, and the bulk of Marian teachings in the Christian tradition have more to do with refining ideas about her son than anything about Mary herself. In the fifth century, Mary is defined as *Theotokos* (God-bearer) rather than merely *Christokos* (Christ-bearer) by the Council of Ephesus by route of affirming that Christ does not have two distinct persons (one human and another divine), but rather that he is one unified person both human and divine. In the seventh century, Mary is defined as *Aei-parthenos* (ever-virgin) at the Lateran Council of 649, that is, she is virgin before, during, and after the birth of Jesus Christ.[1] This Marian teaching serves to strengthen the divine nature of Christ. And, in the nineteenth century, Pope Pius IX proclaims *ex cathedra* the Immaculate Conception of Mary, affirming that she was conceived without the stain of original sin and, consequently, Jesus's own conception is all the more pure. Erik Borgman argues that this papal pronouncement, not without foundation in the devotional life of the faithful but also not without formal theological controversy, is fueled by an ecclesial antagonism toward modernity, particularly secular political State authority. He explains, "Mary's miraculous preservation from original sin, as the only one of the human race, symbolized the infinite difference between the sin which holds the world in its grasp and the redemption from it represented by the church."[2] This combative orientation toward the world, bolstered by martial Marian imagery,[3] is precisely what the Second Vatican Council will try to avoid. As we will see below, Schillebeeckx's work contributes substantially to this shift, as he gradually develops his own conviction, "no salvation outside of the world."[4]

In the twentieth century, Pope Pius X warns that rationalism is an enemy of the faith which must be "torn up by the roots and destroyed"[5] and heralds the incomprehensible and irrational nature of the dogma of the Immaculate Conception as an appropriate "weapon against the rejection of 'reverence and obedience to the authority of the Church.'"[6] In 1950, Pope Pius XII proclaims the bodily Assumption of Mary into heaven *ex cathedra*. This Marian teaching, unlike others that have preceded it, does not function as a proxy for Christological development but

---

[1] See the Lateran Council of 649, canon 3.
[2] Erik Borgman, *Edward Schillebeeckx: A Theologian in His History*, trans. John Bowden (London: Continuum, 2003), 181.
[3] Borgman explains: "Traditionally, Mary was especially regarded as mother, but in the presentation of the papal documents, above all halfway through the nineteenth century, Mary was by no means primarily gentle and caring. Pius XII himself thought that an 'army in battle order' (*acies ordinata*) was an appropriate symbol for her, though he hastened to add that Mary did not of course have a 'martial disposition', but 'strength of soul'. Mary took on the form of a spiritual leader in the battle which according to this pope the church had to wage against modernity" (181).
[4] Edward Schillebeeckx, *Church, CW*, vol. 10 (London: Bloomsbury T&T Clark, 2014), 12 [12].
[5] Borgman, *Schillebeeckx*, 181.
[6] Ibid., 182, citing Pius X, *Ad diem illum* (February 2, 1904), 22, http://w2.vatican.va/content/pius-x/en/encyclicals/documents/hf_p-x_enc_02021904_ad-diem-illum-laetissimum.html.

rather concerns Mary alone, and, like the Immaculate Conception, is grounded in revelation "which surely no faculty of the human mind could know by its own natural powers"[7] echoing the broader anti-rationalism trend in nineteenth and twentieth century Marian pronouncements. Just three years after Pius XII infallibly defines the Assumption, he declares 1954 a Marian year to commemorate the centenary of the definition of the Immaculate Conception.[8] The year of celebration is punctuated with the institution of the feast of Mary the Queen of Heaven, amplifying the message of political and spiritual triumph over modernity.[9]

## Mary, Christ's Most Beautiful Creation: Early thoughts

On the occasion of the 1954 Marian Year, the Flemish Apostolate of the Rosary appoints Schillebeeckx to write a text to guide and inspire Marian preaching. Schillebeeckx pens *Mary, Christ's Most Beautiful Creation (Maria, Christus' mooiste wonderschepping)*. In 1992, Schillebeeckx will later reflect on the 1954 Marian year as, in the experience of many Catholics, "organized one-sidedly by 'Rome,'" yet he used this writing opportunity to advance an understanding of Mary as one of the people.[10] With the proclamation of the dogma of the Assumption in 1950, Pope Pius XII had nurtured the seeds of Marian maximalism and anti-rationalism planted in the nineteenth century. Yet, in the aftermath of the Second World War, many other theological voices begin to work to counter this trend and to bring about a shift in Catholic language about the church. As Borgman puts it, in postwar Catholic theology, there is a "shift away from the triumphant impregnable church—Mary had always also been an image of the church—to the human life of believers in the midst of the world."[11] Schillebeeckx's first Marian text intentionally reflects this shift, though as we will see, he works to express this new ecclesial paradigm more completely over the course of his career. For him (and many others), the shift from a Marian maximalism emphasizing her unique privileges to a more modest Marian mode of speech emphasizing her relationship with Jesus and what she holds in common with the faithful is not radically new, but rather it is a "renewal" of older, first Christian millennium Marian traditions.[12] Highlighting that redemption comes from God alone in the person of Jesus Christ, Schillebeeckx describes Mary as a redeemed human person whose redemption, in turn,

---

7   Pius XII, *Munificentissimus Deus* (November 1, 1950), 12, http://w2.vatican.va/content/pius-xii/en/apost_constitutions/documents/hf_p-xii_apc_19501101_munificentissimus-deus.html.

8   Pius XII, *Fulgens Corona* (September 8, 1953), http://w2.vatican.va/content/pius-xii/en/encyclicals/documents/hf_p-xii_enc_08091953_fulgens-corona.html.

9   Pius XII, *Ad Caeli Reginam* (October 11, 1954), http://w2.vatican.va/content/pius-xii/en/encyclicals/documents/hf_p-xii_enc_11101954_ad-caeli-reginam.html. See Borgman who highlights the document's hopes for the "triumph of religion" (Borgman, *Edward Schillebeeckx*, 181; *Ad Caeli Reginam*, 47).

10  Edward Schillebeeckx, "Mariology: Yesterday, Today, Tomorrow," *Mary: Yesterday, Today, Tomorrow*, trans. John Bowden (New York: Crossroad, 1993), 12.

11  Borgman, *Edward Schillebeeckx*, 182.

12  Ibid., 182. Elizabeth Johnson, *Truly Our Sister: A Theology of Mary in the Communion of Saints* (New York: Continuum, 2004), 114–23.

affects the redemption of the rest of the faithful.[13] Reflecting on the dogma of the Immaculate Conception, Schillebeeckx argues that Mary's objective redemption by Christ is unique since she had never been marked by original sin, yet her subjective redemption—that is, her subjective appropriation of God's objective redemption—is not unlike ours. She struggled to make sense of God's saving work, she made mistakes (albeit non-moral ones), and she was subject to the typical human processes of spiritual development.[14] In this text, Schillebeeckx offers Mary as a model of faith for all of us. Yet, at this point in Schillebeeckx's understanding, "faith was in fact a matter of being open to God in the midst of the sinful closedness of the world" rather than "the more dynamic, salvation-historical view of faith" that he develops later.[15] Interestingly, the auxiliary bishop of Mechelen-Brussels, Cardinal Leo Joseph Suenens, withheld the episcopal *imprimatur* for this early text until Schillebeeckx revised his point that "the historical Mary did not know that her son Jesus was 'the Son of God' in the later sense of the dogma of Nicaea and Chalcedon" to "Mary had only a very implicit awareness that her son Jesus was the Son of God."[16] Reflecting on this history of conflict later in 1992, Schillebeeckx describes it as a "historical irony" since although this edition was "theologically 'open'" it remained rather "classical" in its approach.[17]

## Mary, Mother of the Redemption: Significant reconsiderations

The following year, Schillebeeckx significantly revises the first edition of this work and retitles it *Maria, moeder van de verlossing: Religieuze grondlijnen van het Maria-mysterie* (Mary, Mother of the Redemption: Religious Basics of the Mystery of Mary). Schillebeeckx self-identifies this revision as the most significant marker of the development of his Marian thought over the course of his career.[18] In this edition (and subsequent editions of the book), he makes three significant changes. As we will see, these are not three isolated points, as much as one coherent development. First, Schillebeeckx develops his description of the historical, biblical Mary. Second, he transforms a static understanding of faith into a more dynamic historical understanding of faith. And third, he clarifies the ways in which Mary is not *co-redemptrix* yet does cooperate with God in bringing about salvation in history. With these changes, Schillebeeckx constructs a portrait of Mary as a fully human woman, living in the midst of the sinful complexity of human history who models to us faithfulness and cooperation with God in bringing about the eschatological salvation of the world.

First, rather than immediately diving into the role of Mary in salvation history, he adds an entirely new opening chapter analyzing the biblical portrait of Mary, highlighting her historical

---

13 Borgman, *Edward Schillebeeckx*, 183.
14 Ibid., 183–84. See Edward Schillebeeckx, *Maria, Christus' mooiste wonderschepping: Religieuze grondljjnen van het Maria-mysterie* (Antwerp: Apostolaat van de Rozenkrans, 1954), 22.
15 Borgman, *Edward Schillebeeckx*, 184.
16 Schillebeeckx, "Mariology: Yesterday, Today, Tomorrow," 20.
17 Ibid., 20.
18 Ibid., 17. This is in large part because Schillebeeckx was influential in shaping Vatican II's Marian proclamations. Therefore, in their formulation of *Lumen gentium,* the Council Fathers take their cues from the intellectual development that Schillebeeckx has already worked through.

identity as a faithful Jewish woman."[19] His intention is to curb exaggerations that "give a false interpretation of true greatness."[20] Her life was not one of a "fairy-tale existence" in which parenting God incarnate came easily and without confusion.[21] Christians can tend to imagine that, with the Annunciation, Mary fully understood God's plan of salvation and her role within it as if she possessed an "intuitive vision of God in miniature."[22] But this is a mischaracterization that belies her true greatness: she could not see the future, she did not fully understand the significance of what was happening in her own life and yet, she trusted in God's promise.[23] The fully human, Jewish Miriam is already glorious; she does not need our maximalist pedestals.[24] The fairy-tale version of Mary, fueled by uninformed Christian devotions, functions as nothing but a "narcotic" that amplifies our own "feeling of inconsolable dreariness" when the high wears off and we confront the reality of our confusions, disappointments, and the challenges of living in a sinful social world.[25] Mary's fully human life lived in the "darkness of a faith which surrenders unconditionally to an uncomprehended mystery and an unknown future [...] is much closer to our own than the pretty pious legends that have gathered around the Holy Family."[26] Mary does not provide us with an escape from the challenges of life but rather roots us more deeply in reality, providing us with a model of perfect faithfulness in a world that is imperfect. She models to us a very human kind of faith, one that cannot "calculate in advance, but rather allows credit for unmeasured quantities and as yet unknown future events."[27]

Second, Schillebeeckx develops his relatively static and abstract understanding of faith as "openness to God" in the first edition into a "more dynamic salvation-historical view of faith."[28] In this second edition of the text, he insists that, because of the Incarnation, salvation is itself historical.[29] As Schillebeeckx explains, "Within this plan of salvation, *facts* are of the utmost importance – events, occurrences and men, both individually and communally, all play a decisive part in the course of the salvation of the whole of the human race."[30] Consequently, the Kingdom of God is not already established (however, hidden from full view) but rather, the Kingdom of God is in a "state of becoming."[31] Mary, with her *fiat*, plays a real part in bringing about of the salvation of the world. She does not merely channel that which has been accomplished

---

[19]   Ibid., 18. Schillebeeckx deepens this line of argumentation in his 1992 Marian work. For example, here he argues that it is not appropriate to refer to Mary as "the first Christian" since "Mary's Jewish observance of the law must be the starting point for all Christian reflections on her" (Schillebeeckx, "Mariology: Yesterday, Today, Tomorrow," 37).

[20]   Edward Schillebeeckx, *Mary, Mother of the Redemption*, trans. N.D. Smith (New York: Sheed and Ward, 1964), xv.

[21]   Ibid., 6.

[22]   Ibid.

[23]   Schillebeeckx clarifies that Mary did intuit something of the significance of God's entrance into human history, but she did not have a developed, "explicit consciousness" immediately with the Annunciation (*Mother of the Redemption*, 19).

[24]   Schillebeeckx, "Mariology: Yesterday, Today, Tomorrow," 19.

[25]   Schillebeeckx, *Mother of the Redemption*, 26.

[26]   Ibid., 7.

[27]   Ibid., 23.

[28]   Borgman, *Edward Schillebeeckx*, 184, 186.

[29]   Schillebeeckx, *Mother of the Redemption*, 3.

[30]   Ibid., 3–4.

[31]   Ibid., 3.

without her. Instead, her active reception of motherhood of God truly cooperates with God in bringing about both her own salvation and the salvation of others.[32] At this point in his career, Schillebeeckx is not as clear as he will become by the mid-1960s that history is open, that God is "the God who is to come," and that salvation is not yet objectively complete.[33] Yet, these eschatological ideas are present in germ in the 1950s. In these 1950s Marian texts Schillebeeckx begins comparing Mary to Abraham. This is especially notable because by the 1960s Abraham will become, for Schillebeeckx, one of his foremost models of eschatological faith.[34] Like Abraham who trusted in God to provide him with offspring in unlikely circumstances and who retained trust in God through a command to sacrifice his son, Mary trusted God's promise to bring about a child in an unconventional fashion and retained trust in God's promise of an "imperishable kingdom" though it seemed impossible in the face of her son's death.[35] In his later writings, where Schillebeeckx develops Abraham as a model of eschatological faith—that is, a kind of faith that both [a] trusts in God to bring about human fulfillment which exceeds that which we can do for ourselves yet, at the same time, [b] generates a deep sense of responsibility for participating in God's plan for human fulfillment—it is his co-agency with God in bringing about salvation that is critical.[36] Abraham actively sets out for the promised land, trusting in God to lead him though not knowing where he would be lead. So too, we can understand Mary as actively participating in God's plan for the salvation of humankind by assenting to motherhood of God, but as unable to calculate in advance what that will entail. In both instances, God's plan of salvation depends upon human cooperation, though salvation extends beyond that which is possible through human action alone.[37] As Schillebeeckx will later put it, this is "paradox of Christianity—we tread in the footsteps of the God who is to come to us from the future and, in so doing, it is still we who make history."[38] Though Mary did not fully understand the significance of God's promise of redemption to humanity nor vision how it would be brought about,[39] she entrusted herself—both spiritually and bodily—to God's purposes over the course of her whole life.[40] Mary's trusting assent to God is not merely an assent to a static reality—a salvation that has already been accomplished apart from her assent—but rather, in a real way participates in the bringing about of salvation history.

Third, Schillebeeckx amplifies his claim present in the first edition that Mary does not play a role in objective redemption yet carves out a clear space to argue that Mary does indeed cooperate with God in the bringing about of salvation history (as indicated above).[41] Thereby,

---

[32] Ibid., 84–86.

[33] Edward Schillebeeckx, *Christ, CW* vol. 7 (London: Bloomsbury T&T Clark, 2014), 9 [25]. See Steven M. Rodenborn, *Hope in Action: Subversive Eschatology in the Theology of Edward Schillebeeckx and Johann Baptist Metz* (Minneapolis, MN: Fortress Press, 2014), 70ff.

[34] Edward Schillebeeckx, "The New Image of God," *GFM, CW* vol. 3 (London: Bloomsbury T&T Clark, 2014), 120 [197]. Julia Feder "The Impossible is Made Possible: Edward Schillebeeckx, Symbolic Imagination, and Escatological Faith," *Philosophy, Theology, and the Sciences* 3 (2016), 201–02.

[35] Schillebeeckx, *Mother of the Redemption*, 23, 121–22.

[36] Schillebeeckx, "The New Image of God," *GFM*, 120 [197].

[37] Edward Schillebeeckx, "Liberating Theology," *Essays, CW* vol. 11 (London: Bloomsbury T&T Clark, 2014), 83.

[38] Schillebeeckx, "The New Image of God," *GFM*, 115 [190].

[39] Schillebeeckx, *Mother of the Redemption*, 99.

[40] Ibid., 75. Schillebeeckx is careful to note that Mary's *fiat* is not concentrated only in the Annunciation but rather encompasses the whole of her life's activity (*Mother of the Redemption*, 114).

[41] Schillebeeckx, *Mother of the Redemption*, 36–37.

Schillebeeckx advances the claim that we all participate with God in bringing about redemption without eclipsing the role of Jesus Christ as sole objective redeemer. He writes,

> Redemption never attacks us by surprise, but is always actively received by us. In this sense, the state of 'being redeemed' always contains an element of human co-operation—man freely consents to receive the redemption which only the God-man Christ can bring. Thus each individual man is, with regard to his own redemption, already his own "co-redeemer."[42]

Like all of us, Mary both plays a role in her own redemption and in the redemption of others. As Schillebeeckx explains, Mary has become "a partner in the redeeming mystery of Christ and a collaborator in our redemption [...] precisely in and through her sublime personal appropriation of her *own* sublime redemption."[43] Just as Mary plays a role in the redemption of others, we all play a role in each other's redemption as vehicles of God's grace for one another.[44] Yet, Mary's active participation in Christ's redeeming activity is more perfect than our own since she is free from original sin. While all believers can, in a sense, be spoken of as "co-redeemers," Mary is co-redeemer par excellence.[45] Later in 1992, Schillebeeckx refers to the way that we redeem each other as the "universal law of Christian solidarity" and argues that this universal law is super-eminently effective in her case as the mother of Christ. The difference between her and us is one of degree, not of kind.[46] Schillebeeckx is being careful to avoid exaltation of Mary as "Co-Redemptrix," a title that some in the 1950s and 1960s want to bestow upon Mary in order to align her role in saving history with that of Jesus's and to distinguish her from the rest of redeemed humanity. Schillebeeckx clearly argues that redemption is only given to us by God in the person of Jesus Christ. Furthermore, redemption is also received and accepted in our name by Jesus alone.[47] Therefore, "co-redemptrix" can obfuscate an important doctrinal parameter: Mary is "on our side" as a member of redeemed humanity.[48] In other words, Jesus, as the God-human incorporates within himself all that is needed for redemption; Mary does not function as the link between divinity and humanity. Consequently, Schillebeeckx suggests that the title "partner in the Redemption" might help to avoid some of the confusions that "co-redemptrix" can impart.[49] While we might all be called partners in our own redemption,[50] Mary's "co-operation in her own redemption was incomparably greater than our co-operation in our redemption" both because of the manner of her co-operation (i.e., without sin) and because of the object of her assent (i.e., motherhood of God).[51] Thus, Mary is both "*within* redeemed humanity"[52] and also "infinitely elevated above the community of her co-redeemed fellows," including other saints.[53]

---

42  Ibid., 39.
43  Ibid., 85. Emphasis original.
44  Schillebeeckx, "Mariology: Yesterday, Today, Tomorrow," 18.
45  Borgman, *Edward Schillebeeckx*, 186.
46  Schillebeeckx, "Mariology: Yesterday, Today, Tomorrow," 18–19.
47  Schillebeeckx, *Mother of the Redemption*, 48.
48  Schillebeeckx, "Mariology: Yesterday, Today, Tomorrow," 18; Schillebeeckx, *Mother of the Redemption*, 95.
49  Schillebeeckx, *Mother of the Redemption*, xiii.
50  Ibid., 71–72.
51  Ibid., 79, 80.
52  Ibid., 109.
53  Ibid., 109, 134. See also p. 124.

Schillebeeckx's careful arguments that Jesus fully incorporates within himself all that is necessary for redemption are somewhat undercut by a gendered argument present in *Mary, the Mother of the Redemption*: God's maternal love cannot be sufficiently expressed in the male person, Jesus, and can only be embodied in the female, Mary.[54] To suggest that Jesus is sole redeemer and recipient of redemption on behalf of humanity while at the same time claiming that Jesus cannot express God's maternal love for humanity suggests that God's paternal care is essential to the divine–human relationship while God's maternal love is accidental to the divine–human relationship. In 1992, Schillebeeckx expresses regret for this earlier claim, though immediately softens his self-critique by arguing that his 1950s gender claims were both "very appropriate" for the time and also "incidental" to the primary thrust of this Marian thought. He explains that his intention was to "base the uniqueness of Mary's being a woman on the insight that God's unique, redeeming love and goodness transcends human male and female love, and in so doing at the same time in an immanent way contains in itself both paternal and male and maternal and female facets of love."[55] Schillebeeckx claims this argument is no longer appropriate given feminist and ecumenical concerns with such a gender essentialist approach. Yet, instead of detailing these concerns, he spends more time highlighting the work of German theologian and psychotherapist Eugen Drewermann, who links Catholic fixation with Mary as mother with pathological forms of male sexuality and compulsory celibacy as a primary reason for his change of heart. As Schillebeeckx simultaneously admits fault with previous claims but also minimizes the relevance of these claims for his broader Marian conclusions, he fails to recognize the ways in which his gendered argument is not merely one isolated aspect of this text.

Indeed, associated patriarchal claims are peppered throughout *Mary, the Mother of the Redemption*. For example, Schillebeeckx argues in *Mary, Mother of the Redemption* that Mary can be considered a type of the church when the church is understood as a "community of grace," but not when the church is considered as a "sacramental, hierarchical institution,"[56] because she "is not a priestess."[57] In particular, as a mother who *received* the primordial sacrament (the Christ-child), she cannot be understood as one who sacerdotally *administers* the sacraments. Schillebeeckx explains, "Mary's mediatorship is not a priestly kind, and for this reason also not of a sacramental kind."[58] Because Schillebeeckx has already laid the foundation for an argument that Mary mediates gendered aspects of God's love that are fundamentally different from the gendered aspects of God's love that Christ is able to mediate, this suggests that the paternal and priestly are synonymous, while the maternal and the priestly are fundamentally incompatible, thereby suggesting that women writ large are incapable of ecclesial leadership. In another place in the text, Schillebeeckx argues that Marian devotion lends a "childlike" and "sweet" quality to Catholic faith, while Protestant Christianity, without the mildness that Marian devotion lends, has a "comparative severity."[59] These remarks only deepen the gendered binary that support Schillebeeckx's assumptions—Jesus communicates God's fatherly love for humanity with all of the virulent severity that entails, while Mary communicates God's maternal love for humanity

---

[54] Ibid., 110, 113–14, 135–36.
[55] Schillebeeckx, "Mariology: Yesterday, Today, Tomorrow," 21.
[56] Schillebeeckx, *Mother of the Redemption,* 124.
[57] Ibid., 125.
[58] Ibid., 127.
[59] Ibid., 111.

with "infinite tenderness"[60] and "gentleness."[61] As Schillebeeckx writes, "Mary is the *dulcedo,* the sweetness in Christianity."[62] His portrait of femininity bears little resemblance to the realities of most women's lives, let alone specific resemblance to the life of the historical Mariam with which he opened his revised version of the text.

## The Second Vatican Council: Making an impact

In the 1960s, the Council Fathers' attempt to say something meaningful about Mary and her significance for Christian theology split the council into opposing factions, coming to a climax in October of 1963 with the debate over whether to treat Mary in a separate schema or to address her in the Constitution on the Church.[63] Schillebeeckx's Mariology played no small part in how the Council Fathers would proceed in the face of substantial disagreement. Though he was not a formal *peritus,* Schillebeeckx had a significant role at the Council advising bishops. As Borgman narrates,

> In this period he became *the* theological spokesman of the Dutch standpoint both
> for Dutch Catholics and for the international press. He came to be regarded as one
> of the important Catholic theologians concerned for renewal, who to a significant
> degree influenced the course of the Council, in the eyes of many people even in a
> decisive way, and who wanted to bring the church, faith and theology into a more
> direct relationship with contemporary culture.[64]

Under the advisement of Schillebeeckx (and others), Cardinal Franz König of Vienna argued on behalf of those who supported the incorporation of the discussion of Mary into the constitution and avoidance of the title "Mary, mother of the church."[65] König argued "Mary is a type of the Church and its *preeminent member* and that she should not be isolated from the unity of the economy of salvation or from the central ecclesiological focus of the council."[66] As Schillebeeckx explains, describing Mary as mother of the church is not *"per se* illegitimate" but this title can suggest that Mary is "too much 'above' and 'outside' the church."[67] Additionally, "Mary, Mother of the Church" is an unknown title for the mother of Jesus in the first millennium of Christianity[68] and presents challenges for Christian unity.[69] Cardinal Rufino Santos of Manila argued for a separate Marian schema because "Mary's role in salvation history transcended her place and

---

[60] Ibid.

[61] Ibid., 112.

[62] Ibid.

[63] As Elizabeth Johnson comments pointedly, "Accustomed as they were to deciding issues with near unanimity up to that point, the bishops were terribly dismayed. How could it be that the mother of God, in whose womb the fundamental union of God and humanity was achieved, had become the source of such great division?" (Johnson, *Truly Our Sister,* 127).

[64] Borgman, *Edward Schillebeeckx,* 2.

[65] Schillebeeckx, "Mariology: Yesterday, Today, Tomorrow," 14–15.

[66] Richard McBrien, *The Church: The Evolution of Catholicism* (New York: HarperCollins, 2008), 186.

[67] Schillebeeckx, "Mariology: Yesterday, Today, Tomorrow," 14.

[68] Ibid., 16.

[69] Ibid. Otto Semmelroth, "Chapter VIII," *Commentary on the Documents of Vatican II,* ed. Herbert Vorgrimler, vol. 1, 285–96 (New York: Herder and Herder, 1967), at 286.

function in the Church."[70] The council voted on October 29, 1963 to incorporate Mary into the constitution on the church by a margin of only 40 votes. The eighth chapter of *Lumen gentium* is the result of the incorporationists' win. As Schillebeeckx notes, however, that while the council indeed "refused to declare Mary 'mother of the church,' [it] nevertheless speaks twice about Mary 'who is called the mother of the church' (*Lumen gentium* I.6; VIII.63)."[71] And, Pope Paul VI declares Mary the mother of the church on his "personal, and thus non-conciliar authority" at the final gathering of the third session.[72] Thus, the incorporationists' win is a tempered one.

The decision to incorporate ultimately affirmed, as prominent Vatican II-commentator Otto Semmelroth explains that "Mary is no less redeemed than the rest of us are. She is a member of the Church, super-eminently and uniquely its member, indeed the archetype who incomparably bodies forth the nature and position of the Church."[73] In many ways, the vote to incorporate echoes the ecclesio-typical interpretations of Mary typical of the first Christian millennium (e.g., Ambrose) and stands in contrast to later tendencies of the second millennium to consider Mary as an isolated mystery apart from the church.[74] The *ressourcement* of a first millennium understanding of Mary in relation to the church and to Christ rather than a portrayal of Mary as an isolated mystery typifies the larger tendency at the Second Vatican Council, as directed by Catholic theologians concerned for renewal like Schillebeeckx, to understand the church in relation to the world and to other religious bodies rather than as an isolated community which stands alone in static perfection.[75] As Borgman argues, these Marian developments reflect "a commitment to a church which realizes itself in the midst of, and in responsibility to, the world and its culture."[76] Mary is not a quasi-goddess figure who grants a salvation parallel to, but not in any way dependent upon, that which is given by Christ. Rather, Mary is a human person who images the church as a community awaiting full, eschatological salvation from Christ. One should note that König's arguments for incorporation had an eye toward the eschatological dimensions of ecclesiology, reflecting the development of eschatological themes cultivated by Schillebeeckx in the 1950s. König argued that treatment of Mariology in the constitution on the church would "complete the ecclesiological vision of the pilgrim Church on earth with the vision of the eschatological fulfillment that awaits it as prefigured in Mary."[77] Thus, the council's vote to side with the incorporationists portrays Mary as one who illustrates the eschatological salvation that awaits all of us (namely, through her bodily assumption) and fleshes out an eschatological vision of the church. She, as an "aboriginal embodiment"[78] of the church, images what the church is as the People of God singularly devoted to the work of God and united as one whole to receive

---

[70]  McBrien, *The Church: The Evolution of Catholicism*, 186.
[71]  Schillebeeckx, "Mariology: Yesterday, Today, Tomorrow," 84, n. 5.
[72]  Ibid., 15.
[73]  Semmelroth, "Chapter VIII," 287, commenting on *Lumen gentium* article 53.
[74]  Johnson, *Truly Our Sister*, 127–28, see also pp. 114–23; Schillebeeckx, "Mariology: Yesterday, Today, Tomorrow," 16–17.
[75]  Anne Carr, "Mary in the Mystery of the Church," *Mary According to Women*, ed. Carol Frances Jegen (Kansas City: Leaven Press, 1985), 25–26.
[76]  Borgman, *Edward Schillebeeckx*, 12.
[77]  Natalia Imperatori-Lee, "The Use of Marian Imagery in Catholic Ecclesiology Since Vatican II," Ph.D. Dissertation (South Bend, IN: University of Notre Dame, 2007), 21; Frederick Jelly, "The Theological Context of and Introduction to Chapter 8 of Lumen gentium," *Marian Studies* 37 (1986), 45.
[78]  Semmelroth, "Chapter VIII," 293.

the truth of God's word and obey it. She models what the church should be and will be when full salvation is realized as one who is "already glorified in body and soul in heaven."[79] Finally, she, as a member of the church herself, models how other members should live as true disciples of Christ.

## II. *Mary. Yesterday, Today, Tomorrow*: A clearer vision

In the 1990s, Schillebeeckx revisits the role of Mary in salvation history on the occasion of an international congress for Dominicans on Mariology, organized by the Dominican generalate in Huissen, Netherlands.[80] His comments are published by the Edward Schillebeeckx Foundation in 1992 in a book titled *Mary. Yesterday, Today, Tomorrow.* Perhaps conscious of Schillebeeckx's need (and desire) to dialogue more closely with Christian feminists, Schillebeeckx's writings take up the first half of the text, while Dutch feminist theologian Catharina Halkes rounds out the second half of the book, though they do not comment on each other's proposals.[81] In his portion of the text, Schillebeeckx proposes "a pneuma-Christological Mariology" constructed "purely on a New Testament basis."[82] In line with previous claims concerning Jesus Christ as sole redeemer, Schillebeeckx does not wish to suggest, as Leonardo Boff does,[83] that Mary and the Holy Spirit are hypostatically united in a parallel fashion to the hypostatic union of Jesus and the Word. (Mary 28) Instead, he foregrounds a special relationship between Mary and the Holy Spirit within what he considers to be a "true, responsibly Christian, authentic christology [*sic*]."[84] The Holy Spirit, not Mary, is rightfully titled Mother of the Church.[85] Yet, Mary is animated by the Spirit in a special way for she is the first to participate in the Spirit's actions in history.[86] For him, this represents "a Mariology centered on Jesus which can speak meaningfully to present-day, even secularized people."[87] He argues that a "modern marian [*sic*] spirituality" must be a "spirituality of the symbiosis of inwardness and outwardness, an attitude of life which is also turned outwards—to others and to the world."[88] Specifically, Mariology should be liberationist

---

[79] *Dogmatic Constitution on the Church: Lumen gentium* (November 21, 1964) 68, http://www.vatican.va/archive/hist_councils/ii_vatican_council/documents/vat-ii_const_19641121_lumen-gentium_en.html.

[80] Schillebeeckx, "Mariology: Yesterday, Today, Tomorrow," 12.

[81] Interestingly, in this text, Schillebeeckx offers a woman's sermon as the ideal preaching on Mary. Though the preacher goes unnamed, he calls attention to her gender. In a Catholic context where women's opportunities for preaching are limited, this detail is significant. Schillebeeckx, "Mariology: Yesterday, Today, Tomorrow," 31.

[82] Schillebeeckx, "Mariology: Yesterday, Today, Tomorrow," 25.

[83] Leonardo Boff, *Ave Maria: Das Weibliche und der Geist* (Dusseldorf: Patmos, 1982); Leonardo Boff, *The Maternal Face of God* (London: Collins Publications, 1987); Leonardo Boff, *The Trinity and Society* (Tunbridge Wells: Burns and Oates,1988).

[84] Schillebeeckx, "Mariology: Yesterday, Today, Tomorrow," 25.

[85] Ibid., 28.

[86] He argues, "In the Gospel, in the New Testament, Mary is the first to share in the history of the Holy Spirit which takes place in our secular history, a real history which is set in motion by Jesus Christ, and her name is associated with his work of salvation." Schillebeeckx, "Mariology: Yesterday, Today, Tomorrow," 26.

[87] Schillebeeckx, "Mariology: Yesterday, Today, Tomorrow," 29.

[88] Ibid.

in which "the poor are raised up by God" according to the pattern of the Magnificat.[89] Marian spirituality must, thus, be fully incarnational—fully fleshed and fully in the world.[90]

Schillebeeckx tracks the relationship between Mary and the Spirit in Scripture highlighting the Spirit's role in the conception of Jesus (as described at the Annunciation) and Mary's role at Pentecost. In Luke's Annunciation (Lk 1:26–38), Mary is described as transformed by God's creative power. The language of overshadowing (Lk 1:35) used in this passage is identical to that which will be used later in Luke's narrative to describe Jesus's transfiguration, another instance of God's creative transformative work (Lk 9: 28–36, see v.34). Luke is explicitly pulling upon imagery from the Hebrew Bible in which cloud and shadow imagery is used to describe God's creative, transformative presence with Israel in the tents in the wilderness in Exodus 40:35 and Numbers 9:17–22.[91] Luke's "overshadowing" language surely is meant to convey a particular kind of power dynamic. When this power dynamic is applied in a context of conception, it can take on a threatening tone that is not present in other contexts because the sustained threat of rape is a "fundamental moment in the production of women qua women."[92] Though Schillebeeckx is not explicitly attentive to connotations of sexual violence in theological language, he is careful to note,

> In this context of Jesus' conception in Mary's womb this certainly does not mean that the Spirit takes over the role of the man in producing a child; what we have here is God's unique presence in the origin of new life, the life of this human child Jesus. Therefore what is coming to be in Mary's womb through God is called "holy," indeed the Son of God.[93]

Thus, he is attentive, if only implicitly, to a significant concern for many feminists[94] in the Annunciation narrative: the Holy Spirit who overpowers the human female Mary does not stand in for a human male in the act of (forced) reproduction. Instead, Mary's special relationship with the Holy Spirit prior to Jesus's birth is one in which she is transformed and empowered by the creative agency of God to participate in God's salvation of the world. This special relationship with the Holy Spirit is critical again at Pentecost when "the Spirit of God, which is the Spirit of Christ" is given to the early community of believers. Because Mary has already received the gift of this Spirit with the conception of Jesus, all other members of the community apart from Mary, receive the gift of the Spirit as a new gift at Pentecost.[95] It is this gift that enables Mary and us alike to hear and hold fast to the word of God, believing in God at work in the world (Lk 8:15; Mary 38–42). Consequently, Schillebeeckx offers, "Mary, the mother of all

---

[89]  Ibid.

[90]  Edward Schillebeeckx, *Church, CW* vol. 10 (London: Bloomsbury T&T Clark, 2014), 70 [72].

[91]  Schillebeeckx, "Mariology: Yesterday, Today, Tomorrow," 27. Schillebeeckx also cites more general "overshadowing" language in the Hebrew Bible in Num 10:34; Isaiah 4:5, Deut 33:12, and Psalm 91:4).

[92]  Ann Cahill, *Rethinking Rape* (Ithaca: Cornell University Press, 2001), 126.

[93]  Schillebeeckx, "Mariology: Yesterday, Today, Tomorrow," 27.

[94]  Mary Daly, *Gyn/Ecology: The Metaethics of Radical Feminism* (Boston: Beacon Press, 1990), 85. Betsy J. Bauman-Martin, "Mary and the Marquise: Reading the Annunciation in the Romantic Rape Tradition," *Sacred Tropes: Tanakh, New Testament, and Qur'an as Literature and Culture*, ed. Roberta Sterman Sabbath (Leiden: Brill, 2009), 217–32.

[95]  Schillebeeckx, "Mariology: Yesterday, Today, Tomorrow," 26.

belief" as the most appropriate Marian title because it highlights the transformative power of her eschatological faith—that is, her steadfast belief in God's promises despite no clear vision of how these promises might be brought about.[96] Mary is, thus, the "living embodiment" of "the model of the true believer."[97]

## Conclusions and future developments: Mary in the twenty-first century

Schillebeeckx's Marian thought typifies the contemporary Catholic theological position—delicately balancing a concern for Marian excess (in particular, Marian forms of maximalism which obfuscate Jesus's role as sole objective redeemer) with a desire to cultivate Marian devotions which uphold the whole human person as graced by God. Schillebeeckx accomplishes this by offering Mary as a model of eschatological faith. Mary is truly one of us and demonstrates how a redeemed human person might hope in God as our future and might work, alongside of God, in bringing about the salvation of the world. Over the course of his career, he works to make Catholic lovers of Mary more conscious that the woman to whom they pray is fully human—her life was conditioned by a particular time, place and (non-Christian) religious tradition; she struggled with confusion and lack of clarity; and she suffered from the complex sinfulness of her world. In the face of these challenges that Mary experienced and we too face in our own times, she cooperated with God in bringing about her own salvation and the salvation of others. With Mary as our model, we too are called to be "partners in the Redemption." She is the "Mother of all Belief" modeling to us how we might live and act in the world for God's good with faith in God's eschatological saving work.

I have noted in this essay the ways in which Schillebeeckx's Marian theology, at times, has failed to be sufficiently liberating for women, particularly to the degree that Schilleebeckx relies upon gendered assumptions about the unique way that Mary can mediate God as a female. There are, however, resources available in Schillebeeckx's own writings—especially his later writings—to develop a more sufficiently feminist Mariology. The space that he provides in his 1992 pneumatological Mariology for describing the creative power of God to transform human beings into co-agents of their own future could be of particular use in this task. This work has already begun, but more needs to be done.[98] The liberationist Mariology which Schillebeeckx himself calls for in 1992 demands not only a greater attention to the concerns of women but also to (related) contemporary concerns for increased racial and environmental justice. One might look to the work of womanists such as Courtney Hall Lee who, upon reflection on police violence toward unarmed black men in the United Sates, refers to Mary as the "Mother of the Movement"

---

[96] Ibid., 41.

[97] Ibid., 40.

[98] See, for example, the work of Catholic feminist Elizabeth Johnson who explicitly judges Schillebeeckx's Marian approach as inadequate in her now classic *Truly Our Sister* since, for him "the female is not allowed to function as an icon of the divine in all fullness but only supplements what remains an overarching male image" (Johnson, *Truly Our Sister*, 86).

dedicated to ending police brutality;[99] or to the work of Black American artist Renee Cox who has photographed herself bare-chested and barefoot holding a naked and apparently dead young black man across her lap in a contemporary reinterpretation of Michangelo's *Pieta*.[100] One might look to the doctrine of the Assumption as a resource utilized by ecological theologians such as Aurelie Hagstrom to insist on the importance of bodies and indeed all material reality in the eschatological vision of salvation. This might be used to fill out Schillebeeckx's own account of the comprehensive nature of salvation[101] expanding his treatment to include the consummation of all creation.[102]

---

[99] Courtney Hall Lee, *Black Madonna: A Womanist Look at Mary of Nazareth* (Eugene, OR: Cascade Books, 2017), 123–24.

[100] For the works of Renee Cox, see: http://www.reneecox.org/flippin-the-script.

[101] Edward Schillebeeckx, *Christ: The Christian Experience in the Modern World*, trans. John Bowden, *CW*, vol. 7 (London: Bloomsbury T&T Clark, 2014), 725–37 [731–43].

[102] Julia Feder, "Directed Toward Relationship: William Stoeger's Immanent Directionality and Edward Schillebeeckx's Mystical Eschatology," *Theological Studies* 78 (2017): 447–61.

# Chapter 22

# Encounters on the Periphery

*Revealing the Reign of God*

Kathleen McManus

I was teaching the required sophomore course on the Bible at my university, and we had finally made it to the New Testament—the Gospel of Mark. I vividly remember the bright, thoughtful student who stopped me as I spoke about the urgency in Mark's portrait of Jesus, a Jesus on the move, "proclaiming the message everywhere." Very politely, she asked, "Excuse me—What was the message?"

She stopped me in my tracks. I was taking so much for granted. At a loss for words, I asked about her religious background, and learned that she had no reference point by which to navigate my language, or the language of the Gospel. But my Christian students were looking at me with expectant faces—they wanted to know, too: What *is* the message? "The Good News of the Reign of God," of course. But what does it mean? Jesus himself never defines that Reign, that Kingdom, that Divine Rule. He describes it, points to glimmerings of it in nature, exhorts people to relate in ways that bring it about, affirms that "it is within you," but just as fervently that "it is among you," "it is in your midst." He tells startling parables that invert conventions and open up spaces where people really do experience the reign of God, however fragmentarily. Most importantly, though, Jesus himself embodies the reign of God, inaugurating it in his person and through his relationships. Even more than in his proclamation, Jesus reveals the reign of God in his diverse human encounters, especially in and through his encounters with those on the margins of his society and his Jewish religious community.

It is no wonder that Pope Francis has spent his papacy thus far urgently seeking to cultivate a "culture of encounter." No wonder he has suggested that the answers to the most pressing questions of our day lie in encounters with those on the periphery of church and society. And no wonder his bold suggestion has stirred up resistance in some arenas of both church and society. Look at what Jesus's own journey of encounter stirred up; look at where it led. I would venture that the "answers" Pope Francis suggests we will find on the peripheries are not airtight definitions, anymore than Jesus's "message" was an airtight definition. In Jesus's case, the medium was the message.[1] I would venture that the "answers" consist in living into

---

[1] "So the gospel came to be the message, directed to the entire world, of which Jesus is the content: his sayings, his acts, suffering and death, as well as the church's identification of this person, expressed primarily in its affirmation that he has been exalted to the presence of God." Edward Schillebeeckx, *Jesus, CW* vol. 6 (London: Bloomsbury T&T Clark, 2014), 90 [110].

the mutual mystery of being human by way of encounter with the "other," encounters that inevitably will stir up varying kinds of resistance.

While this phenomenon of "encounter" is very much in vogue today due to the so-called "Francis effect," it is actually a major category in the theology of Edward Schillebeeckx, whose lifelong project revolved around the "Praxis of the Reign of God." Embedded in the reign of God-motif are Schillebeeckx's seminal themes of creation and salvation—one theme, really, as Schillebeeckx understands salvation to be God's ongoing creation of the world unto the New Creation, which is the arrival of the reign of God in its fullness. At the heart of the New Creation is the *humanum*: the freed and flourishing human person. And this is no anthropocentric vision, but rather a vision that recognizes the enormous responsibility which God has entrusted to humanity vis-à-vis the care of creation, our common home.[2] Schillebeeckx calls this God's "risky trust" in humanity; alternately, he speaks of creation as a "blank check" that God has placed in the hands of free human creatures, a check for which God stands as guarantor.[3] In fact, this is a theocentric vision, one that manifests the nature of God in and through God's manner of relating to what God has created.

Shockingly, Schillebeeckx maintains that creation is the meaning God chooses to give to divinity. Moreover, within creation, *humanity* is the meaning God most explicitly chooses to give to divinity.[4] What this entails is the revelation of God's nature as freely chosen defenseless vulnerability. That is, God chooses to reign in the world by yielding to creation, which, while ontologically "other," is intimately one with God. God maintains sovereignty by infinitely respecting the finite freedom of creation, and of humanity within creation. The earthly fate of Jesus, who is the supreme expression of God's oneness with humanity and creation, reveals the "superior power of God's defenseless vulnerability." The Cross displays the tragic result of religious, political, and social rejection of the encounter with God in the marginalized, suffering, and outcast "other" that Jesus both proclaimed and embodied. At the same time, the Cross reveals God's faithfulness to humanity in and through Jesus's faithfulness to God's cause unto death. The vindication of Jesus's life praxis in the resurrection thus reveals "defenseless vulnerability" to be God's "superior power."[5]

To seek the reign of God is to seek the truth of God's life among us in the encounter with the defenseless and vulnerable of our world today. It is to be willing in our relationships with others to mirror God's own pattern of giving creation space, of making room for our freedom, of honoring our human and divine becoming. Schillebeeckx long maintained that, if experience is the locus of theology, then suffering experience is its privileged, epistemological locus.[6] In

---

2   "The world of creation, our history within the environment of nature, is the sphere of God's saving action in and through human mediation." Schillebeeckx, *Church, CW* vol. 10 (London: Bloomsbury T&T Clark, 2014), 11–12 [12].

3   Schillebeeckx, "I Believe in the Man Jesus," *God Among Us: The Gospel Proclaimed*, trans. John Bowden (New York: Crossroad, 1983), 104; Schillebeeckx, *Church*, 88 [90]; Edward Schillebeeckx, "Doubt in God's Omnipotence: When Bad Things Happen to Good People'," *For the Sake of the Gospel*, trans. John Bowden (London: SCM, 1989), 93.

4   Schillebeeckx, *Church*, 119–21 [121–22]; Schillebeeckx, *Jesus*, 43 [61].

5   A pervasive theme in Schillebeeckx – see, for example, "Doubt in God's Omnipotence: 'When Bad things Happen to Good People'," 88–102. See especially p. 93ff; cf. Schillebeeckx, *Church*, 87–89, 94–95 [90–91, 97].

6   Schillebeeckx, *Christ, CW* vol. 7 (London: Bloomsbury T&T Clark, 2014), 813–17 [817–21]; Schillebeeckx, *Jesus*, 602–05 [641–43].

his later theology, he demonstrated particular concern for those who suffer at the margins of the church as well as society—not only those who suffer literal poverty and oppression but also those who suffer more subtle forms of political, social, and religious oppression. With this in mind, the question at hand in this essay is "How, dialectically, is the reign of God being revealed through the suffering experience of the marginalized?" Our response will first take us through a deeper exploration of "encounter" as theological category. Here, attention to the roles of experience, faith, and knowing will lead us to reflect upon how resistance, variously understood, functions in revelation. The ground will then be prepared to engage representative epistemologies of the marginalized arising from concrete experiences of negative contrast in our contemporary global context. In this engagement, we will be on the lookout for glimpses of the reign of God as envisioned and described in the longings of particular suffering "Others," remembering always the fragmentary and beckoning nature of salvation so revealed, remembering, that is, the "eschatological proviso."

Just as, for Schillebeeckx, the *humanum* can never be positively defined, neither can the reign of God which is its correlate. Yet, Schillebeeckx does venture to lay out a pattern of coordinates or anthropological constants necessary to create the always fluid conditions for the flourishing *humanum*. We will reference these in conjunction with what Schillebeeckx calls the "criterion of the proportional norm," wherein the "proportional identity" between Jesus and contemporary believers mediates revelation. Here, we face more concretely the challenge posed above vis-à-vis God and creation: Are we willing to mirror in our contemporary relationships Jesus's pattern of relating in his own context? Are we, as church, open to the truth about the reign of God that may emerge in such encounters? Ultimately, we will find that the "message" Jesus urgently proclaimed, lived, and died for is one that can only be authentically known and passed on in and through embodied encounters in the diverse contexts of our contemporary world.

# I. "Encounter" as theological category

Saturated as Schillebeeckx was by the philosophical milieu of existentialist phenomenology during his early formation as a theologian, it is natural that he should have emphasized inter-subjective, interpersonal encounter. While this is evident in Schillebeeckx's early works in terms of a primarily individual, sacramental encounter with God, the notion of encounter in his later works gradually evolved to emphasize that encounter with God is primarily mediated through others, especially those who suffer, and in a particular way, those who suffer exclusion and rejection.[7] Highlighting the originality and imaginativeness of Schillebeeckx's contribution, Philip Kennedy elevates encounter as one of "three interwoven notions that stand as the conceptual building blocks of his theology."[8] The other two are humanity and negativity, which will be integral to our considerations of how the reign of God is revealed in encounter with the suffering experience of the marginalized.

---

[7] For an analysis of encounter in Schillebeeckx's theology, see Philip Kennedy, *Schillebeeckx* (Collegeville, MN: Liturgical Press, 1993), 6, 135–36.

[8] Kennedy, *Schillebeeckx*, 136.

# Revelation: Experience, faith, and knowing

Revelation, according to Schillebeeckx, can only be mediated through experience, which itself always "remains *interpretive perception*."[9] Schillebeeckx begins his extensive and painstaking analysis of experience and its authority with reflection on the experience of revelation in everyday human life. He can do this because of his conviction about what it is that is being revealed: reality. And for Schillebeeckx, reality, while variously experienced and interpreted by Christian believers and non-believers alike, is one. Schillebeeckx identifies revelation as "a word that reveals reality to us"—a word that comes to us brought by an experience of recognition, of coming to ourselves, a word which comes to us as grace.[10] This coming to ourselves occurs through a breakthrough process of disintegration and reintegration that "includes conversion."[11]

Schillebeeckx certainly recognizes that there are different "revelatory intensities of human experiences," or a "hierarchy of experiences," but he is convinced that explicitly religious experiences of revelation are dealing with the self-same reality as ordinary human experiences. The experience of the believer, however, differs from that of the non-believer via the contextualization of experience within the horizon of faith.[12] For the believer, the finite boundary or limit situation is the occasion of the actual experience of grace, of God. It is the experience of God's self-disclosure as mercy at the heart of reality—revelation received and responded to in faith—the eternal Mystery within the experience of finitude. Our concern here is primarily with the nexus of the authority of experiences of suffering and the authority of Christian experiences of faith. In particular, we are concerned with how the various forms of resistance incurred by encounters on the periphery both reveal and conceal the reign of God, both open a path of salvation and summon those on the periphery and at the center to distinct forms of conversion.

# Revelation-in-resistance

"Resistance" is a multivalent concept in Schillebeeckx's writing, thus it is important to describe those valences in order to illumine how they are being employed in this essay. Schillebeeckx speaks first of the resistance that arbitrary reality offers to human plans, a resistance which we come up against, and that he maintains brings us into contact with a reality *independent* of us:

> Where reality offers resistance to human plans and thus imperceptibly supports and directs them, we are in contact with a reality which is independent of us … we see that through the alienation and disintegration of our achievements and our plans, truth comes nearer to us. So the principle for the interpretation of reality is not what we take for granted, but the "stumbling block" of a reality which resists us.[13]

---

9  Edward Schillebeeckx, "Experience and Faith," *Essays, CW* vol. 11 (London: Bloomsbury T&T Clark, 2014), 8; Schillebeeckx, *Christ*, 17, 34–40 [31, 49–54].

10  Edward Schillebeeckx, "Experience and Faith," *Essays*, 1.

11  Ibid., 2; cf. Schillebeeckx, *Christ*, 19–21 [34–36].

12  For a careful analysis of the distinction, see Mary Catherine Hilkert, "Experience and Revelation," *The Praxis of the Reign of God*, ed. Mary Catherine Hilkert and Robert J. Schreiter, 2nd ed. (New York: Fordham University Press, 2002), 59–77, esp. 69.

13  Schillebeeckx, *Church*, 27–28 [28]. See also Schillebeeckx, "Experience and Faith," *Essays*, 2–3; and Schillebeeckx, *Christ*, 21 [36].

The truth that draws near through this resistant reality is, for the believer, the one, foundational reality of God who is mercy. Encounter with this reality, which occurs in boundary experiences, leads us through disintegration to a new integration. It implies conversion, and it entails a degree of suffering. Schillebeeckx defines these boundary experiences as negative experiences of contrast. They occur in everyday life, in experiences of failure, threat, and meaninglessness; they occur in the suffering of love. They produce something positive in the opening up of a new dimension of reality, which is the encounter with God experienced as a new future, a future always ahead of us.

On the continuum of negative experiences of contrast, however, there are horrendous conditions of injustice, violence, and oppression that threaten humanity and give rise to indignation and protest, to the instinctive "no" to what should not be. This "no" arises out of a deeper "yes" to God's open future, to the fullness of life humans yearn for but cannot define.[14] It is expressed in resistance to the conditions that threaten human being and becoming, and this is another valence of "resistance" that Schillebeeckx employs—a resistance both on the part of and in solidarity with suffering humanity and the suffering earth. It is a resistance on the way to constructing the positive conditions for a livable humanity and the integrity of creation, a resistance that summons the future.

A heading and sub-heading in Schillebeeckx's book, *Church: The Human Story of God*, aptly capture the essence of what this essay is trying to say about the reign of God and how it is revealed. The heading is "Experiences Subjected to the Criticism of Stories of Suffering," followed by the sub-heading, "Resistance: The Truth and Authority of Suffering and Oppressed Men and Women." Under these headings, Schillebeeckx provides a concise description of the evolutionary movement from the reality which resists, and therefore redirects our life and our plans, to the ways refractoriness and negativity culminate in stories of suffering, to the outright experiences of suffering and oppression that give rise to indignation and protest.[15] All of these dimensions of resistance are important in our consideration, beginning with those encounters with reality which call into question our established ways of thinking, which challenge our presuppositions and even our doctrines.[16] While it may be self-evident that the reign of God arrives through work that resists injustice and summons a new future, it is perhaps less obvious how reality that resists our plans, perceptions, and ways of "knowing" may actually create the conditions for the conversion through which Truth, and therefore the reign of God, might draw near. We turn now to engage representative epistemologies of the marginalized arising from negative experiences of contrast.

# II. Epistemologies of the marginalized

Who are "the marginalized" under consideration here? Their identities are diverse, and their "marginalization" is constituted by exclusion and discrimination precisely on the basis of

---

14  Schillebeeckx, *Church*, 5–6 [5–6].
15  Schillebeeckx, *Church*, 27ff [28ff].
16  Schillebeeckx, *Christ*, 22–23 [37].

those identities; it is constituted by the controlling perceptions and values of a dominant social/political/cultural/economic/ecclesial reality, each of which functions in distinct ways in diverse contexts. The evolution of feminist theology alone in the twenty-first century manifests the bourgeoning diversity of "the marginalized" as women scholars of color from every continent on the globe rise up and give new expression to the age-old Christian Tradition in language and symbols imbued with the experience, especially the suffering experience, of their people. From womanist and *mujerista* theologians in the United States, to African, Latina, Asian, and Australian feminist theologians representing the myriad nations and cultures of each of those continents, including Indigenous traditions, revelation is ongoing in a multifaceted key.[17] And there is more, as the feminist emphasis on relationship and embodiment encompasses relationship with creation, rendering every feminist today an ecofeminist, at least implicitly.

Decades ago, women theologians in Europe and the United States were asking, "Whose experience counts? And who is doing the counting?"[18] The question is even more applicable today, as it challenges discrimination and oppression on the basis not only of gender but also of race, class, and sexual orientation. More cogently, however, it challenges the presuppositions and epistemologies of the ones who are "doing the counting." Edward Schillebeeckx has said that, "truth is to be found not so much in our responsive language as in that which causes us to ask questions, and in our conscious ignorance."[19] And in his later theology, Schillebeeckx expressed increasing concern with the particular suffering of groups experiencing marginalization in and by the church. As we narrow our focus to representative "epistemologies of the marginalized," we will attend explicitly to the negative experiences of contrast of precisely these groups. Our concern is to ferret out what is being revealed about the reign of God in those places where the reality of the "Other" comes up against ecclesial positions, stimulating and directing an ever-widening search.[20]

## Of peripheries and centers: The suffering of women and the encounter with patriarchy

While the church publicly decries sexism and champions the equality and dignity of women in the face of forces that subjugate women throughout the world, its institutional structures, symbols, and sacramental practices loudly proclaim the superiority of men as the only acceptable

---

[17] Recent representative anthologies include Maria Pilar Aquino and Maria José Nunes, eds., *Feminist Intercultural Theology: Latina Explorations for a Just World* (Maryknoll, NY: Orbis, 2007); Kwok Pui-Lan, ed., *Hope Abundant: Third World and Indigenous Women's Theology* (Maryknoll, NY: Orbis, 2010); and Elizabeth A. Johnson, ed., *The Strength of Her Witness: Jesus Christ in the Global Voices of Women* (Maryknoll, NY: Orbis, 2016).

[18] See, for example, Mary Catherine Hilkert, "Experience and Tradition – Can the Center Hold? – Revelation," *Freeing Theology: The Essentials of Theology in Feminist Perspective*, ed. Catherine Mowry Lacugna (San Francisco: HarperSanFrancisco, 1993), 59–82.

[19] Schillebeeckx, *Christ*, 32 [47].

[20] Ibid., 21 [36].

"official" representatives of Christ.[21] In spite of itself, the church's patriarchal mode of being at best neutralizes its global work on behalf of women; at worst, it inadvertently reinforces cultural patriarchies that contribute in myriad ways to the suffering of women in the two-thirds world.[22] Frequently, this assertion leads people to leap to the issue of women's ordination, and cynically to question whether this is even on the radar of women suffering poverty and oppression, women struggling to survive domestic abuse, women trapped in the slavery of trafficking, women who are displaced, and exiled. Women, who, as refugees and immigrants, bend under the strain of keeping their families together, of keeping them in life. The answer is, "of course not." At least not explicitly, not consciously, not while in the grip of the struggle to survive. But does it ultimately matter to their future and their fate? Absolutely. Not only that, it matters to the future and fate of the created world placed in humanity's care. God's blank check requires the ecclesially received and globally promulgated investment of women's actual gifts and callings.

Perhaps it is true that our focus should not be on the single issue of women's ordination. As many feminist theologians have argued, simply ordaining women in the midst of the church's current structures would serve only to co-opt women into the patriarchal system. However, it is incontrovertible that the theological anthropology, the Christology, the ecclesiology, and the sacramental theology that are magisterially wielded in defense of the current prohibition on women's ordination pervade our ecclesial practices and our global presence with subtle and not-so-subtle misogyny. It follows that women's ordination is not merely an issue for first world women who suffer marginalization in the ecclesial rejection and nullification of their vocation to sacramental ministry. It is also an issue for women whose subjugation on account of gender is reinforced and implicitly justified by the theologies on which the public pinnacle of an exclusively male priesthood pivots. The prohibition of women's ordination stands, then, as the symbol of the ecclesial sexism to which women theologians across the globe have testified eloquently. It is the elephant in the room, and within the church, that must be acknowledged. The work of removing it has been ongoing for decades in the transformative theologies being written by women in diverse cultures. Indeed, the "theology of women" that Pope Francis has called for already exists, if we take that phrase to mean a theology done *by* women.[23] It is abundant and rich, but it has not seeped into doctrine, because it has neither been heard nor received by the arbiters

---

[21] See Congregation for the Doctrine of the Faith, "Women in the Ministerial Priesthood [*Inter insigniores*]," *Origins* 6 (Feb. 3, 1977), 518–24; also Mary Catherine Hilkert's critique in "Experience and Revelation – Can the Center Hold? – Revelation," 61; for a critical analysis of the *in persona Christi* argument, see Elizabeth Groppe, "Women and the *Persona* of Christ," *Frontiers in Catholic Feminist Theology: Shoulder to Shoulder*, ed. Elena Procario-Foley and Susan Abraham (Minneapolis: Fortress, 2009), 153–71.

[22] Ann Arabome of Africa emphasizes that, while the pain of exclusion is universal for women in the church, it varies in degree: "In the global North, women are asking for *equality* and full participation in the life and mission of the Church, while women in the global South are struggling to reclaim their *humanity* in the Church and society that have dehumanized them and denied their God-given potential." Recognizing, however, that these are related, she urges solidarity and mutual support. See S.S.S. Ann Arabome, "Gender and Ecclesiology: Authorities, Structures, Ministry," *Concilium* 4 (2012), 112.

[23] Some have expressed concern that the phrase connotes a separate theology, or theological anthropology, of the nature of women, as though that were a monolithic nature standing over against a monolithic nature of men.

of doctrine. And, efficacious symbol that it is, doctrine *functions*. Doctrine arising exclusively from a patriarchal epistemology cannot help but function to oppress women and all who do not conform to the stereotypically male gender.[24] What, then, is being revealed in the encounter between women who suffer from ecclesial oppression and the ecclesial institution itself? How might the reign of God be coming through the negative contrast so differently experienced by these distinct "Others"?

First, it is important to underscore that women typically suffer ecclesial oppression in indirect, socially constructed ways which, as Edward Schillebeeckx observed decades ago, are reinforced by patriarchal doctrine and symbol.[25] In her study of the phenomenon of feminicide in Ciudad Juarez, Nancy Pineda-Madrid develops a social-suffering hermeneutic that "links personal accounts of extreme suffering *to* the social matrix that precipitates them."[26] Among the characteristics distinguishing this hermeneutic is its discernment of the ways in which "core symbol systems and structural discourses" are used to mediate a social suffering experience. While these systems and discourses are social and cultural, they are also religious. And in a Latin American culture, the religious imagination is deeply Christian and predominantly Catholic. Another distinguishing characteristic of this hermeneutic is its recognition of the presence of our interests in the naming of suffering, and the power dynamics at work in the refusal to acknowledge the pain of the "Other."[27] How many are the ways in which the church at large refuses to acknowledge the pain that it inflicts on women when it discounts their experience?

"Feminicide" is the violent killing of women precisely because they are women. As such, it represents all of the more subtle forms of discrimination against women amplified to the *nth* degree. It is a phenomenon that exists throughout the world,[28] but Pineda-Madrid documents and analyzes its very particular manifestation in the disappearance, sexual torture, and murder of

---

[24] In the introduction to her collection of global feminist Christologies, Elizabeth Johnson asserts that, "of all doctrines, Christology is most used to oppress women." Elizabeth A. Johnson, "Introduction," *The Strength of Her Witness*, xi.

[25] In a discussion of how the revelation of God through the symbols of a patriarchal culture have made belief in God more difficult for women, Schillebeeckx asserts that "theological symbolism has in fact intensified social and cultural discrimination against women." Schillebeeckx, *Church*, 60 [62].

[26] Nancy Pineda-Madrid, *Suffering and Salvation in Ciudad Juarez* (Minneapolis: Fortress, 2011), 21.

[27] Ibid.

[28] Writing in 2009, Nicholas Kristoff and Sheryl WuDunn reported that between 60 and 101 million women were currently missing worldwide (according to one study, the number is 107 million), and at least another 2 million girls worldwide disappear every year because of gender discrimination. "It appears that more girls have been killed in the last fifty years, precisely because they were girls, than men were killed in all the battles of the twentieth century. More girls are killed in this routine 'gendercide' in any one decade than people were slaughtered in all the genocides of the twentieth century." Nicholas D. Kristoff and Sheryl WuDunn, *Half the Sky: Turning Oppression into Opportunity for Women Worldwide* (New York: Vintage Books, 2009), xv, xvii. These "disappearances" occur through forced abortion, infanticide, domestic violence and murder, forcing girls into prostitution, and selling them into sex slavery and trafficking. On forced prostitution, See Kristoff and WuDunn, *Half the Sky*, 7; narrative examples fill the pages of *Half the Sky*. For documentation of female infanticide in India and China, see, for example, Namrata Poddar, "Female Infanticide - India's Unspoken Evil," *The Huffington Post UK*, April 26, 2013, http://www.huffingtonpost.co.uk/namrata-poddar/female-infanticide-indias-unspoken-evil_b_2740032.html; and *It's a Girl*, directed by Evan Grae Davis (United States of America: Shadowline Films, 2012), film.

girls and women that has been taking place in Ciudad Juarez, Mexico, since 1993. The examples of the victims that she brings to light reveal heinous, ritual killings of women, often as a sport, as competition between gangs, and as a means whereby members of drug cartels celebrated successful runs, or marked their territories with desecrated female bodies. Law enforcement and political and ecclesial authorities are all complicit in the social matrix that sustains this evil. While Pineda-Madrid emphasizes that the state's role must be foregrounded, she asserts that "Christian church authorities have scandalously remained silent about feminicide or have (like the state and law enforcement) also adopted a blame-the-victim strategy."[29] Our concern here is with how the misogyny of the church's silence and/or blaming is magnified by the patriarchal character of its operations as an institution, an institution meant to be the public instrument of Christ's salvation. The compelling point of Pineda-Madrid's study is that salvation must speak to the evil of feminicide. By viewing this phenomenon through the lens of a social-suffering hermeneutic that privileges a feminist epistemology, she succeeds in recontextualizing the doctrine of salvation. Convinced that the stories we tell ourselves produce the structures that give rise to evil, Pineda-Madrid exposes the deep underpinnings of the stories and worldviews that contribute to machismo, misogyny, and false ideals of the feminine in Mexican Latino/a culture. Women as well as men participate in sustaining this "social imaginary" that renders the idea of violence against women at least tolerable. The antidote is the intentional cultivation of awareness of how conventional norms often conceal "the workings of power that inflict suffering on the vulnerable and innocent among us."[30]

Where the church is concerned, the ecclesial workings of power function pervasively through received doctrines which, if they are to continue to reflect truth, require intentional reinterpretation and reformulation in every age.[31] After demonstrating the myriad ways we are still awash in the myth of redemptive violence, a myth in which women and suffering have been inextricably linked to one another,[32] Pineda-Madrid analyzes the "history of effects" of Anselm's doctrine of atonement which has sustained this myth. In expert systematic fashion, her analysis illumines the network of distorted theological doctrines at play in the doctrine of salvation: Ethics, theological anthropology, Christology, and the Image of God have functioned respectively in supporting a doctrine of salvation that accommodates violence on behalf of the social order, subordinates female humanity, idealizes suffering and death, overlooks the specifics of the historical Jesus's life, and supports the human impulse to unilateral power in the interest of some "greater good." Noting that an Anselmian doctrine of salvation "lacks an eschatological orientation," she asserts in language reminiscent of Schillebeeckx that "a theology of salvation needs to anticipate

---

[29] Pineda-Madrid, *Suffering and Salvation,* 34–35.

[30] Ibid., 25.

[31] Schillebeeckx, *Church,* 43 [44]: "Cultural shifts are … always times of testing, crisis and uncertainty for the Christian churches … the Christian *perception* of the meaning of the offer of revelation comes about in a creative *giving* of meaning or a re-reading of the Bible and the tradition of faith within constantly new situations of every kind. Interpretation and praxis *make* new traditions, in creative fidelity".

[32] Pineda-Madrid, *Suffering and Salvation,* 55–58. For the deep roots of this association, see, for example, Elizabeth Johnson's analysis of the cult of the Virgin Martyrs, in which she inverts the tradition to point out that "Resistance is as much a way of holiness as sacrificing one's life." Elizabeth A. Johnson, *Friends of God and Prophets: A Feminist Theological Reading of the Communion of Saints* (New York: Continuum, 1998), 151–56, at 156.

resurrection."[33] In particular, it needs to anticipate resurrection from within the very conditions of violence and diminishment; it needs to find expression in practices that resist those conditions and the structures, social and ecclesial, that sustain them.

Pineda-Madrid details the practices of resistance undertaken by the women of Mexico in a manner that praxiologically embodies Schillebeeckx's principle of negative contrast experience and vividly reveals the reign of God coming through the suffering experience of these women. Moreover, the witness she unveils begins to answer the further question of what is being revealed in the encounter between women who suffer from ecclesial oppression and the ecclesial institution itself.

The women of Ciudad Juarez enact a genuine "Mysticism of Resistance" by reclaiming and reinterpreting the symbols of their Catholic faith. Religious processions, protests, and vigils in the public square make visible the feminine suffering that the powers sought to render invisible. The Cross that has so often falsely symbolized the sacrifice that women presumably are uniquely meant to bear becomes the symbol of liberation and anticipated resurrection in the very midst of death's dark forces. By erecting pink crosses in memory of victims, the women reclaim the spaces marked out by their dead bodies, vindicating their memory and indicting the perpetrators. Their public testimony to resurrection is at one and the same time an ethical demand for justice in the here and now; it is a proclamation of hope. This feminine embodiment of a transformed theology of the Cross has drawn into being multiple communities of resistance, communities of both women and men making real the Body of Christ in the midst of a sinful world and complicit church. They *are* the church in encounter with the church's institutional trappings and patriarchal distortions, an encounter in which each entity is in some sense "Other." Here, the "periphery" confronts the "center" with its own deepest truth. In Schillebeeckx's terms, the experience of the "center" of the church as tradition-guarding institution is being subjected to the criticism of stories of suffering, and the suffering and oppressed subjects of these stories are authoritative witnesses to truth.[34] Something is being revealed in this difficult and disorienting encounter— something of the reign of God. However, the revelation is not merely one-sided; it occurs in a dialectic—at least, potentially.

In this particular encounter between the church on the periphery and the church at the center, the reign of God is being revealed through the women's re-appropriation of the center's doctrinal symbols in a manner that corrects the patriarchal distortions in which they have been wielded and opens up a path to existential, historical salvation here and now, however fragmentary. Through engaging the symbols of the "center," the women demonstrate groundedness in the deep sources of the tradition, the very tradition that the patriarchal "center" is anxious to guard. By this very fact, they are implied in and related to the ecclesial structures and doctrines upon which their stories of suffering exert an authoritative critique. Early on, we noted that Schillebeeckx identifies revelation as "a word that reveals reality to us"—a word that comes to us brought by an experience of recognition, of coming to ourselves, a word which comes to us as grace.[35] This

---

[33] Pineda-Madrid, *Suffering and* Salvation, 89–94, quote at 91. This demonstrates Schillebeeckx's assertion that "the particular epistemological value of the experience of contrast in suffering is the knowledge that looks for the *future* and opens it up." Schillebeeckx, *Christ*, 814 [818].

[34] Schillebeeckx, *Church,* 28 [28].

[35] See Schillebeeckx, "Experience and Faith," *Essays*, 2.

"coming to ourselves" occurs through a breakthrough process of disintegration and reintegration "that implies conversion."[36]

The women of Ciudad Juarez enacting a mysticism of resistance on behalf of the victims of the feminicide may be said to have experienced a disorienting disintegration first in coming to grips with the horror of what was happening to women, then in their gradually emerging awareness of the extensive, corrupt network of forces involved in this evil, and finally in the realization that they placed themselves under threat by those same forces when they risked organizing, speaking, and acting in solidarity with the victims. And they may be said to have experienced a reintegration in the process of finding their voices, making this evil known, and challenging its sources. The conversion implied here entailed embracing their vulnerability as courage in confronting the powers. It entailed claiming their female humanity and that of the victims in the public square; it entailed demanding justice in the face of overwhelming injustice, regardless. In the process, they experienced and created communities of life resisting death. In documenting this, Nancy Pineda-Madrid ringingly asserts that "community must be a condition of the possibility of our knowing salvation."[37]

The recognition, the "coming to ourselves," the word which comes to us as grace, the revelation of the coming reign of God experienced fragmentarily is on display here in communities of women and their male supporters on "the periphery." By extension, it is on display wherever representative communities of oppressed, marginalized populations speak and act from the depths of their diversely unique humanity, transformatively reappropriating the symbols of their faith, and embracing their vulnerability as courage in the face of the powers. The extended example here of Pineda-Madrid's analysis of feminicide serves as a paradigm of how the reign of God is being revealed through negative experiences of contrast on the periphery. Though there is no space here to substantially engage all of the marginalized groups mentioned earlier, countless theologians belonging to these communities or doing theology in relationship to them are doing so in varied and compelling ways. Among the groups on the "periphery" that this paradigm embraces are African American women and men both inhabited by the memory of slavery and inhabiting a religious and cultural context of racism,[38] Asian and African women struggling with the oppressive vestiges of post-colonial Christianity,[39] members of the LGBTQ community seeking authentic inclusion in the church,[40] and Australian Indigenous peoples seeking to integrate

---

[36]  See ibid.

[37]  Pineda-Madrid, *Suffering and Salvation*, 60.

[38]  See, for example M. Shawn Copeland, *Enfleshing Freedom: Body, Race and Being* (Minneapolis: Fortress, 2010); Bryan N. Massingale, *Racial Justice and the Catholic Church* (Maryknoll, NY: Orbis, 2010); Christopher Pramuk, *Hope Sings, So Beautiful: Graced Encounters Across the Color Line* (Collegeville, MN: Liturgical, 2013).

[39]  Teresia Hinga, "Jesus Christ and the Liberation of Women in Africa," *The Strength of Her Witness: Jesus Christ in the Global Voices of Women*, ed. Elizabeth Johnson (Maryknoll, NY: Orbis, 2016), 131–40; Muriel Orevillo-Montenegro, *The Jesus of Asian Women* (Maryknoll, NY: Orbis, 2006) are examples.

[40]  See Paul G. Crowley, SJ, "Homosexuality and the Counsel of the Cross," *Theological Studies* 65 (2004), 500–29; Charles Hefling, ed., *Our Selves, Our Souls & Bodies: Sexuality and the Household of God* (Boston: Cowley Publications, 1996); Margaret Farley, *Just Love: A Framework for Christian Sexual Ethics* (New York: Continuum, 2006); Luke Timothy-Johnson, "The Passionate Body," *The Revelatory Body: Theology as Inductive Art* (Grand Rapids, MI: Eerdmans, 2015), and Kwok Pui-Lan, "Engendering Christ," *The Strength of Her Witness: Jesus Christ in the Global Voices of Women*, ed. Elizabeth Johnson (Maryknoll, NY: Orbis, 2016), 255–69.

their native earth-reverencing spirituality into Christian Gospel praxis.[41] All of them are bringing their defenseless vulnerability into the public and ecclesial square, banking on God's promise that they have the right to exist, the right to be who they are, the right to flourish. The reign of God is being revealed in myriad ways on the peripheries. But what about the ecclesial "center" in relation to them? Is there a true and engaged dialectic between the periphery and the center, a dialectic with mutual receptivity to the truth that may emerge in dialogue with the "Other"?

The ecclesial center undergoing the critique of these stories of suffering may be said to be resisting the disorienting disintegration of truth drawing near. It may be said that the ecclesial institution experiences the resistance of women and other marginalized people to patriarchal structures and doctrines as threatening to its power, to its authoritative stewardship of "truth." And the suggestion that these structures and doctrines are complicit in misogyny and sexism, as well as in racism and heterosexism, is simply inadmissible, leading not only to impasse, but to increased pain on the part of those "others" who identify, or want to identify, with the church. The negative contrast experience of these "others" inheres in their instinctive "no" to ecclesial structures and positions that minimize or deny their full humanity and flourishing. Their "no" is grounded in a "yes" to what should be, a fragment of the reign of God here and now, though what that looks like is only inchoately known. Nevertheless, the space in which it might begin to come into being is precisely the space of tension between the periphery and the center. And here we want to keep our focus on the center. How might it be possible for those at the center to open themselves to the suffering of the marginalized in such a way that they become vulnerable to precisely the disorientation and disintegration that they fear? A disintegration on the way to a new reintegration?

In some ways, the question is rhetorical. It is clear that the condition for the possibility of such openness implies conversion, *metanoia,* and that cannot be prescribed or legislated. It can, however, be invited by the willingness of those on the periphery to engage the center which is, or should be, their home, too. In a different reference to the "center" that is, nevertheless, intrinsically related to its meaning in this essay, Mary Catherine Hilkert asks, "Can the Center Hold?" Her usage refers to the constellation of doctrines and dogmas comprising the church's deep Tradition, it refers to what is embraced and handed on as orthodoxy. In an essay on revelation written over twenty years ago, Hilkert stated, "As feminist scholarship develops, diversity is unfolding at the center—at the level of fundamental theology."[42] Today, that diversity has increased exponentially. The "intersection of commitments" where Catholic feminists hope to find the revelation of God among us is today far more complex. In *every* arena of theology, the diversity of human experience is giving rise to the most crucial questions having to do with identity, consciousness, and inclusivity. What Hilkert noted then, however, is yet more true now. We are still in need of structures of authentic dialogue for discerning what are authentic developments of tradition, if we believe that the Word of God is *truly* entrusted to the entire church–*sensus fidelium.*

---

[41]  See, for example, Lee Miena Skye, "Australian Aboriginal Women's Christologies," *The Strength of Her Witness: Jesus Christ in the Global Voices of Women,* ed. Elizabeth Johnson (Maryknoll, NY: Orbis, 2016), 162–71.

[42]  M. Catherine Hilkert, "Experience and Tradition – Can the Center Hold? – Revelation," *Freeing Theology: The Essentials of Theology in Feminist Perspective,* ed. Catherine Mowry LaCugna (San Francisco: HarperSanFrancisco, 1993), 59–82.

It is precisely the stretching of the center of orthodoxy that its guardians fear in the encounter with those on the periphery. Many at the center fear the summons to embrace the ambiguity of human experience; they fear the need for fluidity and open-endedness entailed in that embrace. They resist "truth drawing near" in favor of truth propositionally institutionalized. How to discern what is authentic development? Schillebeeckx provides a structure for such discernment, but engaging it requires at least the beginning of the openness to conversion that genuine encounter entails. In the next and final section, we attend to Schillebeeckx's "criterion of the proportional norm" with reference to his anthropological constants.[43]

# III. *Sequela Jesu*: Encountering the vulnerable rule of God

Schillebeeckx's understanding of what it means to follow Jesus Christ and thereby enact the reign of God is not a matter of static imitation, but rather of dynamic re-presentation entailing endless reinterpretation and innovation in the dialectic between the received Tradition and the present context, a dialectic guided by the Word of God which is ever new.[44] The Incarnation reveals the fullness of humanity as both God's nature and God's "cause." Because humanity is a narrative unfolding in history, and because that great narrative is diversified in uniquely unfolding subjects, each of whom is "a situated and thematic freedom," the flourishing *humanum* amidst a renewed creation—reign of God—is an eschatologically open-ended project.[45] The "proportional identity" between Jesus and contemporary believers entails responding in faith to the existential conditions of our historical context in the manner that Jesus responded to his, and that will necessarily look different in our time than it did in his. Moreover, it will look different across the diverse cultural contexts of our own time. The constant for Christians is the flourishing here and now of diversely human icons of the mosaic *Imago Dei*.[46] While our focus on the reign

---

43  Erik Borgman observes that Schillebeeckx's notion of a "proportional identity" between Jesus and contemporary believers is revolutionary because "it introduces the current social-historical context into the very core of revelation itself." Erik Borgman, "Edward Schillebeeckx's Reflections on the Sacraments and the Future of Catholic Theology," *Sacramentalizing Human History: In Honour of Edward Schillebeeckx*, ed. Erik Borgman, Paul D. Murray, and Andres Torres Queiruga (London: Concilium/SCM Press, 2012/1), 21.

44  For Schillebeeckx, the authority of God's word consists "in the relationship between the intentionality of faith and a given (and changing) referential framework." He emphasizes that the criterion for orthodoxy can never be figured out purely theoretically. This criterion always reveals itself in something other than itself: "the future cannot be theoretically interpreted, it must be done … In interpreting the past in light of the present, then, it should not be forgotten that eschatological faith imposes on the present the task of transcending itself, not only theoretically, but as a change to be realized." Edward Schillebeeckx, "Theological Criteria," *UF, CW* vol. 5 (London: Bloomsbury T&T Clark, 2014), 59 [66].

45  My interpretive paraphrase of Schillebeeckx: "In his very essence, man [*sic*] is a narrative, a historical event rather than a pre-determined fact. He reveals something of this essence nowhere but in the course of his historical passage: in the very history of humanity. Man is situated and thematic freedom ...." Edward Schillebeeckx, "Questions on Christian Salvation of and for Man," *Toward Vatican III: The Work That Needs to Be Done*, ed. David Tracy, Hans Küng, and Johann Baptist Metz (New York: Gill and MacMillan, 1978), 30.

46  An image beautifully employed and illustrated by Christopher Pramuk in *Hope Sings So Beautiful*.

of God is Christian, Schillebeeckx situates this "language of faith" within a universal human longing for healing, wholeness, and fulfillment. He offers a set of anthropological constants which reveal human values, point to lasting human impulses and orientations, but do not provide us with concrete norms and ethical imperatives. Rather, they provide constitutive conditions. These constants are coordinates that are interrelated and which reveal the interdependence of our relationships to our own bodiliness, to one another and to the earth, to social and institutional structures, and to historical and social location and culture; the dialectical relation between theory and praxis, and the human religious and "para-religious" consciousness. The seventh constant affirms the irreducible synthesis of these six dimensions, cautioning that the undervaluing of any one of these throws human culture out of balance.[47]

The Christian imagination "fills in" these coordinates with the fragments of salvation envisioned and described in the longings of those who suffer under conditions which threaten their humanity. It reaches to improvise a contemporary enactment of Jesus's encounters with the oppressed and dispossessed of his own day, creating a praxis of solidarity and justice that becomes a living proclamation of the Gospel to which God will give a future. But where particular ecclesial structures and doctrines impede the experience of salvation here and now, these representations of the "center" must respond to the critique from the peripheries. Those who would be guardians of the "center" are summoned to the humility of giving priority to the "epistemological privilege" of the suffering experience of the marginalized; they are exhorted to take to heart Jesus's own preference for the excluded "Other"; they are invited to receive and respond to the Gospel word being proclaimed on the peripheries, to bring it to the heart of the church and allow its grace to enrich and transform both doctrine and structure. In Schillebeeckx's terms, those in "ministerial authority" are called to model the "vulnerable, even helpless, rule of God."[48]

We are all summoned to seek the reign of God and the truth of God's life among us in encounter with the defenseless and vulnerable of our world. We are all called to mirror in our relationships God's own pattern of giving creation space, of making room for human freedom, of honoring our divine and human becoming. At the center, on the peripheries, and in between, we are called to both exercise and honor the "vulnerable rule of God."

---

[47] See Schillebeeckx, "Questions on Christian Salvation." See also Schillebeeckx, *Christ*, 725–37 [731–43].

[48] Schillebeeckx, *Church*, 220 [221].

# Chapter 23

# Magisterium and Authority

Daniel Speed Thompson

"Ecclesiology in a minor key."[1] In the long second phase of his theological career (from 1966 until his death in 2009), Edward Schillebeeckx used this phrase from time to time to advocate for a Catholic Church that shifted the focus from itself back to the center of Christian faith: God's gracious salvation effected in the life, death, and resurrection of Jesus. The inspiration for this shift in emphasis was expressed succinctly in the famous phrase from the Dogmatic Constitution on the Church (*Lumen gentium*) from the Second Vatican Council (1962–1965): "[T]he Church is in Christ like a sacrament or as a sign and instrument both of a very closely knit union with God and of the unity of the whole human race."[2] With particular regard to the last clause, Schillebeeckx joined other Catholic theologians of this period in emphasizing common service to human flourishing as a concrete sign of the Kingdom of God. In turn, this shift to a model of church as servant in and of the world led Schillebeeckx to criticize the emphasis on ecclesiology that still dominated the Second Vatican Council. The future of Christian faith in the modern world, Schillebeeckx argued, will depend not on the church's talk about itself but on its practical enactment of God's salvation in the here and now. An understanding of faith not linked with this critical praxis will only be an empty ideology.[3]

If, according to Schillebeeckx, ecclesiology needs to move from a major to a minor key, then one might easily conclude that his later theology would downplay theological discussions of the magisterium and authority even more, making them an occasional minor chord heard in the background of a piece emphasizing the major themes of Christology and salvation. In one sense, this is true; Schillebeeckx's treatments of these topics are occasional and usually brief, often sparked by a particular situation in the local or global church or by his own encounters with magisterial criticism. On the other hand, these treatments, considered in combination with the major themes of his theology, offer a provocative if incomplete reconsideration of these classic Catholic doctrines. This chapter will offer the reader an outline of his theology of the magisterium and authority. After an abbreviated overview of these topics in his earlier thought, I will examine in more detail his later theology. I will place an emphasis on connecting his views on the magisterium and authority with the shifts in method that he embraced after 1966,

---

[1]   Edward Schillebeeckx, *Church, CW* vol. 10 (London: Bloomsbury T&T Clark, 2014), xxvii [xix]. See also, Edward Schillebeeckx, *I Am a Happy Theologian: Conversations with Francesco Strazzari*, trans. John Bowden (London: SCM Press, 1994), 74, and, Edward Schillebeeckx, *On Christian Faith: The Spiritual, Ethical and Political Dimensions*, trans. John Bowden (New York: Crossroad, 1987), 31.

[2]   *Lumen gentium* (November 24, 1964) 1 (hereafter cited in text as *LG*), http://www.vatican.va/archive/hist_councils/ii_vatican_council/documents/vat-ii_const_19641121_lumen-gentium_en.html.

[3]   Edward Schillebeeckx, *UF, CW* vol. 5 (London: Bloomsbury T&T Clark, 2014).

and on the way in which his relationships with different ecclesiastical authorities influenced his theology. Finally, I will close with a suggestion about the relationship between Schillebeeckx's theology and the practice of Pope Francis.

# I. Preserving the apostolicity of the church in Schillebeeckx's early theology

The first period of Schillebeeckx's theology is no mere short phase. Beginning with his training with the Dominicans in the 1930s and concluding after the Second Vatican Council, these decades saw Schillebeeckx engaged in developing what biographer Erik Borgman has termed "a Catholic theology of culture."[4] For the purposes of this essay, this approach can only be sketched in a brief outline. On the level of fundamental theology, Schillebeeckx, following the inspiration of his teacher Dominicus De Petter, attempted to interpret the Thomistic metaphysics of the day in such a way that would overcome its narrow focus on concepts and allow for a richer language of personal encounter and historical context. On the level of ecclesiology and sacramental theology, Schillebeeckx used this language of encounter to ground an understanding of the sacraments in the context of the church, which in turn concretely serves as the ongoing locus of encounter with the risen Christ. As the title of his 1959 book states, Christ is the sacrament of the encounter with God. The church is then Christ's ongoing sacrament in history and the sacramental rituals of the church, the ongoing making present of Christ in the church's life and in the life of individual believers.[5] For Schillebeeckx, this presence of the glorified Christ is constitutive of the church, both head and members.[6]

Although expressed in the "descending" Christology and ecclesiology of the day, Schillebeeckx's view of the church was not clericalist or triumphalist. As much as was possible at the time, he gave emphasis to the idea that the *whole* church, both laity and clergy, was the sacramental body of Christ in history. Using language that will also be adopted by the bishops at the Second Vatican Council, Schillebeeckx describes the whole church as the "People of God." He in no way denies that the laity and the hierarchy have different roles in the church as a result of Christ's relationship to it, but he also makes clear that the hierarchy consists of believing members within the church, not another class of persons above it.[7] The church's divine origin— indeed its fundamental reality as the mystical body of Christ in history—does not exempt it from failures and the constant need for reform. The church that reveals Christ can also conceal him; the church that is a motive for faith and an object of faith can also be a trial for that faith.

Schillebeeckx roots his understanding of both ecclesial indefectibility and infallibility in this twofold conception of Christ's presence and veiling within the church. As I will outline below,

---

[4] Erik Borgman, *Edward Schillebeeckx: A Theologian in His History*, trans. John Bowden (London/New York: Continuum, 2003), 6.

[5] Edward Schillebeeckx, *Christ the Sacrament, CW* vol. 1 (London: Bloomsbury T&T Clark, 2014).

[6] Schillebeeckx, *Christ the Sacrament*, 5–28 [7–46]. See also, Henricus Edward Schillebeeckx, s.v. "Sacrament," *Theol. Woordenboek*, vol. 3 (Roermond/Maaseik: J. J. Romen & Zonen, 1958), cols. 4200–02.

[7] Schillebeeckx, *Christ the Sacrament*, 20–30 [48–49].

his theology of authority and the magisterium will follow from this more general ecclesiological claim. I will also argue that this dialectical orientation toward church authority will carry over into his later theology, even as his changes in methodology will create some difficulties for his thought to consistently maintain this dialectic.

Considered as a whole, the church is the sacrament of encounter with Christ. Yet, following an interpretation common at the time, according to Schillebeeckx, the church's sacramental representation as Christ's body in the world is twofold, with the hierarchy sacramentally representing Christ's headship in relation to the church.[8] The preeminent form of this office or ministry, which is also the paradigmatic priestly office in the church, is held by the bishops as the successors of the apostles.[9]

Since bishops possess the fullness of the "*sacerdotium*" given to the church by Christ, they are primarily responsible for both the word and sacrament. To use language from his discussions of revelation and salvation, Schillebeeckx describes the bishops as those commissioned to continue the apostolic task of transmitting and keeping alive the dialectic of "revelation-in-reality" and "revelation-in-word" which culminated in Christ.[10]

From their primary task of oversight over word and sacrament flows their teaching authority, which Schillebeeckx characterizes as simply an organized and official exercise of this task.[11]

Hence, the *source* of authority in the church is Christ, who mediates his own authority to the bishops who then enact it in the historical church.[12] This characterization of the source of ecclesial authority also foreshadows the language of *Lumen gentium* (*LG* 21) that states episcopal authority derives from the sacrament of orders and not simply by jurisdictional power of the pope. This concept of authority also coincides with Vatican II's doctrine of episcopal collegiality. The *subjects* or bearers of this authority are then the bishops who themselves are under the authority of the bishop of Rome, the pope. Schillebeeckx distinguishes but does not separate *types* of authority exercised by the episcopacy and the pope, that is, powers conferred by ordination and the power of jurisdiction. This distinction in turn rests on different aspects of Christ's headship over the church, that is, that he is the "offering principle of all grace on the basis of his *cultus* to the Father" and he is the "*exousia* or sovereign power leading the Church, and thus as the normative principle of our actions in life, our response to grace."[13] Bishops hold these powers in their fullness (with the pope exercising them in an ultimately authoritative way over the whole church). Priestly powers of liturgical presidency are real but dependent on episcopal power; in a similar way, priestly ordination does not convey the power of jurisdiction or teaching authority in itself, except as derived from episcopal mandate.[14]

Schillebeeckx at this point accepts the distinction between the extraordinary and ordinary magisterium and between the episcopal and papal exercises of magisterial authority. The

---

8   Henricus Edward Schillebeeckx, s.v. "Priesterschap," *Theol. Woordenboek*, cols. 3981–84.

9   Ibid., col. 3982. See also, Edward Schillebeeckx, "Het apostolisch ambt van de Kerkelijke hierarchie," *Studia Catholica* 32 (1957), 258–90.

10  Schillebeeckx, "Priesterschap," cols. 3983–84.

11  Schillebeeckx, *Christ the Sacrament*, 98 [170].

12  A side note: Without lapsing into modalism, Schillebeeckx can also assert that the Spirit is a source of authority in the church but in a different sense. See the discussion of ecclesial indefectibility below.

13  Edward Schillebeeckx, "Dogmatiek ambt en lekenstaat," *TvT* 2 (1962), 275.

14  Ibid., 282–88.

extraordinary magisterium of the church only occurs when the pope himself makes an infallible dogmatic definition under certain particular circumstances or when a properly convened ecumenical council does so under papal authority.[15] This extraordinary magisterium of the pope with the bishops is a specific form of the ordinary and universal teaching authority of the whole hierarchy, whose infallibility Schillebeeckx also accepts.[16] Likewise he agrees with the classical distinction between episcopal teaching authority and the particular teaching office of the pope, although he also recognizes that papal infallibility also occurs only under restricted circumstances and only in relation to the fundamental reality of revelation.[17] Schillebeeckx carefully nuances the various levels of authority of church statements and argues, on the basis of his revised Thomist epistemology and understanding of language, that even dogmas are not in themselves simply the truths of revelation. In so doing, he takes an orthodox but minimalist posture toward the magisterium.

In this early period of Schillebeeckx's thought, however, one should note that because the episcopal authority over the laity involves the power to make judgments on the doctrinal language, liturgical practice, and ethical behavior of the other members of the church, the laity ultimately do not have an independent "power" of interpretation, judgment, or action. Although Schillebeeckx is an early advocate for the more complete participation of the laity in their own mission in the church, this activity does not yet include a share in the teaching ministry or office that is the prerogative of the hierarchy.

Schillebeeckx shares with the Catholic theologians of his time the assumption that the *object* of magisterial authority is not only the doctrinal language of the church, but also its ethical teachings and liturgical practice. For example, his own treatment of sacramental theology and his extended reflections on marriage work within the boundaries established by the magisterium on these topics, which he nevertheless attempts to rethink in the light of the pastoral needs of the day.[18]

Within the limits allowed by pre-conciliar theology, Schillebeeckx argues for a complementarity between the magisterium, theologians and laity in the development of the understanding of faith. This complementary interplay ultimately stands under the protection of the Holy Spirit, who is the final guardian of the church's preservation in truth. In both his earlier and later work, Schillebeeckx affirms that the Spirit is the ultimate source of authority in the church, even if that authority is also mediated through the apostolic office of the hierarchy. However, this mediation of the Spirit also has a dialectical aspect; the teaching office, and indeed the whole church itself, is both *sancta* and *semper reformanda*. Instead of describing the teaching office as simply the direct mediator of the Spirit's presence, Schillebeeckx prefers to speak about the Spirit's preservation of the church in truth (or indefectibility), despite the errors and limitations of the church's members, even its officeholders.[19] This presence of the Spirit means that the church, in head and members,

---

[15] Henricus Edward Schillebeeckx, s.v. "Kerkvergadering," *Theol. Woordenboek*, vol. 2, cols. 2773–76.

[16] Ibid., col. 2775.

[17] See Henricus Edward Schillebeeckx, s.v., "Ex cathedra," *Theol. Woordenboek*, vol. 1, col. 1481, for the more specific conditions under which the pope can make an infallible declaration.

[18] See Schillebeeckx, *Christ the Sacrament*, and, Edward Schillebeeckx, *Marriage: Human Reality and Saving Mystery*, trans. N.D. Smith (New York: Sheed and Ward, 1965).

[19] Edward Schillebeeckx, "The Reformation of the Church," *The Mission of the Church*, trans. N.D. Smith (London: Sheed and Ward, 1973), 12.

is not the completely fulfilled presence of Christ in the world, but rather the community that is being drawn forward into the eschatological future. As the principle of renewal, the Spirit's impulse therefore cannot be reduced to the official or structural element in the church.[20]

The early phase of Schillebeeckx's work concludes with the Second Vatican Council, which marks the fruition of many of its themes and also creates the conditions for the transition to the later phase of his thought. The Council, according to Schillebeeckx, reformed Catholic ecclesiology both internally and externally. The Dogmatic Constitution on the Church, *Lumen gentium*, promulgated in 1964, is the cornerstone of both forms of renewal. The Constitution's famous twofold sacramental analogy for the church echoes Schillebeeckx's earlier work and sets the direction for his future forays into ecclesiology. The church is a sacrament not only of communion with God, accomplished fully in Christ, but also of the "unity of all men." Naming this second aspect of the church's sacramentality signifies to Schillebeeckx a shift in ecclesiology of momentous proportions. No longer will the world simply be the implicit field of God's action that the church's teaching and life make explicit. The world no longer exists simply to be drawn into the church; rather, the church exists to be a sacrament of what the world should become in its graced autonomy. Schillebeeckx sees this changed understanding of the relationship between the church and the world in *Lumen gentium* continue and develop in the other groundbreaking ecclesiological document from the Second Vatican Council, the Pastoral Constitution on the Church in the Modern World, *Gaudium et spes*.

In this text, Schillebeeckx notes the new spirit of acceptance of the historicity of human nature, and the willingness both to give to the world and to receive from it. Of paramount importance is the constitution's embrace of the autonomy and goodness of secular reality; it is the end, as Schillebeeckx puts it, of the "'syllabus mentality' of Pius IX."[21] In his view, this changed relationship between the church and the world is the most revolutionary result of the whole council. He wrote not long afterward: "The characteristic of Vatican II is that its basic theme concerns the question of religious existence in a world that is changing, abandoning sacral for human forms."[22] This new understanding of the world—which is at heart really a changed understanding of God's salvation and revelation in the context of all human history—undergirds the many other ecclesiological changes that mark the Second Vatican Council. While still affirming the uniqueness and fullness of the revelation given in Christ and its preservation within the Catholic Church, the Second Vatican Council also says that the other Christian communities and the other great traditions of the world bring salvation to their members. The Catholic Church at the Second Vatican Council, according to Schillebeeckx, abandons any claim to possess a monopoly on all forms of religiousness, all forms of Christianity, all forms of the church. Furthermore, it abandons all claims to control over every aspect of ordinary human life, recognizes the proper autonomy of the world, and the right of persons to organize their lives according to their deepest convictions. Yet because the church is still the bearer of the fullness of revelation, the tension of church and world is not eliminated; this theological question will continue to frame Schillebeeckx's later work, including his more occasional ecclesiological works.

---

[20]  Ibid., 13.
[21]  Edward Schillebeeckx, *The Real Achievement of Vatican II*, trans. H.J.J. Vaughan (New York: Herder and Herder, 1967), 49.
[22]  Ibid., 56.

# II. Preserving the apostolicity of the church in Schillebeeckx's later theology

For Schillebeeckx, the close of the Second Vatican Council was the beginning of a new era both in Catholicism and in his own work. Especially in its later documents, the Council had reconsidered the church's relationship with the world and reoriented its task toward the concrete service of that world. It is here that the church as a subject of theology begins to move from a major to a minor key. Therefore, in order to understand Schillebeeckx's theology of the magisterium in this later period, it is first necessary to set out, however briefly, the more fundamental shifts in Schillebeeckx's thinking which occurred after the Council.

## The Hermeneutical and Critical Turns

Not long after the conclusion of the Council, as Schillebeeckx recalled it years later, he came to the conclusion that the so-called "perspectivalist" reading of Thomas which had heretofore served as the framework of his theology was no longer adequate for the task of expressing an understanding of faith adequate for the modern world. As he put it, he made a "clear break with the 'implicit intuition' of the meaning-totality maintained by the classical philosophy like that of D. De Petter, L. Lavelle, and the French *philosophes de l'Esprit*."[23] In a situation marked by widespread human suffering, greater pluralism, and the breakdown of a single Christian culture, Christian pretensions to knowledge of the total meaning of history must now "be replaced by the idea of the anticipation of a total meaning amid a history still in the making."[24] To articulate the understanding of faith in this changed historical situation with its deeper historical consciousness, Schillebeeckx turns his focus to the central topic of Christian theology and embarks on a reappraisal of the meaning of Jesus of Nazareth for the modern world.

In order to do this, Schillebeeckx pursues a nearly decade-long exploration of contemporary theology, biblical exegesis, and philosophy. His reading in philosophy touched on nearly every school of twentieth century Western thought: semiotics, structuralism, linguistic analysis, critical theory, the thought of Ludwig Wittgenstein and Emmanuel Levinas, as well as other philosophical approaches.[25] However, immediately after his "clear break" with perspectivalist Thomism, Schillebeeckx turned first to the hermeneutical school represented in the thought of Martin Heidegger, Hans-Georg Gadamer, and Paul Ricoeur.

As a result of this reading, Schillebeeckx came to argue that human beings understand the world through interpretative experience. The interpretative act always exists in a dynamic, historical circle of pre-understanding or horizon, new experience, and reshaped horizon. Within this irreducible circle, human beings come to know the objective world interpretatively as this world presents itself to the human knower. In other words, human beings do not experience the

---

[23] Edward Schillebeeckx, *Jesus, CW* vol. 6 (London: Bloomsbury T&T Clark, 2014), 580 [618].

[24] Ibid., 580–81 [618–19].

[25] Philip Kennedy lists eighteen intellectual sources for the post Vatican II thought of Schillebeeckx and names the four most important as hermeneutics, biblical studies, philosophy of language, and critical theory. See Philip Kennedy, *Schillebeeckx* (Collegeville, MN: Liturgical Press, 1993), 36–37.

world in a "raw" state and then make interpretations of what they experience. Rather, human experience is co-constituted by interpretation; interpretation makes real experience both possible and expressible.

Schillebeeckx refines this hermeneutical analysis of human experience over the course of the two decades after the Council, particularly in response to criticisms of his book *Jesus: An Experiment in Christology* (1974). Space again will not permit me to describe in detail this analysis; for the purposes of this essay, one should note two key claims that Schillebeeckx maintains in this hermeneutical turn. The first is that human historicity and linguisticality, so to speak, serve as the inescapable media for encounter with reality, taking the place of perspectival concepts. Second, that despite the concern that such a turn will immerse the human subject in contingent history and language to such an extent that objective reality becomes inaccessible, Schillebeeckx (particularly when he first adopts this stance) insists that hermeneutics does not entail this epistemological subjectivism.

Yet, on the other hand, Schillebeeckx also increasingly comes to see the limitations of the purely hermeneutical approach for refashioning a contemporary understanding of faith.[26] Although he never breaks from hermeneutical language in the same way that he claims to do from his earlier perspectivalist Thomism, he nevertheless layers this approach with an additional rethinking in the light of the critical theory of the Frankfurt School, particularly Adorno, Horkheimer, and the early Habermas. In the light of these new conversation partners, his early concern with experience becomes a focus on negative contrast experiences; the importance of linguistic pre-understanding becomes a focus on ideological critique; the historicity of human existence becomes a focus on human suffering.

More formally stated, Schillebeeckx takes the position that human knowledge of objective reality comes through practical mediation and the theoretical expression inseparably attached to it. Privileged moments in this circle of praxis and theory are "negative contrast experiences," where knowledge of reality comes both through reality's resistance to human expectations and human, active resistance to that which destroys human flourishing. Because of the narrative structure of human experience, the history of human suffering is an especially privileged source of knowledge. Truth in this view cannot theoretically be possessed under the conditions of human history because of human finitude and possible distortion: it can only be enacted in an anticipatory way. The practical and proleptic nature of truth becomes the new framework for understanding.

With occasional lapses in consistency, Schillebeeckx uses this multi-layered approach to knowledge as a lens for his rethinking of classic Christology and other theological subjects, including church and magisterium, until the end of his career. At the same time, he resists reducing his theology to the limits outlined by his philosophical conversation partners. The Christian narrative carried forward by Christian communities also reinterprets and reframes philosophy, and adds its own distinctive elements.

---

[26] See Edward Schillebeeckx, *Collegedictaat hermeneutiek 1978–1979*, ed. Frank G. Bosman (Nijmegen: Stichting Edward Schillebeeckx, 2004).

# Experience and authority

This dialectic becomes apparent when considering how Schillebeeckx's later theology considers the question of experience and authority. As sketched above, his work not only shifts the mediation of the experience of truth from concepts (rightly understood) to historical narrative, it privileges the narratives of experienced suffering. Furthermore, I would suggest that he no longer can locate absolute authority in any one place, nor, given his shifts in epistemology and fundamental theology, can he even define "authority" in any sort of traditional sense. Rather, he redefines "authority" as the critical, cognitive, and productive force of an experience or a tradition of experiences.[27] Those experiences have authority that rests on the truth in such a way that they unmask ideological distortions (the critical aspect), they provide a disclosure of meaning (the cognitive aspect), and they bring about a liberating praxis (the productive aspect). If this is a correct reading of Schillebeeckx, then in his view authority comes from experiences that have these qualities and does not inhere in people (or in offices themselves for that matter) in an "essentialist" way. Rather, it resides in the dialectical relationship between persons and offices that can create these experiences. In a way which Schillebeeckx himself never fully sketched out, his later view of the authority of church office implies that such offices only have authority *in potentia*; that is, they exist to create and preserve the conditions in the church for believers to experience and enact truly authoritative events. However, for Schillebeeckx, this view of authority and church office does not eliminate the appropriateness and necessity of such office. Nor does it eliminate an idea that he holds consistently throughout his career: the Holy Spirit is the ultimate source of authority in the church. Instead, Schillebeeckx argues that the development of church office over time is both the result of human decision and the ongoing influence of the Spirit.

Nevertheless, his reconception of experience and authority, when applied correctly, de-centers the magisterium in the Catholic imagination and reduces it (appropriately in Schillebeeckx's view) to the role of one dialogue partner in the church's ongoing conversation about orthodoxy and orthopraxy. Like the church as a whole, the magisterium registers in a minor key in Schillebeeckx's later thought; both take on the role of servant to the cause of the suffering *humanum,* which is God's cause as well.

# Rethinking the church

Because of this shift in emphasis, Schillebeeckx does not construct a systematic ecclesiology in his later theology. In my own work, I have attempted to synthesize what such an ecclesiology might look like from his occasional forays into this topic.[28] Without imposing more systematic structure or consistency than his works call for, I argue that Schillebeeckx translates his early view of the church as the sacrament of encounter with Christ into a theology of the church as anticipatory sign. If Christ is "concentrated creation," to use his phrase,[29] the concrete expression

---

[27] See, for example, Edward Schillebeeckx, *Christ, CW* vol. 7 (London: Bloomsbury T&T Clark, 2014), 29–37 [13–23], 817–18 [812–14].

[28] Daniel Speed Thompson, *The Language of Dissent: Edward Schillebeeckx on the Crisis of Authority in the Catholic Church* (Notre Dame, IN: University of Notre Dame Press, 2003), 84–94.

[29] Edward Schillebeeckx, *IR, CW* vol. 8 (London: Bloomsbury T&T Clark, 2014), 109–12 [126–28].

of God's salvific intent for humanity and its ultimate eschatological fulfillment, then the church is the historical community dedicated to remembrance of Christ, actualization of his praxis of the reign of God in the present, and hope for the future.[30]

Adapting and extending the language of *Lumen gentium*, the church remains "the sacrament of Christ" and the "sacrament of the unity of humanity." However, in the context of the hermeneutical, critical, and narrative turns in his theology, Schillebeeckx moves away from describing the church's participation in Christ through a quasi-metaphysical reading of Scriptural images, for example, the church as Body of Christ with the accompanying distinction between Christ's headship in the church represented by the hierarchy and the role of the laity. Rather, the church actively remembers, reenacts, and anticipates this participation in Christ across different eras of history and in many different forms.

# Criteria for apostolicity

How does the church, so understood, preserve its apostolic nature, according to Schillebeeckx? After the publication of the first two parts of his intended Christological trilogy, Schillebeeckx turned his attention to a more extended consideration of ministry and leadership in the church, although he had also written on the topic several times in the wake of the Council.[31] For Schillebeeckx, the decades after the Council had actually become the period of the "anti-Council,"[32] where reactionary forces in the church had defeated the implementation of the Council's vision in favor of returning to an older ecclesiology and understanding of the church's relationship to the world. In this contested situation and in the light of experiments in alternative forms of ecclesial life in the Netherlands and elsewhere, Schillebeeckx takes particular pains to define carefully the apostolicity of the church and the role of ordained ministry in preserving that apostolic nature.

In a relatively early text (1969), Schillebeeckx locates the apostolic succession of office within the context of the whole church.

> The foundation of the apostolic succession in the office of the Church is, in the first place, the apostolicity of the community itself, because it is precisely in the apostolic Church that the Holy Spirit is active. The apostolicity of the Christian community implies the apostolic faith and an office which proceeds from the apostolic Church. The pneumatic character of the apostolic community of the

---

[30] Schillebeeckx, *On Christian Faith*, 41.

[31] See, for example, Edward Schillebeeckx, "Het concilie en de dialogale strukturen," *De concilieboodschap voor de Kerk in Vlaanderen*, Ontmoetingen "Kristendom en Wereld" (Leuven: Davidsfonds, 1966), 43–62; Edward Schillebeeckx, "The Catholic Understanding of Office in the Church," *Theological Studies* 30 (1969), 567–87; Edward Schillebeeckx, *The Mission of the Church*, trans. N.D. Smith (New York: Seabury Press, 1973); Edward Schillebeeckx, "The Problem of the Infallibility of the Church's Office: A Theological Reflection," *Truth and Certainty*, ed. Edward Schillebeeckx and Bas van Iersel, *Concilium* 83 (1973), 77–94.

[32] Edward Schillebeeckx, *For the Sake of the Gospel*, trans. John Bowden (London: SCM, 1989), 137.

Church is therefore also the primary basis of the apostolic succession and thus of the validity of the office of the Church. The apostolicity of the community of the Church, that is, belonging to one of the empirical communities of the Church which, in mutual "ecclesial recognition," claim to be the "Church of Christ," is the basis of the apostolicity or validity of the office of the Church.[33]

Some years later, in response to criticisms of his *Ministry* (1980) book, Schillebeeckx refines his understanding of the elements of the church's apostolicity. First, he regards as "the fundamental dimension of the apostolicity of the churches the fact that these churches are founded or built up 'on the apostles and prophets (Eph. 2.20; 4.7–16).'" Second, "There is above all the apostolic content of 'tradition,' *paratheke*, the gospel of the pledge entrusted, in other words the apostolic tradition. Here the New Testament writings are a permanent foundation document." Third, "There is also the apostolicity of the Christian communities of believers themselves, as called to life by the apostles and prophets on the criteria of the apostolic content of faith, which is handed down .... The *sequela Jesu* or the praxis of the kingdom of God is an essential part of this, i.e., following Jesus in his message, his teaching and his actions." Finally, "There is the apostolicity of the church ministries, the so-called apostolic succession."[34]

This broadening of the definition of apostolicity allows Schillebeeckx to argue that the whole church has a commission to carry forth the apostolic tradition and this commission is fundamentally prior to the ministerial office and its specific task. Indeed, according to Schillebeeckx, the ministerial office, as it develops historically into the combined functions of presidency at the Eucharist and magisterial authority over Christian doctrine and practice, should only be seen as a concrete instance (or "crystallization") of the apostolicity of the whole Christian community, given to it in its baptism by the Spirit.[35]

The consequences are the following: for Schillebeeckx ministerial offices are a legitimate and even necessary development in the life of the church. However, such offices are also necessarily connected to and counterbalanced by other elements in the church. Their form is also *contingent*; types of ministry and office which developed in one period of the church's life may no longer serve the apostolic mandate in a new era and may require change in order to do so. And, if my hypothesis about his later view of authority is correct, such contingent offices in the church possess authority only in a secondary fashion; they exercise authority only insofar as they help to bring about the truly critical, cognitive, and practical experiences that have deeper authority in the life of the Christian and the Christian community.

With this rethinking of the notion of apostolic succession comes an analogous reinterpretation of the notion of orthodox transmission of the apostolic faith. The early Schillebeeckx locates this continuity in the development of dogmas that truly express, however inadequately, the mystery of salvation and revelation contained in the deposit of faith. This continuity in development is guaranteed by the church's magisterium whose task it is to preserve, define, and teach these

---

[33]  Schillebeeckx, "The Catholic Understanding of Office in the Church," 574. Emphasis original.
[34]  Edward Schillebeeckx, *CHF, CW* vol. 9 (London: Bloomsbury T&T Clark, 2014), 106 [116].
[35]  Ibid., 111 [122].

doctrines, and ultimately by the Holy Spirit, whose guidance preserves the magisterium and overcomes the fallibility of the church's human members. The later Schillebeeckx distances himself from this developmental model in favor of *a hermeneutical, critical and practical translation of Christian experience from one historical era to the next.* In *The Understanding of Faith* (1972), Schillebeeckx makes a first attempt to name criteria for this translation. These are: the criterion of the proportional norm, the criterion of orthopraxis, and the criterion of reception by the whole People of God.[36] Briefly, the first criterion states that continuity in the understanding of faith comes from the act or intentionality of faith itself in relationship to the various referential contexts in which that act occurs:

> ... the fundamental identity of meaning between successive eras in Christian interpretation of tradition does not refer to corresponding *terms,* for instance between the biblical situation and ours ... but to corresponding *relations* between such terms (message and situation then and now).[37]

The second criterion states that the transmission of the apostolic faith is primarily a matter of its reenactment by Christians in the life of the church and the world; orthopraxis, tested against the memory of Jesus and the eschatological hope of the reign of God, makes orthodoxy concrete and effective in the world. The third criterion states that the whole church community is the subject sustaining the practical translation of the faith from one generation to the next and that within this community there are various roles which interact with each other through a "tested dialectical process" to ensure the orthodoxy of the transmission of faith. These interactions comprise a series of mutually critical relationships, including those between theologians and the magisterium, between the local church and the other local churches of the wider community, and also between local churches and their leaders, including the pope. Even if the local community must see itself always in relationship with the wider church and ultimately under the judgment of the bishop of Rome in his capacity as successor of Peter, this does not mean that the local church may not be a source for a new interpretation of faith for the entire church:

> The local communities of God are therefore essentially subject to the criticism of the other local churches and, ultimately, to that of all the leaders of the local churches with the "president of the bond of love" among them—the bishop to whom the office of the primacy of Peter is entrusted within the college of bishops. Assuming this, then, the consciousness of faith of one local church which accepts a given interpretation of faith may well be a *locus theologicus*, a source for theology within the universal church, an indication of the Holy Spirit, on the basis of which the given interpretation may be regarded as a safe guiding principle.[38]

---

[36] Edward Schillebeeckx, "Theological Criteria," *UF, CW* vol. 5 (London: Bloomsbury T&T Clark, 2014), 50–64 [55–72].

[37] Edward Schillebeeckx, "Theological Interpretation of Faith in 1983," *Essays, CW* vol. 11 (London: Bloomsbury T&T Clark, 2014), 62. Emphasis original.

[38] Schillebeeckx, "Theological Criteria," *UF*, 64 [71].

# III. Ministry and magisterium: Ecclesial, episcopal, papal

This exposition on apostolicity and the criteria of orthodoxy will serve to frame my presentation of Schillebeeckx's understanding of the role and authority of the magisterium within the church. His understanding of the latter flows from his understanding of the former; the magisterium, theologians, and believers all participate in the "tested dialectical process" referred to above which, under the ultimate guidance of the Holy Spirit, allows the church as a whole to preserve, enact anew, and hope for the fulfillment of the message of Jesus's life: God's salvific will for all humanity.

With regard to the magisterium, Schillebeeckx in his later theology will continue to affirm its necessary role in the translation of Christian experience. However, he will always locate its authority within the broader context of the apostolicity and current experience of the whole church. This placement of the magisterium, coupled with his epistemological shifts, will accentuate his earlier "minimalism" with regard to official church authority to such an extent that, especially with regard to the issue of infallibility, Schillebeeckx will have difficulty affirming this authority in any traditional sense. He will struggle to preserve the language of earlier pronouncements on magisterial authority but will use increasingly metaphorical language to explain it.

As I discussed above, Schillebeeckx sees the ministerial office, including its teaching functions, as a legitimate "crystallization" or concentration of the apostolic "pledge" and task given to the whole church.[39] The magisterium's role is therefore subordinated to the service of this "entrusted pledge." This grounding of the magisterium within the broader context of the apostolicity of the whole church also means that the magisterium is not the sole or even immediate norm of the orthodoxy of the church. The church's teaching office is not one of the three criteria of orthodoxy, although it does have a role to play in maintaining orthodoxy. In distinction from his earlier thought, Schillebeeckx will now criticize the magisterium when it pretends that it itself is the *"regula proxima"* of faith.[40]

This move is significant, because now Schillebeeckx does not see the magisterium (and its official teachings) as belonging primarily to the *interpretandum* of the Gospel that the theologian must take into account, but as part of the process of interpreting the Gospel within the whole church. The magisterium hence is not a purely independent source of dogmatic teaching; it is not primarily a source for the church's language and theological expression, but the office charged with the pastoral obligation to watch over the church's language. As such, the magisterium should only bring to definitive expression the belief of the whole church; its role is not to create new doctrines but to evaluate critically the language and practice of the church in order to discern if it really proceeds from the *sensus fidei*.[41]

This shift in the understanding of the magisterium comes to its clearest expression when Schillebeeckx confronts the idea of ecclesial and papal infallibility. As I suggested above, he will

---

[39] Edward Schillebeeckx, "The Magisterium and Ideology," *Authority in the Church*, ed. Piet F. Fransen, Annua Nuntia Lovaniensia 26 (Leuven: Leuven University Press, 1983), 12. See also, Schillebeeckx, *Church*, 214–15 [216].

[40] Edward Schillebeeckx, "Magisterium: An Interview with Edward Schillebeeckx," interview by Manuel Alcalá, trans. Anthony M. Buono, *America* 144, no. 12 (March 28, 1981), 255.

[41] See Edward Schillebeeckx, "Is the Church Adrift?" *The Mission of the Church*, trans. N.D. Smith (London: Sheed and Ward, 1973), 34–35.

not directly deny either doctrine, but he will take two approaches to understanding infallibility that cumulatively lessen its claims. First, he will argue that infallibility, particularly that of the pope proclaimed at Vatican I, cannot be understood as an isolated power divorced from the wider church. In this regard, he is following a line of moderate or minimalist thinking about Vatican I that begins there and that receives particular expression in Vatican II's doctrine of the *sensus fidei* of the whole church.[42]

However, even with Vatican II's more balanced ecclesiology, Schillebeeckx after the Council will have more difficulty in affirming even the moderate traditional language used in this doctrine, because his epistemological and theological presuppositions will make it nearly impossible to do so. As time progresses, Schillebeeckx's language will become more and more fragmentary and metaphorical with regard to infallibility, particularly the papal variety.

Like magisterial authority in general, Schillebeeckx locates the infallibility of the magisterium, particularly papal infallibility, within the general indefectibility and infallibility of the church. In this way, he consistently argues that the infallibility decree of the First Vatican Council can only be rightly understood in the light of the ecclesiology of the Second Vatican Council, which more clearly spoke about the infallibility of the *sensus fidei* of the whole church. But the infallibility and indefectibility of the church rest on the Holy Spirit's continual renewing power working in and through it and therefore cannot be considered as an inherent or "static" quality of the church itself.

Rather, the indefectibility and infallibility of the church flow from God's promise to preserve the church in truth; this promise in turn extends to the magisterial office in the church.[43] However, this promise does not mean that the magisterium's authority works automatically or quasi-magically or that magisterial statements are somehow exempt from historical location and the possibility of critical distortion. With regard to the first point, Schillebeeckx argues that the magisterium's location within the community of faith and the very humanity of its members means that even infallible decisions can only be reached through "the free will, understanding and experience of the human office bearers."[44] This fact also leaves open the possibility that this mediation of the Holy Spirit can be distorted either through the manipulation of those in office or through their negligence. In either case, this means that the magisterium can produce poorly formulated or one-sided doctrines that need correction in the context of the wider Christian tradition.[45]

Beyond even the possibility of distortion or one-sidedness on the part of the office bearers, ecclesial or papal infallibility, according to Schillebeeckx, cannot exceed the bounds of human language and knowledge. In a 1973 *Concilium* article, he invokes both his (earlier) perspectivalist and (later) hermeneutical circles as parameters for any dogmatic language and argues that the traditional doctrine of infallibility itself can only be affirmed through the following reinterpretation:

---

[42] See, for example, the carefully worded official *relatio* of Bishop Vinzenz Gasser on papal infallibility at the First Vatican Council, which describes both the powers and limits of the pope's authority. Vinzenz Gasser, *The Gift of Infallibility: The Official Relatio of Bishop Vincent Gasser at Vatican Council I*, trans. James T. O'Connor (Boston: Daughters of St. Paul, 1986), 40–55.

[43] Schillebeeckx, "The Problem of the Infallibility of the Church's Office," 80.

[44] Edward Schillebeeckx, *Theologisch testament: Notarieel nog niet verleden*, 2nd ed. (Baarn: Nelissen, 1995), 73. See also, Schillebeeckx, *Jesus*, 21 [39].

[45] Schillebeeckx, *Theologisch testament*, 73.

In its offices or ministries (the papacy, the episcopate, etc.), the Church is able, at a given moment and within a concrete historical context of understanding, to express the Christian confession of faith *correctly, legitimately, faithfully* and with authoritative *binding* force. It can do this even though such concepts as "infallible," "irrevocable" and *ex sese* are disputable as historically situated terms implying a certain view of truth and belonging to a certain ecclesiological context. It can also do it although no concrete formulation or articulation (*enuntiabile*) can claim to stand up to the test of time.[46]

This qualified definition says much. Schillebeeckx here demonstrates again a dynamic that goes back to the earliest stages of his work: the dialectical interrelationship of objective truth and subjective knower. In this case, the objective truth of God's revelation can be expressed through the subjective context of the members of the church's teaching authority. Yet even as Schillebeeckx accepts this idea of infallibility, he also continues his "minimalist" approach by locating that "power" in the context of a whole series of "withins." It must be exercised within the perspectival and hermeneutical limits of language, within the thought forms and questions of a particular historical period, within the context of the whole church's *sensus fidei*, within the dialectic of past tradition, present actualization, and future hope, and within the very human possibilities of willful distortion, ignorance, and negligence.

With all these hedges around the law, so to speak, it is not surprising that Schillebeeckx will argue that the very terms of the traditional doctrine that seem to imply that infallibility reaches beyond these "withins" are themselves highly problematic and should possibly fall into disuse. The term "infallibility" is itself the most problematic, because it is "surrounded by ideological and sociological difficulties which seem insoluble."[47] At a later point, he will argue that "freedom from error" or, better yet, simply "true" are more adequate qualifications for dogma than "infallible," a term that adds nothing real to the quality of judgment about a doctrine, save a questionable "heightened appearance of certainty."[48] For this reason, the use of "theological notes" to qualify dogmas and doctrines almost entirely disappears in his later thought.

The problematic nature of this term becomes even greater when set in the context of the First Vatican Council's definition of *papal* infallibility. As I noted above, Schillebeeckx argues that Vatican I can only be properly understood within the ecclesiology of the people of God and the doctrine of collegiality promulgated at the Second Vatican Council. This ecclesiological framework, however, coupled with his epistemological parameters, makes the terminology of Vatican I, especially the phrases "*irreformabilis ex sese*" and "*non autem ex consensu Ecclesiae*," particularly difficult to accept in any maximalist sense.[49] Since this combination of changes raises problems for the whole idea of infallibility, Schillebeeckx in his later work argues in an increasingly forceful manner against the idea of an independent (or specific) papal infallibility:

> It would therefore be better that we no longer speak of "papal infallibility" (the expression is elliptical and misleading), but rather of the "infallibility" of

---

[46] Schillebeeckx, "The Problem of the Infallibility of the Church's Office," 91. Emphasis original.

[47] See Schillebeeckx, "Magisterium and Ideology," 13, where Schillebeeckx names the ways in which even an infallible statement is "relative to" a variety of different limiting conditions.

[48] Schillebeeckx, *Theologisch testament*, 78.

[49] Ibid., 76–77.

the world episcopate together with the pope as head of that college, and this therefore only in specific, determined actions. Moreover, Vatican II places all this in a still greater perspective, but this council did not work this out further; namely—and now I am citing from the theologian Ratzinger before his career as bishop and cardinal—as follows: this vision involves a moral bond between the pope and the world episcopate and the voice of the people of God. The pope with the bishops must also listen seriously to the voice of all the community of faith before solemnly promulgating a dogma. I would add: in order also to rightly give this form in concrete structures, particular organs of representation of the people of God would have to be called into existence.[50]

Because of his location of papal infallibility within the infallibility of the whole church, and his location of infallibility as a whole within the epistemological conditions of all human knowledge of the truth, Schillebeeckx will treat this idea generally speaking as he literally does in the previous quotation: he will put it in quotation marks. He does accept the idea of the magisterium and its decision-making ability but restricts the proper usage of such magisterial authority to very rare and specific circumstances, and only as last resort for the sake of the preservation of the whole Christian message. Even these rare pronouncements also are only boundary markers or "road-signs" for a particular era; since dogmas are the linguistic expression of a critical translation of Christian experience, even an "infallible" dogma can never completely or permanently capture that experience for all time. Even "infallible" dogmas are open for further reflection, reinterpretation, and criticism.[51]

Schillebeeckx's bracketing of the traditional language of infallibility results in his use of more metaphorical language for that doctrine as well as for the function of the magisterium in general. For example, "[p]articular papal or conciliar decisions taken in the name of the whole church community at the level of challenges which are vital for Gospel faith can indeed be 'infallible', that is, in a more or less happy way they nevertheless give historical expression to Christian truth."[52] Or, similarly, the magisterium "in *very exceptional and definite cases* is gifted with the *same* 'infallibility', that is, stability of the exchange rate, as that with which the whole Christian community of faith is gifted."[53]

Because of the rare nature of these interventions (and perhaps, in Schillebeeckx's mind, because of the epistemological doubts he has about the possibilities of such statements), the magisterium, especially in its Petrine office, should normally be the court of last appeal, not the sole or first voice heard in the church:

> I agree that it is good that the local church of Rome has a leader, its bishop, who has the function of Peter and ultimately sees to it that there is unity between the

---

[50]  Ibid., 78.

[51]  Edward Schillebeeckx, "Theological Interpretation of Faith in 1983," *Essays*, 66.

[52]  Schillebeeckx, *Church*, 197 [199].

[53]  Edward Schillebeeckx, "The Teaching Authority of All: A Reflection on the Structure of the New Testament," *The Teaching Authority of Believers*, ed. Johann-Baptist Metz and Edward Schillebeeckx, *Concilium* 180 (1985); reprinted in *The Language of Faith: Essays on Jesus, Theology and the Church.* (Maryknoll: Orbis, 1995), 234–35. Emphasis original.

other local churches. But that is the only function of the church of Rome—to be a kind of appeal court, so that, in the last resort, the local churches can make an appeal to the Petrine office.[54]

Similarly, the magisterium's chief function, along with its regulation of the language of the church, is actually to facilitate communication and institutional freedom in the church so that the consensus of all believers can emerge:

> In view of the new situation in which the Christian community is placed since the emergence of so many different interpretations of faith, the teaching office must above all serve as a means of communication within the community itself and guarantee an institutional freedom in which open dialogue can take place and in which all views can be heard. Any attempted manipulation must be prevented by that teaching authority so that a free consensus of opinion can come about within the community of believers.[55]

One must say that as time progressed, Schillebeeckx became less and less sanguine about the possibility that this vision of the magisterium would become a reality. Nevertheless, even if his later language about the actual exercise of authority by the Roman administration of John Paul II became harsher, he strove to maintain the idea, based on his understanding both of the Second Vatican Council and the nature of dogmatic language, that the magisterium is a necessary pole in the ongoing dialectic of preserving the apostolic witness in the church. Yet, as but one element in the process, the magisterium in Schillebeeckx's later thought always works within a series of dialectical relationships with other elements in the church, including theologians and the general experience of believers.

## Schillebeeckx and the magisterium: Relationships and cases

Schillebeeckx's theology of authority and the magisterium reflects not only the changes in his intellectual posture over the course of his career but also his own relationships with church authorities. In order to avoid too easily reducing Schillebeeckx's view of the magisterium to a narrative of his interactions with its representatives, I have separated those biographical details from his theological writings up to this point. However, of course, his relationship with church authorities does play a part in the development of his thought. In my view, these relationships offer him living models for both the proper and disordered functioning of the magisterium.

As the above presentation hoped to illustrate, instead of describing Schillebeeckx as a radical or dissenting theologian constantly pitted against the magisterium, it is far more accurate to describe him as a fundamentally ecclesial theologian, both confident in his Catholic faith and optimistic about the church's ability to translate that faith into the language of a new era and new culture. This twofold confidence underlies all of his early work as Schillebeeckx both rethinks

---

[54] Edward Schillebeeckx, *God Is New Each Moment*, trans. David Smith (Edinburgh: T&T Clark Limited, 1983), 83–84.

[55] Schillebeeckx, "Theological Criteria," *UF*, 66–67 [74]. See also, Edward Schillebeeckx, "The Church as Sacrament of Dialogue," *GFM, CW* vol. 3 (London: Bloomsbury T&T Clark, 2014), 71–84 [117–40].

Catholic doctrinal positions and asserts their continued truth even in changed circumstances. In this optimism and confidence, Schillebeeckx found allies in the reformist wing of the episcopacy in the Netherlands and later in the so-called "progressive" majority of bishops at the Second Vatican Council. In my judgment, the model for Schillebeeckx for positive relationships among community, theologians, and bishops could be found in the career of Bernardus Cardinal Alfrink, Archbishop of Utrecht from 1955 to 1975 and cardinal after 1960. Not long after Schillebeeckx's appointment to the faculty at the Catholic University of Nijmegen and Pope John XXIII's surprising announcement of the convocation of a new ecumenical Council, Cardinal Alfrink and the Dutch bishops embarked on an ambitious program both to solicit opinions about the Council from all the members of the Dutch Church and to prepare the community to receive the results of the Council once completed. In this effort, the Dutch episcopate consulted widely with theologians; Schillebeeckx soon took on a pre-eminent role among them. In popular presentations, such as his "The Grace of General Council" (1959) and the Dutch Bishops' famous Christmas Pastoral Letter (1961, authored chiefly by Schillebeeckx), he offered an ecclesiology strikingly prescient of both *Lumen gentium* and *Gaudium et spes*.[56] When the seemingly radical nature of the latter document caused Schillebeeckx to be blocked from assuming the role of conciliar *peritus* (theological expert), Cardinal Alfrink brought him to Rome as the theological advisor to the Dutch bishops.

During the tumultuous period of the Council, and the even more tumultuous post-conciliar decade in the Dutch Church, Cardinal Alfrink advanced a reforming and dialogical agenda. Starting with the controversy over the publication of *The New Catechism* (1966) through the experiment with ecclesial collegiality in the National Pastoral Council (1966–1972), Alfrink, no radical himself, faced the increasingly difficult task of keeping the different wings of his local church in communion with one another, as those on his right saw the Dutch Church sliding into heresy and disobedience, while those on his left saw the message of the Second Vatican Council as only a starting point for a much more radical process of reform. With the publication of *Humanae vitae* in 1968, the appointment of conservative successors to vacant Dutch episcopal sees, and the marginalization of the Pastoral Council's conclusions and process, Alfrink's agenda and his model of leadership seemed defeated in the Dutch Church. The center did not hold.

Even if Schillebeeckx's own positions often fell to the left of Alfrink's—whom he also felt free to occasionally criticize—he nevertheless shared with Alfrink the idea of the need for communion and mediation between all parties in the church.[57] In his own work, he rarely directly discusses "theological dissent," but on the occasions when he does, he both allows for it and also hedges it in with the same qualifications that circumscribe the power of the magisterium. To repeat a passage from above, theologians too must exercise their scholarly service to the church

> within the perspectival and hermeneutical limits of language, within the thought forms and questions of a particular historical period, within the context of the whole church's *sensus fidei*, within the dialectic of past tradition, present

---

[56] Edward Schillebeeckx, "De Genade van een Algemeen Concilie," *De Bazuin* (February 7, 1959); Nederlandse Bisschoppenconferentie, "De bisschoppen van Nederland over het concilie," *Katholiek Archief* 16 (1961): 369–84; Borgman, *Edward Schillebeeckx*, 316–20.

[57] See Schillebeeckx, *I Am a Happy Theologian*, 20–23.

actualization and future hope, and within the very human possibilities of willful distortion, ignorance and negligence.

Nevertheless, even with this caveat, Schillebeeckx argues that burden of blame for conflicts in the post-conciliar church does not rest on progressive theologians but on those who remain ensconced in a non-historical view of the church's language and practices and who connect this view with a non-dialogical view of the whole church community. In his own case, the major *causes célèbres* of his theological career all result from this conflict in fundamental orientations toward language and community.

For example, the conflict over Eucharistic theology, which took place during the latter stages of the Council and resulted in Pope Paul VI's *Mysterium Fidei*, sees Schillebeeckx arguing for a nuanced acceptance of currents in contemporary Dutch theology that attempted to rethink the scholastic doctrine of Eucharistic transubstantiation in terms of "transsignification" or "transfinalization."[58] According to him, the Council of Trent asserted both the reality of Christ's presence in the Eucharist and the appropriateness of naming this transformation "transubstantiation." He argues that the truth of the doctrine can and should be preserved for the contemporary believer, but this can only be done if it can be restated in a language different from the Aristotelian metaphysics of the past. Paul VI's encyclical, on the other hand, insisted on the necessity of the use of "transubstantiation" as the explanation for the sacramental presence of Christ in the Eucharist. After the appearance of the encyclical, Schillebeeckx notes, he met with Pope Paul VI on December 4, 1965. During the meeting, Pope Paul praised Schillebeeckx's most recent lectures on the subject (offered after the appearance of the encyclical) and seemed to suggest that the theologian had joined the orthodox camp against those with erroneous views on the Eucharist. Recalling the interview much later, Schillebeeckx expressed dissatisfaction with the conversation, both because he was not given much opportunity to speak and because he was unsure about whether the pontiff had understood the meaning of his lectures.

> The Pope told me: "They've reported that you've become one of us." I didn't understand what he meant. I had the sensation of not having been clear. Why should I have become "one of us"? I am one of the church. Who are these "us"?[59]

Even though Schillebeeckx was still working within his pre-conciliar "perspectivalist" model, he approached the subject of doctrinal reinterpretation as a "both/and," that is, he saw himself as able to preserve the ontological truth of a doctrine while offering a different philosophical interpretation. Paul VI in this instance seems to have seen the choice as "either/or."

The first formal process against Schillebeeckx took place in 1968. The great Jesuit theologian Karl Rahner informed his Dominican colleague that the Congregation had begun an investigation and that he had been appointed Schillebeeckx's advocate in the matter. Although such processes at the time were secret—even from the accused—Rahner made a decision in conscience to inform Schillebeeckx about the investigation, which concerned his views on secularization and revelation and was based on little more than interviews and articles that had appeared in American theological publications. After the French newspaper *Le Monde* made the investigation public

---

[58] Edward Schillebeeckx, *The Eucharist*, trans. N.D. Smith (New York: Sheed and Ward, 1968); Borgman, *Edward Schillebeeckx*, 337–45.

[59] Schillebeeckx, *I Am a Happy Theologian*, 24.

knowledge, officials in Rome summoned Rahner for a lengthy interrogation, in which he denied leaking the information to the press. At another meeting not long afterward, Rahner defended Schillebeeckx's views and criticized the closed process itself. In the post-conciliar season of *Humanae vitae,* the backlash against such inquisitorial procedures against such a prominent theologian led to revisions in the rules for such encounters. At first "terrified" by the news of the investigation, Schillebeeckx was never informed of its conclusion; no formal condemnation was ever issued.[60]

Schillebeeckx's major works on Christology in the 1970s led to a more direct and protracted conflict with the Congregation for the Doctrine of the Faith. In a more explicit way, this controversy, which lasted from 1976–1980—including a three day long "conversation" with representatives of the CDF on December 13–15, 1979—involved not only the substance of Schillebeeckx's Christological "experiment," but also his methodological claims about theology and his understanding of tradition and the magisterium. As Herwi Rikhof has pointed out, as the exchange of correspondence continues, these latter issues come to the forefront.[61] As they do, the differences between the two parties also become clearer. Schillebeeckx continues to advance a historically minded reading of the Christian sources with an idea toward offering a Christology consonant both with contemporary scholarship and with his estimation of the needs of contemporary people. Not naïve about power in the church, he nevertheless interacts with members of the CDF in a way modeled on his relationship with Cardinal Alfrink, that is, dialogically and with an expectation of an open process. His interlocutors for their part base their assessment of Schillebeeckx's work on the criterion of the preservation of the (supposedly) clear language of the tradition, on the power of the magisterium to insist upon this continuity and clarity in a theologian's work, and on the magisterium's representatives to conduct this process in their own manner. In the end, even the results were contested. The Congregation published a summary of the final conversation and Schillebeeckx's responses which did not square with Schillebeeckx's own account of the events. The former saw it as a series of concessions and retractions on Schillebeeckx's part.[62] Schillebeeckx describes the conclusion in this way:

> On 20 November 1980 I received a letter from the Congregation inviting me to clarify some points and to remove some ambiguities. There was no condemnation in the letter. Some questions remain open on matters which are not in accord with the doctrine of the church, but they are in accord with the faith. That is very important.[63]

Not long after this, Schillebeeckx ran afoul of the CDF again over his books on ministry. Both *Ministry: Leadership in the Community of Jesus Christ* and its revised form in *Church with a Human Face: A New and Expanded Theology of Ministry* continued Schillebeeckx's twofold

---

[60] Schillebeeckx, *I Am a Happy Theologian,* 34; Fergus Kerr, *Twentieth-Century Catholic Theologians: From Neoscholasticism to Nuptial Mysticism* (Oxford: Blackwell, 2007), 55–57.

[61] See Herwi Rikhof, "Of Shadows and Substance: Analysis and Evaluation of the Documents in the Schillebeeckx Case," *Journal of Ecumenical Studies* 19 (1982), 244–67.

[62] See Ted Mark Schoof, ed., *The Schillebeeckx Case: Official Exchange of Letters and Documents in the Investigation of Fr. Edward Schillebeeckx, O.P. by the Sacred Congregation for the Doctrine of the Faith, 1976–1980,* trans. Matthew J. O'Connell (New York: Paulist Press, 1984), 137–58.

[63] Schillebeeckx, *I Am A Happy Theologian,* 36–37.

approach. Responding to a current question—in this case, the growing shortage of priests and the emergence of alternative forms of community in world Catholicism—Schillebeeckx embarked upon an historical examination of ministry with the purpose of offering legitimate new paths for the church in this new situation. With the change in both pontiff (John Paul II in 1978) and head of the CDF (Joseph Ratzinger in 1981), magisterial authorities raised critical questions about both the method and conclusions of Schillebeeckx's work, particularly *Ministry*'s endorsement of the possibility of using extraordinary ministers to preside over the Eucharist. After Ratzinger declared such an option impossible, Schillebeeckx argued for the possibility of an appropriate ordination for pastoral workers in certain circumstances.[64] In 1984, Schillebeeckx met Ratzinger in Rome for an informal colloquium about his views on ministry. Schillebeeckx recalled the meeting in this way:

> The Master General told me to go to Rome for a colloquium with Ratzinger. Ratzinger's secretary was also there, and we talked in English, which Ratzinger speaks well. The colloquium lasted about three quarters of an hour and was very cordial. This was not a process in accordance with the 1971 norms, but a simple colloquium, quite informal. It is a worse procedure than a regular process.
>
> For me this form of colloquium can work well because I am of a certain age, but for younger people it's a gentle form of torture. They can't know what lies behind his kindness and affability.[65]

After the colloquium, and in a way similar to the conclusion of the process on Christology, a final note from the Congregation appeared which distinguished disagreements about church doctrine from those about matters of faith. Noting this distinction, Schillebeeckx states that he was never condemned in any of these processes.

For Schillebeeckx, the long period of the "anti-Council" found personification in the careers of John Paul II and Joseph Cardinal Ratzinger in his time as head of the CDF. Despite his dialogical and mediating style (or perhaps because of it), Schillebeeckx in his later career can reserve his most trenchant language for the pope and cardinal who, in his view, had betrayed the promise of the Council.[66] Yet in response, Schillebeeckx never advocated for radical disobedience or schism. He sympathized with the reform movements in the church, particularly in the Netherlands, and spoke of their right to exist and to be the "human face" of a church whose leadership had turned away from the crucial task of reinterpreting and reliving the Gospel in the world.[67] He argued as well for the creation of democratic structures in the church that would bring the voice of the whole People of God to expression.[68]

---

[64] Edward Schillebeeckx, "Offices in the Church of the Poor," *La Iglesia Popular: Between Fear and Hope*, ed. Leonardo Boff and Virgil Elizondo, *Concilium* 176 (1984), 98–107; reprinted in *The Language of Faith: Essays on Jesus, Theology and the Church* (Maryknoll: Orbis, 1995), 211–24; Schillebeeckx, *Ministry*, 139–40; Schillebeeckx, *CHF*, 249 [266].

[65] Schillebeeckx, *I Am A Happy Theologian*, 38–39.

[66] Ibid., 38, 42.

[67] See, for example, Schillebeeckx's addresses to the Acht Mei Beweging (The Eighth of May Movement) in 1985–1986, in *For the Sake of the Gospel*, 151–64.

[68] Schillebeeckx, *Church*, 185–226 [187–228].

# A Franciscan epilogue

Schillebeeckx died in 2009, aged ninety-five, during the fifth year of Benedict XVI's pontificate. His former adversary surprised the church and the world by resigning from the papal office in 2013. Benedict's successor, Francis, has surprised everyone even more by his humility, simplicity, compassion, orientation toward the poor, and ecological consciousness. Although I know of no direct link between Schillebeeckx's work and Francis's career, it is striking to note the similarities between Schillebeeckx's call for an "ecclesiology in a minor key," and Francis's exercise of his office. He has decried pomp and careerism in the Curia and episcopacy and has called all in the church to reach out in mercy to those in the periphery. He has called the church to the concrete practice of encounter with the marginalized as the preferred method of discipleship and evangelization today. For Francis, reality is greater than ideas, and this includes even theological ideas. He has asked theologians, whose work he values, to also "smell of the sheep" and to always refer themselves to the Second Vatican Council and to the religious lives of those in their communities as the context for their work.[69] He reaffirms the classic doctrines of the church—while noting the need for their reinterpretation—and he makes frequent use of the teachings of his predecessors and brother bishops, while rarely making any calls to obedience or claims to authority. He criticizes fundamentalism in all its forms. Their connection may only be by analogy, but Francis's papacy seems like the embodiment of Schillebeeckx's theology of the church, authority, and magisterium. If this is granted, one can then suggest that the current papacy is also a practical test of the strengths and weaknesses of Schillebeeckx's ecclesiological vision.

---

[69] Francis, "Discorso del Santo Padre Francesco all'Associazione Teologica Italiana" (December 29, 2017).

# Chapter 24

# Mutual Responsibility for the Gospel

## *Schillebeeckx's Later Theology of Ministry and Its Implications for Today*

### Mary Ann Hinsdale

When the Belgian Dominican Edward Schillebeeckx gathered together several of his previously published essays on priesthood and ecclesial office in 1980 and reworked them into the book entitled (in English translation), *Ministry: Leadership in the Community of Jesus Christ*, the ministry situation in Roman Catholic church in the Netherlands was in crisis.[1] A critical shortage of priests,[2] questioning on the part of many Dutch Catholics who were unconvinced that leaving the priesthood to get married should be an impediment to ministry (and who also asked, "why celibacy was required for priesthood anyway?"), increased pressure for the inclusion of women in ordained ministries, along with the general malaise for what appeared to be a retreat from the *aggiornamento* of the Second Vatican Council—all created considerable tension among Dutch Catholics.[3]

Today, some forty years later, the Roman Catholic church, not only in the Netherlands, but globally, is again experiencing a crisis in ministry and church leadership. The number of ordained clergy continues to decrease. In response, parishes are being closed or "linked," resulting in disenfranchised communities. Since the turn of the millennium, clerical sex abuse cases have

---

[1]  Edward Schillebeeckx, *Ministry: Leadership in the Community of Jesus Christ* (New York: Crossroad, 1981). The Dutch title of this work is *Kerkelijk ambt: Voorgangers in de gemeente van Jezus Christus* (Baarn: Nelissen, 1980). For a review of *Ministry* and its successor, *The Church with a Human Face*, see Mary E. Hines, "Ministry: Leadership in the Community of Jesus Christ," *The Praxis of the Reign of God*, ed. Mary Catherine Hilkert and Robert J. Schreiter, 2nd ed. (New York: Fordham University Press, 2002), 149–66.

[2]  This global situation of the shortage of priests was described by Jan Kerkhofs, the Secretary General of *Pro Mundi Vita* in "From Frustration to Liberation? A factual approach to ministries in the church," *Minister? Pastor? Prophet" Grassroots Leadership in the Churches*, trans. John Bowden (New York: Crossroad, 1981), 5–20.

[3]  For general background on the Dutch church during the post-conciliar years, see Michel van der Plas and Henk Suèr, eds., *Those Dutch Catholics* (New York: The Macmillan Company, 1967); and John A. Coleman, *The Evolution of Dutch Catholicism, 1958–1974* (Berkeley: University of California Press, 1978). William Portier suggests that the Dutch Catholic experience during this period is "required reading" for anyone who wants a contextual understanding of Schillebeeckx's theology. See, William L Portier, "Ministry from Above and/or Ministry from Below: An Examination of the Ecclesial Basis of Ministry According to Edward Schillebeeckx," *Communio* 12 (1985), 173–91.

rocked the local churches of the North Atlantic, notably the United States, Canada, Ireland, and Great Britain, but cases have also appeared in Central and South America, and the Pacific Rim.[4] In the summer of 2018, the state of Pennsylvania issued a report detailing years of abuse and cover-ups by bishops; Theodore McCarrick, the former Cardinal of Washington, DC, was forced to resign after a credible report of sexual abuse of a minor brought to the surface revelations of years of inappropriate sexual behavior with seminarians.[5] Thirty-four Chilean bishops offered an unprecedented mass-resignation in the wake of years of cover-ups regarding sexual abuse by their clergy; in Australia, Cardinal George Pell was convicted of five charges of "historical sexual offenses" and will stand trial in another case in early 2019; in Europe, Africa, and Asia so many similar reports of abuse and cover-ups have been reported that Pope Francis, in a "Letter to the People of God" on August 20, 2018, was prompted to name "clericalism" as a central cause for hiding and abetting the cover-up of such cases.[6]

Although "zero tolerance" efforts on the part of the hierarchy in many countries have ameliorated the numbers of such cases, the latest scandals to erupt in the United States and Australia have revealed the extent of the complicity of the episcopacy in covering up abuses and the bishops' inability to police themselves. In addition, there has been increasing pressure on the part of *ad hoc* groups in the church, particularly from women, who have called the inclusion of women in all ordained ministries. Indeed, one movement, officially condemned under pain of excommunication, the Catholic Women Priest Movement, has sought a retired bishop to ordain women priests and bishops in "illicit," if not invalid, ordinations.[7] Less confrontational groups (although they might espouse the same agenda), such as *Catholic Women Speak*, continue to agitate for change regarding the inclusion of women in ministries that now require ordination.[8] While Pope Francis has established a commission to investigate whether women might be accepted into the diaconate, many are skeptical whether such a move can address the real issue of how women can be included in leadership and decision-making in the church. They argue that the church is once again in need of reform, particularly with respect to its understanding and praxis of ministry and church office.

---

4   See also: Cindy Wooden, "Clericalism: The Culture That Enables Abuse and Insists on Hiding It," *Crux*, August 22, 2018, https://cruxnow.com/vatican/2018/08/23/clericalism-the-culture-that-enables-abuse-and-insists-on-hiding-it/. Sigal Samuel, "The Sex-Abuse Scandal Is Growing Faster than the Church Can Contain It," *The Atlantic*, September 14, 2018, https://www.theatlantic.com/international/archive/2018/09/catholic-sex-abuse-pope-francis/570208/.

5   The nearly 900 page report of the Pennsylvania Grand Jury is the largest and most comprehensive report of clerical sexual abuse in the Catholic church: Joshua Barajas, Courtney Norris, and Patty Gorena Morales, "How Catholic Churches in Pennsylvania Hid Decades of Abuse," *PBS NewsHour*, August 15, 2018, https://www.pbs.org/newshour/nation/how-catholic-churches-in-pennsylvania-hid-decades-of-abuse.

6   Pope Francis, "Letter to the People of God," (August 20, 2018) (hereafter cited in text as *Letter*) http://w2.vatican.va/content/francesco/en/letters/2018/documents/papa-francesco_20180820_lettera-popolo-didio.html. Even Schillebeeckx's native Flanders has not escaped this plague. See, John Allen, "Belgium a 'perfect storm' on sex abuse crisis," *National Catholic Reporter*, June 20, 2010, https://www.ncronline.org/news/accountability/belgium-perfect-storm-sex-abuse-crisis.

7   The history of this movement can be found on the organization's US website: https://www.romancatholicwomenpriests.org/.

8   Founded by theologian Tina Beattie, *Catholic Women Speak* began as a Facebook site "for all women's voices in the Catholic church." See: https://catholicwomenspeak.com/.

I find interesting parallels between the situation of the Dutch church in the 1980s when Schillebeeckx was writing his books on ministry and the situation in the North American church (and many other local churches) today which are reeling from the scandal of clerical sex abuse and its cover-up by church authorities. In Schillebeeckx's terms, both of these situations can be characterized in as negative experiences of "contrast"—that which should not be! The goal of this chapter is to examine Schillebeeckx's later theology of ministry in light of some of today's contrast experiences to see how [1] it might illumine our path toward understanding the present crisis and [2] how we might address the necessary, concrete reforms of patterns of communication and ecclesial structures that are needed to alleviate it. I will examine his later theology of ministry in three sections. First, I will give a brief review of Schillebeeckx's early theology of ministry and the ensuing controversy he experienced as a result of his historical investigations into the development of ecclesial office. Second, I will examine the shifts beginning in the mid-1980s and continuing throughout the 1990s in Schillebeeckx's theological method which affected his approach to issues of ecclesial leadership and ministry. In the third section, I will draw attention to key aspects in his overall theology that can prove helpful for envisioning and enacting some specific reforms needed in church office and ministries as we near the end of the first quarter of the twenty-first century.

# I. Schillebeeckx's historical investigations of church office

Schillebeeckx's book, *Ministry*, unleashed a firestorm of responses, notably from the Congregation for the Doctrine of the Faith (CDF), but also from fellow theologians.[9] In this book, Schillebeeckx presented an historical investigation of the development of office and leadership functions in the early church. He began experientially and contextually, with sociological data drawn from the present situation: the shortage of priests, the increasing secularity in the Netherlands which had gradually encroached upon other traditionally Christian European nations, and the growing dissatisfaction with the pace of change in ministerial roles for the laity, and especially for women in the church.

Schillebeeckx's research revealed that over the course of two millennia, ordained ministry gradually became sacerdotalized, ontologized, and increasingly identified with the power of being able to preside over and "confect" the Eucharist, and giving the priest a primary cultic role as dispenser of the sacraments.[10] While it is beyond the scope of this essay to review completely the historical scholarship that led Schillebeeckx to this determination, a few highlights from his research and a review of his methodology are of interest for how his early theology of ministry developed and the possibilities he saw for change. For example, Canon 6 of the Council of Chalcedon (451 CE) had declared the "absolute consecration" of priests to be invalid: "No one may be 'ordained' priest or deacon in an absolute manner (*apolelymenos*) … unless a local community is clearly assigned to him."[11] This view of ministry which, according to Schillebeeckx, was held by the early church up to the twelfth century, stressed a strong link between the community and

---

9. These theologians included Yves Congar, Georges Chantraine, Bernard Cooke, Pierre Grelot, Walter Kasper, Kevin Irwin, William Portier, and many others.
10. The Dutch term *ambt*, which is translated as "ministry," refers mainly to "office" or, the service of leadership in the church.
11. Schillebeeckx, *Ministry*, 38.

its leader, so strong that it was impossible for the leader to be moved to another community except on compassionate grounds. Moreover, a minister who for any reason ceased to be the president of a community returned to the state of being a layman. Thus, he concluded, "[t]he distinction between jurisdiction, i.e., having specific charge over a community, and *ordo*, the power of ordination in itself, did not exist at that time."[12] Furthermore, Schillebeeckx points out that during this period, "[t]he minister is defined essentially in ecclesial terms and not as an ontological qualification of the person of the minister apart from the determinative context of the church."[13]

A second example is that Schillebeeckx's investigation of the historical development of ecclesial office in the church was motivated by the "grassroots communities" which had developed in the Dutch church after the Second Vatican Council. Often ecumenical in character, these communities modeled themselves on the *Communidades de Base* that had developed in Latin America. Schillebeeckx saw these "critical communities" as laboratories, experimenting with new ways of being ecclesial and being community, "which must lead to new forms of leadership and ministry, which in fact they did."[14] Schillebeeckx had been disappointed by the 1971 Synod of Bishops which, in addition to producing the document on *Justice in the World*, considered the role and place of ministerial office in the church. In his estimation, the bishops, fearing that the synod would only consider the role of the priesthood sociologically, "refrained from rethinking episcopacy and priesthood in the light of the mission of the Church." For Schillebeeckx, to neglect the mission of the church, which he saw as "the sacramental presence of God's salvific presence in the contemporary world," was a serious omission.[15] The bishops at the synod started from texts in *Lumen gentium* that stressed continuity with Trent and Vatican I; thus, they could only think of "adapting" the priestly office to what was simply a changed situation.[16] For Schillebeeckx, this was a backward way of proceeding. Since "the very mission of the church was to be 'like a sacrament' in the world," the synod needed to respond to the world as it actually is—not as an afterthought, but as a starting point.

A third issue informing Schillebeeckx's writing of *Ministry* was his concern for the pastoral workers in the Netherlands who were educated theologically (some of them his own students) and had *de facto* responsibility for parishes. Their position was "juridically unclear ... and sometimes economically uncertain."[17] Many of them were women. Schillebeeckx was disturbed by the church's resistance to the presence of women. In 1980, he wrote, "... as long as women are left completely outside of decision-making authorities in the church, there can be no question of real women's liberation."[18] He observed that the 1976 CDF declaration (which, according to its own words attempted to cast itself as making a contribution to the struggle for women's liberation) in fact indicates "a certain hesitation on the part of the Pope to make a 'definitive' pronouncement on the question" since it emanated from the CDF rather than a *motu proprio* from

---

[12] Ibid., 41.

[13] Ibid., 40.

[14] Erik Borgman, "Introduction to the New Edition," in Edward Schillebeeckx, *CHF, CW* vol. 9 (London: Bloomsbury T&T Clark, 2014), xx–xxi.

[15] Borgman, "Introduction to the New Edition," *CHF*, xx.

[16] Schillebeeckx had argued that given the particular circumstances of Trent (the East was not present and they were responding to specific challenges of the Reformers, rather than undertaking a complete theology of ministry), we cannot look to Trent for a complete doctrine of the Catholic conception of ministry.

[17] Borgman, "Introduction to the New Edition," *CHF*, xxi.

[18] Schillebeeckx, *Ministry*, 97.

the pope.[19] This, of course, was the Roman way of "keeping a matter open, though provisionally, a kind of 'magisterial statement' on the issue has been made."[20] Schillebeeckx observed that "in a pre-conciliar way, the connection between church and ministry is again broken in favour of the relationship between Eucharist (sacred power) and ministry."[21] He noted that "all kind of feminine 'impurities' have unmistakably played a part throughout the history of the church in restricting women's roles in worship" and (during the era when priests were allowed to marry) requiring abstinence from sex the night before partaking of the Eucharist.[22] Schillebeeckx regarded such taboos as "prohibitions of a pseudo-doctrinal kind that are to be found in the ontological and sacerdotalist conception of the ministry in the Western Latin Church."[23]

Finally, in the chapter in *Ministry* on the tension between church order and "alternative practices," Schillebeeckx discussed the requirement of clerical celibacy for priests and the possibility of non-ordained persons (both male and female) serving as "extraordinary ministers" of the Eucharist in order to insure the right of a community to the Eucharist and to have leaders.[24]

The CDF investigated both *Basis en Ambt* (1979) and *Kerkelijk ambt: Voorgangers in de demeente van Jezus Christus* (1980) during the first half of the 1980s. Schillebeeckx sent two letters in response to their questions, on November 26, 1982 and July 20, 1983, respectively. However, he received no response until June 13, 1984 when the CDF voiced their conclusions specifically about the whether, under certain circumstances, communities without priests could select someone from their own community to preside at the Eucharist. Schillebeeckx had referred to such a possibility as "an extraordinary form of ministry." The CDF, citing *Sacerdotium ministeriale*, "On Certain Questions Concerning the Ministry of the Eucharist,"[25] said that this proposal was not an open question (as Schillebeeckx had maintained) and that his views could not be reconciled with the teaching of the church.[26] The following month, in the presence of the Dominican Master General, Schillebeeckx met with Cardinal Ratzinger and gave him an oral reply, informing him that a new book which was about to be published would meet the

---

[19] Congregation for the Doctrine of the Faith, "Introduction," *Declaration Inter Insignores on the Question of the Admission of Women to the Ministerial Priesthood* (October 15, 1976) Introduction, http://www.vatican.va/roman_curia/congregations/cfaith/documents/rc_con_cfaith_doc_19761015_inter-insigniores_en.html: "Along the same lines, the Second Vatican Council, enumerating in its Pastoral Constitution *Gaudium et Spes* the forms of discrimination touching upon the basic rights of the person which must be overcome and eliminated as being contrary to God's plan, gives first place to discrimination based upon sex. The resulting equality will secure the building up of a world that is not leveled out and uniform but harmonious and unified, if men and women contribute to it their own resources and dynamism, as Pope Paul VI recently stated."

[20] Schillebeeckx, *Ministry*, 96. In 1994, Pope John Paul II would reiterate that the exclusion of women from the priesthood was in fact "definitive." This was followed up with a "Dubium" from the CDF which has occasioned a great deal of contestation concerning whether the pope's statement was infallible or not.

[21] Ibid., 97.

[22] Ibid.

[23] Ibid., 98.

[24] Ibid., 75–99.

[25] Congregation for the Doctrine of the Faith, *Letter to Bishops of the Catholic Church on Certain Question Concerning the Minister of the Eucharist* (August 6, 1983), http://www.vatican.va/roman_curia/congregations/cfaith/documents/rc_con_cfaith_doc_19830806_sacerdotium-ministeriale_en.html.

[26] B.M.F. van Iersel, "Judgment on Schillebeeckx, (1) What Ratzinger Said," *The Tablet* 239, no. 7541 (January 19, 1965), 62–63.

demands of the Congregation. He followed up with a letter on November 8, 1984, confirming that the forthcoming publication, *The Church with a Human Face* (1985), would also expand and clarify the criticisms made by historians and some theologians, and that there would be no further talk of a "minister extraordinary" of the Eucharist or anything that contradicted *Sacerdotium ministeriale*. Schillebeeckx added, "In the hope of avoiding from now on all misunderstanding, the theme of apostolic succession has been analysed more fully."[27]

Six months later, then-Prefect Joseph Ratzinger, made public the CDF assessment on January 11, 1985 in *L'Osservatore Romano*.[28] Incredibly, Ratzinger's public assessment begins by thanking Schillebeeckx for his responses, and says that the phase of dialogue with the author was now closed. However, according to the CDF's assessment, it did not seem that Schillebeeckx had modified his position. Thus, they reiterated that "the last word has been said" in *Sacerdotium ministeriale* which had been published on August 6, 1983 (apparently not noticing that the two books of Schillebeeckx which were being investigated were published in 1979 and 1980) and that to envisage any exceptions to this statement "prejudices the whole apostolic structure of the church and deforms the sacramentary economy of salvation."[29] In response to the *L'Osservatore Romano* article, Professor Bas M.F. van Iersel, in consultation with his colleagues at Nijmegen issued a letter of protest.[30] While acknowledging that not every theologian might agree with Schillebeeckx, he pointed out that Schillebeeckx was not unique in terms of his intent and conclusions. For example, theologians such as Henrich Fries, Karl Rahner (who had died the previous year), and Leonardo Boff were of a similar mind concerning the topic of ministry. Adding that the CDF examination procedures had created a such climate of fear that some colleagues would only discuss the matter in private, not in public, van Iersel opined:

> It is, after all, clear that the last thing the Catholic authorities want is a public discussion of the points in question—quite understandably, since continued discussion can only have consequences for the existing structure of the Church with its centralistic and hierarchical concentrations of power and authority.[31]

Finally, he questions how the CDF could maintain its statement was the "last word" on this issue, for this raises the question of "who *is* empowered to pronounce 'the last word'?"[32] After all, such pronouncements are not made lightly, but are surrounded by careful safeguards and furthermore, such matters have always been the province of a general council, which makes it quite clear that any particular pronouncement has to be justified as binding. Most importantly, it has never been the case that "so important a matter be settled by such a simple act, by papal approval appended to a letter from one of the Vatican's senior civil servants."[33] As I discuss in the

---

[27] Ibid., 63.

[28] Ibid., 63–64.

[29] Ibid., 63.

[30] B.M.F. van Iersel, "Judgment on Schillebeeckx, (2) A Protest," *The Tablet* 239, no. 7541 (January 19, 1965), 63–64.

[31] Ibid., 64.

[32] Ibid.

[33] Ibid. Van Iersel continues: "Let there be no doubt about it, it is generally held that the Congregation for the Doctrine of Faith has no authority to speak the 'last word', any more than the Pope has the authority to do so in this way." Although, one must add here, that in fact, such procedures continued during the pontificate of Pope John Paul II and the Prefecture of the CDF of Joseph Cardinal Ratzinger.

next section, Schillebeeckx would have much to say about the reforms needed in the operations of the ministry of the church's teaching office!

True to his word, *The Church with a Human Face* expanded his book on ministry. There, Schillebeeckx answered his critics, but he also offered a clearer understanding of his hermeneutical, theological method.[34] This is especially illustrated in the book's introduction. For Schillebeeckx, theology has both a dialectical and a mediating role, consisting of the relating of the two poles of "tradition" and "situation." Tradition comprises a multilayered, meaning-disclosing or "meaningless-transforming" model of truth. It is not primarily a theoretical disclosure of meaning, but a *narrative* revelation that is "consistently accompanied, even in the Old and the New Testament, by at least preparatory theological reflection."[35] Additionally, Schillebeeckx claimed that other religious traditions are "fraught with religious meaning *that possesses transformative, innovative liberating, ultimately redemptive power*" and that they also promise people "salvation and liberation through their disclosure of meaning: the *truth* of what human life is all about."[36]

However, in the most complete presentation of his theological method, what began as the "critical correlation" of the two poles of experience and tradition, would eventually become "a *mutually critical interrelationship*" of revelational experience and experiential, interpretive tradition.[37] This was first expressed two years earlier in his first "theological testament," his valedictory lecture entitled "Theological Interpretation of Faith in 1983" (*Theologisch geloofsverstaan anno 1983*), which Schillebeeckx gave upon the occasion of his retirement from the University of Nijmegen.[38] As Lieven Boeve points out, this lecture presaged *Church: The Human Story of God*, which Schillebeeckx had intended to be the third volume of his *Jesus*-trilogy, a volume concerning pneumatology and ecclesiology.[39] However, by the time of its publication in 1989, *Church* had become "the promised final installment of Schillebeeckx's liberating hermeneutic theology" and thus represents his mature thinking on ecclesiology, church office and ministry.[40] According to this method, what is always key for Schillebeeckx are the questions: What is the Holy Spirit doing *now* in the church and in the world? What does the *sequela Jesu* require?[41]

---

34  But, without really capitulating any of his basic theses in the two previous editions. The Dutch title, A "Plea for People in the Church: Christian Identity and Offices in the Church" (*Pleidooi voor Mensen in de Kerk Christelijke Identiteit en Ambten in de Kerk*) is especially revealing considering the impasse Schillebeeckx was trying to address.

35  Edward Schillebeeckx, "Theological Interpretation of Faith in 1983," *Essays, CW* vol. 11 (London: Bloomsbury T&T Clark (2014), 54–55.

36  Ibid., 55. Emphasis original.

37  Lieven Boeve, "Introduction to the New Edition," in Edward Schillebeeckx, *Church, CW* vol. 10 (London: Bloomsbury T&T Clark, 2014), xix.

38  Schillebeeckx, "Theological Interpretation of Faith in 1983," *Essays*, 51–68.

39  Boeve, "Introduction to the New Edition," *Church*, xvii. For Schillebeeckx's original intention concerning the third volume of his trilogy, see Edward Schillebeeckx, *Christ, CW* vol. 7 (London: Bloomsbury T&T Clark, 2014), 835 [840].

40  Boeve, "Introduction to the New Edition," *Church*, xvii.

41  Schillebeeckx's use of the phrase, *sequela Jesu*, "the following of Jesus," appears in several places. For example, in 1985 in the international journal *Concilium*, and it refers to how the people we read about in the New Testament reacted to the historical appearance of Jesus and how they began to lead a new life. The New Testament is the source which enables us to discover the essential features of Jesus:

In his early theology of the church, Schillebeeckx understood the ecclesial community as the place where revelation, the "encounter" with God in Christ, took place. This *sacramental* understanding of church gradually broadened as his convictions grew about "reality" being where revelation takes place (*nulla salus extra mundum*).[42] Such revelation however was always understood as "mediated immediacy."[43] This is an important idea in Schillebeeckx's philosophical knapsack, though it is not unique to him. William Hill describes it this way: "while all contact with the divine is mediated through creatures, at the very heart of that mediation, God mysteriously gives us nothing less than God's uncreated self."[44]

# II. Shifts in Schillebeeckx's theological method and their implications for office and ministry

In many ways, *Church: The Human Story of God* is a comprehensive work of fundamental theology.[45] Its five chapters cover Schillebeeckx's doctrine of God, Christology, ecclesiology, and the relationship between faith and culture. In Boeve's view, Schillebeeckx created a new synthesis in this book that updated his correlational theological method to such an extent that it can be regarded as the concluding part of his construction of a liberating form of hermeneutic theology which "engages in dialogue with the late modern secular world, of which it is also a product." In correlating

---

who he was, how he lived, what motivated and inspired him. "We have no writings from his own hand and no direct 'documents' by him. It is only in the reflection provided by his followers that a portrait of Jesus has been handed down to us. The Church's *sequela Jesu* is the only document that Jesus has left us. It is *par excellence* the 'icon' of Christ in our midst." See, Edward Schillebeeckx "The Teaching Authority of All: A Reflection about the Structure of the New Testament," *The Language of Faith: Essays on Jesus, Theology and Church* (Maryknoll, NY: Orbis Books, 1995), 226. For a discussion of the origin of the "typically Dominican" use of the term *sequela Jesu* (or *sequela Christi*), see Fergus Kerr, *After Aquinas: Versions of Thomism* (Oxford: Blackwell Publishing, 2002), 167. See also Martin G. Poulsom, *The Dialectics of Creation: Creation and the Creator in Edward Schillebeeckx and David Burrell* (London: Bloomsbury T&T Clark, 2014), 144–49.

42    Schillebeeckx uses the phrase *nulla salus extra mundum*, "no salvation outside the world," frequently in his later theology.

43    For his conception of "mediated immediacy" see Schillebeeckx, *Church*, 68 [70], 78 [80], 97 [99].

44    William J. Hill, "A Theology in Transition," *The Praxis of the Reign of God*, ed. Mary Catherine Hilkert and Robert J. Schreiter, 2nd ed. (New York: Fordham University Press, 2002), 7. Philip Kennedy also discusses God's accessibility in human history under this rubric, noting that it presupposes a relational ontology which does not locate God's presence among human beings in a separate sector, but that God is present to humans because they are part of the reality created by God. Schillebeeckx thus argues that from human beings' point of view, there is no unmediated relationship with God, but from God's side, there is an unmediated relationship. Nevertheless, "a mutual relationship exists between God and people because people live in God's creation which mediates God's immediate presence." See Philip Kennedy, *Deus Humanissimus: The Knowability of God in the Theology of Edward Schillebeeckx* (Fribourg: University Press Fribourg Switzerland, 1993), 251. Kennedy points out that both Rahner and John Baillie have such a concept as well.

45    Here, I am following the interpretations of Lieven Boeve, "Introduction to the New Edition," *Church*, xvii–xx; and O.P. Philip Kennedy, "Human Beings as the Story of God: Schillebeeckx's Third Christology," *New Blackfriars* 71 (1990), 120–31.

"revelational experience" with "experiential tradition," it is clear that his primary category is still experience. However, he moves beyond Gadamer's "fusion of horizons" to posit a "fundamental identity of meaning" among successive, historically situated forms of tradition in relation to their respective socio-historical contexts. Thus, "the relation between Jesus' message and its historical context [that] was reproduced for the first time in the New Testament writings in relation to their historical context" is "constantly reproduced anew in later phases as the tradition developed."[46]

Philip Kennedy describes *Church* as "an attempt to present a constructive vehicle for keeping alive the meaning of the original Christian gospel within contemporary experiences."[47] Far from ignoring Christian tradition, Kennedy says, Schillebeeckx is "striving to weld ancient wisdoms with a new structure for theology so as to render more intelligible what Christian language about God may mean."[48] Thus, as in previous works, Schillebeeckx begins by stating that revelation is mediated by human experience, but now he is careful to point out that revelation includes "secular" experience (*extra mundum nulla salus*) and that world history is also salvation history. For Christians, Jesus is experienced as the supreme density of revelation in a whole history of experiences of revelation. In expressing their experience, believers

> do not just want to say something about themselves … i.e. how *they* see Jesus …. they want to say something about *Jesus himself*: that he is the supreme expression of God, and that precisely for that reason they have experienced salvation in him and continue to do so.[49]

In *Church*, one clearly sees the shifts in Schillebeeckx's theological method that are described in his valedictory lecture cited above.[50] Schillebeeckx was influenced by his forays into historical research, the hermeneutics of Paul Ricoeur, his critical dialogue with the Frankfurt school of critical theory, and the influence of Johann Baptist Metz's anamnestic political theology. As a result, Schillebeeckx's understanding of the dialectic relation between tradition and situation necessitates [1] an appreciation that the interrelationship between past and present is an encounter between different cultural forms of Christian religious understanding; [2] that analyzing the interrelationship of these various cultural forms involves prior structuralist or semiotic work; and [3] that arriving at communicable revelation requires an ideologically critical hermeneutics:

> … if Christian theologians seek to be true to the binding core of biblical and ecclesiastic pronouncements in their authentically evangelical scope, they have to conclude that ideologically critical analysis is an essential element of hermeneutic theology if it is to accord with God's word. The history of theology, too, often reflects a history of victors and powers, who marginalized evangelically feasible alternatives or even silenced them as vanquished in that era—albeit only temporarily: forgotten truths have a way of resurfacing once more.[51]

---

[46]  Boeve, "Introduction to the New Edition," *Church*, xix. Schillebeeckx uses a diagram in *Church* on p. 41 [42] that he used in in his farewell lecture of 1983 in order to illustrate how this functions. See, Schillebeeckx, "Theological Interpretation of Faith 1983," *Essays*, 62–63.

[47]  Kennedy, "Human Beings as the Story of God," 122.

[48]  Ibid.

[49]  Schillebeeckx, *Church*, 26 [27].

[50]  Schillebeeckx, "Theological Interpretation of Faith in 1983," *Essays*, 51–68.

[51]  Ibid., 57–67.

Even before *Church*, Schillebeeckx sought to investigate not only the saving content of Christian faith but also the historical context in which it was set. This involves

> the pre-suppositions of the New Testament authors, the movements and tendencies in the environment of early Christianity, the "spirit of the time" which was also breathed by the New Testament Christians … (in order to) arrive at an exact understanding of the way in which these Christians continually gave new expression to the traditional message of the gospel or apostolic faith on the basis of new experiences and demands with which they themselves were in critical solidarity.[52]

Following the passage just cited above, Schillebeeckx asked a question which could serve as a perennial inquiry for the church in any age, but which is especially pertinent given the present situations of "negative contrast" in the church of the third millennium, where practices of exclusion continue: based upon race/ethnicity, gender, and sexual orientation; the continued exclusion of the laity (especially women) from important decision-making roles and in the church's ordered ministries; and especially the sinful situation of clerical sexual abuse and its widespread cover-up which has become an international scandal. Thus, we might likewise ask,

> … what are the historical circumstances in which we, in the year 1980, must pick up the treads of apostolic belief? Where must our *critical solidarity* find its critical point today, taking into account present-day experiences and demands? In what new experiences today do Christians hear an echo of their remembrance of Jesus Christ and in which new experiences and demands do they see a distortion, blindness, paralysis or even alienation in their Christian identity?[53]

Schillebeeckx observed that it is natural for Christians to embrace historical decisions for which good reasons can be advanced, and which appear to express Christian responsibility here and now, even if history alone will judge whether or not they were in fact the most responsible decisions. However, he also warned that, "to refuse at a particular moment in our history to choose one of the possible historical alternatives can be tantamount to surrendering the impulse and the orientation of the gospel."[54]

Above all, it is the experiences of "meaninglessness, of injustice and of innocent suffering that have a revelatory significance *par excellence*."[55] According to Schillebeeckx, such "negative experiences of contrast" are pre-religious experiences that are basic and accessible to all human beings.[56] They summon a "no" to the world as it is and foster our "indignation." The human response, "this should not be," has the possibility of becoming an "open yes" in the process of liberation:

---

[52] Schillebeeckx, *Christ,* 643 [653]. It is helpful to recall that in *Christ,* Schillebeeckx's intention was to recast traditional Christology as *story,* so that "truth" has a *narrative* character.

[53] Ibid. Emphasis original.

[54] Ibid.

[55] Schillebeeckx, *Church,* 28 [28].

[56] Schillebeeckx, *Church,* 28 [29]. With the notion of "contrast experiences" Schillebeeckx broadened his understanding of theological hermeneutics, by radicalizing what he means by "important human experiences." See, Edward Schillebeeckx, "Liberating Theology," *Essays, CW* vol. 11 (London: Bloomsbury T&T Clark, 2014), 78–84. He then summarizes his growing clarity about "fundamental contrast experiences" in the 1994 essay, "Theological Quests," *Essays, CW* vol. 11 (London: Bloomsbury T&T Clark, 2014), 154–58.

The fundamental human "no" to evil therefore discloses an unfulfilled and thus "open yes" which is as intractable as the human "no," indeed even stronger, because the "open yes" is the basis of that opposition and makes it possible. Moreover, from time to time, there are fragmentary but real experiences of meaning and happiness on both a smaller and a larger scale, which constantly keep nurturing, establishing and sustaining the "open yes." Both believers and agnostics come together in this experience. That is also a rational basis for solidarity between all people and for common commitment to a better world with a human face.[57]

In *Church,* as in *Ministry* and *Church with a Human Face,* Schillebeeckx appealed to historical and sociological investigations in order to show that the developments in church leadership that occurred in the past were sociologically and theologically intelligible, but not unchangeable. In the next section, I continue to draw upon *Church: The Human Story of God*, as well as Schillebeeckx's second "theological testament," written in 1994, more than a decade after his valedictory lecture, in order to examine how the changes Schillebeeckx saw as necessary then might be worth resurrecting in light of the current "contrast experiences" in church office and ministry today.[58]

# III. Confronting clericalism and the practices of exclusion

Schillebeeckx argues that while we can speak in speculative terms about the church, we also can speak "performatively" about the church. It is important to remember, however, that

> in neither case can we by-pass the empirical, specific historical manifestations of the church. For alongside all the gifts and favours of a material and spiritual kind … at the same time, in the past, it has tended to exclude people, cultures, other religions, and I might say, "alternative Christians," even devastating, destroying and overwhelming them. All this has happened, not on the basis of the church's own gospel which it has preached … but in fact with reference to its own, ideological and imperialistic claim to be right.[59]

---

[57] Schillebeeckx, *Church*, 6 [7] Some theologians have expressed concern that Schillebeeckx is too optimistic about the negative contrast experience and ask: "Is it, in fact, the case that the spontaneous human response to the violation of the dignity and integrity of others is protest and resistance?" Mary Catherine Hilkert refers to Johann Baptist Metz and M. Shawn Copeland's work in raising this question and suggests that Bernard Lonergan's concept of "dramatic bias" might offer a helpful corrective to Schillebeeckx's notion. See Mary Catherine Hilkert, "The Threatened *Humanum* as *Imago Dei*: Anthropology and Christian Ethics," *Edward Schillebeeckx and Contemporary Theology*, ed. Lieven Boeve, Frederiek Depoortere, Stephan van Erp (London: T&T Clark, 2010), 132–34. See also, John Dunn, "Negative Contrast Experience and Edward Schillebeeckx," *From North to South: Southern Scholars Engage with Edward Schillebeeckx*, ed. Helen F. Bergin (Adelaide: ATF Theology, 2013), 65–84.

[58] Edward Schillebeeckx, *Theologisch testament: Notarieel nog niet verleden*, 2nd ed. (Baarn: Nelissen, 1995). Part II is translated as Schillebeeckx, "Theological Quests," *Essays*, 111–61.

[59] Schillebeeckx, *Church*, 186 [188].

Regarding exclusionary practices in the church, which are usually based upon a "clericalism" that sees a divide between laity and the ordained due to the sacerdotalizing of priestly ministry that Schillebeeckx has laid out in his early writings on ministry, Schillebeeckx says:

> In many ecclesiologies, both older and more modern ones, no mention is made of the negative side of the empirical churches, which in the language of faith are called the 'community of God," or at any rate this side is not made a theme in the theology of the church. [...] Things must change, not for fear that we Christians will be confronted with our own past by others, historians, but because as Christians—not in pathological self-accusation [...] but simply by being "honest to God" and acting in accordance with human worth—we cannot live our own Christian identity here and now except by at the same time explicitly dissociating ourselves from what an ideological kind of Christianity has done to people up to the present time and still continues to do.[60]

In the section of *Church* entitled, "Towards Democratic Rule of the Church," Schillebeeckx reviews the drafting history of *Lumen gentium* and notes that its ecumenical attempts "go a long way towards the other Christian churches without being unfaithful to the centuries-old self-understanding of the Catholic Church."[61] He further remarks that the Council's rejection of the pre-conciliar draft "was a specific reaction against the one-sided and indeed triumphalistic accents of the encyclical *Mystici corporis*" in three ways. First, it clearly distinguished between the church on earth and the kingdom of God. Second, it made a carefully qualified identification of the biblical *mystery* (emphasis mine) of the church in which the Roman Catholic church "subsists in" (*subsistere in*), but also that the same biblical mystery of the church is also present in other Christian churches in a varied way. Third, it distinguishes between the institutional element in the church and the eschatological community of faith and grace (between the church as "a saving institution" and the church as "the fruit of divine redemption"), although Schillebeeckx laments that this is done inadequately. Nevertheless, he reminds his readers that in Chapter Two of *Lumen gentium,* we read:

> All those, who in faith look towards Jesus, the author of salvation and the principle of unity and peace, God has gathered together and established as the church, that it may be for each and everyone the visible sacrament of this saving unity—a statement that is clearly inclusive of all Christians.[62]

In emphasizing the mystery of the church, "the community of God," Schillebeeckx asserts that the council did not have in mind an "idealistic, or unreal vision." Rather, this mystery is present in our concrete history, "in a very concrete community" with all its distortions, shadows, and deficiencies.[63] Yet, these "blemishes" do not make it impossible for this mystery to become

---

[60] Ibid., 187 [189].
[61] Ibid., 192 [194].
[62] Ibid., 193 [195]. Interestingly, in a later footnote, Schillebeeckx comments on the language used in *Lumen gentium* 2.9, which he finds "over-pious and unctuous, remote from the prayer of most people, even Christians. If it is to be understandable and capable of being experienced, what is meant must be expressed in everyday language, even for Christians." See *Church*, 194, n. 23 [196].
[63] Schillebeeckx, *Church* 192 [194].

transparent in the church. It is important for him that the church took over the Protestant theme of *Ecclesia semper reformanda*. This phrase was bandied about in the pre-conciliar, preparatory period, but ultimately the council documents used the phrase *Ecclesia semper purificanda*. In a footnote, Schillebeeckx acknowledges this was done for liturgical reasons, since this is the phrase used in the Roman Missal.[64] Nevertheless, it still betrays a reluctance of some bishops to use a phrase so closely associated with the Reformation. Thus, Schillebeeckx emphasizes that "in its own way the council is accepting a Reformation view when it says that the church is *sancta simul et purificanda*; it is holy, but must constantly be purified; it must arrive at *metanoia*, repentance and renewal."[65]

In this same section of *Church*, Schillebeeckx reviews the intensification of the centralized hierarchical character of the church and its corresponding anti-democratic face which took place between the French revolution and the period just before the Second Vatican Council. This is a helpful review, particularly for the generations of people for whom the Second Vatican Council itself today is "past history." He emphasizes how in the official church's hierarchical view, "being the church" could not be reconciled with the modern history of freedom and democratic process. However, after giving a detailed history of the authoritative statements issued during "the Pius tradition,"[66] Schillebeeckx points out that, after the century and a half of official opposition, the church recognized "the good achievements of bourgeois liberalism (leaving aside the violence and force that the French Revolution brought on Europe, which are in no way to be trivialized)." One must concede that the Second Vatican Council accepted with open arms the "achievements of the French Revolution (in retrospect, at some points rather naively), after having opposed them for a century and a half with solemn fulminations."[67] He thus concludes,

> [w]e must therefore unmistakably place the Roman Catholic church's break with its feudal past in the period between 1962 and 1965: the time of the Second Vatican Council, though this was the official church expression of what had long been felt among many Catholics and theological spokesmen.[68]

Schillebeeckx admits that for many theologians (here, he has in mind political and liberation theologians), this is perhaps a somewhat compromising remark. But in retrospect, he assesses the Second Vatican Council as a "liberal council" in the sense of the liberal values that were emphasized in the French Revolution. For him, the Second Vatican Council was, especially mindful of "the peoples' theology," espoused by liberation theologians from many continents, and in this sense it represents a "catching up manoeuvre of a church which had come too late (in relation to what was happening in the world)."[69]

Schillebeeckx goes on in this section to blame the "compromise" character of the Second Vatican Council as having impeded the "free play of the Holy Spirit among lay believers."[70]

---

[64] Ibid., 193, n. 22 [195].

[65] Ibid., 194, [196].

[66] So-called because they were issued by nineteenth- and twentieth-century popes, beginning with Pius IX and ending with Pius XII.

[67] Schillebeeckx, *Church*, 204 [206].

[68] Ibid.

[69] Ibid., 205 [207].

[70] Ibid., 206 [207].

Nevertheless, the Council's understanding of the church as the People of God safeguards those "who are called together by God into a community in which all believers are believing subjects of equal worth 'living from the Spirit,' free children of God."[71] At the same time, while the Council said ministries are "a special charisma of the Spirit," it did not say anything about the concrete institutional regulation of them, or the possibility of control that believers have over the official ministers of the church. Being a "charism of the Holy Spirit" does not tell us anything about how the ministers must be appointed.

Here, Schillebeeckx is especially critical of what he calls a

> "predetermined harmony" [that] is postulated between the "believed faith of the whole church community" and what the hierarchy proclaims and formulates as faith and policy, while believers are not involved in either the expression of the faith or the government of the church.[72]

The argument is that "the object of the people of God is the 'revealed mystery' and the object of proclamation, worship and government by the hierarchy is that same mystery." The only limits on the hierarchy are the limits of revelation. Thus, there is a pre-established harmony, with the result being that any conflict—whether between believers and the hierarchy, or the local church and Rome—is labeled "sinful" or "disobedience." This "idyll of internal harmony" has ominous implications for the institution, especially in terms of psychological consequences, conjuring up feelings of helplessness or futility and disappointment. Furthermore, the "declaration that any conflict in the church is either non-existent or sinful puts the hierarchy in an immune or storm-free zone."[73]

The point of Schillebeeckx's long disputation toward the end of the section "Towards Democratic Rule of the Church," concerns how "stemming the tide of the breakthrough at Vatican II" was legitimated by appealing to the idea of "the church as mystery." He wants to clarify that the church community "cannot be found behind or above concrete, visible reality. The church community is to be found in this reality which can be pointed at here and now."[74] He then goes on to discuss Jesus and the Holy Spirit as the source of all authority in the church and how ministerial authority must be organized in such a way that "the liberating authority of the Lord Jesus, which is abidingly present, can come into effect time and again in the life of the Christian community."[75] The "norm" in the church, according to Schillebeeckx, is not the formal authority of the ministry (viz., office), but the *paratheke* ("the entrusted pledge"), in other words, "the gospel, as interpreted by the apostles (the *didaskalia*)."[76] This is the source of what we have come to call "the apostolic succession": the unbroken succession of the apostolic tradition. The teaching authority of the church is subject to this apostolic content as ministerial service, but the one also calls for the other. Moreover, the content of the gospel is the very life of the Christian communities. It is not found somewhere in canonical books but in the hearts of believers, so that the ministry of the teaching authority has to rely on the actual life of the church communities of

---

71  Ibid., 206 [208].
72  Ibid.
73  Ibid., 209 [210].
74  Ibid., 212 [213].
75  Ibid., 215 [216].
76  Ibid.

faith at the grass roots. Above all, "there may be no master-servant relationships in the church," nor should there be any structures of domination—and most shocking of all "there really is no *hierarchy*"—although there is certainly authority and leadership in the church.[77]

Schillebeeckx traces the roots of hierarchy to influences such as adoption of the social status symbols of the Roman Empire, which were taken over by the Constantinian church, and the Neo-Platonism of Pseudo-Dionysius. These allowed the various services of ministry to be organized in a pyramidal, hierarchical structure with the result that the laity, at the base of the pyramid, were devalued and became "merely the object of episcopal and priestly pastoral care."[78]

Schillebeeckx then turns to the "category mistake" made by the church hierarchy with regard to its argument against democratic forms of governance. The argument (which in many ways amounts to "because we've always done it this way") runs as follows:

> The church, as founded by God has its own special form. This is by divine right and therefore … is non-democratic … just as the Pope is not the delegate of the universal church, so the bishop is not the delegate of his see. Pope and bishops have their authority direct from Christ and not from a mandate which is given to them by the people of God or by the diocese. Of course as "hierarchs" they are at the service of the people of God, local and world-wide, but this service is a function of truth and love, the final aim of which is that the people of God should experience God's call. And this call is not dependent on the people. It is God's own initiative.[79]

The nub is that precisely because the church has practically no experience with "democratic" forms of government (at least as the modern world understands it), such an exercise is rejected, "while an authoritarian exercise of authority has been, and is, approved with enthusiasm."[80] Furthermore, where the mistake lies, for Schillebeeckx, is the fact that democracy is the fruit of the American and French revolutions and represents the foundations of human rights. Just as the state is not the proprietor of human rights, neither is the church the proprietor of the word of God.

> Why should the church not be able to democratize its model of government and rule without in so doing harming its subjection to the word of God? As if an authoritarian government agrees better with the subjection to the church to God's word than a democratic government, in which the voice of the whole people of God is listened to more clearly and accurately![81]

In summary, Schillebeeckx views the argument that democratic governance harms subjection to God's revelation—which is expressed in all the official documents of the Roman Catholic Church—is tacitly based on the ideological view that the authority in power (because guided by the Holy Spirit) is always right; authority does not need to be unnecessarily hindered in its actions by contributions from below. This argument is what sociologist Peter Berger calls the "positivism of tradition"—that a non-democratic church is in fact merely a reference to the fact

---

77  Ibid., 215 [216–17].
78  Ibid., 216 [217].
79  Ibid., 216–17 [218].
80  Ibid., 217 [218].
81  Ibid., 217 [219].

of twenty centuries of non-democratic cultures, from which the church took the form of its own government. Yet, here there is also an irony in how the church could, with great self-assurance, take over the civil forms of feudalism for its government, and later, those of an absolute monarchy, while being completely closed to modern, democratic forms of authority.

In terms of positive arguments, Schillebeeckx first cites the working of the Holy Spirit which occurs throughout the life of the church in differing historical mediations and in which both believing people and church leaders are involved. He points out that if the ministerial teaching authority overlooks these mediations, especially the mediation by and through ordinary believers, it will run the risk of not listening to the Holy Spirit. The upshot is, thus, that "the democratic participation of everyone (for which a form of organization has to be found) in a theologically responsible way could … and must play a role at precisely this level, without harming the distinctive responsibility of the hierarchy."[82] Second, he reminds us that God's action in the world is to be found *within* human history. It is from the story of Jesus of Nazareth that Christians learn how God rules, and that this rule is one of faithfulness, justice, and love. Thus, based upon the model of the risen Crucified One, who had a special love for the poor and oppressed, we are provided with a model for ministerial authority: that of a vulnerable God. Third and finally, Schillebeeckx discusses the interplay of the official teaching authority and the teaching authority of believers and their theologians. Schillebeeckx gives a historical survey of the relationship of the ministerial teaching authority—which is always meant to be pastoral—and the academic-theological teaching authority. He explains that in the first millennium, the role of the teaching authority and the role of theologian often overlapped. Bishops were both ministers of the church and theologians. During the Middle Ages, the cathedral schools came into being, followed by the first universities with doctors or magisters in theology. Here, we see the teaching office become part of church governance, the *magisterii authenitca*, along with the *magistralia*, the theologians. During this period, tensions mainly arose among the various theological "schools," although theologians like Bonaventure and Albert could boldly say that the Pope was in error on a specific point. By the time of the late-Middle Ages, the theological faculties were making doctrinal decisions. At Trent, however, things tightened considerably, with a sharper definition of roles between bishops and theologians.

During the nineteenth century, Schillebeeckx describes the emergence of "a completely new type" of theologian who some theologians called "party ideologists." In the reign of the "Pius Popes," this model involved a form of theologizing that simply repeated the ministerial teaching authority, which itself become more dogmatic and "exercised a kind of totalitarian claim on the theologians," who no longer held a form teaching authority in themselves.[83] Schillebeeckx recognizes that "there is always a tension in the life of the church between the pastoral-legal teaching authority of the ministry and the academic 'magisterium' of the theologian" and that this is normal and healthy. However, theological witch-hunts and widespread discontent among the intellectual believers for whom the theologians are often the spokespersons will not solve the problem in the name of "protecting the faith of the simple believers."

---

[82] Ibid., 220 [221]. Given the present crises in the church in the first quarter of a century of the third millennium, the issue of finding a proper form of democratic organization seems most critical.

[83] Ibid., 223 [226].

The question here is really whether or not there is room for the working of the Holy Spirit. Schillebeeckx is quite clear:

> the hierarchy indeed has authority in the church, but it does not have control over the Holy Spirit (any more, of course than does the church people of God) .... we should rather learn the lesson that the teaching authority of the ministry, church theology and the believing community are dependent on one another and are so in a new way, different from what was the case earlier. Community, ministry, theology: these three are themselves fundamentally dependent—in a process in which they are relativized—on the living God, who brings his creation in Jesus Christ, through our history, to a final consummation after history.[84]

In 1994, five years after *Church*, Schillebeeckx published his *Theologisch testament*.[85] Here, Schillebeeckx considered several contemporary problems in the church and does not mince words concerning issues connected with ministry. The first consideration involves "office," or the institutional nature of the church in general. The second concerns the papacy, or the office of Peter. Third, in the context of the infamous *Nota praevia* added to *Lumen gentium*, Schillebeeckx raises the issue of governance in the church, wondering whether a democratic exercise of authority would be possible.[86] Fourth, he reviews the understanding of the church as an eschatological community whose institutional dimension exists as a service "to safeguard God's children and hence to curb all willful anarchy, but not to oppress or humiliate them."[87] Finally, he also considered the issues of voluntary, versus mandatory, celibacy as linked to holy orders, women's ordination, and the future of religious life.[88]

# Conclusion

To return once again to Pope Francis's 2018 "Letter to the People of God," written in response to a seemingly never-ending onslaught of clerical sexual abuse cases and their pervasive cover-up by episcopal authorities, I referred to this situation as a "contrast experience," using Schillebeeckx's

---

[84] Ibid., 226 [227].

[85] Schillebeeckx, "Theological Quests," *Essays*, 111–61.

[86] The *Nota explicative previa* (Preliminary explanatory note) was issued by Pope Paul VI on November 16, 1964 as an appendix to *Lumen gentium*, The Dogmatic Constitution on the Church. The fierce and unrelenting opposition to episcopal collegiality by a small, but powerful minority at the Council provided its impetus. What had been taken for granted for centuries and surfaced as part of Vatican II's *ressourcement*, stirred the fears of conservatives who thought that papal primacy was being threatened. See, John O'Malley, *What Happened at Vatican II* (Cambridge, MA: Harvard University Press, 2008), 244–45. Schillebeeckx called it "the last convulsion" of the era of absolute monarchies and regarded it as "a non-conciliar document" that was imposed on the assembly "from above" in authoritarian fashion without permitting plenary discussion." See, Schillebeeckx, "Theological Quests," *Essays*, 147.

[87] Ibid., 148.

[88] Schillebeeckx covered these same five issues in his original interview with Francesco Strazzari. See, Edward Schillebeeckx, *I Am a Happy Theologian: Conversations with Francesco Strazzari*, trans. John Bowden (London: SCM Press, 1994).

term for "that which should not be." In his letter, the pope began by acknowledging the suffering endured by the young persons who experienced this abuse of power, as well as the wounds suffered by their family members and the larger community of both believers and non-believers. He acknowledged that such wounds "never disappear and that they require us forcefully to condemn these atrocities and join forces in uprooting this culture of death (*Letter* 1)." Incredibly, the pope went on to name the cause of this contrast experience as "clericalism":

> Indeed, whenever we have tried to replace, or silence, or ignore, or reduce the People of God to small elites, we end up creating communities, projects, theological approaches, spiritualities and structures without roots, without memory, without faces, without bodies and ultimately, without lives. This is clearly seen in a peculiar way of understanding the Church's authority, one common in many communities where sexual abuse and the abuse of power and conscience have occurred. Such is the case with *clericalism*, an approach that "not only nullifies the character of Christians, but also tends to diminish and undervalue the baptismal grace that the Holy Spirit has placed in the heart of our people." *Clericalism*, whether fostered by priests themselves or by lay persons, leads to an excision in the ecclesial body that supports and helps to perpetuate many of the evils that we are condemning today. *To say "no" to abuse is to say an emphatic "no"; to all forms of clericalism.* (*Letter* 2)[89]

In his later writings on ministry and office in the church, Schillebeeckx has presented us with a roster of "contrast experiences" specific to the church. Most of these involve some form of exclusion or oppression, including attempts to stifle the stirrings of the Holy Spirit regarding needed change in the church. Nearly all of these, at least in terms of where they represent a negative experience of contrast, can be seen in relation to clericalism or what can be termed "clerical culture." Such a culture entails what Francis describes as reducing the People of God to elite, "authoritative" groups. As Schillebeeckx continually reminds us in speaking about contrast experience, the positive element that is contained within such experiences is *indignation*: the refusal to acquiesce in the face of existing oppression or to accept the status quo. This indignation spurs people to change the situation and therefore provides a potential instance of the inbreaking of the Holy Spirit in history. As a site for the work of the Holy Spirit, such experiences should call for dismantling "clerical culture" which artificially divides the People of God and therefore also diminishes the abilities of those who legitimately exercise authority within it. It is important to recall that the historically constructed structures of ecclesial governance were meant to adapt to a context and to meaningfully unite the People of God, but these structures need to be reevaluated when they fail. As Schillebeeckx reminds us:

> God still offers a future when liberating human praxis fails. History remains an open adventure; here there is no room for naïve Enlightenment belief in progress, but there is eschatological hope that inspires us to establish fragments of salvation here and now.[90]

It is up to each person in each new situation to accept that offer.

---

[89] My emphasis.
[90] Schillebeeckx, "Liberating Theology," *Essays*, 83.

# PART IV
# Theology of Culture

# Chapter 25
# Christ and Culture

Roger Haight

The Second Vatican Council has been credited with facilitating a transition of the Roman Catholic Church from the premodern to the modern world. Where the Modernist movement failed, the Second Vatican Council succeeded with its decree, "The Pastoral Constitution on the Church in the Modern World." But theologians notice that just as that transition came to term, decidedly postmodern sensibilities began to eclipse the modern world. This chapter will show ways in which the Christology of Edward Schillebeeckx engages the culture of postmodernity. To make this case, I will first provide a loose definition of the meaning of "postmodernity" as I am using it here. The body of the chapter then develops the principal elements that distinguish Schillebeeckx's Christology. I conclude with a summary of the ways in which his Christology helps Christians today appropriate aspects of our inescapably postmodern culture. Let me turn, then, to a brief description of postmodernity as it is understood in this discussion.

It is possible to construct a set of beliefs or philosophical positions that define a postmodern view of the nature of the human or the structures of human knowing. Various thinkers, writers, critics, philosophers, and social scientists offer postmodern précis of human existence and history. I distinguish the following impressionistic account of postmodernity from a collection of objective truths. The postmodernity I envisage resembles a culture, a diffuse set of interrelated ideas, values, opinions, and impressions that together create a milieu which pervades the universities and all ranks of the educated population of Western developed nations and can be found in all the cities of the world where critical education is promoted. Young people all over the world are educated into this culture or learn it on the Internet. This intellectual culture takes on so many different forms and becomes internalized in such different genres and means of expression that any description of it cannot but be abstract and vague. With that stipulation, I raise up four qualities of this postmodern intellectual culture that most will recognize.

First, contemporary science has generated a new picture of the universe and the world that differs from the imaginative framework underlying the tradition of Christian language. Theologians, of course, know that theological language is symbolic, and many educated Christians gradually learn that the object of Christian faith transcends the quotidian worldly meaning of our concepts. Nevertheless, if the plain speech of a religion does not make sense in the imaginative framework that structures everyday reality, if it can only be appreciated after studying a whole set of distinctions, it will probably strike people as archaic and tend to be ignored. The problem here far transcends specific issues such as reconciling creation and evolution; the holistic view of reality carried by doctrines that presuppose or use ancient philosophical and mythical language creates a world of meaning that frequently compromises the Christian message. For some, Christian language is hopelessly dated and intrinsically alienating.

Second, passing from the fact of contrasting imaginative frameworks for understanding reality, one should consider the methods that generate and nourish them. Whereas the medieval synthesis was able to integrate faith and reason, Enlightenment and modernity were typified by a tension between the authority of science on the one hand and religion on the other. Modern theologians from Schleiermacher to Tillich and Rahner recognized the autonomy of different forms of reason, but were able to draw these different forms of reason into a synthetic understanding of the human. But today secular science probes the universe and the human person with an empirical method that requires evidence. The antithesis between an autonomous secular reason, sometimes militantly atheistic, and faith has put Christian academics on the defensive, at least when it comes to truth claims. In the academy and more generally in literary and scientific circles, religion, at best, is regarded as a cultural phenomenon or, at worst, an object of anthropological curiosity. The autonomy of science and scientific reason is leaving religion and the churches behind.

Third, postmodern culture carries a consciousness that all ideas and values remain wedded to certain times and cultures, and this leaves people with a confusing picture of irremediable plurality. For some, this amounts to no more than a "system" of cultural relativism. This conviction causes or is augmented by a sense of the value of individuality, of uniqueness, and of difference. "Difference" outweighs the thin, abstract lines of "sameness" that connect individuals in groups, societies, or nations. One finds historical consciousness wherever awareness of being in history prevails. But it varies greatly in its radicality or the perception of the depth of the problems it entails. Christian consciousness has internalized a sense of its own developmental and changing history. But it has yet to come to terms with the radicality of randomness and a new appreciation of the positive character of change and diversity. Unmovable sameness still remains the highest value and the implicit norm of truth. While fundamentalist Christians revel in this, educated Christians can be deeply embarrassed, if not scandalized, by their own churches' narrowness and unwillingness to change.

Fourth, despite the movements of liberation within the churches and the development of coherent theologies of liberation, Christian spirituality still seems to be clinging to an interiority that abets an escape from the chaos of history and uncontrollable historical events. At least this remains a permanent temptation, so that the case for Christian responsibility in and for the world has to be made continually. Is there a rudimentary Christian ethic that defines Christianity as intrinsically concerned with society and forbids a spirituality of escape from the world? Or, in the end, is Christian faith a quiet, safe zone protected from the terror of history?

These four points do not exhaust the intellectual culture of postmodernity. But they help set up a problematic to which the later Christology of Schillebeeckx responds. That later Christology begins formally with the writing of his book *Jesus: An Experiment in Christology*, which was published in the mid-1970s, but it depends on premises internalized during the 1960s.[1] Although Schillebeeckx did not write a systematic Christology, his essays contain most of the elements for

---

[1]   Schillebeeckx, *Jesus, CW* vol. 6 (London: Bloomsbury T&T Clark, 2014). In this, chapter I focus on texts of Schillebeeckx written after Vatican II. Others have traced the development of Schillebeeckx's theology in the periods before Vatican II, a middle period following the council, and his later writings beginning in the early 1970s. I do not develop but build into this representation of Schillebeeckx's Christology his post-Vatican II embrace of secularity, historicity, critical sociology of knowledge, and critical exegesis.

a coherent representation of Jesus Christ in the face of postmodernity. I will represent that thesis in five stages: (1) Schillebeeckx's Christology rests on a platform of a theology of creation. (2) Three principles derived from historicity, negativity, and praxis consistently channel the flow of his thinking. (3) Systematically Schillebeeckx's Christology begins with a consideration of Jesus of Nazareth. (4) He then exhaustively studies how Jesus's disciples interpreted him as savior in the light of the resurrection.[2] (5) Finally, addressing the formal Christological problem of the divinity of Jesus Christ, Schillebeeckx calls Jesus "concentrated creation."

# I. Theology of creation

I turn now to a consideration of some points in Schillebeeckx's creation theology which play a major role in his later Christology. Because Schillebeeckx did not write a systematic Christology, any representation of a holistic framework for such a project, if he thought it valuable at all, becomes a matter of interpretation. A clue to his mind on this, however, lies in the elemental structure of the basic doctrines that Schillebeeckx thinks carry the essential Christian vision. These are creation (anthropology), Christology, church, and eschatology.[3] The outer skeleton of this framework is made up of the source and the destiny of reality and human history within it. In between lie Jesus the revelation and concentrated presence of God to history and the continuing story of Jesus in the community of his disciples. In this holistic vision, faith in creation assumes a fundamental grounding role.

"Belief in God the creator is never an explanation, nor is it meant to be."[4] The symbol of creation represents faith in the nature and character of God and is the result of a revelation of God that takes place within religious experience. This experience is mediated through a recognition of the radical contingency of oneself and the larger existence in which we participate. "Nature and history are the authorities in which and through which God discloses himself as creator, in and though our fundamental experiences of finitude."[5] Schillebeeckx shows that the experience of contingency can be interpreted in faith as an opening up to a transcendent ground of being and meaning.

More precisely, the possibility of speaking of a creator God is founded in a "basic trust" experienced within a person and directed toward the human project itself. Basic trust in existence, life, and history operates within conscious human achievement as the basic drive and condition of its possibility. This fundamental trust engages difficulties and frustrations; it asserts that the future of human existence is meaningful. The Christian interpretation of this secular trust names it a hope for salvation. This does not prove anything.

> The so-called proof of the existence of God which is based on the experience of contingency is therefore only the reflective justification, made afterwards, of the

---

[2]   Schillebeeckx also formulated a rudimentary pluralistic theology of religions that is discussed in another chapter. It is important to note here, however, that positions on the theology of religions have arisen out of our contemporary situation, and they enter into thinking about more narrowly conceived Christological issues.

[3]   Schillebeeckx, *Christ, CW* vol. 7 (London: Bloomsbury T&T Clark, 2014), 621–33 [631–44].

[4]   Schillebeeckx, *God Among Us: The Gospel Proclaimed* (New York: Crossroad, 1983), 91.

[5]   Ibid., 91.

conviction that this unconditional trust in the gift of a meaningful human future is not an illusion, not a projection of frustrated wishful thinking …"[6]

Once internalized this conviction wields critical power. Creation is not God; no one should relate to finite reality as something divine. Creation faith, recognizing the finitude and contingency of created reality, realizes that nothing created can be absolutized.[7]

Creation faith also means that God is immediately present to all reality. "From a Christian perspective, the world and human existence are totally other than God, but within the presence of the creator God."[8] As transcendent creator and absolute being, God is not distant and absent from God's creation. Creation out of nothing implies that there is no medium between God and creation. God is directly present to God's creation as its cause and ground. "The boundary between God and us is our boundary, not God's."[9] God creates out of love, and God is immanent and present to God's creation. All things exist within God's creative power so that God in turn is the within of all creation.[10]

Human beings participate in God's creating. Creation is not an event of the past, but an always actual, ongoing process. The significance of creation not being an explanation is that one cannot look backwards and say that the creator established a preordained order of things that cannot change. Rather creation includes a constant process of change through contingent events and chance. Human existence emerged in this creative process so that human freedom and intelligence now participate in the process itself. "God creates man as the principle of his own human action, who thus himself has to develop the world and its future and bring them into being within contingent situations."[11] In this way, creation has become a task for human freedom; it is something that human freedom is intended to take up. "This does not do away with the saving presence of God, God's immanence in creation. But this creative power of God never breaks in from outside. God's power is inwardly present."[12] For Schillebeeckx, creation in human beings has become history. It is open to the future and is changing. God and creation, therefore, cannot be used to canonize past events and arrangements as static norms for the future. Life is a narrative; it moves out of the past and into the future; to live is to look ahead and continually draw the past forward to illumine the future. In sum, creation faith translates through freedom into commitment to this world and history.[13]

---

6  Schillebeeckx, "Secularization and Christian Belief in God," *GFM, CW* vol. 3 (London: Bloomsbury T&T Clark, 2014), 45–46 [74–75 at 75].

7  Schillebeeckx, *God Among Us*, 94.

8  Ibid., 93.

9  Ibid., 94.

10 Dorothy Jacko, *Salvation in the Context of Contemporary Secularized Historical Consciousness: The Later Theology of Edward Schillebeeckx* (Th.D. Dissertation, Toronto: Regis College, University of Toronto, 1987), 94–99. See Schillebeeckx, *Christ*, 799–17, esp. 805 [804–21, esp. 809]. Schillebeeckx's position can be called panentheism, which holds the radical distinction in being between creator and creature, but the mutual interactive presence of creator and creatures to each other. This closeness of a personal and creating God of love is foundational to Schillebeeckx's theology. Creation is the symbol for God's presence to reality, the world, and human existence.

11 Schillebeeckx, *God Among Us*, 95.

12 Schillebeeckx, *For the Sake of the Gospel* (New York: Crossroad, 1990), 93.

13 Schillebeeckx, "Secularization and Christian Belief in God," *GFM*, 46–47 [76].

Freedom in modernity and postmodernity is understood as creativity; it is more than the power to choose; it transcends existentialist commitment; it is also the power to construct new reality. As creator God created this human power. Therefore, God desires that it be used. And God has confidence in it. God has entrusted creation to human beings not merely as caretakers of a past condition, but as co-creators with God of the future.

> Man himself is responsible for earthly history and will have to make order and *shalom* out of chaos … The world and history are entrusted to [humanity] within creaturely limits, human beings are entrusted with the world and history, and in that context Yahweh bestows on [humans] God's complete confidence.[14]

# II. Three basic principles

Moving from an all-encompassing creation faith as a bridge to the content of Schillebeeckx's Christology, it will be helpful to signal three principles which continually manifest themselves in his understanding of Jesus Christ. These principles were internalized in Schillebeeckx's middle period; they help define further the logic of his constructive Christology.

## One reality in two languages

The phrase, "one reality in two languages," represents a fundamental characteristic of Schillebeeckx's later theology. To speak of one reality and two languages about this reality allows both ontic identity and real distinction in interpretation between meanings that are secular-historical on the one hand and theological on the other. For example, it allows Schillebeeckx, in creation faith, to identify human liberation from bondage and Christian salvation. "Universal resistance to alienation, inhumanity and the absence of freedom assumes, in Christianity, the form of a redemption by God which can be realized in and through the faith of people in history."[15] The problem of human fulfillment, of this-worldly freedom and its final destiny, is a secular question, which at the same time, from a religious point of view, elicits the language of salvation. They are the same reality, from two different perspectives and in two different languages.[16] Human

---

14  Schillebeeckx, *IR, CW* vol. 8 (London: Bloomsbury T&T Clark, 2014), 96 [109].

15  Schillebeeckx, "Correlation Between Human Question and Christian Answer," *UF, CW* vol. 5 (London: Bloomsbury T&T Clark, 2014), 81 [93]. It may be important to note here that, against the idea of two parallel economies of history, Schillebeeckx maintains a single history of creation and salvation. God the creator is savior; God's saving action is not other than God's loving creative action; the two are one. Perception from different perspectives may account for premodern postulating two distinct orders of God's interaction with the world.

16  Schillebeeckx, "Correlation Between Human Question and Christian Answer," *UF*, 85 [98]: "In this consideration of reality from the point of view of man's questions about the authentic fulfillment of his life, about salvation, I see the only explicitly non-religious context within which it is meaningful to speak correlatively about God according to the criteria of the religious language game."

reality can be experienced as meaningful in secular terms and in secular praxis, and Christianity should be construed as the support and guarantee of this worldly project. Outside the world, no salvation; salvation is salvation of the world.[17]

This principle defines a fundamental outlook on religion and God's action in the world for human salvation. Ontologically, God does not operate overtly or empirically in the world. Therefore, epistemologically, all one sees and touches is a secular world.[18] The key is not to separate salvation off to another sphere; salvation consists in liberating and humanizing events in this world and a particular faith experience and interpretation of them that perceives God immanent to the world and at work in them.

# Negative experience of contrast

Schillebeeckx learned from critical theory what he called "a negative experience of contrast," which became an important category for explaining several of his positions. A negative experience of contrast is an experience of something that is wrong and should not be, a kind of direct intuitive awareness and conviction that something is evil. This experience is accompanied by two intrinsic dimensions. The negative experience presupposes an awareness of the positive because one would not be able to grasp negativity except against the background of an intuition of the way things should or could be. Also, this negative experience is accompanied by an impulse and consistent desire to resist the negativity in whatever way is possible and appropriate.[19]

Negative experience, resistance to the negativity, and a fundamental positive conception of what should be including a hope that it will come to be achieved, together form a kind of anthropological and ethical groundwork for Schillebeeckx's theology. They explain an openness to revelation and a desire for salvation that always accompany the many forms of human suffering. The negative basis for a question about God comes from a common human impulse to repair the constantly damaged *humanum*.[20] Resistance to the threat to humanity is a human universal. Thus, he writes: "This critical negativity, or negative dialectics, is the universal pre-understanding of

---

[17] Schillebeeckx, *Church, CW* vol. 10 (London: Bloomsbury T&T Clark, 2014), 12 [12]: "[*E*]*xtra mundum nulla salus*, there is no salvation outside the human world."

[18] Schillebeeckx, "God the Living One," *New Blackfriars*, 63 (1981), 364: "God-given redemption and salvation do not lie next to or beyond and on the other side of self-liberation, but lie inside liberation in the same way as what is called in Christian faith the *divinity of Jesus* is located inside Jesus's humanity and not next to it or on the other side of it." Schillebeeckx applies this principle to the study of the church: the political and sociological organization is also the community of the people of God. Schillebeeckx, *Church*, 208–12 [210–13].

[19] Schillebeeckx, "Church, Magisterium and Politics," *GFM*, 92–94 [154–56]; *Church*, 5–6 [5–6]. A concise account of Schillebeeckx's negative experience of contrast can be found in Patricia McAuliffe, *Fundamental Ethics: A Liberationist Approach* (Washington, DC: Georgetown University Press, 1993), 1–38.

[20] Schillebeeckx, "Correlation Between Human Question and Christian Answer," *UF*, 79–80 [91].

all positive views of man."[21] The dialectic of the negative, the positive, and the hope implicit in resistance relate to the basic trust seen earlier.

> All our negative experiences cannot brush aside the "nonetheless" of the trust which is revealed in man's critical resistance and which prevents us from simply surrendering man, human society and the world entirely to total meaninglessness. This trust in the ultimate meaning of human life seems to me to be the basic presupposition of man's action in history.[22]

# Christianity is a praxis

Schillebeeckx's attention to creation theology was developed within an eschatological framework and in response to a God who summons human beings from out in front of us. Recognition of how the future is always at work in human freedom requires that we shift to a concept of God that connects with human beings as agents of what is to come. Life into the future spontaneously introduces the language of praxis and orthopraxis. The way to the future passes through action. Like secularity, a concern for the future and for the action that leads to a new future was in the air in the 1960s. This was especially evident in the Christian–Marxist dialogues, and it blossomed into political and liberation theologies. It easily finds a place in Schillebeeckx's new theological vision. The spontaneous urge toward praxis flows directly from negative experiences of contrast.

> Based on and stimulated by such 'contrast experiences,' i.e. experiences of inhumaneness or meaninglessness in certain situations, there arises an attitude of opposition or critical solidarity with regard to the human values one sees permanently threatened, with the common purpose of removing the threat.[23]

Schillebeeckx consistently writes as one guided by the principle that Christianity is not about knowledge but about praxis, that revelation is *for* praxis.

These three principles suffuse Schillebeeckx's later theology. They are therefore operative when he turns to an appreciation of Jesus of Nazareth. The themes of "contrast experience" and "praxis" show that his emphasis on God's presence to history as creator is balanced with a concern for praxis, the future, and ultimate meaning that is God's promise of our destiny. The drama of salvation mediated in Jesus transpires within the created present and the promised future.

---

[21] Ibid., *UF*, 80 [92]: "I regard these negative dialectics coming within a positive sphere of meaning which is, however, in its universality only implicit (it is a call to the *humanum*) as the universal pre-understanding not only of the pluralist answers that man gives to this call, but also of Christian talk about God, in other words, of the gospel."

[22] Ibid., 83–84 [96–97]. In sum, the dialectical structure of the negative experience of contrast explains why suffering assumed such a large place in Schillebeeckx's later theology. See Kathleen Anne McManus, *Unbroken Communion: The Place and Meaning of Suffering in the Theology of Edward Schillebeeckx* (Lanham, MD: Rowman and Littlefield, 2003).

[23] Mark Schoof, "Masters of Israel: VII. The Later Theology of Edward Schillebeeckx," *Clergy Review* 55 (1970), 957. See especially Schillebeeckx, "The New Image of God," *GFM*, 101–25 [167–207].

# III. Jesus of Nazareth

With the metaphysical vision produced by creation faith as a presupposition, Schillebeeckx begins the formal discipline of Christology with a consideration of Jesus of Nazareth. What follows reports on what he is doing (method) and some of the salient points about Jesus that he emphasizes (content).[24] Because Schillebeeckx begins by turning his attention to Jesus of Nazareth and to exegesis, his Christology can be called "Christology from below," or a "genetic Christology," or a "narrative Christology." Each one of these designations builds on the principle that, in order to understand the community's confession of Jesus as the Christ, one has to study how it emerged, that is, its origin and development. All Christology is ultimately about, or reaches back to, Jesus of Nazareth. Therefore, Christology has to consider what can be known about the Jesus who is the historical referent of the discipline.

Much could be said about the thoroughly debated method and character of any interpretation of "the historical Jesus" and what exactly that phrase means. But Schillebeeckx's Christology posits a construal of the Jesus of history as the starting point for understanding the meaning of the interpretive titles that are assigned to him. Actually, interpretation proceeds in both directions, so that the opposite thesis is also true: the titles interpret Jesus as well. But the point of the initial thesis is clear: since Jesus is the subject matter or object of interpretation, interpretation cannot negate and should be guided by the actuality of the historical person.

Turning to the content of Schillebeeckx's interpretation of Jesus of Nazareth, given the sources, one does not have the data to write a biography of Jesus. Although one knows little in detail about his life, the synoptic gospels give a significant portrait of his public ministry. Jesus is subject of innumerable different interpretations through the course of history, and this interpretation is intrinsically fraught with problems. But interpretation cannot be escaped. The influence of human imagination about the actual person accompanies every understanding of him. How does Schillebeeckx appreciate this historical figure? I will return to his theological appreciation further on.

Several standard but key themes structure Schillebeeckx's interpretation. First of all, the central historical datum about Jesus is that he preached the kingdom of God. "Centrality" here means that for Schillebeeckx everything else we know about Jesus should be understood within the context of Jesus's preaching the kingdom of God. What does the kingdom of God mean? It certainly refers to the will and rule of God. More concretely, its meaning comes from the other accumulated teachings and actions of his public ministry.

The principal teachings of Jesus on the kingdom of God in the New Testament are cast in the form of parables. But besides the parables, one has a more general sayings tradition from Jesus consisting in the beatitudes and other aphorisms, and ethical teachings or interpretations of Jewish tradition. Schillebeeckx consistently interprets Jesus as preaching God's cause as the cause of human flourishing against injustice and human diminishment and for life in its fullness.

---

[24] The major source for Schillebeeckx's representation of Jesus of Nazareth is his *Jesus*. Schillebeeckx synopsizes his investigations of Jesus in *Church*, 101–42 [102–44]. A short presentation of the theological logic of this historical account is found in Edward Schillebeeckx, "The 'God of Jesus' and the 'Jesus of God,'" *The Language of Faith: Essays on Jesus, Theology, and the Church* (Maryknoll, NY: Orbis, 1995), 95–108.

The other major source for determining the meaning of God and the kingdom of God as Jesus represented them can be gleaned from his praxis: his exorcisms, the stories in the wonder-working tradition, his acceptance of sinners, his reaching out to those marginated in Jewish society are revelatory of the God whose kingdom he represented. Schillebeeckx also tried to formulate an aspect of Jesus's experience and conscious relationship with God. These considerations revolve around the fact that Jesus spoke of God as Father and presuppose that Jesus must have had some powerful experience of God. Schillebeeckx builds on the position of Joachim Jeremias some decades ago who argued that Jesus's use of the term "Abba" indicated an intimate, personal relationship. Although Jeremias's position has been called into question, Jesus obviously related to God consciously, but it is notoriously difficult or impossible to define the psychological contours of this experience with the data we have.

That Jesus was executed as a criminal is one of the most solid pieces of historical data about him. There is a good deal of interest in the historical reasons for Jesus's death; and Christian theology has devoted considerable theological attention to his death in the belief that his death was the saving moment par excellence. Schillebeeckx is one among many theologians today who wishes to include more emphasis on Jesus's public ministry and his resurrection in the interpretation of salvation.

It is significant to note that Schillebeeckx's historical approach shifts attention to the disciples after Jesus's death. Historically, the question focuses on the Easter experience: how did the disciples, confused and scattered at the death of Jesus, come to the recognition that Jesus was alive, risen, and exalted? In his *Jesus* book, Schillebeeckx approaches this issue slowly and methodically. More important than his theory of the Easter experience, however, is his firm affirmation that Jesus is risen and the significance of this as a promise of our own resurrection. The Easter experience is also significant because it represents the condition *sine qua non* of the development of formal Christology. As an opening door draws one into another room, interpretation of Jesus as the Christ must pass through the Easter experience that Jesus was raised from death. Salvation is the key term for that interpretation.

# IV. The salvation mediated by Jesus

Schillebeeckx wrote a great deal about salvation, and it is impossible not to oversimplify his reflections in a brief statement. However, I can still indicate the structure of his thinking here by noticing how his treatment of salvation in the *Christ* book relates to his portrait of Jesus as savior in the *Jesus* book. In the book *Christ*, Schillebeeckx analyzes the idea of salvation or grace in every book in the New Testament except the synoptics. He then presents a summary of his findings in a synopsis of the various images, metaphors, and concepts expressing the experience and meaning of the salvation mediated in the event of Jesus Christ. Jesus is or wins salvation for us as the one who redeems from servitude and slavery; he is a ransom for our release; Jesus effects reconciliation between human existence and God and between human beings; our redemption is satisfaction for sin; it brings justice and peace; redemption is expiation, and it is forgiveness; sinners are justified; they are sanctified; salvation in Jesus is legal aid; it is freedom to love;

salvation is freedom itself or freed freedom; salvation renews human existence and the world; it is victory over demonic power; it is life lived to the fullest.[25]

How does one handle the extravagant pluralism of the interpretations of Jesus and salvation that one finds in the New Testament? Schillebeeckx's response to this question has three dimensions: first, one can determine where the common element of all the interpretations lies. They all reflect one core conviction that God is encountered in Jesus in a saving way. He shows that "a fundamentally identical experience underlies the various interpretations to be found throughout the New Testament: all its writings bear witness to the experience of salvation in Jesus from God."[26]

Second, to get closer to the kernel of this common experience, one should focus on Jesus the person who is the one subject of all the interpretations. Jesus of Nazareth interprets the interpretations. Third, one then must try to express this datum in a way that is understandable in today's world, a way that is analogous to the way the various interpretations of the first century did the same in those cultures.[27]

Turning to Jesus, his public ministry was his saving activity. Jesus is savior by being the parable of God and the revelation of the mystery of human existence. Jesus's "going around doing good" was his mediation of this-worldly salvation: his wondrous works for people's benefit, his acceptance of the marginalized, his table fellowship with those shunned, his bias toward the poor. In attending to human suffering Jesus "reveals a universally relevant manner of being human," one which by its alignment with the kingdom of God also mediates salvation.[28] Salvation should not be associated exclusively with Jesus' death.[29] Jesus himself is savior because he reveals God and is the pioneer of human existence; Jesus is parable of God and paradigm of human life. His resurrection is a promise of eternal life and a guarantee that our contributions to human history in this world will count for eternity. Jesus saves by revealing the character of God and the nature and destiny of human existence.

## Jesus Christ as concentrated creation

Schillebeeckx's formal Christology contains his appropriation of the councils of Nicaea and Chalcedon. The teaching of those councils states that Jesus as a single person is both truly human and truly divine. This doctrine symbolizes for Christian tradition the classic content of Christian faith in Jesus Christ. Where does Schillebeeckx's Christology stand in this tradition? Schillebeeckx shifted his language about this central doctrine and a brief outline of the first two stages in his development will help shed light on his third and final position.

Before the Second Vatican Council, in his *Christ the Sacrament of the Encounter with God*, Schillebeeckx used traditional objective trinitarian terminology of a divine Word or Son descending and becoming incarnate in this world by assuming a human nature or humanity

---

[25] Schillebeeckx, *Christ*, 457–501 [468–514].
[26] Ibid., 451 [463].
[27] See Schillebeeckx, *Church,* 39–43 [40–43]
[28] Jacko, *Salvation,* 184, citing Schillebeeckx, *Jesus,* 553–54 [593].
[29] Schillebeeckx, *Christ,* 621–23 [632–33].

that constituted Jesus of Nazareth. Jesus was God acting in history in an overt but empirically unrecognizable way.[30]

Schillebeeckx's book, *Jesus*, contains a second stage. After his extensive reflection on the historical ministry of Jesus, Schillebeeckx added a reflection on the classical doctrinal language, as an afterthought, mainly because he thought people would expect it. He did not want to leave his discussion of Jesus without saying something about his divinity and the traditional language about it.[31] In this reflection, he proposed that traditional theology adopt the conception of a mutual and simultaneous "enhypostatic union" between the Logos and the human person Jesus. While his conceptual analysis sharply clashes with the historical method of the book, Schillebeeckx explains the relationship between the two kinds of reflection in terms of primary and secondary religious language. Primary religious language is the more or less proximate expression of primal Christian experience. Such experience usually relates to the person of Jesus, either the memory of him as a concrete person or an image of him. Secondary reflection, what Schillebeeckx calls reflection to the power of two, consists of critical appropriation of primary expression and, as such, is tied to the primary language which relates back to Jesus. Primary language is normative for secondary; and Jesus is normative for primary Christological language because it refers to him. The purpose of second order reflection is to explain and, by critical grounding, to protect these first-order assertions. The relation between these two languages is a way of situating the meaning of "enhypostiatic union" about which I will say something further on.

In 1974, Schillebeeckx published the short essay, "The 'God of Jesus' and the 'Jesus of God,'" in which he characterized the primary experience that Christians had of Jesus.[32] This experience is simultaneously an experience of God mediated through Jesus and an interpretive experience of Jesus. Jesus is encountered as one who reveals God as savior, a God who as creator is intrinsically and by nature savior. At the same time, especially in the experience of Jesus risen, Jesus is interpreted as of God, as sent by God, as a representative of God and God's salvation. This short essay gets at the heart of the experience of Jesus as mediator of salvation from God as the basis of all Christology.

Moving to secondary language, Schillebeeckx says that Jesus is both "parable of God and paradigm of humanity."[33] God was acting in Jesus in such a way that Jesus is the focus and medium for this twofold revelation. Jesus reveals God narratively; faith can read the character of God as authentically represented in Jesus's preaching and his acts of love.[34] And one can experience in his ministry as well the model of what human existence should be. If a theoretical or second-order Christology explains and protects such an experience of and relation to Jesus, it

---

30  Schillebeeckx, *Christ the Sacrament of the Encounter with God,* displays this understanding well. See Schillebeeckx, *Christ the Sacrament, CW* vol. 1 (London: Bloomsbury T&T Clark, 2014), 9–24 [13–39].

31  See Schillebeeckx, *Jesus,* 599–633 [636–74].

32  Schillebeeckx, "The 'God of Jesus' and the 'Jesus of God,'" *The Language of Faith,* 95–108.

33  Schillebeeckx, *Jesus,* 587 [626].

34  The key to the first *Jesus* book is narrative: the basic model is that Jesus is the parable of God. Jesus expresses God in a narrative form suited to a dynamic life in this world. The deep motive of this Christology is "promoting eschatological hope and practical action." See Steven M. Rodenborn, *Hope in Action: Subversive Eschatology in the Theology of Edward Schillebeeckx and Johann Baptist Metz* (Minneapolis: Fortress Press, 2014), 156.

is orthodox. In other words, this basic religious proposition is the norm and criterion for second-order theology and doctrines. This makes the idea that Jesus is the parable of God and the paradigm of human existence a contemporary translation of the Chalcedonian formula of truly divine and truly human.[35] Schillebeeckx's proposal of a mutual or simultaneous enhypostatic union means a co-inhabitation of the individual Jesus in God and of God as Word in the individual Jesus. Schillebeeckx says that this is possible because it does not generate two individuals as it would in two finite subjects being united. In the case of creator and creature, there is no parity; the creature is already in the creator, and the creator is immanent in the creature sustaining it. Thus, on the level of Jesus's freedom and autonomy as a creature there is no competition but a mutual indwelling. This formulation is a theoretical construal that allows Jesus his individual personhood and thus protects his status as a human creature and at the same time his real mediation of true God.

The third stage in Schillebeeckx's development is stated at the end of the *Interim Report* where he poses this question, is Jesus God?[36] He does not answer this question straightforwardly the way a neoscholastic theologian might. A direct "Yes" to such a misguided question would compromise the tension of the Chalcedonian formula: Jesus is both human and divine. Rather his answer is twofold and consistent with his whole interpretation of Jesus. On the one hand, the significance of Jesus is that he really reveals God, he points away from himself so that one encounters God and God's salvation in and through him. Salvation from God is revealed in Jesus. But the medium or person Jesus in whom this saving God is revealed cannot be separated from the revelation. "We cannot separate God's being from his revelation. For this reason, the man Jesus, in the definition of what he is, does indeed have something to do with the being of God."[37]

Schillebeeckx's formula for this final position is that "'Christology' [*sic*] is *concentrated* creation: belief in creation as God wills it to be."[38] I take this to mean that God's creative and saving presence is so active in Jesus that Jesus mediates that power and presence; it both empowers him and mediates it to others in a conscious and efficacious way. Jesus is not the Christ because he strives harder and thus becomes the sacrament of the encounter with God. It is God at work within him that makes him Christ and savior.

# V. Contributions of Schillebeeckx to Christology

Schillebeeckx negotiated a remarkable transition in his mode of thinking in the course of the 1960s.[39] One could say he reinvented himself as a theologian. I have condensed part of that transition into his turn to creation theology, his embrace of secularity and history, the dialectics of negativity, and a concern for praxis leading to the future. These premises open up a synthesis that allows his Christology to address the postmodern world.

---

[35] Jacko, *Salvation*, 189, drawing on: Robert Schreiter, "Jezus als parabel van God en paradigma van menselijkheid," *Meedenken met Edward Schillebeeckx*, ed. Herman Häring, Ted Schoof, and Ad Willems (Baarn: H. Nelissen, 1983), 158–70.

[36] Schillebeeckx, *IR*, 121–24 [140–43].

[37] Ibid., 123 [142].

[38] Ibid., 111 [128].

[39] Steven Rodenborn provides an incisive guide to this development in *Hope in Action*, 69–198.

# The new imaginative framework

The new interpretive framework proposed by Schillebeeckx results from a turn to experience, in this case the postmodern disenchanted experience of the world and time. Even the most radical humanism, however, must ask the question of the meaning and relevance of human activity itself. In response, the basic trust exhibited in the human project suggests that the secular and religious questions of salvation share something in common. Grounded in basic trust but ultimately the result of religious experience, creation faith offers a more satisfactory alternative than nihilism and relativism; it opens human imagination to hope for an absolute future. On the basis of creation faith, God can be seen as mediated in and through a finite and contingent world; God is not up there or out there, but the within of things. The one physical reality that we perceive can be interpreted as existing within the embrace of a benevolent and loving author and finisher of life. This allows people to grasp what should and perhaps can be within the negative; it empowers human freedom to resist the negative and build new structures for human flourishing. Creation is good, and human freedom is partly responsible for its future. Creation faith is intrinsically pragmatic, hopeful, and activist in its response to a world that is always in the process of becoming, now more than ever through human agency. In the light of Jesus risen, Christian faith offers a promise of an absolute future. How does this imaginative framework reappropriate and present Jesus Christ to a postmodern world?

# Christology in a postmodern key

Schillebeeckx's interpretation of Jesus Christ responds to the four challenges of postmodernity noted at the outset while at the same time remaining faithful to the biblical and conciliar teachings of the tradition about him. He has negotiated a fundamentally new Christology along the following lines. First of all, he has moved Christian understanding out of the framework of "double gratuity" and resituated it in a continuous process of evolution and history. The idea of double gratuity has determined the language of the tradition of Christian theology in the West most decisively since Augustine. The first gratuitous grace of God is creation; God freely creates. The second gratuity is the grace of salvation usually formulated within the context of sin. The encompassing framework for the Christian story is creation, fall, and redemption; grace, responding to sin, is a second gratuity. Augustine was convinced that if salvation could be accomplished in the created order, then Christ came in vain. The second gratuity, the grace of Christ, either restores creation or is added to it.

Schillebeeckx proposes a single gratuity; all that can be said of God in the light of Jesus's saving activity applies to the loving creator. Jesus Christ dramatizes and reveals the object of creation faith. There is no supernatural order or order of redemption beyond the created order. The mythological framework of fall and redemption vanishes. More dramatically, Schillebeeckx has moved Christian imagination from a Christocentric universe to a theocentric view. Christian faith in God remains Christomorphic because it is mediated and schooled by Jesus Christ; the Christian encounters the creative-salvific power and presence of God precisely in Jesus. But it is universally present and accessible; it has always been there and is experienced fragmentarily by all; it is decisively revealed in the life, death, and resurrection of Jesus of Nazareth. The

Christian language of salvation in Christ correlates with the continuity of the scientific picture of the universe.

Second, on the level of principle and method, Schillebeeckx opens up the Christian imagination to the secular, scientific, and evolutionary interpretations of reality by finding God within the world.[40] One reality in two languages; the God of the universe is the "within" of things and can only be so because of God's absolute transcendence. If God is creator, God does not come to creatures from outside creatures because God's loving presence and power makes creatures to be. Jesus, as the bearer of God, then, does not cease to be a human being but is the perfect response to God precisely because of God's power within him. Incarnation is the name of the nature of the creator God, and the love to which Jesus testified further defines God's character. In this scenario, God, the grounding source of the world, is totally *for* the world and its flourishing. There is nothing about the world that science can discover and, with evidence, assert that can in principle contradict Christian faith. Quite the contrary, Christian faith affirms that whatever is real must be integrated into one's understanding of God. Schillebeeckx's understanding of Jesus Christ and Christianity, far from being defensive against the dynamics of science, appeals to it as a manifestation of the search for what Jesus reveals.

Third, Schillebeeckx's Christology also embraces historical consciousness. The experiences of contingency and finitude, which implicitly are experiences of creation in the sense of complete dependence in being on a transcendent source, are perfectly human experiences. From within creation faith finitude is good. Each limited thing is good. The anthropological constants that Schillebeeckx predicates across all appreciations of the human are not a priori assumptions but observed characteristics.[41] Within the one, huge, and mysterious phenomenon of the human, differences are valuable and to be cherished as ongoing creation continuously generates new forms of being and being human. In a world of historical process, unchanging sameness is not a value but a principle of decline, entropy, and ultimately death. Many of the problems of Christology lie in fixating on past doctrines *about Jesus* instead of allowing Jesus to release his message about God, human life, and history. In Schillebeeckx's Christology, the positive revelations and truths found in the religions help us to look at Jesus with new eyes, and a re-examination of Jesus and the God of Jesus enable us to see these religions with new eyes. The pluralism that Schillebeeckx embraces is not sheer plurality or relativism, but the one salvation from the God of creation experienced in the many religions.

Fourth and finally, Schillebeeckx's Jesus Christ provides no grounds for passive or escapist Christianity. God, working through evolution, has gifted human beings with intelligent freedom so that human beings participate in the very process of creation itself. His stress on eschatology and praxis integrates engagement with the world, society, and the political realm into the heart

---

[40] Much of Schillebeeckx's analysis and appropriation of secularization can be applied, *mutatis mutandis*, to a critical dialogue with evolutionary sciences.

[41] Anthropological constants are constitutive aspects of the human. They form a formal system of coordinates revolving around personal identity and social culture that help define the human. He enumerates six: relationship to environment, relationship to other human beings, connectedness to institutional structures, location and definition by space and time, the connection of theory and practice, and religious consciousness. A seventh factor is the original synthesis in each case of all six. Schillebeeckx, *Christ*, 728–37 [734–43].

of Christian spirituality. Negative contrast experiences lay a foundation for ethical judgment concerning the direction action should take. Humans know when a given event or situation is radically wrong, and they experience the universal impulse is to resist it, to protect life, to create richer forms of being for human flourishing. The prophetic dimension of Jesus's ministry provides an analogous guide for human response: where he saw human defilement, he sought to reverse it and promote human integrity and reconciliation.[42] In Schillebeeckx's Christology, the mission to follow Jesus in engaged service to the world defines the project of God. In short, he has integrated ethics and responsibility for the world into the Christian spirituality of salvation and following Jesus Christ.

---

[42] This should not leave one with the impression that Schillebeeckx promoted a spontaneous intuitive ethics for complex ethical problems. These common impulses drive toward wide consultation, critical analysis, and conversation.

# Chapter 26

# Schillebeeckx and the Path to a Liberation Theology

Michael E. Lee

As part of the larger historical "irruption of the poor" ushered in during the post-colonial period following the Second World War, liberation theologies gave voice to those who had been previously outside of theological consideration or discussion.[1] By bringing the reality, concerns, and hopes of marginalized peoples to theological reflection, liberation theologies challenged and upended many assumptions asserted by the dominant theological discourses. With the rise of liberation theology, realities such as global poverty, gender, and racial discrimination, and structural violence could no longer be ignored theologically. For decades, liberation theology has functioned as an empowering theology that unmasks the ways that oppressive social systems have been legitimated religiously. No longer do those who are marginalized need to hear about a God who condones widespread malnutrition or who offers a reward after death for patient endurance of repressive torture states. To paraphrase the Gospel of Luke, liberation theology has been a sign of hope to "lift up the lowly" and to empower them with the good news of salvation—one whose future fullness has an anticipatory presence in a more just and peaceful world in the present (cf. Lk 1:52).

Of course, the opposite side of the coin that lifts up the lowly is that the mighty are cast down from their thrones. Indeed, inasmuch as liberation theology has served as an empowering agent to voices in Latin America, Africa, and Asia, and those on the underside of societies around the globe, it has confronted the powerful and those theologies that either justify their position or ignore it as privilege. As the understanding of the interconnectedness of the world has increased, the reality of this "global village" demands that all of its members realize how they are implicated in structural inequalities, coloniality, and exclusion. For theologians who are located in the centers of power, this demand is a call to transform the method and content of their theologies to respond to this reality.

Edward Schillebeeckx represents one of the foremost European interlocutors of liberation theology. Over the course of his career, he engaged the thinking of liberation theologians and considered the implications of liberation theology for his own work in the elite academic setting of the European university. Indeed, commentators agree that along the many turns in Schillebeeckx's intellectual journey (formation in neo-scholasticism, philosophical influence of Dominicus De Petter, exposure to *la nouvelle théologie*, engagement with phenomenology,

---

[1]    Virginia Fabella and Sergio Torres, eds., *Irruption of the Third World: Challenge to Theology* (Maryknoll: Orbis, 1983).

hermeneutics, critical theory, etc.), his mature work resonates with liberation theology as "more politically responsible, eschatologically oriented, and resolutely attentive to suffering."[2] The affinities are many, and certainly no account of Schillebeeckx's extraordinary career can overlook his interaction with liberation theology. Yet, examining Schillebeeckx's relationship to liberation theology possesses several difficulties that must be overcome.

# I. Itinerary for a Catholic liberation theology

As an entity, "liberation theology" poses a challenge because of its diversity along a number of lines including: social locations, contexts of oppression, religious affiliations, and national origins. As Leonardo and Clodovis Boff have helpfully distinguished, liberation theology has operated at a "popular" and "pastoral" level in addition to the well-known "professional" work of scholars that have produced a significant bibliography.[3] Though he accompanied the Dutch "critical communities" that have been likened to the Latin American *comunidades eclesiales de base*, Schillebeeckx's work is most fruitfully understood by comparing it with those "professional" liberation theologians who shared his academic calling. However, even restricting oneself to the work of academic liberation theologians, there still exists a wide plurality of material.[4] Liberation theology is not a static entity, nor is it monolithic in its appearance. In reality, it is more proper to speak of liberation *theologies* that, much like a school of art or a style of music, possess certain shared characteristics or family resemblances.

The sheer diversity and scope of liberation theologies demands limits to any interesting study of Schillebeeckx's thought. To compare his thought to all liberation theologians would involve cherry picking in too large an orchard. Interesting candidates include US scholar James Cone, who published *A Black Theology of Liberation* at the time that Schillebeeckx's work showed significant changes of its own.[5] Because liberation theologies can now be found around the globe, it would be possible to compare his thought to theologians in Asia, Africa, or Australia/Pacific Islands as well.[6] Finally, as liberation theology itself has matured and engaged different contexts and critical questions, Schillebeeckx could be analyzed from a number of perspectives including feminist and ecological liberation theologies as well as those that emerge from marginalized

---

[2]  Philip Kennedy, *Schillebeeckx* (Collegeville, MN: Liturgical Press, 1993), 50–51. See also William J. Hill, "A Theology in Transition," *The Praxis of the Reign of God: An Introduction to the Theology of Edward Schillebeeckx*, ed. Mary Catherine Hilkert and Robert J. Schreiter (New York: Fordham University Press, 2002), 1–18.

[3]  Clodovis and Leonardo Boff, *Introducing Liberation Theology*, trans. Paul Burns (Kent: Burns & Oates/Search Press, 1987).

[4]  Compendia of Latin American liberation theologies in English include: Alfred Hennelly, *Liberation Theology: A Documentary History* (Maryknoll: Orbis, 1990) and Jon Sobrino and Ignacio Ellacuría, eds., *Mysterium Liberationis: Fundamental Concepts of Liberation Theology* (Maryknoll: Orbis, 1993).

[5]  Originally published by the J. B. Lippincott Company in 1970, it is currently available in a fortieth anniversary edition as: James Cone, *A Black Theology of Liberation* (Maryknoll: Orbis, 2010).

[6]  Helen Bergin, ed., *From North to South: Southern Scholars Engage with Edward Schillebeeckx* (Adelaide: ATF, 2013).

populations within developed countries like US Latinx theologies.[7] Although any of these approaches and figures could be fruitful, the chronological, cultural, and geographical differences would be limiting factors as well.

Over his career, Schillebeeckx engaged directly with the "first generation" of Roman Catholic Latin American liberation theologians, whose writings in the 1970s and 1980s established liberation theology as deserving of international recognition. More importantly, perhaps, he shared a similar intellectual and vocational formation. Just like figures such as Gustavo Gutiérrez, Leonardo Boff, Jon Sobrino, and Ignacio Ellacuría, Schillebeeckx was a Roman Catholic priest, formed in the mid-twentieth century neo-scholastic manuals, who critically expanded his theological thinking in the period during and subsequent to the Second Vatican Council. Even beyond a series of ideas that they might share, Schillebeeckx and his Latin American counterparts map an intellectual and theological itinerary that blossoms into liberationist theologies. Thus, this chapter will document Schillebeeckx's relationship to liberation theology as a series of insights, a developing trajectory of thought emerging in three important periods of his career, that [a] illuminate how modern Catholic theology turns liberationist and [b] substantiate the claim that Edward Schillebeeckx can be called a European liberation theologian.

The first period, his early work through the end of the Second Vatican Council, meant exposure to *la nouvelle théologie* and the events of the Council. Key developments in his thought, which include a greater historical consciousness, a reconfigured theological understanding of the world, and a renewed idea of the church's mission in the world, are ones shared by liberation theology as it gets initially formulated. In the second period, from the middle 1970s to the early 1980s, Schillebeeckx enters into direct critical dialog with liberation theologies, identifying what he sees as their strengths and the areas that needed more attention. Finally, from the middle 1980s on, in his most mature work, Schillebeeckx articulates a contextual liberation theology that deploys the central concepts shared by liberation theologies: the centrality of praxis and the preferential option for the poor.

# II. Different soil, shared ground

At one level, Schillebeeckx's theology originates from a completely different context than that of Latin American liberation theologians. The world of European university intellectual life is literally and figuratively miles away from the poor communities where the Latin Americans did their work. Gustavo Gutiérrez, who spent decades doing pastoral ministry in a poor parish in the Rímac district of Lima, did not accept a university appointment until 1999.[8] While Clodovis and Leonardo Boff conducted university teaching, they would use time between terms to work in the jungles of Amazonia.[9] Despite these basic geographical and cultural differences, Latin American seminarians in the early-to-middle twentieth century were often sent to Europe for theological

---

[7] See, for example, Benjamín Valentín, ed., *In Our Own Voices: Latino/a Renditions of Theology* (Maryknoll: Orbis, 2010).

[8] For more on his early biography, see Robert McAffee Brown, *Gustavo Gutiérrez: An Introduction to Liberation Theology* (Maryknoll: Orbis, 1990).

[9] Clodovis Boff, *Feet-on-the-Ground Theology: A Brazilian Journey* (Maryknoll: Orbis, 1987).

formation in places such as Rome, Paris, Munich, and Leuven.[10] Thus, as a consequence of their being exposed to the same theological methods and content, European and Latin American Roman Catholic theologians of this generation would share important negative and positive responses to their formation.

Negatively, both Schillebeeckx and the liberation theologians react against the neo-scholastic theology dominant in their theological formation. The rigidity, abstraction, and dualisms inherent in the "manual" theology presented in seminary training represent a mutual target against which their theologies would be aimed. Without taking this context into account, especially the drive for historical awareness, greater accounting for the reality of lived Christian experience, and attention to the aspiration for liberation, these theologians' works cannot be understood.

That negative context notwithstanding, the theological formation that Schillebeeckx and the Latin Americans experienced in the 1950s and 1960s was not entirely negative. Exposure to the pioneering work of the so-called *nouvelle théologie* and the experience of the Second Vatican Council gave them important shared theological themes that would ground and animate their work. For example, both Schillebeeckx and Gustavo Gutiérrez have identified Marie-Dominique Chenu as their greatest theological influence. As has been well documented, it was in Chenu's classes at the École des Hautes Études in Paris (1945–1947) that Schillebeeckx was won over by the Dominicans' historical contextualization of medieval theology.[11] In contrast to the idealized and context-free presentation of scholastic theology in the manuals, here was recognition of the diversity in ancient Christian sources and the dynamism in Aquinas and his medieval contemporaries—and a case for carrying out contemporary theology with the same kind of dynamism. As William Hill has noted, "That [Chenu and Congar's] historical approach to Aquinas's writing allowed his thought to reemerge in a way that challenged the rationalistic and conceptualist interpretation being put upon it by neo-Thomism."[12]

Gustavo Gutiérrez came to know Chenu while studying in France, seeking him out when the latter was banned from teaching. In the early chapters of *A Theology of Liberation*, Gutiérrez gives evidence that he too was shaped by the historical studies of the Dominicans. He frames liberation theology in a historical lineage of different epochs in Christian theology marked by distinct spiritualities—from the wisdom theology of early Christianity, to the theology as "rational knowledge" of the scholastic period, and concluding with the need for a liberation theology as "critical reflection on Christian praxis" in the present.[13] In addition, it was Chenu's insistence that theology spring from the lived experience of believers that would prove a cornerstone for both Gutiérrez and Schillebeeckx. In A *Theology of Liberation*, Gutiérrez expresses a sentiment that resonates with Schillebeeckx's work,

---

10  For example, Leonardo Boff (Brazil) and Juan Carlos Scannone (Argentina) studied in Munich. Hugo Assmann (Brazil) studied in Rome. Pablo Richard (Chile) and Ronaldo Muñoz (Chile) did licentiates in Rome and then doctoral studies in Paris at the Sorbonne and Institut Catholique, respectively. Juan Luis Segundo (Uruguay) did his licentiate at Leuven before moving on to the Sorbonne. Clodovis Boff and Gustavo Gutiérrez also studied in Leuven. An excellent overview of these theologians is Juan José Tamayo, *Para comprender la teología de la liberación* (Estella, Spain: Editorial Verbo Divino, 1990).

11  Jürgen Mettepenningen, *Nouvelle Théologie – New Theology: Inheritor of Modernism, Precursor of Vatican II* (New York: T&T Clark, 2010), 119.

12  William J. Hill, "A Theology in Transition," 9.

13  See Gutiérrez, *A Theology of Liberation*, 3–13.

Regarding the participation of Christians in the important social movements of their time, Chenu wrote insightfully more than thirty years ago, "They are active *loci theologici* for the doctrines of grace, Incarnation, and the redemption ... Poor theologians who, wrapped up in their manuscripts and scholastic disputations, are not open to these amazing events, not only in the pious fervor of their hearts but formally in their science; there is a theological datum and an extremely fruitful one, in the presence of the Spirit."[14]

Just as he had for Gutiérrez, Chenu helped Schillebeeckx to recognize the separation of theology and lived faith (or what he would call "scholarly" and "kerygmatic" theology) as it was being carried out at the time and turned his attention to the importance of Christian experience for theology. Schillebeeckx recalled Chenu saying, "I always begin by listening—opening all my ears ... I want to listen to people's experience and only then do I apply critical analysis."[15] This listening would prove to be at the heart of both Schillebeeckx's and Gutiérrez's theological approaches.

It is difficult to underestimate the importance of the Second Vatican Council (1962–1965) for this generation of theologians. Though the documents of the Council often contain ambiguities and compromises between competing theological visions, the landmark event served to coalesce the fruit of the *ressourcement* affected by *la nouvelle théologie*, along with a number of other theological currents, including the historical-critical investigation of the Bible and the contributions of liturgical studies. While the influence of the Council is vast, two particular themes shaped the intellectual trajectories of Schillebeeckx and liberation theologians: [1] a new understanding of the theological significance of the world and [2] the Christological and ecclesiological ramifications of a revised soteriology. These two insights will allow these theologians to move decisively away from Roman Catholicism's dualisms and to concretize the historical and experiential priorities cultivated in their formation.

# III. A Church at home in the modern world

Schillebeeckx's 1957 move from Leuven to his professorship in Nijmegen meant a transformation of his pedagogical and theological methods. While he had once begun his teaching by explaining a dogma and its history before turning to what it might mean to contemporary believers, Schillebeeckx "began more resolutely to reflect theologically by taking human experiences as a methodological point of departure."[16] As he became involved in the preparations and then actual discussions of the Second Vatican Council, his reflection on the relationship between the church and the world developed and was marked by several important characteristics.

Repeatedly in his work of the 1960s, one finds Schillebeeckx identifying the *"fuga mundi"* mindset as dominant in Catholic theology and spirituality, and in the Council, the catalyst for

---

[14] Here, he is citing Chenu's "La théologie au Saulchoir" (1937 text). See Gutiérrez, *A Theology of Liberation*, 6–7.

[15] Schillebeeckx, *God Is New in Each Moment*, trans. David Smith (New York: Seabury Press, 1983), 16.

[16] Kennedy, *Schillebeeckx*, 26.

leaving it behind.[17] Surprisingly, in his efforts to articulate a more engaged sense of faith that seeks to transform the world instead of fleeing it, he turns to eschatology. However, Schillebeeckx's eschatology examines "the end" not to dwell on the post-historical future, but rather to envision the church's present mission in relation to humanity's future path. In the midst of the social upheavals of the 1960s, he asks, "Are [humans'] great expectations for this earth, which are at present in a state of fermentation, therefore really alien to the essence of [humanity's] theologal life in union with the living God?"[18] Answering this question affirmatively involves significant soteriological and Christological ramifications.

Just as a historical view changed the nature of eschatology for Schillebeeckx, it also meant a shift away from the typical framing for Christology in the neo-scholastic manuals. While prior to the full turn to hermeneutics and critical exegesis that would characterize his subsequent great works, the conciliar period shows Schillebeeckx taking incipient steps toward it in a historical Christology that informs an engaged ecclesiology. Indeed, he emphasizes:

> [t]he *locus theologicus* or source of all reflection about faith and also of the theology of the relationship between church and world is the historical event of salvation in which God gave himself to us in an absolute and gratuitous manner in Jesus Christ.[19]

Rather than framing the hypostatic union of Jesus, the God-man, as the vehicle by which human beings attain a supernatural end, Schillebeeckx recognizes Jesus Christ as historical event, as the historical revelation of God in human worldly existence. Thus, the world is not a vale of tears or the menacing sea of chaos from which Christians must turn their backs, but the important location for the self-revelation of God.

Just as Schillebeeckx's historical-theological framework shows renewed eschatological and Christological ideas, his ecclesiology takes on a historical character in this period as well, particularly in his use of the conciliar image of the church as sacrament of salvation.[20] Though certainly the image of church as the "people of God" dominated much of post-conciliar ecclesiology, both Schillebeeckx and liberation theologians find a richness in "sacrament of salvation."[21] Rather than ushering souls into the afterlife or serving as the gatekeeper of sacraments, the church as Schillebeeckx describes it, is called to be the historical epiphany of grace's reality. He argues that the church "makes explicitly clear and explicitly confesses the wealth ... present in the reality

---

17  For his extended analysis of *Gaudium et Spes* and its implications for theology and spirituality, see Edward Schillebeeckx, *The Mission of the Church*, trans. N.D. Smith (New York: Seabury Press, 1973), 43–89. Latin Americans who also articulate a spirituality rejecting the *fuga mundi* include Gutiérrez, Jon Sobrino, and Segundo Galilea.

18  Edward Schillebeeckx, "Church and World," *WC, CW* vol. 4 (London: Bloomsbury T&T Clark, 2014), 73 [96]. The book is a translation of Edward Schillebeeckx, *Wereld en kerk*, Theologische peilingen 3 (Bilthoven: Nelissen, 1966), but this citation comes from a chapter that had previously appeared as an article in *Tijdschrift voor Theologie* in 1964.

19  Schillebeeckx, "Church and World," *WC*, 75 [98].

20  See *Lumen gentium*, 48.

21  Ignacio Ellacuría speaks of the church as the "historical sacrament of liberation" in the effort to articulate the historical dimension of salvation and the church's role. See Ignacio Ellacuría, "The Church of the Poor, Historical Sacrament of Liberation," *Essays on History, Liberation, and Salvation*, ed. Michael E. Lee (Maryknoll: Orbis, 2013), 227–53.

of every human experience of existence in the world."[22] In light of this connection between church and the human experience of grace, the image of church as sacrament of salvation proves most compelling to Schillebeeckx. As a sacrament, the church links to God's plan of salvation, manifesting the mystery of God's love for all humanity. Yet, this mysterious manifestation of grace need not lead to a triumphalistic, exclusivist ecclesiology typified in the pre-conciliar phrase "*extra ecclesiam nulla salus*" (outside of the church there is no salvation).

Schillebeeckx recognizes a "dialectical tension" in the documents of the Second Vatican Council regarding the role of the church that retain elements of the pre-conciliar exclusivism, but also inaugurate a more inclusivist vision. On the one hand, the Council Fathers do not move away from the traditional notion of the church as a vehicle of salvation. It is necessary for the salvation of all humanity. However, the exclusivist triumphalism inherent in the *nulla salus* formulation recedes in favor of a more inclusivist vision where the possibility of salvation is open to all human beings, whether members of other religious traditions or of no religious affiliation. Moreover, while in this period Schillebeeckx frequently describes the church as the manifestation of God's plan or will for salvation, he does so while also noting the concomitant shadow—the church always needs purification.

Taken together, the renewed sense of the relationship between the church and world, and the notion of the church as sacrament of salvation provide a springboard from which Schillebeeckx and Latin American liberation theologians will do their reflection. In Schillebeeckx, the realization of the church-world relationship would direct his attention to a deepened and critical account of human experience, represented in his turn to phenomenology and hermeneutics. This turn results in a greater awareness of the social and structural dimensions of human experience. With those elements of experience in place, attention to the experience of human suffering would lead him to formulate negative contrast and more explicitly political and social engagement.

# IV. Moving to a social and structural awareness

As the late 1960s saw Schillebeeckx incorporating the insights of critical hermeneutics in his work and pursuing the implications of the Second Vatican Council for the life of the church, the seeds of liberation theology were beginning to bear fruit in Latin America. During the years of the Council, there had already been important theological conferences.[23] In Petrópolis, Brazil (1964), Gustavo Gutiérrez first used the description of theology as a "critical reflection on praxis." The following year saw meetings in Havana, Cuba; Bogotá, Colombia; and Cuernavaca, Mexico.[24] However, 1968 proved to be the pivotal year. In May, the Latin American Jesuit provincials met in Brazil and defined their apostolic mission as "liberation of persons from every sort of servitude that oppresses them."[25] In July, Gutiérrez would deliver a lecture in Chimbote, Peru

---

[22]  Schillebeeckx, "Church and World," *WC*, 76 [100].

[23]  On this early period, see Christian Smith, *The Emergence of Liberation Theology: Radical Religion and Social Movement Theory* (Chicago: University of Chicago Press, 1991).

[24]  Main presenters at these meetings besides Gutiérrez include: Segundo Galilea, Juan Luis Segundo, Casiano Floristán, and Ivan Illich.

[25]  Provincials of the Society of Jesus, "The Jesuits in Latin America," in Hennelly, *Liberation Theology: A Documentary History*, 78.

that he entitled "Toward a Theology of Liberation." The following month came the landmark meeting of the Conference of Latin American Bishops (CELAM) in Medellín, Colombia. Its final documents, particularly those on justice, peace, and the poverty of the church, would be the foundation upon which Catholic liberationists would build their work. Finally, in 1971, Gustavo Gutiérrez published the book that would enshrine the name given to this theology, *Teología de la liberación*.[26] It was not long before this Latin American theology began to garner international attention—both positive and negative.

By the time that Schillebeeckx began to engage liberation theology explicitly, there had already been some contact with other European theologians and institutions. As early as 1969, SODEPAX (the Commission of Society, Development, and Peace created jointly by the Pontifical Commission on Justice and Peace and the World Council of Churches) held a meeting in Cartigny, Switzerland where Gutiérrez presented the basic outline of his forthcoming book as, "Notes for a Theology of Liberation." The 1972 Congress, "Christian Faith and the Transformation of Society in Latin America" had the leading Latin American theologians meet in El Escorial, Spain. Schillebeeckx was on the board of the leading Catholic journal, *Concilium*, when it dedicated its June 1974 issue to liberation theology.[27] During the next few years, Schillebeeckx would comment on liberation theology and begin explicitly to think through its implications for his work.

A 1976 conference on "Faith and Society" provided Schillebeeckx the opportunity to engage with liberation theology by speaking about the significance of redeeming and liberating activity. His starting point is the idea that the present situation shows us our distance from salvation. There is a basic intuition that springs from this experience of alienation—we do not know who we are, but we do know that we are not what we are supposed to be. This realization might be addressed by a preconceived notion of salvation (that in fact operates from a preconceived notion of the human) that simply demands the proper strategy to be worked out. However, for Schillebeeckx, this is insufficient. Christian theology should respond in a more complex manner to the intuition of alienation, and rather than a pre-definition of humanity, this response should contain several "anthropological constants." It should take into account: the relation of our bodies to the environment, the notion of gathering or common humanity, humanity's relation to social structures, the relationship between nature and history, and the connection of theory and practice.[28] At this point, there is no trace of the old deductive theological methods in Schillebeeckx's thought.

In this period, Schillebeeckx demonstrates a deepening awareness of the implications of human sociality. He recognizes the dangerous abstractions in those theologies that encourage a

---

[26] In English: *A Theology of Liberation: History, Politics, and Salvation*, trans. Sister Caridad Inda and John Eagleson (Maryknoll: Orbis, 1973). The 1988 fifteenth anniversary edition has been revised with a new introduction.

[27] Claude Geffré and Gustavo Gutiérrez, eds., *The Mystical and Political Dimension of the Christian Faith, Concilium*, no. 96 (New York: Herder and Herder, 1974). The volume included essays by Segundo Galilea, Enrique Dussel, Leonardo Boff, José Comblin, Juan Luis Segundo, Raúl Vidales, Ronaldo Muñoz, and Jose Miguez Bonino.

[28] Edward Schillebeeckx, "God, Society and Human Salvation," *Faith and Society/Foi et Société/Geloof En Maatschappij: Acta Congressus Internationalis Theologici Lovaniensis 1976*, ed. Marc Caudron, BETL 47 (Gembloux, Belgium: Éditions J. Duculot, 1978), 89.

flight into interiority and prioritize the personal sphere, and how that relegation of religion to the private sphere represents a de facto political choice in favor of the status quo. Thus, Schillebeeckx arrives at an insight the Latin Americans knew all too well in their colonial Catholic context: for all of its abstraction and willful ignorance of historical human existence, the old manualist theology reveals itself to be profoundly political. In the name of personal faith and spirituality that avoids politics, it legitimates an often oppressive status quo.

Schillebeeckx finds a more authentic theological turn when the human person and social structure are not opposed. On the contrary, he argues that the realization of humanity's social character has a direct impact on how Christians must connect salvation and liberative activity. He declares that, "Christian freedom or deliverance is dependent on political and social liberation as a condition of its own possibility."[29] If Christian belief supposes and discloses freedom, then it would follow that the acknowledgment of others means that salvation cannot be thought in terms of an escapist deliverance; it is dependent on a social liberation.

While the deepened awareness of sociality leads Schillebeeckx to recognize the important role that political and liberation theologies possess, he also pushes them to consider how they might make an authentically religious contribution. They cannot, in a sacralizing of political change or revolution, simply be the opposite of those theologies that legitimize the status quo. In that case, by contributing nothing new or distinct, they guarantee their own uselessness. Rather, Schillebeeckx argues for the "unique critico-hermeneutical force and impulse of religion as religion" in liberation theologies.[30] In this view, people of faith provide their own form of knowledge and awareness. Specifically, "[r]eligion judges man [sic] and world in terms of its experience of the Holy and the Divine."[31] To Schillebeeckx, not only is every statement on the Holy also a statement about the human and world, but every statement on humanity or the world is also one about God. Building on the Heideggerian insight that every manifestation is simultaneously concealment, he sees a double implication that both justifies liberation theologies and cautions them. God's simultaneous manifestation and concealment means that contempt for the world is incompatible with Christian faith. However, it also means that no image of the world or specific political program may be idealized. Perhaps, the most striking insight that flows from Schillebeeckx's realization of sociality consists in its turn to the structural causes of human suffering and the need for a praxis to overcome them:

> If the human is the fundamental symbol of God then that place where he is shamed, wounded, and enslaved, both in his own heart and in suppressive society, is at once the privileged place where religious experience becomes possible in a living praxis that intends to give shape to that symbol, to heal it, and restore it to its own identity.[32]

In the subsequent years, Schillebeeckx would prioritize the praxis that heals humanity and give voice to a theology that is at once mystical and political.

---

[29]  Schillebeeckx, "God, Society, and Human Salvation," 91.
[30]  Ibid., 95.
[31]  Ibid., 96.
[32]  Ibid., 98.

# V. Salvific theology as mystical-political

The 1970s witnessed the first significant assessments and criticisms of liberation theology around the globe, and these years provided several occasions for Schillebeeckx to comment directly on Latin American liberation theology. In 1977, the International Theological Commission issued the first Vatican statement concerning liberation theology.[33] Even-handed in tone, the document praised liberation theology for recognizing, "the profound unity that links the divine history of salvation accomplished through Jesus Christ to efforts undertaken for the welfare and rights of humankind."[34] The more important development of this period was CELAM's preparations for its first conference since Medellín. Bishop Alfonso López Trujillo, an ardent opponent of liberation theology, had assumed leadership of the conference and hoped that the meeting scheduled for 1978 in Puebla, Mexico could mean a reversal of Medellín's commitments. The outlook was not hopeful for liberation theologians when the preparatory document for the meeting, the so-called "green book," was distributed to the different national bishops conferences. It looked to restore the colonial role of the church in legitimizing political authority and sacralizing neo-liberal economics.[35]

Recalling his own experience with how the initial drafts for the Second Vatican Council were rejected by the Council Fathers, Schillebeeckx delivered a lecture in which he notes the shortcomings of Puebla's preparatory document and evaluates liberation theology.[36] This discourse is important because Schillebeeckx prioritizes certain "common elements" that he views as liberation theology's most important contributions—elements that Schillebeeckx himself would absorb into his own theological reflection. He notes that liberation theologies, at their root, begin with the notion that all injustice must be denounced. This means a priority is placed on conscientization—the process in which awareness of misery and injustice is heightened so that economic changes might be made. Liberation theologies demand a (freely chosen) solidarity with the poor and a protest against oppressive societal and church power structures. These theologies flow out of praxis and are explicitly contextual so that the church's identity is discovered within the horizon of experience in the world. In sum, liberation theology, in Schillebeeckx's eyes, is the attempt to make God's word more "actable" by critically reading the signs of the times in light of the gospel.[37]

Beyond the general description of common elements, he identifies the contributions of specific liberation theologians to the wider theological discourse. He praises the Jesuits in El Salvador, Jon Sobrino and Ignacio Ellacuría, for promoting a political Christology that unmasks a "hidden monophysitism" wherein the human heart must change but not socio-economic structures. They also articulate a radically Christian social critique that unmasks a "hidden Nestorianism" in which social transformation is relegated to the purview of humanist or Marxist ethics. In the

---

[33] International Theological Commission, "Declaration on Human Development and Christian Salvation," in Hennelly, *Liberation Theology: A Documentary History*, 205–19.

[34] Ibid., 207.

[35] See Penny Lernoux, "The Long Path to Puebla," *Puebla and Beyond: Documentation and Commentary*, ed. John Eagleson and Philip Scharper (Maryknoll: Orbis, 1979).

[36] It was published as Edward Schillebeeckx, "Liberation Theology Between Medellín and Puebla," *Theology Digest* 28 (1980), 3–7.

[37] A task that Schillebeeckx likens to Paul VI's *Populorum Progressio*.

work of Gustavo Gutiérrez, he lauds an ecclesiology in which the church functions as the visible sign of the Lord's presence. Contrary to its critics, Schillebeeckx does not think that liberation theology politicizes the gospel, but it rather "combines the political and the mystical dimension of Christian faith praxis."[38]

In 1979, when the University of Nijmegen awarded an honorary doctorate to Gustavo Gutiérrez, Schillebeeckx delivered the promotion address. Given in the form of a letter to Gutiérrez, he takes the opportunity to praise the Peruvian theologian for a number of theological insights— again, insights that Schillebeeckx himself was incorporating into his work. He lauds Gutiérrez for stressing that theology should be a critical reflection on praxis. However, his highest praise lies in the declaration, "You are the first person in modern history to re-actualize the great Christian themes of theology, starting from a fundamental option for the poor."[39] That option means that the poor are not simply addressees of the Christian message of salvation, but they are its carriers and active subjects. Indeed, in Gutiérrez's writings, Schillebeeckx sees a new spirituality of solidarity with the poor. The theology and Christian discipleship that flow from this solidarity take on a newly found depth and interpretive force in understanding the demands of the Christian faith:

> To my mind, liberation theology and "salvific theology" (*heilstheologie*), a term that I have been using ever since 1945[,] are synonymous. Theologically liberation and salvation have both mystico-theologal and socio-political significance. The problem centres on what we Christians would and may call liberation and salvation in the full sense of both words: mystico-theologal, socio-political, individual-corporeal, psychosomatic and ecological.[40]

In contrast to his work of the 1960s, Schillebeeckx comes to recognize how the question of human suffering supersedes that of unbelief or secularization as a priority for Christian theology. This marks a split between two important trajectories following the Second Vatican Council. As Gustavo Gutiérrez has articulated it, the first trajectory, evident in documents such as *Lumen gentium, Nostre aetate*, and *Ad gentes*, wrestled with the role of the church vis-à-vis the "non-believer" in the modern world. However, a second trajectory, that of the developing world and found in *Gaudium et spes*, prioritized the role of the church in relation to the "non-person."[41] Schillebeeckx, praising the liberation theologians on the latter, declares that the task for Christianity today is "no longer Bonhoeffer's 'how to proclaim God in a world come of age,' but rather 'how to proclaim God in a world that is not human, and what implications might be of telling non-humans that they are children of God.'"[42]

Thus, Schillebeeckx's direct engagement with liberation theologians in the 1970s reveals several intersecting lines of thought and areas of resonance between their works. The general sense of the church needing to be involved in the world has been concretized and specified by the particular suffering of the majority of humankind. There is no room for a privatized or escapist

---

[38] Schillebeeckx, "Liberation Theology," 5.

[39] Edward Schillebeeckx, "Dear Gustavo," *Faust* 1, no. 5 (1979), 45–48, at 46.

[40] Schillebeeckx, *God is New Each Moment*, 124. See also, Edward Schillebeeckx, "Liberating Theology," *Essays, CW* vol. 11 (London: Bloomsbury T&T Clark, 2014), 69.

[41] See the discussion of this theme in Gutiérrez's work in Robert McAffee Brown, *Gustavo Gutiérrez* (Maryknoll, NY: Orbis, 1990), 86–90.

[42] Schillebeeckx, "Dear Gustavo," 46.

personalism that ignores or legitimizes the status quo. The massive poverty and oppression that characterize global reality, now understood in its structural complexity as sin, demands a Christian theology that flows from a transformative praxis. Though it remains wary of the temptation to sacralize a politics of revolution, Schillebeeckx's theology would be marked from this point on by what he calls in Gutiérrez's work an "evangelical militant compassion." Its highest ideal is a mystical-political faith in which prayer and political action mutually inhere:

> Prayer … without social commitment becomes reduced to mere sentimentality, and commitment to society without prayer often becomes grim and even barbaric. I think what I would like to see most of all is a unity between mysticism and commitment, just as I would like to experience unity between quiet reflection and active commitment in politics.[43]

## VI. Schillebeeckx's European liberation theology: Option for the poor and praxis

With the publication of the Jesus trilogy, Schillebeeckx's theology not only reaches its full maturity, but the fundamental insights he shares with liberation theologies permeate his work. Noting how the Dutch title of the second volume (*Gerechtigheid en liefde: Genade en bevrijding* = Justice and Love: Grace and Liberation) more clearly indicates his commitments, Philip Kennedy affirms that in this period, "he [Schillebeeckx] acknowledges the political ramifications of Christian faith and sees his work as a Western form of a theology of liberation."[44] Much has been written on Schillebeeckx's mature theology, but this study can conclude by highlighting two themes that he incorporates into his work that best reflect his theology's liberationist character: the preferential option for the poor and the role of praxis.

Perhaps, no more important idea has come from liberation theology than the preferential option for the poor. In Schillebeeckx's work, it points to both the defining characteristic of Jesus' eschatological ministry and the orienting element of the church's mission on earth, the primary mode by which the "good news" of the gospel is proclaimed today.

> Jesus, the eschatological prophet, is present among the poor and brings them the joyful message here and now. What is at issue is not a hereafter but God's lordship and rule being realized already in the ministry of Jesus: the eschatological reversal is about to happen now.[45]

The option stems from the recognition of poverty as a grave social-structural problem, and this recognition demonstrates how the inductive, historical approach that Schillebeeckx had embraced culminates in a concrete specificity.

---

[43] Edward Schillebeeckx, *God Is New in Each Moment*, trans. David Smith (Edinburgh: T&T Clark, 1983), 124.

[44] Kennedy, *Schillebeeckx*, 68.

[45] Schillebeeckx, *Jesus, CW* vol. 6 (London: Bloomsbury T&T Clark, 2014), 151 [174].

> Poverty in its most oppressive form is in fact the social condition of by far the majority of the world's population. Moreover, we know that this is not a matter of fate or natural law, but the consequence of all kinds of interactive human factors of a cultural, socio-economic and political kind – of a system which can, however be changed.[46]

Though some would critique liberation theology's preferential option for the poor as either restricted to a very particular historical context or an exclusivist misunderstanding of God's love. Schillebeeckx, however, notes that the church has often universalized those aspects that are actually non-universal, things that are bound to a certain culture or time.

> Thus universal must, moreover, be incarnate in each and every one without all the potentialities and virtualities of the universal being exhausted in these particular incarnations. Now within the context of grinding structural world poverty, the universal openness and universal challenge of the message of the gospel takes on a very specific social dimension and as it were a new context. I am inspired to say this above all by Latin American, Asian and African forms of liberation theology, and for a long time this has also been a theme of my own theological quest.[47]

Because the preferential option for the poor demands particular actions from the church, it has always been tied to a robust notion of praxis. As Bradford Hinze has noted,

> The anchor of the church's ethics, in Schillebeeckx's view, must be commitment to solidarity with the marginalized and the suffering, the praxis of justice and love. The preferential option for the poor provides the biblical basis for a Christian ethics of political responsibility; it is a datum of revelation.[48]

Though the modern usage of the term "praxis" cannot escape the influence of its importance in the Marxist lexicon, it does not mean that any invocation of praxis must necessarily be opposed to Christianity. For Schillebeeckx, Christian praxis is simply the response that flows from the double commandment to love God and neighbor.[49] As such, it is a measure of Christian fidelity to the gospel, an orthopraxis. Moreover, while this orthopraxis cannot be dismissed as materialist reductionism vis-à-vis Marxism, it must also not be understood in opposition to orthodoxy. Rather, true orthodoxy and orthopraxis mutually inhere in a vibrant, historical faith.

---

[46] Schillebeeckx, *Church, CW* vol. 10 (London: Bloomsbury T&T Clark, 2014), 53 [54].

[47] Schillebeeckx, *Church*, 167–68 [169]. See also his essay, Edward Schillebeeckx, "The Religious and the Human Ecumene," *Expanding the View: Gustavo Gutiérrez and the Future of Liberation Theology* (Maryknoll: Orbis, 1989), 136.

[48] Bradford E. Hinze, "Eschatology and Ethics," *The Praxis of the Reign of God: An Introduction to the Theology of Edward Schillebeeckx*, ed. Mary Catherine Hilkert and Robert J. Schreiter, 2nd ed. (New York: Fordham University Press, 2002), 179. Hinze cites Edward Schillebeeckx, *The Language of Faith: Essays on Jesus, Theology, and the Church*, Concilium Series (London: SCM Press, 1995), 260–63, and Schillebeeckx, *Church*, 85–87 [80–99] as representative texts of this point.

[49] He notes, "Love of humankind and love of God are one and the same theologal virtue in the Christian tradition … love of humanity as disinterested commitment for fellow human beings is at the same time the hallmark of the truth of love towards God." Edward Schillebeeckx, *On Christian Faith: The Spiritual, Ethical, and Political Dimensions* (New York: Crossroad, 1987), 70.

Above all a common concern in solidarity for the poor and oppressed reunites men and women in the "ecumene of suffering humanity" and this action in solidarity can then bring us back to theory; in other words, through orthopraxis we can again confess and express in new worlds an authentic and living orthodoxy.[50]

# Conclusion

From the *fuga mundi* to the recognition of the world; from the historical and critical analysis of the world's problems to a faith response rooted in praxis and the preferential option for the poor, Schillebeeckx's theological journey mirrors a larger theological *intinerarium* adopted by Catholic liberation theologies in the twentieth century. Indeed, with the election of the Argentinean Jorge Mario Bergoglio to the papacy, the fruits of this journey have become incorporated into the universal church's self-understanding moving forward. Even if the theological language or categories change from generation to generation, the realities of poverty and marginalization continue in the world today and demand a response from Christians.

Liberation theologies have opened the door for those at the peripheries to raise their prophetic voices and call the church to proclaim and incarnate a truly good news to the poor. The response to that cry has been mixed, but Edward Schillebeeckx has provided a theology that calls the center to a kenotic, political faith that demands a concrete praxis and a preferential option for the poor. Certainly, historical awareness and the structural realities of our times make our circumstances different from Christians of generations past. Yet, the adoption of a historical, political faith need not mean an abandonment of spirituality and the wisdom of generations past. Ultimately, Edward Schillebeeckx's life and theology remind us to draw from the wells of prayer and the Christian tradition to cultivate a mystical-political faith that is both contemplative and active:

> That political form of Christian love of God and neighbor, albeit in another area of experience, knows the same conversion and metanoia, the same ascesis and detachment from self, the same suffering and dark nights, the same losing of oneself in the other as was the case in contemplative mysticism in times past.[51]

---

[50]  Ibid., 83.
[51]  Edward Schillebeeckx, "Christian Praxis in the World," *The Schillebeeckx Reader*, ed. Robert J. Schreiter (New York: Crossroad, 1984), 273.

# Chapter 27
# Religious Pluralism

Edmund Kee-Fook Chia

Even as the phenomenon of religious pluralism has been around for centuries and millennia, it was only in the recent decades that it has featured prominently in academic discourse, especially in the West. To be sure, globalization and enhanced information technology have increased people's awareness and contact with the many religions of the world and have led scholars to examine the phenomenon from a variety of perspectives. For Christianity, which makes claims for the uniqueness and universality of its faith, the encounter with the other religions can indeed be a challenge as the other religions also have similar but often contradictory claims to truth. In fact, the very continued presence of these other religions, despite centuries of Christian missionary activity, is already unnerving. As David Griffin puts it: "This is because the tendency to religious absolutism has been strong among Christians and also because Christians have in recent centuries had far more power—militarily, economically, and culturally—than adherents of other religions."[1]

Thus, it is not surprising that religious pluralism has been on the radar of the Vatican, the response of which is the declaration *Dominus Iesus* (*DI*), issued in 2000 to caution Catholics of its threat especially to the church's evangelizing mission: "The Church's constant missionary proclamation is endangered today by relativistic theories which seek to justify religious pluralism" (*DI* 4).[2] The declaration's aim was to "reassert the definitive and complete character of the revelation of Jesus Christ" (*DI* 5) so that Christians are able to unequivocally proclaim "the unicity and salvific universality of the mystery of Jesus Christ and the Church" (*DI*,3). These are very strong claims made in an Internet age where practically everyone, including those of other religions, have access so such pronouncements almost instantaneously. To be sure, the document did elicit a lot of negative reaction from within and without the church and Christian theologians had a field day commenting on it.[3]

While Edward Schillebeeckx, who was already in his late 80s then, did not exactly respond to the document in a full-length book or article, it turned out that he had already done so, albeit

---

[1]  David Ray Griffin, "Religious Pluralism: Generic, Identist, and Deep," *Deep Religious Pluralism*, ed. David Ray Griffin (Louisville, KY: Westminster John Knox Press, 2005), 4.

[2]  Congregation for the Doctrine of the Faith, *Declaration Dominus Iesus: On the Unicity and Salvific Universality of Jesus Christ and the Church* (August 6, 2000) (hereafter cited in text as *DI*), http://www.vatican.va/roman_curia/congregations/cfaith/documents/rc_con_cfaith_doc_20000806_dominus-iesus_en.html.

[3]  See Stephen J. Pope and Charles Hefling, eds., *Sic et Non: Encountering Dominus Iesus* (Maryknoll, NY: Orbis, 2002); and also this volume of the Indian theological journal *Jeevadhara* 31/183 (May, 2001).

indirectly and some decades earlier. His trilogy, sometimes referred to as his Christological tome, was basically his way of offering "the Lord Jesus" (*Dominus Iesus*) to the late twentieth century Christian. Moreover, it did address many of the same issues and questions raised by the declaration *Dominus Iesus*. It could, therefore, be regarded as Schillebeeckx's response or, better still, his own rendition of *Dominus Iesus* or the proclamation that Jesus is Lord, except that it takes a very different stance from that taken by the Vatican's declaration to the new situation of religious pluralism.

This is what I will examine in this chapter. I will take as starting point the concerns raised by the Vatican's *Dominus Iesus* to religious pluralism and examines how Schillebeeckx as well as other contemporary theologians have themselves responded. Specifically, I will focus on theologians from Asia and also the Asian pastoral magisterium as the situation is by no means new to Christians in Asia. Besides, as will be seen later, *Dominus Iesus* seems to have been particularly concerned about the theologies of religious pluralism arising from Asia, the cradle of all the major religions of the world with whom Christianity has been living as neighbor for many centuries.

# I. Problem of religious pluralism and Asian theology

The term religious pluralism has often been used interchangeably with religious diversity "in discussions about the variety and multiplicity of religions in the world."[4] But there are actually significant differences between them. More accurately, religious pluralism can be used [i] to signify a fact of history, that is, that there is a diversity of religions and [ii] one's attitude toward that fact. David Griffin offers a useful differentiation: "Whereas 'religious diversity' refers to the simple sociological fact that there are many religious traditions, often within a single country, 'religious pluralism' refers to beliefs and attitudes."[5] *Dominus Iesus* uses the terms *de facto* and *de iure* (in principle) to distinguish the two and, while it is resigned to the former, is apprehensive about how the acceptance of the latter will inevitably raise questions about the truth claims of Christianity. Griffin's elaboration on what is entailed in the acknowledgement and acceptance of religious pluralism *de iure* sheds light on the Vatican's concerns: Negatively, it would be "the rejection of religious absolutism" and positively, it would be "the acceptance of the idea that there are indeed religions other than one's own that provide saving truths and values to their adherents."[6]

Thus, *Dominus Iesus* fears that the "Christian revelation and the mystery of Jesus Christ and the Church [will] lose their character of absolute truth and salvific universality, or at least shadows of doubt and uncertainty are cast upon them" (*DI* 4). Religious pluralism has, therefore, become a problem as "certain indispensable elements of Christian doctrine" are being questioned and so the declaration's aim is to guide "theological reflection in developing solutions consistent with the contents of the faith and responsive to the pressing needs of contemporary culture" (*DI* 3).

---

[4]    Chad Meister, "Introduction," *Religious Diversity*, ed. Chad Meister (Oxford, UK: Oxford University Press, 2011), 4.
[5]    Griffin, *Deep Religious Pluralism*, xiii.
[6]    Griffin, "Religious Pluralism," 3.

To that end, the declaration proposed that a steadfast response is necessary: "As a remedy for this relativistic mentality, which is becoming ever more common, it is necessary above all to reassert the definitive and complete character of the revelation of Jesus Christ" (*DI* 5).

In presenting the declaration at a press conference, the then-Cardinal Joseph Ratzinger, who was Prefect of the Congregation for the Doctrine of the Faith (CDF), singled out what he believes is the underlying problem, namely, the mistaken notion that "all religions are equally valid ways of salvation for those who follow them," and identifies its source, namely, "relativism."[7] Ratzinger posits that "such a relativist philosophy is found at the base both of post-metaphysical Western thought and of the negative theology of Asia" and that they can only be "accompanied by a false concept of tolerance," which in turn is "connected with the loss and the renunciation of the issue of truth." "Without a serious claim for truth," Ratzinger advises, "even an appreciation of other religions becomes absurd and contradictory, since one has no criterion to determine what is positive in a religion, distinguishing it from what is negative or the fruit of superstition and deception." He concludes by reiterating that "esteem and respect for the world's religions [...] does not diminish the originality and uniqueness of the revelation of Jesus Christ and does not in any way limit the missionary task of the Church."

Ratzinger was actually repeating what he had said about the problem of religious pluralism a few years earlier. In an address to the presidents of the Doctrinal Commission of CELAM held in Mexico in May 1996, he pronounced that "relativism has thus become the central problem for the faith at the present time."[8] Ratzinger said that "the so-called pluralist theology of religion has been developing progressively since the '50s. Nonetheless, only now has it come to the center of the Christian conscience." He continues:

> On the one hand, relativism is a typical offshoot of the Western world and its forms of philosophical thought, [...] on the other it is connected with the philosophical and religious institutions of Asia especially, and surprisingly, with those of the Indian subcontinent.

That the fingers of the Vatican were pointing toward Asia can also be gleaned from a statement made by Cardinal Josef Tomko, the then-Prefect of the Congregation for the Evangelization of Peoples in a 1991 address to his fellow cardinals where he hinted that interreligious dialogue seemed to be leading toward "doctrinal confusion" and that "although India is the epicenter to this tendency and Asia is its principal camp, [...] these ideas already circulate in Oceania, in some African countries and in Europe."[9] The focus on India as the "epicenter" was subsequently repeated by other curial officials. Ratzinger himself, in a 1993 address to the presidents of the member-conferences of the Federation of Asian Bishops' Conferences (FABC) and episcopal

---

[7]   Joseph Ratzinger, "Reasons for the Christian Claim," *Remarks made by the Prefect of the Congregation for the Doctrine of the Faith at the Presentation of the Church document Dominus Iesus"* (Press Room of the Holy See, September 5, 2000), http://www. traces-cl.com/archive/2000/ottobre/ratzing.htm. All of Ratzinger's comments in this section are from this source.

[8]   Joseph Ratzinger, "Relativism: The Central Problem for Faith Today," *Address delivered During the meeting of the Congregation for the Doctrine of the Faith with the presidents of the Doctrinal Commissions of the Bishops' Conferences of Latin America'* (Guadalajara, Mexico, May 1996), http://www.ewtn.com/library. All of Ratzinger's comments in this section are from this source.

[9]   Josef Tomko, "Proclaiming Christ the World's Only Savior," *L'Osservatore Romano* (April 5, 1991) 4.

chairpersons of their doctrinal commissions, also explicitly mentions the country by name: "The problem which arises in India, but also elsewhere, comes to expression in [Raimon] Panikkar's famous phrase: 'Jesus is Christ, but Christ is not (only) Jesus.'"[10]

In fact, when the Vatican declaration *Dominus Iesus* was issued, many immediately sensed that the targets were the theologians from Asia in general and India in particular. It is certainly not a coincidence that just a few days before the declaration's release, the Belgian Jesuit Jacques Dupuis, who had served for more than thirty years in India, was summoned to a meeting with Ratzinger and other CDF officials as the final step before a notification of error was issued about his book *Toward a Christian Theology of Religious Pluralism*.[11] The notification that eventually came out had *Dominus Iesus* as basis for the "errors, ambiguities or harmful interpretations" Dupuis was alleged to have committed.[12] Likewise, the investigation of Vietnamese-American theologian Peter Phan also took *Dominus Iesus* as basis for judging that it "is notably confused on a number of points of Catholic doctrine and also contains serious ambiguities" for his book *Being Religious Interreligiously: Asian Perspectives on Interfaith Dialogue*.[13]

In view of Schillebeeckx's own run-in with the CDF in an earlier era, he would certainly have been considered among the "post-metaphysical" Western theologians, especially given his sympathies for theologies coming out of Asia and also Latin America. That is actually what some doctoral students from India studying in a particular Catholic university in Europe are reporting; they claim that some of their professors allege that the Christian faith in Europe went on a decline in the 70s and 80s because of the liberal and relativistic views promoted by theologians such as Schillebeeckx. This, much like the notifications, is disingenuous at best, if not overestimating the influence theologians have on the lives of the ordinary Catholics or, worse still, underestimating the independence and judgment of the latter. Schillebeeckx's response to such a charge, like how he sees the clear break between the Jesus of history and the Christ of faith, is that this situation has arisen simply as a result "of the loss of the church's grip or influence on society and culture."[14]

## Methodological pluralism

It is rather obvious that, methodologically, the declaration *Dominus Iesus* takes the basic teachings of the church as starting point, which it insists must be *"firmly believed"* (*DI* 5, emphasis in original). The declaration elaborates:

---

[10]  Cardinal Joseph Ratzinger, *Christ, Faith and the Challenge of Cultures* (Hong Kong, March 2–5, 1993), http://www.ewtn.com/library/curia/ratzhong.htm.

[11]  See "Justice Denied, Delayed, Truth Exposed: The inside story of the unfair dealings with J. Dupuis, in a free-wheeling interview exclusively given to ICAN," *Indian Currents Associate News* (April 15, 2001), 10–16. See also the book Jacques Dupuis, *Toward a Christian Theology of Religious Pluralism* (Maryknoll, NY: Orbis, 1997).

[12]  Congregation for the Doctrine of the Faith, *Notification on the Book Toward a Christian Theology of Religious Pluralism (Orbis: Maryknoll, New York 1997) by Father Jacques Dupuis, S.J.* (Vatican City, January 24, 2001), http://www.vatican.va/roman_curia/congregations/cfaith/documents/rc_con_cfaith_doc_20010124_dupuis_en.html.

[13]  Peter C. Phan, *The Joy of Religious Pluralism* (Maryknoll, NY: Orbis, 2017), 175. See also Peter C. Phan, *Being Religious Interreligiously: Asian Perspectives on Interfaith Dialogue* (Maryknoll, NY: Orbis, 2004).

[14]  Edward Schillebeeckx, *Church, CW* vol. 10 (London: Bloomsbury T&T Clark, 2014), 104 [105].

> The proper response to God's revelation is "*the obedience of faith* (Rom 16:26; cf. Rom 1:5; 2 Cor 10:5–6) by which man freely entrusts his entire self to God, offering" the full submission of intellect and will to God who reveals "and freely assenting to the revelation given by him." (*DI* 7, emphasis original).

This, of course, is the neoscholastic method for theological reflection, with its cognitive and intellectualist approach to faith, as well as its apologetic stance. Moreover, it is quite unashamedly explicit in invoking the church's authority to posit the finality of particular church teachings and insists, about ten times, that they must all be *firmly believed*.

For Schillebeeckx, whose primary concern was enabling the ordinary Catholic faithful to continue making sense of the Christian faith amidst the challenges of secularism (as was his context in the 1960s and 1970s) and religious pluralism (the challenge that has come to the fore since the 1980s and which he wrote about only in his later writings), the methodologies that he employs differ significantly. The foreword to his *Jesus* book indicates that his aim was to "bridge the gap between academic theology and the concrete needs of ordinary Christians."[15] Moreover, his starting point was that the church's magisterium was simply missing the point:

> It is clear that Christian revelation in its traditional form has ceased to provide any valid answer to the questions about God asked by the majority of people today, nor would it appear to be making any contribution to modern man's real understanding of himself in this world and in human history. It is evident that more and more people are becoming increasingly unhappy and dissatisfied with the traditional Christian answers to their questions. It is their questions about God himself which are involved above all, and there is unmistakable evidence of a growing desire everywhere for new answers to be given to new questions concerning him. The situation requires us to speak of God in a way quite *different* from the way in which we have spoken of him in the past. If we fail to do this, we ourselves shall perhaps still be able to experience God in outmoded forms, but clearly our own witness of and discussion of God will be met with headshaking disbelief as mumbo-jumbo.[16]

To be clear, Schillebeeckx is not saying that Christian revelation has become irrelevant. All he is saying is that the way the official church has presented it is outmoded and does not accurately reflect how God reveals Godself to people. In the context of the sense of disillusionment among ordinary Catholics, no amount of shoving will be able to force the church's teachings and doctrines down their throats. Instead, faith in God is affirmed or tested through their day-to-day experience of life. God's revelation, Schillebeeckx believes, is mediated through the concrete and visible in human history: "Revelation does not drop out of the sky as a series of truth; it comes to us in experience in concrete, existential encounter."[17] Experience is, therefore, the medium through which God speaks: "God's revelation follows the path of human experiences … Apart from any experience, there is no revelation either."[18] It is against this backdrop that

---

[15]   Edward Schillebeeckx, *Jesus, CW* vol. 6 (London: Bloomsbury T&T Clark, 2014), xxv [5].
[16]   Edward Schillebeeckx, "Secularization and Christian Belief in God," *GFM, CW* vol. 3 (London: Bloomsbury T&T Clark, 2014), 31 [53].
[17]   Robert Schreiter, ed., *The Schillebeeckx Reader* (New York, NY: Crossroad, 1984), 17.
[18]   Edward Schillebeeckx, *IR, CW* vol. 8 (London: Bloomsbury T&T Clark, 2014), 10 [11].

Schillebeeckx speaks of Christianity: "it began with an experience."[19] Experience is the source and foundation of Schillebeeckx's theology. Christian faith, then and also now, is not primarily a body of truths that one submits to in obedience, but takes a particular experience as starting point and continues in the form of the many experiences of the believers: "Christianity is not a message which has to be believed, but *an experience of faith which becomes a message* and, as lived message, wants to offer a new experiential possibility of life to others who hear of it from within their own life experience."[20]

Schillebeeckx warns that,

> present-day theology, both conservative and progressive, will render the problem of faith more acute if it does not devote itself first of all to a serious search for a real hermeneutics of history which analyzes the ontological conditions making possible the retention of an authentic identity of faith *within* the reinterpretation of faith, a reinterpretation which in turn is necessary because of man's situation in history.[21]

He further posits that the hermeneutical process is one entailing a mutually critical correlation between Tradition and contemporary experience: "On the one hand we have the whole tradition of the experience of the great Jewish-Christian movement, and on the other hand the contemporary, new human experiences of both Christians and non-Christians." Furthermore, this second source, the contemporary situation, represents "an intrinsic and determinative element for understanding God's revelation in the history of Israel and of Jesus, which Christians have experienced as salvation from God for men and women, the first source."[22]

This is exactly the method employed by the church in Asia in its theological reflections. Since its inception, the Federation of Asian Bishops' Conferences (FABC) advanced the doctrine of the Triple Dialogue, which effectively means that Asian Catholicism has to be expressed in terms of how Catholics engage in dialogue with the cultures, the religions, and especially the poor in Asia. This is a typically Asian approach and has since come to be known as the contextual approach. Malaysian-American theologian Jonathan Tan offers a description of what this means:

> From the various official documents of the FABC, one sees the development of a new way of doing theology with Asian resources in multireligious, multiethnic, multilingual and pluricultural Asia, which may be described as the contextualization of the salvific message of the Gospel in the diverse and pluralistic Asian *Sitz-im-Leben.*[23]

The FABC Office of Theological Concerns expands on this in a document entitled "Methodology: Asian Christian Theology" where it asserts that "context or contextual realities are considered resources of theology (*loci theologici*) together with the Christian sources of Scripture

---

[19] Schreiter, *The Schillebeeckx Reader*, 129.

[20] Schillebeeckx, *IR*, 43 [50].

[21] Schillebeeckx, "Secularization and Christian Belief in God," *GFM*, 53 [86].

[22] Schillebeeckx, *IR*, 3 [3].

[23] Jonathan Tan, "Theologizing at the Service of Life: The Contextual Theological Methodology of the Federation of Asian Bishops' Conferences (FABC)," *Gregorianum* 81 (2000), 565.

and Tradition."[24] The document then significantly extends the meaning and understanding of contextual resources, the raw material for the task of theology, by the following explicit definition:

> The cultures of peoples, the history of their struggles, their religions, their religious scriptures, oral traditions, popular religiosity, economic and political realities and world events, historical personages, stories of oppressed people crying for justice, freedom, dignity, life, and solidarity become resources of theology, and assume methodological importance in our context. The totality of life is the raw material of theology; God is redemptively present in the totality of human life.[25]

As is clear from the quick survey of differences in theological method above, theology is a function of the method used in the theologizing process. One expects therefore that the teachings that are the outcome of each method will also differ significantly from one another. Employing the neoscholastic method in addressing the phenomenon of religious pluralism, the Vatican declaration *Dominus Iesus* insists on "the definitive and complete character of the revelation of Jesus Christ" (*DI* 5), the distinction between Christianity's "*theological faith*" as compared with the "*belief*" of other religions (*DI* 7), and states that "the designation of *inspired texts*" is applicable only "to the canonical books of the Old and New Testaments" (*DI* 8). With that as premise, it then "reasserts that Jesus Christ is the mediator and the universal redeemer" (*DI* 11) and that the unicity and universality of Christ presumes the unicity and universality of the church, leading to the conclusion that "the Church, a pilgrim now on earth, is necessary for salvation" (*DI* 20). In ruling out "in a radical way, that mentality of indifferentism 'characterized by a religious relativism which leads to the belief that one religion is as good as another'" (*DI* 22), it also asserts that

> if it is true that the followers of other religions can receive divine grace, it is also certain that *objectively speaking* they are in a gravely deficient situation in comparison with those who, in the Church, have the fullness of the means of salvation. (*DI* 22, emphasis original)

# II. Schillebeeckx's theology of religious pluralism

For Schillebeeckx, on the other hand, who employs a hermeneutical method for theological reflection, his theologies and conclusions are more charitable with regard to other religions. Within his *Jesus* trilogy, the problem of religious pluralism is addressed only in the third volume, *Church: The Human Story of God*:

> This book is about the life of men and women and their bond with God as God has become visible above all in Jesus of Nazareth, confessed as the Christ by the

---

[24] "Methodology: Asian Christian Theology," in *For All the Peoples of Asia: Federation of Asian Bishops' Conferences, Documents from 1997 to 2001*, vol. 3, ed. Franz-Josef Eilers S.V.D. (Quezon City, Philippines: Claretian, 2002), 356.

[25] Ibid., 355–56.

Christian churches—which are increasingly aware that they live in a secular world amidst other religions.[26]

Beginning *Church* with a section entitled "A Guide to the Book," Schillebeeckx advances the "doctrine" of *extra mundum nulla salus* ("outside the world there is no salvation") which is a spin on the age-old adage *extra ecclesiam nulla salus* ("outside the church there is no salvation"), which was officially embraced by the church at the Council of Florence.[27] Thus, if salvation is achieved in and through the world, then "the religions are the place where men and women become explicitly aware of God's saving actions in history."[28] He points to the Second Vatican Council's *Nostra aetate* which reminds us that men and women look to different religions for the "message of salvation and the opening of a way of salvation."[29] It follows that those who belong to religions other than Christianity find salvation not so much "despite" their religion but precisely "in" and "through" them.[30]

This in no way suggests that Schillebeeckx lends himself to the theses that "all religions are equal, or all equally relative, or all equally wrong."[31] He strongly admonishes such perceptions which he regards as a "particular new form of modern 'indifferentism'".[32] Such indifferentism, rooted in the post-Enlightenment disdain for claims to truth and universality, is "basically wrong" and a "cheap form of tolerance." This is where, according to Schillebeeckx, it is important that the religions be a form of "criticism and provocation of this spirit of the time." They do so without tending toward the other extreme, which is that of absolutism: "we shall have to look in a direction in which both absolutism and relativism are avoided in connection with what is called 'religion.'"[33] Each religion has to allow itself to be "challenged by the other religions and which, on the basis of its own message, also challenges other religions"[34] No single religion—not even Christianity—can claim monopoly to nor exhaust the whole meaning of truth. God is the only absolute.[35] As historical particularities, religions are relative in relation to God and to one another. They have to be brought into a critical correlation and confrontation with each other, so as to better discern truth from that which is untrue.

Hence, the question for Christians is certainly not about whether Christianity is superior to other religions. Instead, it is about how Christianity can "maintain its own identity and uniqueness and at the same time attach a positive value to the difference of religions in a non-discriminatory sense." Accordingly, "what is relevant to Christianity is not what is common to many religions,

---

[26] Schillebeeckx, *Church, CW* vol. 10 (London: Bloomsbury T&T Clark, 2014), xxi [xiii]. He does address the theme elsewhere but basically says the same as what he carefully expounds in *Church: The Human Story of God*. So, this article will quote solely from this source. See, for example, Edward Schillebeeckx, "The Religious and the Human Ecumene," *The Language of Faith: Essays on Jesus, Theology, and the Church* (Maryknoll, NY: Orbis, 1995), 249–64.

[27] Schillebeeckx, *Church*, xxv [xvii].

[28] Ibid., 12 [12].

[29] Ibid., 158 [160].

[30] Ibid., 160 [161].

[31] Ibid., 166 [167].

[32] Ibid., 161 [162].

[33] Ibid., 162 [163].

[34] Ibid., 162 [164].

[35] Ibid., 164–65 [166].

but precisely that difference between them which forms their uniqueness and distinctiveness." It is in view of this that Schillebeeckx deems it important that we explore anew Christianity's self-definition, including its claims to uniqueness and universality, as well as its foundation, which must lead to an "open and not-intolerant attitude," in order to put Christianity in its place while giving it its rightful place.[36] He posits that all religions are unique in and of themselves.[37] Each manifests a different face of God who is "ultimately the invisible and unnameable One."[38] Christianity's distinctiveness is in identifying God, of whom Jesus is the definition. The God of creation, who wills the salvation and love for all, is revealed in Jesus of Nazareth, the "historical, culturally located expression of this universal message of the gospel."[39] On the basis of his historical and hermeneutical investigations, Schillebeeckx proposes that the distinctiveness, uniqueness, and foundation of Christianity "lies in Jesus' message and praxis of the kingdom of God, with all its consequences."[40]

If this message and praxis of Jesus is to see its fruition in God's kingdom, then "the history of Jesus' career must be continued in his disciples." Without this continuity by the Christian community, the church, Jesus's proclamation and praxis will remain in "a purely speculative, empty vacuum."[41] "Christ" will be no more than an honorific title if the redemption began in "Jesus" is not continued but ends with his death and resurrection. If God's offer of salvation in Jesus is to be truly universal, then the churches have to be active in continuing Jesus' mission by following his way of life. This means that Christians, the community of disciples, have to "take upon themselves the aspirations of the wronged of this world and [be] in solidarity with the call for justice of poor and voiceless people."[42] As justice and peace are the entitlements of all persons, and not only for Christians, the salvation in Jesus has to be universalized through Christian praxis. It is the mission of Christians, "called to be God's holy people," to "confess freedom from evil," to undertake "the task of bringing justice," and to be filled with "the courage to love." Schillebeeckx is emphatic that "the transformation of the world to a higher humanity, to justice and peace, is therefore an essential part of the 'catholicity' or universality of Christian faith; and this is *par excellence* a non-discriminatory universality."[43]

# III. Asian theology of religious pluralism

Asian Theology presumes the method and theology advanced by Schillebeeckx and takes it further with its emphasis on the Triple Dialogue with the poor, the cultures, and the religions of Asia. It does not compare the church with other religions, much less pass any form of negative judgment upon them. At most, as in its first plenary assembly, the FABC affirms the Christian

---

36  Ibid., 163 [165].
37  Ibid., 181 [182].
38  Ibid., 177 [179].
39  Ibid., 178 [179].
40  Ibid., 163 [165].
41  Ibid., 167 [168].
42  Ibid., 168 [169].
43  Ibid., 168 [170].

faith in Jesus as the way, the truth and the life (*FABC I*, no. 7).[44] But in so doing, it does not in any way suggest that other religions or their "savior-figures" are less true or less perfect. Instead, the Asian bishops are explicit in testifying that other religions are indeed "significant and positive elements in the economy of God's design of salvation" (*FABC I*, no. 14). They are also conscious that these religions of Asia have been the source and inspiration for generations of peoples and have helped in the spiritual development and growth of an entire continent for millennia. In light of this they ask, albeit rhetorically: "How then can we not give them [the other religions] reverence and honor? And how can we not acknowledge that God has drawn our peoples to Himself through them?" (*FABC I*, no. 15).

In its publication *Theses on Interreligious Dialogue* (*Dialogue*), the FABC suggests that it is on account of the Asian bishops' own personal experience with persons of other religions that they have a "positive appreciation of [the role of other religions] in the divine economy of salvation" (*Dialogue*, no. 2.2).[45] This experience, in turn, relies upon the theological conviction that "God's plan of salvation for humanity is one and reaches out to all peoples" (*Dialogue*, no. 2.3). It is therefore inherent upon Christians to discern how God's saving activity is in operation and made manifest in the other religions. Interreligious dialogue is the mode of this Christian duty, "a demand of the Church of its very life as mission" (*Dialogue*, no. 2.5). Because God's action in the world is beyond the grasp of the church, the church discerns God's will through dialogue as well as proclamation. Dialogue allows the church to listen and to learn from the other religions while proclamation enables it to share with others God's presence and action as experienced and discerned by the church. Christians believe the church is the sacrament of this kingdom, "visibilizing it, ordained to it, promoting it, but not equating itself with it" (*Dialogue*, no. 6.3). The kingdom, therefore, is certainly wider than the institutional church. Nevertheless, the building up of the church is still necessary as it is at the service of the kingdom. By extension, the building up of the other religions is also as necessary. It can be surmised from here that FABC accepts the phenomenon of religious pluralism as not only *de facto* but also very much *de iure*. The plurality of religion is not only tolerated but accepted as part of God's design of salvation of human beings: "The great religions of Asia with their respective creeds, cults and codes reveal to us diverse ways of responding to God whose Spirit is active in all peoples and cultures."[46]

Like Schillebeeckx's theology, FABC theology also does not tend toward relativism. To be sure, the issue was specifically addressed in *Methodology: Asian Christian Theology*, where the bishops acknowledge that "any discussion of pluralism must reckon with the question of how we understand pluralism in theology in relation to the threat of relativism."[47] While emphatically rejecting theological positions which claim that all religions are the same or of equal value, the Asian bishops also assert that "just because certain persons and groups are misled in their

---

[44] "Evangelization in Modern Day Asia," in *For All the Peoples of Asia: Federation of Asian Bishops' Conferences, Documents from 1970 to 1991*, vol. 1, ed. D.D. Gaudencio Rosales, and C.G. Arévalo (Quezon City, Philippines: Claretian, 1992), 13.

[45] Theological Advisory Commission of the Federation of Asian Bishops' Conferences, "Theses on Interreligious Dialogue: An Essay in Pastoral Theological Reflection," in *FABC Papers No. 48* (Hong Kong: FABC, 1987), 7.

[46] Seventh Bishops' Institute for Interreligious Affairs on the Theology of Dialogue, *BIRA IV/7* (1988), in *For All the Peoples of Asia*, vol. 1, 310, no. 12.

[47] "Methodology: Asian Christian Theology," 333.

search for truth, and just because they tend to relativize all reality, we cannot conclude that all pluralism leads to relativism."[48] The document then quotes from the Eleventh Bishops' Institute for Interreligious Affairs on the Theology of Dialogue which argues that

> diversity is not something to be regretted and abolished, but to be rejoiced over and promoted, since it represents richness and strength. Harmony is not simply the absence of strive, described as "live and let live." The test of true harmony lies in the acceptance of diversity as richness. (*BIRA IV/11*, no. 15)[49]

That notwithstanding, it must also be emphasized that Asian Christians are fully committed to their faith, just as they are very clear about their mission. With *Dominus Iesus* they believe the Christian's mission is the preaching of the Gospel of Jesus, "the proclamation of the mystery of God, Father, Son and Holy Spirit, and the mystery of the incarnation of the Son, as saving event for all humanity" (*DI* 1). However, they do not agree with *Dominus Iesus* on how this preaching is to be done. The crux of the problem is not with the "who" of mission, but the "how."[50] Asian Christians are in agreement that Jesus is the subject of their proclamation and, indeed, he has to be proclaimed. They differ on the approach that Christians ought to take in proclaiming Jesus. In this regard, as the article shows, Schillebeeckx's approach to the same "how" question, especially in the context of the many other religions, seems to resonate more with the Asian approach. Employing hermeneutical or dialogical approaches enables both to be more open to religious pluralism, as Schillebeeckx insists: "the multiplicity of religions is not an evil which needs to be removed, but rather a wealth which is to be welcomed and enjoyed by all."[51] Likewise, the Asian bishops suggest: "What is needed is a vision of unity and harmony, and a language of reconciled diversity that will enable people of different communities to work together for peace and the building of a more just society."[52] Such a vision facilitates the authentic acceptance of pluralism, including religious pluralism. As Michael Amaladoss puts it: "People then learn to relativize their own belief systems without in any way relativizing the Absolute to which they are committed and which they witness to and proclaim."[53]

## Schillebeeckx's *Dominus Iesus*

As can be seen from the exposition above, the Vatican declaration *Dominus Iesus* was concerned with the Christian faith in the context of religious pluralism. Specifically, it insists that Christians remain staunch in their faith especially with regard to questions raised about the identity of Jesus Christ (Christological question: who do you say that I am?), his salvific value (Soteriological question: what does salvation in Jesus mean?), and the church's mission and its relation to

---

[48] Ibid.
[49] Eleventh Bishops' Institute for Interreligious Affairs on the Theology of Dialogue (1988), *For All the Peoples of Asia*, vol. 1, 321.
[50] John Prior, "Unfinished Encounter: A Note of the Voice and Tone of *Ecclesia in Asia*," *East Asian Pastoral Review* 37 (2000), 259.
[51] Schillebeeckx, *Church*, 165 [167].
[52] "Methodology: Asian Christian Theology," 330.
[53] Michael Amaladoss, "The Church and Pluralism in the Asia of the 1990s," *FABC Papers No. 57e* (Hong Kong: FABC, 1990), 12.

the world and to other religions (Ecclesiological question: what is the church's response?) Schillebeeckx, in his trilogy, actually did address every single one of those questions in the three volumes of *Jesus, Christ,* and *Church.* The *Jesus* book explored the question "Who do you say that I am?," the *Christ* book examined "What does salvation from God in Jesus mean to us?," and the *Church* book developed on the question "What is the Church's response to this offer of salvation?"

These are questions centered upon the foundation of one's faith. They are questions as relevant to the early Christians as they are to contemporary Christians. One could say that in the trilogy Schillebeeckx had more or less anticipated the questions raised by the declaration *Dominus Iesus,* or that the trilogy constitutes his response to the document. The trilogy could therefore be regarded as Schillebeeckx's own *Dominus Iesus,* his confession of faith that "Jesus is Lord" and, with Irenaeus, he underscores that salvation for all of humankind lies in the living God, the creator of all (*vita hominis, visio Dei*) as well as the conviction that God's glory lies in humankind's happiness, salvation, and wholeness (*Gloria Dei, vivens homo*): "Glory for God and peace for men."[54]

---

[54] Schillebeeckx, *IR,* 142–43.

# Chapter 28

# Creation Faith and the Politics of Nature

## Reading Schillebeeckx in an Ecological Age

Elizabeth M. Pyne

This chapter undertakes a reading of Schillebeeckx's theology in the context of contemporary ecological concerns. The analysis that follows proceeds from three interrelated features of Schillebeeckx's theology. The first is the prominent role of creation in his thought. Insofar as the doctrine of creation remains the key starting point for Christian consideration of the interconnectivity that ecological issues bring into view, Schillebeeckx's rich understanding of the ontological and ethical import of a vision of the world as God's creation recommends itself as a point of ecological dialogue. Moreover, not only the meaning of creation as such but also its connection to salvation represents a crucial area of eco-theological inquiry.[1] The Christian narrative of creation, redemption, and eschatological fulfillment shapes a theological sense of nature that is dynamic—transformed, for good and for ill, by sin and grace.[2] Here, too, ecological interpreters may draw on Schillebeeckx's keen interest in carefully articulating points of continuity and discontinuity between present human experience and its salvific wholeness, that is, between what is and what is hoped for. Along with these two structural features of Schillebeeckx's theology, a third point of ecological connection is more explicit. In the latter part of his career, Schillebeeckx began to exhibit the environmental awareness that was increasingly entering social consciousness and ecclesial discussion. While he cannot be considered an ecological theologian in a comparable way to thinkers who consistently reflect on the natural world as a central theme, his attention to ecological matters was not a negligible development.[3] In significant ways, he began to weave an interest in what is other-than-human into his critical engagement with modernity, concerning questions of subjectivity, suffering, and hope.

---

[1]   For two examples, see Willis Jenkins, *Ecologies of Grace: Environmental Ethics and Christian Theology* (New York: Oxford University Press, 2003), 13–14, and Ernst Conradie, *An Ecological Christian Anthropology: At Home on Earth?* (Burlington, VT: Ashgate, 2005), 18–20.

[2]   See David Albertson and Cabell King, eds., *Without Nature?: A New Condition for Theology* (New York: Fordham University Press, 2009), 12.

[3]   For a sampling of representative texts published in the time frame of Schillebeeckx's major works, consult the historical survey in Peter W. Bakken, Joan Gibb Engel, and J. Ronald Engel, eds., *Ecology, Justice, and Christian Faith: A Critical Guide to the Literature* (Westport, CT: Greenwood Press, 1995). The field of ecological theology has grown rapidly since the new millennium.

The main task of this chapter is to examine in greater detail the picture of human identity in relation to the natural world that emerges out of Schillebeeckx's efforts to address the human cause in conjunction with the cause of all creation.[4] The specific contours of his ecological turn, as it were, merit careful attention on their own terms. Thus, the majority of this reading focuses on the means by which Schillebeeckx extended, adapted, and developed his thinking about human-nature relations in light of the ethical and theological issues raised by the ecological crisis. The balance of the chapter then shifts from an exegetical to a constructive mode. Convinced of the new questions that face Christian believers, Schillebeeckx both affirmed and modeled the need for theology to adapt.[5] A wide range of constructive projects "*sequela* Schillebeeckx" attests to the generativity of this invitation for contemporary theology, especially at sites of creative friction in his thought.[6] The concluding part of this chapter proposes the politics of nature as one such location of indeterminate, yet fruitful insight, and argues for the ongoing value of creation faith in addressing the dilemmas of our ecological age.[7]

# I. A developing ecological perspective

The volume of Schillebeeckx's writing precludes a comprehensive treatment of all references to the environment or ecology in his corpus. Undoubtedly, the pivotal discussion of human-nature relations occurs in the epilogue to the third volume of his *Jesus* trilogy: *Church: The Human Story of God*. This text has rightly garnered scholarly attention as evidence of the "growing emphasis" on ecological issues in Schillebeeckx's thought.[8] In what follows, I will situate the key passages in *Church* in the context of his engagement with ecological matters in the preceding two volumes of his Christological trilogy and two later essays. When taken together, these three snapshots present a composite picture of his developing perspective on humanity's place in and with the wider sweep of creation. Insofar as they are roughly chronological, they also allow for

---

[4] Mary Catherine Hilkert employs this parallel phrasing—the human cause and the cause of *all* creation—in "'Grace–Optimism': The Spirituality at the Heart of Schillebeeckx's Theology," *Spirituality Today* 44, no. 3 (Fall 1991), 220–39.

[5] See Edward Schillebeeckx, *I Am a Happy Theologian: Conversations with Francesco Strazzari*, trans. John Bowden (London: SCM Press, 1994), 80.

[6] Martin G. Poulsom adopts Schillebeeckx's use of *sequela*—originally in the context of "following after" Jesus in new situations—to refer to ongoing theological engagement with Schillebeeckx's work, in "Concentrating on Creation: Following Christ in the Context of Climate Change," *Grace, Governance, and Globalization*, ed. Stephan van Erp, Martin G. Poulsom, and Lieven Boeve (London: Bloomsbury T&T Clark, 2017), 127–28. For one recent volume demonstrating the enduring constructive potential of Schillebeeckx's work, see Lieven Boeve, Frederiek Depoortere, and Stephan van Erp, eds., *Edward Schillebeeckx and Contemporary Theology* (London: T&T Clark, 2012).

[7] "Ecological age" is now widely used, although its exact meaning differs. For two theological examples, see Sallie McFague, *Models of God: Theology for an Ecological, Nuclear Age* (Philadelphia: Fortress Press, 1987) and Norman Wirzba, *The Paradise of God: Renewing Religion in an Ecological Age* (Oxford: Oxford University Press, 2003).

[8] Mary Catherine Hilkert, "Introduction," *The Praxis of the Reign of God: An Introduction to the Theology of Edward Schillebeeckx*, ed. Mary Catherine Hilkert and Robert J. Schreiter, 2nd ed. (New York: Fordham University Press, 2002), xxi.

an analysis of lines of continuity and change.[9] We will see that Schillebeeckx employs several distinct and sometimes competing strategies as he seeks to express human beings' ecological responsibility and ecological belonging, as well as God's loving concern for the well-being of the natural world.

## The promise of salvation: "A new heaven and a new earth"

In the 1970s, Schillebeeckx's Christological project contributed to the sea change in theological appraisal of the connection between socio-political liberation and a religious understanding of salvation. Along with *nouvelle théologie* and liberation theologians, Schillebeeckx directed his energies to charting a course through the contested terrain surrounding human effort and divine grace, intersubjective relationships and structural forces, and scriptural authority and contemporary experience. However, he was neither unaware of nor unaffected by the import of environmental issues. One can observe the beginnings of Schillebeeckx's ecological consciousness taking shape within the defining commitments of his "practical-critical soteriology."[10]

Scattered references to the harm wrought by planetary mistreatment occur in his writing from this period. They tend to be laconic, yet unflinchingly grave. For instance, a footnote in *Jesus: An Experiment in Christology* (1974) refers to widespread apocalyptic expectation in the first century as "a fitful but powerful phenomenon at that time (rather like the end of the world by means of hydrogen bombs and pollution of the environment in our time)."[11] Again in *Christ: The Christian Experience in the Modern World* (1977), he identifies "the setting at naught of ecological principles of life by our technocratic and scientifically directed industrial society" as one of two "macro-dangers"—along with atomic energy—posing a threat to the entirety of human existence.[12] The resolutely incarnational bent of Schillebeeckx's mystical-political theology means that such a hazard to worldly well-being cannot be sloughed off as the responsibility of governments or scientists; or rather, inasmuch as it concerns them, it is at one and the same time a matter of sincere theological concern.

Attention to the natural environment follows from Schillebeeckx's determined effort to explicate the proposition *extra mundum nulla salus* ("outside the world, there is no salvation"), as he would later put it.[13] The scope of the ecological threat to human well-being, and indeed, to

---

9   As Poulsom observes, however, the question of whether Schillebeeckx's perspective on these issues manifests continuity or change partakes of broader debates about his theology and is somewhat complicated by his own assessment in *Church* that, rather than being "a fashionable adaptation to later trends … I was already writing substantially the same thing in 1974 and even in 1960." See Schillebeeckx, *Church, CW* vol. 10 (London: Bloomsbury T&T Clark, 2014), 234 [263] and Poulsom, "Concentrating on Creation," 131.

10  Derek J. Simon, "Salvation and Liberation in the Practical-Critical Soteriology of Schillebeeckx," *Theological Studies* 63 (2002), 494–520. Simon summarizes, "Practical-critical soteriology develops the claim that liberation is intrinsic to and constitutive for the experience and interpretation of eschatological salvation" (p. 494).

11  Edward Schillebeeckx, *Jesus, CW* vol. 6 (London: Bloomsbury T&T Clark, 2014), 422, n. 84 [719, n. 144].

12  Edward Schillebeeckx, *Christ, CW* vol. 7 (London: Bloomsbury T&T Clark, 2014), 651 [660].

13  Edward Schillebeeckx, *On Christian Faith: The Spiritual, Ethical and Political Dimensions*, trans. John Bowden (New York: Crossroad, 1987), 8; Schillebeeckx, *Church*, xxvi [xix].

the possibility of human life, will continue as a theme in Schillebeeckx's commentary over the next two decades.[14] If environmental destruction is a menace to human integrity, then it follows that action on behalf of a healthy environment must be an element of a liberating theological anthropology. In working out the implications of his Christological studies, Schillebeeckx comes to affirm the inclusion of an ecological dimension among the constituents of Christian faith. Salvation always concerns wholeness and fulfillment. Whereas in *Jesus* its sphere is restricted to the "being in wholeness" of humanity and history, Schillebeeckx later extends its reach:

> If Christian salvation is salvation of and for human beings … this means that Christian salvation is not simply the salvation of souls, but the healing, making whole, wholeness, of the whole person, the individual and society, in a natural world which is not abused. Thus, Christian salvation also comprises ecological, social, and political aspects.[15]

This trend becomes increasingly clear in his references, in works throughout the 1980s, to the "[t]hree great metaphors" of salvation. They include: first, the kingdom of God as an image of human persons liberated to live in true community; second, the resurrection of the body, which affirms the integrity of the individual person; and, third, "the consummation of the undamaged 'ecological milieu' which human beings need to live in is suggested by the great metaphor of 'the new heaven and the new earth.'"[16] While Schillebeeckx may be spare in his elaboration of the scientific details, insofar as human beings are undeniably dependent on the capacity of earth, such dependence cannot be considered merely incidental or temporary. Albeit in this bare form, then, he positions the reality of the ecological crisis, as a matter of human salvation, near to the heart of Christian faith.

## The anthropological constants and ecological implications

A closer look at Schillebeeckx's discussion of the "anthropological constants" in *Christ* further demonstrates a nascent ecological concern within his soteriology. In their partial and fragmentary way, the constants seek to orient ethics toward conditions of "livable humanity" by protecting broad values without determining specific norms.[17] In this, they also point in the direction of the "complete and undamaged humanity" that exists in the fullness of God's salvation.[18] The first

---

[14] Parallel comments about the scope of the ecological threat occur in major lectures and essays from the early and mid-1980s, e.g., Schillebeeckx, *God Among Us: The Gospel Proclaimed*, trans. John Bowden (London: SCM Press, 1983), 250; and Schillebeeckx, *On Christian Faith*, 83. Among later examples, see Schillebeeckx, "Liberating Theology," *Essays, CW* vol. 11 (London: Bloomsbury T&T Clark, 2014), 80, and the two essays treated below.

[15] Schillebeeckx, *God Among Us*, 100; compare the more anthropocentric version in Schillebeeckx, *Jesus*, 585 [624]. A parallel passage to the former in Edward Schillebeeckx, *IR, CW* vol. 8 (London: Bloomsbury T&T Clark, 2014), 49–50 [58], does not include the phrase "a natural world which is not abused," but does clearly state the ecological aspect. For later affirmations of an ecological dimension within the fullness of salvation, see Schillebeeckx, *On Christian Faith*, 65 and Schillebeeckx, "Liberating Theology," 69.

[16] Schillebeeckx, *On Christian Faith*, 29.

[17] Schillebeeckx, *Christ*, 727 [733].

[18] Ibid., 731 [737].

anthropological constant is the most topical; it identifies the "relationship to human corporeality, nature, and the ecological environment" as a constituent element of the well-being and wholeness of the *humanum*.[19] The value of ecological care is affirmed within this zone of sustaining and environing importance for the human beings for whom God wills salvation.

Schillebeeckx's discussion of the ethical implications of human embodiment occasions broader reflection on human–nature relations. The signal features called upon in this discussion are dependence, limits, and balance. He notes that human beings depend in myriad ways on nature for their livelihood. Disavowal of any body-soul dualism means that this dependence must be seen as an enduring fact of human existence. Humanity's material constitution entails respect for certain limits inhering in the natural world, presumably related to finite resources and the ability of ecosystems to function naturally, as well as the limitations on human capabilities.[20] But the exact quality of this dependence is malleable, as is the mode of engaging natural limits. Thus, Schillebeeckx pairs his claim about respecting and protecting the natural environment with an affirmation of the role of culture and the call to humanize nature; people do not and cannot live in a "purely natural world."[21] A similar posture of balance characterizes his assessment of science and technology. Humans need to employ instrumental and technological reason, which involves intervention in and transformation of nature. Yet, such activity must be situated within the many dimensions of what it is to be a human being; science and technology do not answer the question of meaning or purpose and must always be employed in light of what is "worthy of our true humanity."[22] "The concern," Schillebeeckx writes, is "on the one hand to emancipate man from nature without on the other hand destroying his own ecological basis."[23] The first constant sketches a picture of human interaction with (non-human) nature in which the premium placed on the humanization of nature bespeaks the *relative* autonomy of culture or history from nature. However, this is true only to the extent that the meaning of "humanize" recalls that nature, as a finite domain, *to some degree* resists overweening human designs and thus, by its difference, makes visible the normative and physical circumscription of human freedom and rationality.

The second and third anthropological constants pertain to interpersonal relations and relations to structures and institutions, respectively.[24] They showcase Schillebeeckx's resistance to the individualizing as well as spiritualizing terms of certain historical and contemporary notions of salvation, especially when such ideas serve to reinforce an unjust status quo.[25] While Schillebeeckx

---

[19]  Ibid., 728 [734].

[20]  Schillebeeckx seems to suggest that boundaries in the natural world are rather more straightforward to determine than those inhering in human life; of the latter he writes, "Although we may not be able (or perhaps may not yet be able) to establish by an empirical scientific method precisely where the *limits* of the mutability, conditioning and capability of humanity lies, we may be sure that such inescapable limits do exist"; ibid., 728 [734].

[21]  Ibid., 729 [735].

[22]  Ibid., 728 [734–35]. Typically, Schillebeeckx leaves "science and technology" at this level of generalization, rather than specifying certain scientific disciplines or technological products. Likewise, he often juxtaposes a scientific mode of engaging nature to an esthetic or contemplative approach.

[23]  Ibid., 729–30 [735].

[24]  Schillebeeckx introduces the seven constants with the comment that their overall purpose is to situate "personal identity within social culture"; ibid., 728 [734].

[25]  Ibid., 730, 739–41 [736, 744–46].

does not elaborate the precise relationship of the ecological, personal, and social dimensions of life, he holds that salvation is a synthesis of the six constants; the multi-faceted unity they form is itself a seventh constant.[26] On this basis, Dorothy Jacko argues that Schillebeeckx's soteriological framing of the liberative socio-political involvement of Christian believers is a root-bed for "an ecological spirituality," the content of which is "both mystical and political–ecological activity."[27] She maintains that the universality of the concrete ethical demand indicated in constants two and three also obtains with respect to the cosmic relationships outlined in the first;

> It therefore is legitimate to extend their concerns beyond human society in itself to include the disadvantaged and oppressed of other species and the endangered cosmos itself within the realm of one's concern for a commitment to the communitarian life and well-being of the whole.[28]

Such an interpretation draws from Schillebeeckx's soteriology a significant resource for an ecologically inflected vision of human personhood and for environmental ethics.[29]

The conviction that salvation is the being in wholeness of humanity and indeed of all creation is a powerful, if only schematic, claim in favor of the ethico-religious import of human interaction with the natural world. This interaction partakes of the revelatory dynamic in which negative affronts to the goodness of God's creation enable positive glimpses of its fulfillment, and thus an ecological dimension may rightly be linked to the "critical and productive force" of creation faith.[30] At the same time, it should be noted that Schillebeeckx does not, at this juncture, consider whether the well-being of "the ecological milieu" beyond or apart from its role in human habitat ought to be taken up as a theological matter. This is unsurprising given that ecological concern emerges as a corollary to theological anthropology. To be clear, there is never a sense that the God of creation is anything other than the God of history *and* nature.[31] Nevertheless, close inspection of this architectonic structure of creation—as both nature and history—reveals a persistent tension regarding the relationship of personal and socio-political wholeness to ecological wholeness.

As much as Schillebeeckx explicitly affirms the material-spiritual unity of human beings and upholds the need for a healthy environment, nature continues to function as a difference-defining boundary that illuminates human exceptionalism. Suggestions of this difference were already

---

[26] Ibid., 736 [741–42].

[27] Dorothy Jacko, "Schillebeeckx's Creation-Based Theology," *An Ecology of the Spirit: Religious Reflection and Environmental Consciousness*, ed. Michael Barnes, The Annual Publication of the College Theology Society vol. 36 (Lanham, MD: Catholic University of America Press, 1994), 157.

[28] Ibid., 150. She argues that this extension is in keeping with Schillebeeckx's intentions; see ibid., 153, n.12.

[29] For a parallel judgment, see Erica Olson-Bang, "Edward Schillebeeckx's Creation Theology as a Resource for Ecological Ethics," *Horizons* 38 (2011), 263: "The inclusion of ecological wholeness in Schillebeeckx's understanding of salvation encourages Christians to broaden their soteriological perspective to envision the healing of the whole world and to work for the good of the world – its humans, plants, and animals."

[30] Schillebeeckx declares, in no uncertain terms, that "to damage and harm this world is a sin against the creator of heaven and earth, against the one whom, under whatever name, many people call God: the mystery that has a passion for the wholeness of nature and history, of society and human beings"; Schillebeeckx, *On Christian Faith*, 31.

[31] E.g., Schillebeeckx, *Christ*, 504–05, 518 [516, 530].

evident in the first anthropological constant. Human corporeality has a share in nature insofar as physical existence depends on habitat, food, and so on, but, as we have seen, Schillebeeckx depicts the exercise of human reason as a project of emancipation from nature; by this he does not mean a separation, but rather the transformation of nature for human well-being according to proper respect of human and natural limits.[32] Nature is provisioning, but also conceptually represents a zone of determinism and order, a kind of weight that bears upon the human project to encounter God in the freedom and creativity of history. In this vein, a sense of the capacity for culture as both gift and burden unique to humankind pervades the second half of the anthropological constants. It is precisely the "dialectical tension between nature and history which is irremediable even by the best possible social structure" that establishes human existence as a "*hermeneutical* undertaking," invested in the "question of the *meaning* of humanity" across its varied temporal and geographical contexts (fourth constant).[33] Humanity remembers its past and imagines its future (fourth and sixth constants) and aims to instantiate the conditions that support a meaningful existence through the "mutual relationship of theory and practice" (fifth constant). Schillebeeckx articulates the fifth constant by way of a contrast between self-critical human judgments about culture and the instinct-based struggle for survival that obtains at the "sub-human level, i.e. in the animal world."[34] Within these comments on the enduring facets of a truly human life, assertions of human difference from the animal and natural world casually slide into assumptions about superiority.

Schillebeeckx's language regarding the "humanization of nature" should be read in the context of its time and the particular struggles in which he was engaged.[35] Even so, the viability of this framing may well surface critical questions from contemporary ecological interpreters who desire a more robust account of humanity's creaturely belonging. Despite the real impetus to incorporate environmental responsibility into the praxis of the reign of God, it is premature to find in this phase of theological articulation a "foundation for a spirituality which avoids the dangers of anthropocentrism."[36] Such a claim would, minimally, have to acknowledge that the way in which Schillebeeckx describes human identity—and thus the human cause that is also God's cause—hinges on a constitutive and categorical difference from nonhuman nature. Although he mobilizes that theological anthropology to attend to the reality of ecological threats and, by extension, to support the inclusion of an ecological dimension in the wholeness of salvation, this wholeness has its center of gravity in an ideal of human fulfillment that places the natural world on the sidelines of the story of salvation in created history.

---

[32] Interestingly, he also describes the ability to shape a human environment as a compensatory measure for humanity's deficit in "the refined instincts and the strengths which animals possess." Cultural transformation of nature "rescues man from his animal limitations and offers an opening for new possibilities"; ibid., 729 [735].

[33] Ibid., 733 [739].

[34] Ibid., 734 [740].

[35] E.g., ibid., 810 [814]. In arguing for the relevance of politics to mysticism, Schillebeeckx took pains to defend "humanization" as worthy goal over and against critics who claimed that it was reductive horizontalization of faith; see, for example, Schillebeeckx, *IR*, 114 [131].

[36] Jacko, "Schillebeeckx's Creation-Based Theology," 148.

# II. "One dimension was forgotten …":
# Co-humanity and co-creatureliness

The trajectory of Schillebeeckx's engagement with environmental responsibility as a component of Christian faith indicates that he continued to grapple with the meaning of creation in regard to historical human experience and did so with an awareness of the need for nuance. The sustained discussion of human–nature relations in *Church* signals the increasing visibility of the environmental movement in public consciousness and ecclesial deliberation. Schillebeeckx's reference to the "conciliar process" with its principles of "justice, peace and the integrity of creation" indicates the role of this context for his own theological consideration of a renewed emphasis on creation and the environment.[37] Of course, creation was never absent from his theology; Schillebeeckx's soteriology maintains a firm connection to the abiding integrity of creation.[38] Yet, as we have seen, the ecological potential in affirmations of creation's deeply relational eschatological destiny can remain hamstrung by the structural importance of human difference from other creatures and of history from nature in the economy of grace. There are signs of a new approach to human–nature relations in Schillebeeckx's work by the late 1980s. Erica Olson-Bang observes that his theology of creation, far from assuming a new importance per se, nevertheless became a productive forum for contending with ecological questions in this period.[39]

In the closing chapter of *Church*, Schillebeeckx seeks to show how creation faith can meaningfully illuminate secular and religious interpretations of the question of salvation in the contemporary Western world.[40] In this first section of his comments "by way of an epilogue," one aspect in particular attracts the attention of an ecological interpreter. It is clear that the primary creator–creation distinction enfolds all others, including that between humanity and the rest of the natural world. Schillebeeckx contends that finitude "applies to everything in our world, in nature, history and society … Nothing of all this is not contingent. That means that even matter, as an interplay of chance and necessity, need not have been or could have been quite different."[41] The doctrine of creation, he reiterates, is not meant to explain why worldly phenomena are the way they are or to assign them predetermined meaning. But, as was evident in the interaction of human

---

[37] Schillebeeckx, *Church*, 232, 236 [235, 238]. He is referring to the World Council of Churches, which adopted this process at its Vancouver Assembly in 1983.

[38] The connection of salvation to creation is expressed succinctly and powerfully in the idea that Christ is "*concentrated* creation: belief in creation as God wills it to be"; Schillebeeckx, *IR*, 111 [128], emphasis added. This is, to be sure, an ecologically promising idea; however, I would argue that what Schillebeeckx means by it is strongly colored by the way in which he concentrates the identity of creation in human history, rather than nature. In the background is the sense that "nature" represents either chaos or immutability; both are suspect in regard to the work of human liberation.

[39] Olson-Bang, "Schillebeeckx's Creation Theology," 255, 257. While agreeing in part with Philip Kennedy's emphasis on the longstanding importance of creation in Schillebeeckx's theology, Olson-Bang insists that something new is at stake in this theology when Schillebeeckx draws from it a burgeoning ecological commentary; cf. Philip Kennedy, "God and Creation," *The Praxis of the Reign of God: An Introduction to the Theology of Edward Schillebeeckx*, ed. Mary Catherine Hilkert and Robert J. Schreiter, 2nd ed. (New York: Fordham University Press, 2002), 57–58, and Edward Schillebeeckx, "Theological Quests," *Essays, CW* vol. 11 (London: Bloomsbury T&T Clark, 2014), 124.

[40] For a general discussion of the concept of creation faith, see Kennedy, "God and Creation," 37–58.

[41] Schillebeeckx, *Church*, 228 [230].

freedom with nature in Schillebeeckx's earlier work, he strives to preserve a delicate balance. On the one hand, his resistance to creation-as-explanation affirms that real change happens— "for better or for worse," he adds—and must often be sought over-against stifling injustice that masquerades as inevitable; moreover, the notion of contingency protects the idea that human beings relate to God as "*absolute* origin of our humanity" rather than to a divine puppeteer.[42] On the other hand, a chastened version of order still remains. In a classically Catholic register, Schillebeeckx asserts that freedom entails responsibility as well as choice. So, because human beings are created by God as "the principle of their own human lives," they must act freely in the world "within contingent situations and given boundaries, and therefore with respect for both inanimate and animate nature."[43] This move to connect the core convictions of creation faith (i.e., creaturely finitude and contingency) with the constellation of dependence, limits, and balance implies a support for restraint and moderation in the interest of human dignity and ecological health—what Schillebeeckx elsewhere terms a "collective ascesis."[44]

The second section of the epilogue marks a more conspicuous environmental pivot. Schillebeeckx reviews the global political scene from the 1950s through to the present and observes that an important concern for "co-humanity" has taken root; this orientation would characterize his own starting point for theological correlation during this period and the subject matter of the preceding inquiries into culture and politics.[45] Schillebeeckx now wishes to join those seeking to show where the "cosmic aspect of Christian redemption and liberation" comes in.[46] This perspective detects a lacuna in the emphasis on human solidarity: "But God is not just a God of human beings. Or rather, one dimension was forgotten; the fact that with inorganic and organic creatures we share in the one creation."[47] The explicit articulation of this fundamental continuity sounds a new note in his thinking. It suggests that in bringing the wider natural world into the foreground—or at least recognizing the need to do so—Schillebeeckx understands himself to be marking a difference from the perspective he has previously taken. The pages that follow are a loosely organized combination of cultural commentary and biblical exegesis in a homiletical style. They demonstrate his attempts, under the shadow of "the catastrophe to the environment," to renegotiate the character of human–nature relations within the parameters of his primary theological and ethical commitments.[48]

His primary route for addressing human–nature relations runs through theological anthropology; as he puts it, "The decisive question is: what image of human beings do you opt for?"[49] Schillebeeckx summarily dismisses the critique from "some circles" that Jews' and Christians' origin story—particularly the dual injunction in Genesis 1:28 to "[b]e fruitful and multiply …

[42] Ibid., 228–29 [231].

[43] Ibid., 228 [231].

[44] Schillebeeckx, *IR*, 106 [121]; see also Schillebeeckx, *God Among Us*, 99.

[45] A representative passage in *God Among Us* draws out a link between finitude and human solidarity through the notion of "co-humanity": "The Christian tradition thus sees co-humanity as a dimension with religious depth which has to do with the insight of faith that finitude is not left in isolation but is supported by the absolute presence of the Creator God. And this presence remains an inexhaustible source which can never be secularized." See Schillebeeckx, *God Among Us*, 101.

[46] Schillebeeckx, *Church*, 232 [234].

[47] Ibid., 234 [236].

[48] Ibid., 237 [239].

[49] Ibid., 237 [240].

and have dominion over ... every living thing"—is the root cause of the environmental crisis.⁵⁰ If there is blame to be laid on his account, the culprit is a distinctly modern vision of the human person that glorifies rational and technological capacity at the expense of all else. Schillebeeckx, as before, reminds readers that science and technology must take the ethical horizon into account. Likewise, the excesses of consumer society need to be genuinely critiqued. The seriousness of the situation marks, for Schillebeeckx, a qualitatively new moment of ecological concern.⁵¹ He seeks to offer a corrective anthropological vision over and against a model of one-sided control and an exploitative desire for unceasing progress. Echoing the discourse of restraint and limits from above, Schillebeeckx appeals to the co-inherence of natural and rational boundaries in the human. An appreciation of nature's structure not only encourages a gentler relationship to earth and its creatures, but also enables humanity to enjoy the esthetic dimension of the natural world. Such a perspective also facilitates the ability to name the dangers to it; Schillebeeckx mentions "modern ecological experiences of contrast," which contravene the integrity of creation.⁵²

It is the creation stories in Genesis 1–3 that occupy him most in *Church* and furnish the strongest warrants for both extending ethical regard to nature and rethinking the creaturely status of human beings. In his interpretation, Schillebeeckx introduces two new notes into his ecological thinking. The first of these is that "the earth is more than just the human world" and has, in the parlance of environmental ethics, intrinsic as well as instrumental value. In several places, Schillebeeckx affirms "God's bond with the earth" (although it is, as we will see, a bond that "is mediated by the unique position of human beings as the image of God").⁵³ Especially evident in the first, Priestly story is that God's creation includes the provision of "an appropriate environment for every living being." Whereas "nature" in the two earlier Christological volumes comes across as somewhat flat, here nature is populated: a world of creatures, "a cosmic community in solidarity," deemed "very good," in which "[God] wills the life of the living and the survival of things."⁵⁴ Such passages amend others where Schillebeeckx's language suggests that the value of the ecological environment (in the singular) is judged only in reference to human well-being.⁵⁵ The New Testament, he contends, presents a decentered ethical perspective

---

⁵⁰ In his words, "It is indeed a fact that (not in antiquity and in the Middle Ages but) with the rise of bourgeois capitalism among Western Christians this biblical text has often been misused to legitimate the exploitation and pollution of nature. But that is a very recent, ideological legitimation which has little or nothing to do with the biblical roots and meaning of these texts"; ibid., 238–39 [240–41]. Schillebeeckx's unnamed opponents voice the famous attack on biblical anthropocentrism made by Lynn White in "The Historical Roots of Our Ecologic Crisis," *Science* 155 (1967), 1203–07.

⁵¹ He compares the modern situation to a more generalized environmental awareness in the pre-industrial period; Schillebeeckx, *Church*, 238 [240–41].

⁵² Ibid., 237 [239]. This provocative claim is not unpacked. Presumably he intends to suggest a category of *human* experience in which the witness of specifically ecological harm or injustice illuminates a contrast to a sense of what ought to be; skies polluted by factory smoke, for instance. But it is not entirely clear in this brief formulation whether the suffering at issue—a constitutive element of the negative contrast experience—is limited to that of humans or extends, in a more radical move, to some analogous experience on the part of nonhuman nature.

⁵³ Ibid., 236 [238].

⁵⁴ Ibid., 242–43 [245].

⁵⁵ With respect to the status of the natural world, Olson-Bang maintains, "For Schillebeeckx, the created world is valuable in itself, and while humanity has a unique responsibility to creation, it is not the source of creation's value," in "Schillebeeckx's Creation Theology," 269.

in which more is asked of human beings than simply "the preservation of nature to ensure self-preservation."[56] Nonhuman nature is undoubtedly part of the creation God brings into being with love and for which God wills salvation, along with human beings and world history. The more direct affirmation of this truth in *Church* as compared with his earlier work is one of the ways Schillebeeckx seeks to expand the socio-political framing of his theology.[57]

Another essential facet of his anthropological corrective is a stress on the "parallels between human beings and nature," for which he finds support in biochemistry as well as the Bible. Both biblical accounts of creation situate the distinctive features of human identity within an essential and prior unity (recall the image of creation as "a cosmic community in solidarity"). The first narrative tells that there is no separate day of creation for human beings, who come into existence with "the cattle, the creeping things and the wild beasts."[58] The second narrative, as noted above, speaks to God's generous provisioning of environments and vitality for plants and animals as well as humankind. Schillebeeckx thus understands the biblical witness to go against separative and hegemonic anthropologies based on the fundamental conviction that "[t]o be a creature is at the same time to be an 'ecological' being."[59]

In each instance, however, Schillebeeckx promptly qualifies an assertion of commonality by a statement of differentiation. Thus, alongside the level of existence as "living chemistry" shared by humans, animals, and plants, "on the other hand anthropology rightly stresses that there is something in human beings that cannot be reduced to nature. There is a 'surplus.' In human beings there is also an element that is not nature."[60] Biblically, he holds that the creation of human beings "in the image of God" affords a unique trait: "[i]n contrast to animals … a somatic spiritual awareness, something transcendent" which in turn bestows a unique position of creaturely response to God. In a fascinating exposition of Psalm 104, he endeavors to recoup the ecological value of creation's praise while strongly affirming the unavoidability of human perception and narration of that praise. He takes this dynamic to support his thesis that "nature transcends itself in human beings, who are themselves part of nature."[61] For Schillebeeckx, it is this delicate balance of "likeness" and "difference" that must undergird the possibility of an ethical and genuinely Christian relation to nonhuman nature. While aspects of that dynamic are broadly familiar from the previous section, the framework here shifts in a subtle but significant way. Rather than a perpendicular intersection between nature and history—two entities that meet

---

[56] Schillebeeckx, *Church*, 236 [238]. Schillebeeckx reaches this conclusion by way of an interpretation of the sacrifice of the cross, which he links to the abolition of the institution of animal sacrifice in the New Testament and then to the salvation of the animal world.

[57] Likewise, in his prologue to a secondary introduction to his theology written around the same time, he refers to "God, the most holy mystery, who holds to his heart everything of life, from the heights to the depths, from ant and aphid to elephant and human being," See Edward Schillebeeckx, "Prologue," *The Praxis of the Reign of God: An Introduction to the Theology of Edward Schillebeeckx*, ed. Mary Catherine Hilkert and Robert J. Schreiter, 2nd ed. (New York: Fordham University Press, 2002), xvii.

[58] Schillebeeckx, *Church*, 234 [236].

[59] Ibid., 243 [245].

[60] Ibid., 236 [238]. It is not clear whether he means here theological anthropology, specifically, or would contend that this claim is supported by secular cultural anthropology. The text's subsequent turn to prayer supports the former; "Nature itself cannot pray: as material, inorganic and biologically living creatureliness it needs human beings to come to the praise of God."

[61] Ibid., 236 [238–39].

only in the human—Schillebeeckx presents something like the traditional pyramid with humans on top, or perhaps a circle encompassing all of creation that is brightest at its center.

The rendering of human uniqueness in *Church* always points back to care for creation and creatures as well as to human need and it emphasizes humanity's co-existence with the natural world rather than conflict with it or emancipation from it. In the first creation account, the creation of human beings in the image and likeness of God means that they "must *take after God*" in the sense that they, too, "must act creatively in their environment" through attempts to control chaos, foster life, and pursue justice for others.[62] Schillebeeckx refers in several places to the steward's role as that of a regent or representative acting on earth in God's stead while always reminding us who this God is. He does not shy away from asserting the superiority of human beings in creation, but emphasizes at the same time the responsibility incumbent on such a position: human beings are "servants of creation" and accountable to God.[63] In its socio-historical and scriptural context, he contends, the "dominion" mandate in Genesis 1:28 emphasizes a divinely willed "stable community" of individuals and peoples on and with their lands and of humans who conduct themselves toward other living beings "as God wills to act towards them, as friends."[64] A similar pattern emerges in Schillebeeckx's interpretation of the second creation story, wherein the prophets' vision of an eschatological state of creaturely harmony shapes their protological narrative. Again, a mandate to responsibility and loving concern characterizes the distinctive human task of fostering peaceful co-existence through thoughtful management; Schillebeeckx glosses the command to till the land and keep it as an "expression of something like a concern for the ecological environment."[65]

Yet with this responsibility comes the very real possibility of sinful mismanagement on the part of human stewards.[66] Isaiah laments the violence of those who were meant to be a blessing but instead become a curse; Paul notes the "groaning of creation." With them, Schillebeeckx indicts contemporary engines of devastating negativity.[67] Nevertheless, he displays his characteristic framing of Christian hope as a fragile yet persistent pull from the God who is faithful to creation in the promise of what is to come. Therefore, even as "human beings seem more often to fail than to succeed in their task of creation, this in fact opens up space for a truly human ethic governing our attitude to the world and nature."[68] Schillebeeckx declines to say that the Bible offers specific norms for ecological or bioethical issues, but insists that it presents a much-needed vision of reconciling human–nature relations for people in an era of ecological catastrophe.[69] The primary modality for Schillebeeckx's effort to better incorporate ecological responsibility into his

---

[62] Ibid., 234 [236–37]. Emphasis original. The contrast is to animals and plants, who are created "each after its kind."

[63] Ibid., 235 [237]. He communicates the ideal vision of humankind a few pages later in this way: they are "beings who in peaceful fellow-creatureliness with all other existing beings nevertheless have a somewhat privileged position" (ibid., 242 [244]).

[64] Ibid., 240 [242–43].

[65] Ibid., 242 [244].

[66] Here, the second (Yahwistic) account, Schillebeeckx says, is unlike the first creation story, "which knows no 'original sin' (but a growing human history of sinfulness and murder)"; ibid., 243 [245].

[67] Ibid., 235 [237].

[68] Ibid., 243 [245–46].

[69] Ibid., 239 [241].

mystical-political theology is an anthropological expansion: "universal involvement in creation, not just co-humanity, is the task of human beings as creatures for whom God is concerned."[70]

In *Church*, there are evident shifts of tone and substance in Schillebeeckx's position on human–nature relations in the face of the ecological crisis. An anthropology that emphasizes human co-creatureliness is key to his energetic articulations of environmental responsibility and ecological solidarity; as he says, "Being creatures among many other nonhuman creatures and being human beings must go hand in hand."[71] Nonetheless, Schillebeeckx's reading of these texts indicates that one must carefully parse *two* asymmetrical aspects of identification here; we recall that he understands nature's inner transcendence in humanity to refer to an irreducible surplus, "an element that is not nature." Olson-Bang also acknowledges a "tension in Schillebeeckx's thought" regarding humanity's co-creaturely yet distinctive position. But it is one she seems willing to resolve in the same terms that Schillebeeckx does: by stressing the functional over the ontological meaning of this distinctiveness.[72] The task of the *imago Dei* becomes an asset to motivate human beings' ethical obligations to the natural world. Olson-Bang goes on to argue, the aforementioned tension notwithstanding, that in fact Schillebeeckx "disallows an anthropocentric worldview" and "explicitly decenters humanity in creation."[73] While this assessment of the ecological material in *Church* has credibility, I would maintain that even as he integrates a more capacious perspective on ecological belonging, Schillebeeckx is still working within the contours of a theological project characterized primarily by the "question of who God can be for human beings" and who human beings are to become in response.[74]

## III. "The earthly soil of all possible culture": Humans and animals, culture and crisis

The epilogue to *Church* remained Schillebeeckx's most wide-ranging discussion of the human responsibility to enact a different manner of relationship with nature. He continued, nevertheless, to treat the ecological crisis as a grave issue; although his output slowed as he aged, articles from the final decade of his publishing life include several prominent statements concerning environmental degradation as a source of enormous suffering.[75] Two of his final pieces also include

---

[70]  Ibid., 242 [244].

[71]  Ibid., 235 [237].

[72]  Olson-Bang, "Schillebeeckx's Creation Theology," 261, n. 33.

[73]  Ibid., 268.

[74]  Hilkert, "Introduction," xx. The tension between ecological expansion and homocentric concentration is reflected in a subtle way at the level of Schillebeeckx's language. For instance, he writes in *Church* of the Bible's "[f]our great metaphors" for salvation which "suggest to us the way towards what, according to God's dream for the happiness for men and women *and all their fellow creatures*, humankind will eventually be." See Schillebeeckx, *Church*, 131 [133], emphasis added.

[75]  In a striking passage in "Liberating Theology" (1990), he aligns "Auschwitz, Hiroshima, Bergen-Belsen and the rest, and the stranglehold on our ecological environment," referring parenthetically to them all as "symbols of the 'demonic' in our history" (p. 80). In the context of this essay's focus on the possibility of a liberation theology in the first-world, he also acknowledges global inequity in ecological degradation, namely "the suffering that Western people have inflicted on virtually all cultures and the planet" (p. 72).

reflections on religious faith in the context of the contemporary world that call upon scientific inquiry as a resource for understanding culture and nature in relationship to one another. They furnish additional insight into the ways in which Schillebeeckx's theology might be brought to bear on a rethinking of theological anthropology in an ecological age.

In a lecture entitled "Culture, Religion and Violence" (1996), Schillebeeckx's opening comments on the postmodern search for meaning between dogmatism and relativism lead to a stinging reminder of the material and ecological context of such inquiry:

> This postmodern process is moreover running its course on an exhausted planet, because humans are gradually poisoning the actual matrix, the humus, the earthly soil of all possible culture. I once heard a Flemish engineer resident in America say, "Nature is very forgiving." Humanly degraded nature appears to forgive us a lot, on its own steam it raises itself up from all the havoc and pollution. But there are limits to nature's endurance and forgiveness, and that sets off alarm bells. Culture seems to pose a threat to nature, and as a result to humans and authentic, respectful human culture. That makes us enquire about culture as a perennially ground-breaking movement in the service of truly human liberation and wellbeing, respecting the autonomy of what we call earth and all that live on it.[76]

This passage is a fascinating indication of the way in which Schillebeeckx's recognition of human responsibility for ecological degradation prompts two simultaneous reactions: first, the move to affirm human *likeness* to nature (recalling the language of Genesis 1) and, second, a call to respect nature's *otherness*, however compromised that autonomy has become in practice. These impulses go hand in glove, it would appear, inasmuch as nature mediates culture to itself, at least if it is to be "authentic, respectful human culture." Schillebeeckx's linkage of the fruitfulness of human liberation to the well-being of its earthly matrix is, by now, perceptible as a genuine development in his mystical–political theology.

Implicit in this passage seems to be another principle stated more directly in *Church*, namely that domination and exploitation of the natural world—leading to "an exhausted planet"—follow from a flawed anthropology. Schillebeeckx does not explicitly advocate for the theory of culture that he develops in the essay as a corrective response, but it could well be understood as an alternative anthropology. Culture is, for Schillebeeckx, a uniquely human enterprise, "the human world against the backdrop of nature ... what people can produce ... from or with pre-existent nature through their own technical and artistic, physical and mental endeavors."[77] Yet, perhaps consistent with the trend in his thought toward a better-articulated sense of humans' ecological belonging, he seeks to ground the particularity of cultural endeavors in an earthly commonality. His account discloses a basic ambivalence about this belonging; he writes:

> For *despite or because of* the fact that humans as natural beings share the mineral, chemical and biochemical makeup of all natural beings, ultimately they are

---

[76] Edward Schillebeeckx, "Culture, Religion and Violence," *Essays, CW* vol. 11 (London: Bloomsbury T&T Clark, 2014), 164. See also Schillebeeckx, "Theological Quests," *Essays*, 154.

[77] Schillebeeckx, "Culture, Religion and Violence," *Essays*, 165.

above all 'cultural' manifestations on this planet, however barbarically—even inhumanly—these cultural beings may behave.[78]

Schillebeeckx pursues a non-dualistic account of the "reason for and source of all culture," which seeks to soften the boundary between culture and nature. His thesis is that "[h]uman sense perception includes cultural activity."[79] To this end, however, comparisons between human and nonhuman animals re-emerge. As in previous writings, his perspective seeks to toe a fine line between differentiation from nature and embeddedness in it, now accented by this enigmatic "despite or because of." He contends that, in contrast to a certain shortsightedness on the part of many cultural anthropologists, the classical philosophical and Christian traditions rightly affirm the unity of the human person as "mind-in-body." On this basis, Schillebeeckx argues for the origin of culture in an "inner mental spark" that animates human corporeality and opens up a world—of visions, dreams, theorizing and so on—above and beyond mere survival. Notably, the material-spiritual anthropological unity Schillebeeckx advocates rests on a division of human animality from nonhuman animality, for the "soul-spark" imbues human sense perception with something "more than what animals see, hear, taste, touch or smell, even when looking at the same thing a human being does."[80] There is a transformative quality to human seeing such that, for instance, earth becomes landscape in the presence of the interpretative human gaze. However, Schillebeeckx cautions that this should not be taken to imply "anything either for or against anthropocentrism in the universe." As ever, he stresses the profound ambiguity of this human calling to beauty and creativity, which can be betrayed as easily as it can be exercised.[81] The innovation in this text is that nature's transcendence of itself in human consciousness is now accounted for with reference to a scientific paradigm of evolutionary emergence.[82]

Schillebeeckx's dialogue with cultural anthropology continues in his final published article, "Towards a Rediscovery of the Christian Sacraments: Ritualising Religious Elements in Daily Life" (2000). Here, Schillebeeckx returns to the subject of his earliest work, still pursuing his unwavering commitment to seek the divine in the genuinely human.[83] A broadly Thomistic theology of creation that he has now made his own replaces the technical discussion of

---

[78]  Ibid., 163. Emphasis added.

[79]  Ibid., 167.

[80]  Ibid., 167. In support of this point, Schillebeeckx offers, "[a] biologist once told me that people differed from animals in that they not only lived in the world of their everyday needs and interests, but also in another, new world"; Schillebeeckx dramatically contrasts this "life world" to the "world that simply is there, cumbrous and massive, as it were *an sich*, a dark, stagnant, murky, dank watery waste comparable to primeval chaos, the *tohu wa bohu* of the Hebrew creation story, or a swamp that we can point to and whose actuality can even be tested scientifically" (p. 168).

[81]  Ibid., 168–69.

[82]  Schillebeeckx claims that "in evolution as a whole the animal kingdom heralds the emergence of the human race as a kingdom of cultural beings" (pp. 167–68). This unilinear framing is not borne out by biological anthropology, which tends to stress the multidirectional emergence of complexity and novelty, even if certain features coalesce in the human species. For a creative pairing of Schillebeeckx's theology of hope with contemporary biological anthropology, see Julia Feder, "The Impossible is Made Possible: Edward Schillebeeckx, Symbolic Imagination, and Eschatological Faith," *Philosophy, Theology and the Sciences* 3 (2016), 188–216.

[83]  Edward Schillebeeckx, "Towards a Rediscovery of the Christian Sacraments," *Essays, CW* vol. 11 (London: Bloomsbury T&T Clark, 2014), 183–210.

hylemorphism from the 1950s, with insights from the field of ritual studies informing his effort to show that rituals are not simply re-enactments of texts or performances of disembodied myths, but rather flow from human corporeality, "the soil in which ritual as such (and that includes the Christian sacraments) is rooted."[84] Although Schillebeeckx does not broach the topic of ecological degradation in this essay, the language of ecological belonging colors his analysis of "both profane and religious" rituals; he refers readers to "the real matrix of all ritual, namely the human body with its natural and cultural-historical ecosystem."[85] Schillebeeckx is intent to say that the ecological character of human corporeality and rituality comprises "both natural and cultural elements."[86] Part and parcel of his exposition of the biological basis of human ritualizing are several passages discussing the continuity of ritual in human and nonhuman animal behavior. Animals engage in rites—that is, fixed patterns surrounding certain mundane occurrences—accompanied by particular movements and communicative sounds; in a manner that at first blush seems to modify his parsing of human from animal traits in the previous essay, here he grants that "through stylisation and repetition certain actions become 'symbolic' even among animals, in codes that are intelligible to members of that species."[87] A certain hierarchy of human over animal nonetheless persists, even if Schillebeeckx comes across as slightly less confident about its basis.[88] While holding to the basic structure for ritual inclusive of human and nonhuman animals, he also argues that a "cultural dimension" obtains in human ritual, because in humans "that which, among animals, primarily serves biological needs becomes the vehicle and expression of meaning and sense…"[89] Overall, then, the back-and-forth motion that characterizes his reflections on the natural basis for culture and ritual results in a softening of the boundary between culture and nature without erasing it. This last pair of essays reflects the movement we have traced in Schillebeeckx's thought toward a theological anthropology in an ecological key as well as the quandaries that inhere in such an endeavor.

## "Humble humanism" and the cause of creation

Schillebeeckx's treatment of ecological issues is largely occasional; it does not constitute a general theory of human–nature relations. This examination of three chronological snapshots reveals the addition of layers and shifts in emphasis in his thinking, rather than definitive transitions

---

[84] Ibid., 197.

[85] Ibid., 194; cf. 193, 197. Schillebeeckx also deploys the ecosystem as a metaphor for "the overall liturgical field with all its dimensions," which expresses the unity of differentiated elements (e.g., the eucharistic institution formula) within "the complex whole"; ibid., 199.

[86] Ibid., 193.

[87] Ibid., 192.

[88] See ibid., 192: "Even though humans are 'more' than just members of the animal species …"; and ibid., 193: "… as human beings belonging to the ritualising animal species we are also 'programmed' and embedded in a society with a distinctive, unique culture, with an immediate worldly context and its own notions about people and reality, whether bound up with transcendental powers and forces or not."

[89] Ibid., 194; 195–96. The qualifier "primarily" opens the possibility of understanding the difference between humans and other animals as one of degree rather than kind.

from one phase to the next. What Schillebeeckx modifies is his manner of parsing the relations between creation, nature, and humanity; especially crucial is his turn to defining humanity in terms of co-creatureliness and to a more dynamic view of the interaction between nature and history or culture. With the introduction of an ecological horizon, Schillebeeckx explores the plasticity of creation as a relational vehicle; the formal assertion that creatureliness is something human beings share with everything that exists (i.e., nature and history) develops into a more textured view of co-creaturely relation and the specific traits that humans share with animals. What endures are core convictions regarding the goodness of all creation, the universal scope of salvation, and the "critical and productive force" of praxis that orients itself to God's desire to make the creation whole. In seeking to articulate this transformation and what threatens it—both increasingly understood to have a cosmic as well as personal and socio-political dimension—Schillebeeckx preserves the unique role of grace-filled human activity as he contends with a pivotal question for ecological theology: in what way are human being creatures among other creatures?

Martin Poulsom contends that Schillebeeckx's "humble humanism" has considerable ecological relevance in that it challenges both anthropocentric and ecocentric renderings of the human place in nature; rather than claiming either difference from or sameness to nature, creation faith enacts a vocabulary of "distinction-in-relation" that calls us to "rearticulate what it means to be genuinely human, so that the good of humanity is not defined in opposition to the good of the earth."[90] Other ecological interpreters are less sanguine about the prospect that even the humblest of humanisms can truly serve the cause of all creation.[91] Interpreting the demands of co-humanity together with those of co-creatureliness remains a live issue in ecological theology, surfacing difficult questions about how best to negotiate humans' social, cultural, political, and religious identity in regard to ecological belonging and responsibility. To tug at threads of tension in the way Schillebeeckx undertakes this complex negotiation is not, however, to unravel the ongoing potential of his thought for eco-theological reflection.

---

[90]   Martin G. Poulsom, "The Place of Humanity, in Creation," *Faiths in Creation*, The Institute Series 8, ed. Catherine Cowley (London: Heythrop Institute for Religion, Ethics and Public Life, 2008), 26. Poulsom adopts the phrase "humble humanism" from one of Schillebeeckx's early essays; see Schillebeeckx, "Humble Humanism," *WC, CW* vol. 4. (London: Bloomsbury T&T Clark, 2014), 15–24 [19–31]. For another succinct framing of the pitfalls of both anthropocentrism (i.e., personalism) and ecocentrism (i.e., naturalism), see Peter Scott, *A Political Theology of Nature* (Cambridge: Cambridge University Press, 2003), 63–66.

[91]   Deep ecology, which Poulsom identifies as the exemplar of an ecocentric approach, is indeed the paradigmatic critique. Yet scholars equally critical as he of deep ecology also challenge the humanist framework. For one example that draws on poststructuralist philosophy, see Laurel Kearns and Catherine Keller, eds., *Ecospirit: Religions and Philosophies for the Earth* (New York: Fordham University Press, 2007). For a critique that dialogues with patristic theology, animal studies, and posthumanism, see Eric Daryl Meyer, *Inner Animalities: Theology and the End of the Human* (New York: Fordham University Press, 2018).

# IV. Toward a mysticism of creation on contested ground

Given the surge of eco-theological writing in recent years, what would be the distinctive value in returning to Schillebeeckx's work to approach the problematic of human–nature relations? I suggest that the contribution of an approach "*sequela* Schillebeeckx" emerges in the extent to which the meaning of creation faith can illuminate and engage—without resolving—a series of paradoxes that characterize the current eco-political context.

Elizabeth Johnson observes the first of these paradoxes with respect to the emergence of an ecological awareness that has come to the fore in recent decades. On the one hand, there is "the wonder" informed by modern scientific inquiry into the extraordinary dynamism of cosmos and earth; on the other hand, there is "the wasting" of the natural world—habitats polluted and destroyed; massive losses of biodiversity; accelerating rates of extinction; warming temperatures and extreme weather. This dire situation imbues the topic of human–nature relations with an imperative character; for many, it is apparent that we must *do something* to change course. While the wonder of creation may be no less real, the reality of its wasting increasingly conjures images of apocalypse.[92]

Against the background of this freighted urgency, the transition from knowledge to effective action presents a second paradox, no less harsh than the first. A half-century on from the inception of the environmental movement and several decades since the World Council of Churches pronounced, "The stark sign of our times is a planet in peril at our hands," too many responses have been adaptive, incremental, and anemic instead of radical, swift, and comprehensive.[93] If anything is "too big to fail," surely it is our very planetary home. Somehow, in lockstep with widespread recognition of the ecological destructiveness of dominant modes of politics, transportation, consumption—in a word, life as usual—these patterns seem only to become more entrenched, determined, defensive. Enfolded in this recognition is a third contradiction, namely that increased human power over nature is bound up with a slew of new vulnerabilities and negative repercussions; unprecedented advances in the movement of people and goods, for example, rely on a fossil fuel-driven economy that wreaks havoc on ecosystems and climate.[94] The prospect that a sustainable future (let alone salvation) will be administered by scientific ingenuity and an invisible hand has a remarkable staying power, but the accuracy of this claim is gainsaid by any fair and comprehensive assessment of "market logic" and the instrumental approach with which globalized late capitalism utilizes the planet's inhabitants and its resources.[95]

---

[92] See, for example, Henry Fountain, "Apocalyptic Thoughts Amid Nature's Chaos? You Could Be Forgiven," *New York Times*, September 8, 2017. https://www.nytimes.com/2017/09/08/us/hurricane-irma-earthquake-fires.html.

[93] World Council of Churches, *Signs of the Spirit: Official Report, Seventh Assembly, Canberra, Australia, 7–20 February 1991*, ed. Michael Kinnamon (Geneva/Grand Rapids, MI: WCC Publications/Eerdmans, 1991), 55.

[94] Andrew Biro, ed., *Critical Ecologies: The Frankfurt School and Contemporary Environmental Crises* (Toronto: University of Toronto Press, 2011), 4–5, 7.

[95] See Naomi Klein, *This Changes Everything: Capitalism vs. the Climate* (New York: Simon and Schuster, 2014) and, on the seepage of such a mentality into putatively environmentally-friendly solutions, Heather Rogers, *Green Gone Wrong: Dispatches from the Front Lines of Eco-Capitalism* (London: Verso, 2010).

These first three claims begin to indicate that the meaning of an ecological age is inseparable from social dynamics. The "politics of nature"[96] signifies that experience of the natural world—that variegated entirely that comprises our homes, our sustenance, our jobs, our neighbors, our enemies, our very selves—is always suffused by relations of power. Nature is never encountered in the abstract absolute, rather it is mediated by political decisions, social institutions, and cultural symbols. As Catholic social thought recognizes, the separation between political economy and scientific ecology is illusory and often ideological.[97] The recent encyclical, *Laudato Si'*, by Pope Francis represents an incisive example of attention to a fourth paradox shaping our ecological age: matters of planetary ecological concern are at the same time highly differentiated, both in terms of who holds responsibility and who suffers the consequences.[98] They illuminate enormous disparities in access to basic resources, wealth, and political agency between the global north and south, the burden of which typically falls most heavily on groups such as women, children, and ethnic and religious minorities.

The politics of nature also extend to the normative function of the concept of nature in the social sphere. "Nature" is a category that forms and regulates human identity in ways that have very material implications for people's lives. Sometimes these are damaging and even violent; to deem certain behaviors, forms of life, and persons "unnatural" or "against nature" remains a powerfully charged indictment. How does one make sense of the need to defend nature's limits in some contexts (e.g., in regard to warming temperatures in the Arctic) and to deconstruct the discourse of respect for nature's boundaries in others (e.g., when contesting oppressive notions of race, gender, or sexuality)? Can nature be a foundation for a liberative and integrative ecological politics? This fifth paradox names the tension surrounding the status of nature as constructed and/or given, and the ethical stakes of how that status is defined and expressed at the intersection of social and ecological concerns.[99]

## Schillebeeckx's contribution and the ongoing crisis

In light of this partial yet daunting sketch, what can Schillebeeckx's understanding of creation faith contribute to the gospel proclamation of flourishing life in an era of rampant ecological degradation and severe social injustice? The following suggests several points where the

---

[96] Bruno Latour, *Politics of Nature: How to Bring the Sciences into Democracy*, trans. Catherine Porter (Cambridge, MA: Harvard University Press, 2004).

[97] See Francis, *On Care for Our Common Home: Laudato Si'* (May 24, 2015) 139 (hereafter cited in text as *LS*), http://w2.vatican.va/content/francesco/en/encyclicals/documents/papa-francesco_20150524_enciclica-laudato-si.html. Here, Francis writes: "We are faced not with two separate crises, one environmental and the other social, but rather with one complex crisis which is both social and environmental." In addition to the whole of Chapter Four on "integral ecology," see *LS* 118, 189–98.

[98] The notion of an "ecological debt" is perhaps the most striking statement of this differential; see *LS* 51 and 93, 170–72. See also Biro, *Critical Ecologies*, 5, 7–8.

[99] See Crina Archer, Laura Ephraim, and Lida Maxwell, eds., *Second Nature: Rethinking the Natural Through Politics* (New York: Fordham University Press, 2013); Kate Soper, *What Is Nature? Culture, Politics, and the Non-Human* (Malden, MA: Blackwell, 1995). For a theological consideration of this question, see Catherine Keller, "Talking Dirty: Ground Is Not Foundation," *Ecospirit: Religions and Philosophies for the Earth*, ed. Laurel Kearns and Catherine Keller (New York: Fordham University Press, 2007), 63–76.

mysticism of a "critical, productive and liberating power of authentic belief in creation" might be brought to bear on the politics of human–nature relations.[100]

Although Schillebeeckx does not develop the idea of "ecological experiences of contrast," this paradigm is apposite to a situation where the "wasting" of the natural world stands in stark contradiction to its capacity to inspire "wonder." Building on the fundamental goodness of reality, faith in creation encourages celebration of nature's beauty, intricacy, and diversity, while prioritizing the critical, revelatory power of protest against the destruction of nature.[101] There is no direct path from a changed worldview to behavior, but thinking differently is essential to effective eco-political action.[102] Between entrenched fantasies of human mastery over nature and self-exculpatory claims of helplessness, Schillebeeckx's formulation of finitude gets to the heart of the paradox concerning human power and human vulnerability. His counsel to embrace our creaturely status energizes practices of restraint—a "collective ascesis"—but it also underscores the imperative for transformative engagement in and with nature. Moreover, to accept finitude is never to acquiesce to unnecessary suffering, especially that which passes under the guise of what is "natural," unchanging, or universal.[103] While the scale of ecological issues redoubles interest in finding a common ground for a global ethics (recall, in this vein, Schillebeeckx's comment on the "earthly soil of all possible culture"), careful attention to the radically differentiated contexts in which human and nonhuman interact is warranted. In an ecological age, an emphasis on the mystery of finite wholeness may help to navigate a shared creaturely reality in its indelibly particular configurations.[104]

As ever, critical negativity directs ethical attention to those configurations that cause suffering.[105] Although other criteria are needed to mediate between competing needs, creation faith insists, as an orienting axis, on commitment to vulnerable populations and fragile habitats. Creation faith knows that such commitment comes up against the refractory reality of the powers-that-be.[106]

---

[100] Schillebeeckx, *Church*, 231 [233].

[101] One might consider protests in 2016–2017 by indigenous water protectors and allies against the construction of an oil pipeline near the Standing Rock Reservation in North Dakota, USA.

[102] On this point, see Klein, *This Changes Everything*, 23, 61. Cf. Jenkins, *Ecologies of Grace*, 10–15.

[103] See Schillebeeckx, "Secularization and Christian Belief in God," *GFM, CW* vol. 3 (London: Bloomsbury T&T Clark, 2014), 32–33 [55]; Schillebeeckx, *Christ*, 730, 832 [736, 836]; Schillebeeckx, *God Among Us*, 91–102.

[104] See Daniel Minch, "Re-Examining Edward Schillebeeckx's Anthropological Constants: An Ontological Perspective," *Salvation in the World: The Crossroads of Public Theology*, ed. Stephan van Erp, Christopher Cimorelli, and Christiane Alpers (London: Bloomsbury, 2017), 113–30. An ecological context places a new accent on whether and how Schillebeeckx's project succeeds in holding together "hermeneutical" and "creation-ontological" approaches to theological anthropology. See also Lieven Boeve, "Introduction: The Enduring Significance and Relevance of Edward Schillebeeckx? Introducing the State of the Question in Media Res," *Edward Schillebeeckx and Contemporary Theology*, ed. Lieven Boeve, Frederiek Depoortere, and Stephan van Erp (London/New York: T&T Clark, 2010), 1–22.

[105] In seeking to mobilize the "critical and productive force" of creation faith, theology can find a partner in political ecology. Though diverse in its methods, this field endeavors to fuse empirical study of the natural world and critical social theory in order to support liberative intervention in the politics of nature. See Paul Robbins, ed., *Political Ecology: A Critical Introduction*, 2nd ed. (Hoboken, NJ: John Wiley and Sons, 2012) and Tom Perreault, Gavin Bridge, and James McCarthy, eds., *The Routledge Handbook of Political Ecology* (New York: Routledge, 2015).

[106] Schillebeeckx, *Christ*, 32 [35–36].

Acting differently in the interest of eco-social justice and earthly well-being must overcome not only the inertia of the status quo but also its resistance. Therefore, a Schillebeeckxian "mysticism of ecological praxis" must be agonistic.[107] Genuine ecological solidarity, like authentic humanity, is a task that includes adventure and risk; trust in creation does not furnish a blueprint for living well together in co-creatureliness.[108] So, respect for creation's integrity must understand this integrity to be, in part, the product of struggle, striving, and imagination. To affirm the co-mediation of nature and history/culture in creation speaks to the accumulated effects of complex and contingent networks of agency, rather than to a metaphysical difference between the given and the constructed (or the natural and the political). An ecological age calls for a pliable, historicized, and critically adept vision of human beings' ecological belonging and political subjectivity. New interpretations of Schillebeeckx's creation faith may be counted among the resources with which Christian theology can address the meaning of finite human creatureliness and the contested politics of nature, toward the glory of God and the cause of all God's creation.

---

[107] The quoted phrase is from Denis Edwards, *Ecology at the Heart of Faith* (Maryknoll, NY: Orbis, 2006), 117, who formulates it in view of Schillebeeckx's fusion of mysticism and politics. "Agonistic" here refers to struggle and conflict as a vital democratic practice, an idea that has been advanced in political theory (especially in the work of Chantal Mouffe, among others) and adopted in political theology. For two examples of the latter, see Bradford E. Hinze, "Decolonizing Everyday Practices: Sites of Struggle in Church and Society," *Proceedings of the Catholic Theological Society of America* 71 (2016), 47–61, and Mark Lewis Taylor *The Theological and the Political: On the Weight of the World* (Philadelphia: Fortress Press, 2011).

[108] Schillebeeckx, *God Among Us,* 98.

# Index